Fundamentals of Communications and Networking

MICHAEL G. SOLOMON AND DAVID KIM

World Headquarters
Jones & Bartlett Learning
5 Wall Street
Burlington, MA 01803
978-443-5000
info@jblearning.com
www.jblearning.com

Jones & Bartlett Learning books and products are available through most bookstores and online booksellers. To contact Jones & Bartlett Learning directly, call 800-832-0034, fax 978-443-8000, or visit our website, www.jblearning.com.

Substantial discounts on bulk quantities of Jones & Bartlett Learning publications are available to corporations, professional associations, and other qualified organizations. For details and specific discount information, contact the special sales department at Jones & Bartlett Learning via the above contact information or send an email to specialsales@jblearning.com.

Production Credits
Chief Executive Officer: Ty Field
President: James Homer
SVP, Chief Technology Officer: Dean Fossella
SVP, Chief Marketing Officer: Alison M. Pendergast
SVP, Curriculum Solutions: Christopher Will
VP, Design and Production: Anne Spencer
VP, Manufacturing and Inventory Control: Therese Connell
Editorial Management: High Stakes Writing, LLC, Editor and Publisher: Lawrence J. Goodrich
Managing Editor, HSW: Ruth Walker
Editor, HSW: Cynthia Hanson
Reprints and Special Projects Manager: Susan Schultz
Associate Production Editor: Tina Chen
Director of Marketing: Alisha Weisman
Associate Marketing Manager: Andrea DeFronzo
Cover Design: Anne Spencer
Text Design and Composition: Mia Saunders Design
Cover Image: © Oriontrail/ShutterStock, Inc.
Chapter Opener Image: © Rodolfo Clix/Dreamstime.com
Printing and Binding: Malloy, Inc.
Cover Printing: Malloy, Inc.

ISBN: 978-1-4496-4917-3

6048
Printed in the United States of America
15 14 13 12 11 10 9 8 7 6 5 4 3 2 1

Contents

Preface

Fundamentals of Communications and Networking is a resource for understanding today's networks and the way they support the evolving requirements of different types of organizations. Networks have long been regarded as methods to connect resources. While this is still the case, today's networks are required to support an increasing array of real-time communication methods. Video chat, real-time messaging, and always-connected resources put demands on networks that were previously unimagined. Networks must respond to user requests in ways that require sub-second round-trip times. Such demands mean that network designers must rethink how they set up topologies. Reliance on higher layer flexibility is not good enough. Performance often rises above flexibility in design priority.

This text covers the critical issues of designing a network that will meet an organization's performance needs. You will learn about how businesses use networks to solve business problems—not just technical problems. Today's networks must not only be technically proficient—but also perform to a degree that they support an organization's ability to conduct operations as effectively as possible.

You will learn about network basics, beyond just the formal technology coverage, and how to build functionality to support business demands. The focus of the topics is both on the technology and how the technology meets business goals. A functional network is one that allows an organization to meet its goals—regardless of the technology it employs. You will learn how to choose what works for your organization.

This text is organized to describe the basics of how networks work, how they support increasing demands of advanced communications, and how to map the right technology to the organization's needs.

To my wife and best friend, Stacey
—Michael G. Solomon

Acknowledgments

I would like to thank David Kim, Ron Price, and Jim Cavanagh for providing content for this book, as well as the book's technical reviewers, David Kim and Mike Coker, for ensuring the content was accurate and complete. I would also like to thank Danny Schmidt and Ryan Werner for providing our great-looking graphics, Cynthia Hanson for tackling the arduous task of editing our work, Mia Saunders for laying out the book, and Ruth Walker for serving as our project manager to ensure we produced a quality product. All of your input has really made this a better book. And thanks to my dad, who retired from AT&T with a ton of knowledge of how communications work, and passed a fair amount on to me. He helped put things into perspective with stories and some great analogies.

Michael G. Solomon

I would like to thank Michael Solomon for always being there late at night and early in the morning. His commitment to his work and his family is something to behold. And a special thank you to my wife, Mi Young Kim, who is always by my side.

David Kim

About the Authors

MICHAEL G. SOLOMON, CISSP, PMP, CISM, is a full-time security speaker, consultant, and author who specializes in achieving and maintaining secure IT environments. He is a former instructor in Kennesaw State University's computer science and information sciences (CSIS) department, where he taught courses on software project management, C++ programming, computer organization and architecture, and data communications. He holds an MS in mathematics and computer science from Emory University (1998) and a BS in computer science from Kennesaw State University (1987); he is currently pursuing a PhD in computer science at Emory University.

DAVID KIM is president of Security Evolutions, LLC, and chief technology officer for vLab Solutions, LLC (*www.vLabSolutions.com*), both located in North Carolina. Mr. Kim's IT and IT security experience encompasses more than 25 years of technical engineering, technical management, and solutions selling and sales management. This experience includes LAN/WAN, internetworking, enterprise network management, and IT security for voice, video, and data networking infrastructures. Previously, Mr. Kim was chief operating officer of $(ISC)^2$ Institute, located in Vienna, Virginia.

PART ONE

Evolution of Communications

CHAPTER 1

Today's Personal and Business Communication Requirements

COMMUNICATION HAS CHANGED TREMENDOUSLY in just the past century. In fact, it has changed more than in the previous several thousand years. People communicate in ways few could imagine several years ago. The new options and methods to carry on conversations have changed the ways we interact with one another and how we conduct business. Good communication is essential to business. The most innovative organizations include new communication methods in their ongoing business plans. Consumers often find that the organizations that communicate most effectively deserve their repeat business. In this chapter you will learn how personal and business communication requirements have changed and how these changes affect our daily lives.

Chapter 1 Topics

This chapter covers the following topics and concepts:

- What being hyperconnected means
- The pervasiveness of Internet and IP connectivity
- How unified communications (UC) connect people and businesses
- How snail mail, store-and-forward messaging, and real-time messaging compare
- How the World Wide Web transformed business
- The importance of customer service as a primary business driver

Chapter 1 Goals

When you complete this chapter, you will be able to:

- Describe what it means to be hyperconnected
- Explain the benefits of Internet connectivity
- Define and describe some benefits of unified communications (UC)
- Contrast snail mail, store-and-forward messaging, and real-time messaging
- Explain how the World Wide Web changed the way businesses operate
- Explain how customer service drives business communications

Today's Hyperconnected World

The common experience of always being connected to the rest of the world is fairly recent. Until about 20 years ago, almost all electronic communication used **analog** media. Analog devices transmit data using continuously variable signals. The analog devices had limitations that made it difficult to do much more than engage in voice conversations and slowly transmit other types of data. Of course, before telephones, most communication occurred either through face-to-face interaction or written documents. Letters were the primary method for communicating when face-to-face meetings were not practical. At that time, the transmission speed depended entirely on how fast the sender could deliver a letter to the recipient. This practice that has lasted for thousands of years is still the main communication method for formal and legal correspondence (see Figure 1-1). Businesses have just recently improved the process that enables any sender to transport a document to virtually any recipient overnight.

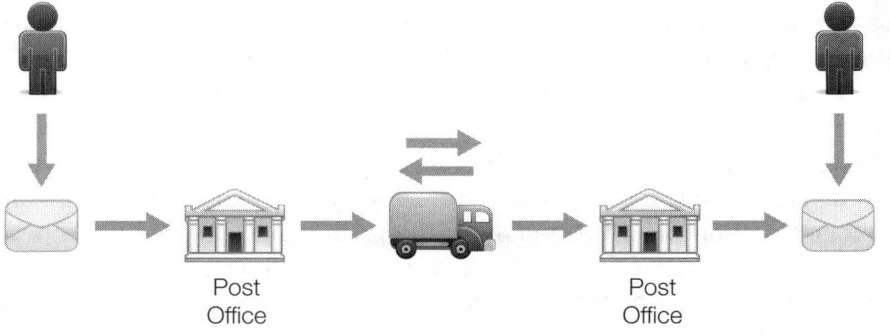

FIGURE 1-1
Transporting written communication.

The introduction of the telegraph, and then the telephone, in the 19th century started a steady communication revolution. The electrical telegraph, commonly just known as the telegraph, was the first successful electronic communication device. The telegraph can send electrical signals over long distances using simple cables. Samuel Morse developed a code made up of long and short signals that could represent the alphabet. Humans who knew this Morse code could send and receive text messages. Alexander Graham Bell developed the telephone late in the 19th century. The telephone allowed people to talk to one another across long distances using simple cables.

Once the basic infrastructure was in place to support telephones, people and businesses quickly adopted the new invention. They began to replace many face-to-face meetings with telephone conversations. As long as both parties had access to telephones, this type of communication filled the need for many informal conversations. Businesses embraced this new way to communicate. Telephones allowed workers to carry on conversations with associates and customers without having to leave their workplace. Businesses increased worker efficiency and extended the area they could serve. The new invention gave them the ability to talk with more people in any given day. Location became less of an issue, and the world began to seem a little smaller.

Answering machines became popular in the early 1970s and started another wave in the communication revolution. Prior to the common use of answering machines, it was possible to communicate using a telephone only if both parties were at their respective telephones. During this time, nearly all telephones were hard-wired and could not move more than a few feet. The first approach to handling missed calls was to route all calls through a central person. The switchboard operator would intercept all calls and take messages when a recipient was not able to answer the call. This approach worked well, but it required at least one person who was dedicated to the task of handling telephone calls and messages. Answering machines made it possible to leave a recorded message for someone who was not available to answer a telephone call. While this did not substitute for a complete conversation, it did allow parties to send messages that the recipient could retrieve later. This practice was one of the first electronic versions of sending complete messages.

In the last 40 years, the range of communication options has exploded. **Facsimile devices**, better known as fax machines, became popular in the 1980s. These devices allowed nearly anyone to send and receive printed documents in addition to voice communication. Fax machines could scan multiple page documents and transmit the document image over regular analog telephone cables. Users didn't need any special hardware other than the fax machine. Anyone could receive a faxed document as long as they had a fax machine connected to their telephone line. The quality wasn't great, and large documents took minutes to transmit, but the process was much faster than mailing a document.

Beepers, also called **pagers**, and **mobile phones** emerged to allow people to maintain communications without the restriction of wires. The first pagers only received messages. Anyone could call a specific telephone number associated with the pager to cause the pager to sound an alarm. Second-generation pagers supported two-way conversations.

The messages could only be a few characters long, but two-way pagers gave users the first taste of freedom from telephone wires. They made it possible to reach people regardless of where they were. These devices made it possible to carry on simple conversations while engaging in unrelated activities. Users participate in personal activities and still provide input for business matters. Mobile phones provided the next step toward full communication freedom. Mobile phone users could carry telephones with them wherever they went without any wires. They could make and receive calls with other mobile phones or any regular telephones. These technologies gave the average person the ability to stay connected with anyone else in many locations throughout the world. Most pagers and early generation mobile phones still relied on analog communication and had to contend with its limited speed and quality.

The latest group of technology advances focused on the transition from analog to **digital** communication. Advances included digital wireless access and readily available **broadband**, or faster-access Internet connections. Easy access to digital networks means devices with any electronic components are candidates to connect to one another. This type of connection supports easy access for remote users. Today we routinely see computers, **personal digital assistants (PDAs)**, scanners and printers, soft drink dispensing machines, automobiles, refrigerators, security systems, entertainment systems, and many other devices already able to connect to digital networks. There is almost no limit to what you can do remotely now. Anyone can interact with many devices in their home or place of business without actually being there. It also means that people are connected to their homes and offices more than ever before. We live in the era of **hyperconnectivity**. The increasing reliance on digital documents and always being connected means that few transactions require a physical presence. You can do most of what you need remotely. This remote ability applies to both personal and business activities.

Hyperconnectivity does have its drawbacks. Always being connected tends to breed its own expectations. Most people who rely on their smart phones tend to develop the need to frequently "check in" to fetch the latest e-mail or social network messages. Many find it uncomfortable, or even difficult, to put the phone down and focus on a single face-to-face conversation. Hyperconnectivity easily provides access to more information than any human can digest and interpret. One of the greatest challenges for today's networks is not to provide more connections. The real challenge is to use available network resources to present useful information to users and limit the growing volume of useless data.

Internet and IP Connectivity Are Pervasive

The global network we know as the **Internet** grew from a network created in the 1960s by the United States Department of Defense. In the early days, only military facilities and some academic research labs could access the network. Users began to rely on the network resources and often suggested adding more organizations to the growing network. Each time new groups of computers and users joined the network, the nature of the network changed to meet their needs. By the mid 1990s, the Internet had grown to include many businesses and private users. The **World Wide Web** was brand new, and it was clear this new phenomenon had staggering potential to change the way we understand and use networks. More and more small networks and computers connected to the Internet around the world and accelerated its growth.

In the early years of the Internet, many segments of the network used analog media. That meant network devices translated messages from analog to digital and back again many times as the messages traveled to their destinations. The ability for such a large network to operate on both analog and digital media made it easy to use existing telecommunication equipment. The ease of connecting to the Internet generated more demand for services—and more speed. Engineering techniques allowed service providers to use the maximum **bandwidth** of existing cabling and transmission technologies. But it was not enough. Network users demanded a faster solution.

The next step in solving the Internet's performance problems was to replace the analog segments with digital segments. That meant upgrading network access hardware and laying new cable in many cases. But the result was a global network supported by newer hardware with far greater bandwidth than before. Expanding the digital components of the Internet and its supporting networks made it possible to support far more users than was ever possible using analog components. These new changes made an even greater impact in highly populated areas. Today's Internet can provide network access to large groups of users in population centers and still allow access using analog components to service more remote areas, as shown in Figure 1-2.

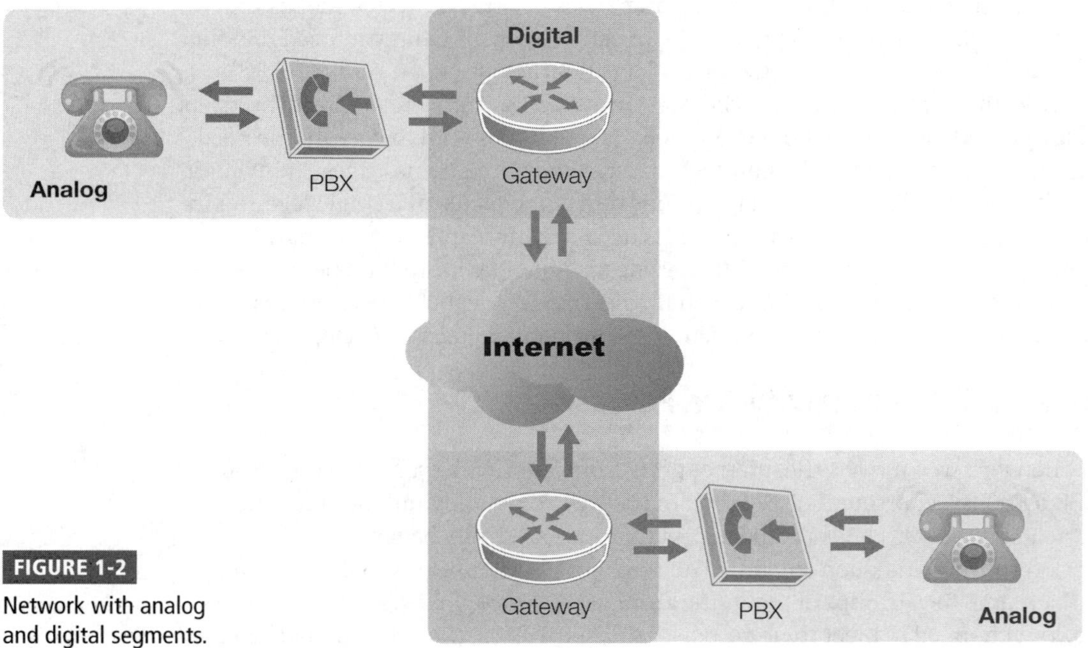

FIGURE 1-2

Network with analog and digital segments.

The digital network revolution made it possible for billions of devices and computers to attach to the Internet. The only requirement is to get an **Internet Protocol (IP)** address from a recognized **Internet service provider (ISP)**. ISPs provide a unique **IP address**, or range of IP addresses, for their customers. The customer connects to the ISP's network and uses the assigned IP address to exchange messages with other computers and devices on the Internet. Any computers or devices connected to the customer's network can potentially access the Internet's resources using the single ISP connection. The original IP address format, called IPv4, provides unique addresses for approximately 4.3 billion devices. The existing 4.3 billion IP addresses are not enough to keep up with the Internet's rapid growth. Internet users are in the process of transitioning to a new IP address format, IPv6, to solve the address exhaustion problem. IPv4 uses a 32-bit address and is commonly expressed as a group of four bytes, separated by a period. For example, an IPv4 address would appear as 192.168.1.254. IPv6 addresses are 128-bit numbers. The new format provides the ability to uniquely address 2^128, or 3.4 × 10^38 devices. IPv6 addresses are expressed as a group of eight 2-byte numbers (using hexadecimal notation) separated by colons. A new IPv6 address would appear as 3ffe:1700:45a5:3:200:f8bf:fe21:67cf.

>  **NOTE**
>
> IPv6 is more than just bigger numbers. Although IPv6 does dramatically expand the number of available IP addresses, it attempts to improve IP network efficiency as well. The new format makes it easier to aggregate subnets using routing prefixes. When this subnet routing occurs at routing nodes, it can reduce overall traffic. The new format should reduce the Internet's bandwidth use and make it more efficient.

The original designers of the Internet Protocol addressing standards wisely set aside a range of **private IP addresses**. These private addresses made it possible for devices to connect to the Internet without having to have a globally unique IP address. Private IP addresses are non-routable. That means that the addresses are valid only for private networks and not the Internet. These addresses provide organizations with the ability to create their own networks with standard IP addresses. All an organization needs is a single public IP address from their ISP. All of the other IP addresses can be private addresses. IPv6 calls private IP addresses **unique local addresses (ULAs)**. All ULAs use the routing prefix of fc00:/7. That means any IPv6 address in the range fc00 through fdff is a ULA, or IPv6 private IP address. The ranges of private IP addresses are:

- IPv4: 10.0.0.0 to 10.255.255.255
- IPv4: 172.16.0.0 to 172.16.255.255
- IPv4: 192.168.0.0 to 192.168.255.255
- IPv6: fc00:0:0:0:0:0:0:0 to fdff:ffff:ffff:ffff:ffff:ffff:ffff:ffff

Organizations can assign IP addresses in the private address ranges or can set up a server or device to dynamically assign private IP addresses as needed (see Figure 1-3). Dynamic addressing uses the **Dynamic Host Configuration Protocol (DHCP)** to request and assign IP addresses.

Historically, a network connection required a physical cable. The last 10 years have seen tremendous growth in wireless network capabilities and numbers of wireless devices. It is common to find Internet connectivity using either Wi-Fi or cellular wireless networks. Most of today's home and business networks include both wired and wireless segments. Wireless networks make connecting computers and devices much easier than in the past. It has always been easy to plug a network cable into two computers. However, it has generally been difficult to ensure that there are appropriate cables in place to connect all computers. Wireless networks make it possible to connect computers and devices to home or business networks and the Internet where no network cables exist.

The ease of wired and wireless connections to the Internet made it possible to connect any device to a global network. But the Internet did not expand alone to just wait for new devices. The Internet expanded at the same time products began to appear that needed Internet access. Manufacturers of all types had been preparing their products for Internet connectivity. Many of today's products either rely on an Internet connection or provide features that depend on an Internet connection. For example, many home and business security systems allow remote users to arm, disarm, and check the status of the system. Remote users access the system by connecting to the security system through an Internet connection. This ability allows users to monitor and manage their security system from anywhere in the world.

FIGURE 1-3

Network with DHCP server.

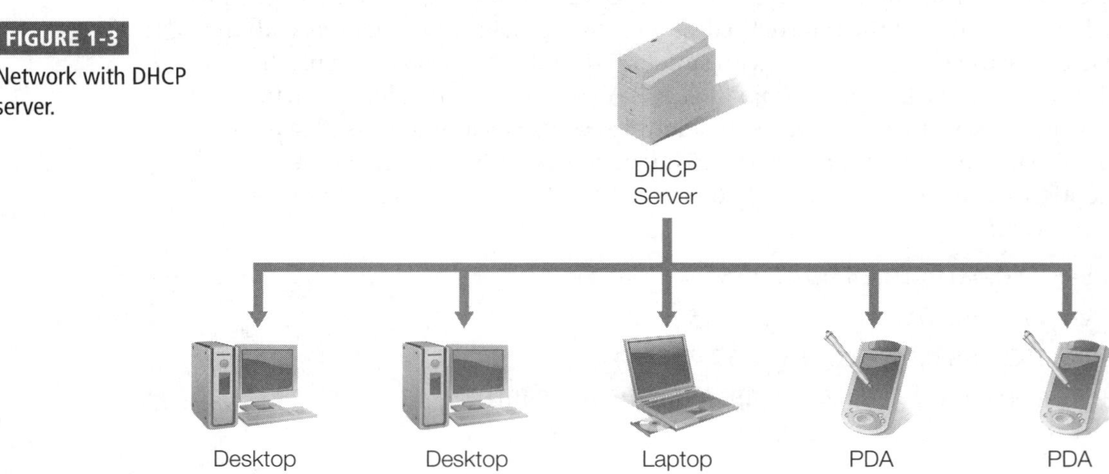

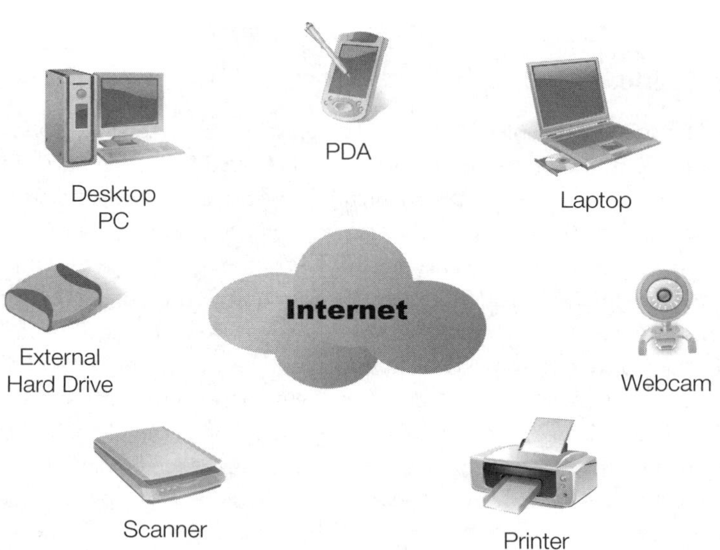

FIGURE 1-4
Devices using wired and wireless connections to the Internet.

Most standalone devices or those connected to an organization's internal network are now potential candidates to support remote Internet users. Printers, copiers, scanners, storage devices, and computers are common examples of network resources users can access using the Internet (see Figure 1-4). Of course, organizations must implement solid security controls to limit use to authorized users.

Today is it easy to connect to the Internet with little regard for location. While there are still some places with no easy Internet access, the list of such locations is rapidly shrinking. You don't have to go very far in any direction to find Wi-Fi or cellular access to a network that provides Internet access. Most existing coverage requires connection fees, but free access points are growing in numbers daily. The easily available Internet connections and large number of IP-enabled devices have made Internet access a common feature of many electronic devices.

How Unified Communications Connect People and Businesses

There are a growing number of devices connected to the Internet—and easier access to the Internet than ever before. This means that users have access to an unprecedented amount of information. While "more is better" sounds good, having lots of data often means that useful information gets lost in the noise. As users receive more and more information, it becomes difficult to manage all of the devices and streams of data. In the past, organizations suffered from the inability to make timely decisions due to a lack of

Information Overload

The McDonnell Douglas F-4 Phantom II jet entered service in the United States Navy in 1960. By the mid-1960s, the United States Air Force and United States Marine Corps were flying the versatile jet as well. This new aircraft carried many new electronic devices and dramatically increased the workload of its crew. During combat, the F-4 pilot would encounter a large volume of input, including the voices of the Radar Intercept Officer (RIO) in the back seat, the wingman, a Forward Air Controller (FAC), Combat Information Center (CIC, or Red Crown), and other aircraft on the same frequency. He also would hear various tones and sounds from incoming threats and his own infrared (IR) and radar-guided weapons. On top of all this, he had to read the primary instruments and a map while flying the aircraft. Keep in mind they didn't have GPS during the Vietnam War! The real challenge was that all this information was important at some point during the flight. There were multiple documented cases of information overload—pilots missed crucial inputs because they just had too much information to process and prioritize. The US military began to study the problem and developed guidelines to streamline the information pilots received. They learned that too much information is sometimes worse than too little.

accurate information. Now it seems that the large volume of information is just too much: Making timely decisions is still difficult due to the time it takes to identify and interpret the good information.

One of the best ways to avoid information overload is to streamline business processes and minimize the amount of information users receive. Make sure you don't send information to users unless they ask for it. Emphasize process flow, required information, and process automation. This focus can reduce the amount of human input required to complete many business functions. Reduced user input allows personnel to focus on absorbing and interpreting smaller amounts of important information. This reduced workload allows users to focus on making good decisions, not on processing lots of data. Aligning business processes and mapping each one to software applications and IT solutions is called **business process management (BPM)**, shown in Figure 1-5. BPM empowers organizations to be more productive and effective. It relies on reducing redundancy and increasing automation throughout the enterprise. The goal of BPM is to streamline business processes and create an environment that promotes competitive advantage and customer responsiveness.

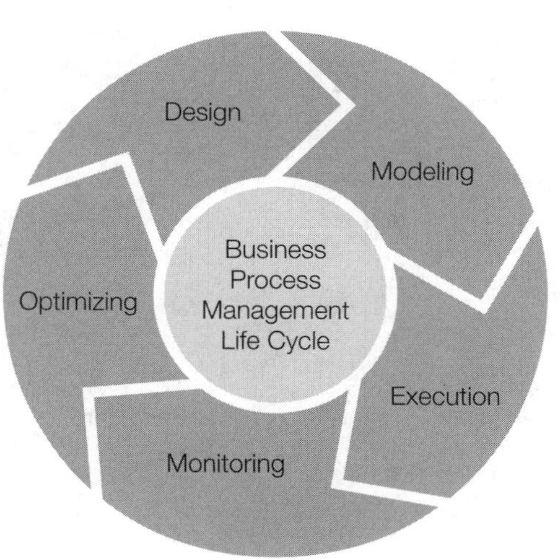

FIGURE 1-5
Businesses process management (BPM) life cycle.

Developing effective communications methods is a central focus of many BPM implementation projects. The BPM process often attempts to bring all communication mediums together into a unified structure. The final result of this effort is called **unified communications (UC)**. UC refers to combining multiple technologies to provide the most effective real-time and non-real-time communication with the correct individual. UC isn't just one technology. It combines the best of the many **real-time communication** methods with non-real-time methods. Common real-time communication methods that UC solutions use include:

- Telephony
- Presence/availability
- Instant messaging
- Video conferencing
- Collaboration

An effective UC solution integrates real-time communication methods with other methods, such as voice mail, e-mail, and fax, to provide the best all-around solution, as shown in Figure 1-6. A solid UC implementation involves automation to identify the best target and medium to use when a person or application needs to communicate. UC can dramatically reduce the time spent searching for a person to answer a critical question. UC processes can automatically identify the correct resources and decide the best way or ways to contact them.

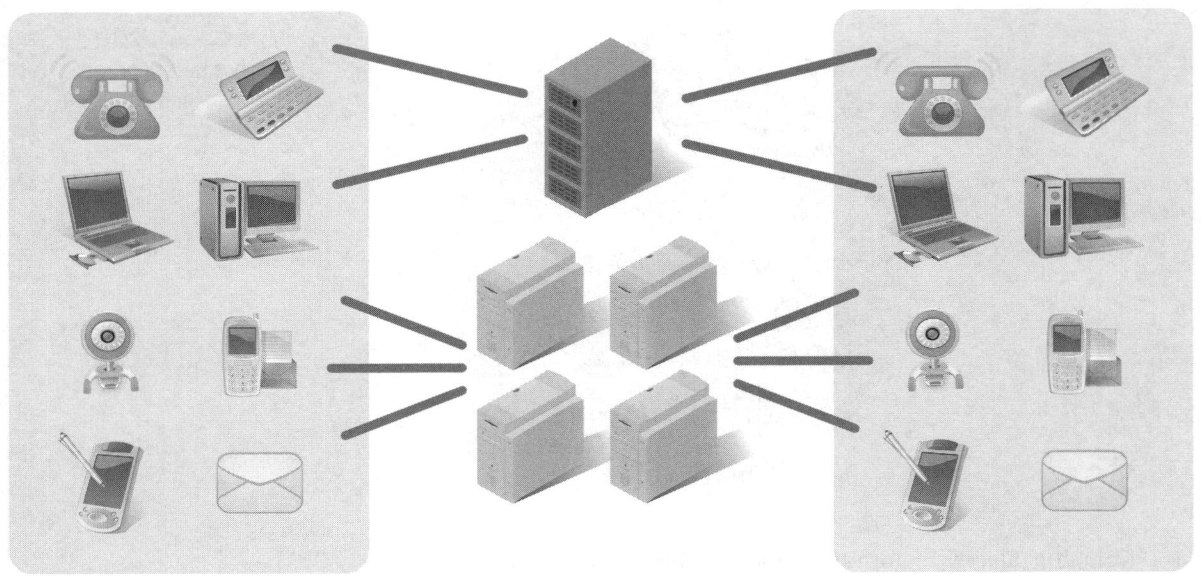

FIGURE 1-6 Unified communications.

Organizations can implement UC throughout the enterprise. UC has many benefits, including the clarity gained just from examining existing processes. The UC analysis process often identifies outdated and inefficient processes. This process of planning for UC helps to ensure that the organization only keeps the communication processes it really needs. UC can improve communication efficiency in many areas, including:

- Reducing communication between modules and streamlining critical software applications
- Making communication less time-consuming and increasing customer service effectiveness
- Reducing wasted calls when managing customer relationships
- Targeting critical decisions in the enterprise resource planning (ERP) process
- Automating tedious portions of supply chain management (SCM) and sales force automation (SFA)

UC can't solve all of an organization's problems, but it does provide a process to make communications more effective. Analyzing current communication and using technology to unify communication methods can make an organization far more effective. If nothing else, UC generally reduces the number of messages sent and received. UC helps to ensure that each message goes to the correct recipient and contains just the information necessary to continue the business process. Organizations that use UC generally see a drop in the number of duplicate or meaningless messages. That makes users happy. UC also means that the organization and its personnel require fewer devices and less network bandwidth to communicate. This means that equipment costs may go down.

There are many benefits to UC. Organizations may realize some, or many, cost and effort savings. The list of potential UC benefits includes:

- Better support of remote and mobile users reduces the number of workers that need a physical office. This can reduce the facilities an organization must maintain.
- Increased ability to conduct teleconferences and video conferences can reduce travel expenses for meetings and training.
- Higher worker productivity and retention as remote worker support provides more flexibility to conform to personal needs and schedules.
- There is a reduced sales cycle timeline due to more effective communication with all parties involved in the sales effort.
- Shortened project timelines occur due to a reduced lag time in communications. There is better identification of communication paths to resolve questions and issues.
- Increased customer satisfaction occurs due to more effective communication throughout the issue resolution process.

UC provides organizations with an approach to communication that leverages existing technology and makes business processes more effective. The key to a solid UC plan is to understand the organization's process and communication needs. Once the organization understands these needs, analysts can develop a UC plan that makes the overall organization more effective.

Snail Mail, Store-and-Forward, and Real-Time Communication

One of the advantages of UC is the effective use of blended communication methods. UC combines real-time communication with other methods. In most organizations the sender of a message chooses the delivery method before sending the message. It is the responsibility of the message sender to compose the message, select the best recipient, and then select the best delivery method. This approach requires that every message sender understand the communication process and make the best delivery decision. While this approach may sound good, it has several flaws.

First, not all message senders fully understand the impact of their delivery method decisions. For instance, is there any real difference between an instant message and an e-mail message? In some cases there isn't any major difference. Questions that don't require an immediate response aren't extremely time sensitive. In other cases, there are huge differences. Time-sensitive messages such as "Our primary database has crashed. What do we do?" require an immediate response. If the recipient is frequently monitoring the email in-box, the e-mail message will arrive shortly after the instant message. The recipient won't immediately receive either message if he or she is not near the computer. In fact, instant message clients may not even deliver messages if the recipient is not logged in. Message senders in legacy environments must determine how sensitive a message is and whether the chosen method is the right one.

Second, most message senders have more to do than just monitor messages they send. It is more efficient to send a message and continue working until a response arrives. This efficient method of exchanging messages depends on a **reliable communication** process, shown in Figure 1-7. A reliable communication process is one in which senders have verification that recipients received all sent messages. Few communication methods provide such assurance without some type of monitoring. In most classic communication methods, senders must monitor sent messages for errors or potentially missing messages. Errors are generally easier to detect and handle. Many errors in the communication process result in some type of sender notification. Dropped or missing messages are more difficult to handle. How do you know when a message doesn't reach its intended recipient? That problem is one of wait-and-see. The simplest response is for the sender to wait for some period of time and try to contact the recipient again if there is no response. This method is inefficient and relies on an arbitrary amount of waiting time. Reliable communication provides sender feedback that verifies message receipt.

Third, most communication methods require that the sender know the recipient to send a message. In some situations the sender knows the message contents but not the recipient. The sender may not even know the role of the recipient. For example, suppose a Web site user wants to know if a specific food product contains allergens, such as gluten. Many Web sites provide generic request pages that send messages to a "catch all" e-mail address. Someone must read these messages and determine the best recipient. UC solutions may pass generic customer requests to a software program that analyzes the message content and determines the most likely recipient (see Figure 1-8). An automated UC process gets the message to the selected recipient faster than a process that requires human input. The UC process may determine that the best recipient for the allergen-related request may be the organization's automated response system. The system may be able to find an answer in a knowledge base and provide an immediate response to the original question. In many cases, UC can provide valuable, timely information without requiring human interaction.

You learned in the previous section that UC involves multiple technologies. UC isn't all about real-time communication. Each of the three classic communication methods has a place in UC. A robust UC strategy should include **snail mail**, **store-and-forward**, and real-time communication. Each communication method has advantages and disadvantages in an enterprise communication model.

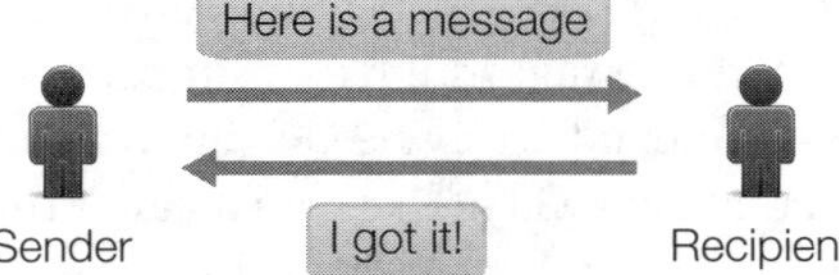

FIGURE 1-7
Reliable communication.

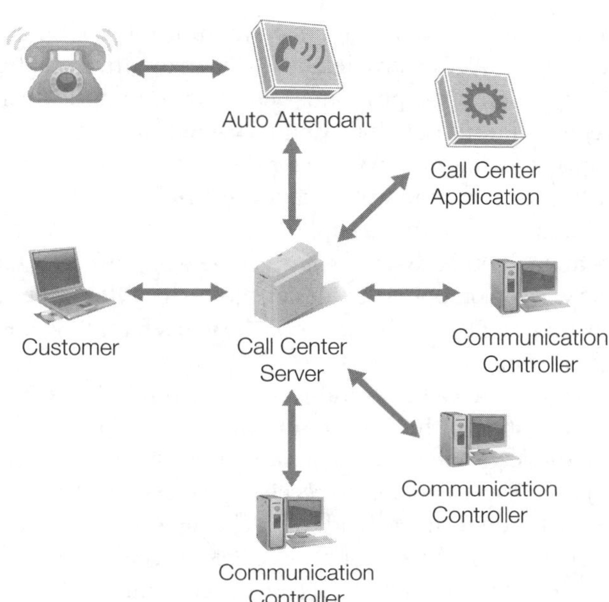

FIGURE 1-8
Automated knowledge base response system.

Snail Mail

The oldest and arguably slowest form of communication is written documents. The sender creates the document and sends the physical paper to the recipient. The sender can write the message using long-hand or print the message using a computer printer. The sender either delivers the document directly or gives the document to a delivery person in the first step of the delivery process. This type of physical document delivery has been around for thousands of years and is still the most common method for legal and official documents.

In the simplest case, the sender delivers the document to the recipient directly. A more common approach involves some type of delivery service. The simplest delivery service is a courier service. Couriers generally work in metropolitan areas to deliver documents and packages directly from senders to recipients. Deliveries involving more distance between the sender and the recipient generally involve more complex delivery organizations. The specialized organizations include government postal services, United Parcel Service (UPS), and Federal Express (FedEx). There are many more delivery organizations of all sizes. Some are regional and others have a global reach. Regardless of the size or scope of the delivery organization, they normally deliver letters and small packages in a matter of hours or days. Since this type of delivery is the slowest of the modern methods available, it is often referred to as snail mail.

Store-and-Forward Messages

Once computers joined even the earliest networks, users came up with new and unique ways to use them to communicate. Early network users appreciated the ability to use computer communication to support human communication. They simply created an electronic model of snail mail. The problem was that computers and humans communicate in different ways. Computer programs generally communicate in pairs. A common strategy was to create a communication channel something like a telephone conversation. The initiator sets up a connection and waits for the target to complete the connection. Once both sides of the conversation were ready, the sender started sending messages. This model worked well between two computers but didn't work as well with two people who may not be near each other. In fact, some people who needed to communicate using computer networks worked on opposite sides of the earth. Different time zones meant that there were few times where both parties of the conversation would be at their computers at the same time.

Software developers created a store-and-forward method of message delivery to address the ineffective nature of human communication and interaction. The message sender could send a message to a recipient at any time. The message delivery didn't depend on the recipient being available to receive the message. Actually, the sender only has to send a message to the recipient's address. The delivery agent program would deliver the message to the recipient's address, but the recipient wouldn't immediately receive the message. The recipient would have to access the contents of the agent's mailbox to extract any delivered messages.

This model was built on the snail mail model of message delivery. Think of how you receive a letter. The letter carrier picks up mail from the main post office and delivers it to your mailbox. You don't actually receive your letter until you visit your mailbox after the letter carrier delivers the letter. The letter carrier doesn't wait for you. She just drops the letter into your mailbox and then leaves to deliver other mail. The store-and-forward method of electronic mail, often just called e-mail, follows this same approach, as shown in Figure 1-9. When you send an e-mail message, you actually send it to an e-mail server. The e-mail server decides where to send the message to get it to the recipient. The recipient is actually a mailbox on another e-mail server. The target e-mail server doesn't actually deliver the message to the final recipient until that recipient connects to the server to collect any delivered messages. The e-mail server stores messages until the recipient connects, then forwards any messages to the recipient.

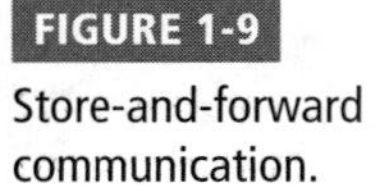
FIGURE 1-9
Store-and-forward communication.

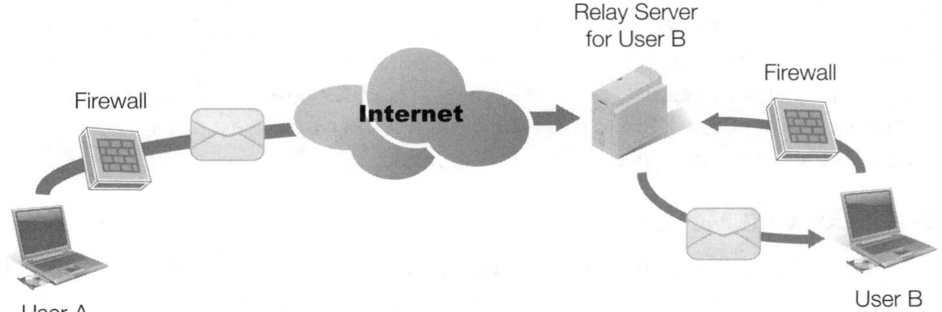

TABLE 1-1 Real-time communication.

TYPE	ADVANTAGES	DISADVANTAGES
Face-to-face meeting	Full spectrum of communication, including voice inflection, non-verbal cues, and expressions.	Requires all parties be present. Generally more expensive when travel is necessary.
Video conference	Most of the advantages of a face-to-face meeting except visual cues limited by camera field of view and quality.	Not as intuitive as face-to-face meetings—participants can easily miss non-verbal cues. Requires hardware, software, and network support for each participant's location.
Telephone conversation	Easy for all participants. Low cost to set up.	Absence of non-verbal cues. Less personal than previous options.
Instant messaging	Easy to participate in an informal conversation—especially when the messages are generally simple and time-sensitive. Enables multi-tasking during conversations.	Low attention requirement often means conversations may be fragmented when participants are multi-tasking. Very difficult to convey tone.
Short Message Service (SMS) text messaging	Easy to carry on conversations anywhere. Good when communicating simple messages quickly.	Difficult to convey tone or complex concepts. Most supplemental cues are missing.

Real-Time Communication

The last common type of communication is similar to face-to-face or telephone communication. This type of communication depends on immediate feedback and response. In nearly all cases, real-time communication is less formal than snail mail or store-and-forward communication. Telephone conversations are a common type of real-time communication. All real-time communication simulates face-to-face conversations to some degree. The advantage over other forms of message exchanges is immediate feedback and the opportunity to engage multiple messages in a short period of time. This type of message exchange lends itself well to conversations that are less developed than formal documents. It encourages a back-and-forth style of exchange that allows conversations to develop. This format also works well when conversations depend on answers to questions earlier in the conversation.

Real-time conversation has changed somewhat in the electronic age. While it is easier to connect and carry on an electronic real-time conversation, these formats often lack some of the important cues to detect message tone and intended impact. Table 1-1 lists common real-time communication options along with their advantages and disadvantages.

Although real-time communication is the latest form of informal electronic communication, it may not always be the best method. This is particularly true when dealing with transmission of real-time communication such as **Voice over IP (VoIP)** and **Session Initiation Protocol (SIP)**, which are used by unified communications applications throughout an IP networking infrastructure. Real-time communication is subject to the following time-sensitive requirements:

- **Bandwidth**—The amount or capacity of the number of bits transmitted per second. VoIP and SIP protocols usually require from 24 kbps to 90 kbps.
- **Time delay or latency**—The total amount of time elapsed (queuing, contention, serialization, etc.) from source to destination through the IP network infrastructure, normally measured in milliseconds (mSec). VoIP and SIP protocols usually require from 100 mSec to a maximum of 150 mSec **latency** end-to-end for acceptable speech quality.
- **Packet loss**—The **packet loss** is measured as a percentage of total packets sent. VoIP and SIP protocols can endure packet losses of 1 percent or less, and above that, the degradation of speech quality enters.
- **Packet jitter**—The measure of the average of the deviation from the mean latency of a network. Consistent network performance means low **packet jitter** values. Quality of service or traffic prioritization can help mitigate packet jitter through an IP network to achieve less than 400 mSec end-to-end latency.

The use and deployment of VoIP and SIP as time-sensitive protocols will dictate the need for real-time communication and support for these protocols through an IP network. It is this commingling of real-time communication with store-and-forward communication that requires unique solutions for end-to-end networking and communications connectivity. This is particularly true given that VoIP and SIP are both inherently insecure protocols.

The World Wide Web's Impact on Business

Easy and reliable access to the Internet and the World Wide Web changed more than just how people communicate. It also revolutionized how organizations conduct business. Physical places of business, often called brick-and-mortar stores, now have global reach by extending business to remote customers. The practice of doing business with remote customers over the Internet is commonly called **e-commerce**. E-commerce changed how organizations sell, and the World Wide Web changed how organizations market their goods.

E-commerce Business Models

Today's customers can use e-commerce to buy goods and services from a vendor online. In current business environments, the vendor's presence on the Internet is almost always a Web site. A Web site makes it easy for customers to interact with organizations using generic, standard software and the Internet. Customers can exchange information and

TABLE 1-2 E-commerce business models.

MODEL	DESCRIPTION	FEATURES
Business-to-Consumer (B2C)	Also called business-to-customer, this model describes business activities that involve providing products or services directly to end consumers. The most common B2C activities involve retail sales.	• Typically low volume • Fixed or limited pricing • Little integration with customers' systems
Business-to-Business (B2B)	Describes activities that involve doing business with other businesses. B2B interactions often occur in the supply chain prior to B2C. Common B2B interactions include manufacturers and wholesalers.	• Much higher volume • Price negotiation is common • Integration generally desired or mandatory between participants' systems
Business-to-Government (B2G)	Describes activities that support business activities between commercial organizations and government agencies, also called public sector organizations (PSO)	• Request for proposal (RFP) provides the relationship basis • Prenegotiated price • Strict constraints on allowed products, services, and activities

conduct business activities that used to require a physical presence. They can exchange information of all types, including private data such as checking account or credit card information. The potential for private data exchange means that organizations that conduct e-commerce must take measures to protect the security of their customers' data.

E-commerce provides organizations with more than just the ability to interact with their customers. In fact, e-commerce supports three primary business models. The first model, **Business-to-Consumer (B2C)**,model focuses on conducting business with customers. The second model, **Business to Business (B2B)**, focuses on conducting business with other organizations. The third model, **Business to Government (B2G)**, focuses on doing business with government agencies. Table 1-2 describes the three common e-commerce models.

Solving E-commerce Business Challenges

The World Wide Web elevated the Internet from a large network to a global online market in just a few short years. Very few people could foresee the long-range impact and how it would affect the methods of conducting business. Organizations of all types must now consider the online aspects of advertising, sales, marketing, and customer/partner management. These activities extend the traditional methods of reaching and interacting with customers and partners. Television, radio, print media, and telephones are no longer sufficient to reach out to find customers and meet their changing needs. Today's business demands an online presence, and organizations must respond to these demands to remain competitive. The new challenges that face organizations in today's connected business environment include:

- How to expand business offerings using the World Wide Web
- Converting an existing organization to conduct e-commerce
- Ensuring data security for online customers
- Incorporating online technology into the organization's core business activities
- Using online resources and capabilities to reach new customers

It takes more than just a Web site to solve the many challenges of transforming a traditional business model to an e-commerce model. There are many things to consider and pitfalls along the way. The first important decision is which model will be the primary model. Will the organization become primarily an online entity or will e-commerce support the traditional activities? How will you continue to interact with existing customers? How will you find new customers? These are just some of the questions to get the process started. Organizations have a lot to learn when transitioning to an online model. They have to understand how to use online resources to find new customers and business partners. Once they find new prospects, it is important to understand how to provide the right services to convert them into repeat customers or long-term business partners. Far too many organizations jump into the online world without a plan.

Today's population is generally Internet savvy. That means that they are comfortable using the Internet and the World Wide Web to find products and services. They routinely make online purchases and communicate online. Everyone is not an Internet guru, but most people can tell the difference between a good Web site and one that is difficult to use.

FIGURE 1-10

Transforming a traditional business model into an online model.

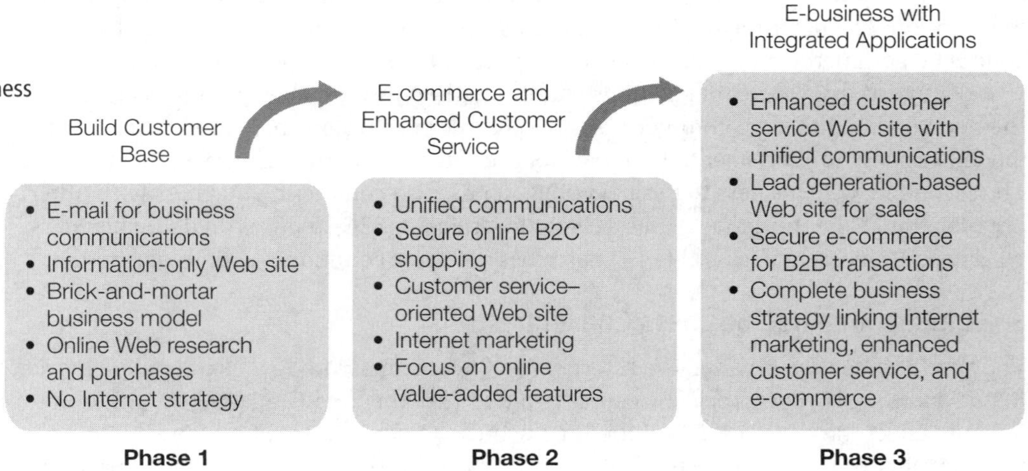

Phase 1 — Build Customer Base
- E-mail for business communications
- Information-only Web site
- Brick-and-mortar business model
- Online Web research and purchases
- No Internet strategy

Phase 2 — E-commerce and Enhanced Customer Service
- Unified communications
- Secure online B2C shopping
- Customer service–oriented Web site
- Internet marketing
- Focus on online value-added features

Phase 3 — E-business with Integrated Applications
- Enhanced customer service Web site with unified communications
- Lead generation-based Web site for sales
- Secure e-commerce for B2B transactions
- Complete business strategy linking Internet marketing, enhanced customer service, and e-commerce

Creating a good Web site to conduct e-commerce can be very difficult. Organizations have to understand their customers and partners and ensure their Web site meets their current needs. A good Web site also should anticipate future user needs and provide the flexibility to change based on demand. The overall goal of a good online presence is really quite simple: "Attract as many people as possible, interest them enough to keep them there, and meet their needs to encourage them to return in the near future." Figure 1-10 shows the process of transforming a traditional business model to an online model.

Customers and partners who find what they want at an organization's online presence will likely continue to do business with that organization. If they can't find what they're looking for, or they find the Web site awkward, they will likely leave the Web site and search for a better one. Retention is the main goal of conducting online business.

Customer Service as a Business Driver

The current trend is to move traditional customer interaction to online interaction. The goal is to use automation to replace as much human interaction as possible. This trend toward a self-service model is one that has developed for over 30 years. Drive-through windows at fast-food restaurants and ATMs at banks gave consumers a taste of low-impact service and self-service. More recently, grocery stores are adding more and more self-service lanes that allow customers to check themselves out and pay for goods. This trend directs online activities as well.

Many of the interactions that large organizations have with the public and their established customers do not require a human. Organizations that automate repetitive customer interactions can reduce the number of humans required to conduct business. Recent years have seen a surge in the number of organizations that rely on automated telephone response systems and online Web-based interactions. Automating interactions with humans can be efficient. However, it also can leave customers and prospects with the impression that the organization doesn't really care about human interaction. In some situations the perceived lack of care ends up resulting in lost customers.

An automated public and customer interaction system that avoids being too impersonal can help organizations to be more effective. Many organizations find the appeal of automated customer support systems too good to pass up. Customer service is an important priority of many organizations as a critical factor to being productive. Implementing online software applications, along with UC components, can help solve much of the customer service challenge. Every organization must keep customer service as a main focus when transitioning to an online presence. Although purely automated systems seem attractive, there is still a need for traditional person-to-person communication. Organizations that pay attention to their customer and partner needs generally end up developing transition plans that include simplified processes and support real-time information exchange.

There is no single plan to transition from a traditional business model to an online model. Each organization is unique and has specific needs. However, there are some common customer service challenges many organizations face. The following list presents some of the more common customer service challenges and goals organizations must address:

1. **Increase organizational revenue (and the bottom line)**—Increase the customer base and retain new and existing customers to increase overall revenue.
2. **Measure customer service effectiveness**—Develop a strategy to monitor, measure, and store trending data related to customer satisfaction, retention, and repeat business.
3. **Increase customer service offerings through using multiple types of communication**—Customers and partners may want to use different types of communication at different times and for different reasons. Provide multiple communication paths that use different types of communication to help meet specific needs with different priorities. Multiple types of communication can include priority methods for high-volume customers and customer-driven choices based on desired response time.
4. **Increase customer service system effectiveness**—Incorporate automation when appropriate to help route customer service calls to the best destination. The goal is for a customer to find a resolution without navigating through several support options or making several calls. First-call, first-destination resolution means the customer gets to the correct answer directly. Call monitoring and feedback help identify calls that do not provide first-call, first-destination resolution.

Many organizations such as Amazon, DELL, Apple Computer's iTunes, Western Union, eBay, Priceline.com, Domino's Pizza, and UPS have created e-business models. Each organization uses Web sites as the main way to reach customers all around the world. Their customers make purchases with enhanced customer service delivery built into the Web sites. Most of these companies leverage self-service to reduce the need for customer service personnel. Users can accomplish many regular activities, such as ordering products and managing their accounts, all using self-service actions. Real-time access to customer service agents through voice or video chat, and IM chat can enhance the experience for high value customers.

E-commerce has introduced new ways to conduct business. Customers can carry out many traditional business activities from a company's Web site. The list of available activities is long, but here are just a few of the actions customers can accomplish online:

- **Buy a computer**—Customers can browse many computer products, configure a computer to meet specific needs, purchase the computer, and have it shipped to any address with different delivery speed options. Online computer sales represent the majority of all computer sales.

- **Purchase music and videos**—Customers can purchase and immediately download digital copies of nearly any music or video product in existence. Retail music and video stores still exist, but their numbers are declining.
- **Rent movies and video games**—A fairly recent group of companies offer online movie and video game rentals. Customers can request that physical copies of media be sent to their home or that they watch some video titles online. Either way, customers don't have to visit a physical store to rent media.
- **Send money electronically to anywhere in the world**—Anyone can send money to another person with only a credit card. Online companies will send money to an individual or organization using one of several different delivery options.
- **Purchase travel**—Many travelers now use travel Web sites to purchase airplane tickets and make hotel and rental-car arrangements. Online travel sites give consumers and businesses the ability to find options for their specific needs without involving a human travel agent.
- **Shop for real estate**—Many real estate listings now appear on the Internet. Customers can review pictures and videos before e-mailing a real estate agent to see a property.

Organizations can't survive very long without customers. Customer service must be a primary focus for any organization that plans to survive and grow. While online customer service offerings aren't the only way to find and keep customers, they are becoming nearly indispensable. A solid online customer service strategy is becoming more important as consumers demand online solutions. Organizations that ignore this trend likely will find their customers migrating to organizations that embrace online presence and effective customer service.

CHAPTER SUMMARY

Communication technology has changed in dramatic ways in just the last century. These changes have had far more impact than just giving us more options. The new technology of communication has transformed the ways in which we interact with one another. Online capabilities have made it possible to stay in touch with people all over the world. This allows relationships to exist with little or no face-to-face interaction. The new communication methods reach far beyond personal relationships as well. Hyperconnectivity has revolutionized the way we conduct business. Businesses are more connected with each other and their customers. They can be more responsive and more in tune with what their customers want and need. In short, the technological advances in communications have essentially rewritten the rules on how to conduct business. Understanding the technology of communication is mandatory to running a successful business in today's economy.

KEY CONCEPTS AND TERMS

Analog
Answering machine
Bandwidth
Beeper
Broadband
Business process management (BPM)
Business to Business (B2B)
Business to Consumer (B2C)
Business to Government (B2G)
Digital
Dynamic Host Configuration Protocol (DHCP)
E-commerce
Facsimile device
Hyperconnectivity
Internet
Internet Protocol (IP)
Internet service provider (ISP)
IP address
Latency
Mobile phone
Packet jitter
Packet loss
Pager
Personal digital assistant (PDA)
Private IP address
Real-time communication
Reliable communication
Session Initiation Protocol (SIP)
Snail mail
Store-and-forward communication
Unified communications (UC)
Unique local address (ULA)
Voice over IP (VoIP)
World Wide Web

CHAPTER 1 ASSESSMENT

1. Prior to 1990, nearly all electronic communication used analog communications and transmission techniques.

A. True
B. False

2. Which device became popular in the 1970s that enabled the first electronic version of storing messages for playback at a later time?

A. Telephone
B. Fax machine
C. Telephone answering machine
D. Pager

3. Which device became popular in the 1980s that enabled users to send and receive printed documents using analog telephone lines?

A. Telephone
B. Fax machine
C. Answering machine
D. Pager

4. Who was the originator behind what we know of as the Internet today?

A. IBM
B. US Department of Defense
C. US Federal Communications Commission
D. AT&T

5. Which of the following IP address ranges is *not* a private IPv4 address range?

A. 10.0.0.0 to 10.255.255.255
B. 152.0.0.0 to 152.255.255.255
C. 172.16.0.0 to 172.16.255.255
D. 192.168.0.0 to 192.168.255.255

6. A network's ________ server provides private IP addresses to devices dynamically.

A. Authentication
B. DHCP
C. Office automation
D. Syslog

7. The formal process of aligning business processes and mapping each one to software applications and IT solutions is called configuration management (CM).
   A. True
   B. False

8. Unified communications (UC) is the process of bringing all communication mediums together into a unified structure.
   A. True
   B. False

9. ________ communication is faster than snail mail but slower than immediate or ________ communication.

10. Which of the following is *not* a unified communications application and service?
    A. SMS text messaging
    B. Video conferencing
    C. Collaboration
    D. IM chat
    E. Audio conferencing

11. Which of the following impacts real-time communication on an IP networking infrastructure?
    A. Bandwidth
    B. Time delay or latency
    C. Packet loss
    D. Packet jitter
    E. All of the above

12. Why must you handle VoIP and SIP protocols uniquely through an IP networking infrastructure?
    A. IP networks have latency and packet loss when congested
    B. They are insecure protocols
    C. They are used for real-time communication and applications
    D. End-to-end time delay and latency will degrade voice quality performance
    E. All of the above

13. Which of the following is *not* a typical e-commerce model?
    A. B2B
    B. B2C
    C. B2D
    D. B2G

14. Which of the following business drivers can be addressed with unified communications?
    A. Driving incremental services revenue
    B. Implementing managed services revenue
    C. Enhancing customer service delivery
    D. Lowering operational costs

15. Businesses that transform to the World Wide Web with an Internet presence and an e-commerce solution require an e-customer service and self-serve customer service delivery strategy.
    A. True
    B. False

CHAPTER 2

Solving Today's Business Communication Challenges

PEOPLE TODAY HAVE VERY DIFFERENT COMMUNICATION EXPECTATIONS than they did even a few years ago. Today's public expects immediate responses to questions. They expect that their concerns will be addressed just as fast. They want to feel their situation is worth an organization's undivided attention. Organizations must be more responsive. They must provide the reassurance that they are ready to meet customer needs. They also must support effective communications with increasingly responsive personnel and business partners.

All types of organizations must interact with people to meet their objectives. They have to be in touch with their employees, partners, and customers. In short, they need to communicate to get anything done. Each type generally encounters challenges that are specific to that business. In this chapter you will learn about the major types of organizations. You will also learn the communication problems unique to each one. This chapter also covers how to solve them and create technical requirements to empower each solution.

Chapter 2 Topics

This chapter covers the following topics and concepts:

- The enterprise business communication challenges found in many organizations
- Communication problems unique to government agencies
- How small and medium-sized business (SMB) communications differ from those of other organizations
- Small office/home office (SOHO) communication challenges
- How to transform communication requirements into network requirements

Chapter 2 Goals

When you complete this chapter, you will be able to:

- Recognize top-of-mind enterprise business communication challenges
- Identify communication problems unique to government agencies
- Address communication challenges common in small- and medium-sized businesses
- List communication problems frequently found in small offices and home offices
- Transform communication requirements into technical and connectivity requirements

Solving Enterprise Business Communication Challenges

An **enterprise business** faces more challenges today than ever before. The growth of **small- and medium-sized business (SMB)** has forced enterprises to use their size to compete. But these businesses cannot rely on their size alone. They can use their greater resources to meet problems in ways that other organizations cannot. In some cases, bigger is better. For example, larger enterprises may be able to negotiate lower unit prices for network products or services. This is due to increased use volume. Larger size provides both advantages and disadvantages. Larger organizations may benefit from economies of scale—volume pricing, for instance—but they are often more geographically spread out than smaller organizations. This means that they may require more creative solutions to communicate effectively throughout the organization.

Enterprise businesses—those with 500 or more employees—often encounter unique challenges due to their size. They generally have more than one office. In fact, most have multiple offices. They often are spread across the world. It often means that offices operate in different time zones. They also draw workers from different cultures. One problem they face is simply ensuring that communication is effective. This means effective communication within the organization and with the many customers and partners. Technology can help achieve this goal if used carefully to solve challenges.

These organizations encounter three main operational challenges:

- Reducing costs
- Improving team collaboration
- Providing better customer service

Organization Classifications

This section focuses on communication problems that are specific to enterprise organizations. Later sections in this chapter will address other types of organizations. There are many ways to classify these entities. Different regions use different numbers to separate the types. This chapter uses the following categories to classify organizations:

- **Enterprise organization**—An organization with more than 500 employees
- **Medium sized organization**—An organization with more than 100, but fewer than 500, employees
- **Small organization**—An organization with fewer than 100 employees
- **Small office/home office (SOHO)**—A home office or location with fewer than 10 employees
- **Government organization**—A government agency

Each of these problems is at least partially related to communications. They are also interrelated. It is difficult to address one of the challenges without impacting at least one other challenge. The goal is to address all three problems with minimum effort and disruption to normal business operations.

You learned about unified communications (UC) in the previous chapter. UC can address three of the most important business challenges. It addresses them by making communication more efficient. Organizations that use multimodal forms of communication (see Figure 2-1) often find new ways to improve business processes. For example, cell phones and personal digital assistants (PDAs) integrate many workstation features and functions. Many cell phone and PDA users can surf the Web as easily as workstation

FIGURE 2-1
Today's multimodal business communication options.

users. Current PDA user interfaces may not have as many features. But the experience is improving all the time. Likewise, today's desktop phones have matured to support more than just phone calls. This type of integration is easier and more common due to a standardized signaling protocol, Session Initiation Protocol (SIP). UC and applications such as Yahoo Messenger utilize the SIP protocol for presence, IM chat, collaboration, and audio/video conferencing.

The SIP protocol makes it possible for organizations to combine different communication features and functions. This approach helps enterprise businesses identify new opportunities. One common technology solution is to use IP networks to carry voice conversations. Instead of using standard analog lines, many organizations now use voice over IP (VoIP) for telephone traffic. VoIP makes it easier to focus on a single network to handle all communications. An enterprise business can benefit from a VoIP and UC solution that combines its communications. This results in smaller network hardware requirements. Using multiple modes of business communications gives the enterprise the ability to break up different processes into smaller parts. This encourages reusing software in newer applications. In personnel response-oriented organizations, such as health care or military agencies, decreased response time could be the difference between life and death.

The overall business goal for enterprise organizations is to address their most important challenges. They must identify their specific problems. Then they must select the best solutions. UC provides the flexibility and power to develop a blended solution that fits a specific enterprise. A solution that works in one will likely not work as well in another. Each business must start the process with a clear understanding of the challenges that organization faces. The best approach identifies the problems and then formulates business solutions. Then you can develop technical solutions to satisfy the business solution.

Each type of enterprise organization runs into different kinds of challenges. The following sections look at some of those problems.

Banking and Financial Services Challenges

Banking and financial services enterprises provide a wide range of customer services—see Figure 2-2. Most involve money or investments. Services can include any of the following:

- Maintaining bank accounts
- Managing investment portfolios
- Trading in securities
- Making loans and mortgages
- Financial planning

Government regulations control many of the activities of banking and financial services enterprises. They drive many of the interactions between these entities and their customers. Regulations also affect how they communicate among themselves.

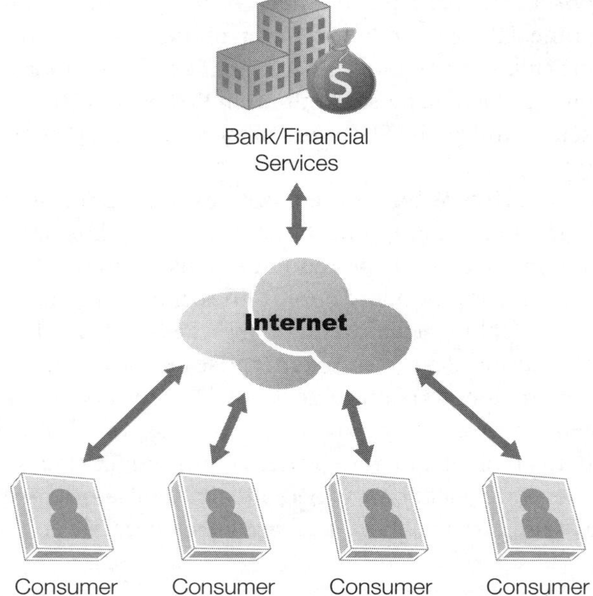

FIGURE 2-2

Banking and financial services business.

For example, suppose a public company decides to split its stock. It may choose to do so to allow more investors to buy shares. Regulations set communication requirements to make sure all stockholders are aware of the proposed change. Banking and financial services enterprises must make sure they include all regulations in their communication plan. But there is more to a successful plan than just meeting regulations. Successful enterprises in any market understand their customers. Then they adopt solutions to meet their needs.

These financial services enterprises have to satisfy several specific customer needs in their communications. Since they handle their clients' money, **confidentiality** and **integrity** are very important. Confidentiality is the assurance that only authorized users can access, or view, data. Integrity is the assurance that only authorized users can modify data. In fact, customer communications should address the following:

- **Timeliness**—Information should be as current as possible. Financial information can be very volatile. Any old information can cost customers money.
- **Security**—Much of the information these enterprises store and exchange with customers is private. They must make sure that only authorized users view or modify private information.
- **Clarity and reliability**—Banking and financial services generally handle large amounts of market data. The volume is too large for most customers to understand or digest. One of the greatest challenges in their communications is to provide summarized data. It needs to be easy to understand and reliable.

These problems can be difficult to address. One of the most promising strategies to satisfy all communication requirements is well-planned UC. It makes it possible to combine several simpler methods to deliver a complete communication solution. The banking and financial services market is moving to online transactions. UC makes it possible for them to meet their changing customer needs. Some examples of UC solutions for these customers include:

- **Chat or audio/video conferencing at automated teller machines (ATMs)**—Traditional **ATMs** offer limited menu options. UC-enabled ATMs can offer audio and video communications with a customer service representative. UC makes it possible to extend a full-service experience to ATMs. Embedding UC within ATM menus provides integrated real-time access to customer service and customer banking information.
- **Integrated analysis training and tools**—Banking and financial services customers are starting to make more of their own financial decisions. They need tools to analyze market conditions. They also need training to use the tools. UC solutions can make it easy for customers to use analysis tools, and view online, context-sensitive instructional videos. They also can initiate chat sessions with customer service representatives to answer time-sensitive questions.
- **Multimodal trade alerts and execution**—Many investors define alerts to let them know about certain market conditions. Multimodal communication makes it easier to decide how the enterprise sends alerts and receives responses. Users can choose to create alerts from an interactive Web page. They can also send them directly to a PDA. Likewise, users may choose to include response links in alerts. These make it easy to respond to an event. One response may be to immediately enter a buy or sell stock order.

UC provides the flexibility to construct a solution that meets customer needs. Well-planned UC can also reduce costs and increase collaboration. Planning to achieve clear goals is the key to a successful UC solution.

Health Care and Patient Care Services Challenges

In some ways, health care and patient care services, as shown in Figure 2-3, are similar to banking and financial services. The same three main concerns apply. Information related to health care and patient care must be:

- **Timely**—Health care involves life-threatening situations. It demands real-time access to key persons and health care information. The information should be as current as possible. It needs to be accessible in real-time. Patient status changes over time and as a patient responds to treatment. Old information may cause incorrect decisions. These can have disastrous results.

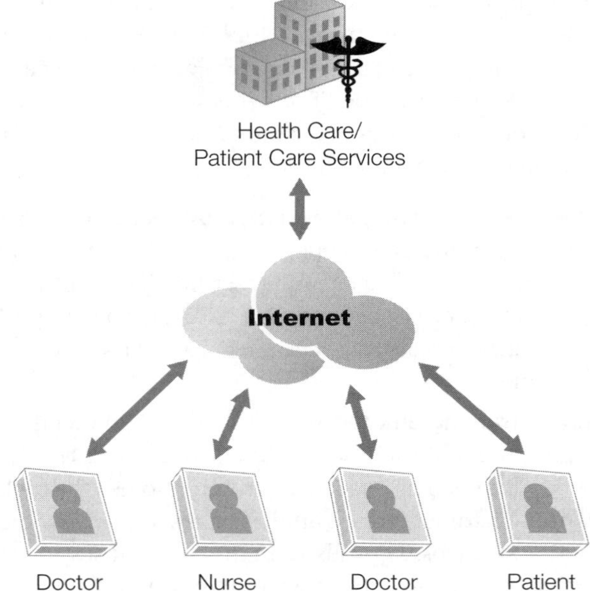

FIGURE 2-3
Health care and patient care services business.

- **Secure**—Much of the information these organizations handle is private. Governments are adding more regulations to protect medical data privacy. Organizations must make sure only authorized users can view or modify private information.
- **Clear and reliable**—These businesses generally handle large amounts of medical and patient data. The volume is too large and technical for most patients to understand or digest. To be effective, they must try to give summarized and accurate data to patients and practitioners. Making it reliable and easy to understand is one of the greatest communication challenges in this industry.

A primary goal of these organizations is to enhance patient care services. One way to do this is to provide the right medical expert with the right information when it is needed. Another common goal is to eliminate human delays in life-threatening situations. Removing them can help minimize medical diagnosis and treatment errors. UC can support secure, real-time medical and patient care services. It can help save lives.

Medical professionals, including first responders, doctors, and nurses, can benefit from UC solutions. They can gain unprecedented access to critical information. UC can empower the following real-time communication capabilities to enhance patient care services:

- Access to accurate and pertinent patient health care information and status
- Access to medical specialists and experts to provide critical, time-sensitive input
- Self-service patient services delivered via Web applications

The Cost of Poor Communication

The Yale School of Medicine estimated in 2006 that there was a 14.9 percent chance of medical error when there were human delays in distributing medical information. The same school also stated that as many as 44,000 to 98,000 deaths per year in the United States are partially due to preventable medical error. Health care and patient care organizations want to lower these numbers as much as possible. UC can help achieve those goals.

UC solutions can provide many benefits to these organizations. They range from saving lives to making patient record maintenance easier. UC helps solve problems that enhance the organization's bottom line and the quality of its patients' lives.

K–12 and Higher Education Services Challenges

The communication challenges in educational organizations (see Figure 2-4) are unique as well. The data they handle is not as time-sensitive as financial or medical data. Yet its integrity and confidentiality are just as important. As with the previous two types of organizations, regulations place limits on how they handle some types of data. Much of the information K–12 and higher education services businesses handle is **Personally identifiable information (PII)**. PII is any data that can uniquely identify a specific person. Many local and federal regulations define PII. They limit what PII is accessible and who can access it.

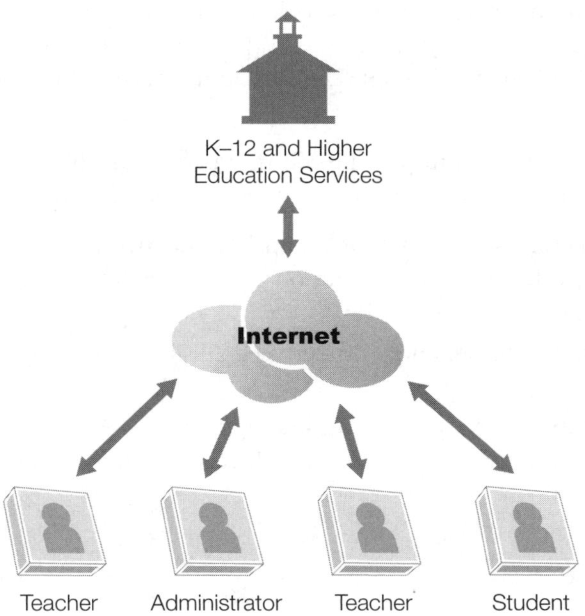

FIGURE 2-4
K–12 and higher education services business.

Educational PII is data that relates to individual performance. Careful control is necessary to prevent disclosure. It can also prevent misuse of the information. Integrity is important as well. Missing educational information can be just as much of a problem as good information that leaked out. For example, suppose a person applies for a position as a college professor. The prospective employer would want to verify that the applicant holds the degree required for the position. The prospective employer likely would contact the school from which the applicant received the degree. The school could verify the degree only after verifying their own stored graduation records. Missing or altered data could cause problems for the applicant.

K–12 and higher education services businesses have several unique communication issues. As with the previous types of enterprises, this information must be available when needed. They also must make sure that their information is:

- **Accurate**—Information should reflect the student's current educational status. An individual's status changes over time. Up-to-date information provides the basis for accurate assessments. Old information can lead to misunderstandings and poor decisions. For example, some institutions exempt students with certain grade averages from final exams. Accurate grade averages for all students help determine who is exempt.
- **Secure**—Much of the educational information is PII and must be protected from disclosure or changes. Organizations must make sure that only authorized users can view or modify PII.
- **Clear and available**—Having accurate and secure educational information is only the first step. Authorized individuals must be able to access data summaries of educational information. This is necessary to determine status and make future decisions. One of the biggest challenges to these businesses is to securely provide the level of summary or detailed information. They also must make it easy for authorized users to access data.

There are several ways to use multimodal communication to address the needs of students and other educational system users. Some innovative ideas include:

- **IM chat and audio/video conferencing during registration**—Students often need extra help to get through the registration process. Such help can reduce later schedule changes.
- **Real-time remote advisement**—Students can discuss course options with advisers remotely.
- **Automated response system for common questions**—A Web-based method to quickly answer common questions can reduce stress. It also can lighten a customer agent's workload.

- **Automated student/faculty interaction application**—Applications that automate interactions between students and faculty provide documentation of conversations. These same applications can automatically handle issues that arise. They can make it easy to dispute a response and involve a moderator. In many such cases, manually working through the process of resolving disputes is more time consuming than resolving the actual dispute. UC solutions can help streamline the process.
- **Interactive grade distribution and explanation**—Centralized systems to distribute grades make it easy for students and parents to see all the grades in one place. Integrated explanations can provide any necessary additional data. They use prerecorded videos and real-time communications with counselors.

UC solutions can make it easy for users to get answers to their questions. Unlike other enterprises, educational organizations may provide second-hand information. Especially in K–12 organizations, the primary information requesters are often not the students. In many cases, the parents are the more frequent requesters. Systems must maintain required security while still allowing authorized users access. A well-planned UC solution can automate many of the controls and access paths. It can make it easier for users to get what they need at any time.

Commercial Retail Products and Services Challenges

Commercial retail products and services businesses, as shown in Figure 2-5, are probably the most familiar of the businesses in this chapter. All businesses of this type perform the same basic task. They provide a product or service to a customer. They also encourage the customer to return in the future. It sounds simple. But it takes a lot of planning to get it right.

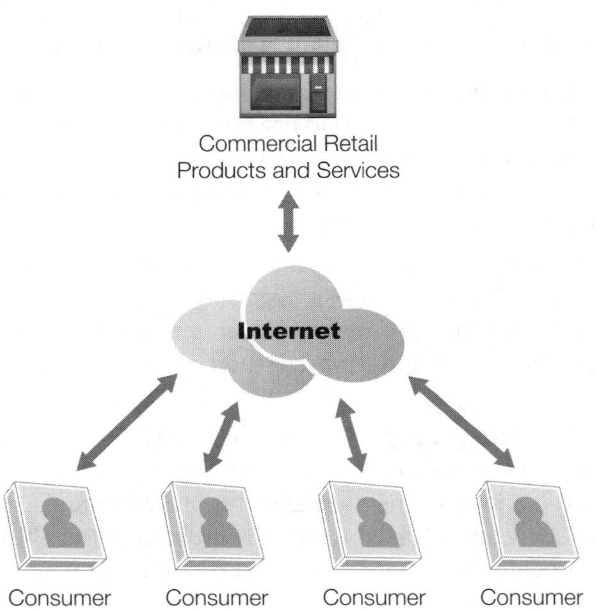

FIGURE 2-5
Commercial retail products and services business.

These businesses operate in a crowded market. There is intense competition for customers. Today's businesses have found that the pursuit and retention of customers is the primary goal.

Retail businesses focus as much on customer service as any other type of organization. As the business environment changes, these organizations must change with it. The alternative is to be left behind in a shrinking market. In the past, a **retailer** could advertise in a few newspapers and on the radio or TV. Those efforts were enough to bring in the customers. Today's consumers do a lot more research before making a purchase. It is common for consumers to shop online for the best price before buying even moderately priced products or services. The final purchase decision depends on several factors, including:

- **Purchase price**—The product or service price is a large factor in the buying decision, but not the only factor.
- **Availability**—A great deal is a great deal only if the product or service is available when you want it. If you need a clothes dryer door seal today, you can't wait another week to get a cheaper product.
- **Shipping cost**—Even if you find a better price online than the price at a local retail store, shipping costs may push the total higher. Consumers are becoming more careful to factor in the cost of shipping into their buying decisions.
- **After-sales support**—This is where businesses can show how they are different. Consumers like to feel good about purchasing from a business. Many businesses invest substantial effort to make customers feel secure when they purchase products or services from them. This is where customer service contributes to the bottom line.

Retail businesses have found that UC solutions allow them to provide more sophisticated customer service. Better customer service is often a selling point. It allows businesses to attract and retain more customers. The main challenges to retail businesses are:

- **Reaching out to new customers**—Traditional methods of advertising are no longer good enough. Today's retailers have to use new methods to reach out to a connected world. Social media and network-based communication can help reach more potential customers. The most successful businesses work to identify new prospects. Then they convert them into customers.
- **Standing out from other businesses**—Innovation draws attention. Having the "best" Web site is an honor that doesn't last very long. It won't be long before competitors mimic the innovative parts of a successful Web presence. The truly innovative businesses constantly improve their processes to stay ahead of the competition.
- **Meeting existing customer needs**—Customer needs are not static. They change as the environment changes. For example, several years ago shipping information became easy to access. Customers realized this. They demanded that shipping rates and delivery times be integrated into online purchasing Web sites. Retailers have to continually update their processes to meet current customer needs.

- **Keeping customers informed of news and updates**—The most innovative features don't mean much unless prospects and customers know about them. Businesses have to reach out to new and existing customers to keep them informed of the latest news and updates. Businesses can use e-mail, social networks, and even traditional methods to keep the public informed.

The good news for retail businesses is that technology can help meet these problems. UC provides a flexible framework that allows businesses to create solutions that meet the needs of customers. It helps to attract a steady stream of new customers. Some UC offerings to meet customer service challenges include:

- **IM chat, audio, or video conferencing to provide live customer service**—Many Web sites offer visitors the option to interact with a live customer service agent. Sites are starting to offer self-service browsing combined with live audio, video, and IM chat. Retail businesses are combining communication methods more frequently. Businesses commonly send messages to new and existing customers using multiple methods. Some methods include e-mail, phone messages, and SMS text messages. Customers that receive the same message multiple times, such as a sale or special pricing alert, may view it as being more important.
- **Online ordering with flexible delivery options**—Customers can order a meal online by simply visiting a restaurant Web site. They can securely purchase the meal with their credit card and then have the meal delivered to their door. UC-oriented Web sites can keep the customer updated on the status of the order in real time. The application can trigger an e-mail or SMS text message to the customer when the driver leaves the restaurant with the order. An automated delivery notification system can provide updates to the customer's e-mail or text message device as often as desired. Some restaurants are asking for real-time customer feedback. They want to know how they are meeting the customers' needs at the time of service.
- **Extensive purchasing assistance to increase add-on sales**—Retail Web sites can direct and increase online sales. These applications are already suggesting additional purchases based on related items and customer preferences. Integrating UC allows retailers to combine suggested products with related product information Web pages and video. They also can integrate immediate access to customer service representatives via chat or audio/video conference and comparisons of selected products. Many consumers respond well to add-on suggestions. They increase their purchases to include more than what they intended. Today's biggest online retailers already make add-on suggestions. Look for the "others also purchased" or "you may also like" sections of shopping sites.

Consumers want their shopping experience to be easier and faster. Retail businesses can use UC to meet customer needs in new and innovative ways. Customers demand information at their fingertips. They want Web sites that are easy to use. The most successful retail businesses use communication technology to meet their customer needs. It increases their opportunities to expand and grow.

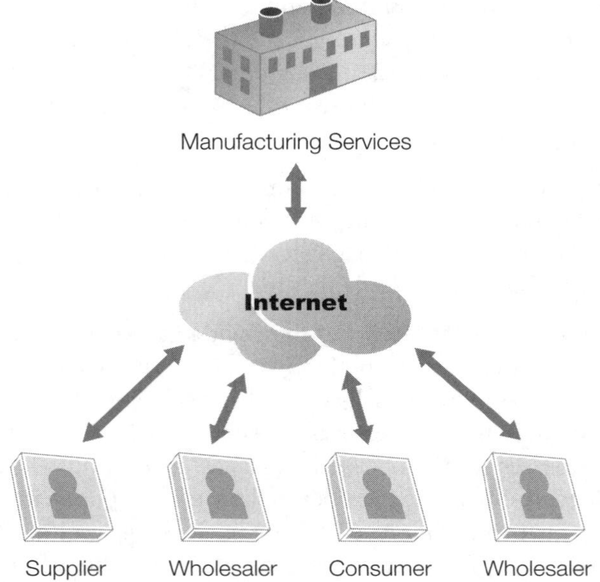

FIGURE 2-6
Manufacturing services business.

Manufacturing Services Challenges

Manufacturing services businesses—see Figure 2-6—transform raw materials or components into finished goods. They generally either assemble or make new products. Their customers can be just about any type of organization, including:

- **Manufacturer**—A component **manufacturer** may provide finished goods to other manufacturerss. For example, an electric motor manufacturer may sell motors to another manufacturer that makes vacuum cleaners. This kind of relationship generally focuses on price, quality, and schedule. Packaging and promotion generally aren't as important when the customer is another manufacturer.
- **Wholesaler**—Many manufacturers sell their finished goods to a **wholesaler**. The wholesaler then distributes the goods to retailers, who in turn sell to consumers. This type of relationship depends on having a good price, a quality product, and keeping up with wholesaler demands. Since the product may end up in a retail setting, packaging is more important. Many manufacturers also provide promotion materials intended for retailers. Manufacturers generally provide a large volume of product and materials to a small number of wholesalers.
- **Retailer**—Manufacturers that sell directly to retailers generally have more work to do than when selling to other manufacturers or wholesalers. Communication and customer service is more important since the number of contacts is likely much larger than with the previous two models.

- **Consumer**—Selling directly to the consumer is a model that requires the same amount of effort as a commercial retail product or services business. Effective customer service is crucial to keep customers satisfied. This type of relationship often only exists in high-value products, such as industrial generators or aircraft.

All of the product and service delivery options require good communication. One of the most important functions of manufacturers is to produce products. Their customers depend on being able to get their finished product. UC can enhance process flow efficiency by incorporating real-time communications throughout the manufacturing, supply chain, and sales order entry inputs. Organizations can streamline the operational process by automating and linking individual activities, such as:

- Sales order entry
- Purchasing
- Supply chain management
- **Just-in-time (JIT)** inventory that the organization purchases or makes when it is needed, and not before
- JIT manufacturing processes

UC and business process management can help eliminate manual and redundant tasks. This can reduce required human input to make decisions. Manufacturers can use technology to develop a system based on policies and decision criteria to streamline processes. Automatic processes can make manufacturing more efficient and reduce sales cycle time. Product sales and manufacturing businesses follow a linear sequence of steps that typically include the following:

1. **Sales**—Before the customer signs a contract, the manufacturer has to complete several important tasks. These background and planning tasks include:
    - Sales proposal
    - Statement of work
    - Solution mapped to IT and UC enablement
    - Calculating total costs (include parts, labor, service, maintenance, and ongoing support)
2. **Get the order**—The customer purchasing department generates a purchase order or requisition to commit the funds for the order.
3. **Enter the sales order**—Enter the confirmed customer order into the computer system and schedule for manufacturing.
4. **Just in time (JIT) make or buy decisions**—Integrated sales order systems can maximize manufacturing schedules by purchasing or making components when needed.
5. **Manufacture products**—Combine raw materials and other components to create or assemble a new product.

Streamlined Sales Order Entry

Manufacturing organizations can streamline the order-to-delivery process. They can do so by using technology in several different ways. For example, they can use UC to provide salespeople with real-time access to pre-sales support specialists and subject matter experts. The goal is to provide the most accurate and timely answers to customer business challenges. UC-based customer service and integrated processes that support remote salespeople can speed up order processing. Remote order processing allows salespeople to manage the sales process in the field instead of waiting until they return to the office.

Organizations can have an advantage when they transform manual tasks into fully automated processes. The benefits of UC and process automation include shortening the order lead time and incorporating JIT inventory and manufacturing. This increases efficiency and reduces costs. Speeding up sales, manufacturing, and delivery increases revenue and gross profit margins.

6. **Package and ship the product**—Package the manufactured product for shipment. Then arrange for product delivery to the customer. This stage also includes final quality assurance activities.
7. **Create invoice and collect payment**—Invoicing generally coincides with completing products. Organizations manage invoices and payments as part of the customer management life cycle.
8. **Post sales and ongoing customer service**—Manufacturers must continue to interact with customers to retain them.

These processes are common in modern manufacturing operations. Many of these steps that are not automated introduce human delays because they require humans to make decisions. Organizations can reduce these delays: They can automate or streamline more of these steps through a faster and easier communications solution.

Travel and Transportation Services Challenges

The last type of enterprise business is travel and transportation services. Although these businesses run into many of the same challenges as commercial retail businesses, they have unique problems. They generally specialize in one of two areas:

- **Travel arrangements**—These organizations make travel arrangements for individuals or groups of people. The most common types involve transportation and lodging. Different organizations may work with clients directly or may provide travel services to those who work for a specific company. The latter generally encounter more restrictions from corporate travel policies. In these cases, the organization has to satisfy the client and sponsoring organization. Trying to please two customers at the same time makes customer service more difficult.

- **Transportation and shipping**—Transporting cargo presents its own challenges. These organizations arrange to transport goods from one location to another. They may handle shipping a large amount of product between two locations. They also may participate in distributing products from one location to many different destinations. These services businesses must satisfy both the shipper and recipient. In one sense they have two customers for each transaction.

Travel and transportation services businesses, shown in Figure 2-7, are commonly brokers. Travel services businesses almost always sell services that connect a service provider with a service consumer. Transportation services businesses may use third parties to transport goods. They also may own their own transportation network, such as UPS and FedEx. Both types of businesses depend on effective customer service to attract and maintain customers. UC solutions can help businesses stay connected with their customers. They also can help respond to their changing needs.

Here is an example of how one of these businesses can use connected technology to meet customer needs. A business traveler visits a hotel Web site to make a reservation. The customer has a frequent traveler account with the hotel chain. The customer's travel preferences are stored in an online profile. The hotel uses the traveler's preferences to set up the reservation with the customer's unique requirements and requests. The hotel reservation system sends a confirmation to the traveler's chosen multimodal communication options. The traveler can choose to receive the confirmation via e-mail or SMS text message, or even have the reservation details sent to a shared online calendar. The hotel also can pre-authorize access to the property's facilities. All the traveler has to do is use a frequent traveler card for that hotel.

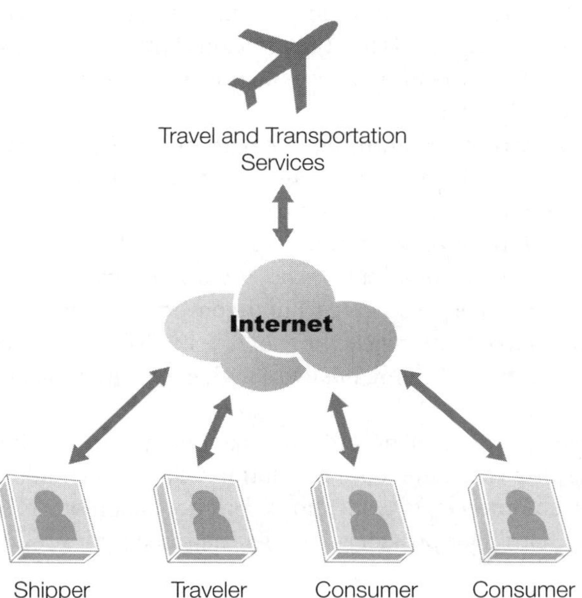

FIGURE 2-7
Travel and transportation services business.

On arrival, the traveler can bypass the registration desk. This hotel allows frequent travelers to use their card with an embedded **radio frequency identification (RFID)** chip. This allows them to complete the automated check-in process at a VIP self-service kiosk. The traveler uses the special card and the unique code sent with the reservation confirmation to complete the check-in process. The kiosk application provides the room number. The traveler uses the same card as the hotel room key.

When the traveler enters his or her room, the hotel automation system configures the room to the desired preferences. For example, the preferences can include Internet access restrictions, television stations, and environmental controls. Preferences also can include having VoIP and UC calls directed to the traveler's laptop via the Internet. They would no longer need to be forwarded through the hotel's telecommunications system. VIP hotel customer service with UC can instantly link to the hotel room phone. This provides real-time access to VIP customer service agents.

This is just one example of how UC and network-related applications can be used for personalized customer service. The organization focused on their customer throughout the entire process, from reservation to fulfillment. Such enhanced delivery drives a positive customer experience.

Solving Government Business Communication Challenges

Conducting business with government agencies requires a different approach. It has its own challenges. Enterprise organizations emphasize a customer service model in which they normally are in touch directly with their customers. They set most of their own policies and rules governing their communication efforts. In some cases, such as health care and patient care services organizations, regulations place limits on communication. Health care information regulations limit the information an organization can release. However, most of the communication between enterprise organizations and customers is governed by the organization.

Government business organizations operate with more restrictions. Regulations govern nearly all aspects of the way they conduct operations. Good communication is still important. In fact, it may be more important than with other types of organizations. The reason for more emphasis on communication is the nature of doing business with government agencies. Government services businesses receive money from government agencies. That means they derive income from taxpayer money, as shown in Figure 2-8. The cost of receiving taxpayer money is the increase in visibility and validation requirements. In short, every aspect of doing business with government agencies is subject to inspection.

Mandatory visibility ensures all organizations doing business with government agencies do so according to the agency's regulations. The government life cycle process differs from the way commercial organizations conduct business. Enterprise business customers generally search for providers to meet their needs for products or services.

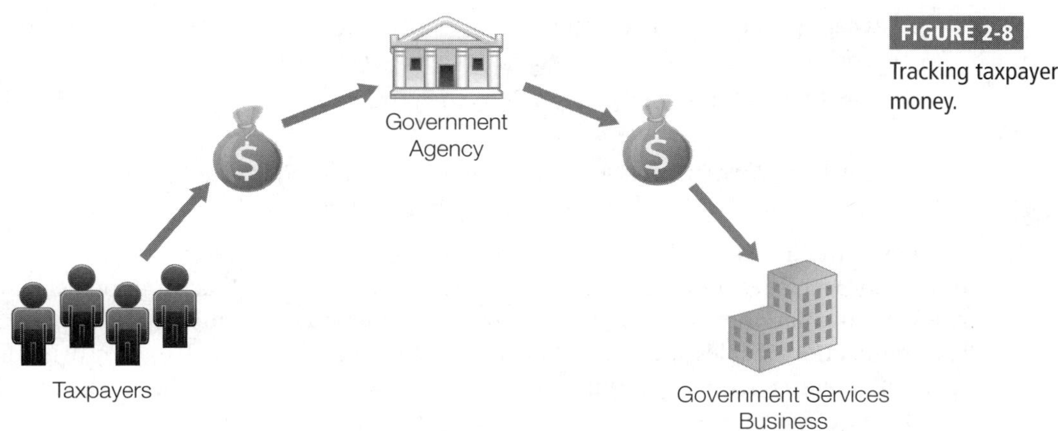

FIGURE 2-8

Tracking taxpayer money.

They conduct the search using any available methods. In many cases, consumers respond to marketing efforts of one or more vendors. The emphasis is on the consumer's response to the vendor's initial efforts. Government agencies do not operate using the same model. Each step in the procurement process follows a set sequence. Government services businesses must comply with this process.

The overall procurement process for government agencies follows the **request for proposal (RFP)** model—see Table 2-1. The RFP model varies from agency to agency, but it shares many common steps. The general steps in the RFP model include:

1. **Identify a need**—An agency formally identifies a need for a product or service. The requirements documents provide an explanation and justification of a problem and its solution.
2. **Acquire funding**—After the agency validates the need, personnel must request approval to fund the solution. This process can be lengthy and may span multiple years. Government agencies have limited budgets. Any procurement must have allocated budgets before it can proceed.
3. **Issue the RFP**—Once the agency allocates funds, it can issue an RFP. The RFP is a formal document that describes the problem and identified solution. It asks organizations to submit proposals to meet the RFP's requirements. The RFP sets the scope and rules that organizations must follow to conduct business with the agency. This document governs many of the communication interactions between the government services businesses and the agency.
4. **Communicate with prospective respondents**—Agencies generally hold formal meetings and provide methods for prospective RFP respondents to ask questions and receive answers. This communication process helps potential respondents develop their proposals.

5. **Accept proposals**—The agency receives all proposals that meet schedule and performance guidelines. It then assesses each proposal.
6. **Select a vendor**—The agency selects the vendor whose proposal best meets its needs.
7. **Post-RFP procedures**—Once the agency selects a vendor, it notifies other respondents. It then moves forward with the proposed project.

The entire RFP process helps avoid wasting taxpayer money. The process requires much more formal communication than other business models. It depends on defined rules and regulations. UC can help government businesses stay compliant. Multimodal communication enables government businesses to communicate with agency personnel without violating necessary regulations. A UC-enabled environment can make sure all contact with agencies is authorized. The UC system can deny unauthorized contacts and redirect authorized contact to authorized individuals. The system can also automatically document each contact and even alert appropriate people when mandatory action is approaching. Many RFPs include mandatory deadlines for many types of communication. A UC system can integrate with a scheduling system to help manage the RFP project.

UC can help organizations manage government projects they have won as well. The increased communication requirements do not stop with the RFP process. Awarded contracts come with additional requirements as well. In fact, agencies may require more communication with vendors once business processes start. Remember that all funds coming from government agencies originate from taxpayers. Agencies must set strict communication requirements for an organization with which they conduct business. UC can help make sure that both the agency and the government business stay compliant with communication regulations.

TABLE 2-1 Request for proposal (RFP).

PHASE	STEPS
Preliminary	• Identify need • Acquire funding
Active	• Issue RFP • Communicate with respondents • Accept proposals
Award	• Select a vendor • Award contract • Manage

Verified Communication

RFPs and subsequent contracts with government agencies often limit communication to specific parties. This helps to avoid any undocumented information exchange. For example, many RFPs specify one or more contacts in the government agency that are authorized to release information that relates to the RFP. UC can help make sure all communication occurs only with the authorized individuals. Unauthorized connection requests can be logged and rejected. In this way, UC can help the organization avoid non-compliance with RFP requirements.

On the other hand, UC can make authorized communication far easier. UC systems can help speed up communication by making sure it selects the best message recipient and contact method. When contracts limit your communication options, it is helpful for a UC system to find the best option. For example, a UC system could determine that an authorized government agency worker be available via IM or video chat. That could save a lot of time if the user had planned just to send an e-mail.

Solving SMB Business Communication Challenges

Small and medium sized businesses (SMBs) generally have fewer than 500 employees. (See Figure 2-9.) They differ from enterprise businesses in their size and the way they conduct business. Although SMBs may have more than one place of business, they generally have far fewer physical locations. SMBs also tend to focus their business activities more narrowly. Their focus may be confined to a geographic region, a specific industry, or even a limited line of products or services. In any case, the limited size and scope of SMBs means they have slightly different communication challenges.

SMBs employ fewer people than enterprise businesses. The culture of a smaller organization tends to be more personable and a little less formal. The smaller size often means there are fewer people between the upper management and entry-level workers. The smaller numbers of employees and business locations make it easier to make informal communication decisions. On the other hand, fewer employees mean that there are fewer people to be in touch with customers and vendors. SMBs face many communications problems due to the way they conduct business, including:

- **Comprehensive customer service**—SMBs do not have the resources that enterprises have. However, they still must provide customer service that meets their customer needs.
- **Marketing reach**—SMBs often compete with larger organizations for customers. Smaller organizations have to leverage their marketing efforts to remain competitive.

FIGURE 2-9

Small and medium sized business (SMB).

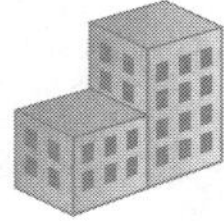

Medium-Sized Business
100 to 500 employees

Small Business
Fewer than 100 employees

- **Limited customer base**—SMBs can normally carry only a fraction of the customers that large organizations can. Smaller customer bases mean successes, and setbacks, tend to be more visible.
- **Competing demands for budget**—Smaller budgets and fewer budget categories mean every expenditure competes with other business needs. A major SMB challenge is to make sure that budget dollars provide the highest return on investment (ROI) possible.
- **SMB perception**—Even though the SMB is smaller than the enterprise business, it is important that it not appear small or limited. Customers and partners need to perceive that the SMB can meet their needs.

UC solutions can help SMBs solve many of the challenges that are unique to this type of organization. Combining communication methods provides the SMB with the ability to leverage limited resources. UC isn't a simple solution to all problems. But it can provide a vehicle to solve the most visible issues. A well-planned UC solution can help the SMB in many ways, including:

- **Multimodal communication**—Providing employees, partners, and customers with the ability to be in touch in multiple ways makes communication easier. Employees can initiate a quick group IM chat and seamlessly switch to a video conference to address issues as the conversation becomes more complex. Customers can send an e-mail asking for support. They can receive a response with a link to a prerecorded video of a solution. The video also could contain a link to initiate a live chat session for additional information.

- **Comprehensive customer service**—UC can help SMBs address a wide range of customer needs with limited customer service personnel. Integrated automation leverages personnel to service more customers. The customer and partner perception of good service and support is historically an important factor in retaining customers and partners.
- **Reach more prospects**—Integrating automation makes reaching a wider range of prospects possible. It is easy to send out thousands of e-mails that advertise a product or service. The trick is in sending the e-mails to the right recipients and then handling the responses efficiently. UC can help in both situations. A good UC environment helps assure prospects that the SMB is ready to handle their needs and questions.
- **Maximize resources**—UC environments exist on the concept of using networks for multiple modes of communication. Empowering the SMB network to carry all communication traffic maximizes the investment in the network infrastructure. At the same time it relieves the need for multiple communication solutions. SMBs can focus budget resources on an infrastructure that serves multiple needs.
- **"Large company" perception**—UC can make an organization appear much larger than it really is. Customers who can find solutions to issues anytime and anywhere are likely to perceive that the organization employs enough people to meet their needs. The reality may be that their customer service application is largely automated. Regardless of the actual size, effective customer service gives the impression that the company is a large organization.
- **Measurable feedback**—UC makes the process of monitoring communication easier. Monitoring interactions and resolutions makes it possible to evaluate how well the organization meets its customer needs. Feedback is an important part of the customer service model. Providing advanced customer service is important. Getting informative feedback is better. Even negative feedback helps the organization make changes that improve the overall process.

Despite the unique challenges of SMBs, UC solutions can help them compete in a dynamic market. A solid UC plan can empower SMBs to focus on their customers and meet their changing needs. Effective customer service makes it possible for SMBs to compete with the larger enterprises. UC provides the ability for SMBs to service their customers as effectively as any other organization.

Solving SOHO Business Communication Challenges

The **small office/home office (SOHO)**, shown in Figure 2-10, consists of a small number of people in a single location. SOHO organizations have 10 or fewer employees. SOHO locations are growing in numbers as telecommuting and remote access become more popular. The SOHO is an attractive model for new businesses or independent contractors.

FIGURE 2-10
Small office/home office (SOHO) business.

The flexibility of inexpensive and lightweight office equipment and easy Internet access make SOHOs accessible and popular. It doesn't take much money or effort to set up a SOHO. All you need is an Internet connection, a computer, and a few office supplies to get you started.

The ultimate lightweight office is the neighborhood coffee shop. Many small business owners and independent contractors run their initial operations from a laptop using the coffee shop's wireless Internet connection. While this model is the extreme SOHO, it is a model that is becoming more common. The SOHO model provides unparalleled flexibility. It also presents new challenges. The compactness and lightweight nature of the SOHO causes them to encounter many of the same problems of SMBs, plus some unique communication challenges, including:

- **Competing with the enterprises and SMBs**—The challenge of the SOHO competing with the larger organizations is an important one. Most of the SOHO activities focus on satisfying customer needs without appearing too small. SOHOs compete for the same customers as the enterprise and SMB organizations.
- **Reaching the customer**—Limited capabilities can make reaching customers difficult. SOHOs have to focus their efforts on methods that provide the greatest positive response to their marketing efforts.
- **Managing time**—Spending time on mundane or unproductive tasks can rob a SOHO of valuable productive time. An organization with very few people is extremely sensitive to the impact of wasted time. Managing time well directly relates to profitability.
- **Operating on a limited budget**—SOHOs generally do not have large budgets and cannot absorb much waste. These organizations have to carefully decide how they spend their limited budgets. Each expenditure should have a direct impact on the organization's success.
- **Meeting customer needs**—The SOHO's success ultimately depends on how well it meets customer needs. While this goal is the same as all other types of organizations, the small SOHO size and limited resources make this a crucial primary goal.

Today's SOHO can exist due to technology. It is possible to carry all of the items necessary to run a business in a single container. More and more small business owners carry their primary business environments around in a backpack or messenger bag. Many businesses start as single-person endeavors. They grow to respond to the business's success. This growth normally starts by adding one or two people and establishing a permanent location. The early locations for growing businesses often have few of the amenities of larger offices. The SOHO's limited budget often allows only minimal infrastructure. This shoestring environment can benefit from a solid UC solution in ways that other organizations may not. Technology and UC solutions can help SOHOs solve their unique problems in many ways, including:

- **Extending organic communication**—Many SOHOs grow from single-person businesses or small partnerships. These organizations started with very informal communication that likely occurred face to face. Growing companies often lose the richness of informal communication. UC can provide easy communication using different modes, such as IM or video chat, to encourage informal communication. UC makes this possible even as personnel separate into different office spaces.
- **Providing a professional appearance**—Many small organizations provide a small organization appearance. Most customers want to conduct business with professional organizations. UC solutions can provide a large organization professional appearance. Customers and partners contact the SOHO via a UC solution that looks like a large enterprise. Multiple communication options and the ability to reach the right person present the image of professionalism.
- **Leveraging limited resources**—UC solutions can help maximize limited personnel and processing resources. Automated UC components can handle some of the customer and prospect inquiries without human interaction. That allows personnel to focus on the most productive activities. Customers like the ability to get direct answers to their questions. That's the case even if the answers come from automated resources.
- **Responding to customer needs**—The most effective result of UC solutions is the ability to respond better to customer needs. Customer service focuses on meeting customer needs and retaining customers. Every organization is different. It must use different measures to meet its customer needs. The SOHO has limited resources but is generally in more direct contact with customers. This direct contact means they generally have a better idea of what their customers want and need. UC helps the SOHO deliver the right solutions by making it easier to stay connected to customers.
- **Reaching new customers**—Integrated UC solutions can automate much of the process of reaching out to new prospects. Automated e-mail and social network messages help reach targeted prospects. Web sites with demonstration videos, interactive activities, and online customer service make even the smallest SOHO appealing to prospective customers. As is the case with all organizations, reaching new prospects and then turning them into customers is crucial to long-term survival.

UC can use existing resources to provide exceptional levels of customer service. Smaller organizations that wisely use technology can compete with the customer-care offerings of much larger organizations. The SOHO organization can enter the market and compete with organizations of any size. The results aren't automatic, and they take substantial planning and effort. But the positive results are possible. A well-planned UC solution can enhance limited resources to provide full customer service in any industry. The key is to understand the organization's customer needs. Then develop the right solutions to meet those needs.

Transforming Communication Requirements Into Networking Requirements

Organizations of all sizes and purposes have communication problems. These challenges differ among organizations. All result in a need for better internal and external communication. Effective communication helps ensure an organization's health and ongoing growth. UC can offer many solutions to various problems. However, a poorly planned UC solution is not really a solution at all.

UC provides a technology solution to a business problem. It is crucial that organizations not view UC as a solution to a technology problem. In fact, UC can create its own technology problems. The best strategy for implementing the best communication solution is to follow these steps, shown in Figure 2-11:

1. Identify the business problem.
2. Formulate a business solution.
3. Develop or acquire a technology solution that enables the business solution.

Many organizations skip the second step. Some even skip the first step! Technology is not the solution—it is a vehicle toward a solution. Organizations that fully understand their business problems first can develop solutions to those problems. Solutions to business problems may involve technology. There also may be nontechnical solutions.

FIGURE 2-11

Transforming business requirements into technical solutions.

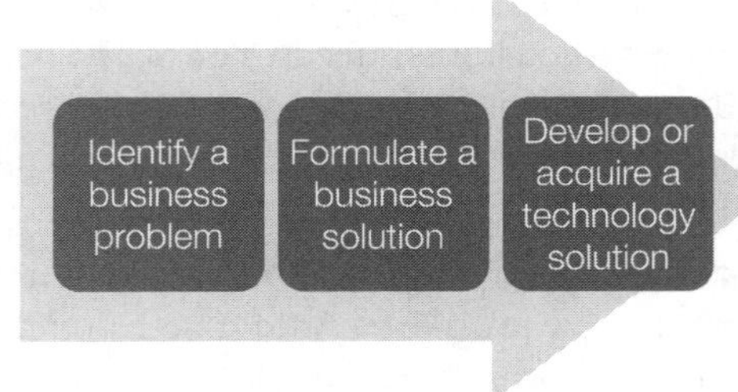

FYI

Suppose a SOHO has three employees. On several occasions voice mail messages from the night before were not discovered until lunchtime. Several customers had become frustrated with the slow response. The organization could implement a UC solution. It could use multiple methods to alert employees that voice mail messages were waiting. The UC system could send e-mail alerts as well as SMS messages whenever someone leaves a voice mail message. While this option would work, a simple procedure would solve the problem as well. In this case, a simpler solution would be to remind every person to check voice mail before checking e-mail each morning. This simple procedure would help reduce stale voice mail messages. While this low-tech approach isn't as elegant, it is effective. Always choose the most effective solution for a business problem first.

The communication challenges in this chapter are really business problems. They each require a business solution that may be addressed through the use of technology. In fact, most of the solutions in this chapter rely on UC solutions. Do not assume that UC solves all communication challenges. UC is a powerful solution in the right environment. An effective plan will make sure any UC solution provides a business solution to a specific business problem. In the correct context, UC solutions can include many technologies. They also can provide benefits to many applications, including the following:

- **Service-oriented architecture (SOA)**—Modular and reusable applications that integrate people-to-people communication, processes, and data distribution into specific business applications.
- **Customer service (CS)**—Integrating multimodal contact center with UC-enabled Web site to provide enhanced customer service delivery solution.
- **Customer relationship management (CRM)**—Application that combines customer service modules with historical purchases data and extended customer demographic data. CRM provides support for data mining and analysis to identify trends and needs.
- **Supply chain management (SCM)**—Integration of UC solutions with processes and decisions to reduce human-related lag time and increase efficiency. SCM focuses primarily on communication between suppliers and organizations. It can benefit from UC features that encourage automation.
- **Enterprise resource planning (ERP)**—UC solutions integration can help organizations make financial and resource planning decisions more timely.
- **Sales force automation (SFA)**—Integrating UC solutions with internal and external pre-sales communications can help shorten sales cycles and increase revenue.

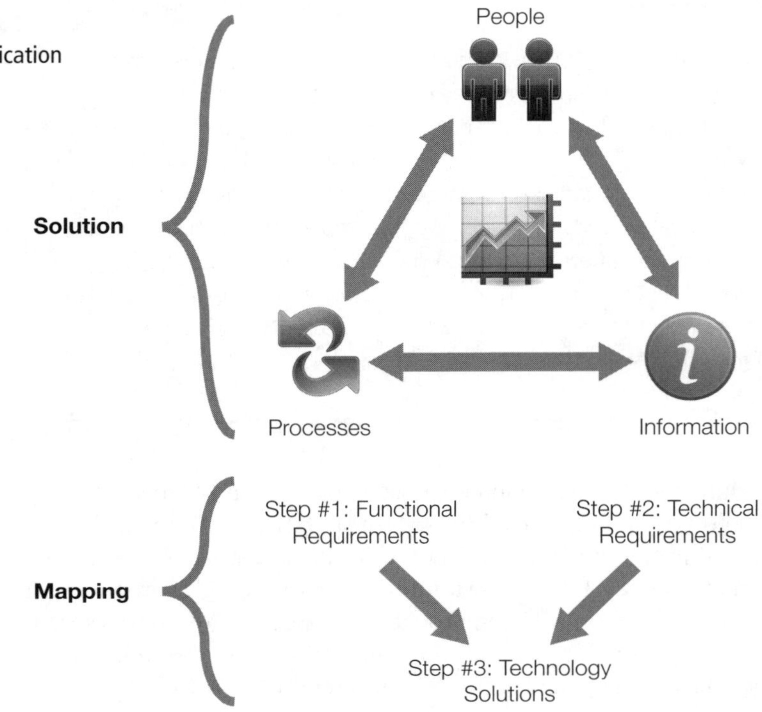

FIGURE 2-12
Solving communication challenges.

Applying a complete solution to business problems extends the process described at the beginning of this section. Figure 2-12 shows the steps involved in mapping technology solutions to business problems.

Mapping UC technology solutions to business problems typically includes the following initial three steps:

1. **Functional requirements**—Input from business process owners who define the business problem and requirements to solve the problem.
2. **Technical requirements**—Input from technical personnel who define technical needs for solving each of the business (functional) requirements.
3. **Map requirements to technical solution**—Relationship between each technical requirement and the functional requirement it satisfies, along with the components necessary to deploy each solution.

These three steps provide the crucial planning phase of any communication solution project. Skipping any of these steps will likely result in a solution that falls short of the expected functionality and probably will waste resources. The next steps are consistent with many other projects:

1. **Define the scope of work**—Determine what the project will and will not accomplish. Decompose the total work product into manageable units.
2. **Schedule activities**—Assign resources and time expectations to each work unit. Arrange the sequence of activities to maximize resource use and minimize conflicts.
3. **Execute the plan**—Follow the schedule. Manage issues as they arise.
4. **Monitor the solution**—Evaluate the resulting UC solution to make sure it meets the organization's goals and operates as expected.

Applying UC solutions can help all types of organizations. They can enjoy lower operational costs through process improvements and get rid of expenditures. Businesses in all vertical markets can also realize financial benefits and returns through increased revenue and profitability. The key to a good UC solution is thorough planning. Know your organization's needs. Then apply only the solutions necessary to meet those needs.

Solving a Communication Challenge

A large grocery store chain wanted to reduce labor costs. One of their highest labor costs was in keeping idle cashiers on the daily schedule. The company had introduced self-service kiosks. Customers weren't using them as often as expected. A customer survey found that the main reason customers avoided the self-service kiosks was that any problem left them stuck at the register waiting for help. The company researched the problems. It found that most of the problems were related to two issues. First, customers had problems when items didn't scan properly. Second, they had to wait for an ID check when they tried to purchase alcohol. The company identified a business problem. It then decided to make remote customer support representatives available to help resolve issues quickly.

The company changed their self-service registers to include a "Let me talk with a real person" button. They also changed the software to quickly alert customer service when these problems occurred. The company added video cameras to each register. It provided direct access to a centralized customer call center. Customers can now initiate a video chat with customer service and resolve most self-service problems. Customers do not have to wait for on-site help in most cases.

CHAPTER SUMMARY

Today's businesses encounter many challenges. The demands of the hyperconnected world place new expectations on organizations of all sizes. Customers demand immediate access to information and assistance. Organizations that want to meet these problems and flourish must understand their customers and their needs. They also must learn emerging techniques and tools to address the ever-changing needs of connected customers. UC can provide solutions to most communication challenges. This is the case only if they are applied in the correct context. Applying the right solution to the wrong problem only makes matters worse.

Organizations of all sizes must follow a formal approach to solving these problems. Identify a business problem, formulate a solution, and then map a technology solution to the business solution. In this way all types of organizations can use technology to address even the toughest communication issues. From enterprise businesses to SOHOs, UC solutions applied in the correct context can provide elegant and effective communication solutions.

KEY CONCEPTS AND TERMS

Automated teller machine (ATM)
Confidentiality
Enterprise business
Integrity
Just in time (JIT)
Manufacturer
Personally identifiable information (PII)
Radio frequency identification (RFID)
Request for proposal (RFP)
Retailer
Small- and medium-sized business (SMB)
Small office/home office (SOHO)
Wholesaler

CHAPTER 2 ASSESSMENT

1. Each type of organization, enterprise, SMB, SOHO, tends to compete for different customers.
   A. True
   B. False
2. Which of the following terms could describe a company with five employees? (Select two.)
   A. Enterprise
   B. SMB
   C. Commercial
   D. SOHO
3. Which of the following is *not* a common business challenge for enterprise organizations?
   A. Reduce costs
   B. Improve team collaboration
   C. Manage time resources
   D. Provide better customer service
4. Which property of data security makes sure that only authorized users can modify data?
   A. Confidentiality
   B. Integrity
   C. Availability
   D. Nonrepudiation
5. ________ inventory describes materials used in the manufacturing process that an organization makes or buys to have it available when it is needed, and not before.
6. Which communication challenge do enterprise and SMB organizations encounter that SOHO organizations generally *do not* encounter?
   A. Using UC to empower internal communications
   B. Operating with a small office footprint
   C. Finding local suppliers
   D. Communicating among geographically diverse offices
7. Which term describes a critical step in the government agency procurement process?
   A. Equal Access Bid (EAB)
   B. Purchase Order (PO)
   C. Request for Proposal (RFP)
   D. Authorized Contractor List (ACL)
8. Why do government agencies require so much oversight and open communication?
   A. Government agencies are managed by elected officials
   B. All budgeted funds originate with taxpayers
   C. Government projects are generally larger than commercial projects
   D. Government agencies are more sensitive to internal politics
9. Which of the following communication challenges do SOHO organizations normally encounter that enterprise organizations generally *do not* encounter?
   A. Finding local suppliers
   B. Avoiding appearing small
   C. Reaching new customers
   D. Keeping existing customers happy
10. Every technical solution should start by identifying a ________.

CHAPTER 3

Circuit-Switched, Packet-Switched, and IP-Based Communications

THE CONCEPT OF CONNECTING COMPUTERS is simple. Getting them to communicate with one another is not. Organizations must carefully consider how they want to use networks. More important, they need to consider how the devices on the network are to communicate. A network that connects many computers but doesn't allow its users to access resources they need isn't a useful network. Networks that provide mainly local services differ from those that support large numbers of remote users. Local services can include file sharing and internal communications while external services can include Internet Web applications and remote database access. Networks must be designed to handle the type of traffic and growth requirements of the organization. Finally, networks must be affordable while meeting all the functional and technical requirements of the organization. This chapter presents the evolution of networking from circuit-switched to packet-switched and IP-based communications.

Chapter 3 Topics

This chapter covers the following topics and concepts:

- What network topologies are
- How networks connect and interconnect
- What switching concepts networks use
- How networks use circuit switching
- How networks use packet switching
- What IP-based communications and convergence are

Chapter 3 Goals

When you complete this chapter, you will be able to:

- Describe network topologies
- Explain how to connect networks
- Describe switching concepts used by network technologies
- Distinguish how circuit switching and packet switching is used
- Describe how IP-based communication works in today's networks

Network Topology Overview

A computer network is how computers, servers, printers, and users share information and communicate with one another. The public Internet is a computer network allowing individuals to share information, send e-mail, and communicate in real time via VoIP or **instant message (IM chat)** or via store-and-forward messaging such as e-mail. Networks interconnect network attachable devices. A network attachable device is a device that can physically connect to the network and has an assigned IP host address such as:

- A computer
- A printer
- A scanner
- A server
- A Web server
- A local area network (LAN) switch
- A router

Devices can connect to networks in several different ways; see Figure 3-1 for an example a simple network. Some devices use wires and others do not. In fact, it is common for some devices to support several connection modes. Most laptop computers can connect to standard networks using a wired or wireless connection. The layout of how devices connect to a network is the **network topology**. The network topology is a map of the network that shows how devices connect to one another and how they use a **connection medium** to communicate.

FIGURE 3-1

Simple network diagram.

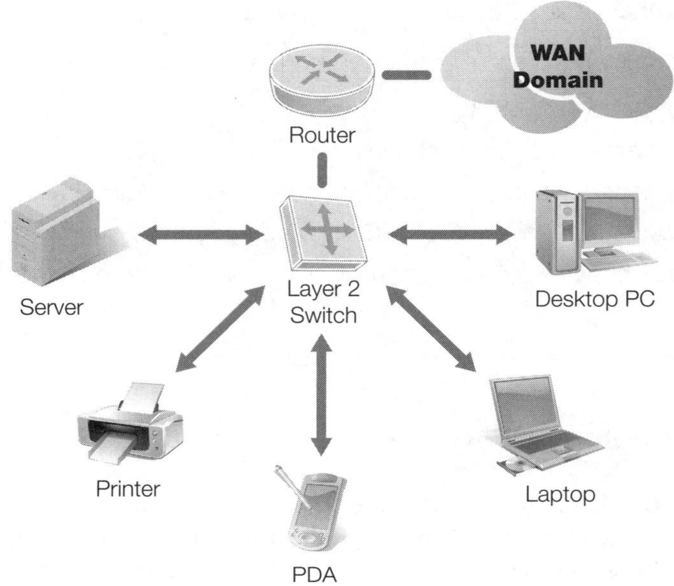

Home Electrical Wiring Map

Think of a network topology like a map of your home's electrical wiring. The wiring and outlets don't just appear in the walls. Someone had to decide where to place the electrical components. Many of the walls in a home contain electrical wires. The wires carry electricity from the main supply to outlets and fixtures. An architect should decide where the wires should go based on the residents' needs. For example, the wiring plan should include a high voltage cable and outlet in the laundry room for the electric clothes dryer. The plan should also ensure there are enough outlets to provide a convenient supply of electricity where it is needed. The wiring map is only part of the picture. If you include all of the appliances you plug into outlets, you would see a complete picture of where electricity flows in the house.

A network topology is similar. The topology depicts how the network components connect to one another. The main purpose of the network topology is to help planners ensure the network serves its purpose. Poor network design results in poor network performance.

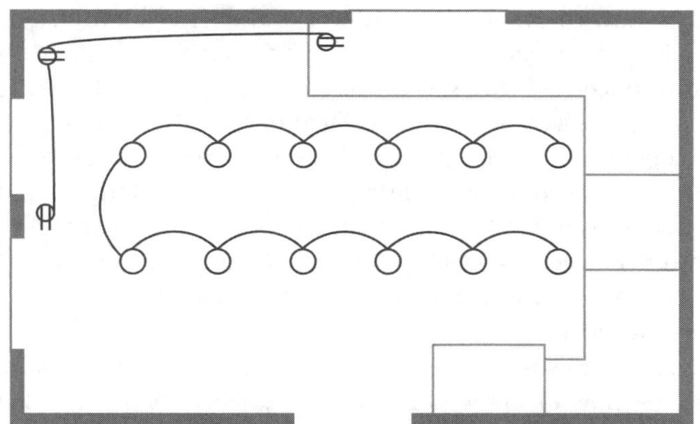

FIGURE 3-2
Home electrical wiring map.

There are two ways to consider a network topology. The **physical topology** is the picture of the actual network devices and the medium the devices use to connect to the network. Each device connects to a network using at least one connection medium. Figure 3.2 shows a typical wiring map for something like your kitchen. A network connection medium is the physical method to link devices together. The connection medium can be wires, radio waves, or even light waves. The physical topology shows how the physical parts of the network connect—see Figure 3-3. Many organizations use the physical topology as a wiring and device diagram. Troubleshooting network problems is difficult without an accurate picture of the physical topology.

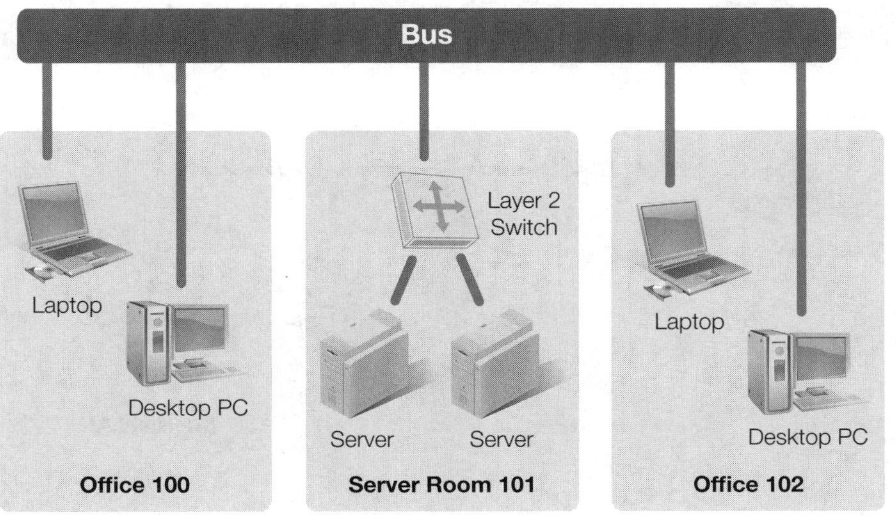

FIGURE 3-3
Physical network topology.

The **logical topology** is how the actual network works and how you transfer data in a network. This topology view focuses more on how the network topology operates. A logical topology is not concerned with specific physical properties of the network. For instance, a physical topology contains precise locations of devices and wiring. You can look at a physical topology and determine the location of a specific device. A logical topology of the same network would not contain precise location information. It would simply show that the device connects to a specific segment of the network and supports certain types of communication. A logical topology (see Figure 3-4) is how the network logically works at the Data Link Layer where the MAC (media access control) and LLC (logical link control) sub-layers reside.

Most topology names refer to shapes. These shapes describe the general organization of the network. The shape may not correspond to the physical design of the devices and medium of the network. The type of network topology generally describes the network's logical topology. A **ring topology**, for instance, is a network layout in which each computer connects to two other computers. The computers connect to one another in a virtual ring. Each type of network topology has both advantages and disadvantages. You will learn about the main topologies that make up most of today's networks. Most networks are made up of one or more of the following topologies:

FIGURE 3-4
Logical network topology.

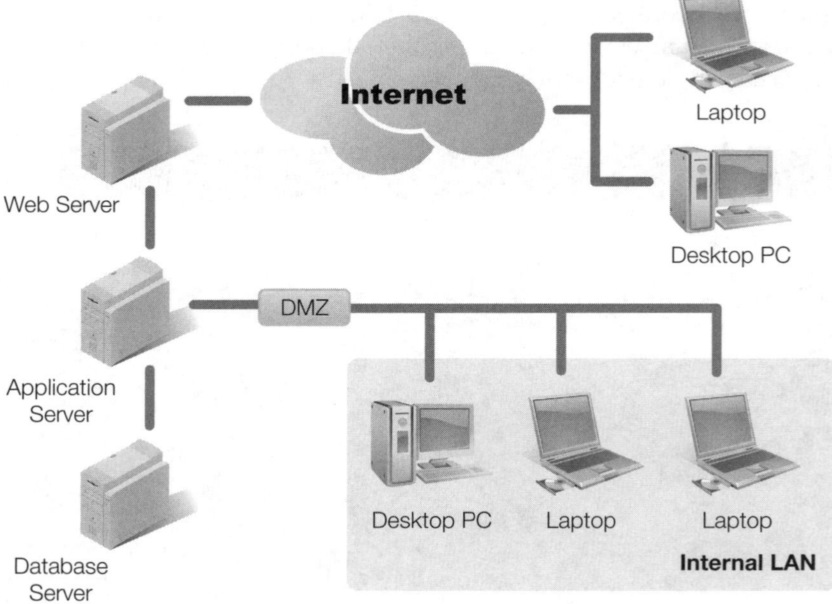

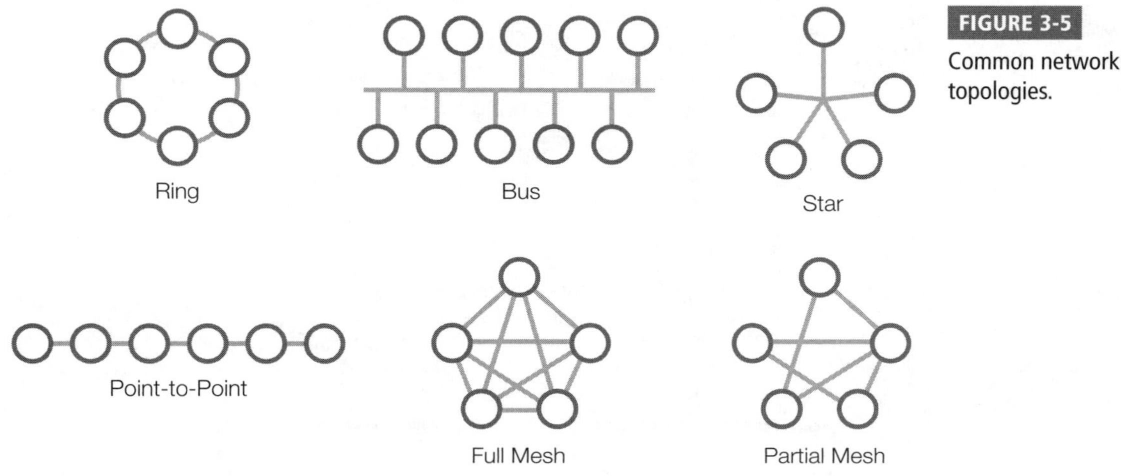

FIGURE 3-5
Common network topologies.

- **Point-to-point**—A direct link or connection between two devices
- **Ring**—A shared ring connecting multiple devices together
- **Star**—A star-wired connection aggregation point, typically from a wiring closet
- **Mesh**—Multipoint connections and direct links between network devices
- **Bus**—A shared network transmission medium allowing only one device to communicate at a single time
- **Hybrid/star-wired bus**—A shared, star-wired connection aggregation point to a LAN switch

The topologies shown in Figure 3-5 are not the only ones organizations use. But they are the most common. In fact, many organizations use several topologies to create their entire network. But before you learn how to connect network segments, you need to know what network topologies are available.

Point-to-Point Networks

Organizations first created networks by simply connecting two computers with a single cable. Legacy computer systems tended to be **host-based** systems. A host-based system is one that consists of a central computer such as a mainframe or minicomputer with many users that connect directly to it. Users accessed the central computer by connecting **terminals** to it. A terminal is a device that has a keyboard and a monitor that can input data to the central computer. Since these early terminals didn't do much more than just send and receive characters to and from the central computer, they were called **dumb terminals**. Most dumb terminals connected to central computers using a **serial communications** connection. Serial communications means that the terminal would send or receive one character at a time (ASCII text, etc.) in a serial fashion.

FIGURE 3-6

Point-to-point topology with legacy mainframe computers.

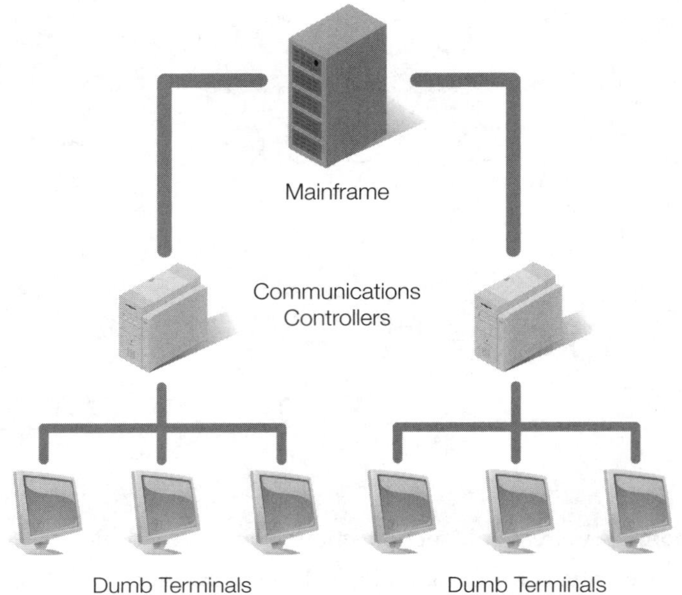

A network that consists of computers or devices that connect directly to one another is called a **point-to-point** network. Point-to-point communications are based on time slots and polling where communication controllers poll each dumb terminal one at a time to provide a time slot to transmit data to and from the mainframe computer. This type of network is difficult to scale. That means that it is difficult to add many devices to the network, since each new device requires some new type of direct connection. You can still find this type of simple network in very small environments that only need to connect two personal computers. These networks, as shown in Figure 3-6 are considered archaic. They are no longer the mainstream in data processing and information processing today.

The standard for serial communications and connectivity was based on a 25-pin connector defined by the **Electronic Industries Association (EIA)** as the **RS-232** serial communications standard. (See Figure 3-7.) The RS-232 standard defines how **data terminal equipment (DTE)** devices communicate with **data circuit-terminating equipment (DCE)**. DTE devices include terminals, printers, and any device that can connect to a computer. Although the RS-232 standard defines as many as 25 connectors at each endpoint, unidirectional devices (devices that send data in only one direction) can use a 2-wire cable. Many bi-directional serial cables and communications signaling use 4-wires for transmit and receive signaling. In fact, today's Ethernet or **IEEE 802.3 CSMA/CD** 10/100/1000 networks require 2-wires for transmit and 2-wires for receive within a 4-pair unshielded twisted-pair (UTP) cable using RJ-45 connectors.

Host-based computers dominated data processing in the 1960s and 1970s. It wasn't until the 1980s that computers were first networked together via a bus network topology and architecture. Thus, the local area network (LAN) was born providing physical and

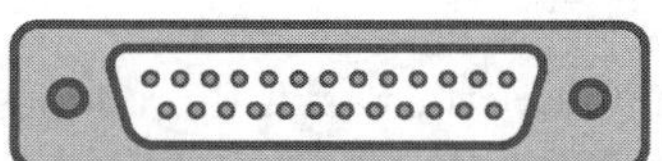

RS232 Pin Assignments	
Pin 1	Protective Ground
Pin 2	Transmit Data
Pin 3	Received Data
Pin 4	Request to Send
Pin 5	Clear to Send
Pin 6	Data Set Ready
Pin 7	Signal Ground
Pin 8	Received Line Signal Detector
Pin 20	Data Terminal Ready
Pin 22	Ring Indicator

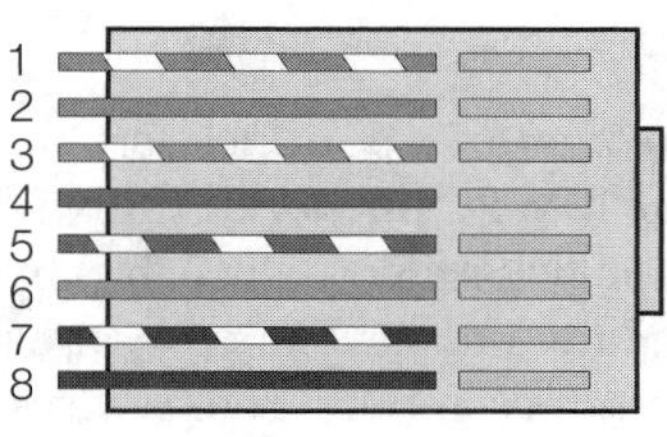

10BaseT Standard Patch Cable	
1	Orange/White
2	Orange
3	Green/White
4	Blue
5	Blue/White
6	Green
7	Brown/White
8	Brown

FIGURE 3-7

RS-232 DB-25 connector and 10BaseT RJ-45 connector.

logical connectivity for personal computers and PCs. LANs allowed organizations to connect their desktop PCs and workstations together for file sharing, printer sharing, and office automation functionality. Now, two or more computers could communicate on the same LAN allowing for greater productivity enhancements among departmental or workgroup users. Users within the same department can share information and access resources connected to either computer through a common file server.

The Rise of Client/Server Computing and LANs

The transition from mainframe computers and minicomputers toward client/server in the mid 1980s into the 1990s was a major driving force for local area networking. Office automation was one thing, but as applications migrated from mainframe and minicomputers using point-to-point communications, deployment of client/server applications and access led the migration toward local area networking. This combination of client/server computing and local area networking helped accelerate the use of the bus and ring local area networking technologies in the mid to late 1980s into the 1990s. This migration was led by IBM, which was a major adopter of the IEEE 802.5 token ring LAN standard, and Digital Equipment Corporation (DEC), which was a major adopter of the IEEE 802.3 CSMA/CD LAN standard. Early adopters of LAN technologies typically followed either IBM or DEC as legacy mainframes and minicomputers transitioned to client/server architecture and applications.

Bus

The most common type of network topology was originated by the first LAN vendors such as the IBM PC Network, ARCNET, and eventually the first IEEE 802.3a CSMA/CD standard for 10Base5 coaxial cable–based bus topologies. The bus network topology provides additional flexibility over previous topologies by providing a linear network throughout the computer room, wiring closets, and externally lying workstations and devices. Organizations need to be able to physically connect to the bus network where the devices are physically located (i.e., factory automation floor, computer data center, workstation locations, etc.). A **bus topology** (see Figure 3-8) is one that starts with a coaxial cable that can support high-speed network communications but is subject to physical distance limitations and maximum number of devices per bus or Ethernet LAN segment. The main cable runs throughout the organization's physical space and provides accessible connections anywhere along its length. Connecting to a bus network is easy. Any network device can attach an Ethernet transceiver to the bus, allowing for physical connectivity to the network-attached device.

A bus topology is simple to construct but requires electrical transceivers to transmit and receive network communications. The flexibility of a bus does come with a performance cost. Communications signaling traverses in both directions where the transceiver connects to the bus or coaxial cable. Because of this, only one device can communicate at a given time. Each network device's transceiver must listen on the network (coaxial cable) to see if it is available before transmitting. When two devices transmit at the same time, a **collision** occurs on the network, requiring both devices to retransmit again when the network is available. This led to the creation of the IEEE 802 Committees focusing on both IEEE 802.3 **CSMA/CD (carrier sense multiple access with collision detection)** and **IEEE 802.5 token ring** standards for local area networking. See Figure 3-9 for more information.

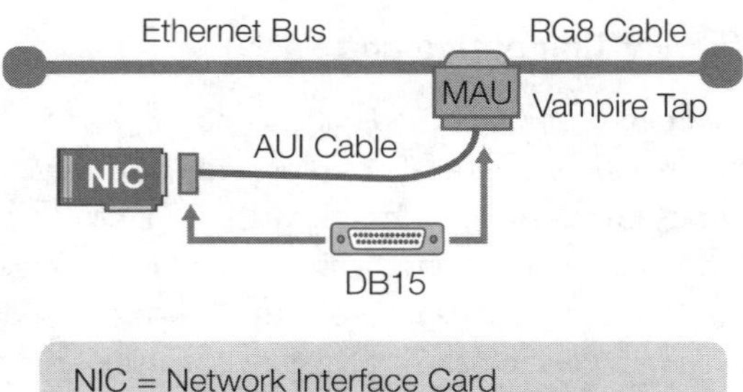

FIGURE 3-8
IEEE 802.3a CSMA/CD Ethernet bus topology.

IEEE 802.3 CSMA/CD Standards

Ethernet was originally developed by Xerox in the early 1970s. Xerox filed a patent application listing Robert Metcalfe, David Boggs, Chuck Thacker, and Butler Lampson as inventors. Robert Metcalfe then left Xerox in 1979 for 3Com Corporation. It was then that DEC, Intel, and Xerox joined forces to create the DIX Ethernet standard. The "Digital/Intel/Xerox" Ethernet standard v1.0 was a 10 Mbit/s Ethernet bus topology and used a 6-byte destination and source MAC addresses and a 2-byte protocol type field. Ethernet v1.0 became known as the Ethernet v2.0 standard in 1982 (Ethernet II). This evolved into the IEEE 802.3 CSMA/CD Standards Committee definition. Today, the term Ethernet is synonymous with IEEE 802.3 CSMA/CD for local area networking.

OSI Model	IEEE				
Data Link Layer	802.2 LLC				
	802.3 MAC—CSMA/CD				
Physical Layer	802.3 10Base5 Thick Coax	802.3a 10Base2 Thin Coax	802.3b 10Broad36 Broadband	802.3e 1Base5 StarLAN	802.3i 10BaseT Twisted Pair

FIGURE 3-9
IEEE 802.3 CSMA/CD standards.

Ring

During the 1980s and early 1990s, one of the other common network topologies that was deployed was the token ring. This networking was made popular by IBM, which adopted token ring as its LAN architecture of choice. IBM integrated token Ring LAN interfaces within its Front-End Processors and Communications Controllers. IBM led the IEEE 802.5 Token Ring standard, which competed directly with IEEE 802.3 CSMA/CD. Within token ring, all stations are connected in a logical ring while being star-wired from a centrally located wiring closet. Token ring-attached devices must have permission to transmit on the network. This permission is granted via a token that circulates around the ring.

Token ring networks, as shown in Figure 3-10, move a small **frame** called a **token**. Possession of the token grants the right to transmit. If the network device that receives the available token has no information to send, it alters one bit of the token, which flags it as available for the next network attached device in line. When a network device wants to send information, it must wait for an available token, transmit information to the next upstream device, wait for the destination device to receive the data, and then a new token is released. Token ring–attached devices can transmit only when they have an available token. Token ring networking eliminates communication collisions. A network collision occurs when two or more computers transmit at the same time on a bus topology. Forcing all communications in a unidirectional manner eliminates network transmission collisions. This is how token ring works.

A cut in the cable will break a ring network. Most organizations install star-wired cabling from a wiring closet to the desktop location. Legacy IBM shops used IBM Type 1 cabling for 4/16 Meg token ring networking. Others migrated to 4-pair, unshielded twisted-pair cabling. Hence, a physical star, logical ring network supported most token ring networks. To mitigate the single point of failure with a break in the cable, multi-station access units (MAU) incorporated a loopback mechanism in the event that a cable pair (transmit or receive) gets cut. Communications occur on the other cable pair in a unidirectional fashion.

FIGURE 3-10

Token ring network—physical star, logical ring.

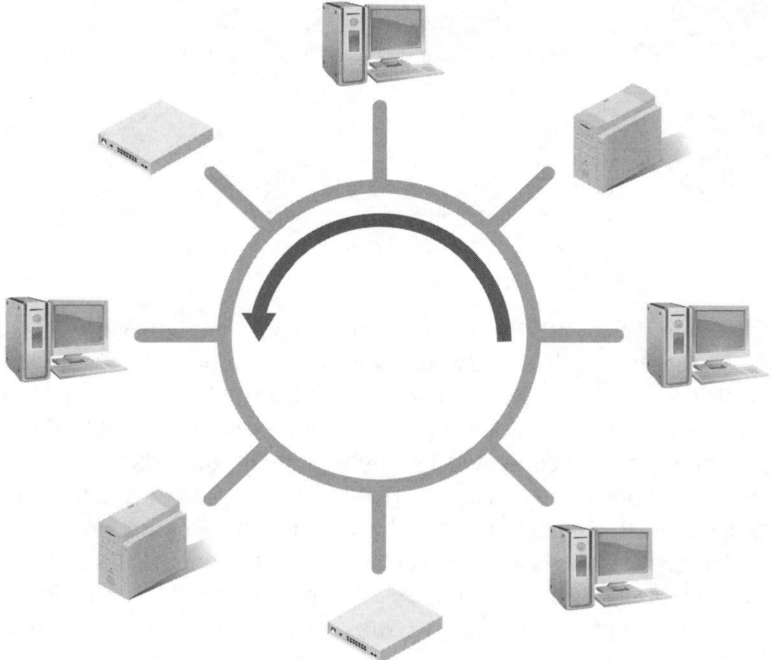

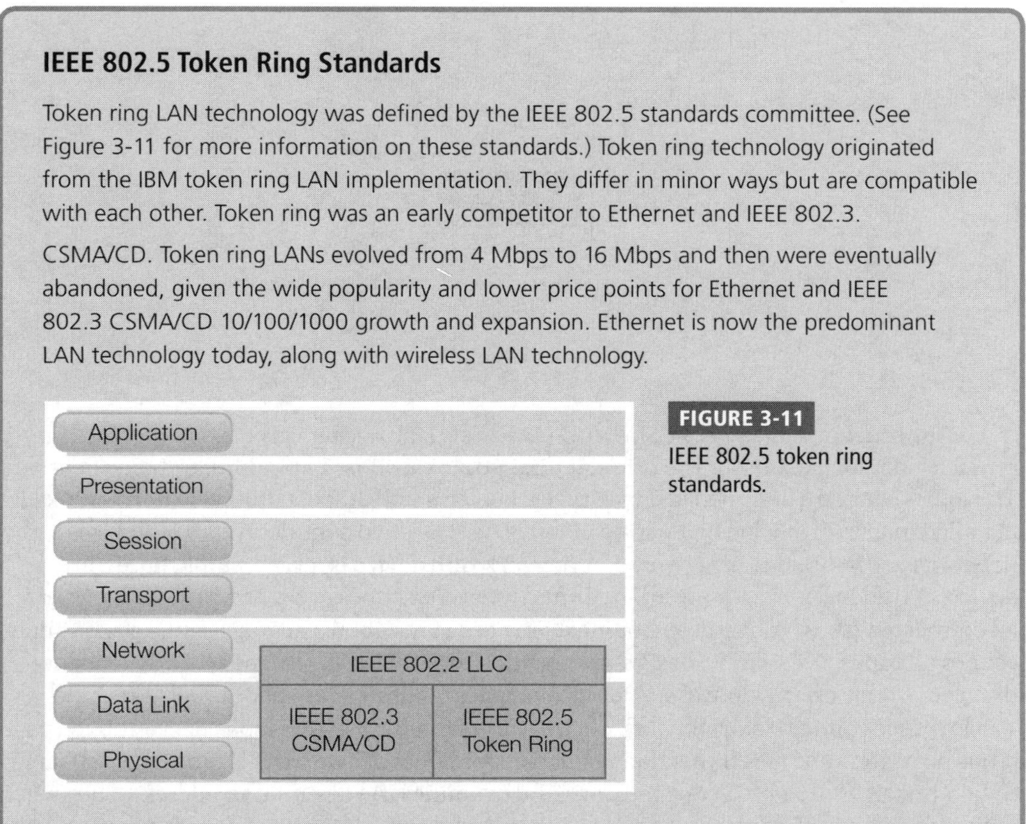

IEEE 802.5 Token Ring Standards

Token ring LAN technology was defined by the IEEE 802.5 standards committee. (See Figure 3-11 for more information on these standards.) Token ring technology originated from the IBM token ring LAN implementation. They differ in minor ways but are compatible with each other. Token ring was an early competitor to Ethernet and IEEE 802.3.

CSMA/CD. Token ring LANs evolved from 4 Mbps to 16 Mbps and then were eventually abandoned, given the wide popularity and lower price points for Ethernet and IEEE 802.3 CSMA/CD 10/100/1000 growth and expansion. Ethernet is now the predominant LAN technology today, along with wireless LAN technology.

FIGURE 3-11
IEEE 802.5 token ring standards.

Star

One of the problems ring networks have is maximum physical **path length**. Path length is the length of the transmission media. Network signaling is subject to signal loss on transmission media. This is also called **attenuation**. Networks are subject to a maximum distance or path length due to signal attenuation. With lots of workstations and devices, maximum distance and path length limits are easy to reach. Network designers needed a simple and easy way to physically connect local area networks together. They needed a way to reduce path length and handle signal attenuation as networks grew in size.

This was solved with star-wiring cabling from a centrally located wiring closet. (See Figure 3-12.) Network-attached devices used this star-wired cabling to physically and electrically connect to an Ethernet or token ring network. This was the beginning of **star-wired topology** deployments for both Ethernet and token ring networks.

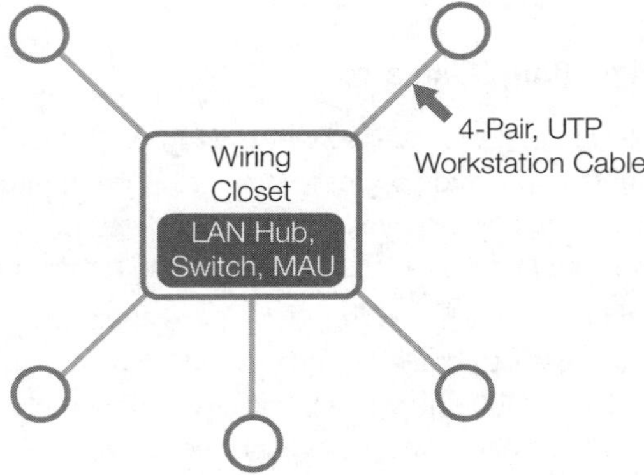

FIGURE 3-12
Physical star—logical ring topology.

For Ethernet or IEEE 802.3 CSMA/CD networks, star wiring was used to provide a physical star, logical bus for the original IEEE 802.3i, 10BaseT standard and specification. The logical bus can be supported by either a **hub** or a **switch**. This hub or switch is typically installed in a centrally located wiring closet. There are two common types of devices networks use to build star networks. A network hub device is a very simple hardware device. A hub has ports for multiple connections and echoes every message it receives to all connected ports. A hub does not make any decisions about message routing—it simply echoes all input. This simple design makes hubs easy and cheap to make. It also means that every node on the network receives messages it doesn't care about.

The other common star network device is the switch. A switch looks like a hub in that it has ports for multiple connections to network devices. However, it is more sophisticated than a hub. A switch receives a message and examines the destination address. The switch maintains a table of connected devices and knows to which port it should forward the message. The switch sends the message directly to the destination. Switches do not send messages to all destinations as hubs do. Figure 3-13 illustrates how a hub echoes any received traffic to all ports, but a switch sends the traffic only to the appropriate port.

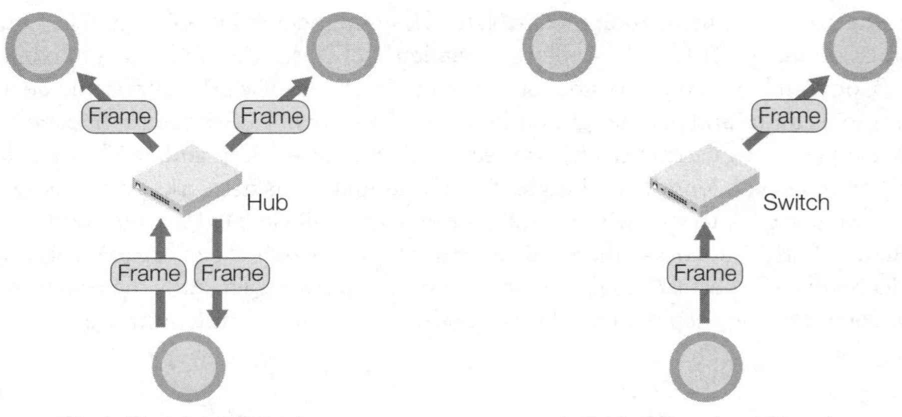

FIGURE 3-13
LAN hub versus LAN switch.

This discrimination ability makes switches more secure. The only devices that can access messages are the switch and the destination. Switches also reduce message collisions and can increase the network's throughput given that each port on a switch is its own dedicated Ethernet LAN or **broadcast domain**. A broadcast domain is the physical cabling that an Ethernet signal or transmission traverses. A hub is a multiport broadcast domain where each Ethernet frame and signal is transmitted through each physical port. A switch is a multiport broadcast domain where each physical port is its own Ethernet LAN segment.

Regardless of the hardware in use, star networks have advantages and disadvantages. They reduce the average path length but do so by centralizing all network traffic. Star-wired LAN topologies are dependent upon LAN hardware electronics (i.e., hub or switch) to terminate the physical cabling. This star-wired topology is common in today's LAN installations. Use of unshielded twisted-pair cabling from wiring closet to workstation location dominated LAN connectivity before wireless LAN technologies were born. As networks grew and expanded, so did the need for connecting LANs together. This is referred to as **internetworking**. You'll learn more about internetworking LANs later in this chapter.

Mesh

You learned that point-to-point networks suffer from a lack of scalability. It is difficult to scale a point-to-point network due to the large number of connections growing networks require. This restriction assumes that every network node would connect to every other node. A **mesh topology** describes the network layout in which all nodes are directly connected to all other nodes. **Metcalfe's law** shows that a mesh network requires $n(n - 1)/2$ connections to directly connect each node to every other node. Actually, there are two different types of mesh topologies, depending on whether all or just most of the nodes are directly connected. Mesh networking is more common in wide area networking, given that alternative paths and redundancy are typically required.

Fully Connected Mesh

A **fully connected mesh** (shown in Figure 3-14) follows the strict definition of a mesh topology. That is, every node directly connects with every other node. A fully connected mesh provides a path length of one for every connection. It also provides the maximum number of alternate paths in case any available paths fail. That means that fully connected mesh topologies have a high degree of **fault tolerance**. Fault tolerance describes the ability to encounter a fault, or error, of some type and still be available. A fully connected mesh topology with IP routing can easily bypass a failed connection and still communicate through the mesh using alternate connections and nodes.

FIGURE 3-14
Fully connected mesh.

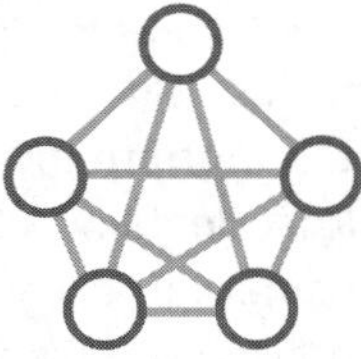

FIGURE 3-15
Partially connected mesh.

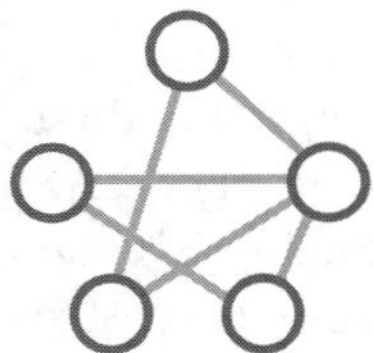

The biggest drawback of a fully connected mesh topology is the required number of connections. This can be cost prohibitive. Organizations must provide a large number of cables, fiber connections, or wide area network circuits to complete a fully connected mesh. This can be cost prohibitive because now you may need more network devices such as IP routers and proper traffic monitoring and controls. For these reasons, fully connected meshes tend to be the most expensive networks to set up and maintain. They work best in environments where connection availability is the highest priority business driver. The extensive fault tolerance of fully connected mesh topologies is hard to beat.

Partially Connected Mesh

A **partially connected mesh** (Figure 3-15) is a network topology in which network nodes connect to only some of the other nodes. Network designers identify the most active or important nodes and ensure those nodes connect to most other nodes. Lower priority nodes do not connect directly. All nodes in the network do connect, but some connections will have a path length greater than one. Partially connected mesh topologies provide more fault tolerance than many other topologies without requiring the expense of a fully connected mesh. This topology can be a good compromise when an organization needs better fault tolerance but cannot afford to set up and maintain a fully connected mesh.

Hybrid

The final network topology is a combination of the previous topologies. A **hybrid topology** is a network that contains several different topologies. Network nodes differ in traffic and use. Nodes that require high fault tolerance may benefit from a mesh topology. Lower usage networks may work better using a bus topology. A hybrid network that combines the two topologies can provide fault tolerance for some nodes while providing flexibility for other parts of the network. Core backbone networks are usually resilient with mesh topologies. Building or access networks can be resilient with or without mesh connectivity.

Regardless of the networking topology selected, the most important requirements that a network must provide include:

- Support for the connectivity needs of the organization
- High-speed connectivity with optimum performance
- Unique support for time-sensitive applications
- High availability (core/backbone, building, access)
- Reliable transport service to support user connectivity
- Security and the ability to encrypt confidential data when required

Internetworking

As LANs grow and expand, so does the need to interconnect them. LANs have a physical distance and node limitation. LANs that support workstations and servers are designed to optimize performance. Workgroup LANs typically share files and information mostly with each other; hence, network traffic should be isolated within the workgroup. Internal traffic that leaves the workgroup LAN traverses the building or campus backbone network to designated servers. External traffic that leaves the workgroup LAN traverses through the public Internet.

Internetworking is a term used to describe connecting LANs together, as shown in Figure 3-16. There are several ways to connect LANs together such that network traffic can traverse between them. LANs communicate using protocols and the **Open Systems Interconnection (OSI) Reference Model**. Different network devices interoperate at different layers of the protocol stack. What is a protocol stack? A protocol stack is how software operates at different layers of the OSI Reference Model. Internetworking LANs must follow the OSI model protocol stack definition. Thus, network devices must operate at either the Data Link Layer or Network Layer.

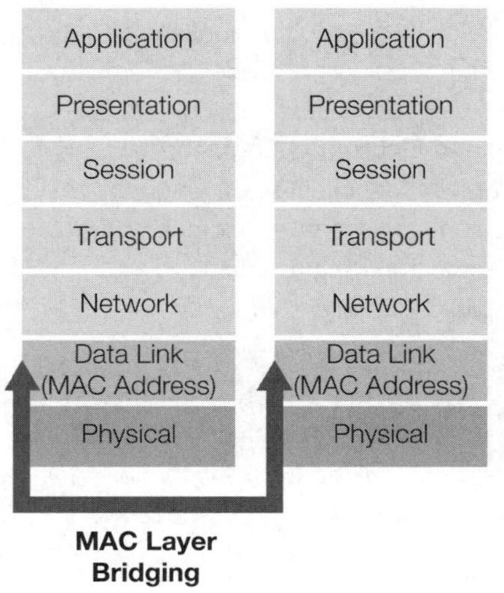

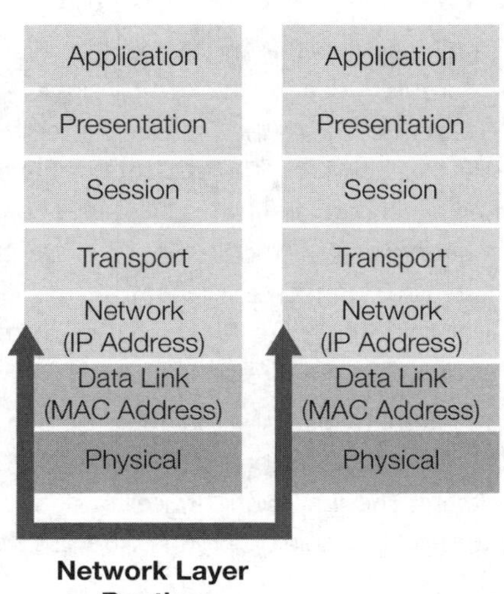

FIGURE 3-16 Internetworking at the Data Link Layer or Network Layer.

Internetworking at the Data Link Layer requires a network device known as a **MAC layer bridge.** The MAC layer implies the media access control layer within the Data Link Layer of the OSI Reference Model. Within this layer, the 6-byte MAC layer address is examined within the Ethernet v2.0 or IEEE 802.3 CSMA/CD frame to make a forwarding or non-forwarding decision. A MAC layer bridge creates the MAC address table by learning where all the MAC layer addresses are of other devices. The bridge listens to received traffic and remembers the port on which the traffic arrived from each MAC address.

Internetworking at the Network Layer requires a network device known as a **router**. The Network Layer implies a Network Layer address must be present within the Network Layer of the OSI model. Within the Network Layer resides a Network Layer address. The Network Layer IP address is like a zip code that is used for routing mail and letters through the US Postal Service. Within this layer, the Network Layer address or IP address is examined within the IP packet found at the Network Layer. Routers build IP routing tables that define path determination for IP packets. A **packet** is a chunk of a message. IP networks are configured on physical ports of the router. Routers forward IP packets based on where that IP network is physically located and the physical port or interface that connects to it.

Network Interface Cards and MAC Layer Addresses

Nearly all of today's computers come with a **network adapter**, **network interface card**, or **network interface controller (NIC)**. Previously, you had to purchase a separate network interface controller or card and physically install it within a computer slot. Then you had to install software drivers to enable the NIC. Now, computer manufacturers embed the NIC within the motherboard of the desktop computer or laptop computer. Because of the popularity of wireless LAN technologies, computer manufacturers have been shipping computers with both a wired NIC and a wireless NIC to support both networks.

The NIC is the device within computers that allows it to connect and communicate on the network. Because it deals with electrical signaling and a physical connection, NICs are also a Physical Layer device. At the Data Link Layer, NICs provide media access using a unique 6-byte MAC layer address. The **Institute of Electrical and Electronics Engineers (IEEE)** has defined a standard and tracks "Organizationally Unique Identifier" (OUI) unique to the original manufacturer of the NIC. The OUI is a unique company identifier (Company_ID) that is three bytes long. The OUI identifies the NIC manufacturer that is unique to a particular piece of hardware. It can be used to create MAC addresses, Bluetooth MAC addresses, or NIC card addresses.

In order to internetwork LANs together, use of a MAC layer bridge or router must encapsulate and utilize Ethernet or IEEE 802.3 CSMA/CD frames to transfer data and information between them. These network devices track and store MAC layer addresses within a MAC layer bridge address table or a router **Address Resolution Protocol (ARP)** cache table.

technical TIP

An internal network that only employees can access is called an intranet. An organization's intranet typically allows users to access internal files and resources pertinent to the organization and its employees only. For this reason, access to an intranet requires proper security controls. The terms Internet and intranet are often confused.

Many organizations maintain their own internal network of connected networks. An internal network is accessible only from locations within an organization (i.e., behind the Internet ingress/egress firewall where the organization's dedicated Internet access link resides).

The public Internet is a global worldwide network that uses the Internet Protocol (IP) for communications. An **intranet** is a private network within that organization's IP network infrastructure. An **extranet** is a remotely accessible network that an organization makes accessible to its business partners and suppliers through the public Internet. An extranet is also a secure network that requires proper access controls and authentication prior to granting access. Figure 3-17 illustrates the differences.

There are several options for interconnecting multiple networks. These options vary based on functional, technical, and security requirements. Each option provides different levels of functionality with varying levels of performance, manageability, and security. Today, manufacturers incorporate MAC layer bridging and Network Layer routing within the same hardware device. In addition, embedded firewalls and security countermeasures also are incorporated into the software functionality of combined bridges and routers. Each organization must carefully select the best product to meet its specific needs and financial parameters.

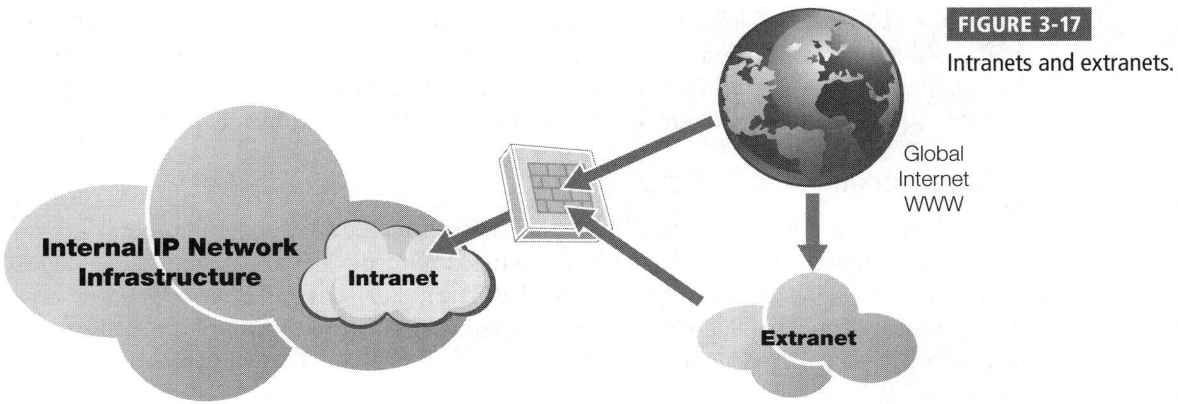

FIGURE 3-17
Intranets and extranets.

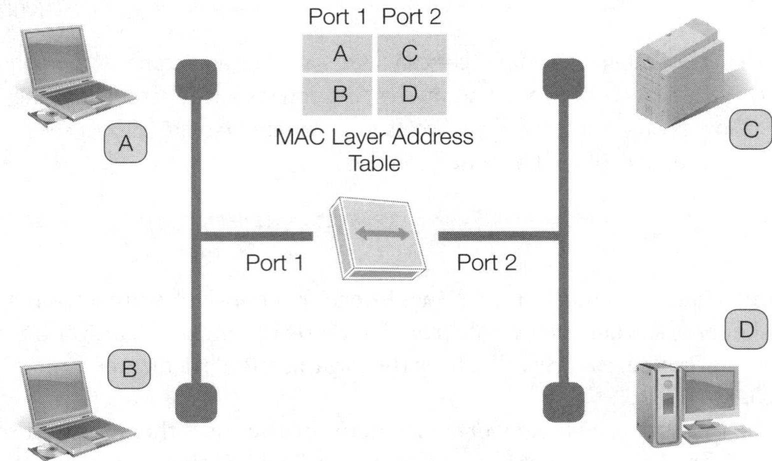

FIGURE 3-18
MAC layer bridge address forwarding table.

Internetworking with MAC Layer Bridges

The easiest way to interconnect two networks is to place a MAC layer bridge in between the two networks. A simple network bridge is a device with two network interface cards so that it can connect to both networks. A MAC layer bridge operates at the OSI Data Link Layer or **Layer 2**. That means it interacts with the Physical Layer and the Data Link Layer. A MAC layer bridge can read the **Media Access Control (MAC) layer address** of each Ethernet frame to make a forwarding or filtering decision. The MAC layer address is a 6-byte address that is burned into a chip on the network interface card. Each MAC layer address is unique. A MAC layer bridge examines the MAC layer address of each frame received. Then it makes a filtering or forwarding decision based on the MAC layer address forwarding table.

Because a MAC layer bridge has two or more network interface cards, it learns where the MAC layer addresses are on each port. The bridge then builds a table of all the MAC layer addresses learned and what port they are located on. This is how a MAC layer bridge filters or forwards an Ethernet frame to an appropriate port. MAC layer bridges (see Figure 3-18) can have static address tables, or they can dynamically build tables.

Internetworking with Switches

A switch is essentially a bridge with more than two ports. A bridge generally connects two networks. A switch often has the ability to connect many devices and networks. Switches operate as an OSI Layer 2 device. They use MAC layer addresses and build address tables of devices connected to each physical port. Switches that connect multiple devices or networks keep track of MAC layer addresses on all ports. When the switch sees an Ethernet frame destined for a specific MAC layer address, it forwards that frame to that port.

There are two kinds of LAN switches. A Layer 2 switch is a device that operates at the Data Link Layer and examines the MAC layer addresses of Ethernet frames. Using this information, filtering and forwarding tasks are performed by the MAC layer switch. Layer 2 switches come in 12-port, 24-port, and 48-port versions providing individual Ethernet LAN segments per port. This maximizes performance and provides a dedicated Ethernet LAN segment per device that connects to that port. A **Layer 3** switch is a device that operates at either the Data Link Layer or Network Layer. Layer 3 switches typically have software that lets them function like a Layer 2 switch or multiport MAC layer bridge. Layer 3 switches usually operate at the Network Layer that examines the network layer address within the Ethernet frame.

The TCP and IP addresses typically are found in the Network Layer of the Ethernet frame. An IP address is like a zip code for mailing a letter. It has both a network number and a host number, which is used to route IP packets to the appropriate destination IP network. By looking up the destination IP network number in the Layer 3 switches IP routing table, a path determination decision can be made by the Layer 3 switch. A Layer 3 switch provides each device connected to its ports with its own Ethernet LAN segment. Layer 3 switches typically have **resiliency** or a redundant path connection to a building or campus backbone network. With Layer 3 switches, routing and alternate paths are typically implemented.

Internetworking with Routers

A router is a device that operates at the Network Layer. A router is the same thing as a Layer 3 switch except it is typically used for wide area network circuit connections, campus backbone connections, and building backbone connections. Routers can make intelligent decisions on where to send packets. Instead of just reading the MAC address and forwarding a packet based on a forwarding table, routers can see the packet's Network Layer address or IP address. The Network Layer address contains information about the destination network number and host number. This is analogous to mailing a letter through the US postal service. The street address acts like a MAC layer address, and the zip code acts as the network routing information. In essence, routers perform a path determination calculation to find the best path for the IP packets to traverse.

Routers are very powerful network devices. Typically they have redundant processors and plenty of memory, and can support lots of network connections. These network connections can be wide area network connections or local area network connections. Of course, this increased functionality has a cost. It takes longer for a router to examine a packet than a Layer 2 switch or MAC layer bridge. High-traffic networks may notice performance issues with multiple routers examining each IP packet to make a path determination decision. (See Figure 3-19.) For lower-traffic networks, a router can help ensure network packets flow only to their destination network. This can reduce overall network congestion and increase security by keeping workgroup LAN traffic isolated. Ensuring packets travel only to their destination networks makes it harder for unauthorized users to intercept the traffic. Many organizations that are concerned with network security often create smaller networks. They use routers to reduce the traffic and distance that network traffic has to traverse.

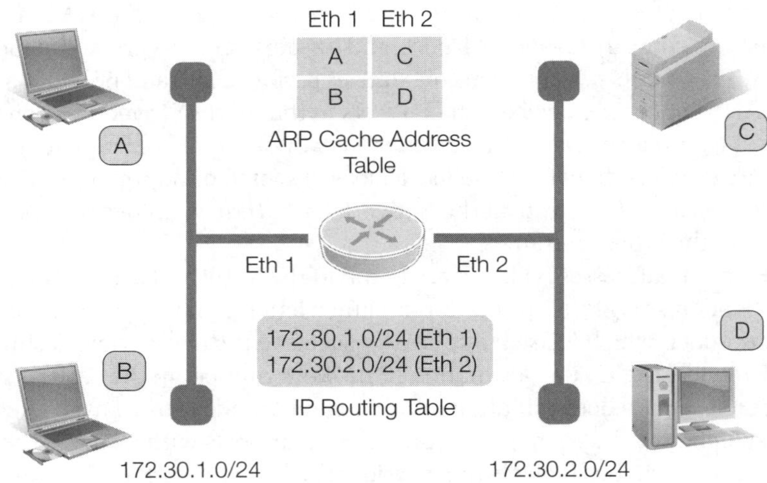

FIGURE 3-19

Router ARP cache table and IP routing table.

Internetworking with a Bridge/Router

One problem with regular routers is that they can examine packets only in formats they understand. That means all nodes on the network must use protocols the routers understand. This makes it harder to connect networks that use different protocols. A device that can act as a MAC layer bridge or router is often called a **brouter**. This is the same thing as a Layer 3 switch with Layer 2 bridging software. Depending on the LAN protocols that exist, networks may need to support non-routable and routable protocols. A non-routable protocol is one that does not have a Network Layer address. A routable protocol is one that has a Network Layer address that is routable. A brouter will then MAC layer bridge Ethernet frames that are non-routable and will route IP packets that are routable. This requires that IP routing be enabled in the device. A brouter is a more flexible and powerful internetworking device for networks, given that it can interconnect LANs as the Data Link Layer or Network Layer.

Internetworking with a Gateway

The final internetworking device found in networks is the **gateway**. A gateway is a device that interconnects two networks that use different protocols. Unlike a brouter, the gateway translates network packets from one network protocol to another. The main job with a gateway is to translate all incoming packets to a protocol compatible with the destination network. Gateways are commonly placed at entry and exit points of a network. Gateways commonly run either as software on a computer or as a device that performs the same functions as a router.

Gateways were common during the IBM SNA mainframe era, when **3270 terminal emulation** was performed in LAN-attached PCs and workstations. IBM's SNA protocol was widely used for mainframe data processing and communications; 3270 terminal emulation was the language that IBM terminals use to communicate to the mainframe computer. Using a common gateway, PCs and workstations could emulate and communicate via the SNA protocol using TCP/IP as a Transport and Network Layer protocol. Gateways allow IP-connected PCs and workstations to communicate with an IBM SNA mainframe device.

Switching Concepts

The main difference between devices to connect networks is how much work they must do to decide where to send each packet. Higher-level devices, such as routers and gateways, operate at the OSI Network Layer or higher. The higher a device operates within the protocol stack, the more processing power and intelligence is needed in the device itself. Software is what powers a bridge, router, brouter, or gateway. However, the more powerful and intelligent the device, the more costly it becomes. It requires more processing power to examine each Ethernet frame of IP packet and then to determine the best path to take. When a packet requires many hops to get from its source to destination, the added work can cause noticeable performance problems.

Store-and-Forward Versus Real-Time Communication

Networks typically support two kinds of network traffic: store-and-forward traffic and real-time traffic. E-mail is a kind of store-and-forward means of communication. Users write e-mails and send them to an e-mail server, and the recipient downloads messages and reviews them. File transfers are performed in a store-and-forward manner, where the file may reside on a user's hard drive and is then transferred to another user or an intermediate server for retrieval by the recipient.

Examples of real-time communication include voice and video. Voice over IP (VoIP), for example, is a real-time voice communication application that requires real-time access and high performance in a network. Traffic prioritization may be required when transmitting VoIP through a wide area network with lower-speed communication circuits. Unified communications use Session Initiation Protocol (SIP), which supports real-time presence, availability, IM chat, audio conferencing, video conferencing, and collaboration with multiple users simultaneously. AOL Instant Messenger, Yahoo Instant Messenger, and MSN Instant Messenger are applications that use SIP-enabled unified communications.

Store-and-forward communications typically send large chunks of data, such as 512 bytes or 1024 bytes, in an IP packet. This puts a performance strain on internetworking devices. Real-time communication sends lots of 64-byte- and 128-byte-sized IP packets, which also can put a performance stress on internetworking devices. The goal is to design and implement the most appropriate internetworking devices that can support the type of network traffic effectively and efficiently.

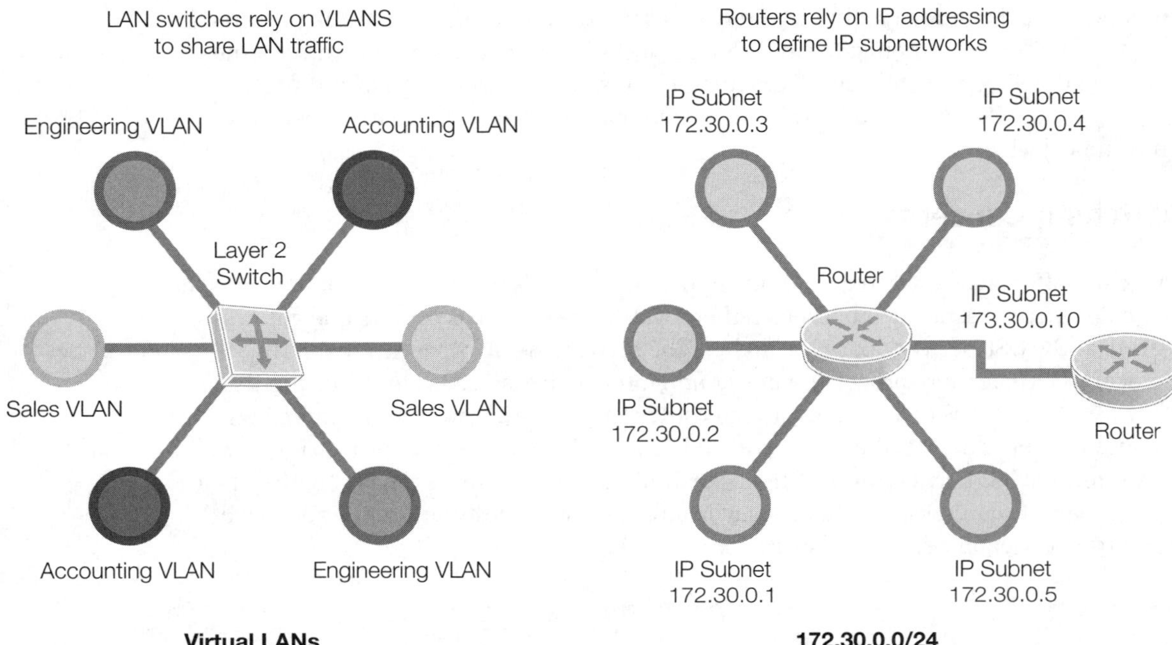

FIGURE 3-20

Physical versus logical network segmentation.

Switching subdivides a network into multiple small networks. Since the bridge or switch only sends packets to their destination network segment, they can help reduce overall traffic and collisions. However, you will only reduce overall congestion with a good network design and proper network segmentation (see Figure 3-20). A bridge or switch that forwards almost all traffic is not optimal. The bridge or switch can become a traffic bottleneck with traffic entering buffer memory, or worse, traffic may be dropped. It is important to monitor network traffic, perform capacity planning, and provide for network growth and expansion. This is discussed in greater detail later in this book.

Switch Functionality

Switches today have been engineered to support some basic functionality that all LANs require. There are six core functions that every network designer must consider when implementing network switches for edge or access connectivity. Edge or access connections refer to the wiring closet connection to the workstation device. The following switch functions must be incorporated into your network design accordingly:

- **Layer 2 versus Layer 3 workstation connectivity**—LAN switches that are deployed in the wiring closet for workstation connectivity typically require a network backbone connection. This usually is provided via fiber-optic trunk cables. Providing resiliency to the LAN switch requires a redundant physical path or second fiber-optic trunk cable. Layer 2 or Layer 3 resiliency is required to provide redundancy and a failover backbone connection.
- **MAC layer addressing tables**—LAN switches build MAC-layer address tables by examining the source MAC address of every Ethernet frame. It checks to see if the source MAC address is already in its address table. If the address is not in the table, it adds the source MAC addresses to the address table for each physical port on the switch. The MAC address table allows the switch to make a rapid filtering or forwarding decision. During the learning process, a switch may receive some Ethernet frames with a destination MAC address that it does not know about. In that case, the switch forwards this frame to every outbound port. Although this practice does cause a flood of packets on all network segments, the real destination node likely will send a reply. When the switch receives the reply, it learns the whereabouts of the new node and updates the MAC-layer address table.
- **Forwarding/filtering**—A switch takes one of two actions for each Ethernet frame when it is received. It forwards the frame for all unknown MAC addresses or for known MAC addresses that have a distinct destination port. If the MAC address entry indicates a frame should be forwarded to the same port on which it was received, the switch drops, or filters, the frame. This action helps isolate local traffic.
- **Prevent broadcast storms caused by loops**—Fault-tolerant networks have a redundant path or connection. This second connection obviously can create a physical loop in the network. Because of this, loop prevention or broadcast storm prevention is required. Depending on the switch, Layer 2 or Layer 3 resiliency and loop prevention techniques can be deployed. These redundant connections can cause loops if switches blindly forward packets between each other. A loop is any complete cycle where packets continue traveling in a circle and never reach a destination. To avoid this possibility, switches commonly use the **Spanning Tree Protocol (STP)** or **Rapid Spanning Tree Protocol (RSTP)** to communicate with one another and identify potential loops. The name of the game with spanning tree protocol is to prevent broadcast storms and provide for a redundant network connection in the event of physical cable or switch failure.
- **Power over Ethernet (PoE) switch ports**—Many LAN switches today can support **Power over Ethernet (PoE)** to power IP phones from the same RJ-45 connector on the switch. For workstations connections that support IP phones, workstations can plug directly into the back of the IP phone using a single 4-pair unshielded twisted-pair cable. From here, the workstation cabling then terminates in the wiring closet for patching directly to the PoE switch. PoE is supported by the **IEEE 802.3af–2003** and **IEEE 802.3at–2009** standards and specifications. IEEE 802.3af–2003 was the original PoE standard specifying up to 15.4 watts of power per RJ-45 port. IEEE 802.3at–2009 or PoE+ provides up to 25.4 watts of power per RJ-45 port.

- **Virtual LANs (VLANS)**—Layer 2 switches create **flat topology** networks. A flat topology means that there is no hierarchy to the network structure. One of the drawbacks to a flat topology is that Ethernet broadcasts frames are sent to all physical ports on the switch. Network segmentation and Layer 3 routers can limit the destination domain for broadcast messages, but not Layer 2 switches. On the other hand, switches work much faster because they operate at a lower network level. To address the problem of global network broadcasts, LAN switches allow the network designer to configure **Virtual LANs (VLAN)**. A VLAN defines a single broadcast domain where the Ethernet broadcast frame is allowed to traverse. Switches can map devices to specific VLANs and limit the scope of broadcasts to the assigned VLAN. As networks grow, VLANs can be configured to shrink the size of the broadcast domain. The **IEEE 802.1q** standard defines how VLANs can be deployed within Layer 2 switches using **Ethernet tagging**. Tagging allows you to send specific Ethernet frames to other switches where members of the same department or workgroup reside. You will learn more about VLANs and how they can be configured later in this book.
- **Layer 2 or Layer 3 switch resiliency**—LAN switches that reside at the edge or access point in a wiring closet may require a redundant backbone connection. This connection can be based on Layer 2 or Layer 3 techniques. The important requirement to consider is how fast must the failover connection converge? **Convergence** is the amount of time it takes for a network to recoup a connection. The answer to this question must be aligned to what applications and time-sensitive protocols must be supported. For example, VoIP and SIP protocols support real-time communication. Hence, sub-second (less than 1.0 seconds) resiliency and failover is critical, otherwise IP packets will be dropped. This can terminate a voice, video, or real-time communication. You will learn more about Layer 2 and Layer 3 resiliencies later in this book.

Switch Forwarding Methods

Layer 2 switches and MAC layer bridges forward Ethernet frames, using one of two common methods, illustrated in Figure 3-21. Each method has advantages and disadvantages for different environments.

- **Cut-through switching**—As soon as the LAN switch reads the destination MAC address, it starts to forward the packet to the destination and does not examine the entire frame. Once the MAC destination address is identified in the MAC layer address forwarding table, off it goes. No additional processing or storage in memory is required. This method of forwarding increases network throughput and performance. Since the Ethernet frame has a **checksum**, frame receipt can be verified, and the integrity of the frame is validated with a valid checksum. A checksum is how a network interface card verifies that the frame integrity is valid when received. In the event of an invalid checksum, the receiving workstation will request a retransmission of the errant frame. This method does not work well when using low-grade unshielded twisted-pair cabling.

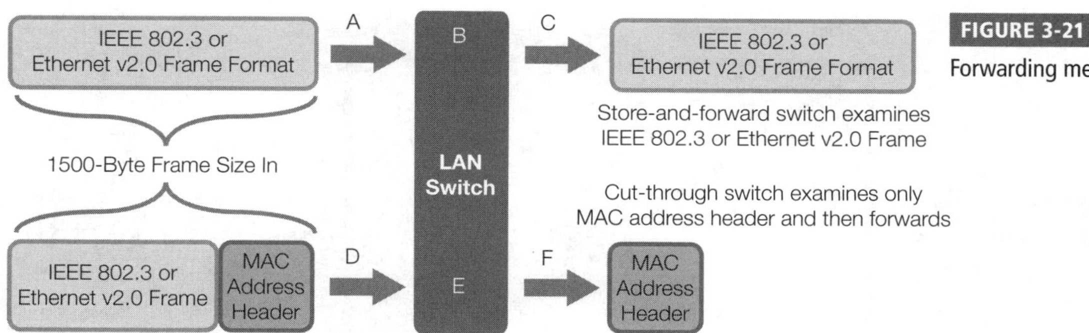

FIGURE 3-21
Forwarding methods.

- **Store-and-forward switching**—LAN switches that use this method must receive the entire Ethernet frame and then make a forwarding decision based on the MAC layer address table. The advantage of this method is that the device can drop any packets with errors prior to forwarding them. This method uses less of a network's capacity since it never forwards partial Ethernet frames, but it increases latency due to the time required to collect the entire Ethernet frame. Store-and-forward switching tends to work best for networks that encounter high error rates.

Circuit Switching

A **circuit-switched** network sets up a path between the source and destination devices. The two devices use the same path, or circuit, throughout the conversation. This is the model the original analog telephone system used. This telephony network, **plain old telephone service (POTS)** or **Public Switched Telephone Network (PSTN)**, carried analog signals. Analog communications work well on circuit-switched networks since the messages are continuous. The devices that participate in the conversation have complete access to the circuit, even when they aren't exchanging messages. Although many circuit-switched networks are analog, they can support digital communications as well.

Circuit-switched networks don't scale well because even idle circuits are unavailable to other devices. A growing number of users may exhaust the number of available circuits. These networks generally have very low latency since intermediate devices use the same path to send messages from the source to the destination. They don't have to decide on the best route with each message, and they don't have to decompose messages into smaller chunks. Network devices can either store predefined circuits or they can set up circuits on an as-needed basis.

POTS used circuit-switched networks when all calls were analog. Today's telephone networks use a different switching method. Any time a caller dialed a number on the POTS network, the network established a dedicated circuit between the caller and the called party. The two parties could talk back and forth uninterrupted until one party hung up and terminated the connection. The network segments dedicated to the call

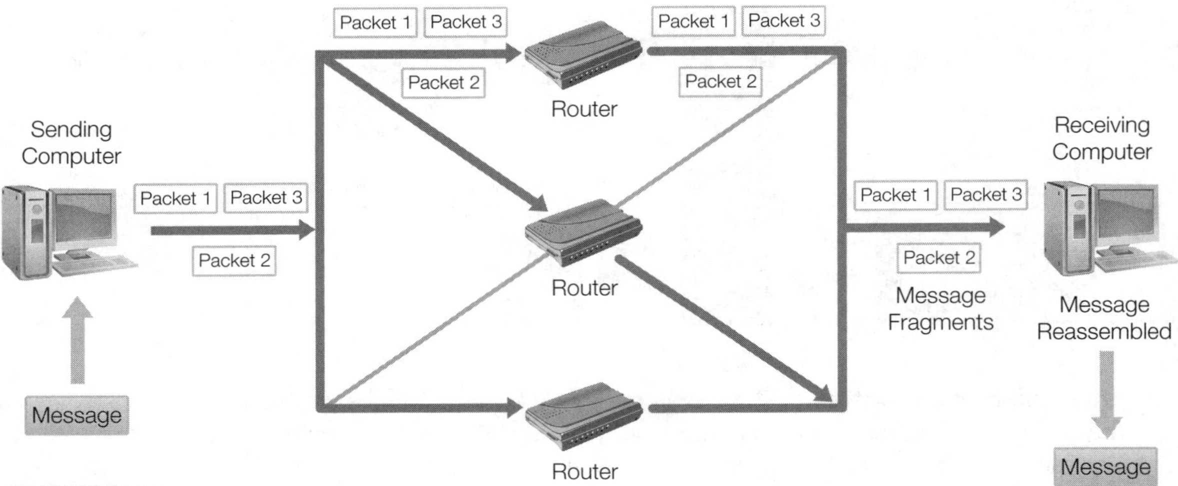

FIGURE 3-22

Circuit-switched network.

would only then be released to participate in other circuits. The next time the same caller called the same number, they would likely get a different physical circuit. The path between source and destination changes between calls, but remains constant during any call.

One advantage of circuit-switched networks, shown in Figure 3-22, is that once you set up a circuit, there is very little overhead in sending messages. That means these networks support real-time communication without many delays. You also know that since both devices own the circuit, all messages travel in the same order until they reach the destination. Collisions and congestion are not issues with circuit-switched networks. Another advantage of circuit-switched networks is the integrity of messages. Circuit-switched networks transmit complete messages instead of separating each message into smaller chunks. The network doesn't have to spend any effort disassembling and then reassembling messages.

On the other hand, circuit-switched communications are expensive. Once the sender and receiver set up a circuit, they own that circuit for the duration of the dialog. Network carriers define supply dedicated service throughout the dialog even if the two parties aren't using the circuit. Telecommunication service providers charge for the use of the circuit. It generally costs more to use circuit-switched networks because fewer users can access the available circuits. In spite of the drawbacks of circuit-switched networks, several popular networks use this technology, including:

- plain old telephone service (POTS)
- Integrated Services Digital Network (ISDN) B-channel
- Circuit-Switched Data (CSD) and High-Speed Circuit-Switched Data (HSCSD) cellular networks
- X.21 network

Packet Switching

The other common switching technique does not establish a circuit for a conversation. It separates messages into smaller, manageable-sized chunks called packets. Packets can vary in size, but are generally between 512 bytes and 8 kilobytes in length. Different protocols may use different minimum or maximum packet sizes. Different software applications may choose to use different packet sizes even when using the same protocol. The packet size should reflect how you use the data from an effectiveness and efficiency perspective.

Networks that transmit packets as individual messages are called **packet-switched** networks (see Figure 3-23). Packet-switched networks send each packet toward the intended destination. Each device along the way examines the packet's destination MAC address and selects the best outbound port. The receiver is responsible for reassembling the packets to reconstruct the full message.

When everything works well, the network can dynamically direct packets around bottlenecks and get the packets to the destination with minimal delay. The receiver reassembles the message and presents it to the application software as a complete message. Packet-switched networks are more scalable than circuit-switched networks. Since each packet travels on its own path, circuits are immediately available for other packets from different messages. Many conversations share the same network connections and use more of the network's capacity. This is more effective and efficient when transmitting large amounts of data from source to destination.

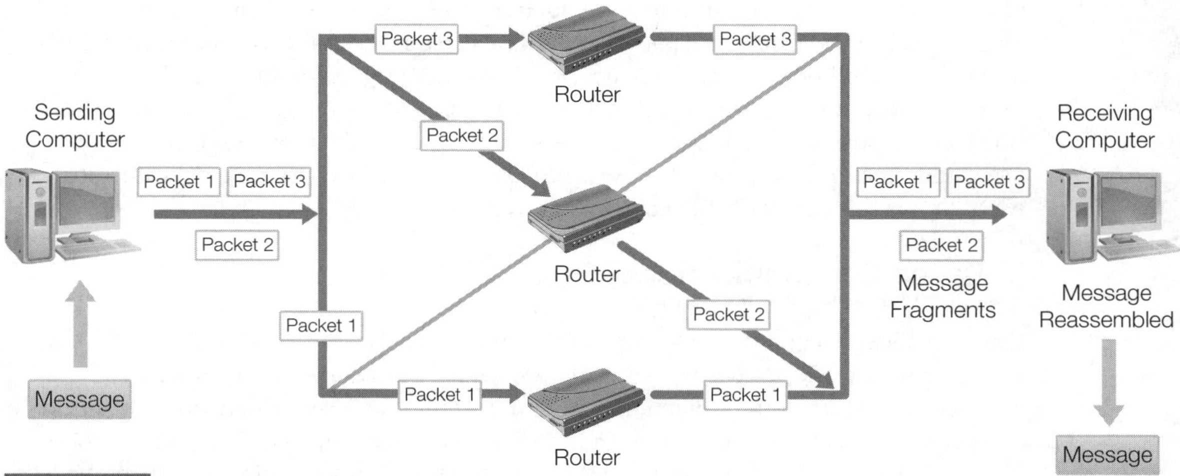

FIGURE 3-23
Packet-switched network.

Packet-switched networks do have drawbacks as well. Transmission delay or latency tends to be higher on packet-switched networks when compared to circuit-switched networks. The source computer must chop the message into multiple packets and send each one to the destination. The source numbers each packet sequentially so the destination knows how to reassemble the message. Each switch between the source and destination must make a decision on where to send each packet. Networks with multiple paths between nodes may use different paths to balance network traffic and load.

The destination device performs most of the work to reassemble the packets into a message. To transform packets into messages, the destination must do the following:

- **Resequence packets that arrive out of order**—Resequencing puts the packets back into the order in which the sender sent them.
- **Identify missing packets and request re-sends**—The destination device notices gaps in packet sequences numbers as lost packets. It examines the time the next packet it received was sent. If the time that has passed since that packet was sent is greater than the timeout period for packets, it requests a re-send for that packet. The destination device has to wait until it receives enough packets in order to reassemble a complete message.
- **Reassemble the complete message**—The destination device must completely reassemble the packets to form the complete message and validate its integrity.

Organizations used both circuit-switched and packet-switched networking throughout the 1970s, 1980s, and 1990s. This has since diminished due to the rise of TCP/IP and IP networking as the predominant means of supporting communications. As organizations move toward IP-based communications such as VoIP and Unified Communications, the need for circuit-switching and packet-switching is reduced. IP-based communications provide new methods to communicate. New and emerging technology has the ability to support advanced communication. Before choosing a technology for your network, consider the business applications that must be supported, the protocols that must be used, and the time sensitivity of these protocols. These design parameters will dictate what kind of LAN switch and backbone network is required.

IP-Based Communications

Growing networks and the ability to connect multiple networks together created a need for a global network standard. Many different vendors developed specifications and products to support communication across many different types of networks. By far the most popular set of standards organizations use today to communicate using networks is the **TCP/IP suite**. This suite, also known as the **Internet Protocol Suite**, takes its name from the two most common protocols at its core: **Transmission Control Protocol (TCP)** and Internet Protocol (IP). They were developed for the Internet's predecessor, ARPANET, in the 1970s. Both have been around for a long time.

These protocols govern how computers and devices send and receive messages across a network. They define the rules of how messages travel from application software on one computer device to the application software on a remote computer or device. Each protocol addresses a different communication problem.

- **TCP**—The TCP protocol guarantees the delivery of a reliable stream of data between two computer programs. TCP isn't the only protocol that organizations use to communicate on the Internet, but it is one of the most popular. TCP operates at OSI Layer 4.
- **IP**—The Internet protocol that makes it possible to deliver packets across a complex network to a destination. IP handles the routing decisions necessary to get packets from their source to destination. IP operates at OSI Layer 3.

IP provides a consistent foundation for communicating across large networks. Although it is commonly associated with the TCP protocol, it stands on its own as a distinct protocol. There are many protocols that operate on top of IP, using it to handle the addressing issues with delivering packets. Some of the protocols that commonly operate at the Transport Layer (OSI Layer 4) above IP include:

- Transmission Control Protocol (TCP)
- User Datagram Protocol (UDP)
- AppleTalk Transaction Protocol (ATP)
- Stream Control Transmission Protocol (SCTP)
- NetBIOS Frames Protocol (NFP)
- Fiber Channel Protocol (FCP)

Today's applications are designed and built knowing that TCP/IP is the transport and protocol of choice. TCP/IP basically wiped out all other network layers and transport protocols used in modern day communication networks. The standard is so prevalent that network presence is often expressed as an IP address. In short, if you have an IP address, you're on the network. While this isn't always true, getting an IP address does generally provide some level of network access. In the past, only computers and network devices had IP addresses. Today, nearly every electronic component can have an IP address. Computers, cell phones, refrigerators, security system controllers, and even cameras often have IP addresses. These devices become nodes on a global network.

An IP address identifies a device or computer to a network as a unique node. Private IP addresses identify nodes within an organization. Public IP addresses identify nodes to the global Internet. Any node with a public IP address is a visible destination and potential recipient of network communication from any other node with a valid IP address. This standard addressing technique makes it possible for any two devices to communicate, regardless of their physical locations or the distance between them.

The Internet Protocol provides location independence. Applications that want to communicate over networks only need to reference the IP address of the destination node. The standard networking software will handle the process of sending the message on its way. The devices connected to the network between the source and the destination handle the process of routing the messages to their proper destinations.

Today's IP-based business communications provide the ability for organizations to save money over legacy solutions. They can also provide far more services than with older networks. The hardware and software required to set up today's IP-based networks is more expensive than older options. However, the ability to use IP-based networks for many applications simultaneously results in lower **total cost of ownership (TCO)**. Organizations used to have to lease telephone lines on circuit-switched networks to provide connectivity. The leased lines were limited in the bandwidth they could support and didn't allow much multi-use. Current IP-based networks can support many more users for the same, or lower, cost.

Many applications exist today that help organizations reduce costs, increase productivity, and improve customer satisfaction. The real power of IP communications is in UC. Recall that UC is the convergence of voice, video, and data applications. The architecture of IP communications allows applications to integrate with an organization's current applications. For example, an organization can integrate e-mail with Web-enabled applications such as sales order entry, or customer relationship management, or electronic medical records, providing greater functionality and streamlined access to applications and data.

One of the first noticeable advantages of IP-based communication was the paradigm shift from circuit-switch voice communications to IP-based communications. This paradigm shift was first led by presence/availability (i.e., buddy list) and IM chat and then VoIP. AOL was one of the first Internet service providers to provide a SIP-enabled presence/availability and Instant Messenger application. This instant messaging application became known as IM chat. This led to VoIP with applications from Skype and Yahoo Messenger. Users with a broadband Internet connection could send and receive telephone calls using the public Internet and a headset. They could bypass the telephone system and talk to friends and family using their home computer. Skype is a popular VoIP and video conferencing application. Skype offers a premium option that allows its users to initiate a local, long distance, or international telephone call. Calls to regular telephone numbers are charged at a rate that is far lower than current telecommunication service providers. The user initiating the telephone call would use VoIP to set up a call to a Skype server that is close to the destination location. The Skype server then connects to the local telephone system in that region to mitigate long distance toll call charges. While this approach doesn't totally bypass the telephone system, it does provide inexpensive long distance calls using VoIP as the transport.

Skype and other VoIP- and SIP-enabled applications provide home users and business users with inexpensive communication options that can support both store-and-forward and real-time communication. Businesses are realizing how valuable video chat and video conferencing can be. Organizations are replacing business travel with audio conferencing, video conferencing, and real-time **collaboration**. Collaboration is an online application that allows multiple users to share and view the same information on a master computer or controller. Webex, HP Virtual Rooms, and Yahoo Messenger support real-time collaboration, allowing multiple users to communicate and share applications in real-time. These options are possible largely due to the growth of fast Internet connections and IP-based networking software. The ability to transport audio, video, and nearly any other type of media and data makes IP-based communication the protocol of choice. Today, IP-based communications and unified communications provide organizations with real-time applications and communications where and when needed.

CHAPTER SUMMARY

The most important goal of any organization is to meet its customer needs. Organizations that fail in this goal tend not to stay in existence. Organizations that migrate to IP-based communications can maximize effectiveness and efficiency when communicating with customers and employees. IP-based communications can help organizations drive VoIP and unified communications into their everyday lives. Support for VoIP and SIP protocols, however, requires unique network designs and resiliency given the time-sensitive nature of these applications and protocols. VoIP and unified communications require VLANs, layered security, and other network techniques to ensure the timely delivery of these IP packets.

This chapter covered the evolution of circuit-switched, packet-switched, and IP-based communications. It examined the evolution of local area networking, or LANs, and how LANs have become the predominant desktop and networking infrastructure for many organizations. It reviewed how Ethernet evolved into the IEEE 802.3 CSMA/CD standard. This led to the creation of 10/100/1000 IEEE 802.3 standards and specifications. From here the chapter covered how different topologies can support different physical and logical connectivity requirements. This led to a discussion on how to interconnect LANs using various internetworking techniques and solutions.

Since today's networks rely on solid addressing and routing, the chapter covered common switching techniques. It discussed how switching differs from routing and how many organizations are returning to switching to support real-time applications and time-sensitive protocols. The chapter then addressed circuit-switched and packet-switched networks and their relative strengths and weaknesses. Finally, it discussed how today's Internet and IP-based communications have become the dominant means of supporting voice, video, and data communications.

KEY CONCEPTS AND TERMS

3270 terminal emulation
Address Resolution Protocol (ARP)
Attenuation
Broadcast domain
Brouter
Bus topology
Checksum
Circuit-switched
Collaboration
Collision
Connection medium
Convergence
CSMA/CD (carrier sense multiple access with collision detection)
Data circuit-terminating equipment (DCE)
Data terminal equipment (DTE)
Dumb terminal
Electronic Industries Association (EIA)
Ethernet tagging
Extranet
Fault tolerance
Flat topology
Frame
Fully connected mesh
Gateway
Host-based
Hub
Hybrid topology
IEEE 802.1q
IEEE 802.3 CSMA/CD
IEEE 802.3af–2003
IEEE 802.3at–2009
IEEE 802.5 token ring
Instant message (IM chat)
Institute of Electrical and Electronics Engineers (IEEE)
Internetworking
Intranet
Layer 2
Layer 3
Logical topology
MAC layer bridge
Media Access Control (MAC) layer address
Mesh topology
Metcalfe's law
Network adapter
Network interface card
Network interface controller (NIC)
Network topology
Open Systems Interconnection (OSI) Reference Model
Packet
Packet-switched
Partially connected mesh
Path length
Physical topology
Plain old telephone service (POTS)
Point-to-point
Power over Ethernet (PoE)
Public Switched Telephone Network (PSTN)
Rapid Spanning Tree Protocol (RSTP)
Resiliency
Ring topology
Router
RS-232
Serial communications
Spanning Tree Protocol (STP)
Star-wired topology
Switch
TCP/IP (Internet Protocol) suite
Terminal
Token
Total cost of ownership (TCO)
Transmission Control Protocol (TCP)
Virtual LAN (VLAN)

CHAPTER 3 ASSESSMENT

1. A network can consist of at least two connected computers.

A. True
B. False

2. Which IEEE standard specifies the 10BaseT specifications?

A. IEEE 802.1q
B. IEEE 802.3i
C. IEEE 802.5
D. IEEE 802.3af

3. Which of the following is *not* an example of a real-time application?

A. Voice communications
B. File transfer
C. Video communications
D. Instant message/IM chat

4. Which of the following is an example of a store-and-forward application?

A. Instant message/IM chat
B. Voice over IP
C. E-mail
D. Collaboration

5. Which network provides the highest level of fault tolerance and redundancy for failed connections?

A. Ring
B. Mesh
C. Point-to-point
D. Hybrid

6. A MAC layer bridge examines the ________ MAC layer address to make a filtering or forwarding decision.

7. A router makes a path determination decision by examining the ________ network number within an IP packet.

8. ________ switching starts forwarding packets as soon as the device reads the destination address.

9. Which term describes how to interconnect LANs and networks regardless of the technique?

A. Bridging
B. Routing
C. Switching
D. Internetworking

10. Why is an IP-based communications infrastructure the best solution for many organizations?

A. It can support voice, video, and data using the same protocol.
B. It is easy to implement.
C. It has inherent security.
D. It can support real-time applications.

PART TWO

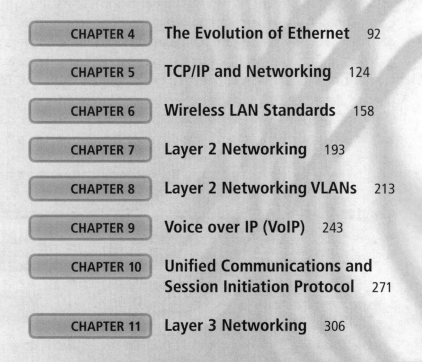

Fundamentals of Networking

CHAPTER

4 The Evolution of Ethernet

ETHERNET AND IEEE 802.3 CSMA/CD LAN TECHNOLOGIES have become the leading LAN and networking technology of the modern Internet era. Ethernet is a family of networking technologies that define how computers and devices communicate on a LAN. Ethernet was introduced to the commercial marketplace in 1980. It has replaced other LAN technologies. Understanding why Ethernet was developed and how it has since evolved is important. It will help you understand how it can empower effective communications. Prior to its introduction, LANs used a variety of protocols and technologies to connect computers and devices. While each technology had its strengths and weaknesses, connecting LANs was a common difficulty. Connecting LANs of different types generally required specialized hardware or software to convert packets from one LAN's format to another. It wasn't long before organizations wanted a standard format that would make connecting LANs easy and efficient. Ethernet filled this need. It has since become the de facto LAN standard for networks of all sizes. In this chapter, you will learn about Ethernet and IEEE 802.3 CSMA/CD. You will also learn how organizations have implemented it over the past 30 years.

Chapter 4 Topics

This chapter covers the following topics and concepts:

- How Ethernet evolved
- What the IEEE 802.3 standard and specifications are
- How multiple nodes share network media
- How to internetwork Ethernet LANs together
- How to design Ethernet networks for workgroups, buildings, campuses, and metropolitan area networks
- What GigE and 10 GigE specifications are

Chapter 4 Goals

When you complete this chapter, you will be able to:

- Describe the history of Ethernet
- Explain the IEEE 802.3 standard and specifications
- Identify shared media capabilities
- Select the appropriate internetworking solution for connecting LANs together
- Describe Ethernet network design best practices
- Incorporate GigE and 10 GigE in backbone network designs

Ethernet Evolution

You previously learned that the DIX **Ethernet** standard became the IEEE 802.3 CSMA/CD standard for 10 Mbps baseband LAN technologies. There are two common Data Link Layer frames used: Ethernet v2.0 and IEEE 802.3 frame formats. Software drivers are required to enable the physical NIC cards and determine which of the frame formats to use. There was a mass migration from coaxial-based workstation cabling to star-wired, unshielded twisted-pair cabling. It transformed LAN connectivity. As the IEEE 802.3 CSMA/CD family of standards evolved into smaller, faster, more energy efficient chips, network connection speeds increased. **10Base5 "Thicknet"** evolved into **10Base2 "Thinnet."** The transition to structured wiring systems drove **10BaseT**, **100BaseTX**, and now **1000BaseT (GigE)** to the desktop and server farm connectivity. These higher speeds allow for **real-time applications** and **time-sensitive protocols** to operate effectively and efficiently.

The speed at which Ethernet-based LAN technologies matured attracted many organizations. The focus of this chapter is the IEEE 802.3 CSMA/CD family of LAN technologies and the way businesses and organizations use them. During the 1980s and 1990s, Ethernet LANs dominated due to the ease of implementation and migration for LANs based on the10, 100, and 1000 BaseT LAN standards. With structured wiring systems now capable of supporting gigabit-plus transmission speeds, networks can support higher-speed applications and time-sensitive protocols.

From here through the remainder of this book, the term "Ethernet" refers to the entire family of Ethernet and IEEE 802.3 CSMA/CD standards and specifications. The book will be specific whenever we need to distinguish Ethernet v2.0 and IEEE 802.3, as when discussing frame formats.

IEEE 802.3 Standards and Specifications

Ethernet LAN technology solved many business communication and connectivity business challenges. And it did this at a lower cost than its early rival, token ring. Businesses and organizations were connecting their PCs and workstations with LANs. This connectivity provided the foundation to build for departmental or **workgroup** applications and client/server applications. Workers needed office automation functionality and the ability to share documents and files quickly and securely. LANs and networking became a primary requirement to support the business needs of many companies and organizations.

Solving Business Challenges

Table 4-1 shows business challenges and solutions, and the technical means to solve problems.

These foundational business challenges were the major business drivers that drove the evolution of Ethernet LAN technology. When first introduced, Ethernet networking was based on the physical requirements of coaxial cabling. Deployment of Ethernet LANs was dependent on distance, integrity of the cabling, and use of electronics to connect to this bus topology. Early deployments of Ethernet LAN technology used Thicknet and Thinnet coaxial cabling to support 10Base5 and 10Base2 LANs respectively. This is shown in Figure 4-1.

TABLE 4-1 Defining the need for a LAN.

BUSINESS CHALLENGE	BUSINESS SOLUTION	TECHNICAL SOLUTION
• Need to connect PCs, workstations, and servers	• Interconnect the PCs, workstations, and servers on the same physical and logical network	• Ethernet switch connectivity via star-wired, unshielded twisted-pair cabling
• Need to share and access applications with other workers	• Install shared applications on servers for all users to access	• Implement LAN servers with enterprise-wide access controls
• Need to share files between workers	• Implement user and shared permission rights for access to drives, folders, and data	• Implement standardized access controls and permission rights as per policy definition
• Need to share printers and other devices among multiple users	• Allow users to access shared servers and printers	• Integrate office automation functionality within departments and workgroups
• Need to communicate with other workers throughout the company	• Support multiple methods of communicating between users—VoIP, e-mail, IM Chat, conferencing, collaboration	• Enable VoIP, SIP, and unified communication solutions for user desktops and mobile devices

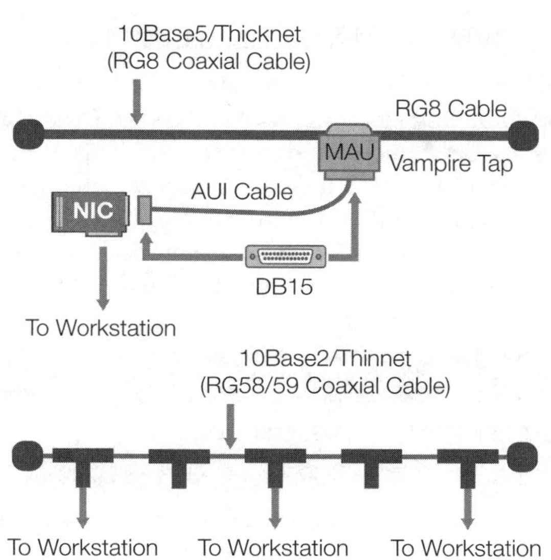

FIGURE 4-1
Early implementations of 10Base5 and 10Base2.

The early adopters of the original Ethernet implemented the baseband bus topology as defined in the original IEEE 802.3 CDMA/CD 10Base5 standard and specification. This quickly evolved to support the easier-to-implement 10Base2 standard and specification. Structured cabling systems emerged that drove the use of 4-pair, unshielded twisted-pair cabling. Cabling options varied from Category 3 (voice-grade cabling) to Category 5 (high-speed data grade) to Category 6 (very high-speed data grade). The 10BaseT standard and specification (Figure 4-2) was a major driving force to encourage the use of unshielded twisted-pair cabling for workstation connections. As Ethernet speeds increased, so did the need for higher-grade unshielded twisted-pair cabling. This dependency led to the installation of structured wiring systems and Ethernet LAN switches in wiring closets for PC and workstation connections.

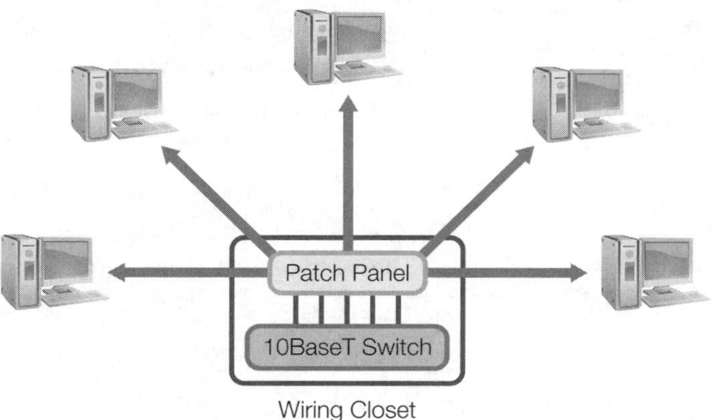

FIGURE 4-2
10BaseT dominated the early installations.

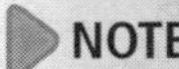
NOTE

You can obtain a complete copy of the 802.3 standards and specifications from the IEEE Web site: *http://standards.ieee.org/about/get/802/802.3.html*

IEEE 802.3 CSMA/CD Standards

You can start learning about the IEEE 802.3 standards by downloading your own personal copy of the original IEEE 802.3 CSMA/CD standard and specification. This document gives you an idea of the level of detail and specifications that are actually defined in an IEEE standard.

The IEEE 802.3 family of standards defines different standards and specifications for the various current Ethernet hardware and

TABLE 4-2 Significant parts of the IEEE 802.3 family of standards

ETHERNET STANDARD	RELEASE DATE	DESCRIPTION
Experimental Ethernet	1973	2.94 Mbps using coaxial bus
Ethernet II (Ethernet v 2.0)	1982	10 Mbps using thick coaxial cable
802.3	1983	(10Base5) 10 Mbps using thick coaxial cable
802.3a	1985	(10Base2) 10 Mbps using thin coaxial cable
802.3i	1990	(10Base-T) 10 Mbps using twisted-pair cable
802.3j	1993	(10Base-F) 10 Mbps using fiber optic cable
802.3u	1995	(100Base-TX, 100Base-T4, 100Base-FX) Fast Ethernet—100 Mbps
802.3y	1998	(100Base-T2) 100 Mbps using low-quality twisted-pair cable
802.3z	1998	(1000Base-X) 1 Gbps using fiber optic cable
802.3ab	1999	(1000Base-T) 1 Gbps using twisted-pair cable
802.3ae	2003	(10GBase-SR, 10GBase-LR, 10GBase-ER, 10GBase-SW, 10GBase-LW, 10GBase-EW) 10 Gbit/s using fiber optic cable
802.3af	2003	PoE Switch standard for up to 15.4 watts of power to IP phone
802.3at	2009	PoE Switch standard for up to 25.5 watts of power to IP phone
802.3ak	2004	(10GBase-CX4) 10 Gbps using twin-axial cable
802.3an	2006	(10GBase-T) 10 Gbps using twisted-pair cable
802.3aq	2006	(10GBase-LRM) 10 Gbps using multimode fiber
802.3bg	2011	(40GBase-SM) 40 Gbps Ethernet Operation Over Single-Mode Fiber

technologies. Each standard conforms to a unique naming convention that identifies the IEEE committee that actually defined the standard. The 802.3 standards range from the original 802.3 standard to include multiple subcommittees and standards. The original 802.3 standard defined Ethernet running at 10 Mbps using Thicknet coax cable. The latest published standard, 802.3bg, includes many revisions to the original standard and now defines Ethernet running as fast as 40 Gbps using fiber optic cabling. Today's Ethernet is faster than the original specification, runs on additional physical media, and supports a variety of networking topologies. Table 4-2 lists some of the milestones of the Ethernet standards.

Ethernet and IEEE 802.3 Frame Formats

Ethernet was originally designed as a method to send and receive data packets using a common shared medium. All of the IEEE 802 LAN standards define a 6-byte, or 48-bit, MAC layer address. This address uniquely identifies each NIC and is burned into the Ethernet chip on the board. It is possible for one computer or device to have more than one NIC. This is true when virtual machines are installed in the same physical workstation. The ability to host more than one NIC allows hosts and devices to be associated with more than one MAC layer address. Although MAC layer addresses generally are defined for each NIC at the manufacturer, many NICs allow installers and even end users to change the MAC layer address through software drivers. MAC layer addresses are added to each Ethernet frame's header to uniquely identify the MAC layer address of the source and destination nodes. Figure 4-3 distinguishes an Ethernet v2.0 from an IEEE 802.3 frame.

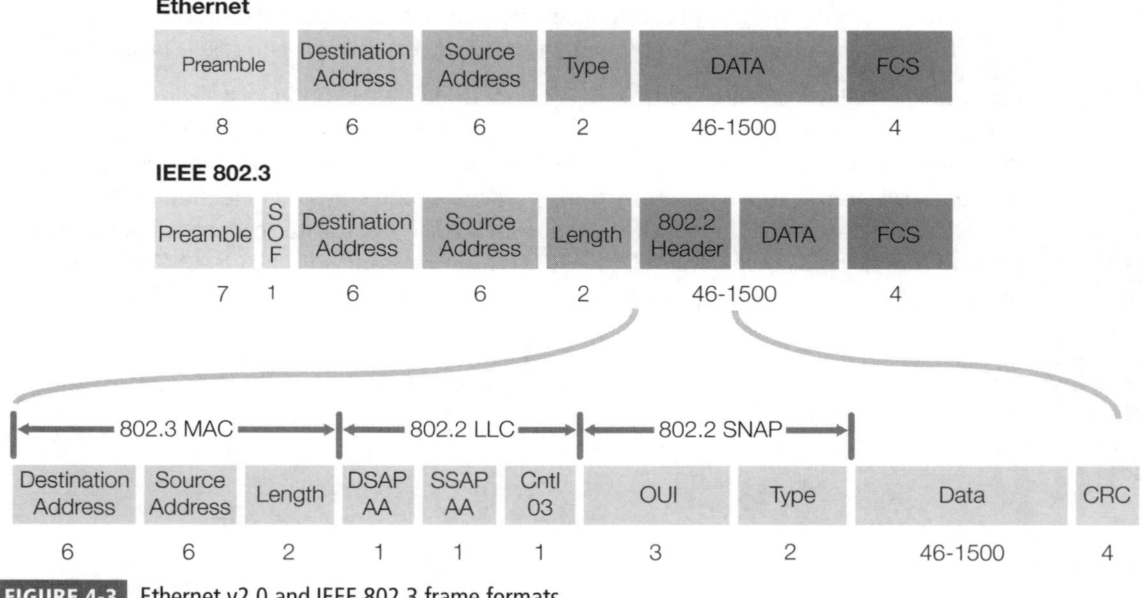

FIGURE 4-3 Ethernet v2.0 and IEEE 802.3 frame formats.

Note the key differences between the Ethernet and IEEE 802.3 frame formats:

- Ethernet v2.0: 2-byte type field that indicates the Network Layer protocol.
- IEEE 802.3: 802.2 Logical Link Control (LLC) sub-layer within the Data Link Layer that indicates service access points and Network Layer protocols.

How Multiple Nodes Share Network Media

How does Ethernet work? How do PCs and workstations send and receive traffic to and from servers? What happens when there are too many workstations trying to communicate? What happens when workstations communicate simultaneously? How did Ethernet evolve to combat these bus topology problems?

Let's break carrier sense multiple access with collision detection (CSMA/CD) down into the following pieces:

- **"Carrier sense"**—NIC cards listen on the physical media for specific voltage levels or carrier signals. If the coast is clear, the NIC can transmit on the network. If someone is already transmitting, you will know because the carrier sense voltage level is different.
- **"Multiple access"**—NIC cards can transmit simultaneously. When this occurs, it causes a collision situation on the physical media. This collision is noticed by the NIC card transceivers that listen to specific voltage levels or carrier signals.
- **"Collision detection"**—NIC cards react to signal collisions by retransmitting after receiving notification that a collision occurred. While this solution solves the initial collision, bus topologies with excessive collisions can cause problems.

Ethernet solved the problem of how to connect multiple PCs and workstations together. Along with it came the most popular method of accessing shared media. Ethernet brought with it a scheme for controlling access to a shared medium. This access control is what's referred to as carrier sense multiple access with collision detection (CSMA/CD). CSMA/CD defines a set of rules that define when a PC or workstation can transmit and how to handle collisions. Behind CSMA/CD is a simple concept. The CSMA/CD rules formalize how humans have talked with one another for thousands of years.

FIGURE 4-4

Carrier sense multiple access with collision detection.

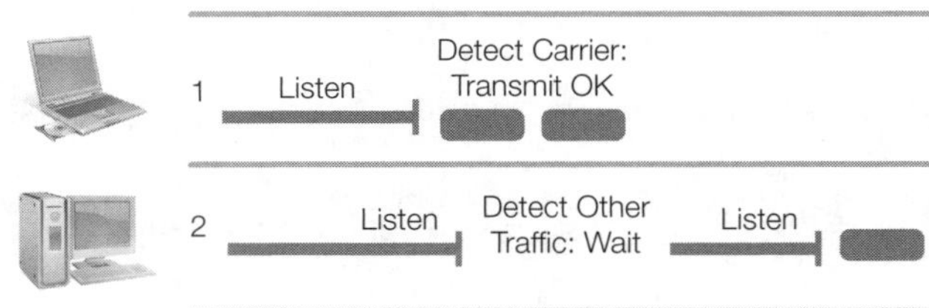

People-to-People Communications

People have used CSMA/CD for many years. Nearly all of it is second nature—we rarely have to think about it. In fact, we generally don't pay attention to the rules at all until someone fails to play by them. In conversation, it all comes down to three basic rules:

- Listen to others so you can hear if anyone else is talking.
- Don't talk when someone else is already talking.
- If you do interrupt someone else, stop talking and wait until they are done.

The telephone network provides a good example of how people use CSMA/CD to communicate. Many rural areas didn't immediately receive direct telephone service to every home. In low population areas, it was common to connect several houses to a shared telephone line. This was called a party line. Anyone who wanted to place a call would pick up the handset and listen for a dial tone. A dial tone meant no one else was currently on the line. If other people were talking, you could join in the conversation as long as you didn't talk over other people. It was good manners to treat a party line like a face-to-face conversation. As more people joined a conversation, it became harder to coordinate who could talk. Think about the last time someone interrupted you or talked over you. It probably interfered with your ability to communicate. The same problem occurs in network communications.

Ethernet uses an **optimistic transmission** approach. Ethernet doesn't try to prevent all collisions. It attempts to avoid some collisions by detecting collisions. Since all of the nodes on an Ethernet network share the same transmission media, there must be some way to handle collisions. Avoiding collisions and incorporating collision detection is the goal of CSMA/CD. Before any node can transmit, it first listens to the media for any current traffic. If the media is available to transmit, it has a specific voltage level that tells transceivers the coast is clear. If the media is not available to transmit, a carrier signal is detected by the transceiver indicating that a transmission is occurring. If the transceiver doesn't detect any current traffic, the node starts to transmit. Figure 4-4 shows how carrier sense multiple access works.

As the NIC transmits onto the media, it continues listening to the medium. If the transmission is valid, the destination node receives the entire Ethernet frame for processing. An invalid Ethernet frame indicates that two frames have collided. When this happens, the transceiver of the transmitting node stops transmitting. The node then waits for a random amount of time and then retransmits when the carrier sense condition is obtained. The random wait time reduces the possibility that the same nodes will transmit colliding frames again simultaneously. Figure 4-5 shows how Ethernet collision detection works.

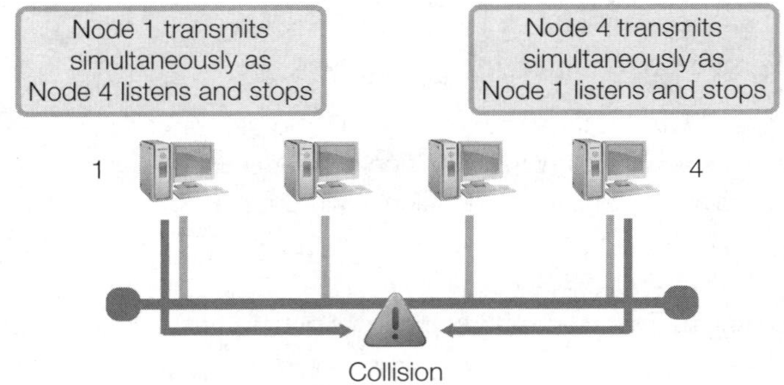

FIGURE 4-5 Ethernet collision detection.

CSMA/CD and the deployment of Ethernet LAN technologies evolved rapidly (Figure 4-6). From 10 Mbps baseband coaxial LAN topologies, to GigE to the desktop, to metro-Ethernet MAN connectivity, Ethernet has become the de facto standard for transporting IP-based communications to the desktop. Ethernet made a huge impact on how IP-based communications and networking is delivered end-to-end to PCs and workstations. CSMA/CD has proven to be more scalable than other LAN technologies. This was driven by the fact that Ethernet technology and chipsets were able to increase Ethernet bandwidth speeds 10 times from 10 Mbps to 100 Mbps to 1000 Mbps or Gigabit speeds. Today, Ethernet supports 40 Gbps trunk bandwidth speeds on single-mode optical fiber. With Layer 2 and Layer 3 LAN switches providing each port an Ethernet LAN segment or broadcast domain, collisions are avoided. This provides PCs, workstations, and servers with their own dedicated switched Ethernet LAN connection. This maximizes throughput and performance for all devices. With structured wiring systems providing high-grade unshielded twisted-pair cabling to the desktop, users can now migrate their LAN connections from 10BaseT to 100BaseT to 1000BaseT or Gigabit Ethernet to the desktop. Layer 2 and Layer 3 LAN switches make it possible for many devices to be LAN attached via Ethernet. Ethernet has proven to be highly scalable at an affordable price throughout its history.

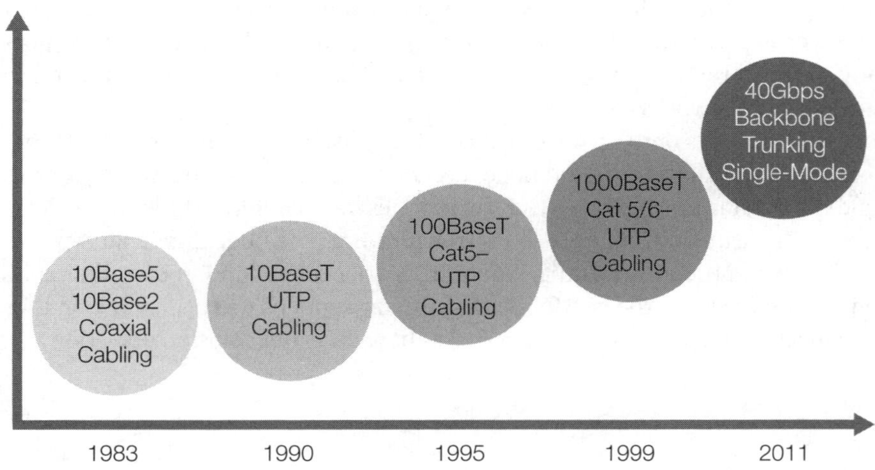

FIGURE 4-6 Ethernet technology bandwidth speed evolution.

Internetworking LANs: Bridging Versus Routing

You read in an earlier chapter that there are multiple ways to interconnect LANs. This was referred to as internetworking. As the popularity of local area networking grew, so did the need to interconnect departmental or workgroup LANs together. Ethernet makes creating small or large networks easy. Using inexpensive hardware, Ethernet could be physically extended using different transmission media and transceivers. With client/server applications migrating to desktop computers and LANs, the need to segment and isolate departmental traffic was born. Security, traffic segmentation, and ease of network management are all reasons to separate and internetwork LANs. Prior to the use of IEEE 802.1q VLAN technology, file servers had to be locally connected to departmental LANs. This provided local access to departmental and shared applications, files, and data.

Today, many organizations cluster servers and application servers within the data center. This puts a burden on designing a proper server farm network within the data center with high-speed **backbone** network trunking. Server access and maximizing performance are key considerations when designing LANs. Where you put servers can impact how you design the network. This is particularly true for real-time applications that have time-sensitive protocols and applications that require heavy client/server data transfers. Hence the need for high-speed backbone connectivity from data center to desktop location is paramount. How Layer 2 and Layer 3 networking can achieve that is the main objective of internetworking.

Ethernet switches have evolved over time to accommodate 10 Mbps, 100 Mbps, and 1000 Mbps Ethernet to the desktop. This era included the introduction of Power over Ethernet (PoE) LAN switches to support IP phone power connections. Finally, support for Layer 2 versus Layer 3 switching within the wiring closet is also of great debate for many network designers. How to provide end-point connectivity for PCs and workstations is dependent on what applications and connectivity requirements are needed by the users.

Let's examine each solution and apply these solutions to real-world examples for Ethernet networking expansion and growth.

Repeaters and Hubs—Layer 1 Forwarding

Physically extending the cabling distances or conversion to other transmission media can be done at the Physical Layer. Because Ethernet LANs were based on thicknet and thinnet coaxial cabling, it was necessary to overcome distance limitations to support growth in the LAN. Depending on the cabling media and the type of physical Ethernet transceiver used, Ethernet LANs can be interconnected via repeaters and media converters. A repeater is a device that regenerates the Ethernet signal subject to signal attenuation. Repeaters are used when converting from one cabling type to another, usually to extend the physical distance of the Ethernet bus topology.

A repeater is a network device that has two ports. The repeater receives signals on one port. It then creates a new copy of the received signal to send to the other port. A repeater echoes everything it receives. By recreating a new digital signal, the repeater

TABLE 4-3 Maximum length of transmission media for Ethernet networks.

ETHERNET SPECIFICATION	CABLE TYPE	MAXIMUM LENGTH
10Base5 (Thick Ethernet)	RG-58 coaxial	500 meters
10Base2 (Thin Ethernet)	RG-58 coaxial	185 meters
10BaseT (Twisted-Pair Ethernet)	Unshielded Twisted-Pair (UTP) (Cat3 and higher)	100 meters
100BaseTX (Fast Ethernet)	UTP (Cat5 and higher)	100 meters
1000BaseT (Gigbit Ethernet over copper)	UTP (Cat5 and higher)	100 meters

enables a signal to travel much farther than without the device. Table 4-3 shows the maximum length of the physical transmission media used for different Ethernet LAN technologies.

A hub is similar to a repeater. The main difference is that a hub has more than two ports. Because an Ethernet hub may have more than two ports on it, it can support multiple physical connections. With hubs, remember, an Ethernet frame traverses out of all ports, since they are all on the same broadcast domain. An Ethernet frame broadcast packet will permeate through all ports on a LAN hub. A hub echoes every frame it receives out of every other port, including the receiving port. A hub allows star-wired connections of PCs and workstations onto the same bus topology. Hubs do not provide individual broadcast domains and are subject to collisions from any device connected to it. For that reason, networks that are connected by repeaters or hubs are part of the same **collision domain**. See Figure 4-7.

technical TIP

Use of LAN hubs provided a cheap and easy way to expand the number of ports onto the same shared logical bus topology. A LAN hub defines a single broadcast domain and a collision domain where all connected devices are part of the same LAN. Hubs were popular in the late 1980s and early 1990s. They are commonly used for home LANs to increase the number of workstations onto the same shared LAN.

The use of LAN hubs in businesses and organizations has been phased out. That is because they represent a security breach by allowing more workstations and devices to connect to the same logical LAN unsuspected.

LAN hubs also do not maximize the use of switched LAN connections. Workstations have to share the bandwidth and bus topology with other workstations connected to the LAN hub.

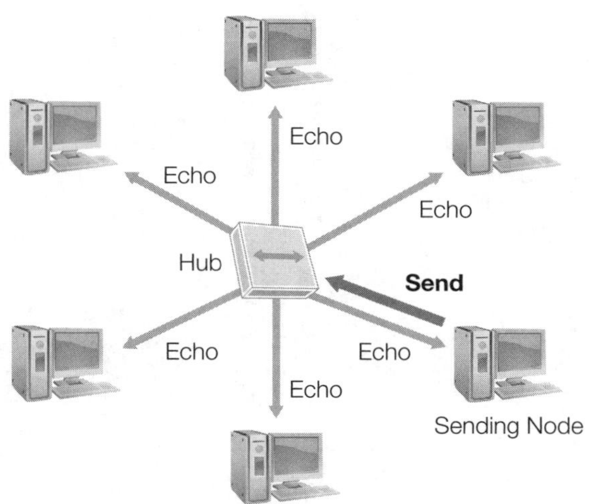

FIGURE 4-7
LAN hub single broadcast domain.

Bridges and Switches—Layer 2 Forwarding

The next step in creating more efficient networks is to minimize collisions. One way to do this is to segment a network into multiple collision domains. This is what bridges and switches do. Each of these devices examines each frame and determines its destination. MAC layer bridges function at Layer 2, which makes filtering and forwarding decisions based on destination MAC layer address. Layer 1 devices simply echo packets. Layer 2 devices make filtering or forwarding decisions based on MAC layer addresses learned. Although this may not seem like a big difference, it is because a network becomes more efficient with a Layer 2 switch.

Bridges and switches perform the same basic tasks. The general difference between the two is how they examine network traffic. Switch ports examine the frame that enters it. They immediately make a filtering or forwarding decision based on destination MAC layer address. A bridge generally runs as a layer of software on a general purpose device or computer. Switches usually have more ports than bridges and come in sizes from 12-port, 24-port, and 48-port switches. Between the two approaches, hardware switching is normally faster than software switching. On the other hand, software provides more flexibility and easier update.

Layer 2 switches, remember, have multiple collision domains, given that they only forward frames out of ports where the destination device resides. When a frame arrives, the bridge or switch examines the destination MAC address and looks for the address in its address table. If it finds the address, it forwards the frame to the port associated with the destination MAC address. The device doesn't echo the traffic to all ports. This packet isolation technique can dramatically reduce the amount of traffic flowing in a network.

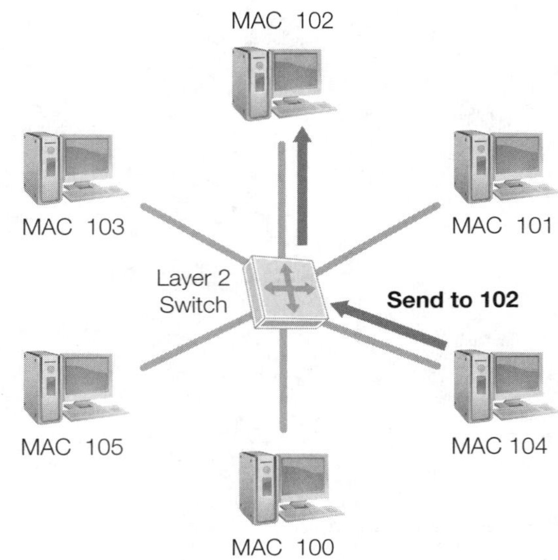

FIGURE 4-8
Multiple broadcast domains with a Layer 2 switch.

Hubs and repeaters flood the network with traffic. Bridges and Layer 2 switches keep traffic away from uninterested nodes. Figure 4-8 shows how Layer 2 forwarding works.

Switches and bridges can make Ethernet networks faster by providing these services:

- Creating multiple collision domains that reduce traffic to uninterested nodes
- Dropping damaged frames
- Isolating traffic between nodes that frequently exchange packets into a common VLAN
- Enabling cut-through switching
- Enabling VLANs to isolate network traffic throughout
- High-speed backbone trunking to server farms

Traffic isolation and segmentation help improve network performance. A good physical network design can have a large impact on network performance. Bridges and switches that isolate and create individual broadcast domains help improve network performance. Workstations and servers that communicate frequently should be connected to the same switch. With data centers and server farms, backbone trunks from the server farm to the LAN switch are required. This may be difficult to accomplish in large organizations, so further network connections may be required.

Routers—Layer 3 Routing

The other means of interconnecting LANs together is based on Layer 3 network routing. Routing is necessary when packets must leave their originating network and travel to another destination network. MAC layer addresses are used to send Ethernet frames from one interface to another. When you need to send IP packets from source to destination, and that destination is beyond the current network, you must route that IP packet. Layer 3 switches or routers operate at the Network Layer of the OSI model. That means the protocol or packet must have a Network Layer address. A Network Layer address specifies a unique network number and unique host number. Layer 3 switches or routers strip off the Data Link Layer or Ethernet frame and examine the IP portion of the packet. Within the IP packet is a source and destination IP address that is examined by Layer 3 switches and routers (see Figure 4-9). Routers make path determination decisions by examining their IP routing table for destination networks. Using this information and the physical interface to send the IP packet, routers encapsulate IP packets with Ethernet frames to send to the next hop IP router.

Routers operate at Layer 3. Routers examine the destination network address of each packet to determine the best path to reach the destination. Layer 3 switches normally direct traffic within a network and send IP packets out to other routers that know where the destination IP network number is.

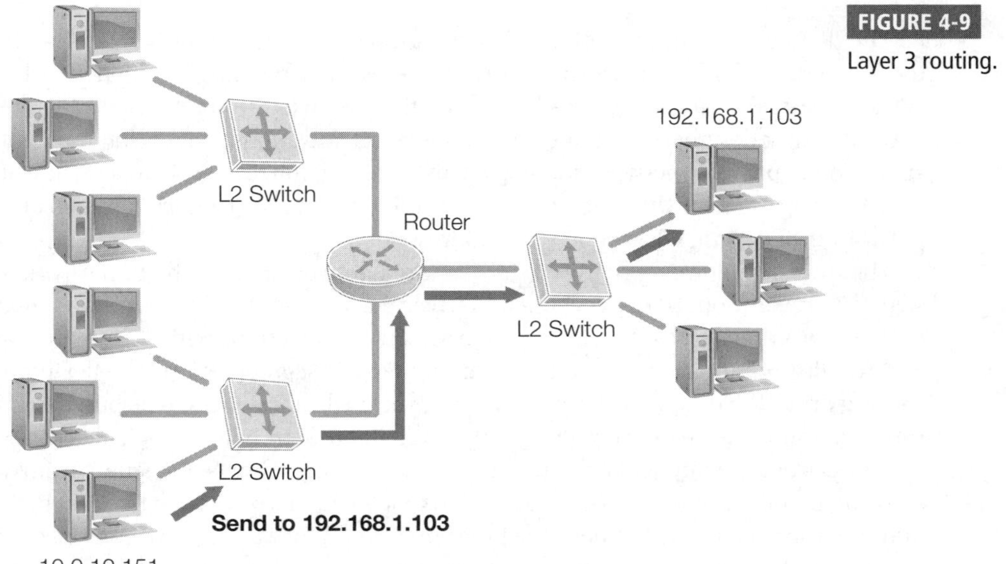

FIGURE 4-9
Layer 3 routing.

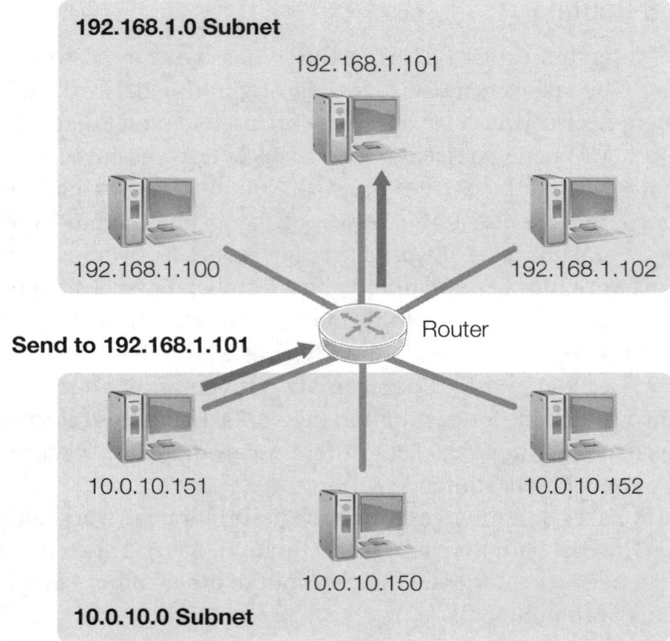

FIGURE 4-10
Layer 3 network addresses and subnetworks.

The IP address contains both a network number and a host number. IPv4 addresses use a different number of bits to identify the network, depending on the network's class. IPv6 addresses use a standard 64 bits to identify a network number. Layer 3 addresses allow network designers to create logical networks and subnetworks that may not correspond to the physical network topology. This flexibility makes it easy to associate devices together regardless of their location. Figure 4-10 shows how routers can help direct network traffic using Layer 3 network addresses.

The Internet, along with growth in wide area networking, led the IP network infrastructure revolution. IP networking and Layer 3 routing dominated wide area networking in the 1990s and early 2000s. Routing provided organizations with the greatest amount of flexibility, redundant paths to networks, and traffic segmentation. The flexibility of routing drove the design of many networks over the last 25 years to be based on Layer 3 routing. Routers gave network designers the ability to separate the logical design of their networks from the physical layout. The ease of creating subnets and small groups of associated nodes increased router workloads. Growing networks started to exhibit performance issues due to the increased reliance on Layer 3 forwarding. Although Layer 3 devices can be very efficient, they take more time to examine Layer 3 addresses than do Layer 2 devices. Layer 3 devices must look deeper into Ethernet frame at the IP packet and make decisions based on a larger set of possible destinations.

technical TIP

Today's network designers are faced with the Layer 2 or Layer 3 network design decision. While wide area networks require IP routing for alternate paths and redundancy, campus and building backbone networks can be designed with Layer 2 or Layer 3 networking. With Ethernet LAN speeds now supporting 40 Gbps trunking with single-mode fiber optic cabling, implementing high-speed LAN connections and Layer 2 switching is a realistic solution for today's LANs.

In spite of the flexibility of Layer 3 routing, many organizations are finding that Layer 2 devices provide superior performance for demanding network applications. Network designers are relying more on physical layout. Layer 2 devices provide the performance they need. In most cases, the more restrictive design decisions are worth the better performance.

Ethernet Network Design

Early Ethernet networks were designed utilizing bus topologies. The original IEEE Ethernet standard, IEEE 802.3, defined a network running at 10 Mbps using thicknet coaxial cable. This was referred to as 10Base5. The 10Base5 standard equals 10 Mbps, baseband transmission, using thicknet with a 500-meter distance limitation. Many organizations first ran thicknet coaxial cabling throughout their office buildings and connected individual workstations to the main cable using Ethernet transceivers. Ethernet bus topologies became a little easier to deploy when IEEE released 802.3a, which defined Ethernet using thinnet coaxial cabling. In 1990, IEEE released the 802.3i (10BaseT) standard and specification, which defined Ethernet using unshielded twisted-pair cabling. The 10BaseT standard dropped the cost of implementing Ethernet LAN technology and simplified the moves, additions, and changes of network connectivity. Nearly every business and organization migrated toward 10BaseT LAN technology. Eventually, token ring LANs were replaced with Ethernet LAN technology. That made Ethernet the dominant LAN technology used globally.

The recent advances in 100BaseT and 1000BaseT (Gigabit Ethernet) utilizing unshielded twisted-pair cabling have changed the landscape of how best to provide high-speed network connections to the desktop. Real-time applications require time-sensitive protocols. Time-sensitive protocols used to traverse Layer 3 routed IP networking infrastructure. Getting packets to their destinations required traffic prioritization and quality of service (QoS) routing. QoS routing prioritizes time-sensitive protocols through an IP-routed network faster. This was the old way of prioritizing IP packets through a routed networking infrastructure.

Today, with GigE and 40 Gbps Ethernet LAN trunking, you can drive high-speed applications and time-sensitive protocols to the desktop at Layer 2 using Layer 2 switching. Now for the first time, network designers can implement Layer 2 network connections to support high-speed applications and time-sensitive protocols. QoS is now only needed for wide area network connections where alternate paths and lower-speed connections are used.

When designing networks, the following physical networks must be addressed:

- **Edge networks**—The desktop workstation LAN connection
- **Building backbone networks**—Aggregations of edge network switches into a collapsed backbone
- **Campus backbone networks**—**Campus backbone** networks are aggregations of multiple buildings on the same physical campus
- **Metropolitan area networks**—Aggregations of remote buildings, but within a regional metropolitan area network service area (usually provided by a metro Ethernet service provider)
- **Wide area backbone networks**—Cloud-based wide area network infrastructures such as Multi-Protocol Label Switching (MPLS) for wide area IP network connectivity

When designing Ethernet networks, the following network design features and functions must be addressed:

- **Port density**—Organizations need high port densities to ensure the lowest cost of connectivity.
- **Power over Ethernet (PoE)**—Support for IP phones is required for VoIP electrical power distribution.
- **Layer 2 versus Layer 3 edge switch**—Depends upon network traffic requirements and whether real-time applications and time-sensitive protocols are required.
- **Layer 2 resiliency and redundancy**—Requirements should be driven by real-time applications and whether sub-second failover is required or not.
- **Layer 3 resiliency and redundancy**—Requirements should be driven by real-time applications and whether sub-second failover is required or not.
- **Layer 2 and Layer 3 trunking**—Backbone trunking, load-balancing, and use of 40 Gbps Ethernet LAN trunks will be required, especially if access to server farms and real-time applications is required.
- **Switch architecture**—Use of application specific integrated circuits (ASIC); high-speed, backplane architectures; dual processors; and cut-through versus store-and-forward switching should be assessed.
- **Switch security**—Use of MAC layer address filtering, Simple Network Management Protocol (SNMP) monitoring and alarming, security lockdowns, and other layered security controls should be implemented to ensure confidentiality, integrity, and availability.

The rest of this chapter will focus on the specifics of Ethernet edge networks, building backbone networks, campus backbone networks, server farm connectivity, and high-speed backbone trunking. Use of Ethernet LANs for these types of networks provides organizations with standardized options to design the best possible networking infrastructure. Use of Ethernet LAN technologies uniquely throughout the physical network infrastructure is covered in the rest of this chapter. Layer 2 and Layer 3 resiliency and redundancy will be covered separately in future chapters.

Edge Network—Workgroup LANs

An **edge network** is one at the last 100 meters or 300 feet from a wiring closet where desktops physically connect to the network. Edge networks can be wired or wireless, but even wireless access points (WAPs) still require physical connectivity to an Ethernet switch in the wiring closet. That said, the workgroup LAN connection at the edge of the network is the predominant method of LAN connectivity used by large, medium, and small businesses and organizations. LANs typically are used to interconnect workgroups together. Because this happens at the wiring closet level within a building, this is referred to as the edge network. Edge network connections are supported by the use of data-grade, unshielded twisted-pair cabling (i.e., Category 5 or 6 UTP) terminated onto an RJ-45 workstation outlet and an RJ-45 patch panel. Workstations, printers, and servers physically connect to the network via an RJ-45 patch cable on both ends (see Figure 4-11).

What is a workgroup LAN? Workgroups typically need to share data and information, and it makes sense to be able to do this within their own workgroup LAN. This is why workgroups are usually located in the same part of their company's building.

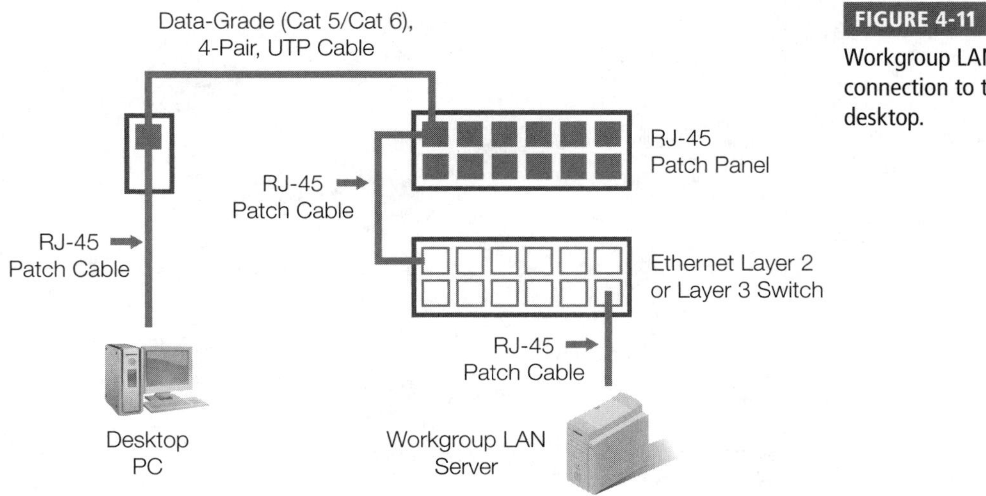

FIGURE 4-11 Workgroup LAN connection to the desktop.

technical TIP

Eighty percent of workgroup LAN traffic stays local to the workgroup. Data and file sharing is accomplished via the workgroup LAN server, where access controls are located and where volume and drive access, as well as folder and data access, are granted.

The remaining 20 percent of workgroup LAN traffic travels outside the workgroup: e-mail, Internet traffic, and remote file or data sharing with other workgroups and users.

Because of this, traffic isolation, broadcast domain containment, and network segmentation are required to separate workgroup LAN traffic. Use of IEEE 802.1q VLAN definitions to extend the broadcast domain to other physical switches and ports may be required.

The term workgroup refers to a group of users and their devices that are needed to perform their job functions. For example, a workgroup could be any of the following functions:

- Ticketing box office
- Accounts receivable group
- Hospital patient admissions
- University bursar office
- Hardware engineering group
- Software development group

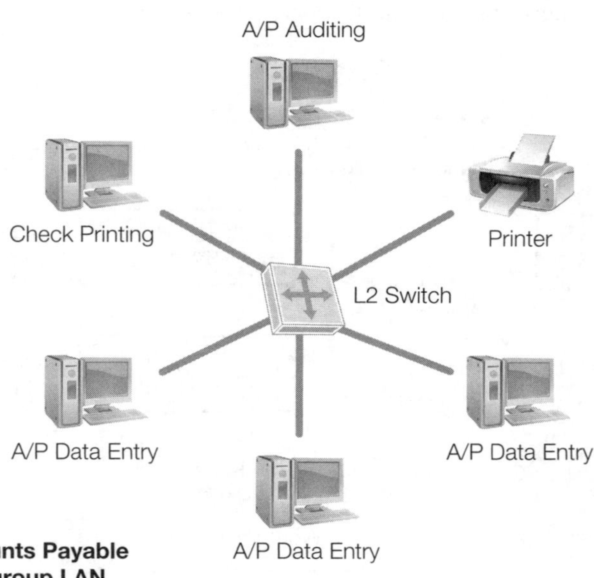

FIGURE 4-12

Workgroup LAN.

Each of these workgroups represents a relatively small group of individuals working together to provide related services. These individuals are likely to need access to workstations and other shared devices such as printers, scanners, and file servers for sharing data and files. Workgroup LANs generally serve to connect groups of devices used by small groups of people who share similar job functions. In many cases, workgroups are subsets of much larger functional departments. For example, an Accounts Receivable workgroup is a subset of the Accounting Department. The hardware engineering and software development groups are subsets of the Information Technology (IT) Department. Figure 4-12 depicts the Accounts Payable Workgroup LAN.

Workgroup LAN Design and Implementation Best Practices

The following present some best practices when designing and implementing edge networks for workgroup LAN connectivity:

- Use structured wiring from a centrally located wiring closet for 10/100/1000BaseT installations.
- Ensure Category 5 or 6 UTP cabling is used to maximize physical distances up to 100 meters or 300 feet.
- Keep workgroup LANs small: generally fewer than 50 devices.
- Connect using layer 2 or Layer 3 GigE switches. This is critical if VoIP, SIP, or other real-time protocols must be supported at the desktop. (Note: If the workgroup LAN intends to deploy VoIP and/or unified communications, you will need a Power over Ethernet (PoE) Layer 2 or Layer 3 switch.)
- Segment or isolate workgroup PCs and workstations within the same physical switch or at least within the same logical VLAN.
- Lock down active ports with a MAC layer address hard-coded into the Layer 2 or Layer 3 switch for enhanced security controls. Disable non-active ports.
- Enable IEEE 802.1q Ethernet VLAN tagging when the workgroup PCs and workstations must physically connect to more than one Layer 2 or Layer 3 switch.
- Connect PCs and workstations via GigE to the back of the IP phone. Physically connect the IP phone to the workstation outlet and cabling via an RJ-45 patch cable.
- Commingle voice and data IP packets within Ethernet frames. Break out a separate voice and data VLAN within the Layer 2 or Layer 3 switch.
- Trunk- or backbone-connect workgroup LAN file servers using GigE, 10 GigE, or 40 GigE NIC cards to maximize performance and throughput for workgroup users.
- Implement Layer 2 or Layer 3 resiliency between workgroup LAN switches and workgroup LAN server connections using dual NIC cards where and when needed.

Note: Each workgroup LAN will require its own unique design, configuration, and security hardening to ensure the confidentiality, integrity, and availability of workgroup LAN and file server access. These best practices should be considered when designing and implementing workgroup LANs using structure wiring systems and LAN switches in the wiring closet.

FIGURE 4-13

PoE LAN switches.

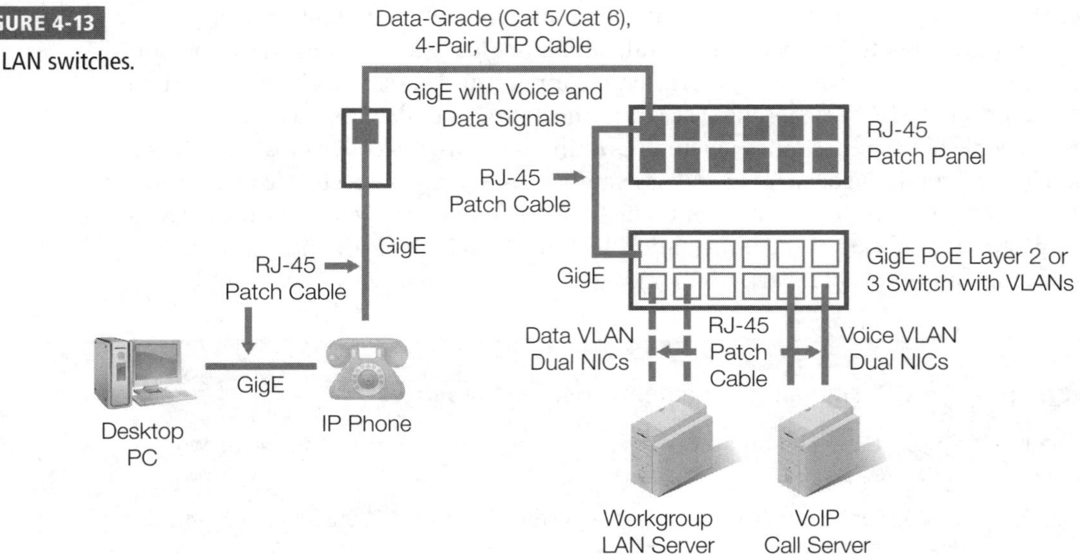

Edge Network—Use of PoE Switches

The deployment of VoIP and IP phones to the desktop has changed how LAN switch vendors manufacture their current Layer 2 and Layer 3 switches. With the proliferation of IP phones now appearing at the desktop, organizations can finally benefit from converged voice and data communications. IP phones today connect at either 100 Mbps or GigE port speeds. They can obtain power from a PoE LAN switch through the RJ-45 connector using the 4-pair, unshielded twisted-pair cabling. This simplifies the electrical power distribution requirements for IP phones at the desktop location. PoE LAN switches can deliver electrical power to IP phones using data-grade 4-pair, unshielded twisted-pair cabling. Ideally, a minimum Category 5 or Category 6 UTP cabling should be installed to support long-term, high-speed data and communications connectivity. (See Figure 4-13.)

There are two different IEEE 802.3 PoE standards:

- **IEEE 802.3af–2003**—Standard that draws up to 15.4 watts of power from the PoE switch port to power an IP phone (IP phones, black-and-white display phones, multiline phones, etc.)
- **IEEE 802.3at–2009**—Standard that draws up to 25.5 watts of power from the PoE switch port to power an IP phone (multiline phones, high-end display phones, color display phones, etc.)

The more powerful the IP phone, the more electrical power it needs. An electrical power distribution analysis and power consumption design for PoE LAN switches must be performed. This is performed by analyzing the total number of IP phones and their aggregate electrical draw that will be accessed from the PoE LAN switch.

PoE Workgroup LAN Switch Best Practices

The following present some best practices when designing and implementing edge networks with PoE workgroup LAN switches:

- Use structured wiring from a centrally located wiring closet for 10/100/1000BaseT installations.
- Ensure Category 5 or 6 UTP cabling is used to maximize physical distances up to 100 meters or 300 feet.
- Commingle voice and data on the same physical 4-pair UTP cable from the workstation outlet to the wiring closet patch panel to save time and money.
- Do not install duplex 110V outlets at the desktop location. Use power supply bricks for IP phones unless on a case-by-case basis.
- Install PoE LAN switches with redundant power supplies or battery backup units to ensure highly available phone service and dial tone.
- Enable separate voice and data VLANs to separate voice traffic from data traffic once it hits the Layer 2 or Layer 3 PoE LAN switch.
- Implement redundant backbone connections to the VoIP call server.
- Enable Layer 2 or Layer 3 sub-second resiliency and failover of backbone trunks to ensure availability of service for VoIP, SIP, and UC at the workgroup LAN.

Note: Workgroup LANs that utilize IP phones should utilize PoE LAN switches for electrical power. This simplifies the installation of voice services. It also eliminates the need for a second 4-pair, unshielded twisted-pair cable to the desktop. Electrical power can be redundant or linked to battery backup systems or on-demand generators to ensure availability of voice communication services, including dial tone.

Edge Network—Departmental LAN

The next common type of LAN is a superset of the workgroup LAN. When organizations better understood the advantages of network communications, they often decided to connect multiple LANs. Connected LANs allowed separate workgroups to communicate with one another. Although it is possible to connect multiple workgroup LANs with a hub or repeater, this only creates a larger workgroup LAN. One of the characteristics of a departmental LAN is that it connects workgroup LANs and keeps them separate. In other words, a departmental LAN is a LAN in which each workgroup LAN is a separate broadcast domain or collision domain. Switches and bridges provide this feature. In most cases, Layer 2 switching efficiently directs packets to the appropriate destinations within the same workgroup and moving Ethernet frames between workgroups. Departmental LANs provide organizations with the ability to separate local traffic from inter-workgroup traffic with very little effort.

Departmental LANs are needed when workgroups are physically located in different wiring closets. This physical separation of workgroup users and departmental users requires network designers to consider how to interconnect these LANs together. The following design considerations must be examined in order to internetwork workgroup LANs together:

- **Total number of workgroup LANs**—Switches come in all sizes and port densities. Fixed-port and chassis-based switches are used for workgroup LAN connectivity.
- **Physical distance between workgroup LANs**—Distance is the enemy to Ethernet. Copper cabling has fixed distance limitations. Fiber optic cabling can support metropolitan area Ethernet connectivity.
- **Transmission media/cabling installed between wiring closets**—Copper transmission media have a physical distance limitation. Fiber optic cabling and use of repeaters can support distances of several miles.
- **Layer 2 or Layer 3 switching**—Layer 2 switching is based on MAC layer address filtering/forwarding. Layer 3 switching is the same thing as routing, and Network Layer addressing path determination is performed.
- **VLANs and Ethernet tagging**—Layer 2 VLANs can be uniquely identified and extend beyond more than one physical switch using IEEE 802.1q Ethernet tagging.
- **Internetworking solution**—Creating small, workgroup LANs that share the same broadcast domain optimizes performance. Internetworking at Layer 2 or Layer 3 can interconnect LANs and VLANs together.
- **Switched LAN aggregation**—Edge switches require high-speed backbone trunk connection. Load-balancing, redundancy, and sub-second failover are all requirements for backbone network connectivity. Workgroup file servers housed in data centers require high-speed backbone connectivity.
- **Network security**—Implementing proper layered security controls starts with locking down switch ports at the MAC layer, enabling Secure Shell Protocol (SSH) for remote access, and implementing internal firewalls and access control lists to filter traffic.

These design considerations should be reviewed when expanding workgroup LANs into departmental LANs. The "best" topology depends on the amount of traffic that travels between workgroup LANs. Remember, 80 percent of workgroup LAN traffic typically stays within the workgroup. Only 20 percent of that traffic needs to traverse to another workgroup LAN or file server. Depending on the business processes and internal functions of the department, it may be important to provide high-speed internetworking between these disparate LANs. Sharing of data, communicating in real-time using VoIP, or collaborating using UC with other workers are all key design criteria to consider.

How do you interconnect these workgroup LANs and switches within the wiring closet? Depending on what you are interconnecting and where your network physically resides, there are many solutions. Because Ethernet frames and use of IP are consistent for 10/100/1000/4000 Mbps Ethernet LANs, interconnecting them is simpler. Workgroup LANs can easily interconnect by connecting to a common backbone network. A backbone network allows workgroup LANs to interconnect along with connecting servers. A backbone network is typically of higher speed than the workgroup LAN, utilizes fiber optic cabling, and is redundant or highly available, given the switch architecture. Backbone networks are like super highways that connect smaller highways that are all transmitting large quantities of IP traffic. There are two common approaches to implementing a backbone network:

- **Multilayered hierarchical backbone**—Each departmental LAN connects to a common chassis-based, high-speed backbone. Traffic bound for other departmental LANs and workgroup LANs must be sent to the department's router for Layer 3 routing and Layer 3 switching.
- **Flat backbone**—Each departmental LAN connects to common chassis-based, high-speed backbone. Traffic bound for departmental LANs is Layer 2 switched via VLANs and Ethernet tagging to direct traffic between departmental LANs.

Flat backbones are more restrictive due to the fact that they must rely on physical device location to isolate departmental LANs from one another. However, Layer 2 switching provides faster traffic direction than the slower Layer 3 routing. Figure 4-14 shows a hierarchical and flat backbone topology.

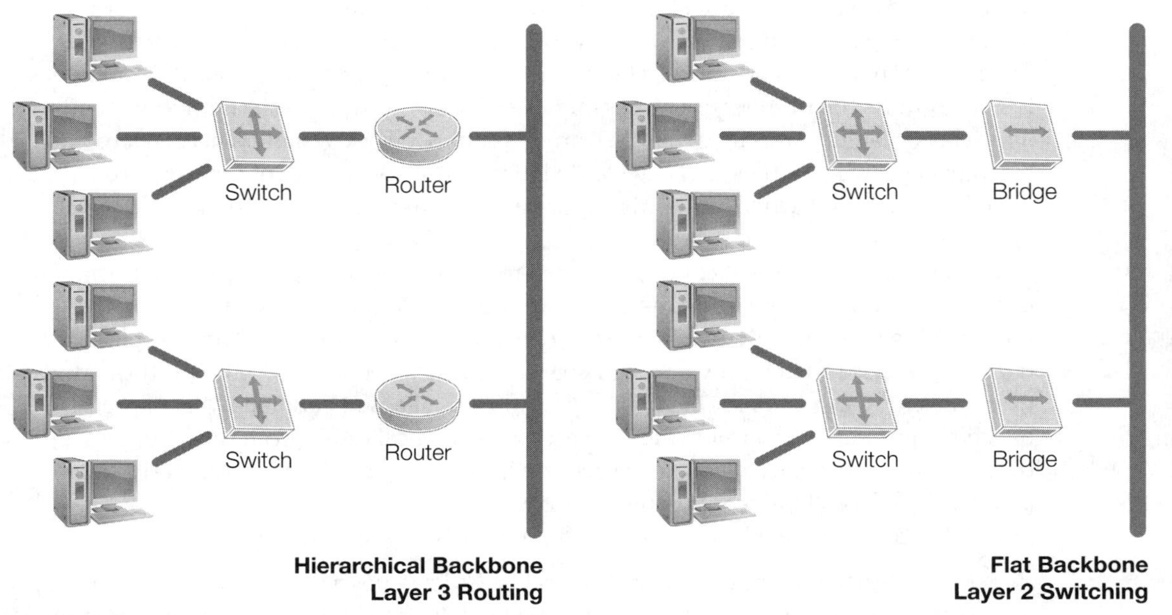

FIGURE 4-14 Departmental backbone LAN topologies.

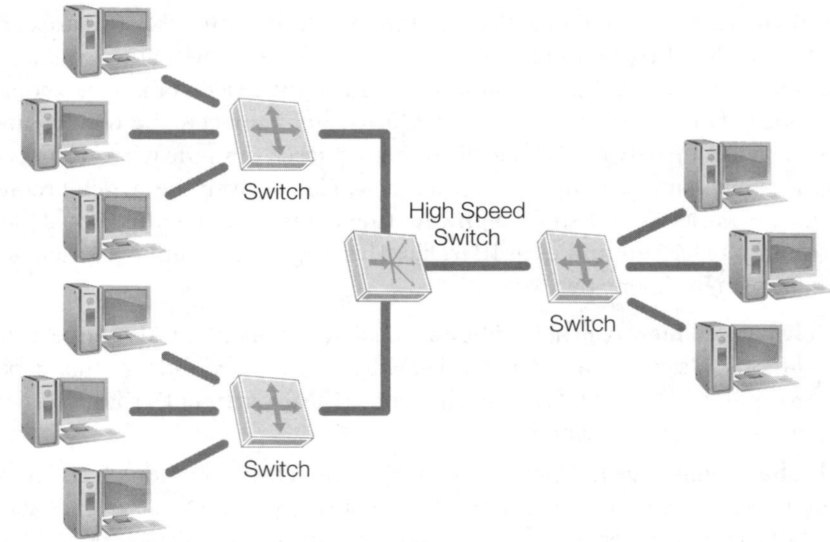

FIGURE 4-15
Collapsed building backbone network.

Building Backbone—Collapsed Backbones

Organizations first started with workgroup LANs. Then they connected them together forming departmental LANs. Then things became more complex as applications commingled with one another on the same physical and logical network. The need to segment and isolate while interconnecting LANs together was needed. The network architecture required to connect multiple workgroup or departmental LANs intensified. The number of devices or switches between source and destination increased, sometimes inefficiently. As the number of devices increased, so did network performance and end-to-end delay or latency in delivery of the transmission. Network designers needed a method to simplify growing networks. They wanted to keep the advantages of separate broadcast or collision domains while minimizing the average number of devices that an Ethernet or IP packet needed to travel.

Larger LANs use a modification to the departmental backbone topology. LANs that cover entire buildings and span multiple departments often utilize the star-wired fiber optic cabling for connectivity to a common Ethernet switch or router. The backplane of the high-speed switch provides high-speed connectivity for 10/100/1000/4000 Mbps Ethernet LAN connections. This topology is called a **collapsed backbone**. A collapsed backbone minimizes traffic flowing between departmental LANs given that they can transfer frames and packets at high speeds on a common backplane. Figure 4-15 shows an example of a collapsed backbone topology.

A collapsed backbone has two main advantages over other topologies:

- Each connection between departmental LANs becomes a department-to-department connection. Using a central switch isolates traffic from other department LANs.
- Central switches reduce the number of devices needed for other backbone topologies. They also make the network easier to manage.

On the other hand, collapsed backbone networks have two main drawbacks over other topologies:

- Fiber optic cabling is required to connect each departmental LAN to the central switch.
- The central switch represents a single point of failure. If the switch fails, no traffic can travel between departmental LANs.

In spite of the drawbacks of collapsed backbone networks, this topology has become popular given that redundant links and switches can be implemented providing resiliency and failover functionality.

Campus Backbone—Collapsed Data Center Backbone

The collapsed backbone topology also provides scalability beyond individual buildings. A backbone that connects other backbones is called a campus backbone. Like the building collapsed backbone, the campus collapsed backbone (see Figure 4-16) is a popular topology

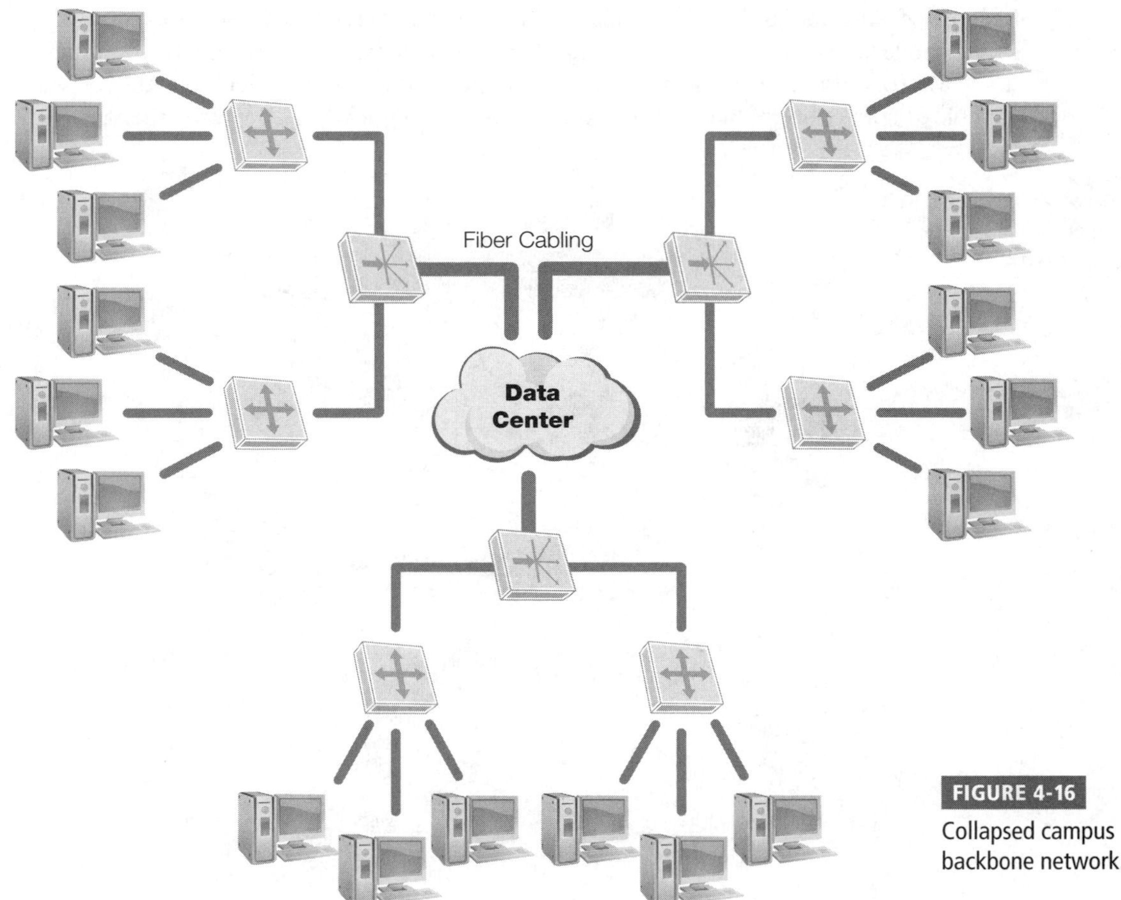

FIGURE 4-16
Collapsed campus backbone network.

to create even bigger networks. A collection of central switches that connect multiple building collapsed backbones can create an organizational campus network while retaining the separation of each workgroup, department, and building. To keep each level separate, network designers often express network connections as levels. The three common network connection levels are:

- **Edge network**—Workgroup LAN supporting PC and workstation connectivity
- **Distribution network**—Building backbone network that connects workgroup LANs into department LANs
- **Core backbone network**—High-speed backbone network that connects building backbones and departmental LANs into a common and shared network. This can be a metro Ethernet MAN, a campus backbone network, or a building backbone network.

Metropolitan Area Backbone—Metro Ethernet Backbone

Because of the popularity of Ethernet, service providers were able to utilize existing single-mode fiber optic cabling to extend the physical distance of Ethernet LAN connections. Metropolitan area networks were now supported by carrier backbone networks capable of supporting Ethernet LAN connections (see Figure 4-17). Metro Ethernet

FIGURE 4-17

Metro Ethernet backbone network.

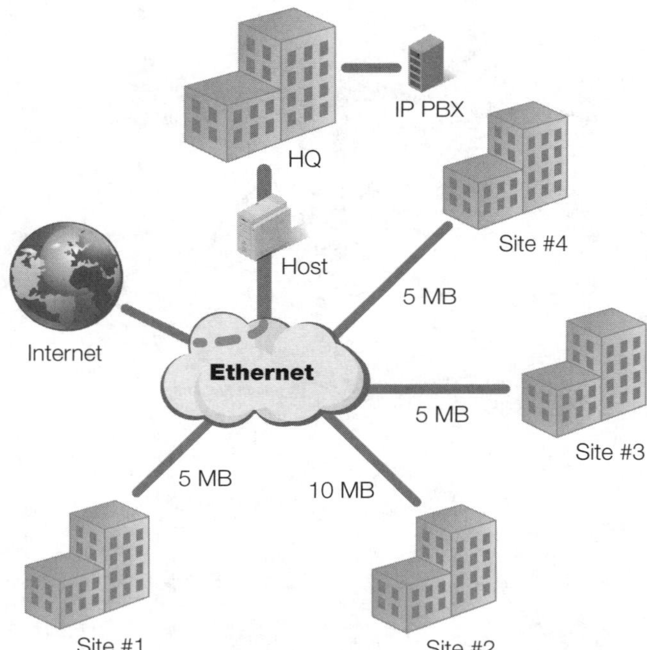

LAN connectivity provided customers located within a single county or region wire-speed LAN connectivity. Metro Ethernet was cost-effective, reliable, and scalable, and provided superior bandwidth just like a local LAN connection.

Metro Ethernet allowed customers such as county and city governments to access LAN connection speeds as an alternative to wide area network circuits. Metro Ethernet LAN services provided businesses and organizations with affordable, high-speed network connectivity with higher availability and performance.

GigE and 10 GigE Specifications

The original IEEE 802.3 specification for Ethernet described LAN communication at speeds of 10 Mbit/s. As Ethernet matured, the speed increased first to 100 Mbps and then to 1000 Mbps or 1 Gbps. Ethernet running at 1 Gbps is also called GigE. Several Ethernet standards define GigE, depending on the physical medium. Since the introduction of GigE, the latest Ethernet standard is 10 times faster, or 10 Gbps. This latest Ethernet standard is called 10 GigE. While the current, most common versions of Ethernet are still 10 Mbps and 100 Mbps, GigE and 10 GigE are rapidly becoming the standard for LANs. GigE was first introduced in 1998 for Ethernet using fiber optic cabling with IEEE 802.3z. Support for GigE soon followed for twisted-pair cabling with IEEE 802.3ab in 1999.

It wasn't long before Ethernet standards for 10 GigE emerged. IEEE 802.3ae in 2003 described 10 GigE using fiber optic cabling. IEEE 802ak in 2004 described 10 GigE for twin-axial cabling, and IEEE 802.3an defined 10 GigE using twisted-pair. Later IEEE standards defined faster Ethernet implementations using specialized hardware specifically for backbone applications. Current Ethernet LANs can run at 10 GigE as long as the individual nodes and intermediate devices, such as switches and routers, support the faster standard. Although the hardware is more expensive than the slower 10 Mbps and 100 Mbps devices, the performance is superior and sufficient to handle the most demanding requirements.

In addition to the added hardware expense, each GigE standard has distance limitations. Different transmission media support different maximum cable lengths. In most cases, media that support longer distances have a higher cost than the more limited media. Table 4-4 lists the different GigE standard names, the media on which they are defined, and their maximum supported distance.

Likewise, 10 GigE has maximum distance limitations based on cabling. Table 4-5 lists the different 10 GigE standard names, the media on which they are defined, and their maximum supported distance.

As prices for GigE chips and NIC cards decreased, GigE has become the predominant speed to the desktop in support of IP phones, UC, and heavy data users. Today's desktop and server farm environments include GigE PoE LAN switches, NIC cards for servers, and copper and fiber backbone connections. High-speed trunking and server connections continue to grow in the current Ethernet landscape. And now with 10 GigE NIC cards, high-speed Ethernet backbone connections and server farm connections are possible.

TABLE 4-4 GigE standards and maximum distances for cabling.

NAME	TRANSMISSION MEDIA	MAXIMUM DISTANCE
1000Base-CX	Twin-axial cabling	25 meters
1000Base-SX	Multimode fiber	220 to 550 meters
1000Base-LX	Multimode fiber	550 meters
1000Base-LX	Single-mode fiber	5 kilometers
1000Base-LX10	Single-mode fiber (1310 nm wavelength)	10 kilometers
1000Base-ZX	Single-mode fiber (1550 nm wavelength)	70 kilometers
1000Base-BX10	Single-mode fiber (mixed wavelength)	10 kilometers
1000Base-T	Twisted-pair cabling (Cat-5 to Cat-7)	100 meters
1000Base-TX	Twisted-pair cabling (Cat-6 to Cat-7)	100 meters

TABLE 4-5 10 GigE standards and maximum distances for cabling.

NAME	TRANSMISSION MEDIA	MAXIMUM DISTANCE
10GBase-SR	Multimode fiber	26 to 82 meters
10GBase-LR	Single-mode fiber	10 kilometers
10GBase-LRM	Multimode fiber	220 meters
10GBase-ER	Single-mode fiber	40 kilometers
10GBase-LX4	Multimode fiber	240 to 300 meters
10GBase-CX4	Copper cabling	15 meters
10GBase-T	Twisted-pair	100 meters

10 GigE and 40 GigE—Server Farms and Backbone Trunking

Organizations utilize both multimode and single-mode fiber optic cabling. With single-mode fiber optics, 40 Gbps Ethernet backbone trunking is now possible. Aggregating 10 GigE backbone connections and interconnecting Ethernet LAN switches with 40 Gbps trunks provide both a resilient and high-speed backbone connection. This is ideal for campus and building backbones that demand higher-speed backbones.

With Layer 2 and Layer 3 resiliency at the forefront, campus and building backbone networks must achieve sub-second failover. In addition, campus backbone connections must be highly available and redundant. Use of active paths on fiber optics is critical to maximize bandwidth and throughput on backbone network connectivity.

High-end servers and databases now have dual NIC cards at 10 Gbps and 40 Gbps speeds providing wire-speed connectivity. Couple this with high-speed backbone connections to departmental or workgroup LANs, and now users have greater access to applications and data at higher speeds. (See Figure 4-18.)

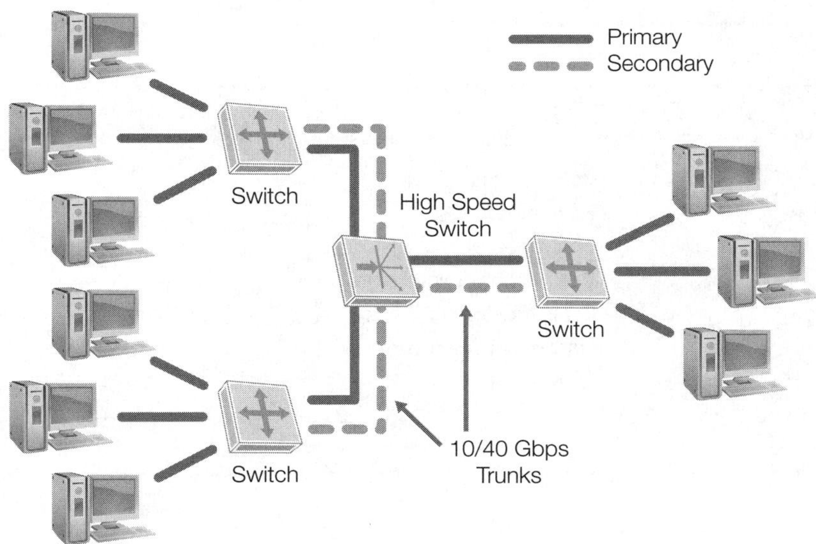

FIGURE 4-18 Server farm and backbone trunking.

CHAPTER SUMMARY

Ethernet became the kind of LANs because it was able to mature and grow along with the needs of the IT world. Ethernet chips allowed for higher-speed NIC cards and LAN switch ports. The flexibility and adaptability of Ethernet allowed many organizations to implement high-speed networking at low costs. Every eight or so years, Ethernet increases its speed tenfold—from 10 Mbps to 100 Mpbs to 1000 Mbps to 4000 Mbps Ethernet LAN speeds. Today's Ethernet networks transfer data as much as 1000 times as fast as the original networks. On top of the incredible speed increases, Ethernet networks today are simpler and less expensive to build and maintain. The Ethernet LAN standard provides flexibility to build networks of nearly any size to meet any organization's communication needs. The increased speed and bandwidth of GigE, 10 GigE, and now 40 GigE allows network designers to plan for future growth and greater network traffic loads. Ethernet has been able to keep pace with the demands of growing network communication requirements.

KEY CONCEPTS AND TERMS

10Base2 "Thinnet"
10Base5 "Thicknet"
10BaseT
100BaseTX
1000BaseT (GigE)
Backbone
Campus backbone
Collapsed backbone
Collision domain
Edge network
Ethernet
Optimistic transmission
Real-time applications
Time-sensitive protocols
Workgroup

CHAPTER 4 ASSESSMENT

1. Early implementations of Ethernet used coaxial cable.
   A. True
   B. False
2. What was the original transmission speed of Ethernet under the 802.3 standard?
   A. 2.94 Mbps
   B. 4.77 Mbps
   C. 10 Mbps
   D. 100 Mbps
3. Which of the following devices only extends the maximum distance between two Ethernet nodes (doesn't provide any other services)?
   A. Router
   B. Bridge
   C. Switch
   D. Repeater
4. Which of the following network devices separate nodes into separate collision domains?
   A. Hub
   B. Repeater
   C. Switch
   D. Router
5. What node identification does a switch use to forward frames to the correct destination?
   A. Network address
   B. MAC address
   C. Node ID
   D. Protocol ID
6. Which switching method starts transmitting a frame as soon as it reads the destination address?
   A. Cut-through
   B. Store-and-forward
   C. Trunking
   D. Aggregation
7. The original Ethernet standard used a software token to avoid collisions.
   A. True
   B. False
8. Which of the following topologies, along with unshielded twisted-pair cabling, transformed LAN connectivity and made LAN access more accessible?
   A. Ring
   B. Bus
   C. Star
   D. Mesh
9. Which simple action does CSMA/CD require to avoid transmitting on a busy channel?
   A. Listen for a clear channel
   B. Wait for a token
   C. Wait for a random amount of time
   D. Listen to the echo of the transmitted message
10. An aggregation of edge networks is called a ________ network.
11. What is the best reason to create a workgroup LAN?
    A. Workgroups are small and require less cabling.
    B. The majority of workgroup traffic stays within the workgroup.
    C. Most switches can't handle more ports than the average workgroup size.
    D. Hierarchical topologies provide the best performance.
12. What was the most common topology used in early Ethernet networks?
    A. Ring
    B. Star
    C. Tree
    D. Bus
13. Real time applications benefit from the higher performance of which type of network devices?
    A. Layer 1 hub
    B. Layer 2 switch
    C. Layer 3 router
    D. Layer 4 stateful firewall

CHAPTER

5 TCP/IP and Networking

FAMILIARITY WITH the Transmission Control Protocol/Internet Protocol (TCP/IP) suite is crucial to understanding how the Internet and IP networking operates. There is no doubt that TCP/IP has become the dominant global protocol used by all. This did not happen by planning. As LANs started to dominate the workstation connectivity landscape, so did the migration from mainframe to client/server computing. When the Internet and telecommunications broadband era was born, organizations flocked to the World Wide Web. Dedicated Internet access, e-commerce, intranets, and extranets became the new way of doing business globally. This foundation led organizations to migrate real-time applications and services such as voice, video, and unified communications (UC) toward IP-based communications and Web applications. Many organizations use IP networking and the Internet to drive business reach globally. This chapter will cover TCP/IP and what you need to know in relation to networking. You will learn about common reference models that help identify protocol services and interactions. Finally, you will learn about the Internet Protocol (IP), IPv4 and IPv6 addressing, and network-related protocols and functions.

Chapter 5 Topics

This chapter covers the following topics and concepts:

- What the OSI Reference Model is
- What the Internet Protocol (IP) is
- How IP devices are addressed using IPv4 and IPv6
- What IP-based communications are
- How connectionless communications compare to connection-oriented communications
- What the TCP/IP Reference Model is
- Essential TCP/IP protocols used in networking

Chapter 5 Goals

When you complete this chapter, you will be able to:

- Explain how computers communicate as per the OSI Reference Model
- Describe the Internet Protocol (IP)
- Distinguish IPv4 and IPv6 addressing schemas
- Describe how IP communications works
- Differentiate between connectionless and connection-oriented communications
- Align the TCP/IP Reference Model with the OSI Reference Model
- Select the appropriate TCP/IP protocol to support various applications

OSI Reference Model

Most discussions of how networks operate include the Open Systems Interconnection (OSI) Reference Model (Figure 5-1). This is foundational to understanding how computers communicate. The OSI model defines seven different layers of communication rules. Each of these rules or layers defines a particular means of communication or **protocol**. The OSI model is used as a reference when explaining how protocols operate. Protocols define how computers communicate in a layered fashion.

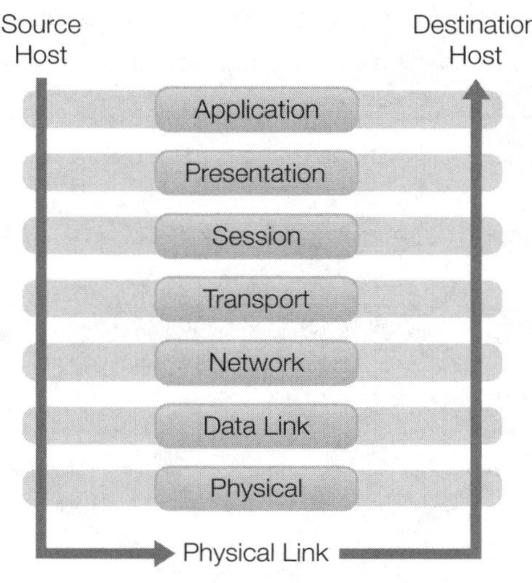

FIGURE 5-1
OSI Reference Model layers.

Layered Protocols in Real Life

The idea of layered protocols sounds complex, but it accurately reflects what happens in normal human-to-human communication. You use layers and translations in subtle ways every time you talk with a different person. Here's an example that demonstrates the obvious need for multiple layers.

Consider how delegates communicate in the United Nations. Assume the United States delegate wants to send a written note to the delegates of China, Russia, and Italy. In this example, the protocol rule in place requires that all written messages be presented in either English or French. To make the illustration clearer, we will assume that the delegate wants his message to go out in French. Here is how the message travels through the U.N.:

1. The U.S. delegate writes a message in English, then hands the message to a translator (the delegate layer passes the message to the translator layer).
2. The translator translates the message into French, then hands it to an aide to take to the mailroom (the translator layer passes the message to the aide layer).
3. The aide makes three copies of the message, addresses each copy, and places the messages in the U.S. outbox in the mailroom (the aide layer duplicates and passes the messages to the mailroom clerk layer).
4. The mailroom clerk picks up the messages from the U.S. out box and places them in the appropriate in boxes for China, Russia, and Italy (the mailroom clerk handles the physical transfer).
5. An aide for each country (China, Russia, and Italy) picks up the message and delivers it to the translator (the aide layer collects a message from the mailroom and passes it to the translator layer).
6. The translator translates the message from French into the country's national language and gives it to the delegate (the translator layer translates the message and passes it to the delegate layer).
7. The delegate for each country reads the message and takes appropriate action.

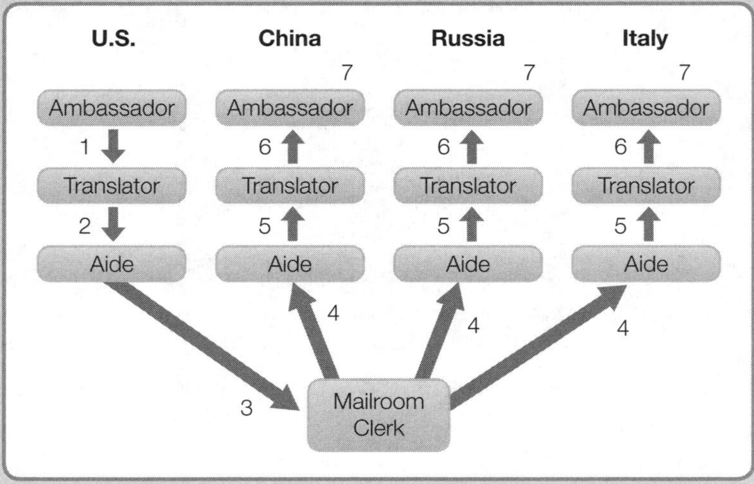

FIGURE 5-2 Message flow in the U.N. example.

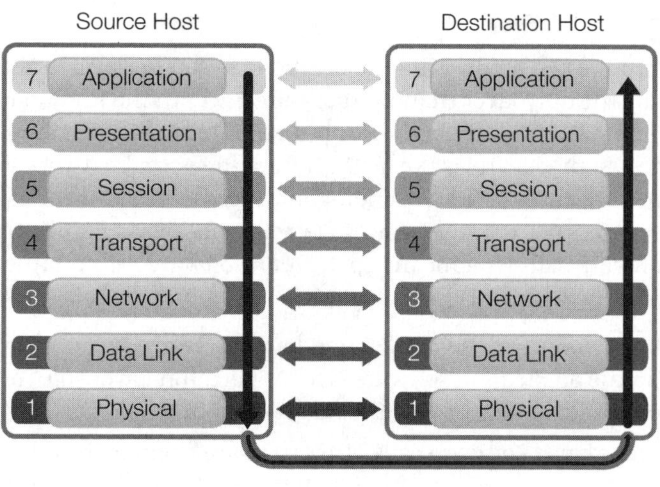

FIGURE 5-3
Logical communication between layers.

The OSI model defines seven layers. Each layer has specific responsibilities and logically interfaces to the layer above or below it. For example, the highest layer is the Application Layer, Layer 7. If the Application Layer needs to send a message to another computer, it sends the message to the Application Layer on the target computer, as shown in Figure 5-3. The networking software on the sending computer handles all of the details to get the message on its way. Today's networking software may combine two or more layers in its functionality. Each layer in the OSI Reference Model provides a different service needed for communication across an IP network and physical media.

The main idea of layered networking is that no one program has to do it all. Using the U.N. analogy from earlier in this section, no single person has to perform every step in the process of getting a message from sender to receiver. All they have to do is perform their assigned tasks. For example, a translator only has to translate messages. As long as there is a process in place and all the participants can perform their jobs, the process works. The process of delivering messages in a network environment is all based on protocols. Protocols are the rules that define how to handle messages. Successful network communication depends on ensuring you have protocols in place that are compatible with one another and fill all the roles in the OSI Reference Model. Remember that you only have to provide the services shown in all of the levels. Your network may not have seven separate levels.

The OSI model is not the only model to describe networks. There are others. You will learn about another popular model later in this chapter. It is important to learn about each of the layers in the OSI model. We will focus on the bottom four layers in this chapter along with the Application Layer from a TCP/IP perspective. These layers are the ones that support IP-based communications and network communications. You have already seen several OSI layer references. Recall from the previous chapter that switches are Layer 2 devices. Layer 2 refers to OSI Reference Model Layer 2. Here is a brief description of each of the OSI Reference Model layers.

Application Layer—Layer 7

The highest layer in the OSI model is the Application Layer. This layer is also called Layer 7. Layer 7 is generally the only layer that interacts directly with the human being. This is where the front-end software interfaces with human interaction. The Application Layer is at the top of the OSI model and is the farthest from the actual network and Physical Layer. It is the software entry point for sending messages to and from an application used by humans. The process to exchange a message with another computer generally starts with a Layer 7 software call. That means application software calls another program or routine that does the following:

- When sending a message, the Application Layer software accepts some message as input from the application software. The Application Layer software adds any additional data, such as address of the target computer.
- The Application Layer software calls other software from the next lower layer and sends the new message (the original message with additional information).
- The Application Layer software may chop the message into smaller chunks before sending each chunk to the next layer.
- The Application Layer software then may wait for a reply.

Once the Application Layer sends the message to the next lower layer, it either continues with other tasks or may wait to receive a response. The Application Layer serves as the primary interface for application software to interact with networks. Protocols define the details of each Network Layer. There are multiple protocols that operate at each layer in the OSI Reference Model. Each protocol provides the required services for a layer and addresses specific needs. Some common protocols that operate at Layer 7 are:

- **Hypertext Transport Protocol (HTTP)**—Primary protocol used in the World Wide Web to deliver hypertext documents
- **File Transfer Protocol (FTP)**—Protocol used to transfer files between network nodes
- **Dynamic Host Configuration Protocol (DHCP)**—Automatic configuration protocol for networks
- **Session Initiation Protocol (SIP)**—Used to control multimedia communication using networks
- **Real-Time Transport Protocol (RTP)**—Defines standard packets for handling streaming media on a network
- **Simple Network Management Protocol (SNMP)**—Protocol used for transferring network management information about IP network devices

The Application Layer is the most visible layer in the OSI model. Most computer users have at least heard of HTTP since they use a browser to surf the Web. HTTP is the most widely recognized Application Layer protocol. The following sections cover the remaining layers in the OSI model.

Presentation Layer—Layer 6

The Presentation Layer, Layer 6, provides the interface between the Application Layer (above) and the Session Layer (below). It is responsible for formatting and coding Application Layer data into a form that is acceptable for transmitting on the network. The Presentation Layer also ensures that the data that reaches the destination computer is acceptable to the destination Application Layer. Some of the most common services the Presentation Layer provides include formatting and encrypting data. Encrypting data can occur at other layers, but the Presentation Layer is responsible for encrypting Application Layer data. Some of the common protocols that operate at the Presentation Layer include:

- **Multipurpose Internet Mail Extensions (MIME)**—Extends e-mail message formats to support multiple character sets, binary attachments, and multipart message bodies.
- **Secure Sockets Layer (SSL)**—Protocol that uses asymmetric cryptography to encrypt connections between network nodes.
- **Transport Layer Security (TLS)**—The successor to SSL.

The Presentation Layer performs the following actions:

- The source Presentation Layer accepts data from the source Application Layer, formats and optionally encrypts it, and then sends it down to the source Session Layer.
- The destination Presentation Layer accepts data from the destination Session Layer, decrypts it if necessary, and formats it for the Application Layer. It then sends the data up to the destination Application Layer.

Session Layer—Layer 5

The Session Layer, Layer 5, controls the conversations between computers. This layer sets up, manages, and terminates connections between applications on source and destination computers. Layer 5 can provide several different modes of operation, including:

- **Full duplex**—In the **full duplex** mode, both ends of a connection can communicate simultaneously.
- **Half duplex**—In the **half duplex** mode, both ends of a connection can communicate, but only one at a time.
- **Simplex**—In the **simplex mode**, the source can only send data to the destination. The destination cannot respond.

Today, many of the Layer 5 functions are built into other protocols that operate at different layers. Layer 5 was included in the OSI Reference Model to highlight the importance of creating and destroying connections in an orderly manner. Some of the common protocols that do explicitly operate at OSI Layer 5 include:

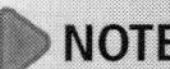

NOTE

Application environments that use remote procedure calls commonly operate using Layer 5 services.

- **Network Basic Input/Output System (NetBIOS)**—Allows applications on different computers to communicate over a LAN.
- **Layer 2 Tunneling Protocol (L2TP)**—A tunneling protocol that supports virtual private networks (VPNs). L2TP operates like a Layer 2 protocol, but actually operates at Layer 5.
- **Point-to-Point Tunneling Protocol (PPTP)**—Another tunneling protocol that supports VPNs.

Transport Layer—Layer 4

The Transport Layer, Layer 4, provides transparent and reliable data transfer between computers. Layer 4 accepts data from the upper layers and handles the details of getting the data to the destination computer. This layer can provide many services, including:

- **Flow control**—Manages the pacing of data transmission to avoid collisions and congestion.
- **Fragmentation/reassembly**—The source computer segments data into packets, adds additional information, and sends packets to the lower layer. The destination computer reassembles the packets into the original data. The destination computer ensures it reassembles packets in the correct order.
- **Error control**—The source and destination computers work together to detect when packets do not arrive within a reasonable time period, and then to retransmit missing packets. Missing packets due to network device or medium failure en route can slow down the reassembly process. The destination has to request that the source resend missing packets.
- **Acknowledgment of delivery**—Acknowledging packet delivery is part of error detection. Packets that are not acknowledged within a specified time period are classified as missing.

The Transport Layer ensures that data from the upper layers make it to their intended destination. Layer 4 relieves the upper layers from being concerned about getting data to the destination. All the upper layers have to do is pass data to the Transport Layer. The Transport Layer handles the rest. Input to the Transport Layer on the source computer either comes from the Session Layer or the Presentation Layer (if the Session Layer is not present). Some of the common protocols that operate at the Transport Layer include:

- **Transmission Control Protocol (TCP)**—One of the two core protocols in the Internet Protocol Suite. TCP is the protocol most major Internet applications rely on. Major applications that use TCP include the World Wide Web, e-mail, and file transfer. TCP provides data transport using persistent connections.

- **User Datagram Protocol (UDP)**—A stateless Transport Layer protocol that allows applications to send data without having to set up a connection first. UDP is useful for sending broadcast messages or simple messages that don't require a persistent connection.
- **Stream Control Transmission Protocol (SCTP)**—Provides services similar to those of TCP and UDP, but with a simpler message structure and fewer restrictions of the more popular protocols.

The Transport Layer is the first layer in the "lower layers." The three layers above the Transport Layer often are called the "upper layers" since they deal primarily with application data. The lower layers deal primarily with getting packets to their destination. Many refer to these layers as infrastructure.

Network Layer—Layer 3

The Network Layer, Layer 3, provides network addressing for packets. Layer 3 provides and supports switching and routing technologies to direct packets to their destinations. Layer 3 is the first layer that addresses issues with how to get packets from the source to the destination. In addition to network addressing, Layer 3 also supports creating virtual circuits. Virtual circuits are predefined paths between two computers.

> **NOTE**
>
> A Network Layer address is different from MAC addressing. A Network Layer address in Layer 3 is a structured address that defines both a network number and host number. A MAC layer address is a Layer 2 address that identifies the NIC card of the device. The MAC address is a hardware address and does not correspond to a logical address.

Network Layer addresses contain structural information about a network. The most revealing information found in a Network Layer address is the arrangement of subnetwork associations. The most common network address is the Internet Protocol (IP) address. IP addresses contain several levels of network and subnetwork identifiers that help isolate the logical location of a device. For this reason, most network design and configuration focuses on Layer 3. Several protocols operate at OSI Layer 3, including:

- **Internet Protocol (IP)**—The main protocol used to transmit packets across networks that support the Internet Protocol Suite. IP handles routing packets that travel outside the boundaries of the source network.
- **Internet Control Message Protocol (ICMP)**—Another core protocol on the Internet Protocol Suite, ICMP provides an easy method to send short messages. Most ICMP use is to send error messages related to devices or network services. Most applications use ICMP messages to query the status of devices or services or to report that devices or services are not available.
- **Internet Protocol Security (IPSec)**—This Layer 3 protocol suite authenticates and encrypts each IP packet to provide secure IP communication.
- **AppleTalk**—A proprietary Layer 3 protocol to exchange packets between Apple computers. AppleTalk is no longer supported in newer Apple operating systems and has been replaced by TCP/IP.

Routers operate at Layer 3. They read the network address to make decisions on the best path to use to deliver the packet. Layer 3 provides the flexibility to select the best route to the destination based on current network conditions. Layer 3 also has the responsibility to meet the quality requirements of Layer 4. As performance degrades along a chosen path, Layer 3 protocols can change future routing decisions to use a faster path. This flexibility allows Layer 3 protocols to react to changing conditions and provide better overall performance.

Data Link Layer—Layer 2

The Data Link Layer, Layer 2, provides the ability to transfer data between nodes on a network. The previous layer, the Network Layer, is more concerned with routing data across a network. The Data Link Layer is more concerned with node-to-node communication. In fact, the original intent of the Data Link Layer was to provide simple point-to-point or point-to-multipoint data transfer. Today's Data Link Layer protocols do more than just transport data from one point in a network to another point. Some protocols provide a layer of error correction for Physical Layer errors.

Data Link Layer protocols operate to provide both LAN and WAN network data transfer. These protocols handle the details of how to transfer packets from one node in a network to another node in the same network. Some of the common Data Link Layer protocols include:

- **Asynchronous Transfer Mode (ATM)**—A switching technique that uses time-division multiplexing to allow multiple applications to share a physical medium. ATM uses a fixed-size cell to transmit data. ATM performs well for networks that must transmit real-time data, streaming data, and large files that require high throughput. ATM uses virtual circuits to reduce the overhead of intermediate switching decisions.
- **IEEE 802.3**—The Institute of Electrical and Electronics Engineers (IEEE) is a global association that defines and publishes standards for many aspects of electronic components and communication. **IEEE 802.3** is a collection of standards that define the Data Link Layer protocol for accessing wired Ethernet. Ethernet has become the most popular LAN technology and is used in some WAN environments.
- **X.25**—A packet-switching protocol primarily used in legacy WAN applications. The X.25 family of protocols implements a WAN using POTS, leased lines, or ISDN. Although X.25 is still in use, many networks use IP instead of the Layer 2 X.25.
- **Point-to-Point Protocol (PPP)**—Layer 2 protocol used to establish a connection between two network nodes that provides authentication, encryption, and compression. Many ISPs commonly use PPP to connect subscribers to the Internet.
- **Network switch**—Network hardware device that operates at Layer 2. Switches examine the destination MAC address to determine the best port to use when forwarding the packet.

The most popular LAN technology, Ethernet, is a Data Link Layer protocol. You read in previous chapters that LAN switches can operate at Layer 2 or Layer 3. Layer 2 LAN switches examine MAC layer addresses—specifically, the destination MAC layer address and examining the forwarding table.

Physical Layer—Layer 1

The Physical Layer, Layer 1, is where data leaves the source computer and travels toward the destination in the form of packets, frames, bytes, bits, electrical signal, etc. It consists of all network media between the source and destination. Layer 1 media can include cables carrying electrical signals, wireless signals, and fiber optic cabling. Regardless of the technology in use, Layer 1 protocols define and control how a packet travels along the media. Layer 1 protocols dictate such specifications, including media and connector requirements, transmission signal characteristics, and device connection details.

The Physical Layer provides three basic services for all active physical connections. These services are:

- Establish and terminate connections with the physical medium.
- Manage the sharing of each physical connection with multiple logical network connections.
- Convert packets from their digital format to a format suitable for physical transmission. This process includes modulating data from a digital representation into a transmission signal.

Layer 1 protocols are closely related to the type of physical media they control. Wireless protocols have to deal with different issues than fiber optic protocols. In fact, Physical Layer protocols differ from other layers. A Physical Layer protocol has to interact with only one entity—its unique type of physical media. Physical Layer protocols generally do not have to deal with multiple physical media types. Physical Layer protocols must be able to transfer data between the Data Link Layer and the physical network media. It is the Physical Layer's responsibility to provide the interface between the physical transmission media and the networking software. Some of the common Layer 1 protocols include:

- **Plain old telephone service (POTS)**—The telecommunications network built to support analog voice communication. The original POTS network consisted of electrical and manual switches and copper wires.
- **IEEE 802.3**—Ethernet physical layer defines the characteristics of transmitting signals across wired Ethernet networks. IEEE 802.3 defines transmission speeds from 1 Mbps to 100 Gbps using coaxial, twisted pair, or fiber optic cables.
- **IEEE 802.11**—Set of standards to implement wireless LANs using radio transmission in the 2.4, 3.6, and 5 GHz frequency ranges. Wireless LANs are commonly called Wi-Fi wireless networks.

- **IEEE 802.15**—Set of standards that define wireless Personal Area Network (PAN) operating characteristics.
- **IEEE 802.16**—Set of standards that define wireless Metropolitan Area Network (MAN) operating characteristics. Wireless MANs are also known as WiMAX networks.
- **Universal Serial Bus (USB)**—Defines the standards to define cables, connectors, and protocols to connect and provide power between computer peripherals and computers.
- **Bluetooth**—Standards that define a wireless technology to exchange data over short distances. Connected Bluetooth devices allow users to easily create a PAN.
- **Network Hub**—Network hardware device that operates at Layer 1. A hub just echoes every packet to all ports. Hubs do not examine packets—they just echo all the traffic they receive.

The Internet Protocol

The primary protocol that relays packets across most of today's diverse networks is the Internet Protocol (IP). IP is the most popular Layer 3 protocol for both large and small networks. The appeal of IP is in its ability to span networks. Network devices can efficiently use switching to direct packets to the correct destination in the same network. However, to direct packets to destinations outside the network, devices must examine the Layer 3 network address and route each packet to its destination. IP provides packet routing and host identification to deliver packets to their destinations. IP treats all packets, also called **datagrams**, separately. It doesn't support the concept of grouping packets together. This means that each packet needs complete address information for the source and destination hosts. Each packet also needs sequence information to tell the destination how to reassemble the packets into the original message.

> **NOTE**
>
> IP does add a sequence number to each packet. However, IP doesn't use the sequence numbers to relate packets in any way when making routing decisions. The sequence number only tells the destination IP layer how to reassemble the packets to construct the original message.

Since IP's primary service is packet routing, the protocol relies solely on the network address to determine each packet's next logical step as it travels to its destination. IP defines methods to address network devices to optimize routing efficiency. Each packet contains a header with the destination's IP address (see Figure 5-4). This address identifies the destination host and provides information about the logical location of the host in its network. IP receives a packet from a higher layer, normally Layer 4, and adds additional data in a new IP header to the packet. The process of adding the IP header data is called **encapsulation**.

IP does more than just address packets. It provides these services:

- **Addressing**—Each IP header contains 32-bit or 128-bit addresses that identify the source and destination hosts. Intermediate routers that use these addresses choose a path through the network for the packet.
- **Fragmentation**—The IP software may chop packets into smaller packets. This process is called **fragmentation**. Fragmentation allows computers to send large packets across a network that can only handle smaller packets. The source computer fragments packets, and the destination computer reassembles packets. Both processes occur transparently.
- **Packet timeouts**—IP adds a Time To Live (TTL) value to each packet header. Each router that handles the packet decrements the TTL value. If TTL reaches zero, the current router drops the packet. This protection mechanism keeps packets from following circular paths and flooding a network.
- **Type of Service**—IP allows software to prioritize network traffic. Each IP packet contains header data that labels the packet with a type of service. Network devices can use these labels to handle packets with a higher or lower priority.
- **Additional Features**—IP supports several optional features, including:
  - **Source routing**—Allow the source to set requirements on the path the packet takes through the network
  - **Record route**—Trace the route a packet takes
  - **Security labels**—Assign security features label to packets

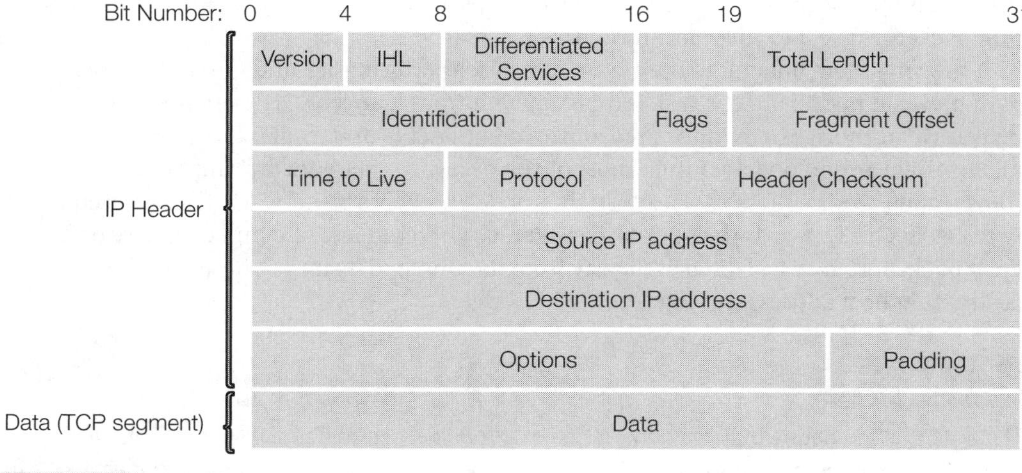

FIGURE 5-4 IPv4 packet header.

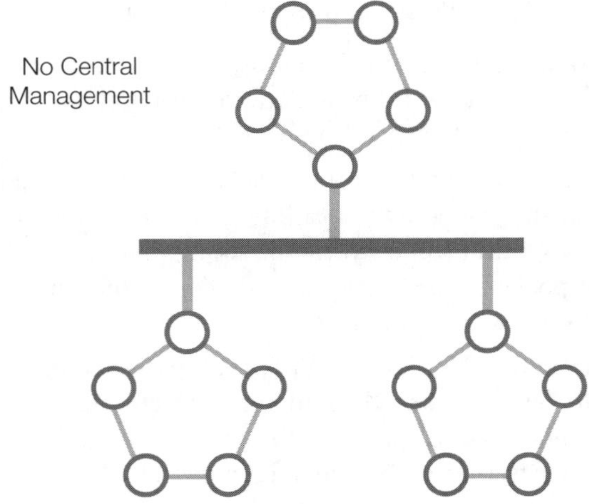

FIGURE 5-5
Decentralized IP network.

Two of the most consistent characteristics of networks are that the components are unreliable, and the best route through the network at any time is dynamic. Although today's network hardware and software are far more reliable than at any time in the past, networks still do fall short of their goals. Components may fail at any time and may cause gaps in the network topology. Excessive use can cause network performance to suffer. In most networks, the best path between any two nodes depends on current conditions. The best path during low use may not be the same path when many applications are using the network. In any case, it is unwise for any software to assume the network is reliable or static all of the time. IP helps address reliability issues and ensures that packets make it to their destination.

It may not seem difficult to monitor a network's performance and to select the best path between nodes, but the task is more difficult than it appears. IP networks have no central authority to monitor and control components and traffic. This design feature means that the end nodes contain most of the necessary network information. The source node sends a message based on that node's view of the network. Each subsequent network device forwards the packets based on its current view of connected networks. Each packet progressively makes its way from its source to its target, based on the destination host address (see Figure 5-5).

FYI

The decentralized nature of IP networks is one of its original design goals. IP was one of the original protocols developed for the U.S. Department of Defense's networks. The designers wanted a decentralized network design that could withstand enemy attacks and still operate. An IP network can do just that. As long as network devices can find a path between a packet's source and destination, the network can still operate.

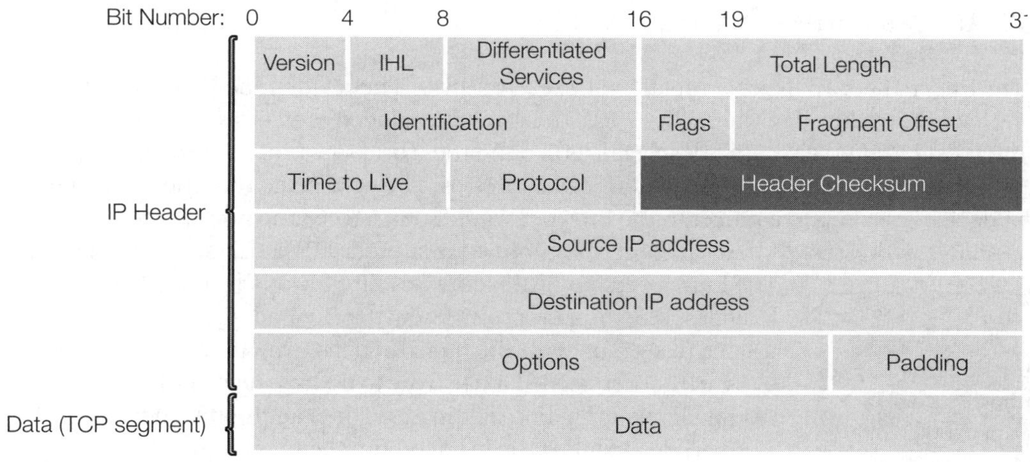

FIGURE 5-6 IP header checksum.

Since IP networks are decentralized and dynamic, there is always the possibility that a packet will not reach its destination node. Even if the packet does reach its destination, it may be different from the original packet. Errors or malicious software can change packets as they travel across a network. Source nodes need to know when a packet does not reach its destination, and destination nodes need to be able to detect when a packet changed during transmission. IP doesn't provide an automatic notification of lost packets. Upper layers handle lost packets.

The earlier IP version, IPv4, does include a checksum for each packet header (see Figure 5-6). The checksum is a numeric value that represents the entire header. The checksum changes when any part of a header changes. Checksums are an easy way for any network node to tell if a header has changed. Each node can calculate a new checksum for a packet header and compare it to the stored checksum. If the two checksums are different, the packet header has changed during transmission. While this method helps nodes detect errors and changes, it does take time to process each header. The newer version of IP, IPv6, does not include checksums. This decision was to increase IP's performance and its ability to quickly route a packet with minimal overhead. Error detection and correction is left to upper layer protocols.

IP earns its place in today's networks by providing a robust method to address nodes, and to route packets between nodes. A node's IP address defines its logical subnetwork. Network IP addresses provide information about how the organization designed the network, and they groups nodes together. They also show how the organization divides nodes into separate logical groups. A good IP addressing strategy can make an IP network more efficient and more functional. Placing nodes that communicate frequently in the same subnetwork can reduce the overhead required to route packets between the nodes. A sensible addressing strategy also makes a network easier to understand and manage. You will learn about different IP addressing options in the next section.

IP Addressing—IPv4 Versus IPv6

The Internet began to grow rapidly in the early 1980s. Then, when the World Wide Web was introduced in the early 1990s, the growth exploded even more. Even before the World Wide Web, network specialists around the world saw that the growth rate would eventually exhaust the available IP addresses. They predicted that the number of devices needing to connect to the Internet would soon exceed the number of available addresses. At that time, there was only one standard IP addressing scheme. The fourth version of IP addresses, IPv4, was the first version in widespread use. Everyone knew the IPv4 addresses were unable to keep up with the rapid Internet growth.

The Internet needed a new way to address devices that would allow many more addresses. These additional addresses were needed to allow the growing number of computers, PDAs, consumer electronics, and hundreds of other types of devices to connect to the Internet. The new addressing format is the sixth version of IP, IPv6. IPv4 is still the more common addressing scheme, but IPv6 is gaining popularity and becoming more common. You will learn about both of these important IP addressing schemes in this section.

> **NOTE**
> The **Internet Assigned Numbers Authority (IANA)** is the organization responsible for coordinating IP addresses and resources around the world. The IANA reported that it exhausted the primary address pool of IPv4 addresses on February 3, 2011.

IPv4

IPv4 is the fourth revision of the IP addressing scheme. It is the first revision to be deployed in most IP networks. IPv4 is the most common version in use today. IPv4 and the newer IP revision form the basis of the standard protocols used across the Internet. The **Internet Engineering Task Force (IETF)**, a global volunteer organization that develops and promotes Internet standards, published the IPv4 description in 1981. The document RFC 791 contains the complete IPv4 specification. This document provides the details of the IPv4 structure and use.

The IPv4 protocol was designed primarily for packet-switched networks. Since the intent of the protocol was to support dynamic paths between source and destination, IPv4 does not rely on existing circuits. It is called a **connectionless protocol**. IPv4 treats each packet as a separate entity and allows each packet to travel along a different path to its destination. Intermediate network nodes can route packets based on current network conditions. IPv4 relies on higher layer protocols, such as TCP, to establish connections, handle errors, and guarantee delivery.

IPv4 addresses are four-byte (32-bit) numbers. This means IPv4 can address 2^{32} or 4,294,967,296 unique devices. Although that sounds like plenty of IP devices, today's Internet has many more than 4 billion potential devices worldwide. To avoid running into the upper limit of IP addresses, the IPv4 specification includes three blocks of private addresses. Organizations can reserve a small number of public addresses and use private addresses for all of their internal IP devices. **Network Address Translation (NAT)** devices map internal addresses to public IP addresses. Many gateways support NAT and make using private IP addresses easy and convenient for organizations of any size. Another common feature that gateways may provide is a Dynamic Host Configuration Protocol (DHCP) server. DHCP is a standard method for internal devices to request and receive IP addresses and configuration information. An organization's DHCP server may be part of a gateway device or be a separate server. DHCP makes it possible to provide network connections to many devices without having to manually configure each one. Organizations that use NAT and private IP addresses made it possible to continue using IPv4 even through the rapid Internet expansion. Even though it is being replaced with IPv6, IPv4 will be around for many years.

IPv4 addresses are not commonly expressed just as 32-bit integers. Instead, they are normally written as four separate 8-bit numbers. Since an 8-bit number can be in the range of 0 to 255, these numbers are easier for people to handle. The standard notation for IPv4 addresses is four 8-bit numbers, called octets, separated by periods or dots. This common IPv4 representation is called **dot notation**. The process of converting from decimal to dot notation is one of repeated division.

TIP

You can find several IP address calculators online. For example, navigate to: *http://www.countryipblocks.net/tools/ip-octet-binary-and-decimal-calculators/*. This Web site provides several IPv4 calculators to make IP address management easier.

Classful Network

The original addressing architecture used for the Internet was called **classful network**. This addressing architecture created five different types of networks based on their required number of nodes. Each class of network was restricted to a range of IP addresses. For example, Class A networks were all networks in which the leading digit on the IP address was 0. Class A networks could contain a large number of nodes. The tradeoff came in balancing the number of networks and the number of nodes. Because of the limited number of bytes in the IPv4 address, the classful network architecture limited the number of larger Class A and Class B networks. On the other hand, classful network allowed many more Class C networks with fewer nodes. The IANA issued IP addresses based on the expected number of nodes a network would support. This strategy limited the IANA's flexibility and ended up wasting IP addresses. Table 5-1 shows how the five classes compare with one another.

TABLE 5-1 Classful network classes.

CLASS	LEADING BITS	SIZE OF NETWORK FIELD	# OF NETWORKS	# OF NODES	ADDRESS RANGE
A (large)	0	8	128	16,777,216	0.0.0.0 to 127.255.255.255
B (medium)	10	16	16,384	65,536	128.0.0.0 to 191.255.255.255
C (small)	110	24	2,097,152	256	192.0.0.0 to 223.255.255.255
D (multicast)	1110	N/A	N/A	N/A	224.0.0.0 to 239.255.255.255
E (future use)	1111	N/A	N/A	N/A	240.0.0.0 to 255.255.255.255

Classless Inter-Domain Routing

The original classful architecture was replaced in 1993. The IETF published new standards for allocating IP address blocks. The new standards are contained in RFC 1518, RFC 1519, and updated in RFC 4632. The IANA now manages network addressing using **Classless Inter-Domain Routing (CIDR)**. CIDR allows IANA to segment any address space to define larger or smaller networks as needed. This new strategy gives the IANA far more flexibility to allocate networks of virtually any size without wasting large blocks of IP addresses. Classful networks were based on fixed network identifiers. CIDR uses **Variable Length Subnet Masking (VLSM)** to allow networks to be fragmented into any size subnetwork.

CIDR defines networks using IP address prefixes. The IANA can allocate a network that consists of any number of binary bits to form the network's address. A CIDR block is a group of addresses that share the same prefix. Classful networks only defined a limited number of network prefixes based on network class. CIDR allows network prefixes of any length, up to the IPv4 address size. The CIDR address format is similar to the IP address dot notation. A network's address is the base IP address in dot notation, followed by

FYI

CIDR address block notation really uses two numeric notations. The IPv4 address part is in dot notation. That means it contains four octets. The second part of the CIDR address block is the number of bits in the network address. That means that to determine whether an IP address is in a specific network, you have to visualize the address in binary form. Then, just compare the leading bits to see if they match the network's address. For example, the CIDR address block 168.12.0.0/16 has a binary network address of:

10101000.00001100.00000000.00000000

Any IP address with the same leading 16 bits (10101000.00001100) would be in this network.

TABLE 5-2 CIDR Block Addresses.

CIDR BLOCK ADDRESS	IP ADDRESS RANGE	COMMENTS
168.12.0.0/16	168.12.0.0 to 168.12.255.255	Same as classful Class B network
201.100.98.0/24	201.100.98.0 to 201.100.98.255	Same as classful Class C network
131.98.80.0/20	131.98.80.0 to 131.98.95.255	Does not map to a classful class—defines a network with 4,096 addresses
222.123.88.80/28	222.123.88.80 to 222.123.88.95	Does not map to a classful class—defines a network with 16 addresses

the number of bits in the prefix. The two values are separated by a slash character (/). Table 5-2 shows several CIDR block address examples.

Subnet Mask

Many networks define a **subnet mask** to serve the same purpose as the prefix length of CIDR address blocks. The subnet mask is a binary number that contains all 1's in the leftmost prefix length positions. All other bits are 0's. For example, the subnet mask for the CIDR address block 168.12.0.0/16 would be:

11111111.11111111.00000000.00000000

This subnet mask contains 16 1's and is followed by 16 0's. The common notation for subnet masks is dot notation. So, this subnet mask would commonly appear as: 255.255.0.0

Networks use the subnet mask to help determine whether an IP address is in the network. This helps make routing decisions to determine where to send a packet. Table 5-3 shows the subnet masks for example CIDR Block Addresses.

TABLE 5-3 Subnet masks.

CIDR BLOCK ADDRESS	SUBNET MASK
168.12.0.0/16	255.255.0.0
201.100.98.0/24	255.255.255.0
131.98.80.0/20	255.255.240.0
222.123.88.80/28	255.255.255.240

Private Networks

You read in Chapter 1 that the IPv4 protocol defines three ranges of addresses for private networks. A private network is one that contains private IP addresses. Private IP addresses are not routable. That means that public routers will not forward any packets with private IP addresses. The purpose of private IP addresses is to allow organizations to assign their own device IP addresses from the private network ranges. This practice allows organizations to consume only a small number of public IP addresses. The organization's perimeter network devices will use NAT to map internal private IP addresses to external routable IP addresses. The ranges of private IPv4 addresses are:

- 10.0.0.0 to 10.255.255.255
- 172.16.0.0 to 172.16.255.255
- 192.168.0.0 to 192.168.255.255

Resolving Addresses

You have seen only IP addresses used to identify hosts so far. However, it is more common to use host names to identify hosts in many applications. Host names are more meaningful than IP addresses. For example, the host name amazon.com is more descriptive than one of Amazon's IP addresses: 72.21.211.176. Since applications and users like to use host names, it is important to look up the IP address for a given host name. The process of finding an IP address for a host name is called **address resolution**. The **Domain Name System (DNS)** is a hierarchical naming system that allows organizations to associate host names with IP address name spaces. DNS servers store these associations and make the tables available for network users. DNS servers return an IP address when given a known host name. DNS is a simple service, but it is crucial to making the Internet a usable network. DNS servers keep up with the changing host names and make it easy to react to any organization that changes its IP addresses.

IPv6

In spite of the efforts to reduce the number of IP addresses organizations required, IPv4 addressing was not able to keep up with the explosive demand. Today's wide range of network-ready devices need IP addresses to be truly useful. Many of these devices are always on and connected to the network. That means any strategy that depends on sharing IP addresses likely will not work. As demand for Internet connections increased, so did the need for a new way to address the new devices. The IETF published a new standard for IP addresses in RFC 2460. The new standard, IPv6, makes several changes to the older IPv4 standard.

The primary motivation for creating IPv6 was to increase the network address space. IPv6 accomplishes this goal by increasing the address size from the IPv4 32 bits to the new 128 bits. IPv4 could address 2^{32}—or around 4 billion devices. Ipv6's larger address size can address 2^{128}—or over 340 undecillion devices!

> **NOTE**
> An undecillion is a very large number that consists of a "1" followed by 36 zeros.

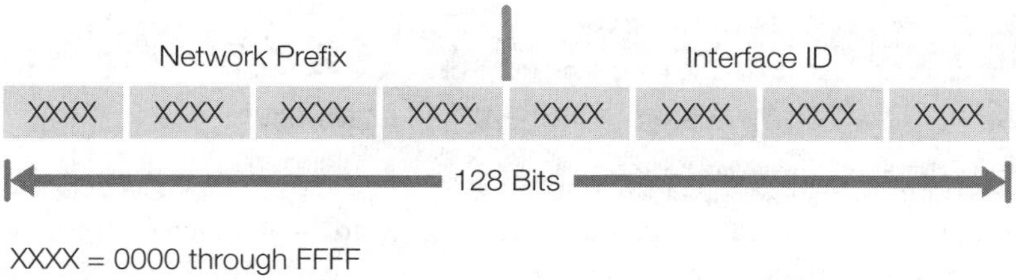

FIGURE 5-7
IPv6 address format.

IPv6 does much more than just switch to a bigger address. In using a bigger address, IPv6 effectively does away with the need for NAT. Recall that NAT was introduced to deal with the eventual exhaustion of IPv4 addresses. With a nearly endless pool of IPv6 addresses, NAT is no longer needed to reuse network addresses. IPv6 also has several additional features, including:

- Making assigning IP addresses easier
- Simplifying renumbering networks
- Standardizing the host identification part of the address
- Integrating network security into the protocol
- Defining multicasting as part of the specification

Since IPv6 addresses are 128 bits in length, they need a different notation. The classic IPv4 dot notation would require 16 octets and may be awkward to use. IPv6 addresses are expressed as eight groups of four hexadecimal digits. Each group is separated by colons. For example, you would write an IPv6 network address as:

2002:0:0:0:0:0:a80c:502b

IPv6 addresses that specify a unique device are called **unicast addresses.** IPv6 unicast addresses are logically divided into two 64-bit segments. The first 64-bit segment (the first four groups of hexadecimal digits) represent the network prefix. The network prefix identifies the network. IPv6 uses a fixed length network prefix, as opposed to CIDR in IPv4, which used a variable length network prefix (see Figure 5-7). Fixed length network prefixes make it easier for network devices to quickly route packets. The second 64-bit segment (the second group of four hexadecimal digits) represents the interface identifier or host. Each device has a unique interface identifier for a given network. In fact, the interface identifier is often generated from the device interface's MAC address.

The IPv6 address format can still be long and sometimes repetitive. For instance, consider the following IPv6 address:

2002:0:0:0:0206:0:a80c:052b

The IPv6 specification offers two rules to abbreviate IPv6 addresses. Abbreviated addresses are smaller and contain less redundant information. The two rules for IPv6 address abbreviating are:

1. You may omit any leading zeros within any group of hexadecimal digits.
2. You may replace one group of consecutive zeros in an address with a double colon.

TABLE 5-4 IPv6 address abbreviation.

FULL IPv6 ADDRESS	COMPRESSED ADDRESS	COMMENT
2002:0:0:0:0206:0:a80c:052b	2002:0:0:0:206:0:a80c:52b	Rule 1—Drop leading zeros
2002:0:0:0:0206:0:a80c:052b	2002::0206:0:a80c:052b	Rule 2—Replace consecutive zeros
2002:0:0:0:0206:0:a80c:052b	2002::206:0:a80c:52b	Rules 1 and 2

These two simple rules allow IPv6 packets to compress network addresses without losing any of the address details. These simple abbreviation rules can have a noticeable impact on network performance. Making packets even a little smaller can have cumulative effects on heavily used networks. Table 5-4 shows several examples of IPv6 address abbreviation.

Network Methodologies

IPv6 supports three different methodologies to send packets. The different methodologies make it easier to send packets to their desired destinations. IPv6 includes methods to send packets to one, several, or many destinations. These methodologies include:

- **Unicasting**—Sending a packet to a single destination
- **Anycasting**—Sending a packet to the nearest node in a specified group of nodes
- **Multicasting**—Sending a packet to multiple destinations

Unlike IPv4, IPv6 does not support **broadcasting**. Broadcasting sends a packet to a complete range of IP addresses. Sending broadcast messages to a large subnet can cause network congestion and allow attackers to affect a network's availability. Each IPv6 address includes a scope value. The scope identifies the part of the network in which the address is valid. Organizations can use IPv6 scope to limit a node's communication to a local subnet or to a larger network.

IPv4 to IPv6

Due to the structural differences between IPv4 and IPv6, each one requires its own layer in the ISO reference model. That means there need to be at least two stacks at Layer 3 to support both versions of IP. Changing from IPv4 to IPv6 is a gradual process that requires operating system support of both versions during the transition. Many current operating systems support a **dual IP stack**. A dual IP stack means that the operating system supports both IPv4 and IPv6 using two separate network stacks for IP. Each operating system can decide to implement dual IP stacks with separate stacks or by using a hybrid approach. Dual IP stacks allow programmers to deploy software that works on either IPv4 or IPv6 without having to be concerned with the networking details. Programmers can write code that specifically uses IPv6 addresses or they can continue to use IPv4 addresses and let the dual IP stack use a special IPv6 address format, the IPv4-mapped address.

IPv4-mapped addresses allow IPv6 to use existing IPv4 addresses. An IPv4-mapped address is composed in the following manner:

- The first 80 bits are set to zero.
- The next 16 bits are set to one.
- The remaining 32 bits correspond to the IPv4 address.

For example, the IPv4 address: 216.12.18.44 would be represented in IPv6 as the IPv4-mapped address:

::ffff:216.12.18.44

Literal IPv6 Addresses

IPv4 addresses are commonly used in network resource identifiers and in UNC path names. Both addressing options include the IPv4 address to identify a host. IPv6 addresses pose a problem. The colon character is a reserved character in both network resource identifiers and UNC path names. The colon character is already used for other purposes. The IPv6 specification contains special handling for each of these situations. Table 5-5 summarizes how IPv6 addresses can be used in each context.

IPv6 provides more addresses, flexibility, and security than its predecessor. The IPv6 specification includes features that ease the process of transitioning to the new standard. IPv6 is the future of the Internet. It is the protocol that will allow the Internet to continue to grow and mature.

TABLE 5-5 IPv6 literal addresses.

ENTITY	RESOLUTION	EXAMPLE
Network Resource Identifier—The colon character already separates the host name and port number.	Add square brackets around literal IPv6 addresses.	http://[2002::206:0:a80c:52b]:8080
UNC Path Names—The colon character is an illegal character.	Convert colon characters to dashes, and append the ".ipv6-literal.net" domain to IPv6 literal addresses.	2002::206:0:a80c:52b would be written as: 2002--206-0-a80c-52b.ipv6-literal.net

IP Communications

The Internet Protocol is a fundamental part of the Internet's success. It has also become the most popular Layer 3 protocol for general communication within LANs. Using the same protocol for LAN and WAN communication makes it possible to expand how we use networks. IP-based networks can carry messages of any type, from e-mail to streaming media. Each type of traffic has its own requirements and provides its own challenges to the network. As more and more applications use IP-based networks to communicate, they use more and more of the available capacity. Newer standards and techniques are necessary to ensure networks are as efficient as possible.

Recall that Layer 3 protocols, including IP, route packets across networks. When a packet enters its destination network, the network stack needs to know the packet's local destination. The Address Resolution Protocol (ARP) is the common protocol in IPv4 networks to provide local MAC addresses. IPv6 networks use the **Neighbor Discovery Protocol (NDP)** to provide a similar service as ARP. To find a local MAC address, the network device would first look up the supplied IP address in its ARP table. A device's ARP table contains the IP address and the corresponding MAC address of known nodes. If the device finds no entry for the IP address, it sends an ARP broadcast query to the network. In IPv6 networks, the NDP discovery request provides similar functionality. If the node is present in the network, it replies with its MAC address. The network device adds the newly discovered MAC address to the ARP table and forwards the packet to its local destination.

ARP and NDP are important protocols for IP-based networks. They make it possible to use IP to transport traffic within local networks and between networks, including those connected to the Internet. Current networks are beginning to rely more on a combination of switching and routing to get packets to their destinations efficiently. You will learn more about how networks operate at Layers 2 and 3 in later chapters. For now, consider how organizations are using IP-based networks to implement UC solutions.

IP networks make it possible to efficiently exchange nearly any type of data between any two nodes on the network. This standard communication method supports many different types of traffic, including:

- E-mail messages
- Telephone calls
- Video conferencing
- Streaming audio and video
- Large file transfers
- Real-time data
- Instant messages

This list is only a representation of the many types of data IP networks can carry. Upper layer protocols carry much of the responsibility of handling different types of messages, but IP gets the packets that make up messages to their destinations. In the past, networks tended to be built for specific purposes. For example, the POTS network was designed to support analog voice data, and it did that very well. The ability to use standard IP networks to transport multiple types of data makes networks valuable assets to any organization. Standard protocols such as IP make UC not only a possibility, but a reality.

Connectionless Versus Connection-Oriented Communications

The Internet Protocol was originally designed for packet-switched networks. That means each packet is handled as a separate message. When IP sends a packet to its destination, it selects the best route based on current conditions. As the state and performance of the network change, so do routing decisions. The most direct path to a destination may not be the best route if it is congested. A longer route with less traffic may be faster. As more and more protocols depend on real-time delivery, speed is often one of the most important delivery measurements. Since IP treats each packet separately, there is no notion of a connection between the source and destination nodes. IP is called a connectionless protocol. The alternative is a **connection-oriented protocol**. In short, a connectionless protocol treats each message separately. A connection-oriented protocol sets up a connection between the source and destination (see Figure 5-8). All messages the two hosts exchange during the conversation use the same connection information. Some connection-oriented protocols go one step further and support virtual circuits.

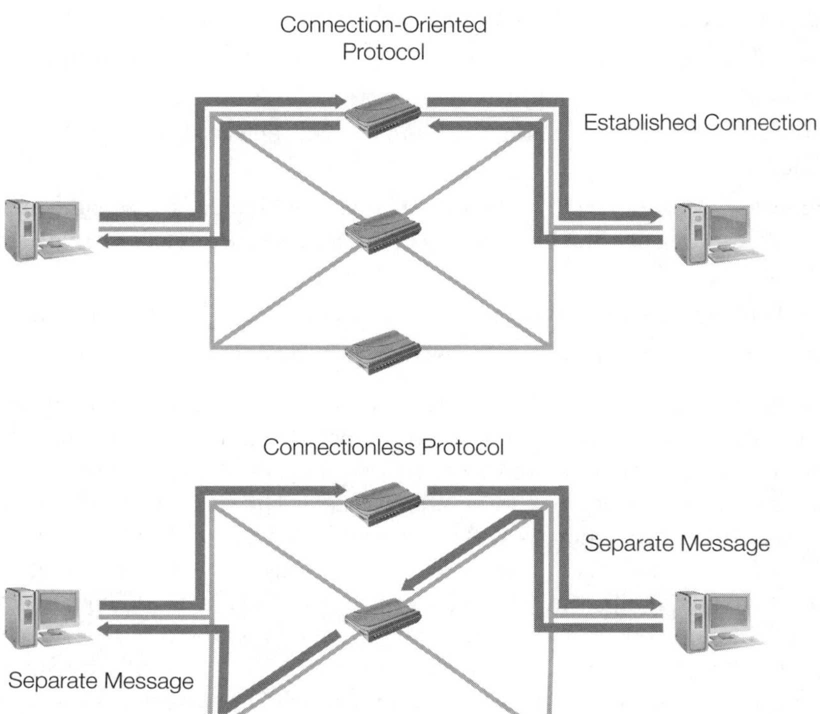

FIGURE 5-8
Connection-oriented and connectionless protocols.

A virtual circuit is a defined path between the two hosts. A connection that uses a virtual circuit uses the same path for all messages in a conversation. Upper layer protocols may need to define and maintain persistent connections to provide a required service.

Layered networking software makes it possible to mix connectionless and connection-oriented protocols. It is possible to use a connection-oriented protocol at Layer 4 or higher and still use IP for Layer 3. The key to using mixed mode protocols is in the way layers work. Recall that each layer in the OSI reference model logically communicates with the same layer on the remote computer. For example, a Layer 4 protocol on the source host talks to Layer 4 on the destination host. If Layer 4 sets up and uses a circuit, or persistent connection, it doesn't really matter how Layer 3 transports the individual packets. IP can, and does, support both connectionless and connection-oriented upper layer protocols.

Two of the most common Layer 4 protocols are Transmission Control Protocol (TCP) and User Datagram Protocol (UDP). These two protocols are at the heart of the Internet Protocol Suite. Many applications that communicate across the Internet use these protocols in normal operation. TCP is a connection-oriented protocol. It takes more work to set up and use a TCP connection. Here are the basic steps required to set up and use a TCP connection:

1. A remote client sends a connection request to the server.
2. The server receives the connection request and replies with an acknowledgment.
3. The remote client replies back to the server with an acknowledgment.
4. The TCP connection is established, and the client and server can exchange messages.
5. At the end of the conversation, the remote client sends a close request to the server.
6. The server receives the close request and replies with an acknowledgment. When the server has finished sending all messages, it sends a close request to the client.
7. The client closes the connection and sends a close acknowledgment to the server.
8. The server receives the close acknowledgment and closes its side of the connection.

Connection-oriented protocols require extra work to set up and maintain connections. However, the additional work is often worth the effort. One advantage of connection-oriented protocols is that they can reduce network traffic. Establishing connections allows the client and server to remember conversation context. The client does not have to send all the details of the conversation with each message. That can make network messages much smaller. Smaller messages mean lower network usage. That translates into better network performance. To illustrate the value of context, consider the following two conversations. In both conversations, Fred Jones is attending an athletic event. He is at the snack bar and is ordering a meal. In the first scenario, Fred talks with the same cashier throughout the conversation. In the second scenario, a different worker answers each of Fred's questions and requests.

Scenario 1—Connection-Oriented Conversation

FRED: Hello, I'd like to order a hamburger and a medium cola.

CASHIER: Certainly. Would you like French fries with your order?

FRED: No, thanks. But could I change that to a large cola?

CASHIER: Yes, sir. Would you like anything else?

FRED: No, thank you. Could I get ketchup and mustard on the hamburger?

CASHIER: Yes, sir. That will be $8.50.

FRED: OK, here is $10.00.

CASHIER: Thank you. Here is your change of $1.50, and here is your food.

Scenario 2—Connectionless Conversation

FRED: Hello, I'd like to order a hamburger and a medium cola.

ORDER CLERK 1: Certainly. Your order number is 123, one hamburger and a medium cola. Your order total is $7.50. Please pay the cashier.

FRED: Hi, I just entered order number 123, one hamburger and a medium cola. Could I change the drink to a large cola?

ORDER CLERK 2: Yes, sir. Order 123 is now one hamburger and a large cola. Your new order total is $8.50. Please pay the cashier.

FRED: Hi, I need to make a change to order 123, one hamburger and a large cola. Could I get ketchup and mustard on the burger?

ORDER CLERK 3: Yes, sir, order 123, one hamburger with ketchup and mustard on the burger, and one large cola. Your order total is $8.50.

FRED: I am paying for order 123, one hamburger with ketchup and mustard on the burger, and one large cola. The order total is $8.50. Here is $10.00.

CASHIER: Thank you. Here is your change of $1.50. Please go to food pickup to get your food.

FRED: I am here to pick up order 123, one hamburger with ketchup and mustard on the burger, and one large cola.

FOOD PICKUP CLERK: Here is your food.

As you can see, the conversation is far easier when Fred only talked with one person. In the second scenario, Fred talked with several people and had to repeat the order details multiple times. These two scenarios show the difference between connectionless and connection-oriented protocols. If your application needs to maintain a conversation and exchange multiple messages with the same host, a connection-oriented protocol may be a good choice. If your application only needs to send occasional messages to a single host or a group of hosts, a connectionless protocol may be faster and easier.

TCP is the most commonly used connection-oriented Layer 4 protocol. Most Internet applications use TCP, along with IP, to support network communications. Some specific network uses do not require the overhead of complete TCP connections. UDP is a connectionless protocol that many applications use to send individual packets to one or more hosts. UDP is a common option when sending service requests to a group of servers. In some networks, a service requester will send a UDP datagram to a group of hosts asking for a specific service. Busy hosts may take longer to respond, so the first host to respond is likely the one that can handle the service request quickest. This strategy uses UDP in simple load balancing.
Other connectionless protocols include:

- **Internet Control Message Protocol (ICMP)**—Used to communicate network health information between network hosts or devices.
- **Domain Name Service (DNS)**—Used to provide a distributed name resolution service. DNS supports converting host names into IP addresses.
- **Trivial File Transfer Protocol (TFTP)**—Generally used to automatically transfer files between network nodes.
- **Simple Network Management Protocol (SNMP)**—Used to monitor and manage networks from remote nodes.

The decision between connectionless and connection-oriented protocols depends on use. Although connection-oriented protocols require more work to set up and manage the connections, they can relieve the network of traffic. The set up overhead can make the network operate more efficiently by reducing message size once you have established the connection. In either case, IP provides a solid foundation for both connectionless and connection-oriented upper layer protocols.

TCP/IP Reference Model

You learned about the OSI Reference Model earlier in this chapter. The OSI Reference Model is not the only layered network reference model. The **Transmission Control Protocol/Internet Protocol (TCP/IP) Reference Model** is another network model that describes how layered network software operates. The TCP/IP Reference Model, with only four layers, is simpler than the OSI Reference Model. It is also closely related to the functionality of the TCP/IP protocol suite. The OSI Reference Model is the most common model used to teach general networking concepts. The TCP/IP Reference Model is more commonly used to model and teach networking concepts specifically related to Internet communications. The TCP/IP Reference Model defines the layers most commonly found in separate Internet-related protocols (Figure 5-9).

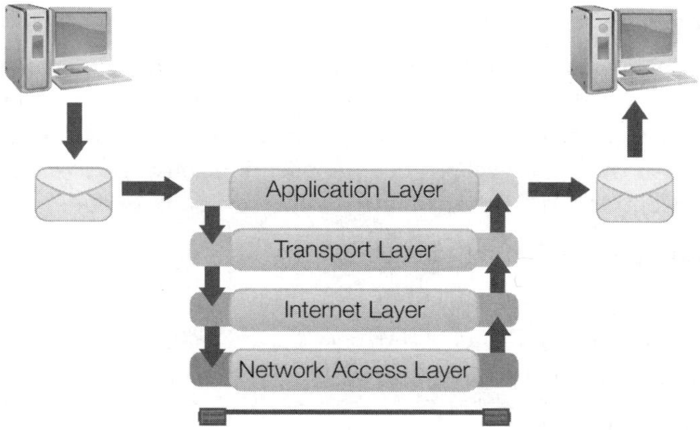

FIGURE 5-9
TCP/IP Reference Model layers.

The biggest difference between the two models is in each model's purpose. Although they are often used somewhat interchangeably, they address different needs. The OSI Reference Model was originally published as a prescriptive model. The OSI Reference Model provides a prescription as to how organizations should develop network software. On the other hand, the TCP/IP Reference Model was created as a descriptive model. The TCP/IP Reference Model describes how the Internet Protocol Suite operates. Since the two models are commonly used to describe networks, it is helpful to compare how the layers in the two models relate. Figure 5-10 shows how each layer in the OSI Reference Model relates to the layers in the TCP/IP Reference Model.

Like the OSI Reference Model, the TCP/IP Reference Model is composed of multiple layers. Each of the four TCP/IP Reference Model layers is responsible for a different phase of communication. At each layer in the network stack, the layer logically communicates with the corresponding layer on the other node. The following sections provide details about each of the TCP/IP Reference Model layers.

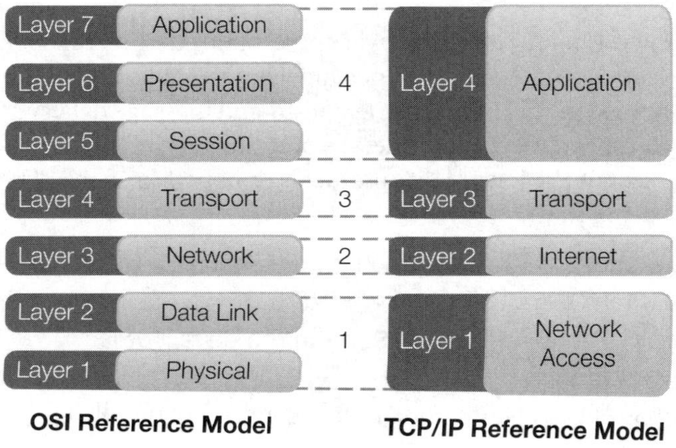

FIGURE 5-10
The OSI and TCP/IP Reference Models.

Application Layer

The TCP/IP Reference Model Application Layer corresponds to three layers in the OSI model. It corresponds to the Application Layer, the Presentation Layer, and the Session Layer in the OSI model. The Application Layer is the highest layer in the TCP/IP model and includes most of the high-level protocols application software uses for network communication. Common TCP/IP Application Layer protocols include:

- Dynamic Host Configuration Protocol (DHCP)
- Hypertext Transport Protocol (HTTP)
- Internet Message Access Protocol (IMAP)
- File Transfer Protocol (FTP)
- Post Office Protocol (POP)
- Session Initiation Protocol (SIP)

The TCP/IP model does not define any layers between the Application Layer and the Transport Layer. The Application Layer generally handles tasks that the Session or Presentation layers would normally handle in the OSI model. For example, encryption may occur in the TCP/IP Model Application Layer. Most OSI Session and Presentation Layer functions are provided as network library calls from the application software.

Application Layer protocols are the most visible protocols in Internet applications. Many other protocols that do not reside in the Application Layer are crucial to the network communication process. These lower-layer protocols are generally hidden from view and accessed as calls from within the operating system's network stack. Application Layer protocols aren't generally concerned with many of the specific details of how messages arrive at their destination. The lower-layer protocols handle the details. All the Application Layer protocols must do is pass a message to the lower-layer protocols, along with the destination's address.

Transport Layer

The TCP/IP Reference Model Transport Layer corresponds to the Transport layer in the OSI model. These layers in different reference models accomplish nearly the same tasks. These protocols are responsible for handling end-to-end message delivery. That means the Transport Layer takes care of all the details of ensuring a message makes it to the destination, regardless of the lower-layer protocols or networks in use. These responsibilities include ensuring that:

- Data arrives in the same state in which it was sent (error correction)
- Missing data is retransmitted
- Data is presented to the Application Layer in the correct order
- Duplicate data is dropped
- Network path problems (congestion or failed links) are handled

TABLE 5-6 Common Application Layer protocols and default ports.

PROTOCOLS	DEFAULT PORT
File Transfer Protocol (FTP)	21
Secure Shell (SSH)	22
Telnet	23
Simple Mail Transport Protocol (SMTP)	25
Hypertext Transport Protocol (HTTP)	80
Secure Hypertext Transport Protocol (HTTP-S)	443

The most common TCP/IP Transport Layer protocols are:

- Transmission Control Protocol (TCP)
- User Datagram Protocol (UDP)

Application and Transport Layer protocols generally connect to remote nodes using specific ports to communicate. Using different ports for different protocols helps to keep individual connections separate from one another. To make communicating as easy as possible, the most popular protocols use well-known default port numbers. The IANA maintains a list of common Application and Transport Layer protocols and their default ports. Most of today's network software adheres to the commonly agreed upon ports list. Agreeing on default port usage helps to make it easy for applications to communicate with one another. Table 5-6 shows a few of the most popular TCP/IP model Application and Transport Layer protocols and their default ports. All of the protocols in Table 5-6 use the same ports for TCP and UDP connections.

TIP

For a complete list of the IANA list of well known ports, visit: *http://www.iana.org/assignments/service-names-port-numbers/service-names-port-numbers.xml.*

Internet Layer

The TCP/IP Reference Model Internet Layer corresponds to the Network Layer in OSI model. This layer is responsible for sending packets across different networks. The Internet Layer examines each packet, determines its destination, and makes the necessary routing decisions to get the packet to its destination. The Internet Layer is primarily made up of the Internet Protocol and other protocols that support IP. Some of the other supporting protocols include ICMP and IPSec. The Internet Layer provides transparency to the upper layer protocols. Any upper layer protocol can send a message to another host without being concerned with any of the details of a specific network. IP provides this level of transparency and makes large-scale network applications possible.

Network Access Layer

The TCP/IP Reference Model Internet Layer corresponds to the Data Link and Physical layers in the OSI model. Network Access Layer protocols ensure packets move between nodes within the same LAN. The Internet Layer handles packets as they leave the LAN. The scope of the Network Access Layer is the current LAN. This lowest layer in the TCP/IP model is the only layer that interacts with the physical hardware. The Network Access Layer takes packets from the Internet Layer and places them on the physical media for transmission to the next node. Network Access Layer devices use switching to direct packets. Common TCP/IP Network Access Layer protocols include:

- Address Resolution Protocol (ARP)
- Layer 2 Tunneling Protocol (L2TP)
- Point-to-Point Protocol (PPP)
- Media Access Control (Ethernet, DSL, FDDI, etc.)

The TCP/IP Reference Model describes how IP-based networks operate. Although the majority of IP-based networks also use TCP, the model supports other Transport Layer protocols. Most Internet applications follow the TCP/IP model fairly closely.

TCP/IP Suite

The collection of protocols that define and enable Internet communication is called the TCP/IP suite. This collection is also known as the Internet Protocol Suite. The TCP/IP Reference Model you learned about in the previous section was designed to describe the TCP/IP suite. From the early beginnings of the Internet and its predecessors, the TCP/IP protocols have played an important role. As the Internet grew and demands on it increased, more protocols were developed. These protocols became part of the standard TCP/IP protocol suite. Today, nearly all Internet-capable operating systems and devices provide support for the protocols defined in the TCP/IP suite.

The protocols in the suite generally are organized into four layers. The TCP/IP Reference Model defines each of the layers and describes protocols that belong to each one. Each protocol logically communicates with its corresponding protocol on the other node. A message actually moves down the TCP/IP networking stack, starting at the Application Layer. The Application Layer sends a message to the next lower layer, the Transport Layer. The Transport Layer protocol may segment the message into smaller chunks. It then adds addresses and other information and sends the new data to the next lower level. This process continues until the source node sends the message fragment to another node using physical media. The packet or frame may be forwarded by several nodes before it reaches its destination. When it does reach its destination, it travels back up the destination network stack until it reaches the Application Layer.

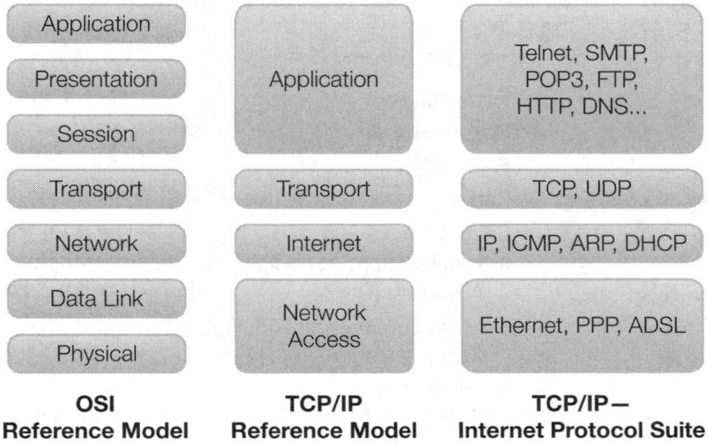

OSI Reference Model	TCP/IP Reference Model	TCP/IP—Internet Protocol Suite
Application	Application	Telnet, SMTP, POP3, FTP, HTTP, DNS...
Presentation		
Session		
Transport	Transport	TCP, UDP
Network	Internet	IP, ICMP, ARP, DHCP
Data Link	Network Access	Ethernet, PPP, ADSL
Physical		

FIGURE 5-11 The main protocols of the TCP/IP suite in relation to the layers of the two reference models.

Taken together, the TCP/IP suite provides all of the protocols necessary for applications to exchange messages and data using IP-based networks. This suite supports communication across networks ranging from small LANs to the Internet. Figure 5-11 shows a list of the main protocols in the TCP/IP suite and the layers at which they operate.

CHAPTER SUMMARY

The TCP/IP protocols make the Internet possible. These two protocols have matured since their introduction over 40 years ago. General network growth created a demand for standards and easy methods to connect networks with one another. As the demand for global connectivity increased, the Internet emerged as the most flexible and dependable infrastructure. The Internet powers today's organizations. In this chapter you read about the two most popular network reference models, the OSI model and the TCP/IP model. You learned about the details of the Internet Protocol, how it supports interconnected networks, and the two current IP addressing options.

You read about the TCP protocol and how it provides services for upper layer protocols. You learned about the differences between connectionless and connection-oriented protocols. And finally, this chapter covered how the TCP/IP Reference Model describes the TCP/IP suite and how the protocols work together to enable transparent network communication.

KEY CONCEPTS AND TERMS

Address resolution
Broadcasting
Classful network
Classless Inter-Domain Routing (CIDR)
Connection-oriented protocol
Connectionless protocol
Datagrams
Domain Name System (DNS)
Dot notation
Dual IP stack
Encapsulation
Fragmentation
Full duplex
Half duplex
IEEE 802.3
Internet Assigned Numbers Authority (IANA)
Internet Engineering Task Force (IETF)
Neighbor Discovery Protocol (NDP)
Network Address Translation (NAT)
Protocol
Simplex
Subnet mask
Transmission Control Protocol/Internet Protocol (TCP/IP) Reference Model
Unicast addresses
Variable Length Subnet Masking (VLSM)

CHAPTER 5 ASSESSMENT

1. The OSI Reference Model is also called the TCP/IP Reference Model.
   A. True
   B. False
2. Which OSI Reference Model layer includes the HTTP and DHCP protocols?
   A. Application
   B. Presentation
   C. Session
   D. Transport
3. Which OSI Reference Model layer is primarily responsible for setting up, managing, and terminating connections between applications?
   A. Application
   B. Presentation
   C. Session
   D. Transport
4. Which of the following OSI Reference Model Transport Layer protocols is a connectionless protocol often used to send simple broadcast messages?
   A. TCP
   B. UDP
   C. IP
   D. PPTP
5. The Internet Protocol (IP) operates an OSI Layer ________.
6. What is the address size of IPv6 addresses?
   A. 32 bits
   B. 64 bits
   C. 128 bits
   D. 256 bits
7. The OSI Model Data Link and Physical Layers correspond to the TCP/IP Model ________ Layer.

8. What does the TTL value in an IP header contain?

A. Time To Live
B. Transport Translation Layer
C. Transport Time Layer
D. Transport Time Left

9. Which class of IP network allows the fewest number of nodes in each network?

A. Class A
B. Class B
C. Class C
D. Class D

10. Which of the following IPv4 addresses is routable (public)?

A. 172.16.0.16
B. 10.0.255.255
C. 192.168.250.16
D. 172.8.0.16

11. Which of the following addresses are valid IPv6 addresses? (Select two.)

A. 2002::206::a80c:52b
B. 2002:0:0:0:0206:0:a80c:052b
C. 2002::206:0:a80c:52b
D. 2002:0:206:0:a80c:52b

12. Which OSI Layer 3 protocol is used to find a MAC address from an IPv6 network address?

A. ARP
B. NDP
C. SNMP
D. ICMP

13. Which OSI Layer 4 protocol sets up a connection before allowing hosts to communicate?

A. HTTP
B. TCP
C. UDP
D. IP

14. The TCP/IP Model Network Access Layer corresponds to which two OSI model layers? (Select two.)

A. Data Link
B. Network
C. Transport
D. Physical

15. In the TCP/IP Reference Model, the Application Layer logically communicates with which layer on the destination host?

A. Network Access
B. Internet
C. Transport
D. Application

CHAPTER 6

Wireless LAN Standards

THE INSTITUTE OF ELECTRICAL AND ELECTRONICS ENGINEERS (IEEE) is a professional organization with members in engineering, science, and education. The IEEE (pronounced "eye triple E") is best known for its standards in the electronics, computer, and networking industries. The IEEE 802.x networking standard has become the de facto industry standard for wired and wireless networks.

The IEEE 802.x standards set guidelines for networks that transmit data using radio frequency (RF) signals. Within the 802.x standards group, the 802.11x standards define the operation, characteristics, and construction of wireless local area networks (WLANs). In this chapter, you will learn about the IEEE 802.11x standards, their capabilities, characteristics, and security. You also will learn about WLAN design and layout and conducting a site survey.

Chapter 6 Topics

This chapter covers the following topics and concepts:

- What standards are contained in the IEEE 802.11 wireless family
- What WLAN security is
- How to design and lay out a WLAN network
- How to conduct an RF site survey

Chapter 6 Goals

When you complete this chapter, you will be able to:

- Identify and differentiate the IEEE 802.11x WLAN standards
- Describe how to implement proper security controls and countermeasures for WLANs
- Explain the processes used to design and lay out a WLAN network
- Review the steps needed to perform an RF site survey

IEEE 802.11 Family of Standards

There have been enhancements made to the initial release of the IEEE 802.11 standard (referred to as IEEE 802.11–1999). The changes resulted in other standards that increased the peak data rates. You will read about the basic IEEE 802.11 protocol model in the following sections. This framework is used by the initial and subsequent releases of the IEEE 802.11 standards. The 802.11 standards that apply directly to wireless networks are listed in Table 6-1.

TABLE 6-1 The IEEE 802 wireless networking standards.

IEEE STANDARD	DEFINES	APPROVAL DATE
802.11 (Legacy)	2 megabits per second (Mbps) wireless networking	1997
802.11a	54 Mbps wireless networking	1999
802.11b	11 Mbps wireless networking	1999
802.11g	54 Mbps wireless networking	2003
802.11i	Security improvements to 802.11x standards	2004
802.11n	100+ Mbps wireless networking	2009
802.11x	Generic name for the 802.11 family of standards	
802.15	Wireless personal area network (WPAN)	2008
802.16	Wireless MAN (WMAN)—WiMAX	2005
802.20	Fixed wireless broadband	2004

The IEEE 802.11 Legacy Standard

The original WLAN standard was released in 1997 by the IEEE as 802.11, which is now referred to as 802.11 Legacy. The 802.11 standard supported two data transfer speeds—1 or 2 Mbps—on either infrared (IR) or RF signals on the 2.4 GHz **industrial, scientific, and medical (ISM) bands**. This standard was later absorbed into the 802.11b standard.

The IEEE 802.11b WLAN Standard

The IEEE 802.11b WLAN standard, also known as 802.11 High Rate or **wireless fidelity (Wi-Fi)**, extends the IEEE 802.11 standard by improving throughput and increasing data transfer rates to 5.5 Mbps and 11 Mbps. IEEE 802.11b operates in the 2.4 to 2.483 GHz unlicensed RF ISM band for either infrastructure or ad hoc mode.

IEEE 802.11b defines the use of a number of technologies and methods, many of which were absorbed into later standards. These technologies include:

- **DSSS—Direct sequence spread spectrum (DSSS)** transmission is a modulation technique that spreads the transmitted signal over an entire bandwidth to fit the transmitted signal on the carrier.
- **CCK—Complementary code keying (CCK)** applies mathematical formulas to DSSS codes so they can represent more data per cycle and achieve the higher data rates defined in the 802.11b standard. CCK works only with DSSS.
- **QAM—Quadrature amplitude modulation (QAM)** combines two amplitude modulation (AM) signals onto a single channel, which effectively doubles the available bandwidth of the channel. The term "quadrature" refers to the 90-degree (one-quarter-of-a-cycle) phase shifts used to differentiate two carriers.
- **DRS—Dynamic rate shifting (DRS)** adjusts the transmission rate lower or higher depending on the signal strength or interference. In an electrically noisy environment, or as devices move into or out of range, an 802.11b transmitter adjusts the transmission speed down from 11 Mbps to 5.5 Mbps, 2 Mbps, or 1 Mbps.

An 802.11b infrastructure network includes at least one wireless station and one access point connected to a distribution system. The distribution system is any access device, such as a wired network interface, an Internet bridge or router, or the like.

Wi-Fi Standards

The four IEEE 802.11 standards, 802.11a, 802.11b, 802.11g, and 802.11n, form the Wi-Fi Alliance's standards for wireless fidelity (Wi-Fi). The Wi-Fi Alliance was formed when the wireless networking industry began cooperating on a single standard to provide interoperability between the networking devices of different manufacturers. The Wi-Fi Alliance also supports IEEE 802.16 under the marketing name of Wi-MAX.

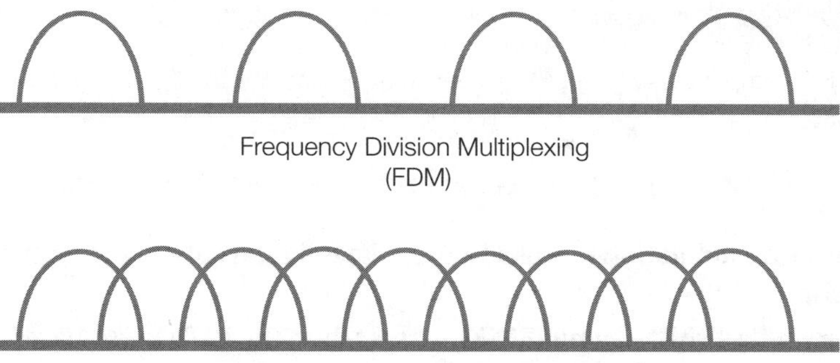

FIGURE 6-1
A comparison of how FDM and OFDM modulate a signal for transmission.

The IEEE 802.11a WLAN Standard

The IEEE 802.11a WLAN standards actually preceded the other standards adapted from the 802.11 Legacy standard. However, the 802.11b standard was more widely adopted by manufacturers. The features that set 802.11a apart from 802.11b and 802.11 Legacy are:

- **UNII**—802.11a operates in the 5 GHz **Unlicensed National Information Infrastructure (UNII)** band, which eliminates most of the interference problems common to 2.4 GHz systems, such as 802.11b, Bluetooth, and many consumer electronics products.
- **OFDM**—**Orthogonal frequency division multiplexing (OFDM)** facilitates up to 54 Mbps of bandwidth, divides a 20 MHz RF channel into 48 narrowband sub-channels and then splits the data signal into 48 separate overlapped carriers, one on each sub-channel. This arrangement, shown in Figure 6-1, enables OFDM to effectively deal with crosstalk and **multipath** propagation, which are transmission problems common to FDM and other 802.11 standards.
- **Multipath propagation**—OFDM supports multipath propagation, which is applied when the RF signal cannot take a clear and direct path between a wireless node and the access point. RF signals may not be able to take direct paths due to objects such as walls, chairs, and desks, which can deflect or diffuse the signal. When this happens, only a portion of a signal arrives at the receiver with the remainder of the signal deflected to an indirect route. This may cause a delay between the two (or more) parts of the signal as much as 50 to 300 nanoseconds, depending on the environment. When multipath propagation occurs, the delayed signal segments may overlap another discrete signal.

NOTE
Frequency division multiplexing (FDM) transmits multiple signals simultaneously over a single transmission medium, each of which travels within its own frequency range.

technical TIP

IEEE 802.11a is incompatible with WLAN systems that operate on the ISM band, including 802.11b and 802.11g.

- **IEEE 802.11a modulation**—802.11a modulates digital data based on the data transfer rate in use:
  - **Binary phase shift keying (BPSK)**—At 6 Mbps, the PMD uses phases to represent binary data on a single carrier.
  - **QAM**—At 54 Mbps, the 802.11a applies QAM to vary the signal on different amplitude levels and phase shifting.

The IEEE 802.11g WLAN Standard

The IEEE 802.11g standard supports high-speed (up to 54 Mbps) wireless networking over relatively short distances as compared to the speeds of the 802.11b standard. The 802.11g standard operates on the same RF bands as 802.11b, but incorporates OFDM to achieve the higher data transfer rates. However, 802.11g can also scale the transmission speeds

Data Speeds Versus Throughput

Don't confuse data transfer speed and throughput. Data speed is a function of both the media and the capabilities of the transmission devices in use. The maximum rate bits that can be transmitted across a medium and supported by the transmitting equipment are the maximum data transfer speed. On the other hand, throughput is the measure of the actual data transfer speed realized by the user.

A network is rarely able to achieve the rated speed of its medium. This is because of the bandwidth requirements of the protocols in use or the overhead (lag time) of the transmission processes themselves. For example, an 802.11b device, with a maximum rated speed of 11 Mbps, typically yields only about 6 Mbps of actual throughput, and this would be true only under the ideal conditions of distance and signal quality. IEEE 802.11a and 802.11g, with data speeds up to 54 Mbps, can deliver throughput speeds of between 18 and 22 Mbps, again in ideal communication conditions.

Distance is perhaps the biggest detriment to throughput. If the wireless station and the access point are sitting side by side, data speed and throughput should be optimal. However, as the two devices move farther apart, the transmission speed lowers and throughput declines right along with it. Other factors can also affect throughput, including wood, metal, concrete, wiring, and other construction materials located between the communicating devices.

back down to the 11 Mbps of the 802.11b standard or even lower when the communication distance increases or the signal becomes compromised. For these reasons, 802.11b and 802.11g devices are compatible within a single WLAN.

The IEEE 802.11n WLAN Standard

The IEEE 802.11n standard increases the throughput of the 802.11g standard to 450 Mbps by utilizing multiple wireless signals and antennas. IEEE 802.11n applies **multiple-input and multiple-output (MIMO)**, an antenna technology that uses multiple antennas (to receive and transmit) at both ends of a transmission. Originally a broadcast radio technology, MIMO was integrated into WLAN communications to improve data throughput and range without changing the nominal bandwidth or transmission power of WLAN devices.

WLAN Security

Wireless networks, and especially WLANs, are by definition not secure. Radio frequency waves are received and transmitted through the air. Anyone with the ability to receive an RF transmission is able to intercept or insert signals to steal data, gain access, and carry out a wide array of evil deeds on a wireless network.

It may seem like heresy to say so, but not all wireless networks need a high level of security. As Gilster's law says, "You never can tell—and it all depends." The need for security depends on the purpose of the network and the sensitivity of the data transmitted across it. A community WLAN hotspot that provides access to all wireless stations within its range has a very low security priority. In contrast, a wireless network in a bank must place network security at its highest priority. For the most part, home networks fall somewhere in between the community hotspot and the bank in terms of their need for security.

As wireless networks became more commonly adopted, securing them became a priority for the industry. In June 2004, IEEE announced the adoption of the 802.11i security standard for WLANs. This standard is aimed at improving security and privacy of data transmitted on a wireless network, protection of SSIDs, and denying access to unauthorized intruders.

A WLAN must meet a number of requirements to be secure. Wireless network security issues can be grouped into two general categories:

- **Authentication and access control**—Authentication should be a two-way street that allows both the originating station of transmitted data and the receiving station to verify each other. Access points (APs) should use authentication and access control to grant access rights to requesting stations.
- **Encryption and data privacy**—Encryption is a method that provides data integrity and privacy.

technical TIP

Security through obscurity means it is best to not broadcast or communicate the SSID signal to others. Users who need to connect to a WLAN can do so by connecting to it on an as-needed basis. Broadcasting the SSID of your WLAN is telling the world you are here. Users that need to connect to your WLAN can do so manually without your broadcasting the SSID. Broadcasting the SSID is unnecessary. It introduces more potential risks and threats to outside perpetrators seeking to find and access WLAN networks.

Authentication and Access Control

Before wireless APs and wireless network adapters are able to begin their exchange of management frames to establish and manage a transmission link, each device must first be aware that the other exists and that it is a safe communications partner. A typical wireless access point broadcasts beacon frames that include its SSID. A wireless station that receives the beacon frame must decide, based on its signal strength, if it wants to associate with the access point transmitting that beacon. To do so, the wireless station transmits a probe frame, which includes its station ID, its configured SSID, and the authentication method to use. The access point receives the transmitted probe frame and responds according to its configuration for establishing an authentication method. The 802.11x standards define two authentication methods: **Open System Authentication (OSA)** and **Shared Key Authentication (SKA)**.

Open System Authentication

The default authentication method for wireless networks is OSA. OSA actually provides for no authentication to be performed at all. Any wireless station is allowed to associate with an access point using a randomly generated shared key.

Authentication implies that a shared key is used to verify that an association exists between two devices. However, in OSA, the station and the access point do not establish a single shared key that remains in use throughout the association. Each station creates and transmits its own randomly generated key. It requests that the receiving station accept the key temporarily to create an association. The key is used only to establish an association. A new key is then generated and used to maintain the association between the devices.

In effect, OSA involves a two-step authentication process in which a station transmits its identity and shared key, and the access point responds with acceptance frames and the data needed to establish an association. The frames used to create the association under OSA are transmitted "in the clear" (not encrypted) as plaintext.

Shared Key Authentication

SKA follows a set sequence of actions to authenticate a station attempting to establish an association with Network Access Protection (NAP). After receiving an association request, in the form of an 802.11 registration request frame, the access point generates a random number challenge key and transmits it to the requesting station. The station then signs (applies) its preset shared key to the challenge key using an XOR operation. It then sends the signed key back to the access point for verification. The access point then performs the same signing operation and compares its key to the signed key sent from the requesting station. If the keys match, the station is authenticated and the association is established.

The danger in SKA, as in OSA, lies in the fact that the challenge key and the signed challenge key are transmitted in open plaintext. This means that a hacker can easily intercept a message frame, extract the IV, and decipher the data payload. With this information, the intruder also gains the ability to respond to any challenge frames and join the network.

Extensible Authentication Methods

The most basic authentication method consists of a user name and a password, which are based on the assumption that only the actual user knows this combination of elements. However, for most network administrators, and generally their organizations, this just isn't enough security. For this reason, the **Extensible Authentication Protocol (EAP)** was developed to add security to point-to-point (PTP) communications. EAP allows standard and proprietary authentication methods to be overridden and other authentication methods to be applied, including passwords, challenge keys, and public key infrastructure (PKI) certificates. As wireless networks became more common, EAP was adapted for use on these networks as well.

On an 802.11x network, authentication and security methods are divided into three primary areas:

- **Authentication framework**—This is the authentication process, including login processing, service classes, protocol support, and the functions that perform user or device authentication. Each authentication type constitutes a different authentication framework.
- **Authentication algorithm**—The 802.11x standards define two primary authentication algorithms: RC4, which is used in WEP and the Wi-Fi Protected Access (WPA) protocol, and the Advanced Encryption Standard (AES) defined in IEEE 802.1x (see "IEEE 802.1x Security" section) and used in most Extensible Authentication Protocols (EAPs).
- **Data frame encryption**—Data frame encryption is the function that applies the encryption key to the data payload of a frame to ensure its secure transmission (see the section "Data Encryption").

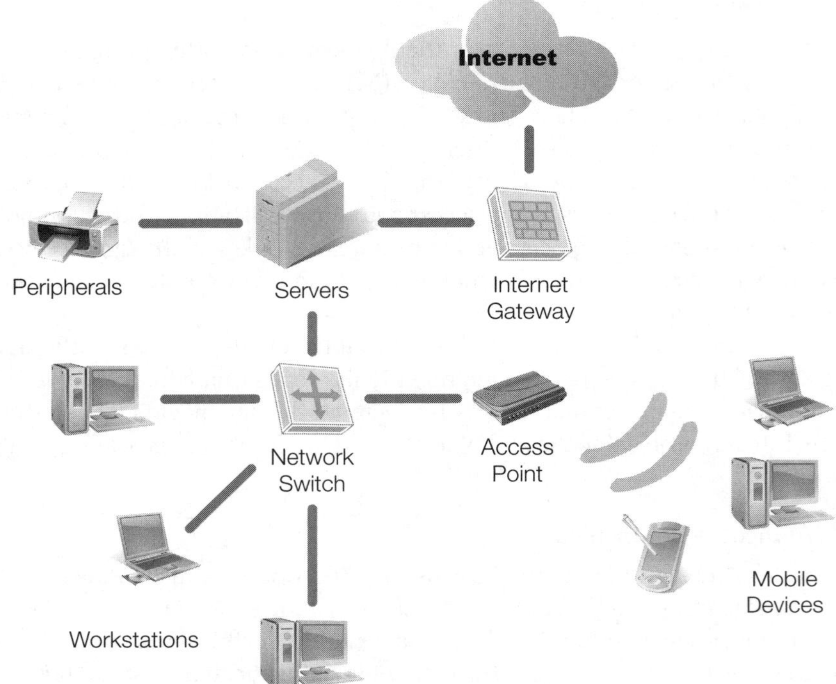

FIGURE 6-2

Risks, threats, and vulnerabilities with WLANs.

Security Threats to WLANs

Because they are wireless, 802.11x networks are uniquely vulnerable to outside attacks and interception. A wired network can be physically secured and its media protected from interference, attack, or inadvertent damage. Wireless media can be attacked from almost anywhere within the range of its RF transmitter, which could be the next cubicle, the next building, the parking lot, or even outside its building in the street.

Attacks on wireless networks come in a wide variety of forms. Not all attacks are particularly dangerous and devastating to a WLAN. Some are frivolous and harmless, but any attack, even one that is harmless, can lead to something far more dangerous. In designing and implementing the security for a WLAN, the more you know about attack threats, the better your chances are of protecting your network.

The network shown in Figure 6-2 illustrates a common network installation. The network has three primary segments: the Internet gateway, a wired network segment, and a wireless segment.

Several types of threats can be made against the wired segment of the network shown in Figure 6-2, but let's focus on the security and the potential threats that can be made against the Internet gateway, the access point, and the wireless nodes. Then let's focus a bit more on the threats that would originate from outside the network.

The threats you should protect your network against the most are not very different from those that threaten a wired network. The most common and frequent of the attacks made on networks are:

- Client-to-client attack
- Denial of service (DoS)
- Insertion and unauthorized access to WLAN by rogue user
- Interception and man-in-the-middle attack
- Unauthorized access to network resources by rogue user

Client-to-Client Attacks

Wireless nodes have the capability to communicate directly with one another and bypass an access point. This capability opens any wireless node for a client-to-client or node-to-node attack. Wireless nodes should be protected from the other nodes on the WLAN. Any node configured with TCP/IP services, such as a Web server or Windows Print and File Sharing, can be attacked by another node on a WLAN.

A common client-to-client attack is a version of the most common attack made on networks, the denial of service (DoS) attack (covered in the next section). A client-to-client DoS attack floods a node with incoming messages to the point that all other functions on the computer are interrupted.

Denial-of-Service (DoS) Attacks

A DoS attack has only one objective: to prevent any access to a network's resources by internal or external nodes. The most common DoS attack involves flooding an Internet gateway, Web server, or internal network server with packets or frames that must be processed. The flood of incoming packets monopolizes the system's resources to the point that all other functions are severely interrupted or prevented entirely.

Types of DoS Attacks. There isn't just one type of DoS attack. A DoS attack can attack a network almost on every layer of the OSI Reference Model. Here is a brief description of the types of DoS attacks that can happen on each layer:

- **Application Layer**—Attacks on the Application Layer typically involve seemingly legitimate requests to a network-ready application running on a server or node. For example, a flood of HTTP page requests is sent to a Web server. The Web server becomes overloaded attempting to fulfill the requests. This prevents other (legitimate) requests from accessing the server.
- **Transport Layer**—Transport Layer DoS attacks typically are launched against a network operating system (NOS) environment, which manages the connections made to network hosts. When a remote device is attempting to establish a TCP connection, it transmits a synchronization (SYN) packet to request the opening of a TCP link. Because most NOS have limits to the number of links they can process per second and the number of established links they can support, a *SYN flood*, as this attack is called, overloads the NOS on one or both of these limits, crowding out requests made by legitimate network nodes and services.

- **Network Layer**—Attacks made on the Network Layer of a wireless access protocol are actually targeting the transmission capabilities of the network. Network Layer attacks flood the transmission media with more packets than it can process effectively. For example, if an attacker continually transmits over 100 Mbps of data to a 10 Mbps network, the network infrastructure would be unable to retransmit all the incoming data to the network. The result is that some of the data in the network queue, including legitimate network traffic, is dropped. The upshot of this type of attack is that network throughput is disrupted, and the collision levels and retransmissions rise, causing further disruption on the network. The most common type of Network Layer attack is a ping flood, in which excessive Internet Control Message Protocol (ICMP) echo request packets are transmitted to the targeted network. This overloads the network's gateway, which denies access to the Internet by network nodes.
- **Data Link Layer**—Data Link Layer attacks target an entire wireless network or can focus on a single network node. The most typical Data Link Layer attack is a flood of empty and invalid frames that the network server then rebroadcasts across the network, tying up the network media. This type of attack is only effective on networks or network segments without a WLAN switch or router, which commonly doesn't forward broadcast messages beyond a single segment. However, if this type of attack is generated from within a network, the network segment of the source device is also affected.
- **Physical Layer**—The Physical Layer of a WLAN is attacked primarily by blocking, jamming, or removing the transmission means. On wired networks, such as wide area network (WAN) links over which Internet requests are transmitted, damage to the physical media can create a DoS situation, although in most cases, inadvertently. The most disruptive Physical Layer DoS situation is "backhoe fade," which means the signal strength has faded to nothing because the main carrier line (typically, fiber optic cable) has been cut. Another common physical layer attack is posed by lightning storms. The best protection against these types of occurrences is redundancy.

WLAN DoS Attacks

Unlike a wired network, where the attacker must have access to the physical medium, and where the evidence of the attack is typically visible, a wireless network's medium can be attacked from a distance with no evidence left behind other than the results of the attack itself. Because the 802.11x PHY standards are readily available and their specific radio frequencies are spelled out, an evildoer is able to flood these frequencies with interference and electromagnetic noise. If enough interference and noise is added to the correct transmission frequencies, the medium becomes unusable. Any wireless nodes within range are effectively blocked.

Insertion Attacks

Also called unauthorized or illicit use attacks, insertion attacks involve adding an unauthorized device to a wireless network to gain access to the Internet gateway or the wired network to which an AP is attached. Insertion attacks are possible only when an attacker is able to bypass the security settings of a WLAN. An insertion attack can happen on two levels: the insertion of a wireless node, such as a notebook computer or a wireless PDA, or the insertion of an unauthorized access point or router. The simplest way to prevent the insertion of an unauthorized node is to require a password before a node is added to the WLAN.

Interception Attacks

Interception attacks are more common on wired networks, especially on those with poor physical security. Because of the general nature of RF transmissions, these attacks are becoming more common on WLANs as well.

There are four general types of interception attacks:

- **ARP spoofing**—Address Resolution Protocol (ARP) is a Data Link Layer protocol used on TCP/IP networks to resolve IP addresses to MAC addresses. ARP provides the MAC address associated with an IP address on the network. In ARP spoofing, an attacker fools the network into addressing packets to his or her computer by supplying its MAC address to the network in response to ARP requests. Once the ARP information is set, packets are routed through the attacker's computer, captured, and then forwarded on to the legitimate recipient. This all happens undetected. ARP spoofing is also called ARP poisoning.
- **Monitoring**—If an AP is connected into a hub on the wired network, all network traffic passing through the hub is also transmitted to the AP and across the WLAN (assuming there are no switches, routers, or bridges on either network, of course). This allows an attacker who has gained access to the network or who is sniffing (see next bullet) the network's traffic to monitor network traffic and potentially view sensitive data flowing across either network.
- **Sniffer**—Wireless sniffers are software programs installed on WLAN nodes or servers that capture transmitted RF traffic for analysis and monitoring. A wireless sniffer captures a transmitted packet as raw data and has the capability to extract addressing information from the packet header. Sniffers are intended for use by network administrators to analyze a network's traffic, but they can be used by an attacker to extract information or to learn the addresses needed for another type of attack.
- **Session hijacking**—An attacker that can view a WLAN's traffic by monitoring or sniffing may also have the capability to insert packets into the network using a legitimate node's identification information.

IEEE 802.1x Security

The authentication methods defined in the 802.11x standards focus more on authorizing an association between wireless devices and less on verifying a user's or station's identity. The authentication method must be scalable (extensible) and robust enough to process all the stations on a WLAN. Scalability is necessary for the focus of the authentication system to be extended to also authenticate, authorize, and verify the relationship of the user and station to the network.

On a network with a single access point, configured in architecture mode, the extensibility of a security method usually is not an issue. However, on large enterprise wireless networks, the authentication method must be extensible enough to provide security to hundreds, perhaps thousands, of wireless stations and users. It also must provide for centralized administration of the authentication process.

To improve security and enhance the authentication methods of WLANs, the 802.11i standard has incorporated the IEEE 802.1x authentication framework. This is the same framework defined for all 802.x networking. The 802.1x standard provides centralized authentication of wireless users or stations and has the capability to work simultaneously with multiple authentication algorithms. Table 6-2 lists the characteristics of many of the more popular 802.1x authentication methods.

The 802.1x protocol, also known as EAP encapsulation over LAN (EAPoL), dynamically applies a multiple encryption key using EAP, which supports multiple authentication methods. Methods supported in EAPoL include Kerberos, one-time passwords, digital security certificates, and public key authentication. IEEE 802.1x authentication starts with an unauthenticated supplicant (meaning a wireless network station) that is attempting to create an association with an authenticator (a wireless NAP). The authenticator responds to the station's registration frame by enabling one of its ports and passing EAP frames between the station and an authentication server, also known as an authentication, authorization, and

TABLE 6-2 IEEE 802.1x authentication methods.

EAP TYPE	DEVELOPER	CERTIFICATES REQUIRED	DYNAMIC WEP KEYS	AUTHENTICATION	SECURITY LEVEL
MD-5	Microsoft	Client/server	No	One-way	Low
PEAP	Microsoft	Server	Yes	Mutual	High
TLS	Microsoft	Client/server	Yes	Mutual	Very High
TTLS	Funk Software	None	Yes	Mutual	High

accounting (AAA) server. An **AAA server** is most commonly on the distribution (wired) network to which the access point is connected. Until the station is authenticated by the authentication server, any frames transmitted by the station will be dropped.

The flow of an 802.1x authentication process on a WLAN is as follows:

1. When a wireless station connects to a WLAN, it transmits an EAP-start frame, which is a request to enter the network over the wireless medium.
2. The access point receiving the EAP-start frame replies with an EAP-request identity frame. In other words, the access point is asking the station to identify itself.
3. The station responds with an EAP-response frame containing its MAC address and other identifying information, which is really intended for the AAA server. After receiving the EAP-response frame and passing it along to the AAA server, the access point blocks any traffic from the station that is not EAP-related.
4. The AAA server then verifies the station's identity information using an authentication algorithm, a digital certificate, or another EAP authentication method.
5. An accept-or-reject frame is transmitted by the AAA server to the access point to indicate that it was able or unable to verify the identity information provided by the wireless station.
6. Depending on the type of frame received from the AAA server, the access point transmits either an EAP-success or an EAP-rejection frame to the requesting station. If the AAA server successfully authenticated the station's identity information, the access point allows the station's normal traffic to pass to the network. However, if the station's information is rejected, its port is locked in EAP-only status.

EAP Types

The 802.1x authentication standard must rely on another protocol or service to perform authentication, such as an authentication server or a service running on the network. On an 802.1x network, the EAP type must be selected and configured as the network's authentication method. On most wireless devices, the EAP types available are typically one of the following:

- **Message-Digest Algorithm (MD5)**—MD5 provides only basic EAP support. In fact, MD5 is not recommended for use on a WLAN because it provides only one-way authentication. This means that it does not include mutual authentication between wireless stations and the WLAN, nor can it generate dynamic WEP keys.

technical TIP

When you are configuring a Windows client for this EAP-TLS, the choice you make from the list in the Wireless Properties dialog box is "Smart Card or other Certificate."

- **Protected Extensible Authentication Protocol (PEAP)**—PEAP has the capability to transport authentication data between wireless devices securely. PEAP, which supports a variety of authentication protocols, creates a virtual tunnel between a PEAP node and the authentication server. PEAP authenticates WLAN stations using server-side certificates, which can simplify the implementation and administration of a WLAN.
- **Transport Layer Security (EAP-TLS)**—EAP-TLS supports both certificate-based authentication and mutual authentication, using client-side and server-side certificates for authentication. EAP-TLS can also dynamically generate user-based and session-based WEP keys. EAP-TLS often is not implemented on large enterprise networks because certificates must be managed on both the client and server side. EAP-TLS authentication is referred to as Smart Card or Certificate authentication.
- **Tunneled Transport Layer Security (EAP-TTLS)**—EAP-TTLS is an extension of EAP-TLS that supports certificate-based mutual authentication of a WLAN station and a WLAN employing an encrypted tunnel. EAP-TTLS uses only server-side certificates.

NOTE

Cisco Systems has its own version of EAP: **Lightweight Extensible Authentication Protocol (LEAP)**. LEAP supports dynamic key encryption and mutual authentication. LEAP is included on Cisco's Aironet wireless devices and on most devices from Linksys (a subsidiary of Cisco) as well.

Server-Side and Client-Side Digital Certificates

Server-side digital certificates verify that the requested data, from a Web site or a WLAN station, is from the source intended and not an imposter. This is done by verifying that the requested source is, in fact, the responding source.

A client-side certificate is essentially the same as a server-side certificate. The difference lies in how it is used. Client-side certificates require that each node or user be issued a unique certificate, which is then used to verify that the user or node is not an impostor but is exactly who they say they are.

Tunneling

A tunnel, channel, or security association (SA) is created through a network by encapsulating the packets of one network protocol inside packets of another network protocol. Tunneling encapsulates (places) unsecured, ordinary packets (such as FTP and HTTP) inside encrypted, secured packets (such as IP). In the context of networking and virtual private networks (VPNs), tunneling refers to the transmission of secured, private data over an insecure transmission medium, such as wireless networks or the Internet, as shown in Figure 6-3.

An encapsulated packet is created by a router or a special-purpose network appliance, such as a virtual private network (VPN) gateway. It moves through the public network, the Internet, as if it is flowing through a tunnel created just for its use.

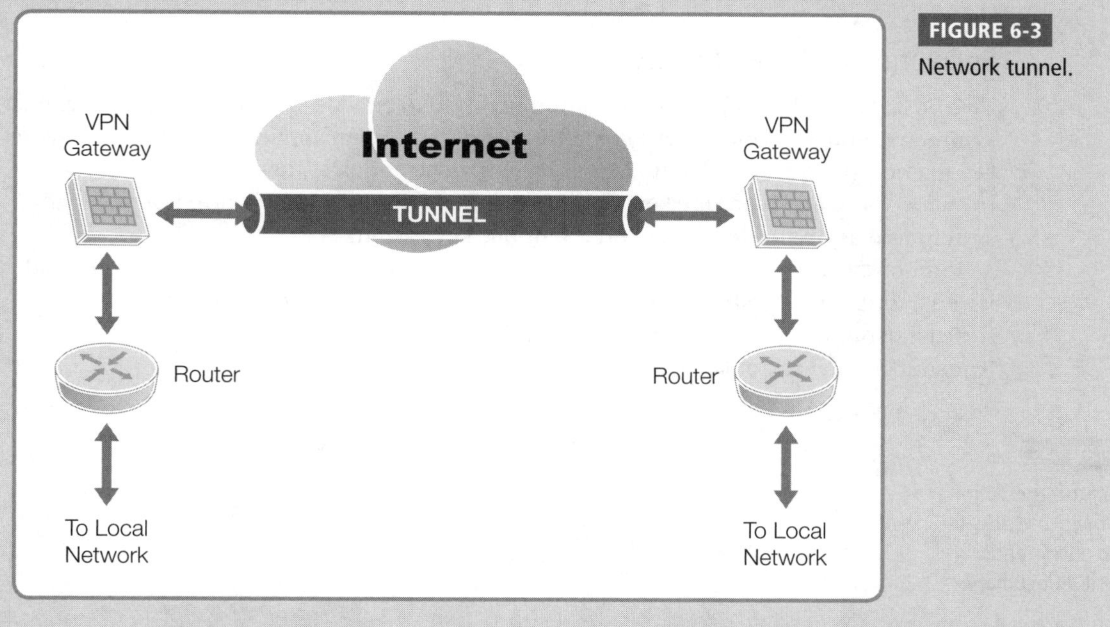

FIGURE 6-3
Network tunnel.

Remote Authentication Dial-In User Service (RADIUS)

Although not actually a secure authentication method, RADIUS (see Figure 6-4) is supported by many WAPs and routers. Included on some EAP systems as a legacy password-based authentication method, RADIUS can provide a minimum level of access security to a WLAN. Its most common use is by dial-up Internet service providers (ISPs) because RADIUS verifies a user name and password against a database of authorized users that is maintained by network administrators.

 **TIP**

Microsoft's implementation of RADIUS is its Internet Authentication Server (IAS).

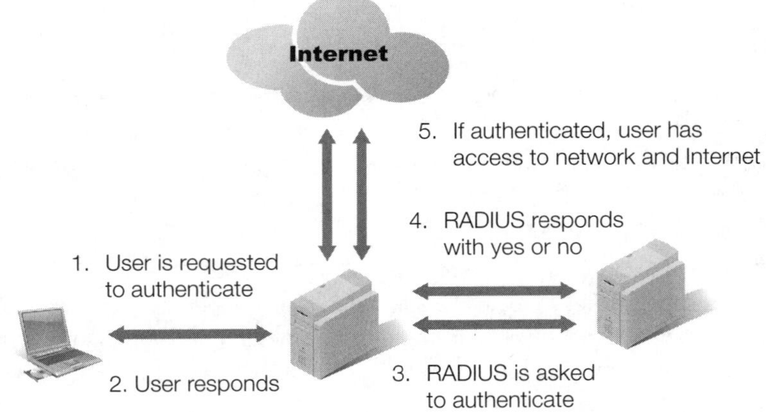

FIGURE 6-4
A RADIUS server provides basic-level authentication on a network.

Encryption and Data Privacy

Two basic types of encryption are commonly used to encode data on computer systems: symmetric and asymmetric. A **symmetric encryption system** applies the same exact secret key to encrypt and decrypt data. An **asymmetric encryption system** uses a public key to encode data and a private key to decrypt data. Symmetric encryption is a secret key system and asymmetric encryption is a public key system.

Public key or asymmetric systems are the most commonly used encryption method for encoding and decoding transmitted data because the encryption key does not need to be transmitted with the data. A major limitation with symmetric key systems is transmitting the secret key without it being intercepted.

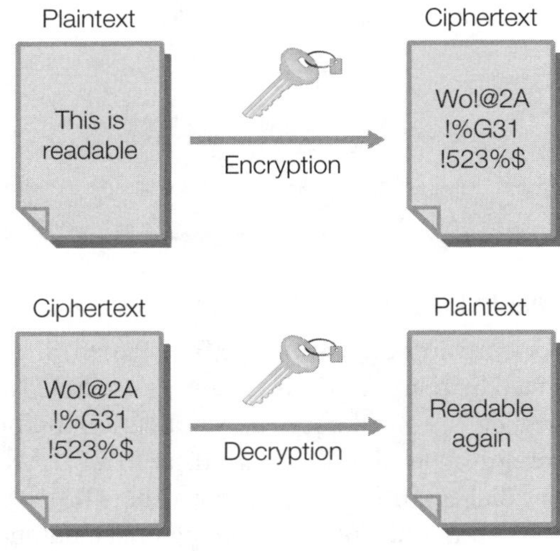

FIGURE 6-5
Symmetric encryption uses the same private key to encrypt and decrypt a document.

Symmetric Key Encryption

Symmetric key encryption, also referred to as block cipher, uses four different encryption modes:

- **Electronic codebook (ECB)**—ECB divides data into 64-bit blocks, and each block is encrypted individually. Because ECB adds no additional encryption steps to standard encryption processes, it is considered the weakest of the symmetric encryption methods.
- **Cipher-block chaining (CBC)**—In CBC, each ECB block of encrypted data is XORed with the next block, so that each succeeding block is dependent on the preceding block. The first data block, which has no precedent block, uses a 64-bit IV instead. CBC adds one additional step to the encryption process, and because of this, it is considered more secure than ECB.
- **Cipher feedback (CFB)**—CFB is used when the data stream is less than 64 bits in length. To pad out the length of the data, dummy bytes are added to the end of the data before it is encrypted. CFB is similar to CBC in security, but because of its additional processing, it is much slower.
- **Output feedback (OFB)**—After the encryption process completes its first pass, OFB passes the encrypted stream back through the encryption process once more. The result is that only the original encrypted data block and the output of the encryption process are needed to decipher a block. This means that because the key is not required to decipher a block, this mode is less secure than the CFB mode.

Figure 6-5 illustrates the process used in symmetric (private key) encryption. The most commonly used symmetric key encryption methods are Data Encryption Standard (DES) with 56-bit key, Triple DES (3DES) with a 112-bit key, and the Advanced Encryption Standard (AES) with a key size of 128, 192, or 256 bits.

Asymmetric Encryption

Asymmetric encryption uses two keys, as shown in Figure 6-6. One is a public key that is not secret, and the other is a private, secret key. The public key is open to anyone, but the private key is known by only the recipient of an encrypted message. For example, if you wish to send an encrypted message to another person, you would use his or her public key to encrypt the message. The person to whom the message was sent would then use his or her secret key to decrypt the message.

The public key and the private key are a part of a public key infrastructure (PKI). The relationship of the two keys is that the public key is used to encrypt data, and only an associated private key can then be used to decrypt it. However, despite their relationship, it is virtually impossible to identify the private key from the public key.

TIP

Wireless network adapters can be assigned a public key manually or have one automatically assigned by the network Basic Service Set (BSS). The best practice is to allow the BSS to assign a public key. This helps to ensure that no mistakes are made when entering the key manually. An error of even one character will cause the encryption and decryption processes to produce different results.

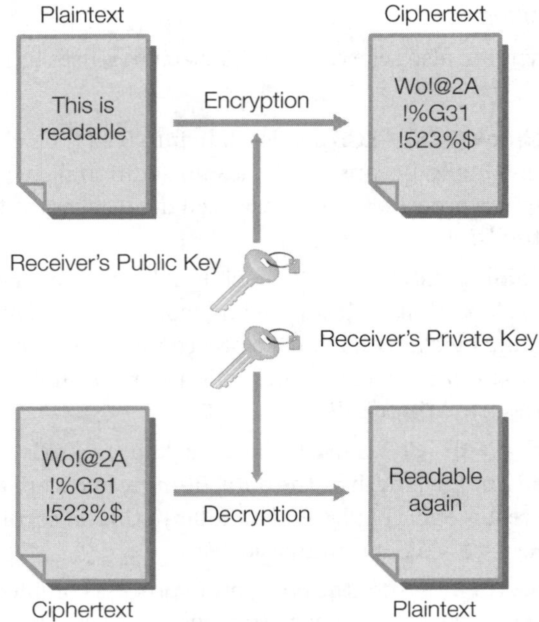

FIGURE 6-6
Asymmetric encryption uses one key to encrypt and another key to decrypt a document.

Digital Signatures

A **digital signature** is a PKI application that is used to verify that the sender of a document, image, or message is a trusted source. Trust means that the public and private keys that are used to encrypt and decrypt a message are verified and have been issued to only one specific person by a certificate authority (CA).

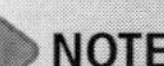
NOTE
For more information on the public key infrastructure (PKI) and a list of public key certificate authorities, visit *www.pki-page.org*.

A CA is a company or agency that issues digital certificates to assure the security and trustfulness of the PKI system. To obtain a digital certificate for a private key, the private key is submitted to a CA. The CA then verifies the identity of the requester and signs a public key with a root key, which is the CA's private key. The signed public key and the digital signature of the CA combine to form a digital signature.

The use of the digital certificate works like this: When a digitally signed document is to be transmitted, a hash total is made of the document and signed with a private key. At the destination, the document's validity and its originator are verified by decrypting the hash total using its public key. The decrypted hash total is then compared to a hash total computed by the receiving station. If there is a match, the receiving station knows that the document is secure.

IEEE 802.11i

The IEEE approved the 802.11i security standard, entitled the "MAC Enhancements for Enhanced Security," in June 2004. IEEE 802.11i defines the security measures for 802.11x wireless networks and includes the Advanced Encryption Standard (AES). AES incorporates the security standards of 802.1x, and it defines the use of **Temporal Key Integrity Protocol (TKIP)** and Wireless Robust Authenticated Protocol (WRAP). The 802.11i standard defines security measures that protect the entire process of association, authentication, and message transmission.

The 802.11i standard consists of three elements arranged into two layers. The lowest layer includes TKIP and a counter mode that defines the Counter Mode with Cipher-Block Chaining Message Authentication Code Protocol (CCMP). The top layer applies 802.1x for authentication processing.

The major features specified as a part of the 802.11i standard are:

- AES
- TKIP
- CCMP

Advanced Encryption Standard. AES was developed to satisfy the high-level standards of the Federal Information Processing Standard (FIPS) required by United States government agencies. The AES encryption algorithm is a symmetric block cipher that can be used to encrypt and decrypt data. AES is capable of processing 128-, 192-, and 256-bit keys to encrypt data block up to 128 bits in length.

Temporal Key Integrity Protocol. TKIP is the new generation of WEP. TKIP provides dynamic encryption keys for each data packet, a message Integrity Check Value (ICV), and a mechanism for periodically assigning new keys to network stations. Each of these features is intended to correct problems of WEP. TKIP uses 128-bit temporal keys that are combined with the wireless station's MAC address and a 16-octet initialization vector (IV) to produce a key used to encrypt the data payload of a frame using the RC4 algorithm. A temporal key is one that is used for just a certain time or a set number of packets. The TKIP temporal key is used for 10,000 packets before it is replaced with a new key.

NOTE

Wi-Fi released an early version of TKIP in early 2003 under the name Wi-Fi Protected Access (WPA), which is replaced with the release of 802.11i. Wi-Fi refers to the 802.11i standard as Wi-Fi Protected Access 2 (WPA2). See "Wi-Fi Protected Access (WPA)" later in the chapter.

Counter Mode with Cipher-Block Chaining Message Authentication Code Protocol. CCMP is a block cipher mode protocol that performs both encryption and authentication. CCMP combines counter-mode encryption with Cipher-Block Chaining Message Authentication (CBC-MAC). The encryption process uses any block cipher, such as AES or DES, in combination with a secret key for that cipher. CBC-MAC is only as strong as the encryption algorithm, but 802.11i specifies it with the strength of AES.

Security Protocols and Access Control

The most commonly used protocols and methods used to secure WLAN transmissions and prevent unauthorized access to the network are:

- Wired Equivalent Privacy (WEP)
- Wi-Fi Protected Access (WPA)
- Wi-Fi Protected Access 2 (WPA2)
- MAC layer address filtering

Wired Equivalent Privacy

To address the apparent need for the security of WLANs, the Wired Equivalent Privacy (WEP) security protocol was included with the 802.11b standard. WEP was designed to provide a security and privacy equivalent to that of a wired network. WEP was introduced as an optional protocol, but when used, it offers more security than no security at all.

The security of a wired network is largely physical in nature and includes controlled building access, locked office doors, and cables in the walls and floors. However, these same measures fail to secure a wireless network because the transmission medium (RF signals) transmits through the air and can pass through walls. To overcome this weakness of wireless network security, WEP secures the data during transmission. WEP encrypts the data payload of a transmitted packet to keep the data secure between network adapters and network access points (NAPs). Adding WEP encryption to passwords and authentication was a first step in securing a wireless network.

A major limitation of WEP is that it uses a symmetric key encryption method. This means that each end of a wireless transmission must use the same key to encrypt and decrypt the message. The problem is that the same encryption key must be stored and used by network adapters and NAPs. This requirement presents a network administration problem. When the encryption keys are changed, they must be distributed to the network's stations. This means that the same keys may be used for extended periods, giving attackers an opportunity to intercept and defeat the encryption method.

WEP was originally intended to provide confidentiality for data transmitted over a wireless medium. However, it was never planned to be the only security measure applied on a wireless network. Even today, many home and small office WLANs use it as their primary security method. WEP is able to prevent the compromise of incidental interception, but because it operates only at the physical and data link layers, WEP cannot provide end-to-end security for transmitted data.

WEP encrypts a packet using a Rivest Cipher 4 (RC4), which accepts encryption keys of arbitrary lengths and generates a pseudorandom number. It then combines that number with the data stream using the Boolean algebra exclusive OR (XOR) function to output encrypted data. The encryption key has two parts: a 24-bit initialization vector (IV), provided by the user or administrator, and a WEP key, supplied by the wireless device, that is either 40 bits or 104 bits in length. The total length of the WEP key is 64 bits or 128 bits.

The 24-bit IV is capable of encrypting 16,777,216 different data streams, regardless of whether 40 or 104 bits are used for the remaining portion of the key. Another of WEP's weaknesses is that it transmits the IV in plain, unencrypted text in each packet. Since the IV is rarely changed, packet filter software should be able to collect enough packets to crack the key.

WEP applies encryption using the following processes:

1. The message to be transmitted, which is in plaintext at this point, passes through an integrity check algorithm to produce the numerical ICV. The ICV is then added to the end of the plaintext message.
2. Next, a 24-bit IV is generated. The IV is then placed at the front of the shared key to create what is called a key schedule (KS). The KS is used to create a seed value using RC4 Key Scheduling Algorithm (KSA).
3. The seed value generated by KSA is passed to the WEP Pseudo-Random Number Generator (PRNG).
4. The PRNG generates the encrypting cipher, which is then merged with the original plaintext message and ICV using a bit-wise exclusive OR (XOR) function to produce the WEP cipher text (encrypted data).
5. The IV (in plaintext) is then added to the front of the cipher text, and the message is transmitted.

When the transmitted WEP encrypted message is received, the process used to decrypt it is just the reverse of the encryption process:

1. The IV (in plaintext) is extracted from the frame and merged with the shared key to recreate the KS, which is then passed through KSA to recreate the cipher stream.
2. The cipher stream and the encrypted frame are "XORed" together, yielding the original data payload in the plaintext.
3. The ICV is then removed from the plaintext and compared against a recalculated ICV.
4. If the two ICVs match, the message frame is accepted, and processing continues. However, if the ICVs don't match, the receiving node either drops the frame or signals the sending station to retransmit the frame.

From a user's point of view, a PC prepares data for transfer and passes it on to a network adapter. The network adapter then applies WEP encryption and transmits the encrypted frame and its IV to a NAP. The access point decrypts the encrypted frame using the IV. If the frame is to be forwarded to a wireless station, the access point applies the WEP encryption process before transmitting it on. If the decrypted WEP message is to be transmitted to anything other than a wireless network, it remains decrypted. WEP only encrypts data frames transmitted between 802.11 WLAN stations.

Wi-Fi Protect Access

To overcome the security weaknesses of WEP, the Wi-Fi Alliance released the WPA protocol. WPA includes most of the IEEE 802.11i standard and specifically TKIP. WPA also incorporates **message integrity check (MIC)**, which prevents an attacker from intercepting, modifying, and retransmitting message packets by checking the integrity of a packet using the ICV.

WPA2

WPA2, an update to WPA, is designed around the Robust Security Network (RSN) processes. RSN adds strong encryption, pre-authentication for roaming devices, and the use of CCMP as an alternative to TKIP. The improvements of WPA and WPA2, which also set a security standard for devices carrying the label of WPA2, are such improvements over WEP that they have become the de facto standard for WLANs.

MAC Address Filtering

Because of its inherent weaknesses, many manufacturers chose not to implement WEP, choosing instead to develop a MAC address-filtering scheme to provide security on a WLAN. Like all 802.x networks, 802.11x WLAN stations are uniquely identified by a 48-bit MAC address.

Defined on the MAC layer, a MAC address contains elements that identify the manufacturer and a globally unique device identification number. The uniqueness of the MAC address led to the concept that because each device contains a MAC address-identified network adapter, WLAN administrators should be able to manage a list of the MAC addresses allowed to access the WLAN.

When a wireless access point or router is installed in a WLAN, it is configured with a list of the allowed MAC addresses. When a frame is received, an access point can scan the allowable MAC address list to verify that a network adapter is on the approved list.

The weakness of MAC address filtering is that the MAC address is transmitted and retransmitted in several administrative and association frames exchanged between two wireless stations. Even when MAC address filtering is combined with encryption, a dedicated hacker can eventually learn one or more of the allowed MAC addresses on a WLAN and gain full access. It should be noted that MAC address filtering is not a part of the 802.11x standards and, as you may have deduced, provides only marginal security to a WLAN.

Security Practices

The security protocols and methods discussed in this section are best used in combination with some common sense configuration items. The following items describe the actions that can be taken to improve the security of and to better control access to a wireless network.

- **SSID broadcast**—Disabling the SSID broadcast feature forces anyone attempting to connect to a WLAN to know the broadcast SSID. However, since the SSID is transmitted in clear text in many administrative frames, it is not all that difficult for a hacker to discover the SSID anyway.
- **Authentication**—Since authentication occurs before MAC address filtering, a WLAN AP should verify requests to connect and authenticate the requesting user.
- **Open authentication**—Frequently used on a public network, open authentication allows any client to connect to a WLAN. Open authentication is often used on networks requiring separate authentications for the Internet or other network access.
- **Preshared keys (PSK)**—The AP and client are configured with the same security key. When a client requests a connection, it encrypts a data block with its preshared key and sends it to the AP. The AP then decrypts the data using its key. If the sent data matches the data received, the keys are in sync, and permission is granted. This is considered to be a one-way authentication because the AP does not authenticate with the host.
- **Extensible Authentication Protocol (EAP)**—The EAP software installed on the client communicates with an authentication server such as a Remote Authentication Dial-In User Service (RADIUS). The RADIUS server maintains a database of users separate from the AP. When the user enters a login and password for the network, the AP forwards the login information to the RADIUS server to check its database for validity.
- **MAC address filtering**—A network security control in which access is granted or denied based on a device's MAC address. An intruder could sniff out an existing and authorized MAC address and then create an insertion attack by spoofing a valid address.
- **Encryption**—An intruder doesn't really need to authenticate to intercept frames from a WLAN. Encrypting all transmissions makes it more difficult for an intruder to retrieve usable data. The most commonly used methods of WLAN encryption are:
  - **Wired Equivalent Privacy (WEP)**—WEP assigns the same WEP static key to every device on the WLAN. However, hacking software can extract the static WEP key. Using WEP alone to secure a network is not an acceptable option.
  - **Wi-Fi Protected Access (WPA)**—WPA uses TKIP to generate new keys and then rotate them on a configurable interval for each communication with the AP. Its dynamic key makes WPA more difficult to crack than WEP.
  - **WPA2 (802.11i)**—An improved version of WPA that uses AES technology for encryption.
  - **IEEE 802.1x**—When implemented on an AP, this standard provides additional EAP security.
- **Filtering traffic on an AP**—An AP can be configured to filter network traffic by source and destination MAC address, source and destination port address, and source and destination IP address.

War Driving and War Chalking

Back in the day when only dial-up modems were used to access a remote network for good or evil, hackers, or rather warriors, would dial a series of random phone numbers looking to find one connected to a modem. This practice became known as war dialing, based on the actions of a young computer hacker in the movie "War Games."

In the wireless network world, it is easy to find networks. One only needs to carry a wireless network-equipped portable computing device and walk around (war walking), drive around (war driving), or fly over (war flying) business areas or residential neighborhoods. Simply being close to wireless networks is sufficient to discover any number of unsecured APs. War drivers, walkers, and flyers then mark the house or building with one of a set of symbols. These symbols were adapted from those used by hobos to mark the houses that would provide food, drink, or shelter. Figure 6-7 illustrates these symbols. The symbols on the left are the original symbols, from the dial-up days; the symbols on the right allegedly are the new set in use. A word or acronym in a symbol indicates where an actual value is inserted to assist in gaining access.

So, if you have a wireless network in your home or office, you may want to see if any suspicious chalk markings are on the building or street curbs. Not all the chalk marks on the street, sidewalk, or the side of your house may be from children. An evildoer may have detected your insecure network and is sharing this good fortune with his or her fellow warriors.

Any wireless networks that use the default SSID or that have lots of open and accessible ports appear vulnerable and will attract attention.

FIGURE 6-7
War driving symbols.

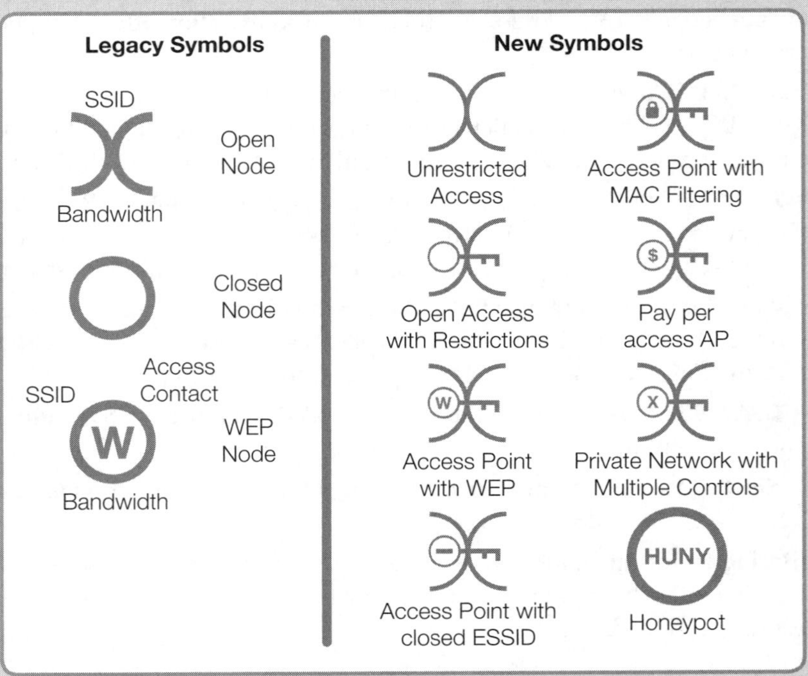

Unauthorized Access to Shared Resources

Another threat to a network is the access to or use of a shared resource on a network. Someone hacking into a network only to use a network-attached printer is not that much of a threat. The same intruder gaining access to a file server containing confidential information could be very serious. The threat also could extend to a wired network to which a wireless network is attached.

A wireless network, because of its relatively easy interception vulnerability, is often the entryway chosen by an intruder to gain access to the resources attached to or those that can be accessed from a wired network to which a WLAN is connected. Additional access authentication and authorization should be placed on the AP to prevent access to a wired network through it.

WLAN Planning and Design

IEEE 802.11x WLANs have a variety of limitations and performance issues that must be considered in the planning and design phases of a WLAN installation project. If not properly addressed, these issues may cause network performance problems ranging from intermittent to complete failure.

The issues that must be addressed during planning and design of a WLAN are, categorically:

- RF design issues
- WLAN site qualification
- Capacity and coverage

RF Design Issues

Perhaps the most important design issue of any WLAN is that it communicates over RF waves. RF transmissions are affected by their environment and surroundings, which may translate into operational problems. Unfortunately, not every space or area is capable of unaffected RF communications.

- **Competing devices**—Because the RF bands on which 802.11x WLANs operate are unlicensed, many other types of wireless devices also use these bands, such as Bluetooth devices, cordless telephones, emergency services (police and fire protection) radio communications, and even some baby monitors. For example, if a company incorporated Bluetooth headsets into its call center operations, it shouldn't be a huge surprise that its 802.11g 2.4 GHz WLAN began to have problems in the call center area.

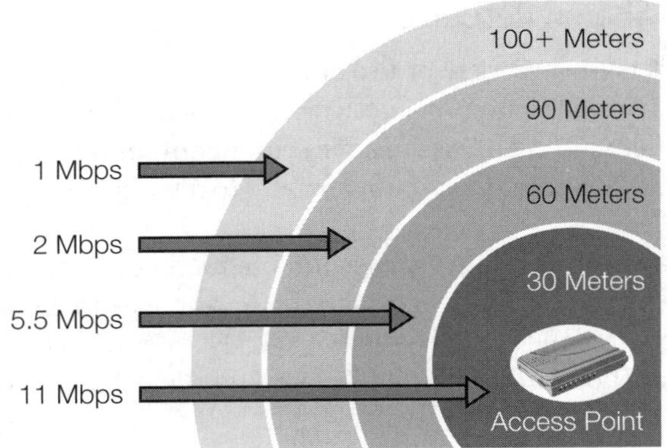

FIGURE 6-8
The bandwidth of an 802.11b signal fades as its distance increases.

- **Distance**—As the distance from an AP increases, RF signals begin losing signal strength and signal quality. As a node approaches the outside edge of a wireless device's effective range, bandwidth and signal integrity decline. Depending on an antenna's power (gain), the distance of its operating range may be wider or narrower, even in comparison to similar devices on the same network. An 802.11b device can provide its full 11 Mbps bandwidth, but only within the first 30 meters (100 feet) around its antenna. Each successive 30 meters in distance experiences a 50 percent decrease in bandwidth (as illustrated in Figure 6-8). This loss of bandwidth continues for each additional 30 meters until, at about 100 meters, bandwidth is decreased to 1 Mbps. Likewise, the 802.11n standard, which is able to transmit on the 5 GHz frequency band, loses around one-third of its bandwidth every 25 meters. Regardless of which 802.11x standard is in use, the reduction in bandwidth is caused by an AP automatically reducing its frequency and data transfer speed when the signal begins to weaken. Lower frequency signals are better able to penetrate interference, which increases as the distance grows. Having only one WLAN node communicating at 1 Mbps can slow the entire WLAN because of the time required for the access point to communicate with the slow node.
- **Metal boxes**—In RF terminology, a metal box is any metallic or magnetic object that blocks or absorbs a transmitted RF signal. A metal box can be a building, air conditioning unit, vault or large safe, large machine, metal partitions, and the like.
- **Stationary objects**—Many types of obstructions can deflect or block RF signals. Some common obstructions include metal boxes, building material, rock walls and fireplaces, trees, large bushes, and other large stationary objects. Different stationary objects create different levels of attenuation in the RF signal. Table 6-3 lists many common objects and their effect on an RF signal.

- **Shared bandwidth**—The bandwidth of WLAN devices is shared bandwidth, which means all active wireless devices are competing for the available bandwidth. As the number of wireless nodes on a WLAN increases, the average available bandwidth can be reduced when multiple nodes compete for the bandwidth. This, in turn, can decrease the performance of the entire network.

TABLE 6-3 Degree of attenuation by common materials.*

OBSTRUCTION	DEGREE OF ATTENUATION	EXAMPLE
Open space	None	Cafeteria, courtyard
Wood	Low	Inner wall, office partition, door, floor
Plaster	Low	Inner wall (old plaster lower than new plaster)
Synthetic materials	Low	Office partition
Cinder block	Low	Inner wall, outer wall
Asbestos	Low	Ceiling
Glass	Low	Untinted window
Wire mesh in glass	Medium	Door, partition
Metal tinted glass	Low	Tinted window
Human body	Medium	Large group of people
Water	Medium	Damp wood, aquarium, organic inventory
Bricks	Medium	Inner wall, outer wall, floor
Marble	Medium	Inner wall, outer wall, floor
Ceramic with metal content or backing	High	Ceramic tile, ceiling, floor
Paper	High	Roll or stack of paper stock
Concrete	High	Floor, outer wall, support pillar
Bulletproof glass	High	Security booth
Silvering	Very High	Mirror
Metal	Very High	Desk, office partition, reinforced concrete, elevator shaft, filing cabinet, sprinkler system, ventilator

*Used with permission from Intel Corporation.

Capacity and Coverage

A WLAN designer concentrates on ensuring sufficient **coverage**, which means he or she attempts to provide the same level of signal strength to all network nodes. However, the goal of the designer should be to strike a balance between **capacity**, meaning the number of nodes and amount of shared bandwidth available to each node, and coverage. If the design focuses solely on coverage, enough bandwidth may not be available across the network to support every node. When the design emphasizes capacity, the WLAN may provide adequate coverage in the near term. However, it may cease to provide adequate coverage as nodes are added.

You should plan for coverage to ensure that all the nodes on the network are able to associate with an AP. Planning for capacity may go against the designer's goal of providing adequate RF signal coverage to all nodes. Equally if not more important is for the WLAN design to ensure that adequate bandwidth is available to support the applications and traffic to be transmitted across the network. Ensuring capacity to every node usually ensures coverage to every node.

Remember, users with wireless nodes expect the same performance as their coworkers with wired nodes. If a WLAN is planned for coverage alone, the resulting network may not consistently provide the necessary bandwidth.

WLAN Coverage

As previously discussed, distance inversely affects the bandwidth of an RF signal. This is because as the distance increases, the bandwidth—and perhaps even more important the throughput—decreases. A typical 802.11g WLAN access point has an RF range of about 100 meters (about 330 feet). To maximize the coverage of the access point, it should be placed in the center of, or at a minimum in, a location that provides the most coverage to the area it is to support.

When it may be necessary to exceed range of a single AP, coverage can be extended by including wireless repeaters or multiple overlapping APs. Overlapping APs provide for seamless roaming within the WLAN's coverage area. However, each overlapping AP should be set to a different channel to prevent crosstalk. Another benefit to multiple APs is a level of redundancy, which means with minor configuration changes, most nodes are able to access the network when its primary AP fails.

WLAN Capacity

The capacity of a WLAN is dependent on the capability of its APs. Because bandwidth is shared by the nodes connecting to an AP, the number of simultaneous users possible depends on what is being transmitted across the network. An AP has the ability to fluctuate its capacity based on its load and the types and amounts of data being transmitted. For example, an 802.11b access point, which has up to 11 Mbps of bandwidth (within 10 meters), can support 50 nodes that are mostly idle, as many as 25 nodes accessing e-mail and mid-sized data files, or 10 to 15 nodes that are active on the network and transmitting or receiving mid- to large-sized data files. The general rule of 20 nodes to an AP is based on the nodes transmitting a mix of traffic.

Planning the capacity of a WLAN must consider the number of non-overlapping channels available from the devices of the various 802.11x standards. IEEE 802.11b/g/n provides only three non-overlapping channels, which should be enough capacity for typical Internet and e-mail activities. Increasing the number of non-overlapping channels available to the network also increases the capacity and potential throughput of the WLAN.

WLAN Mode and Topology

A WLAN can be configured into two basic modes of operation and three standard topologies. WLANs operate in either ad hoc or infrastructure modes, and they can be configured into an **Independent Basic Service Set (IBSS)**, a **Basic Service Set (BSS)**, or an **Extended Service Set (ESS)**. The ad hoc operational mode establishes an IBSS topology. Infrastructure mode requires either BSS or ESS for the WLAN's topology.

Ad Hoc Mode. Ad hoc mode provides WLAN nodes with the capability to connect directly to each other in a way similar to peer-to-peer operations on a wired network. Just as a wired peer-to-peer network doesn't require a central server, an ad hoc WLAN doesn't require a central AP (see Figure 6-9). In most corporate or large business settings, however, an ad hoc WLAN may prove to be chaotic and most likely less secure than required.

Each of the wireless nodes in an ad hoc WLAN is an IBSS. An IBSS can provide access to peripherals, a wired network, a modem connection, and other services, depending on the permissions granted by the IBSS's user.

In some instances, an ad hoc WLAN can be effective for a small area of the overall network, such as in a conference room, an employee break area, or a company-sponsored public hotspot.

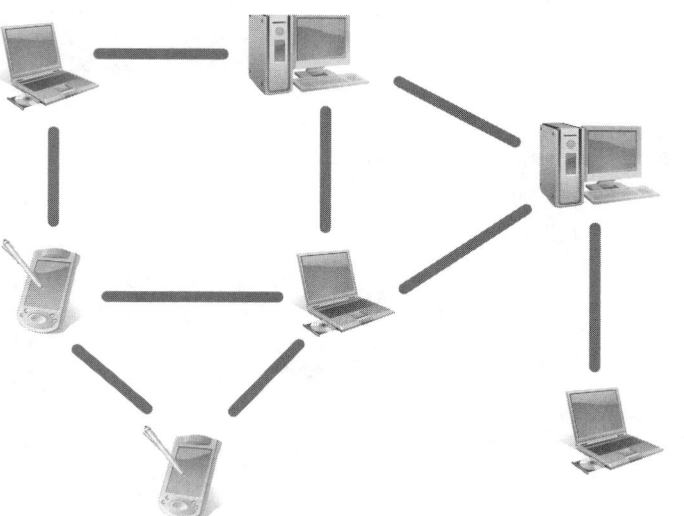

FIGURE 6-9

A WLAN configured as in ad hoc mode.

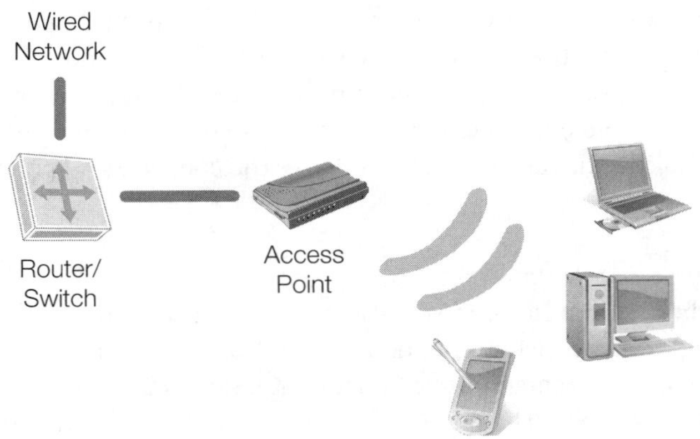

FIGURE 6-10

A BSS requires the inclusion of an access point (base station).

Infrastructure Mode. The most common mode used for larger WLANs is infrastructure. Infrastructure mode requires at least one AP or base station and may be, which it most commonly is, connected to a wired network infrastructure or a WAN gateway. A WLAN implemented with 20 or less wireless nodes and a single access point creates a BSS topology, as illustrated in Figure 6-10.

When multiple APs must interact to access a single wired network connection, as pictured in Figure 6-11, an ESS topology is created. On larger networks that must provide coverage to an area larger than the range of the wireless devices, an ESS topology should be used.

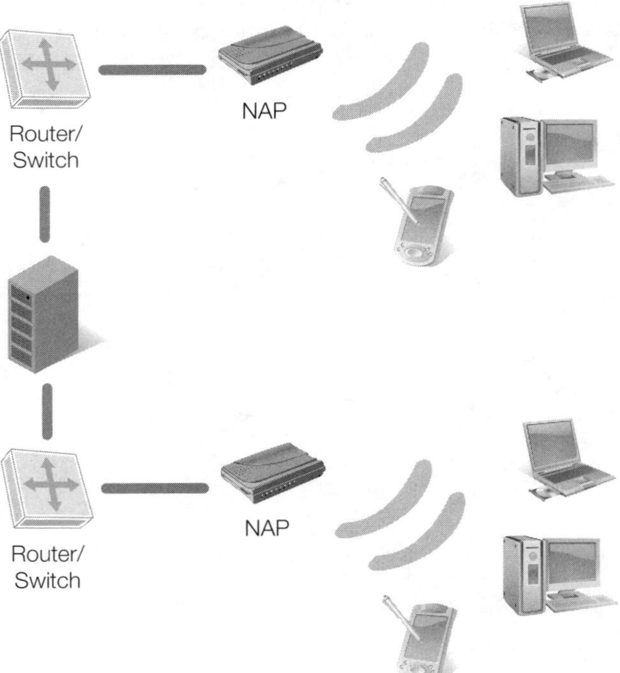

FIGURE 6-11

Multiple access points in a single WLAN create an ESS topology.

Performing a Site Survey

A site survey can be the most important step in the preparation, planning, and installation of a new WLAN. A site survey has three primary purposes:

- **Qualify a proposed site**—Just because it's desired to install a WLAN in a particular space, it doesn't mean the site will actually support a wireless network.
- **Verify coverage**—Ensure that all proposed node locations are able to connect to the WLAN.
- **Verify capacity**—Ensure that all proposed node locations have sufficient signal strength and bandwidth for their network applications.

The complexity of the proposed WLAN determines how extensive a site survey should be. If a WLAN is to be installed in a single room, a small two- or three-room office, or a typical home, it is likely that a single AP can provide the coverage and capacity needed. However, in a multiple-floor, multiple-department WLAN for a corporate office or a similarly complex WLAN situation, a site survey is an absolute requirement to ensure the resulting WLAN meets the users' and the company's requirements.

In essence, a WLAN site survey is a preliminary test of a proposed WLAN site. The site survey tests an area to determine how RF signals will perform in its environment and the amount of RF interference (RFI) or electromagnetic interference (EMI) present. The reasoning behind why you would conduct a site survey is that, regardless of the type of antennas in use, radio waves don't always travel the same distance in every direction. Walls, doors, people, and several other types of obstacles (see the previous Table 8-1) can cause the radiation pattern of radio waves to become irregular and even unpredictable, a condition called multipathing. Therefore, to understand how radio waves will behave in a certain area, a site survey should be performed, certainly before the actual installation of a WLAN proceeds.

Conducting the Site Tests

By assessing the signal strength of an access point in a particular area, you are better able to determine the number and placement of the access points required to meet the design objectives of the WLAN. Using a variety of antenna types and sizes and different combinations of access point configurations, you should be able to identify the right mix of components and configurations required to provide the proper coverage and capacity needs for a proposed WLAN.

In nearly all cases where a site survey is needed, the following steps should be performed:

- **Gather documentation**—Gather all of the relevant documentation available, which should include facility diagrams, drawings, blueprints, wiring plans, and information that identifies the locations of computer systems, existing network infrastructure, power outlets, and where any potential sources of interference are located, such as metal firebreaks, walls, and doors.

- **Walk-through**—Perform a walk-through. Visually inspect the area in which the WLAN is to be installed. Note any building features that may cause performance problems on the network.
- **Use a site survey tool**—Use a device specifically designed for conducting a site survey. Special software can be used to determine the radio coverage and interference patterns in all areas to be included in the WLAN.
- **Place stations**—The results of the site survey should help to identify the best locations for and the positioning of the WLAN's access points and antennas.
- **Place support equipment**—In order to provide even levels of coverage and capacity, the team should identify the areas where additional antennas, access points, or repeaters may be needed to overcome interference, signal loss, or range problems.
- **Locate the available power sources**—Find the locations of any electrical outlets. Also, determine if any existing (or planned) electrical systems are likely to generate interference. You also need to determine if backup power, such as an uninterruptible power supply (UPS), may be required to safeguard against power loss or degradation (highly recommended).

After determining the potential locations for the access points, install an access point in each location and retest the area using the site survey device or software previously used in the process. Test from the location of each of the user stations to be included in the network, noting the data transfer rate, bandwidth, and signal strength of each location. If a location is not supported adequately, adjustments may be needed in the placement of the access point or by adding an antenna or repeater.

Absolutely document every test, finding, and even your suspicions or assumptions during the site survey. If problems arise after the network is installed, you can refer to your notes to see if any warning signs or other red flags occurred that may have forewarned of a potential problem. Knowing the source of the issue, you then can easily correct it.

CHAPTER SUMMARY

The IEEE 802.11x family of standards defines the operational aspects of wireless networks and, in particular, wireless local area networks (WLANs). The primary standards in use are 802.11a, 802.11b, 802.11g, and 802.11n. The IEEE 802.11i standard defines security procedures for a WLAN. WLAN security attempts to protect a wireless network from attacks and intrusions.

The design and layout of a WLAN must take into consideration the needs of the organization, the performance levels needed, and the area into which the WLAN is to be installed. A best practice is to perform a site survey prior to completing the planning and design of a WLAN.

KEY CONCEPTS AND TERMS

AAA server
Asymmetric encryption system
Basic Service Set (BSS)
Capacity
Complementary code keying (CCK)
Coverage
Digital signature
Direct sequence spread spectrum (DSSS)
Dynamic rate shifting (DRS)
Extended Service Set (ESS)
Extensible Authentication Protocol (EAP)
Independent Basic Service Set (IBSS)
Industrial, scientific, and medical (ISM) bands
Lightweight Extensible Authentication Protocol (LEAP)
Message integrity check (MIC)
Multipath
Multiple-input and multiple-output (MIMO)
Open System Authentication (OSA)
Orthogonal frequency division multiplexing (OFDM)
Quadrature amplitude modulation (QAM)
Shared Key Authentication (SKA)
Symmetric encryption system
Temporal Key Integrity Protocol (TKIP)
Unlicensed National Information Infrastructure (UNII)
Wireless fidelity (Wi-Fi)

CHAPTER 6 ASSESSMENT

1. The network security standard for all IEEE networks is ________.

A. IEEE 802.11a
B. IEEE 802.11i
C. IEEE 802.1x
D. IEEE 802.3

2. What did WPA add to improve on the WEP protocol?

A. EAP
B. EAPOL
C. RC4
D. TKIP

3. Which of the following security threats has the primary objective of overloading a network's resources, resulting in the resources becoming unavailable to the network's users?

A. Denial of service
B. Intrusion
C. Interception
D. ARP spoofing

4. ________ is used to provide access to a network to users and networking devices.

A. Authorization
B. Accounting services
C. Authentication
D. Certification

5. A DoS attack is *not* a common security threat to a network.

A. True
B. False

6. What type of protocol does the 802.1x standard prescribe for authentication?

A. TKIP
B. EAP
C. AAA
D. DRS

7. The interference picked up by an RF antenna from other nearby transmitters is ________.
   A. EMI
   B. Metal box
   C. Crosstalk
   D. RFI

8. The capability of a WLAN to support a certain number of wireless nodes is called its ________.
   A. Capacity
   B. Coverage
   C. Mode
   D. Site survey

9. What is the designation of a node in an ad hoc WLAN?
   A. ESS
   B. BSS
   C. IBSS
   D. SSID

10. What is the process used to verify the capability of a site or a space to support a WLAN called?
    A. Coverage
    B. Capacity
    C. Site survey
    D. Mode

11. What is the topology of a WLAN that includes only a single access point?
    A. BSS
    B. ESS
    C. IBSS
    D. RSSI

12. What is the purpose of a site survey?
    A. To perform acceptance testing on a new WLAN installation
    B. To ensure that a WLAN design provides sufficient signal strength and bandwidth for all planned stationary or mobile nodes
    C. To ensure that each node on a WLAN is functioning properly
    D. To verify an existing WLAN meets the requirements for connecting to a wireless WAN

13. The distance between a WLAN node and the AP to which it is associated determines the throughput the node experiences.
    A. True
    B. False

14. What characteristic of the bandwidth of a WLAN is affected by the number of nodes associated with a particular access point?
    A. Bandwidth
    B. Login
    C. Security level
    D. Priority

15. Which of the following does *not* create a serious barrier to the transmission of RF signals?
    A. Concrete
    B. Leaded glass
    C. Open space
    D. Water

CHAPTER 7

Layer 2 Networking

TODAY'S BUSINESS RELIES ON NETWORKING RESOURCES to provide data, access, and connectivity to the outside world. As a part of this reliance, the throughput, response, and transmission times must be as fast as possible. This means that the network medium must provide robust service that minimizes latency and can overcome faults and failures.

Layer 2 of the OSI Reference Model defines the protocols that transfer data between nodes on a local area network (LAN) and in certain cases on a wide area network (WAN), as well. Layer 2 also defines physical addressing and provides a LAN with access control, flow control, and error control for nodes connected to the network media. In this chapter, you will learn about the functions, protocols, structures, and standards of Layer 2 networking.

Chapter 7 Topics

This chapter covers the following topics and concepts:

- What Layer 2 networking is
- Ethernet LAN topologies
- Layer 2 business solutions

Chapter 7 Goals

When you complete this chapter, you will be able to:

- Understand the functions in Layer 2 networking
- Explain Layer 2 addressing
- Identify Layer 2 networking devices
- Define collision detection and Media Access Control on a Layer 2 network
- Describe Layer 2 switching

Layer 2 Networks

A local area network (LAN) is essentially a closed circuit of interconnected devices. These devices are connected for the purpose of exchanging communication and sharing resources. A LAN is commonly thought of in terms of its ability to connect to the outside world, normally by connecting to the Internet. However, a LAN is still a LAN even if it doesn't have an Internet connection. Any LAN is able to operate completely on Layer 2 with some important help from Layer 1. This is true of LANs that connect to the outside world and those that do not. Message frames transmitted on a standalone network are intended solely for another local LAN node. Other LAN nodes can include a file server, an application server, or a PC across the room.

When a message is addressed to a destination that lies outside the LAN, Layer 3, Layer 4, and all of the other OSI Reference Model layers become involved. These higher layers play a part in the process to transmit and display the data contained in the message at the destination node. However, within a LAN, it's Layer 2 that provides all the magic. Layer 2 works very closely with Layer1 to transport frames around a LAN. Most of the technological advancements in Layer 2 are directly related to Layer 1 advances or differences.

Layer 1 and Layer 2 Evolution

You have already learned about Ethernet's history. Recall that Ethernet is the most common LAN technology. It is important to understand how Ethernet's evolution to its current state was affected by Layer 1 changes. Layer 1 in the OSI Reference Model is the Physical Layer. This layer contains the physical transmission media and the hardware to access it. In short, Layer 1 contains the cables and the interfaces. Of course, cables are appropriate only for wired media. Wireless transmission media do not use cabling to transfer frames.

Physical Media Requirements

There are several basic requirements that physical media must meet to be a viable option. Each advance in Ethernet speed occurs when a collection of physical hardware, media, and software converge to meet each of the requirements. A new or improved network solution must meet these requirements to be an attractive option:

- **Availability**—The greatest technology is not much good if you cannot get it. The first requirement for a viable communication option is that the parts be available. That means the transmission media, the interface devices, and the software to use the media are all available. Twisted-pair cabling was around for over 100 years before Ethernet started using it. Neither the quality cabling nor the interfaces were available until the late 1980s.
- **Usability**—A usable solution is one that has all the pieces in place that work together. The overall environment has some impact on usability. For example, using unshielded twisted-pair cabling that runs through an elevator shaft may not be a good idea. The interference created from the elevator's electric motor

will likely cause network disruptions. A usable system is one in which all components work well together in the intended environment. Standards make it possible for products from different manufacturers to work together in a usable system.

- **Affordability**—New technology tends to be higher in price than existing products. There are several reasons for this. First, new technology is often untested in the marketplace. That means it may be accepted, and it may fail. Manufacturers generally do not want to invest large sums of money and resources into unproven products. They generally start off with smaller production runs to see if the product sells. Smaller production runs have higher unit costs than large runs. Second, production processes for new products lack the optimizations of older processes. New products tend to cost more to produce, and new products must be affordable enough for organizations to justify spending the funds. Sometimes that means waiting to deploy new technology until the price comes down.
- **Installability**—A great product will not work well if the organization is unable to install the media to support it. Areas with high amounts of electrical interference may not support unshielded twisted-pair cables well. Buildings that require running cables through many tight corners with limited access may mean coaxial cable, or coax, is not a good choice. Each type of media has its own installation requirements. These requirements make each type of media a good choice in some environments and questionable in other environments.
- **Value**—Any technology solution must provide a greater benefit than its cost. A very costly fiber optic LAN is fast and powerful. However, such a choice is unwarranted if a 10 GigE LAN using unshielded twisted-pair would work just as well. A good technology solution is one that has a favorable price-performance ratio. Make sure all technology choices satisfy a technology need and a business need.

The Perils of New Technology

One small manufacturing facility had a LAN problem in the early 1990s. The company ran shielded twisted-pair cables between two buildings. A small road that connected parking lots separated the buildings. Frequent lightning storms resulted in network disruptions when lightning would travel through the ground. They turned to a new technology, fiber optic cabling, to connect their two buildings. After installing all of the hardware and media, the two buildings could not communicate. After days of troubleshooting, it was discovered that the network interface controllers (NICs) were creating a light signal that was too strong for the cable over such a short distance (less than 100 yards).

It took a few more weeks to figure out a solution. In the end, a high-level engineer who worked for the NIC manufacturer came up with a fix. He suggested diffusing the light signal with a filter. He instructed the on-site technicians to fold a two-ply sheet of tissue paper over one end of the fiber optic cable and reattach the cable. The fix worked. The customer eventually replaced the tissue paper with a real filter, but the company was able to use new technology to solve a problem.

Physical Media Types

Most of the IEEE 802.3 Ethernet standards emerged to support faster transmission, additional features, or just to support new media types. You have already seen how IEEE 802.3 evolved. The use of new media types or the more efficient use of existing media marked the advancement of Ethernet. The most common types of media Ethernet uses include:

- **Coaxial cable**—Oliver Heavinside patented this cable design in 1880 as a way to transmit electrical signals. Coaxial cables have an inner conductor surrounded by an insulating layer. That layer is surrounded by an outer conducting shield, which is surrounded by an insulating cover. The design of coaxial cable, also called coax, reduces internal signal loss and sensitivity to external interference. Common types of coax include standard coax and a thinner, more flexible version called thinnet.
- **Unshielded twisted-pair (UTP)**—Cables that consist of several pairs of individual wires. To help cancel the effects of external electromagnetic interference (EMI), each pair of two wires is twisted together. All of the pairs are then encased in an insulating cover.
- **Shielded twisted-pair (STP)**—Similar to UTP, but wires that are encased in a foil cover to shield them from EMI. Different manufacturers use different techniques to shield cables. Some shield each pair individually, and some just shield the entire bundle of wires.
- **Fiber optic cable**—A cable that contains one or more optical fibers. Fiber optic cables transmit light signals generally across large distances. Since the cable does not use electrical signals, this media type encounters no EMI interference problems. Fiber optic cables tend to be more expensive than other media types.
- **Wireless media**—The vast majority of all wireless Ethernet devices use radio frequency (RF) transmission using 802.11 standards.

Twisted-Pair—The Most Common Media

The first Ethernet installations required coaxial cable. Before 1990, that is all that the IEEE 802.3 standards supported. Coax is much more costly than the twisted-pair cables that telephone networks used. Coax is also stiffer than twisted-pair. The cable stiffness made installing coax more difficult. There were some places that coax was just too difficult to install in a cost-effective manner.

When IEEE published 802.3i in 1990, Ethernet immediately became easier to install and use. IEEE 802.3i defined Ethernet using twisted-pair cables. For the first time, Ethernet operated over a cheap medium that was plentiful and easy to install.

TABLE 7-1 ISO/IES 11801 twisted-pair types.

LEGACY NAME	NEW NAME	SCREENING FOR ENTIRE CABLE (BUNDLE)	SHIELDING FOR EACH PAIR
UTP—Unshielded twisted-pair	U/UTP	None	None
STP—Shielded twisted-pair	U/FTP	None	Foil
FTP—Foil-shielded twisted-pair	F/UTP	Foil	None
S-STP—Shielded/inner shielded twisted-pair	S/FTP	Braiding	Foil
S-FTP—Shielded/foil shielded twisted-pair	SF/UTP	Foil, braiding	None

The number of Ethernet installations began to grow quickly. It was very easy to run twisted-pair cables to nearly any location. Today's Ethernet networks rely primarily on twisted-pair cables. Early Ethernet LANs using twisted-pair cables began to encounter EMI. The older coaxial cables were not as sensitive to EMI as twisted-pair. Manufacturers started adding shielding to their cables to protect cables form EMI. Several types of shielding emerged. In fact, shielding is so important in current wiring applications that the ISO/IEC 11801 standard formally defines different methods of shielding twisted-pair cables. Table 7-1 shows the different methods of shielding twisted-pair cables.

Just as types of shielding differ, so does cable quality. There are several different types of cable available today. The type of cable any organization needs depends on the distance between devices and the desired speed. Of course, higher-quality cables are more expensive than cheaper ones. Ethernet standards that rely on higher transmission speed require higher-quality cables. Table 7-2 lists the main types of twisted-pair cables.

Twisted-pair cabling makes it possible for organizations to easily and inexpensively run cables to nearly every desired node. Combining cheap wiring options with wireless connections makes it possible to extend the LAN to any device that needs it.

Although Cat 5 is by far the most common cable found in Ethernet LANs, many consider it an outdated standard. Today's cable standards define transmission speed far beyond what Cat 5 cables can support. Cat 6a cables currently support 10 GigE connections. With 10 GigE connections to the desktop, the wiring infrastructure has the ability to provide ample bandwidth for nearly any application.

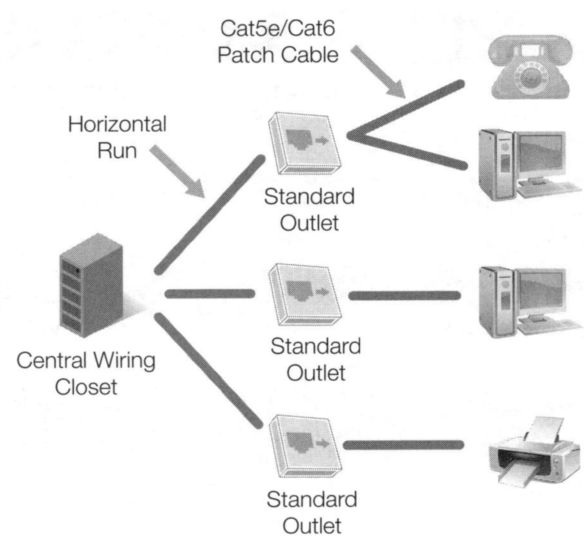

FIGURE 7-1
Structured cabling system.

TABLE 7-2 Major categories of twisted-pair cables.

CABLE CATEGORY	TYPE	BANDWIDTH	DESCRIPTION
Cat 1		0.4 MHz	Telephone wiring—not listed in EIA/TIA recommendations
Cat 2			Legacy terminal cabling—not listed in EIA/TIA recommendations
Cat 3	U/UTP	16 MHz	10BASE-T and 100BASE-T4
Cat 4	U/UTP	20 MHz	Token ring—not normally used in Ethernet
Cat 5	U/UTP	100 MHz	100BASE-TX and 1000BASE-T—most common cable type in use
Cat 5e	U/UTP	100 MHz	100BASE-TX and 1000BASE-T—same as Cat5 with higher testing requirements
Cat 6	U/UTP	250 MHz	1000BASE-T
Cat 6a	U/UTP	500 MHz	10GBASE-T
Cat 7	U/FTP	600 MHz	10GBASE-TX, CCTV, Telephone—standard under development
Cat 7a	S/FTP	1000 MHz	10GBASE-TX, CATV, Telephone—standard under development
Cat 8	S/FTP	1200 MHz	Standard under development

Structured Cabling Systems

High-speed Ethernet segments and faster devices have caused manufacturers to introduce **structured cabling systems**. A structured cabling system is a collection of standard components that connect with one another to provide a complete cabling solution. These systems centralize many of the cable connection points that can make a data center look like a messy group of cables. Structured cabling systems often come in preconfigured modules that connect to one another. Standard modules contain cabling and connectors for the most common data center applications. Figure 7-1 shows a structured cabling system.

Ethernet LAN Topologies

You have already learned about the basic LAN topologies. The **topology** of a network is its physical layout, and so a LAN topology is the physical layout of a LAN. Today's real Ethernet LANs are commonly a series of connected star networks. The way in which organizations connect the stars (or other topologies) can have a huge impact on how well the network performs. Most organizations with more than a few network nodes use structured cabling systems and central data centers or wiring closets. Centralizing network cabling provides several advantages. Bringing network connections into a single location provides network designers with several options. Figure 7-2 shows a centralized wiring closet.

The simplest (and worst) solution would be to connect all cables to a single set of hubs. This solution has one main advantage: It does not matter where a node connects to the network. The node will see the same traffic regardless of where it connects.

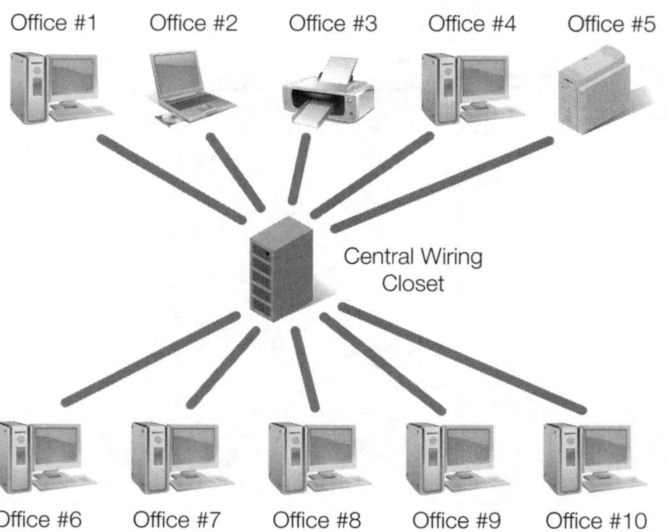

FIGURE 7-2 Centralized wiring closet.

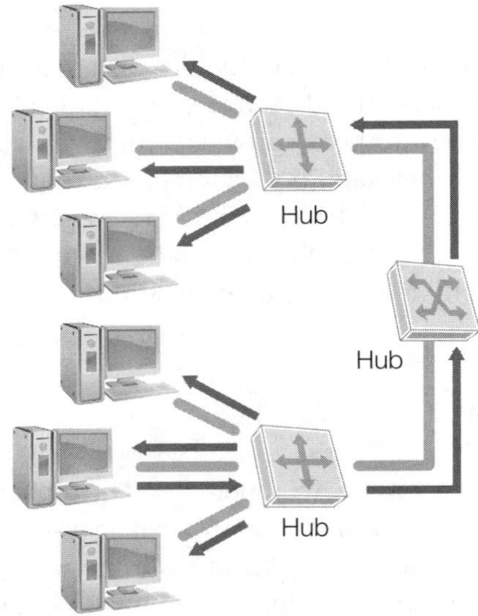

FIGURE 7-3
LAN with centralized hubs.

Figure 7-3 shows a LAN with centralized hubs.

Creating a LAN like the one shown in Figure 7-3 presents several problems. This type of LAN has the same main problem of a bus topology. All nodes are part of a single collision domain. That means every node hears the traffic from every other node. Collisions are frequent in such topologies and can have a dramatic impact on the network's performance. Early LANs were often single collision domains.

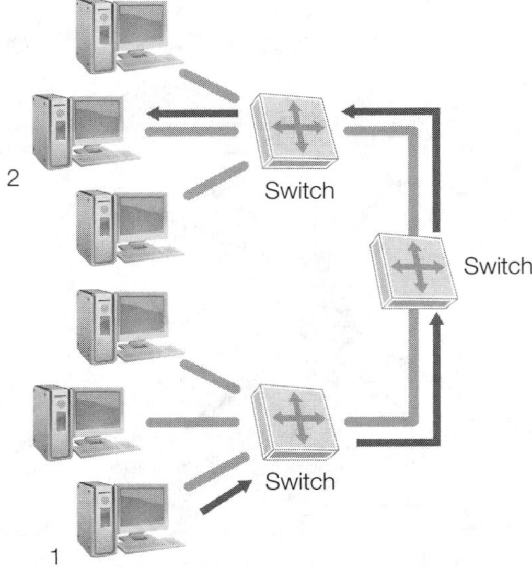

FIGURE 7-4
LAN with centralized switches.

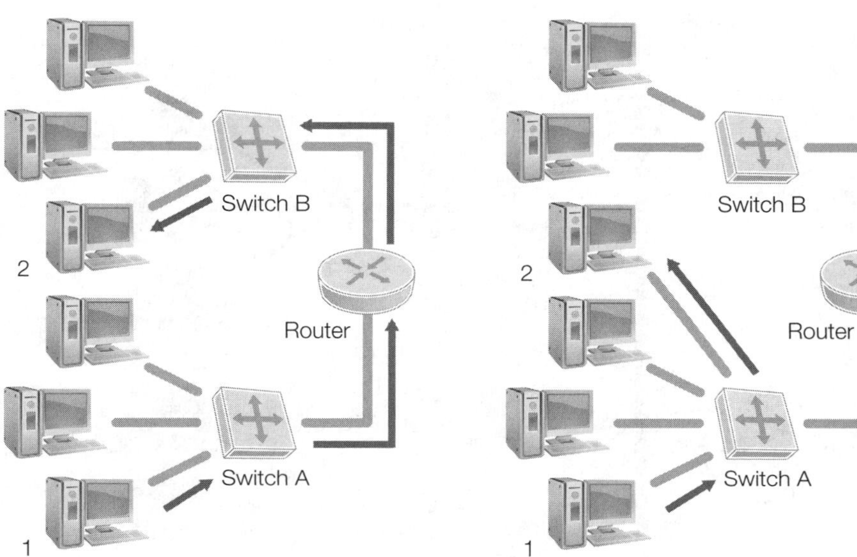

FIGURE 7-5
Moving nodes to the same switch.

The first step in making LANs perform better is to reduce collisions. Collisions degrade performance because each collision causes at least two nodes to wait some period of time before they can attempt another transmission. Avoiding collisions avoids wait times for all nodes. Recall that a switch separates LANs into multiple collision domains. A switch forwards traffic to only a single port. That means a switch does not forward traffic to other ports. The nodes connected to other ports never see the traffic that is not addressed to them. This behavior dramatically cuts down on collisions. Figure 7-4 shows a network with centralized switches.

The main problem with switches and separate collision domains is that poor planning can hurt network performance. Suppose two nodes are connected to different switches. These two nodes, A and B, communicate frequently. It would be better if nodes A and B were connected to the same switch. Connecting them to the same switch means that all traffic between the two nodes has to travel through a single device. Figure 7-5 shows how moving two nodes to the same switch can reduce communication time.

NOTE

Moving nodes for better performance is not the only way to isolate traffic. In the next chapter you will learn about a method to subdivide a LAN into smaller groups of nodes to create a virtual LAN.

Network Backbones

Structured cabling systems and rack-mounted hardware in data centers makes moving nodes easier. The process of moving a node from one switch to another is a simple matter of moving a cable. The ease of central administration makes topologies that use central devices attractive. Such a topology is called a network backbone.

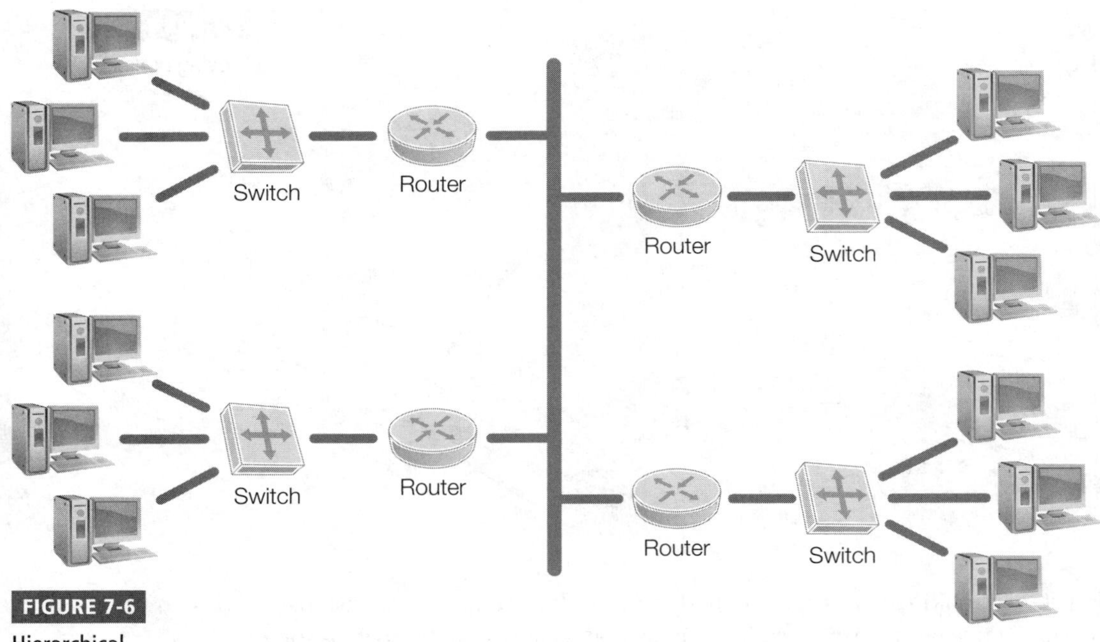

FIGURE 7-6
Hierarchical backbone.

You already have seen several backbone configurations. These networks take advantage of Layer 2 switching to separate collision domains and Layer 3 routing to separate broadcast domains. There are three basic types of backbones:

- Hierarchical
- Flat
- Collapsed

A hierarchical backbone is a topology that depends on Layer 3 routers to separate LANs from one another. Routers are connected to a common medium, such as a bus. This topology is possible with centralized or distributed switches and routers. As long as the bus reaches all of the routers, the hardware does not have to be concentrated in a data center. The main problem with hierarchical backbones is that they rely on Layer 3 routing to communicate between LANs. A message must travel through two routers and the shared medium to reach a destination. Figure 7-6 shows a hierarchical backbone topology.

The next topology was developed to address the performance problems with the previous topology. Instead of relying on Layer 3 routers to connect LAN segments to the shared medium, the flat backbone uses Layer bridges or switches.

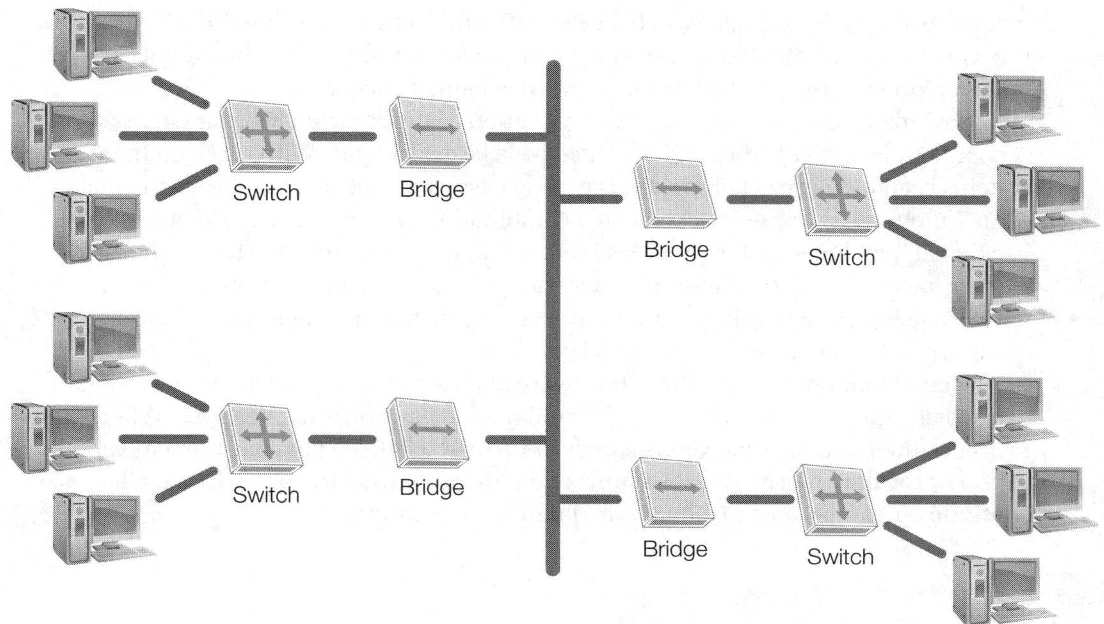

FIGURE 7-7
Flat backbone.

Using a Layer 2 device makes getting frames to their destinations much faster than Layer 3 routing. A side effect of using a flat backbone is that the entire LAN becomes a single broadcast domain. Like the hierarchical backbones, the flat backbone allows bridges to be centralized or distributed. Figure 7-7 shows a flat backbone topology.

The third type of backbone was developed to further increase network performance. This topology relies on switching hardware located in a central location. The advantage of centralized switching is that there is no longer a need for a shared bus. The shared bus could become a source of collisions. The collapsed backbone topology makes each message transfer between segments a point-to-point connection. That speeds up each exchange and reduces overall collisions. A completely collapsed backbone also has fewer devices to manage since all segment connections go through a single switch.

Collapsed backbones do have a few drawbacks. First, the centralized nature of the topology requires that every device be connected to the central switch. There either must be a direct line between each device or to intermediated devices between the central switch and the endpoints. This requirement can cause longer cable runs and potentially result in signal loss. Another drawback is the reliance on a central switch. A single switch for the entire network means that if the switch fails, the whole network fails. Nodes can still communicate within each segment but not with nodes on other segments. Figure 7-8 shows a collapsed backbone.

Today's data centers commonly use a variation of the completely collapsed backbone. A popular alternative is the rack-mounted collapsed backbone. With rack-mounted systems becoming very affordable, it is getting easier to create even small data centers. A rack-mounted collapsed backbone is a combination of a collapsed backbone and a flat backbone. It includes rack-mounted switches that are also connected to a high-speed routing switch. Many rack-mounted switches provide the ability to connect with other switches using extremely high-speed connections, such as fiber optic or on-board bus.

Figure 7-9 shows a rack-mounted backbone.

The combination of centralizing hardware and using high-speed interconnections can provide the performance required by today's media-centric applications. When using rack-mounted switches, backbone speeds of up to 40 GigE are possible. Current vendors also are providing more options to support redundant hardware to make it possible to continue operations during a hardware failure and recovery.

FIGURE 7-8

Collapsed backbone.

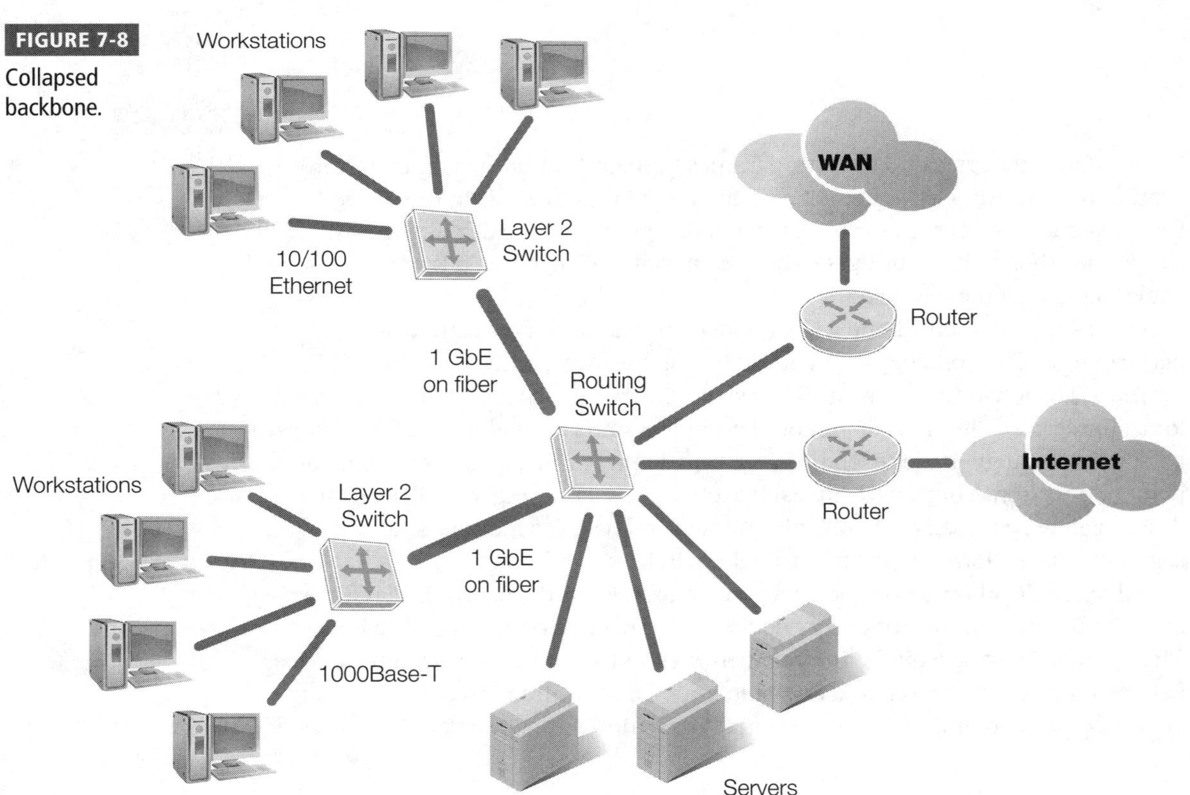

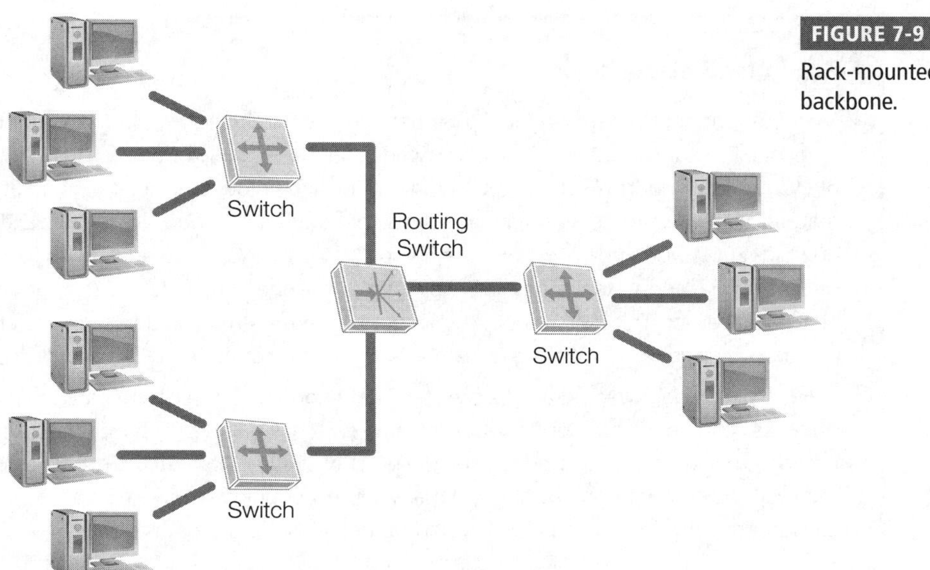

FIGURE 7-9
Rack-mounted backbone.

Network Power

As organizations began to implement networked devices, they began to need more power. Endpoints and network devices all need power to operate. Early Ethernet networks depended exclusively on external power supplies. IEEE 802.3af–2003, and the later updated standard, IEEE 802.3at–2009, describe the technique for providing electrical power with the Ethernet data. The technology is called Power over Ethernet (PoE). The ability to deliver data and power in the same cable meant that PoE-capable devices can operate anywhere that an Ethernet connection is available. PoE provides transportability and flexibility for today's network devices.

Topologies that use centralized architectures make it easy to provide reliable power to Ethernet devices using PoE. Collapsed backbones and rack-mounted backbones provide convenient centralized points to locate power supply units for the rest of the network. Locating these devices in the data center helps to ensure infrastructure support for fault tolerance. Some vendors, such as Cisco, provide hardware options to reduce overall power use by sharing excess power between multiple switches.

Large organizations that provide Ethernet connectivity to remote locations also can provide power for those devices. The ability of organizations to provide power for networked devices can be a huge benefit. They can ensure networked devices such as switches, IP phones, and even thin client devices can operate through power failures or instability. For locations with unstable power, PoE can help to avoid operational interruptions.

PoE in the Enterprise

Many current deployments of Enterprise networks will include some form of PoE. The original IEEE 802.3af–2003 standard allowed for a maximum distribution of 15.4 Watts of DC power per port. As the endpoint devices became more advanced, and additional features were built in, the requirement came for additional power. The next IEEE standard 802.3at–2009, also known as PoE+, or PoE plus, was developed to provide up to 25.5 watts of DC power. A new standard is currently being developed known as 802.az, or Energy Efficient Ethernet. This requirement came about because of the need to save power, and this standard achieves it by lowering the amount of power distributed when the device is idle.

PoE is typically deployed on access switches that endpoint devices terminate to. These switches come in various configurations. Some switches might only have the first few ports on the switch designated for PoE while other switches can utilize PoE on all of the available switch ports. Switches that are densely populated with PoE devices often consume significantly more power driving up utility costs.

Some devices that are typically powered via PoE ports include:

- VoIP phones
- Wireless access points
- Security cameras
- Badge readers
- Wall clocks using Network Time Protocol (NTP)
- Lighting controls
- Intercom and paging systems

Layer 2 Business Solutions

Layer 2 media and devices provide technical solutions to many technical problems. But the only true measure of any technical solution's success is how well it meets a business need. Each type of organization has different business needs and will benefit from different technical solutions. This section explores each type of organization size and the specific types of needs they encounter.

SOHO Organization

Small office/home office locations comprise the smallest type of organization. One of their most important challenges is to provide transparent connectivity between the Internet and each of the few network devices. Although SOHO locations may have more devices, the most common devices include:

- Several personal computers
- Personal digital assistants (PDAs)
- IP phones
- Fax machines
- Printers

In most SOHOs, two devices are able to service most networking needs. The first device connects the SOHO network to the Internet. In most cases, an Internet gateway is an integrated device that includes a Layer 3 router and gateway, and a Layer 2 switch of local ports. Many integrated gateways allow residences or SOHOs to connect to the Internet using asymmetric digital subscriber lines (ADSLs) or cable connections. Some devices even include a wireless access point.

The other common device is a Layer 2 switch with an integrated wireless access point. The wireless access point is not necessary if the gateway provides wireless access. Most gateways have four or fewer local ports. For all but the smallest SOHOs, the additional switch is necessary to allow all of the devices to connect to the Internet and to one another. These two devices create a LAN that can connect to the Internet. Figure 7-10 shows an example of a SOHO network configuration.

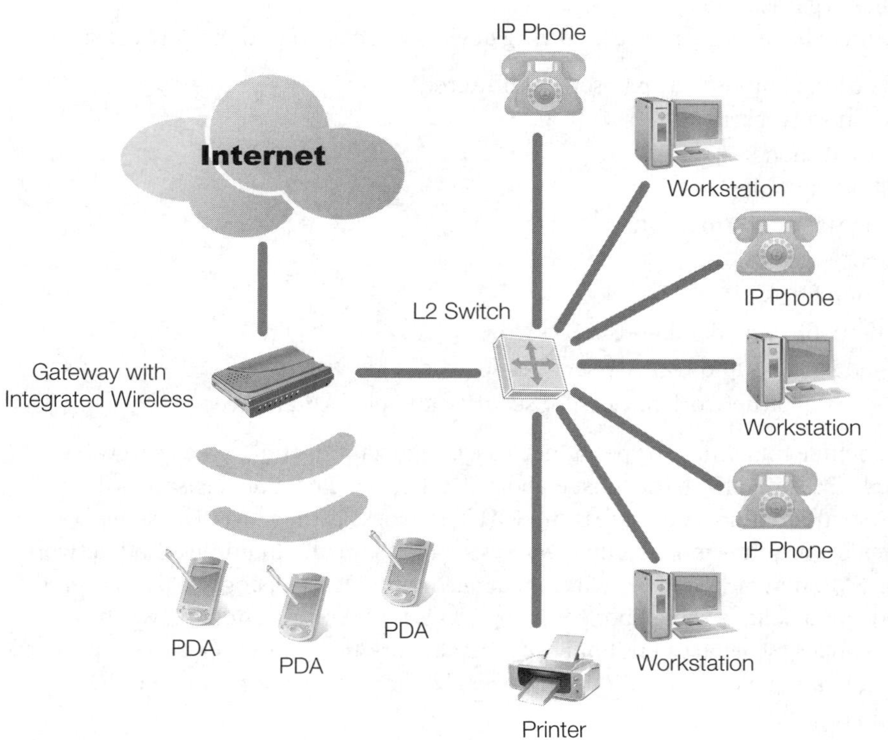

FIGURE 7-10
SOHO network configuration.

technical TIP

One example of a SOHO is a small travel agency. The agency has three travel agents working during the daytime hours. Each agent has an IP phone, a computer, and a PDA. The IP phone and computer use wired connections, and the PDAs connect to the agency's wireless network. The agency connects to the Internet using ADSL service. All three agents share a single color printer. All of the wired devices connect to an eight-port Ethernet switch, and the switch connects to the ADSL modem. The travel agency can share the printer, enjoy low-cost Voice over IP phone service, and connect all computers to the Internet using this simple configuration.

SMB Organization

Small and medium-sized businesses (SMBs) have requirements that put greater demands on an Ethernet network. SMB networks must serve more users and provide more-advanced functionality. They must support more-advanced applications for customers, partners, and workers. SMB networks are the first type of networks to clearly implement the seven domains of a typical IT infrastructure. Most of the seven domains are present in even smaller organizations.

SMBs routinely have many of the following devices connected to their networks:

- Several dozen computers (up to several hundred)
- PDAs for most workers
- IP phones at each desk
- Centralized fax machines
- Departmental or group printers
- Scanners
- Information kiosks
- Application, file, and database servers
- Integrated services and security services servers
- Multiple layers of network devices for security and performance services

This list can include many more types of devices. Organizations that exceed several hundred employees often have the most elaborate networks. The main reason SMB networks are so much more elaborate than SOHO networks is their size. The sheer number of devices requires more complexity to support them and maintain good network performance. SMB networks can benefit from departmental LANs using VLANs (covered in Chapter 9) and a collapsed backbone topology. This LAN organization allows the SMB to group nodes by department but keeps the network traffic at Layer 2 to support streaming media and voice applications. Figure 7-11 shows an example of a SOHO network configuration.

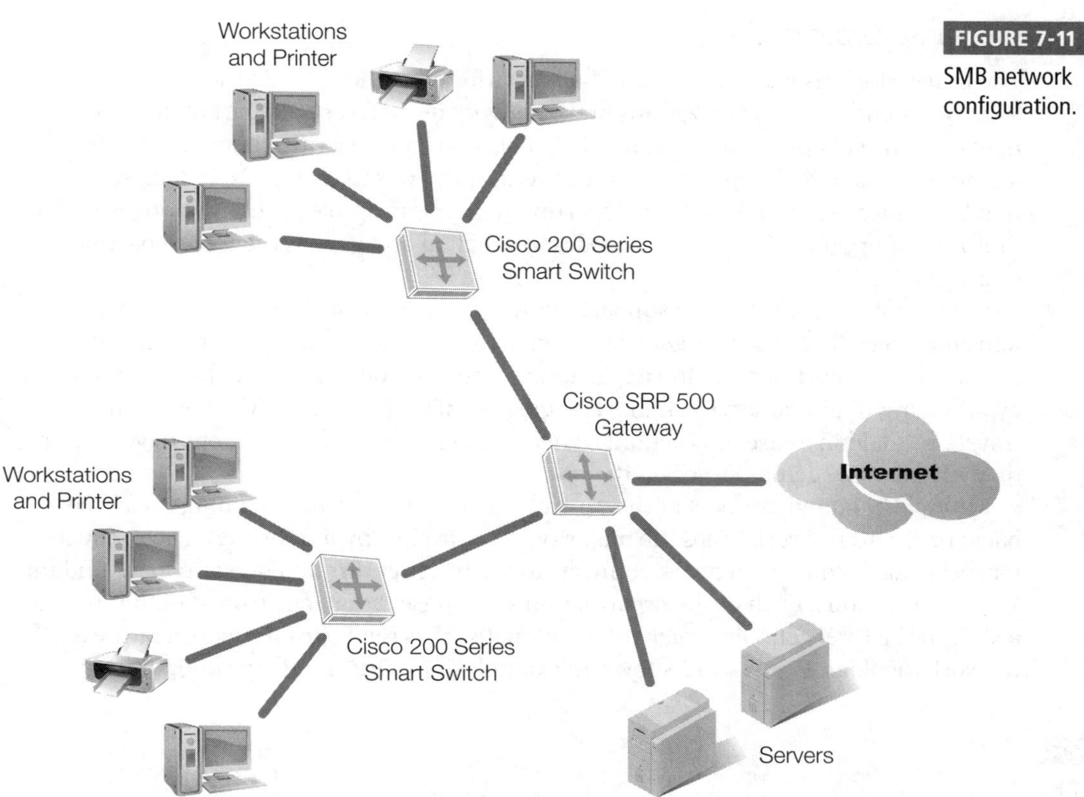

FIGURE 7-11 SMB network configuration.

technical TIP

One example of a SMB is a medical office that specializes in sports medicine. The practice has 10 doctors, 14 nurses, and 23 office employees. Their office has a small central room that houses the practice's two servers and all network hardware. Their network connects to the Internet using ADSL through their Cisco SRP 500 series device. Their wired devices connect to the LAN through one of their two 24-port Cisco 200 series smart switches. The Cisco SRP 500 also provides virtual private network (VPN) access for remote users and IEEE 802.11n for wireless connections. Requests for Internet resources go through the Layer 3 router, but all local requests stay within the Layer 2 switches.

Enterprise Organization

The Enterprise presents the greatest challenges for networks. The size and distributed location of enterprise organizations make network design a crucial part of an effective network. The collapsed backbone topology helps designers create a network that is fast and flexible. Each building throughout the enterprise has its own LAN. In fact, some buildings have several LANs. Each department, and some projects, has their own VLANs. This type of organization separates nodes by building and groups them by department or project.

Enterprise networks have to support many applications for their customers, partners, and employees. The largest organizations generally provide advanced communication options in their customer-facing applications. They also often leverage their IT resources by providing IP phone service, audio and video conferencing, and UC integration to lower travel costs and increase interaction. Networks in enterprise organizations have to keep up with the extra demands put on them.

Multiple buildings connect at the central data center to create a campus collapsed backbone. This network keeps the majority of the traffic flowing through Layer 2 switches for speed. Each campus network connects to the Internet through one of two redundant WAN connections. Each of the organization's campuses connects to one another using a VPN in the Internet. The larger enterprise network is really just a superset of the SMB network topology. Figure 7-12 shows an example of a SOHO network configuration.

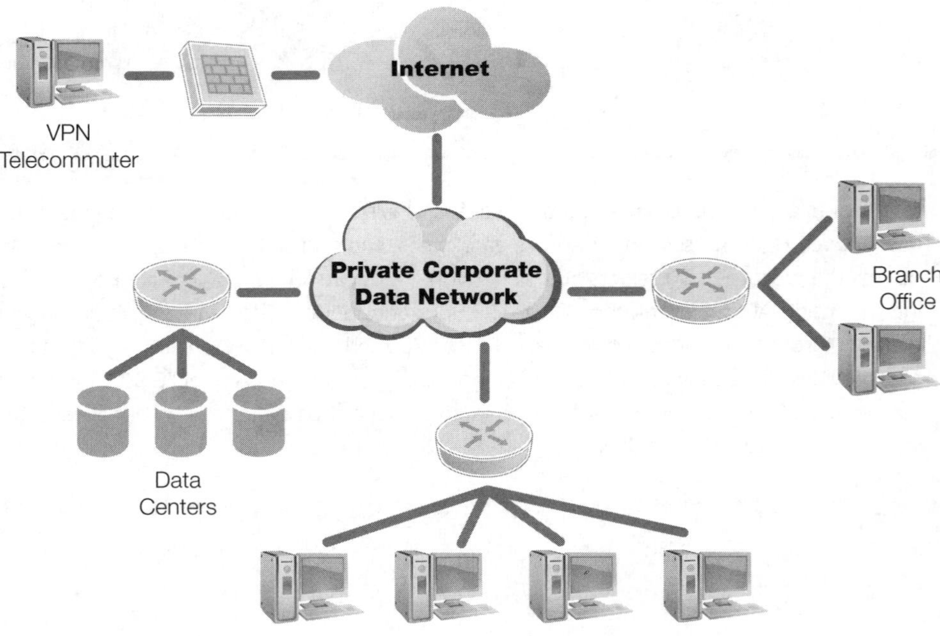

FIGURE 7-12 Enterprise network configuration.

technical TIP

One example of an enterprise organization is a building supply retail chain. The enterprise operates 143 stores in the United States and Canada. The company has its home office in Charlotte and regional offices in Atlanta, Denver, Seattle, Chicago, and Boston. The company employs nearly 3,000 employees and has several thousand network devices. Each store has its own application and communications server. A Cisco SRP 500 series device provides Internet and wireless connections. A single Cisco 200 series smart switch provides connections for all of the stores' computers, printers, and point-of-sale devices. All of the stores connect to the home office data center using a VPN on the Internet. The home office maintains the data center for all of its local employees and devices, as well as all of the organization's servers. Each store is a separate Layer 2 Ethernet LAN. The home office is organized like the SMB architecture, with departmental VLANs and separate LANs per building.

CHAPTER SUMMARY

Layer 2 of the OSI Reference Model, the Data Link Layer, is close enough to the Physical Layer to provide very fast data transfer. However, since it is separate from the Physical Layer, it also can provide flexibility to group and separate nodes based on communication needs. Although Layer 3 has long been used to create networks and subnetworks, routing packets through Layer 3 devices is just too slow for today's demand for real-time data transfer. Layer 2 is the focus of many of today's network designs.

Layer 2 switching provides the speed to deliver real-time data with minimal delays. It also provides the flexibility to construct networks that meet the needs of different types of organizations. In this chapter, you read about different organization sizes and network designs to meet those needs. You also read how Ethernet can help organizations of any size meet and exceed their communications goals.

KEY CONCEPTS AND TERMS

Structured cabling systems
Topology

CHAPTER 7 ASSESSMENT

1. Which of the following is *not* a main requirement that new technology must meet?
   A. Availability
   B. Usability
   C. Expandability
   D. Affordability

2. The original Ethernet specification defined a LAN using which type of cabling?
   A. Coaxial
   B. UTP
   C. STP
   D. Fiber optic

3. Which is the lowest category of twisted-pair cabling that supports 100 Mbps bandwidth?
   A. Cat 3
   B. Cat 4
   C. Cat 5
   D. Cat 6

4. Which type of network device separates segments into different collision domains?
   A. Hub
   B. Router
   C. Firewall
   D. Switch

5. A ________ separates LANs into separate broadcast domains.

6. Which LAN topology uses centralized switches (one for each LAN segment) connected to a central bus?
   A. Tree
   B. Hierarchical backbone
   C. Flat backbone
   D. Ring

7. IEEE 802.3at–2009 defines what capability for Ethernet?
   A. Power over Ethernet (PoE)
   B. Wireless (Wi-Fi) Ethernet
   C. Wi-Fi Protected Access (WPA)
   D. 1 GigE and 10 GigE using twisted-pair

8. A SOHO can often operate an effective Layer 2 network with how many network devices?
   A. 2
   B. 3
   C. 7
   D. 13

9. What are the most common criteria for grouping network devices together for SMB and enterprise organizations?
   A. Workgroup
   B. Team
   C. Department
   D. Division

10. Replacing a hub with a switch immediately reduces which of the following?
    A. Collisions
    B. Broadcasts
    C. False transmission starts
    D. Tokens

CHAPTER

8

Layer 2 Networking VLANs

THE OSI NETWORK REFERENCE MODEL defines a clear division between the Data Link Layer (Layer 2) and the Network Layer (Layer 3). The Data Link Layer handles traffic within a LAN and the Network Layer defines how to connect multiple LANs. There are other differences and layer-specific responsibilities as well. In most cases, the additional features of Layer 3 come with a cost. It takes more time to examine network addresses and make decisions at this layer. Layer 2 decisions to forward frames take less effort and are faster. Legacy networks generally rely exclusively on Layer 2 devices to define LANs and Layer 3 devices to connect the LANs.

In this chapter you will learn about techniques for using faster Layer 2 devices to subdivide LANs. You will learn ways to create logical networks without using Layer 3 devices and without depending on network layer addresses. Designing networks for performance takes more effort, but it can result in a network that better meets an organization's needs. Many current network applications require real-time or near real-time performance. Networks that get messages to their destinations faster are quickly becoming minimum requirements. You will learn how to use Layer 2 features to meet these minimum requirements.

Chapter 8 Topics

This chapter covers the following topics and concepts:

- What LAN broadcast domains are
- How to split switches into separate segments
- How networks implement IEEE 802.1q
- What resiliency features Layer 2 provides
- Understanding spanning trees and VLAN trunking
- What IEEE 802.3ad link aggregation is
- How to put it all together

Chapter 8 Goals

When you complete this chapter, you will be able to:

- Describe LAN broadcast domains
- Explain how to split switches into separate domains
- Illustrate VLAN designs and interconnections
- Describe Layer 2 network resiliency
- Explain use of spanning trees and other bridging techniques
- Describe IEEE 802.3ad link aggregation

LAN Broadcast Domains

Ethernet is a shared transmission medium network. That means network nodes transmit using the same medium. This behavior is part of Ethernet's core design, along with the technique to share the medium CSMA/CD. Simple Ethernet networks are ones in which every node detects all network traffic. Nodes examine the destination MAC address of each detected frame and receive only frames addressed to its MAC. Each node ignores frames that are addressed to any other MAC. You learned about collision domains in an earlier chapter. Recall that a collision domain is a collection of network nodes that are separated from other nodes by a switch. The switch only forwards frames to the destination segment. Creating separate collision domains reduces the number of devices that receive any frame. This behavior reduces unnecessary traffic and reduces collisions. Both actions increase overall network performance. Fewer frames mean less congestion. Hubs and repeaters connect nodes to a collision domain. Switches and bridges create separate collision domains. Figure 8-1 shows the difference between devices and their effect on collision domains.

Normally, the switches forward frames only to their destination segments. A switch examines the destination MAC address for each frame, looks up the address in its address table, and then forwards the frame to the destination segment. In some cases a sender wants to send a frame to all nodes in a network. One reason to do this would be to discover network resources. A node may send a broadcast message to see what other nodes respond. Ethernet uses a MAC broadcast address to handle broadcast transmissions. A broadcast MAC address is an address that consists of all 1s. A 48-bit MAC broadcast address is represented as FF:FF:FF:FF:FF:FF. Switches that receive a frame with a broadcast MAC address send the frame to all network segments. All nodes that receive broadcast frames in a network belong to the same broadcast domain.

A broadcast domain is the collection of all nodes that are connected to the same set of repeaters, hubs, switches, and bridges. An Ethernet LAN is a broadcast domain. Any node in a network can reach all other nodes in the same broadcast domain by sending a Layer 2 broadcast message. Routers and other higher-layer devices separate networks into separate broadcast domains. Routers do not forward Layer 2 broadcast messages. They examine Layer 3 network addresses to determine each packet's destination. Figure 8-2 shows the difference between collision domains and broadcast domains.

Broadcast domain size and scope are directly related to network performance and security. Broadcast messages are common in many networks. They are used to collect information about nodes in a network. One of the most common Layer 2 protocols to use broadcast transmission is Address Resolution Protocol (ARP). Ethernet networks use ARP to determine a MAC address from a network address. The most common network address ARP resolves is an IPv4 address. (The IPv6 specification provides the ability to resolve Data Link Layer addresses by using NDP without broadcast messages.) Suppose a node wants to send a message to a destination IPv4 network address of 10.0.12.88. The node must know a destination MAC address before it can send the frame to its destination.

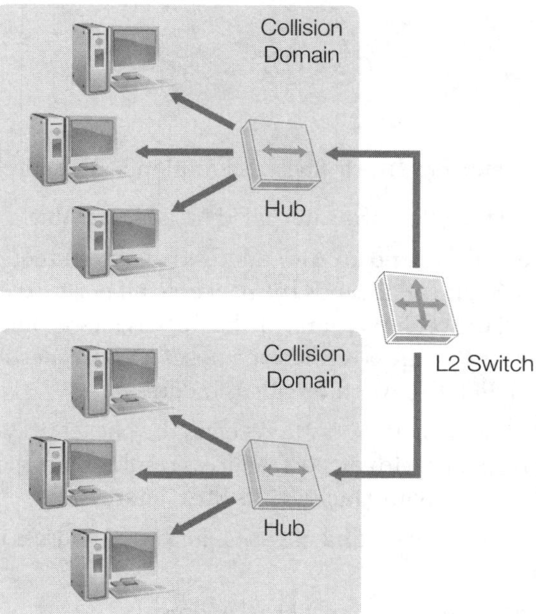

FIGURE 8-1

Collision domains and devices.

In this setup, any device in either collision domain receives the same traffic as any other device in that domain. The switch forwards only traffic that needs to go from one collision domain to the other.

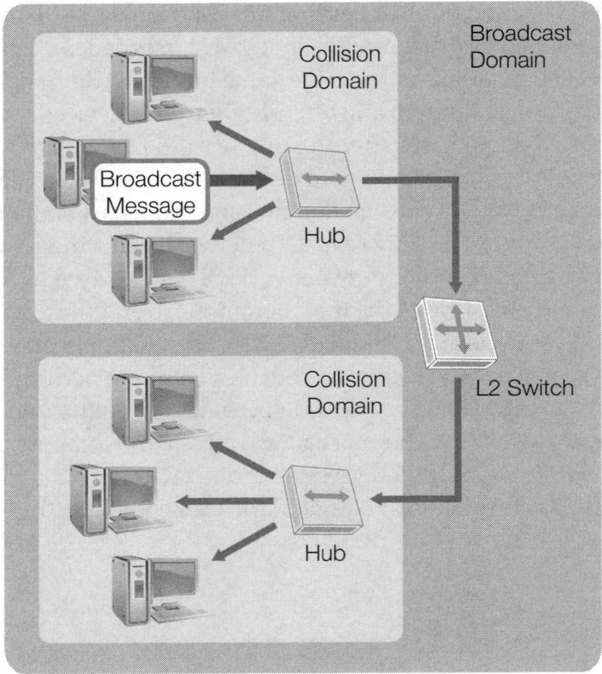

FIGURE 8-2
Collision domains versus broadcast domains.

The node follows these steps to determine the frame's destination MAC address:

1. Look up IPv4 address 10.0.12.88 in the internal MAC address table.
2. If the IPv4 address is not found, send an ARP address resolution request packet for the address 10.0.12.88. The node sends the packet to all ports except the port through which it received the original frame (if the node is forwarding the frame). The node constructs the ARP address resolution packet with the destination MAC address FF:FF:FF:FF:FF:FF (Layer 2 broadcast address).
3. If the node with the IPv4 address 10.0.12.88 receives the packet (it is on the LAN and active), it responds with an ARP address resolution response. The ARP address resolution response includes its MAC address.
4. The node enters the network address and its associated MAC address into its internal address table.
5. The node forwards the frame to the correct MAC address.

All learning network devices, such as learning switches, follow the same series of steps to find the address of unknown nodes. All addresses the node has seen before should be in the internal address table. A node should need to use broadcast transmissions to determine the MAC address only of previously unknown nodes. Figure 8-3 shows the ARP address resolution process using two broadcast domains.

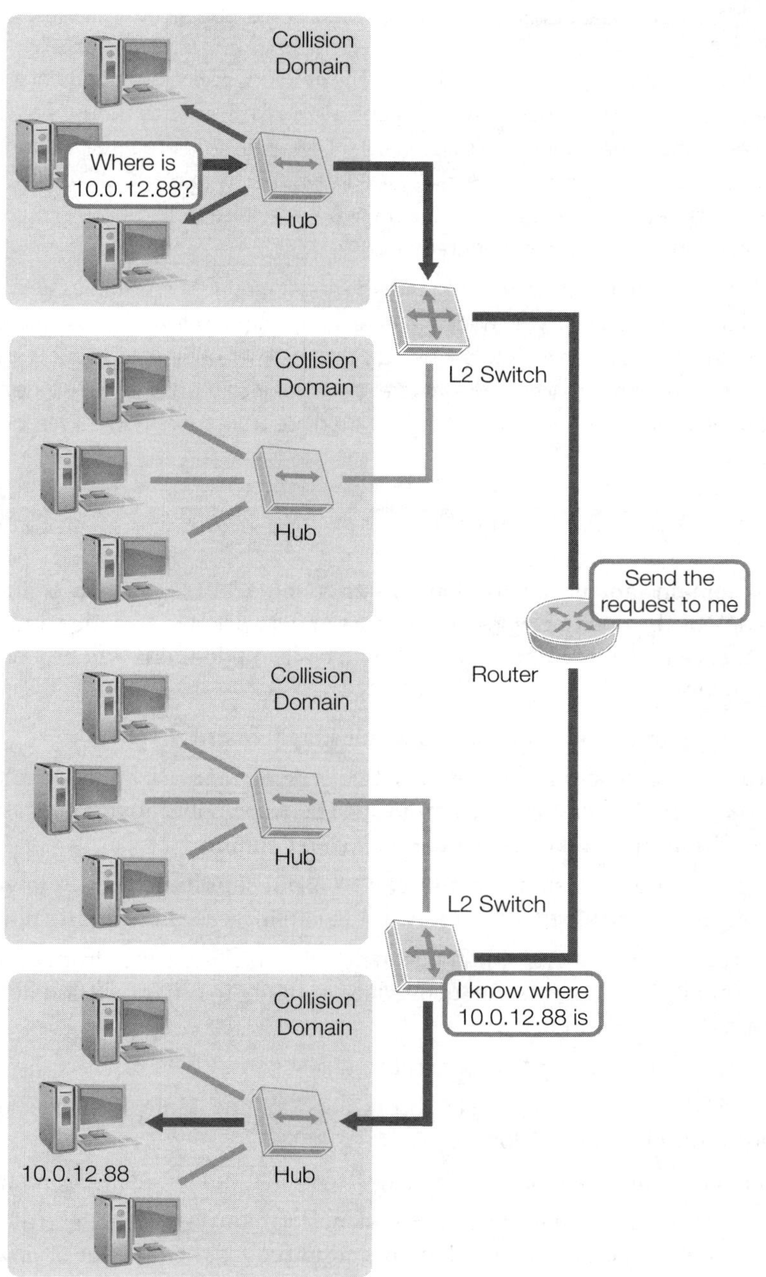

FIGURE 8-3
ARP address resolution using multiple broadcast domains.

FYI

An attacker that can modify the address table for any network device can potentially compromise a network. Modifying the address table with fake entries can cause switches to send frames to the wrong nodes. This action can allow an attacker to intercept traffic and possibly compromise the security of transmitted data. This type of attack is called an ARP table poisoning attack. It is important that network administrators carefully control access to all network devices and configurations.

Likewise, an attacker can masquerade as another device. If a node sends frames with a source MAC address that is not its own, the node pretends to be another device. This is called ASP spoofing. ASP spoofing can make network devices think frames originated at another node. If the network's monitoring devices and software identify the traffic as malicious, they may restrict or block future traffic from the offending node. This is a network's version of identity theft.

Collision domains and broadcast domains are related, but they are two different concepts. Each of the domain types plays a part in network performance and security. The following is a list of different ways in which collision domains and broadcast domains compare:

- Switches separate LANs into different collision domains.
- Separate collision domains increase network performance by reducing frame collisions. Since unicast frames don't travel between collision domains, they can't collide with frames traveling in other collision domains.
- Nodes in separate collision domains can transmit simultaneously. Allowing multiple nodes to transmit without waiting can increase network throughput.
- Separating LANs into multiple collision domains isolates traffic from nodes on other collision domains. Reducing data visibility to other collision domains increases the data's security.
- Routers separate LANs into different broadcast domains.
- Broadcast domains are supersets of collision domains. Many broadcast domains include multiple collision domains.
- Routers limit Layer 2 broadcast messages to individual broadcast domains.
- Broadcast domains can increase network performance by reducing traffic from broadcast messages. Broadcast domains don't reduce the number of broadcast messages, but they do limit the message's scope.

technical TIP

Limit the size of any broadcast domain. Broadcast domains limit how far Layer 2 broadcast messages travel. They also limit the number of nodes that receive Layer 2 broadcast messages. You will learn later in this chapter how to make broadcast domains smaller. However, if a group of workstations and other devices are located close to one another and participate in similar tasks, consider isolating them into their own broadcast domain.

Both collision domains and broadcast domains can affect a network's performance. They can also affect its data and resource security. It is important that network designers consider both domain types as they design networks. Always consider how nodes are physically and logically related. In many networks, devices belong to LANs that correspond to functional use. For example, the accounting department LAN likely has workstations, scanners, and printers that accounting department personnel use. The accounting network is probably also subdivided into subnetworks that correspond to more specific job functions, such as accounts payable and accounts receivable. One design may separate each subnetwork into separate collision domains. Another option is to separate the subnetworks into individual broadcast domains. The difference between the two approaches depends on how frequently nodes need to communicate between subnetworks. Each network has its own unique characteristics and may benefit from a different design than another network. Network designers can increase both the network performance and security by using collision and broadcast domains that work well for their organization's network needs.

Splitting Switches into Separate Segments

All of the ports on a switch belong to the same physical LAN. Recall that switches create multiple collision domains, not multiple physical LANs. In some cases it would be helpful to separate groups of ports within a switch from other ports. Some switches provide the ability to group ports. This ability makes it possible to create two or more virtual LANs (VLANs). A VLAN is a group of devices that communicate with one another as if they were part of a single broadcast domain. VLAN separation occurs at Layer 2, unlike formal Layer 3 broadcast domain separation.

VLANs give network designers the ability to create multiple groups of associated network nodes without having to use Layer 3 routers. Layer 2 VLANs provide much of the flexibility of Layer 3 broadcast domains without the additional performance overhead. Figure 8-4 shows a network with multiple VLANs.

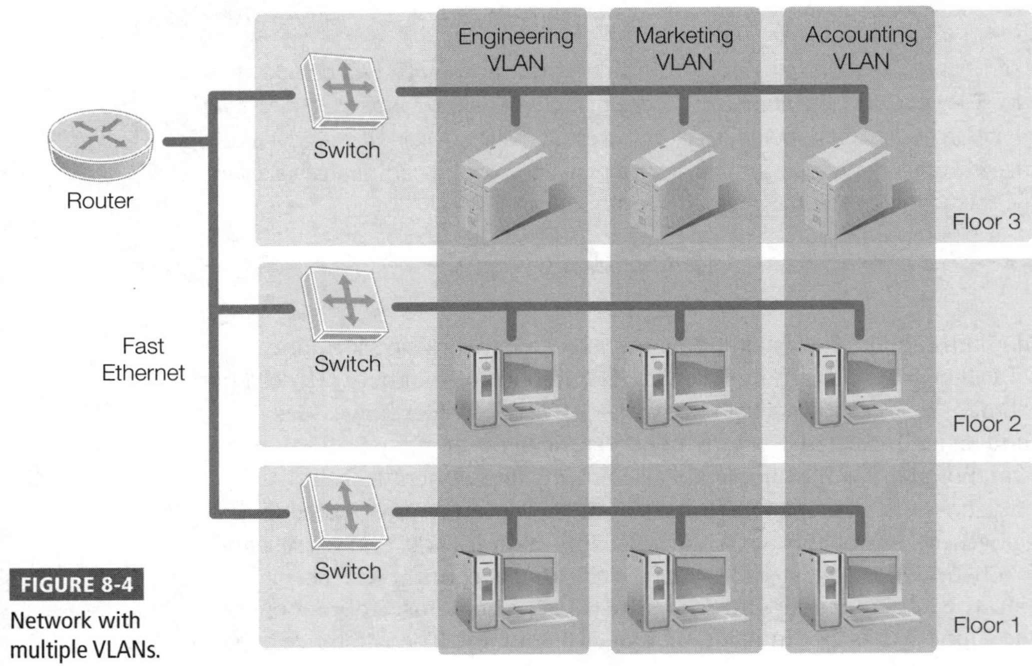

FIGURE 8-4
Network with multiple VLANs.

Many of today's Layer 2 switches support VLANs. In fact, most of the switches define a single VLAN in the default configuration. The standard configuration is for all ports to belong to the default VLAN. The process of creating multiple VLANs consists of removing one or more ports from the default VLAN and creating another VLAN for desired ports. The ability to create multiple VLANs and associate ports with each one makes it possible to create virtual groups of nodes. VLANs give network designers the ability to create virtual broadcast domains. Switches with VLAN support can treat each node as a separate entity or can group nodes together into VLANs. Network designers can add nodes to a VLAN regardless of their physical location.

> **NOTE**
> Many organizations use project management techniques to track and control work products. Projects have beginning and ending dates, and workers often move on to other projects when one finishes. Frequent changes in project focus may mean that workers change their group memberships. Creating VLANs for the duration of a project makes it possible to group project teams together easily and with minimal effort or disruption. While this ability is not a crucial benefit, it does make project team transitions smoother.

Membership in a LAN means a node connects to one of the LAN's devices. Joining a LAN simply means the device connects to a switch or a Layer 1 or Layer 2 device that connects to the LAN. Software controls membership in a VLAN. Layer 2 configuration software defines VLANs and VLAN members. This flexibility makes a dynamic workforce easier to manage and support. It is a lot easier to change a worker's VLAN assignment than it is to move their workstation or re-route patch cables.

IEEE 802.1q and VLAN Design

The concept of creating VLANs is fairly easy to describe. Implementing VLANs also can be straightforward as long as all of the affected devices agree on the details. Switches have to use the same rules to separate traffic between different VLANs. In the early days of LAN segregation, several specifications emerged. Cisco developed their Inter-Switch Link (ISL) protocol and 3Com produced the Virtual LAN Trunk (VLT) protocol. These protocols were proprietary and were primarily supported only on the respective vendors' hardware.

IEEE 802.1q

IEEE wanted to publish a standard that would provide VLAN functionality across multiple vendors' hardware. The IEEE 802 standards committee established the IEEE 802.1 working group to study the problem, along with other LAN and internetworking issues. The 802.1q standard describes virtual LANs. Like other IEEE standards, 802.1q has seen many changes since it was introduced in 1998. The current standard, 802.1q–2011, includes many extensions and additional features over the original standard. Table 8-1 lists some of the more important milestones in the evolution of the 802.1q standard.

Configuring VLANs within a single switch doesn't change the frames that pass through the switch. The switch simply views a VLAN as a group of ports. Traffic flows to other ports in the same VLAN. In this mode, VLANs operate much like Layer 3 subnetworks in which all devices connect to a central device. When VLANs are spread across multiple switches, the sending switch has to add some information to identify the VLAN to the destination switch. IEEE 802.1q and its predecessor, ISL, use explicit tagging to identify VLANs. Each frame that travels between switches can include a tag field that identifies the VLAN to which it belongs. ISL used an external tag. ISL does not modify the internal structure of the Ethernet frame. The 802.1q standard inserts the tag in the Ethernet

TABLE 8-1 Select milestones of the IEEE 802.1q standard.

STANDARD	DESCRIPTION
802.1q–1998	Original virtual LAN (VLAN standard)
802.1s–2002	Multiple Spanning Trees
802.1v–2001	VLAN classification by protocol and port
802.1q–2005	VLAN bridges (Includes 802.1q–1998, 802.1s, 802.1u, 802.1v, and P802.1z standards)
802.1qat–2010	Stream Reservation Protocol (SRP)
802.1qau–2010	Congestion management
802.1q–2011	VLAN bridges (Includes 802.1q–2005 and 802.1ad/ag/ah/aj/ak/ap/Qac/Qaw/Qay standards)

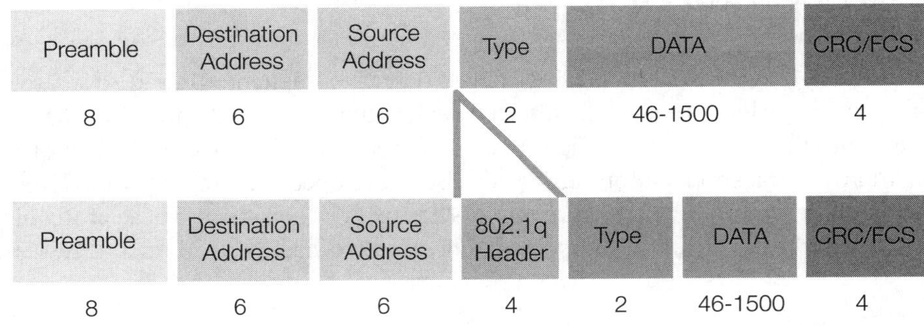

FIGURE 8-5

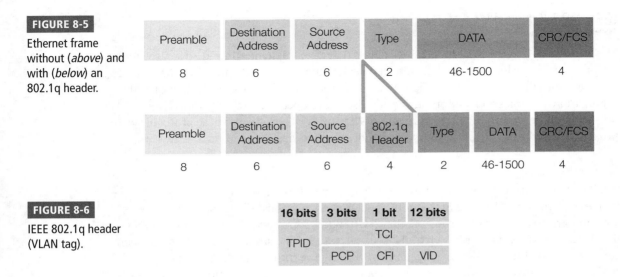

Ethernet frame without (*above*) and with (*below*) an 802.1q header.

16 bits	3 bits	1 bit	12 bits
TPID	TCI		
	PCP	CFI	VID

FIGURE 8-6

IEEE 802.1q header (VLAN tag).

frame, changing its overall format. Since the VLAN tag is most useful in the context of a MAC address, 802.1q places the tag immediately after the MAC address in the frame. Figure 8-5 shows an Ethernet frame without and with the 802.1q header.

The 802.1q header is a 32-bit field that contains several data items. The first 16 bits are the Tag Protocol Identifier (TPID). The second 16 bits are the Tag Control Information (TCI). The TCI itself is made up of three fields, the Priority Code Point (PCP), Canonical Format Indicator (CFI), and VLAN Identifier (VID). Figure 8-6 shows the format of the 802.1q header (VLAN tag).

The 802.1q header contains these fields:

- **Tag Protocol Identifier (TPID)**—16-bit field contains the value 0x8100 to identify a frame as an IEEE 802.1q tagged frame
- **Tag Control Identifier (TCI)**—16-bit field that is made up of three individual fields:
  - **Priority Code Point (PCP)**—3-bit field that specifies the priority of a frame. Values refer to IEEE 802.1p priority standard and can range from 0 to 7. The lowest priority is 1 and the highest priority is 7. A value of 0 represents "best effort." Networks can use PCP to set the priority of different types of traffic.
  - **Canonical Format Indicator (CFI)**—1-bit field to indicate whether the MAC address is in canonical form. Canonical form means the MAC address is transmitted with the least significant bit first. A 0 in CFI indicates that the MAC address is stored in canonical form. Ethernet always uses canonical form. Some other networks, specifically Token Ring, use non-canonical form. CFI would be set to 1 for Token Ring networks.

- **VLAN Identifier (VID)**—12-bit field to identify the VLAN to which a frame belongs. A VID value of 0x000 indicates the frame does not belong to any VLAN. Frames with a VID of 0x000 are called priority frames since the VLAN information only defines the frame's priority.

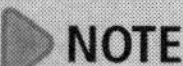

NOTE

IEEE 802.3 sets the maximum Ethernet frame size to 1518 bytes. IEEE 802.1q extends each Ethernet frame by 32 bits, or 4 bytes. That means VLAN tagged frames may exceed the IEEE 802.3 standards. To accommodate the additional VLAN tag, IEEE 802.3ac extended the maximum Ethernet frame size by 4 bytes to 1522 bytes.

VLANs can restrict access to network resources without having to physically move or isolate the resources. VLAN tags make it easy to add or remove nodes to VLANs. VLANs provide network designers and administrators with the tools to reduce the size of broadcast domains and isolate resources from unrelated nodes. They can do all this using Layer 2 devices and MAC addresses. Since VLANs operate at Layer 2, traffic is forwarded more quickly than if the network relied on Layer 3 routing.

VLAN Design

In many networks, VLANs duplicate IP subnetworks. The VLAN provides the speed, and the IP subnetwork provides the flexibility. IP subnetworks often exist to group nodes together that share some common characteristics. For example, the shipping subnetwork may include several workstations, printers, scanners, and scales that shipping department personnel use to ship products. There may be several different shipping locations in the organization. Network designers may want to group all of the shipping nodes into a single subnetwork regardless of where they are physically located. VLANs provide network designers with the ability to do this at Layer 2.

While the shipping department nodes may all have network addresses within the same IP network or subnetwork, they can also all belong to the same VLAN. VLANs do not have to map directly to IP networks. In fact, there is no requirement that VLANs are even similar to IP networks. VLAN membership depends on the

technical TIP

Adding VLANs to your network requires more administrator effort than when using default switch settings. Replacing a failed default switch just requires swapping the hardware and plugging the cables into the new switch. If you use VLANs, you have to enter the configuration settings into the new switch. That means you have to have the current settings in a document that the person making the change can access and understand. Make sure you have procedures in place to document all VLAN settings and all changes to the settings. Good change control procedures will help you keep the information you need to recover up to date. Some switches make it easy to save settings in a file that you can just read into the new switch. Other manufacturers require you to reenter the VLAN settings manually. Know how to replace a switch and enter VLAN settings.

organization's needs. VLANs provide the ability to group nodes by several different criteria. Many newer networks determine VLAN membership by node use. In fact, IEEE 802.1v–2001 standard (rolled up into 802.1q–2005) supports VLAN membership based on protocol and port. This means organizations can define VLANs for VoIP, video conferencing, streaming media, and any other type of traffic. Isolating traffic by VLAN, and setting the priority by traffic type, makes it possible to tune a network for best performance.

VLANs support the practice of grouping nodes by logical association. In fact, that's one of the main reasons for using VLANs. Logically grouping nodes together may mean that workstations, printers, scanners, or other devices may belong to the same VLAN but may not be physically near one another. This physical distribution means that some VLANs may need to span more than one switch. It is a common practice to connect nodes to the nearest available switch. This practice reduces the physical cabling requirements. It is possible to create VLANs across multiple switches to help minimize the cables required to connect nodes to the network.

Connect switches using cables connected to a **trunk port**. A trunk port is a port on a switch that allows VLAN traffic to pass through it. Two switches that are connected by a cable running between two trunk ports can create VLANs spread across the two switches. This type of connection is called a **trunk link**. The switches can still forward frames to the correct destination as long as the switches know where the rest of the VLAN's devices are connected. Suppose a VLAN spans two switches. A switch receives a frame with a destination that is not connected to the switch. Its address tables indicate that the destination is reachable on the trunk port. That means the destination is on another switch. The current switch sends the frame with the VLAN tag to the other switch. The destination switch directs the frame to its destination. Using this method, multiple VLANs can span switches. The VLAN tag inside each frame contains the VLAN ID to identify the VLAN membership to the destination switch. Figure 8-7 shows two VLANs spread across two switches.

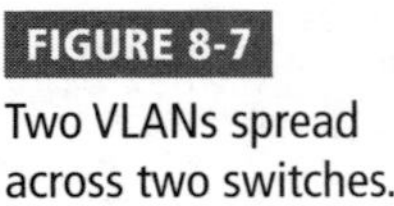

FIGURE 8-7

Two VLANs spread across two switches.

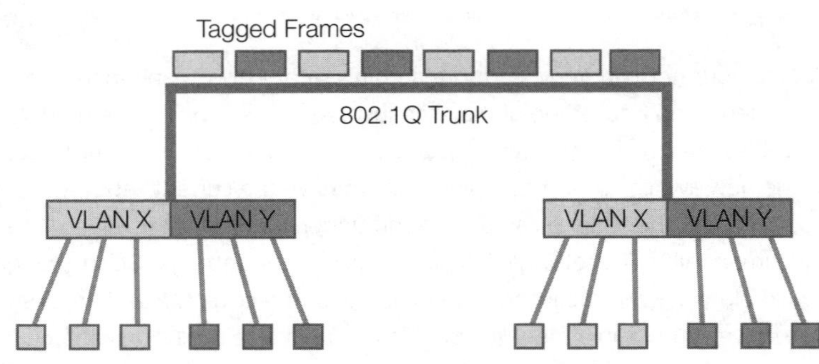

technical TIP

Protocol-based VLAN membership can help network designers segregate different types of LAN traffic. For example, suppose a network carries VoIP and IPX traffic. Such a network can encounter latency issues when mixing the different protocols. Protocol-based VLANs can help segregate the different types of traffic regardless of the originating device. One strategy would be to send all of the IPX traffic to a Layer 3 device for further handling. This action could allow VoIP traffic to flow through the network with less congestion.

VLAN Membership

VLANs operate in and between Layer 2 switches. Nodes don't technically belong to VLANs; switch ports belong to VLANs. The advantage of defining VLANs at Layer 2 is that VLANs are protocol independent. Nodes can send network messages using any higher layer protocols. The switches ensure that the unicast and broadcast messages are forwarded only to other ports in the VLAN. Higher layer devices, such as routers, must handle traffic that flows outside of the originating VLAN. There are two main methods of specifying VLAN membership. Ports can join VLANs based on static or dynamic rules.

- **Static**—An administrator assigns specific ports in one or more switches to each VLAN. Any device that connects to a port "joins" the VLAN to which the port is assigned. The device belongs to the VLAN until an administrator changes the port membership or the device physically connects to another port.
- **Dynamic**—Some switches provide support for dynamic VLAN membership. The VLAN to which a port belongs depends on one of the following criteria:
  - A VLAN Membership Policy Server (VMPS) in supported Cisco switches contains a database that maps devices to VLANs based on the device's MAC address or the currently logged-in user ID. A VMPS allows devices to join VLANs regardless of their physical location.
  - Some switches support protocol-based VLAN assignment. A port's VLAN membership is based on the frame's protocol. This technique allows VLANs to specialize in transporting different types of traffic. Each protocol can have its own VLAN.

Layer 2 Network Resiliency

Today's applications rely on network services more than at any time in the past. It is common for a network to support streaming video and audio, VoIP conversations, and large, time-sensitive file transfers. It is important that these networks be able to handle errors and faults and still deliver content. A network that can survive one or more

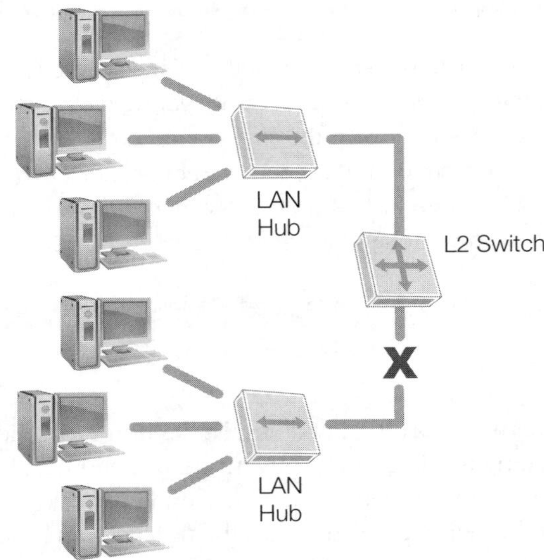

FIGURE 8-8
Non-resilient network.

faults and still support communication is a resilient network. Such networks are also called fault tolerant. A normal, non-resilient network is one that may fail when any component fails. Non-resilient networks generally have central devices and only single paths between critical nodes. A critical node failure or media failure can segment the network or even make it unusable. Figure 8-8 shows the effect of a network that is not resilient.

Networks that deliver time-sensitive content cannot afford to fail when one component fails. For example, cruise ships use networks to deliver digital television and video to their passengers. If the network goes down, many passengers will lose their television and video service. While this doesn't sound like a big problem, the cruise operator likely will receive many complaints and have to offer concessions to make up for the inconvenience.

technical TIP

Many networks in the past have relied on Layer 3 or higher layers to provide resilience. Routers can make more sophisticated routing decisions and possibly work around failed links or hardware. While this option does work, it takes far longer to route traffic using Layer 3 routing. Layer 2 devices are far faster than higher layer devices. They can react to changing network issues faster and reduce latency. However, network designers are finding that flatter network designs, as opposed to deep hierarchies, result in faster, more resilient networks. Today's network diagrams don't look much like organizational charts anymore. But they get the job done. Layer 2 provides several options to ensure frames aren't delayed due to link or hardware problems. But the network designers must consider resiliency from the very start.

Such concessions cost the cruise operator money and can be directly related to the network outage. Another example could be the impact of a hospital's emergency room network going down. The inability to access the network could lead to delayed or inaccurate diagnosis in a critical situation. Any loss that is a result of the network problem could expose the hospital to very large liabilities. Again, there is a cost associated with network outages.

Resilient networks address the availability issue using several methods. Many networks use several of these methods to ensure the content makes it to its destination with as little disruption as possible. Common resiliency methods include:

- Multiple connections between critical nodes
- Redundant critical devices (switches, etc.)
- Quality of service monitoring to react to service slowdowns
- Redirection to avoid congestion
- Analysis of the most efficient use of active connections

One of the most common failures in a network is the medium itself. Any break in the medium between nodes disconnects those nodes. A common practice for critical nodes is to use two network connections. This practice is most common for network devices, such as switches. A node that connects to a network using two connections will still be connected to the network if one connection fails. Figure 8-9 shows three switches that are connected using redundant links.

Any single link in the network illustrated in Figure 8-9 can fail, and the network continues to operate. Every switch is accessible two ways. This network design is more resilient than a purely hierarchical design where a single link failure would segment the network. There is a problem with redundant links. A network design that includes

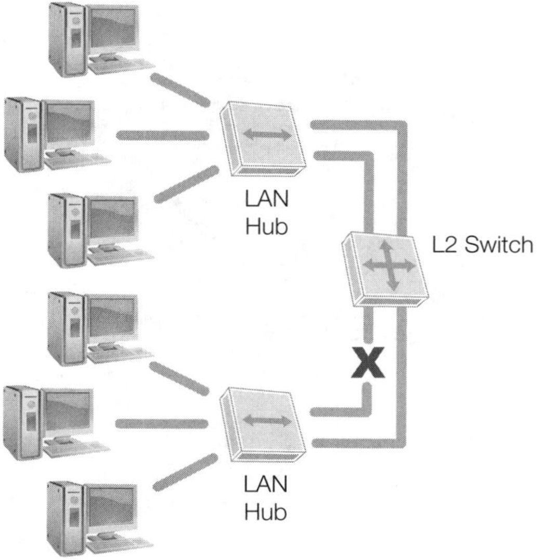

FIGURE 8-9
Redundant links connecting switches.

multiple links between nodes can confuse devices and cause unstable address tables. Multiple paths between switches create a situation called a **switching loop**. Suppose node A in Figure 8-9 sends a Layer 2 broadcast message. Switch 1 sends the message to all other switches. Each switch sends the message to all the other switches (even the switches that have already sent the broadcast message). The result is a **broadcast storm**. A broadcast storm is a situation in which broadcast messages get forwarded and replicated to a point that the network cannot handle all of the traffic. If nothing is done to stop the storm, it eventually will crash the network or make it unusable. Figure 8-10 shows how a broadcast message can cause a broadcast storm.

Switching loops can cause real network problems if they aren't handled. You will learn about a family of protocols in the next section that address the problems with switching loops. For now, just be aware that switching loops provide one type of resiliency.

Another type of resiliency is to place redundant critical devices in a network. Any critical device can become a **single point of failure (SPOF)**. Any SPOF causes a system outage or service disruption if the device fails. Having redundant critical devices can help remove SPOFs and reduce the impact of any single failure. Of course, adding more devices increases the administrator workload. Multiple devices mean more effort to keep configurations current and accurate. Network designers also must address how nodes share the workload when all nodes are operating. Redundant nodes may simply wait in standby mode, or they may participate in normal operation. Each device type may require different configurations to serve as redundant devices. For example, redundant switches can participate in normal network operation. When all switches are operating, the redundant devices can help distribute the traffic and avoid congestion. Redundant network hardware increases the number of connections in a network but provides a more resilient network.

FIGURE 8-10

Broadcast storm in a switching loop.

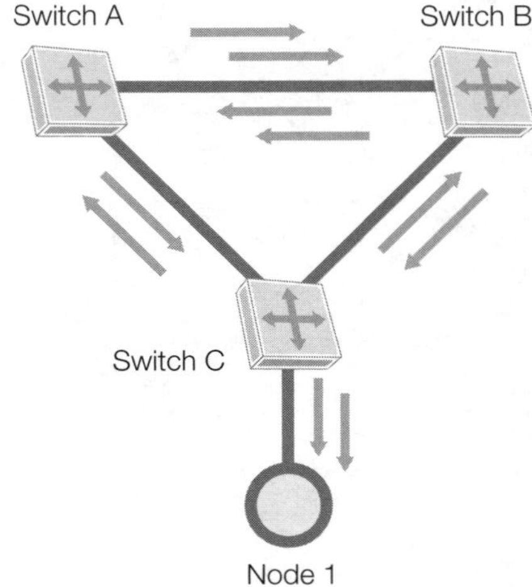

TABLE 8-2 IEEE 802.1p priority levels.

PCP	PRIORITY	ABBREVIATION	DESCRIPTION
1	0 (lowest)	BK	Background
0	1	BE	Best Effort
2	2	EE	Excellent Effort
3	3	CA	Critical Applications
4	4	VI	Video < 100 ms Latency
5	5	VO	Voice < 10 ms Latency
6	6	IC	Internetwork Control
7	7 (highest)	NC	Network Control

Resilience doesn't always refer to service interruptions due to failures. In some cases, congestion or other factors may reduce network performance. The performance reduction may be severe enough that critical traffic cannot reach its destination in a timely manner. In the case of video streams, a congested network may result in jumpy video or video that frequently freezes. Poor quality video is frustrating to watch and may result in loss of business to the providing organization. It is important that the network be able to react to current conditions and deliver content in a timely fashion. VLANs provide another feature that helps to optimize network performance.

Recall that IEEE 802.1q headers include a PCP (priority code point) field. This field allows applications to define the priority of each frame. The PCP refers to priority levels defined by the IEEE 802.1p task group. IEEE 802.1p is not a standard, but it is a recommendation that defines how Layer 2 devices should expedite traffic based on priority. This recommendation was included in the IEEE 802.1d–2004, and later in the 802.1q–2005 standards. 802.1p provides a method of implementing a service similar to quality of service (QoS) in Layer 2. True QoS is a Layer 3 service. The 802.1p task group technique is also called class of service (CoS).

Devices that implement 802.1p ensure that higher-priority frames get to their destinations sooner than frames with lower priorities. 802.1p compliant devices read the PCP field and forward traffic based on the priority value. Each manufacturer can handle different priorities according to their own designs. There is no standard for priority assignments. IEEE recommends the 802.1p priorities listed in Table 8-2.

The overall goal for today's Ethernet networks is to ensure sub-second delivery for network traffic. The use of Layer 2 devices can help decrease overall latency and increase throughput. Networks that add redundant critical devices and links and implement 802.1p priorities can ensure network performance meets the demands of real-time applications.

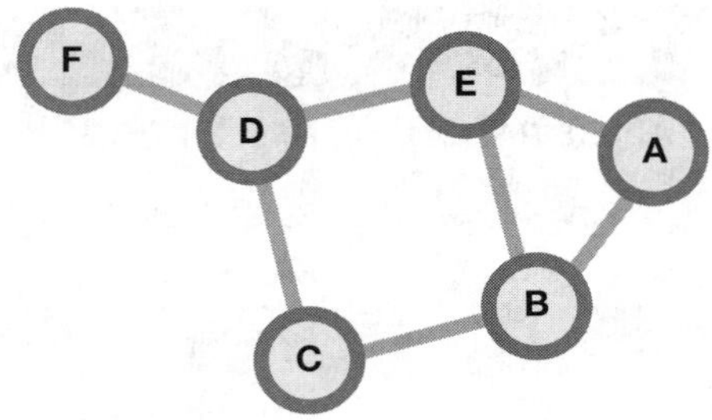

FIGURE 8-11
Graph.

STP, RSTP, and VLAN Trunking

You learned earlier that adding multiple links between switches increases network resilience. If one link becomes unusable, the switches can still communicate using other links. You also learned that unmanaged redundant links can result in a broadcast storm. How can network designers enjoy the benefits of redundant links without risking broadcast storms? The answer lies in using a management protocol that detects switching loops and stops switches from creating broadcast storms.

Graphs and Spanning Trees

The approach to detecting switching loops uses **spanning trees** to determine possible paths through the network. A network diagram includes the same components as a mathematical structure called a **graph**. A graph is a mathematical representation of a set of objects. The graph represents a collection of objects that are connected with links (see Figure 8-11).

In mathematics, the objects in a graph are called vertices or nodes. The links between objects are called edges or lines. Depicting networks as graphs provides several advantages. Graphs are understood well in the mathematics community. There have been many research efforts involving graphs and how their objects are related. From

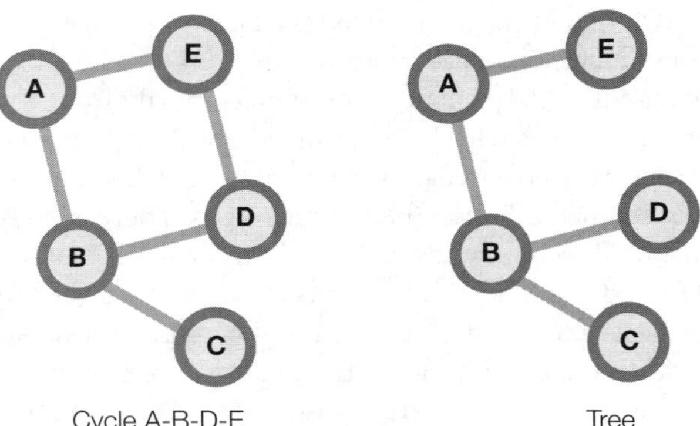

FIGURE 8-12
Graph cycle, tree, and path length.

a network perspective, graphs help determine alternate paths between any two nodes. There are several important concepts to understand when using graphs to represent networks, shown in Figure 8-12.

- **Cycle**—A cycle in a graph is any collection of nodes that are connected by links to form a closed chain. In other words, nodes are connected in a ring topology.
- **Tree**—A graph in which all nodes are connected without any cycles. A star topology would be a tree.
- **Path length**—The number of edges that form a path between any two nodes.

Graphs are useful in networks because they provide an easy way to represent how traffic flows. Suppose your network includes multiple redundant links. Representing the network as a graph gives network designers access to formal methods to calculate potential alternate paths. A spanning tree is a path that starts at one node and visits all of the other nodes exactly once (see Figure 8-13). There are normally several spanning trees for each graph. Each spanning tree represents a separate route between nodes. If a link that connects two nodes fails, all the network has to do is select another spanning tree to get frames to their destination.

Spanning Tree Protocol (STP)

Layer 2 switching is becoming more and more important to high-performance networks. Networks that carry streaming video and other time-sensitive content can't wait for higher layer sophistication. Time-sensitive content needs low-layer forwarding. One of the first obstacles to creating resilient Layer 2 networks is the possibility of broadcast storms. Switch manufacturers realized they needed a way to detect and avoid broadcast storms. They chose to use graph theory to address the problem. Many of today's switches and bridges have the ability to dynamically discover multiple spanning trees in a network. They can tell the difference between a cycle and a tree. Just this ability enables Layer 2 devices to stop broadcast storms.

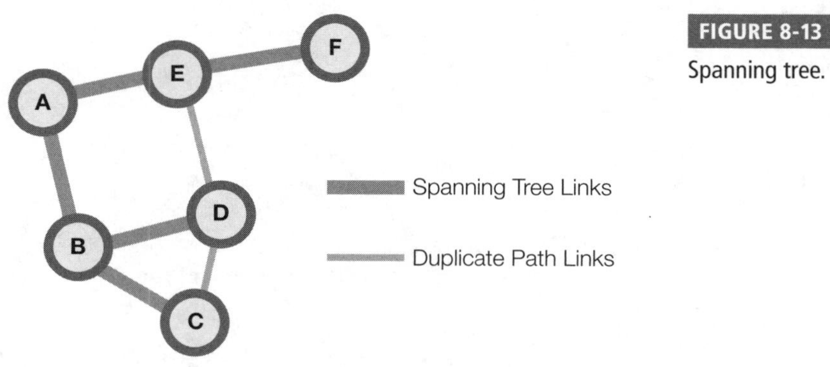

FIGURE 8-13
Spanning tree.

IEEE published the 802.1d standard in 1990 that formally defined how MAC layer bridges operate. Today's switches and bridges are effectively the same devices. The terms are often used interchangeably. The original standard included the Spanning Tree Protocol (STP). In STP, bridges exchange information about detected paths in the network. These messages, called bridge protocol data units (BPDU), can be either of two different types.

- **Configuration**—BPDU that contains detected link information used to compute a spanning tree
- **Topology change notification (TCN)**—BPDU that tells other bridges that something has changed. A change could be a switch or link failure, or a newly detected switch.

STP configuration takes several steps. Each step refines the spanning tree to determine the best path through the network. Bridges (or switches) in a network follow these steps to configure STP:

1. Identify the root bridge.
2. Identify the root port.
3. Elect designated ports.
4. Block other ports.

The first step is to identify a **root bridge** (see Figure 8-14). A root bridge is the first node in the spanning tree. Each bridge or switch has a Bridge ID that consists of a 2-byte priority and the device's MAC address. The default priority value for bridges is hexadecimal FF, or 32768. A lower priority value means the bridge gets a higher priority in the root bridge identification process. In the initial pass, each bridge sets the root bridge ID to its own bridge ID. Then it sends the BPDU broadcast with this bridge ID. Each bridge compares received bridge IDs with its own and replaces its own bridge ID if the received one is lower. Eventually, all devices agree on the lowest bridge ID. That device becomes the root bridge.

FIGURE 8-14
Root bridge identification.

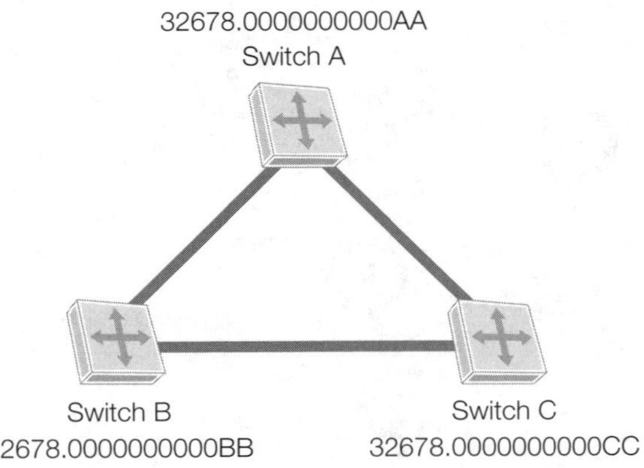

TABLE 8-3 STP path cost by link speed.

LINK SPEED	STP COST
10 Mbps	100
100 Mbps	19
1 Gbps	4
10 Gbps	2

Once all the other switches know who the root bridge is, they need to figure out where they are in relation to the root. Each switch must determine its **root port (RP)**. The root port is the port on any switch that leads to the root bridge and also has the lowest **root path cost**. The root path cost is the accumulated cost of all the links in a path leading to the root bridge. Calculating the path cost starts with assigning a value, or cost, with each link type. The cost of a link is based on its speed. Faster links have lower costs. IEEE 802.1d uses the path costs in Table 8-3.

The root bridge starts the process. Each switch in the network follows these steps to find its own root port:

1. The root bridge sends out a BPDU on each port with a root path cost of 0.
2. Each neighbor receives the BPDU and adds the STP cost (from Table 8-3) to the root path cost for that port.
3. The neighbor then sends out a BPDU on each port to its neighbors.
4. Other neighbors add the STP cost based on the received port speed and sends BPDUs to their neighbors.
5. Each switch keeps track of the lowest root path cost. The port on which the switch received the BPDU with the lowest root path cost becomes the root port. The root port is the best port on the switch to reach the root bridge.

All ports on all switches that are not root ports are candidates for **designated ports (DP)**. A designated port is the port to a network segment with the lowest root path cost. A RP directs traffic toward the root bridge, and a DP directs traffic away from the root bridge toward the leaves of the tree. For each network segment, the DP is the port on the switch connected to the segment with the lowest root path cost. Figure 8-15 shows the process of finding RPs and DPs.

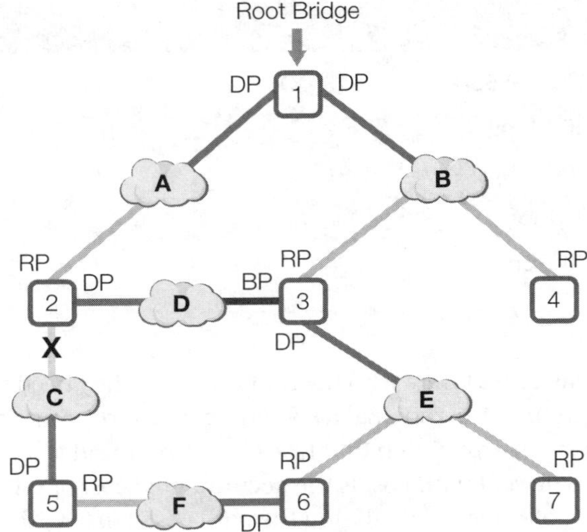

FIGURE 8-15
Finding root ports (RP) and designated ports (DP).

Finally, the switches have enough information to break switching loops and complete the spanning tree. All ports that are not RPs or DPs are blocked. Blocked ports are not used to forward traffic, but they can still receive BPDUs. Blocking ports that are not RP or DP stops broadcast storms in a network. STP defines the port modes listed in Table 8-4.

The STP spanning tree calculation is not a static procedure. Switches will recalculate the spanning tree any time the following events occur:

- A new switch is detected
- A switch fails
- A link fails

TABLE 8-4 STP port modes.

STP PORT MODE	DESCRIPTION
Disabled	• Port is shut down
Blocking	• Does not forward frames • Receives BPDUs
Listening	• Does not forward frames • Sends and receives BPDUs
Learning	• Does not forward frames • Sends and receives BPDUs • Learns new MAC addresses
Forwarding	• Forwards frames • Sends and receives BPDUs • Learn new MAC addresses

technical TIP

Don't assume STP automatically determines the best spanning tree for a network. It is possible that the slowest switch becomes the root bridge! Don't rely on default bridge priorities. Carefully examine your network, and raise the priority (lower the priority value) of the best switches. Good candidates for root bridges are devices that are fast, stable, and close to higher layer routers. Use priority values to specify the best candidates for the primary root bridge and at least one alternate root bridge.

Rapid Spanning Tree Protocol (RSTP)

Frequent network changes can cause delays in calculating new spanning trees. Topology changes can routinely take 30 to 50 seconds to resolve. Convergence time refers to the amount of time it takes for switches to agree on a new spanning tree after topology changes. IEEE introduced a variation to STP in 2001. The IEEE 802.1w standard modified the convergence behavior to make spanning tree convergence much faster. The new standard, called Rapid Spanning Tree Protocol (RSTP), resolves topology changes within 6 seconds by default. It can also respond to link failures within a few milliseconds. This type of performance is necessary to support real-time network applications.

RSTP defines an interactive exchange between switches to converge faster than STP. RSTP provides the ability to define edge ports. Edge ports are ports that do not connect to other switches. Edge ports don't participate in spanning tree calculation. RSTP defines a handshake method to switch synchronization. After the root bridge is identified, the spanning tree is built by each group of switches negotiating at each level. The spanning tree develops as the levels cascade downward away from the root bridge. All other ports are in blocking mode while the higher level switches are negotiating. The result is a faster convergence than STP. RSTP also defines different port roles to make failed link recovery much faster than STP. Table 8-5 lists the RSTP port roles.

TABLE 8-5 RSTP port roles.

RSTP PORT ROLE	DESCRIPTION
Root Port (RP)	Same as STP (802.1d)
Alternate Port	Port with an alternate path to the root bridge
Designated Port (DP)	Same as STP (802.1d)
Backup Port	Alternate port to a segment that connects to the root bridge

technical TIP

Some vendors did not wait for IEEE to publish a standard for VLAN spanning trees. Cisco developed Per-VLAN Spanning Tree (PVST) and PVST+. The main difference between the two protocols is that PVST uses Cisco's ISL protocol and PVST+ uses 802.1q encapsulation. Cisco switches use PVST+ as a default protocol and cannot communicate with many other non-Cisco hardware.

Juniper Networks developed the VLAN Spanning Tree Protocol (VSTP) to provide compatibility with Cisco's PVST protocol. PVST configures a separate spanning tree for each VLAN and makes it possible for Juniper Networks EX switches to include Cisco switches in the same LAN.

Multiple Spanning Tree Protocol (MSTP)

IEEE extended RSTP to include VLANs. The IEEE 802.1s standard included VLANs in the spanning tree protocol. A spanning tree that maps to one or more VLANs is called a **multiple spanning tree (MST)**. STP and RSTP don't segregate ports by VLANs. IEEE 802.1s provides the ability to define spanning trees for either individual VLANs or for groups of VLANs. It also allows network designers to define possible alternate paths within each spanning tree. Each group of VLANs is assigned to an instance of a multiple spanning tree, called a **multiple spanning tree instance (MSTI)**. The **Multiple Spanning Tree Protocol (MSTP)** defines several data structures to create and maintain spanning trees:

- **MST region**—Switches belong to the same region when they share the same attributes
  - MST configuration name
  - MST configuration revision
  - VLAN mapping—which VLANs are represented in this MST
- **Common Spanning Tree (CST)**—A common tree that includes all switches, regardless of MST regions. CSTs provide backward compatibility with STP and RSTP.
- **Internal Spanning Tree (IST)**—Spanning tree that covers an entire MST.
- **MSL Instance (MSTI)**—Group of VLANs assigned to a MST.

VLAN Trunking

Spanning trees make Layer 2 resilient networks realistic. VLANs make it possible to segregate traffic and tune a network for the best performance. Recall that administrators can assign ports to VLANs using static or dynamic methods. Regardless of the methods chosen, some VLAN traffic must travel from one switch to another to reach its destination.

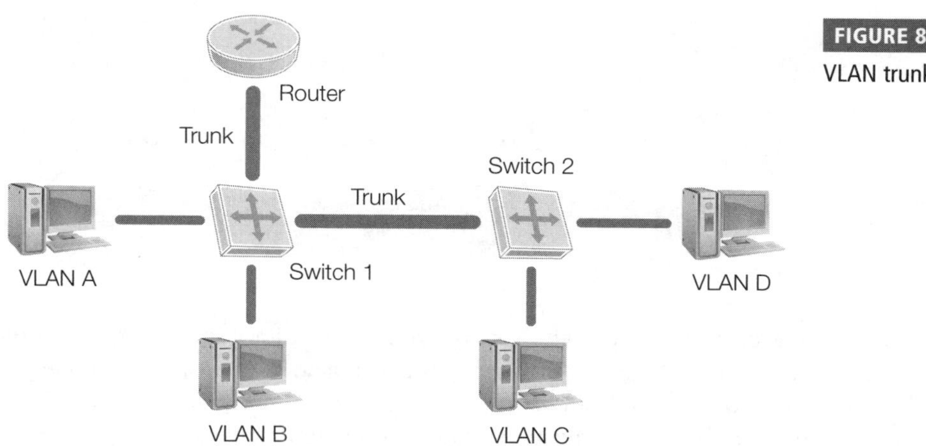

FIGURE 8-16
VLAN trunking.

The process of forwarding traffic within a VLAN from one switch to another is called **VLAN trunking**. A trunk link is a connection between two switches that transports traffic between the switches. VLAN trunking doesn't just forward packets between switches for a single VLAN. A trunk link may transport traffic from several different VLANs.

The VLAN Trunking Protocol (VTP) is a Cisco proprietary protocol that publishes VLAN definitions to the whole network. It defines how switches communicate among themselves about trunking configuration and traffic. Switches could use separate links for each VLAN, but that solution would not be very scalable. Adding more VLANs would require additional ports. Switches have a limited number of ports, and dedicating ports to individual VLANs would eventually require more switches in the network. Transporting multiple VLAN traffic across single trunk links preserves ports and reduces the hardware required for a network, as shown in Figure 8-16.

IEEE 802.3ad Link Aggregation

VLANs provide the ability to segregate network traffic and increase performance. They make it possible to isolate certain types of traffic to their own collection of ports. The idea is to remove other types of traffic that can cause congestion and collisions. For example, an organization may choose to create a VLAN that only transports streaming video content. Creating a separate VLAN and using dynamic membership by protocol removes video traffic from other types of traffic. But in some cases even the entire bandwidth of a single link is not enough. Another important standard, IEEE 802.3ad, defines a standard method to combine multiple physical links together that can be used as a single logical link. This process is called **link aggregation** or **link bundling** and is shown in Figure 8-17.

NOTE
IEEE 802.3ad was originally introduced in 2000. It standardized work that many manufacturers had done to offer proprietary solutions. The standard was transferred to the 802.1 working group in 2008 to resolve discrepancies in protocol stack standard placement. Prior to its move link, aggregation defined a protocol stack standard that operated below 802.1 standards.

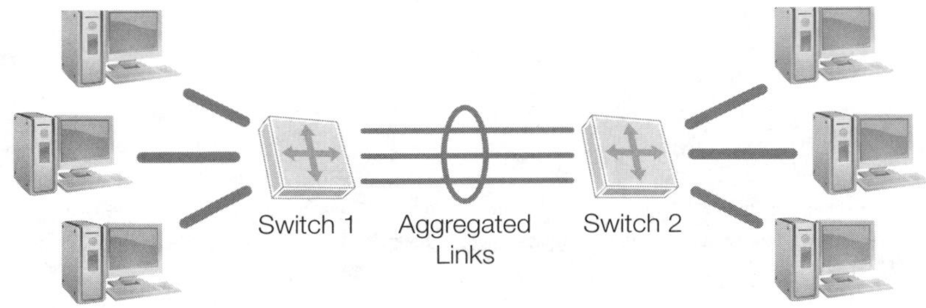

FIGURE 8-17
IEEE 802.3ad link aggregation.

Link aggregation allows switches to communicate along several physical links in parallel. This has the effect of increasing the available bandwidth of a single link. For example, suppose a switch supports ports that use 1 Gbps links. The switch can use link aggregation to combine 4 links to provide a logical link with an effective bandwidth of 4 Gbps. Link aggregation also provides redundancy to protect from a single link failure. If any link in a bundle fails, the other links can still transport traffic. There are two main methods to configure link aggregation: static and dynamic bundling. Table 8-6 lists the advantage and disadvantages to each approach.

The protocol that defines how dynamic link aggregation operates is called **Link Aggregation Control Protocol (LACP)**. LACP provides the ability for compliant devices to negotiate link aggregation. A switch sends LACP frames, called LACPDUs, out to all ports on which the protocol is enabled. If the switch is connected to another device

TABLE 8-6 Static versus dynamic link aggregation.

METHOD	ADVANTAGES	DISADVANTAGES
Static aggregation	• You get what you ask for. • Total control over which ports are bundled together.	• You get what you ask for (may not be optimal). • Any cabling or configuration mistake may make the links unusable. • Link failures may not be detected as down links if there are devices between switches. The sending switch may continue to send data on the failed link.
Dynamic aggregation	• Configuration is negotiated—both ends agree on settings. • Failed links are detected, and the configuration changes to reflect the down link.	• Little control over which links get bundled. • Requires more sophisticated switches.

that has LACP enabled, the remote device will respond with its own identification frames. The first switch examines the responses to detect duplicate links with another device. If the switch detects multiple links with another LACP-enabled device, it aggregates the active links automatically. LACP operates in one of two modes:

- **Active**—Send LACPDUs out to all LACP ports to detect other LACP devices.
- **Passive**—Do not send LACPDUs, but respond upon receiving LACPDUs.

Link aggregation provides inexpensive solutions to increasing bandwidth and resilience. The technique is common when creating backbone networks. Backbone networks can benefit in measurable ways from increased bandwidth. They also rely on resilience to keep the network running. Link aggregation can help networks meet the needs of their users without large expenditures. Many network administrators acquire the fastest hardware their budget can afford and then explore boosting techniques such as link aggregation to make it even faster.

Putting It All Together

Current networks do not use all of the protocols you learned about in this chapter. STP provided the ability to prefer Layer 2 switching over Layer 3 routing. However, STP was far too slow, and it wasted bandwidth in creating the spanning tree. RSTP made convergence much faster than STP, but it still wasted valuable network bandwidth. RSTP was better than its predecessor, but getting the configuration right was complex. MSTP and proprietary protocols such as PVST, PVST+, and VSTP extend the original intent and make sub-second failover for Layer 2 network failure a real possibility.

Link aggregation has received a great deal of attention from network hardware vendors. The IEEE 802.3ad standard is a good idea, but it is too limited. It does a good job of aggregating links between switches. The limitation of switch-to-switch link aggregation means that the protocol is generally most useful in backbone configurations. The idea warranted more attention, so the major network hardware vendors developed their own proprietary protocols to implement link aggregation. Table 8-7 lists some of the approaches vendors used to implement their own link aggregation.

TABLE 8-7 Examples of vendors and their link aggregation solutions.

VENDOR	LINK AGGREGATION SOLUTION
Cisco	• 3750: ISL, Stackwise+, StackPower • 7010: PVST+, Rapid PVST+, ISSU
HP	• IRF (Intelligent Resilient Framework)
Nortel/Avaya	• SMLT (Split Multi-Link Trunking)

Cisco

Cisco common configurations depend on the particular hardware model. Two of the most popular Cisco switches are the Catalyst 3750 series and the Nexus 7010 series. These switches use Cisco proprietary protocols to provide fast and resilient Layer 2 networks.

Cisco Catalyst 3750 switches offer these technologies:

- **ISL**—Cisco Inter-Switch Link. ISL is Cisco's proprietary VLAN tagging protocol. Unlike IEEE, 802.11q. ISL uses external VLAN tagging, meaning that the VLAN tag is added to the Ethernet frame, not embedded in it. ISL can only be used with Cisco switches.
- **Stackwise**+—A Cisco technology that allows up to nine 3750 switches to operate as a single 32 Gbit/s switch. Stackwise+ provides superior resilience and performance. Links among the switches are aggregated for higher bandwidth, and the redundant links provide sub-second failover.
- **StackPower**—A Cisco technology that aggregates available power from all switches in a stack and makes it available to switches that need extra power. Delivering aggregated power is more efficient than adding additional power supplies to each switch to handle increased power needs. StackPower can help organizations save money in equipment and utility costs.

Cisco Nexus 7010 switches offer these technologies:

- **PVST**+ **and Rapid PVST**+—The Cisco 7010 series uses PVST+ or Rapid PVST+ as its spanning tree protocol. Both proprietary protocols are per-VLAN implementations of Rapid Spanning Tree Protocol (RSTP). These protocols create and maintain one spanning tree for each VLAN defined in the LAN.
- **ISSU**—Cisco 7010 series switches also rely on In-Service Software Upgrades (ISSU) to keep switches up-to-date with the latest patches without taking the devices out of service to upgrade. This feature increases overall availability of the network hardware.

HP

HP provides Layer 2 resiliency with its Intelligent Resilient Framework (IRF). IRF defines virtual devices over a collection of connected physical devices. The ability to aggregate physical devices in this way to implement virtual devices makes near real-time failover possible. IRF can respond to physical hardware failures and reconfigure the virtual devices to continue operating.

Nortel/Avaya

Nortel (now Avaya) developed their own link aggregation technology. They developed Split Multi-Link Trunking (SMLT) as an extension to IEEE 802.3ad. IEEE 802.3ad has a limitation that all ports in an aggregated bundle must reside on the same switch. SMLT allows ports in a single aggregated bundle to reside on two different switches. This feature supports more resiliency and greater bandwidth than with ports limited to a single switch.

CHAPTER SUMMARY

VLANs provide the ability to segregate and isolate traffic without having to resort to Layer 3 routing. Current networks must provide real-time performance with low latency and error rate. Generic Layer 2 switches provide the speed, but they lack the ability to handle and group different types of traffic separately. VLANs provide the flexibility for LANs to meet the ever-growing demands of today's applications. They provide the ability to create logical subdivisions of LANs that forward traffic very efficiently. Layer 2 VLANs now allow many of the features, such as resilience and link aggregation, that used to only be available in higher layer protocols. Layer 2 now offers both the speed and flexibility to handle even the most demanding network designs.

KEY CONCEPTS AND TERMS

Broadcast storm
Designated port (DP)
Graph
Link aggregation
Link Aggregation Control Protocol (LACP)
Link bundling
Multiple spanning tree (MST)
Multiple spanning tree instance (MSTI)
Multiple Spanning Tree Protocol (MSTP)
Root bridge
Root path cost
Root port (RP)
Single point of failure (SPOF)
Spanning tree
Switching loop
Trunk link
Trunk port
VLAN trunking

CHAPTER 8 ASSESSMENT

1. The MAC address FF:FF:FF:FF:FF:FF is s special broadcast address the sends a frame to all nodes connected to the same switch.
   A. True
   B. False
2. Which device type separates one broadcast domain from another?
   A. Repeater
   B. Switch
   C. Hub
   D. Router
3. Which statement best describes a VLAN?
   A. Defines a group of devices that communicate as if they were a single collision domain
   B. Defines a group of devices that communicate as if they were a single broadcast domain
   C. Aggregates several collision domains into a larger virtual collision domain
   D. Aggregates several broadcast domains into a larger virtual broadcast domain
4. IEEE 802.1q defines VLAN operation. VLANs are defined at which OSI Reference Model layer?
   A. Layer 4
   B. Layer 3
   C. Layer 2
   D. Layer 1
5. What must a switch add to an Ethernet frame that travels to a VLAN on another switch?
   A. VLAN tag
   B. Trunking address
   C. Destination switch MAC address
   D. Aggregation header
6. VLANs are most closely related to which Layer 3 concept?
   A. Private address range
   B. Broadcast domain
   C. Router group
   D. Subnetwork
7. A ________ port carries traffic to another switch in a VLAN.
8. What term describes multiple paths between switches?
   A. Switching loop
   B. Spanning tree
   C. Graph
   D. Mesh
9. The ________ is the first node in the spanning tree.
10. What is the primary enhancement of RSTP over STP?
    A. RSTP is automatic and STP requires manual configuration
    B. RSTP converges faster than STP
    C. RSTP is fully resilient
    D. RSTP supports VLANs
11. What are the two main benefits to using IEE 802.3ad link aggregation?
    A. Handles more types of traffic (different protocols)
    B. Increases effective bandwidth of switches
    C. Automatically loads balances by moving devices to the fastest switch
    D. Provides resilience
12. The ________ defines how dynamic link aggregation operates.

Voice over Internet Protocol (VoIP)

CHAPTER 9

NETWORKS PROVIDE THE ABILITY for multiple computers to communicate. While this may sound simple, it has far-reaching effects. From the very earliest networks, users have wanted the ability to communicate between computers and do more than just exchange simple messages. Users want their networks to replace older technology and offer new ways to interact with one another. As networks began to mature and get faster, it was normal to compare them to the plain old telephone service (POTS) networks and use POTS as a design basis. It wasn't long before computer networks diverged from the older POTS networks. Network designers started thinking of ways to use newer networks to replace the older analog networks. While many alternatives exist, one approach has become the most popular. In this chapter you will learn about techniques that use modern digital computer networks to carry regular voice traffic. Today's computer networks have reached speeds that allow them to support voice conversations and many other types of more advanced traffic. You will learn about the protocols, techniques, and most successful approaches to implementing voice conversations over IP networks.

Chapter 9 Topics

This chapter covers the following topics and concepts:

- What Voice over IP (VoIP) is
- What the advantages of VoIP over traditional voice communications are
- Which tools VoIP networks commonly use
- Which protocols make VoIP possible
- What the main VoIP challenges are

Chapter 9 Goals

When you complete this chapter, you will be able to:

- Describe VoIP
- Explain the advantages of VoIP over traditional voice communications
- Describe common VoIP tools
- List the most common VoIP protocols
- Explain the most prevalent VoIP challenges

VoIP Overview

Voice over IP (VoIP) is a collection of related technologies, protocols, and techniques used to deliver voice communications using IP networks. Recall that the original telephone network carried analog signals. It was easy to transmit voice over analog circuits since it didn't require any analog-to-digital conversion. The biggest problem with the POTS network was that it set up and maintained circuits for each conversation. As populations grew and telephone use increased, the phone companies realized that their network wasn't as scalable as they wanted. Scalability was one of the primary drivers of the move toward digital networks. Any IP network can carry VoIP traffic, including the Internet. VoIP can operate on scalable networks and provides the same experience to the user as the regular Public Switched Telephone Network (PSTN) or POTS network. There are a few more steps involved in setting up a VoIP telephone call than when using POTS. The steps to set up a VoIP telephone call include:

1. Signaling
2. Setting up the media channel
3. Digitizing the analog voice signal
4. Encoding the message
5. Decomposing the message into network packets
6. Transmitting the packets on the IP network

Figure 9-1 shows the steps in setting up a VoIP call.

The other end of the conversation receives the IP packets and goes through the list above in reverse order to present a voice signal to the other party. The goal is for the people talking on the telephone to be unable to tell whether they are using VoIP or POTS.

The main goal of a VoIP system is to provide transparent telephone calls over an IP network. The end users should not know (or care) how their call works. They just want to enjoy the same reliable telephone service they have used for years. VoIP systems have two main tasks that are necessary to support voice telephone calls over IP networks:

NOTE

You may see the terms **IP telephony** and VoIP used interchangeably. Technically, they are not the same. IP telephony refers to all systems that implement digital telephony over IP networks. There are many implementations from various vendors. VoIP refers to a specific technology used by IP telephony systems to transport phone calls.

- **Setup and teardown of calls**—VoIP systems must first handle creating a virtual circuit and all of the administrative tasks involved in getting a connection ready to transport a voice conversation. At the end of the call, the system also destroys the call and releases resources.
- **Encode and decode speech**—During a call, the VoIP system uses **codecs** to **encode** and **decode** speech data. In a VoIP context, to encode means to convert an analog voice signal into digital data. The decode process converts the digital data back into an analog voice signal on the receiving end. The software that handles the code/decode process is called a codec. Different codecs use different rules and work well in specific environments. Some codecs use compression and work well in limited bandwidth environments. Other codecs depend on highly available bandwidth to transmit high-quality audio.

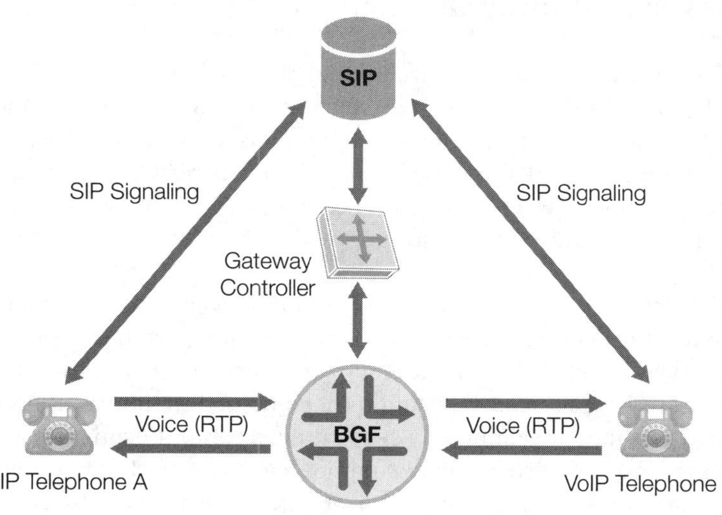

FIGURE 9-1

Steps required to set up a VoIP call.

9 Voice over Internet Protocol (VoIP)

There are three main types of VoIP tools. These different tools provide the endpoints for VoIP calls. In many cases users do not have to use the same type of tools on both ends of a call. As long as the access tool is compatible with the VoIP implementation, the endpoints could use different tools to place and receive VoIP calls. You will learn more about these tools later in this chapter:

- **IP phones**—Devices that look and operate like "normal" telephones, but connect to a network that uses IP to transport call data. This is different from a normal telephone that connects to the PSTN.
- **Software VoIP**—Software VoIP programs use a computer's hardware to provide the same functionality as a regular telephone. Software VoIP includes network calling, audio and video instant messaging, and on-line conferencing.
- **Mobile and integrated VoIP**—VoIP software and hardware support in smartphones, PDAs, and other devices that enable telephone calls over IP networks.

Before 2004, there was not much of a demand for VoIP devices. Networks were still developing and had not yet reached a point where they could support wide-scale use of voice traffic. There were VoIP devices already on the market, starting in 1995, but the technology had not been embraced yet by most organizations. After the turn of the century, networks continued to get faster, and organizations became more cost-conscious. As the first decade of the 21st century drew to a close, organizations looked for any opportunities to save on operating expenses. VoIP provided an attractive alternative to traditional phone service, and acceptance began to grow faster. As of 2008, 80 percent of all new PBX lines were VoIP lines. VoIP provides a high-quality, cost-effective solution to many organizations' telephony needs.

Advantages over Traditional Communications

VoIP supports several advantages over traditional modes of telephone communication. Traditional telephone communication is limited to one type of communication at a time. The most common use of traditional telephones is to carry on voice conversations. Traditional telephone networks can also support fax transmission and computer communication using modems. However, users must choose which mode to use at any one time. In most cases, it is not possible to use multiple modes of communication simultaneously using the PSTN.

VoIP solutions provide the ability to support multiple types of communication at the same time. The ability to transport VoIP networks means that voice, audio, and nearly any type of network message can travel over the network simultaneously. Many organizations have created applications of combined communication methods. These combined methods are commonly called unified communications (UC). UC relies on the ability to transport voice and data communications over the same network. This ability not only makes feature-rich applications possible, but it also can reduce overall infrastructure costs.

technical TIP

VoIP is more than just plugging a VoIP phone into your network and loading some software on a computer. Implementing VoIP means an increase in network traffic. Networks must also be more responsive than when transporting only traditional traffic. VoIP is very sensitive to delays of any type, and networks must be prepared to handle consistently high quality of service. Throughout this chapter, you will learn about how IP networks can provide the level of service VoIP requires.

Operational Costs

Traditional PBX systems were often composed of proprietary hardware and software. The manufacturer created limited quantities of any model, and expansions were often expensive. VoIP solutions operate largely as software programs running on common computers over standard IP networks. VoIP solutions do not require specialized hardware, and most types of computers will run the necessary software. The standardization of the computers and networking hardware means that overall hardware costs are far lower than proprietary hardware solutions.

VoIP can allow organizations to save substantial costs. While VoIP is not an automatically cheap solution, it can help organizations reduce their overall communication costs. VoIP can replace the need for traditional telephone service. For organizations of every size, this means budgets allocated to traditional PBXs, internal communications infrastructure, long distance carriers, and even local telephone service can be redirected. VoIP devices can connect to the network like any other device. Of course, the organization's network has to provide the infrastructure to support the additional devices and traffic.

In most cases there are additional infrastructure costs to ensure a network can handle the additional traffic. In spite of these costs, VoIP can reduce the overall communication and infrastructure costs. Even though you may have to add to your existing IP network, getting rid of a separate telephone system infrastructure can offset that cost. VoIP can help reduce overall costs in several ways:

- Using existing data networks for calls; eliminating the need for a separate voice network infrastructure
- Offering value-added features, such as conference calls, caller ID, call forwarding, and voice messaging, without incurring additional charges from the phone company
- Centralizing network security and support; eliminating the need for separate support groups

VoIP Is Not Free

Many individuals and organizations think that VoIP is a free alternative to traditional phone service. While VoIP can replace most traditional phone service offerings, there are costs associated with it. Think of it like renting a car. Making a traditional telephone call means that you are renting a circuit from the phone company. Renting a car is expensive but hassle-free. You just pick up the car when you want it and provide the gasoline to drive where you want to go. When you are finished using the car, you return it to the rental agency. The car rental agency is responsible for maintaining the car and ensuring that there is a car ready whenever you want to rent another car.

You may decide to save money and buy your own car. Purchasing a car will save you from all future rental fees. However, once you purchase a car, you are responsible for maintenance, repairs, taxes, and insurance fees. The overall cost may be lower than renting, but there are costs involved that are not required with rental cars. VoIP is similar. Implementing VoIP means that you take on the responsibility of purchasing the equipment and ensuring that it operates when you need it. Organizations can do it all themselves or can sign up for VoIP service with a service provider. In short, the VoIP operator takes over the responsibility to ensure everything works as planned.

Feature Flexibility

One of the main advantages of using VoIP is that it is designed to run on a "tried and true" IP network infrastructure. That means it fits into existing network infrastructure. VoIP doesn't need its own separate network. VoIP does require a network that can handle the additional load. The increased reliance on VoIP and related services that rely on real-time protocols is one of the primary drivers toward Layer 2 switching. Although VoIP runs on IP, much of the speed and reliability within LANs comes from a good Layer 2 design. You will learn more about the protocols that make up VoIP as you read through this chapter. As you learn about new features and protocols, always keep the performance and availability requirements of VoIP in mind.

Although cost saving is a primary driver for moving to VoIP, the rich features it can provide are equally appealing drivers. Organizations can do more with VoIP than they could with traditional phone service. The list of VoIP features is constantly growing and differs between VoIP service providers and software offerings. Most VoIP implementations provide these features:

- Ability to carry multiple telephone calls using a single broadband connection
- Built-in provisions to secure telephone calls transmitted over a public network. Many traditional telephone service offerings require additional hardware or software (and a fee) to provide call security.

- Portability and ease of access. All a remote VoIP device needs to establish a call is a connection to the Internet. Smartphones, PDAs, and computers all generally just need a Wi-Fi Internet connection to make a call. Today's ease of Internet access and the rapidly growing number of Wi-Fi hotspots makes VoIP calling easier than ever.
- Communication integration. Since VoIP travels across IP networks with other IP data, it is easy for VoIP software applications to integrate with other applications. Readily available VoIP network packets can easily be combined and integrated with video, text, and data file transfers. This ability makes it possible to conduct video or audio conferences with two or more participants, add data file transfers to conversations, and integrate other ways to exchange information.
- The ultimate approach to integrating multiple modes of communication is UC. VoIP makes UC possible by allowing the most common method of communication, voice conversations, to integrate with other information systems and communication modes. UC enables organizations to provide advanced communications options for their customers and partners that are targeted and aware of the parties' current needs.

VoIP may not be the greatest advancement in networking history, but it can provide impressive benefits. A well-planned VoIP implementation can help any organization save money and provide more advanced communication options.

Common VoIP Tools

The first step in studying a complete VoIP implementation is to understand the most visible parts of the VoIP infrastructure. The VoIP endpoints are the devices people use to initiate and answer VoIP calls. The endpoints are the user interfaces for VoIP calls. You will learn about the three most common VoIP endpoints, or VoIP tools, in this section. As you saw earlier in the chapter, the three most common VoIP tools are:

- IP phones
- Software VoIP
- Mobile and integrated VoIP

IP Phones

An IP phone is a device that looks like a regular telephone but actually is a VoIP endpoint. Regular telephones connect to the standard PSTN network or through a private branch exchange (PBX). Regular telephones transmit and receive analog voice signals. IP phones handle the translation of the analog voice signal to a digital signal suitable for IP network transmission.

IP phones come in many different versions. Some connect to the network using physical cables and others are wireless devices. Single-mode wireless IP phones rely on an available wireless network connection. When you move away from the wireless signal, the phone disconnects any active calls. Multimode wireless IP phones are really two devices in one.

technical TIP

Switching from analog telephones to a VoIP system does not mean you have to throw out all your existing telephones. Organizations can migrate to VoIP more slowly. An **analog telephone adapter (ATA)** is a device that converts an analog voice signal from the analog telephone into a digital signal for the IP network. The existing analog telephones cannot take advantage of all of the VoIP features, but the ATA devices avoid having to immediately replace all existing telephones. If all you need is to make and receive calls at a particular telephone, an ATA could be a long-term solution. Organizations that want to migrate to VoIP and have many existing analog telephones may choose to use a VoIP gateway. A VoIP gateway connects several analog telephones to the IP network.

When they are in range of a wireless network connect, they use that connection to transport calls over the Internet or private IP network. When the phones are out of range, they use a cell phone carrier to connect to the Internet. They operate much like regular cell phones when they are not connected to a wireless network. The advantage of multimode wireless IP phones is that a single call can be handed off from a wireless network connect with low-use cost to a cell connection and back again to a wireless connection as the caller moves around. The caller only has to pay the higher cell network use costs during the time the call was carried on the cell network.

IP phones support many different options. Here are some of the options many IP phones support:

- Optional external microphone and speaker/headphone connections
- Data entry keyboard or keypad, useful to enter VoIP IDs that may include non-numeric characters
- Multiline display for caller ID information and other messages
- Processor to handle application messages
- Analog-to-digital and digital-to-analog signal conversion (necessary to use VoIP connection)
- External network data jack to allow another device, such as a computer, to connect to the data network using the same connection as the IP phone
- Power connector options. IP phones can receive power from a battery, a power adapter, or even through the network connection using Power over Ethernet (PoE).
- Direct analog telephone connection support to allow the IP phone to also directly use a regular PSTN connection

Most IP phones support the advanced features VoIP provides. These features offer the functionality that regular phones cannot. Features that are common to many IP phones include:

- Centrally stored contact directory
- Advanced caller ID, integrated with extended information from the central contact directory
- Ability to create multiple-party audio conference calls. Some IP phones include video cameras or interfaces that support video conferences.
- Ability to transfer calls among VoIP endpoints
- Integration with applications that provide useful information, such as news or weather

Although IP phones have many advantages, there are some drawbacks to the devices. Some of the disadvantages of IP phones include:

- Successful calls require network access between the callers. Internal calls need only internal network access. External calls need access to the Internet or to a gateway device that can use another WAN for the call. PSTN devices use power from the telephone cabling. VoIP phones require some source of power. Even if the organization uses Power over Ethernet (PoE), the networking hardware that carries the network traffic requires power. IP phones and their infrastructure can be more sensitive to power outages.
- Network performance directly affects call quality. Excessive propagation delay, congestion, or just inadequate network design can result in poor call quality.
- Since VoIP travels on IP networks, the infrastructure is vulnerable to the same attacks as any IP application. In the case of VoIP, the most common type of attack is a denial of service (DoS) attack.

Software VoIP

Software VoIP refers to software that runs on general purpose hardware and provides an endpoint for a VoIP call. Unlike IP phones, software VoIP only provides the core functionality to handle a VoIP call. The computer must have the appropriate audio and video hardware installed to meet all of the requirements for a call. The software application generally relies on the computer's operating system to handle the actual hardware. Most current operating systems define default audio and video devices and make those devices available to application software.

There are two general categories of software VoIP—client and server. Client VoIP software handles all of the details of VoIP calls and uses the computer's network connection to connect with the other party. These applications are popular with individuals and small organizations. They are easy to install and easy to use. They require only a network connection to start making calls. They often lack many of the enterprise features of server software, but they provide good options for individuals. There are many software VoIP client applications available today. Table 9-1 lists some of the more popular software VoIP client applications.

The rapid growth in VoIP interest since 2004 attracted many software vendors to the VoIP server market. Today there are several choices for VoIP servers. A VoIP server provides a central connection point for a group of VoIP devices. In many cases the group is a department or entire organization. Organizations that use a VoIP server can enjoy many additional features over individual VoIP clients. The VoIP server can coordinate calls and provide group conferencing and management abilities. VoIP servers can make internal audio and video conferencing easy with central administration. Many VoIP servers provide additional features, including:

- Centralized voice mail
- Call recording
- Instant messaging
- Whiteboarding
- VoIP gateway
- Call accounting and billing
- Authentication
- Remote access support
- Centralized fax services from and to stored documents

Table 9-2 lists some of the more popular software VoIP server applications.

TABLE 9-1 Popular software VoIP client applications.

APPLICATION	OPERATING SYSTEMS	LICENSE TYPE
AOL Instant Messenger	Mac OS, Windows	Freeware
Blink	Linux, Mac OS, Windows	General Public License (GPL)—free
Cisco IP Communicator	Windows	Commercial
Empathy	Linux	GPL—free
Google Talk	Linux, Windows	Free
Linphone	Linux, Windows, Android, iPhone, Blackberry	GPL—free
PhonerLite	Windows	Freeware
Skype	Linux, Mac OS X, Windows, BREW, Android, iPhone, PSP	Freeware
Yahoo! Messenger	Mac OS, Windows	Freeware

TABLE 9-2 Popular software VoIP server applications.

APPLICATION	OPERATING SYSTEMS	LICENSE TYPE
3CX Phone System	Windows	Commercial
CallMax Softswitch	Linux	Commercial
Communigate Pro	Linux/BSD, Mac OS X, Windows, Solaris, HPUX, AIX	Commercial
Elastix	Linux	General Public License (GPL)—free
FreeSWITCH	Linux/BSD, Mac OS X, Solaris, Windows	Open source
GNU Gatekeeper	Linux/BSD, Mac OS X, Solaris, Windows	GPL v2—free
MediaCore Softswitch	Linux	Commercial
Murmur	Linux/BSD, Mac OS X, Solaris, Windows	GPL v2—free
Mysipswitch	Linux	Open source
Revelation LinkLive	Linux, Windows	Commercial

Mobile/Integrated VoIP

Mobile and integrated VoIP refers to VoIP applications that either run on mobile devices or are already integrated into the devices. Most mobile/integrated VoIP devices are smartphones or PDAs. Although cellular service providers originally viewed these devices as competition for regular cell phones, consumer demand has changed their approach. Many cell phone and network hardware manufacturers now sell devices that can connect to cellular networks and IP networks. These devices use Wi-Fi network connections and VoIP when IP networks are available and cellular network connections when Wi-Fi is not available.

Mobile/integrated VoIP devices can operate either as full-featured VoIP clients or they may require a VoIP server to operate. Different devices and service providers result in varying levels of service. More expensive options generally provide better quality calls over a wider coverage area. Less expensive options may only support VoIP when the device is in range of a Wi-Fi network. Service providers are continually offering more capabilities for their users. As reliance on VoIP grows, service providers need to include more VoIP support to avoid losing their customers.

This blended service offering meets both provider and customer needs. Some of the companies that offer dual-band mobile VoIP devices include:

- Alcatel
- Broadvoice
- Cisco
- D-Link
- I-mate
- Motorola
- Netgear
- Nokia
- Samsung
- Vonage

Both network hardware and regular cell phone manufacturers are offering these multimode devices. VoIP is quickly working its way into even the most traditional communication offerings.

VoIP Protocols

You already learned that VoIP is a collection of related technologies, protocols, and techniques used to deliver voice communications using IP networks. In this section you will learn about some of the most important VoIP protocols. Each of the following protocols is responsible for a different aspect of a VoIP call. VoIP is not a single standard. It is made up of collections of protocols from different origins. VoIP operates using both proprietary and open protocols and standards.

H.323

The **H.323** standard is the original signaling protocol for VoIP. The original protocol supported only videoconferencing over LANs and WANs. It is now a packet-based standard that supports audio, video, and data communications across IP networks. H.323 supports point-to-point and multipoint conferencing in a wide range of VoIP devices. H.323 provides several critical functions required by VoIP, including:

- **Call control**—Call setup, admission, tracking, and teardown
- **Multimedia management**—Streaming video and audio
- **Bandwidth management**—Admits calls and selects codecs based on gateway ability to handle the call's bandwidth needs

H.323 is a flexible standard that has long been the chosen standard for audio and video communications. The protocol defines several key components:

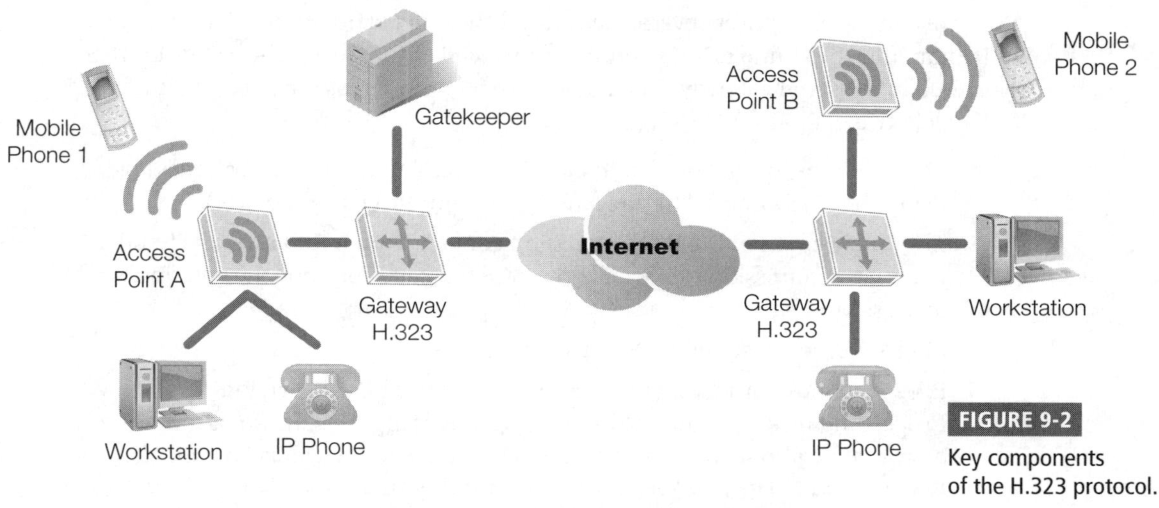

FIGURE 9-2
Key components of the H.323 protocol.

- **H.323 gateway**—Network device that acts as a bridge to the IP network. The H.323 gateway handles the conversion of audio signals to packets suitable for the IP network.
- **Gatekeeper**—Manages components in a logical group, called a gatekeeper zone. Stores the IP addresses of other gatekeepers.
- **Multipoint control unit (MCU)**—Supports conference calls with multiple parties. The MCU accepts the audio stream from the attendees, uses a common signaling format to encode it, and then sends the common signal back to each of the attendees.
- **IP terminal and client**—VoIP endpoints

Figure 9-2 shows the key components of the H.323 protocol.

H.323 defines several protocols and codecs to meet many VoIP needs. The H.323 protocols include:

- **H.225.0 Registration Admission and Status (RAS)**—Used between an H.323 endpoint and a gatekeeper for address resolution and admission control
- **H.255.0 Call Signaling**—Used between any two H.323 devices to establish communication
- **H.245**—Control protocol for multimedia communication
- **Real-Time Transport Protocol (RTP)**—Used to send and receive multimedia information between any two devices

H.323 uses various codecs to encode and decode signals. The most common codecs H.323 uses include:

- **Audio codecs**—G.711, G.729, G.723.1, G.726, G.722, G.728, Speex
- **Text codec**—T.140
- **Video codecs**—H.261, H.263, H.264

A typical call setup requires several steps to get the two parties talking. Assume two VoIP endpoints, EP-1 and EP-2, want to set up a call with one another. They both are registered to the same gateway, GW-1. Here are the basic steps required to set up the VoIP call between EP-1 and EP-2:

1. EP-1 initiates the call by sending a RAS admission request (ARW) message using the RAS channel to the gatekeeper requesting a call to EP-2.
2. The gatekeeper sends a RAS admission confirmation (ACF) message to EP-1 to confirm admission to the call. The ACF message contains the call signaling address of EP-2.
3. EP-1 sends a call signaling Setup message to EP-2.
4. EP-2 responds with a Call Proceeding message to EP1. Receiving a Call Proceeding message causes EP-1 to generate a ring tone. If the user at EP-2 answers the phone, EP-2 sends an ARQ message to the gatekeeper on the RAS channel. The gatekeeper replies to EP-2 with an RAS ACF message to confirm admission to the call. If the gatekeeper denies admission to the call, it returns an Admission Rejected (ARJ) message.
5. EP-2 sends an Alerting message to EP-1 to alert EP-1 that the call is being established.
6. EP-2 sends a Connect message to EP-1 to confirm that the call has been established.

Figure 9-3 shows the steps required to set up a VoIP call using H.323.

The Use of Codecs

Codecs take the VoIP data stream of 64K and compress it down to a certain bit rate. Each codec determines the resulting bit rate. Codecs that use more complex algorithms to compress the data may increase the possibility of additional delay. The standard bandwidth required for each VoIP data stream is between 8K and 64K. An analysis of the network requirements will help in determining which codec to use. Some things to consider are how many VoIP devices will be used, how much bandwidth is allocated toward VoIP traffic, and how much distance or router hops reside between the two endpoints. It is also important to determine what level of voice quality users require. Codecs vary on the level of voice quality produced after compression. Choosing the right codecs can help overall network performance.

It is important to note that codecs vary in their ability to compress data and provide a certain level of voice quality. These codecs use different amounts of resources and add different amounts of delay. Codec providers frequently update and enhance the codecs with new features. It is important to research the current levels of codecs when deploying a VoIP solution to find the best fit for your environment.

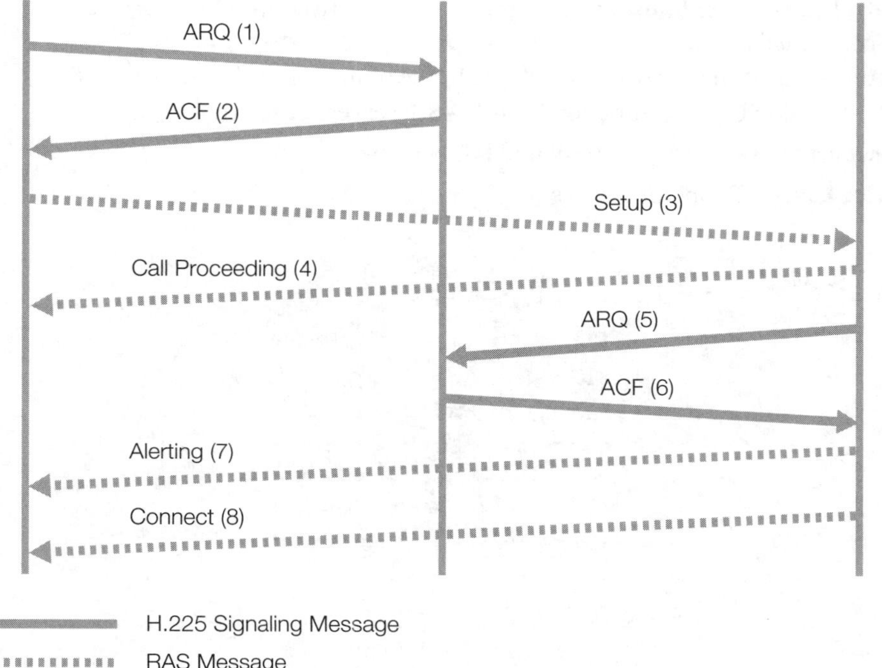

FIGURE 9-3
Steps required to set up a VoIP call using H.323.

IP Multimedia Subsystem (IMS)

IP Multimedia Subsystem (IMS) is a framework for delivering multimedia services over IP networks. IMS originally was designed as a framework for mobile devices to move beyond Global System for Mobile (GSM) Communications. The original version defined an approach to delivering generic Internet services over General Packet Radio Service (GPRS). Later versions expanded the supported networks to include more than just GPRS.

IMS is a framework, or a reference architecture, not a standard. The developers of IMS, Third Generation Partnership Project (3GPP), wanted to introduce a framework that would be accepted as widely as possible. To encourage wide acceptance they use standard (non-proprietary) protocols as much as possible. For example, the IMS framework uses Session Initiation Protocol (SIP) as a signaling protocol. You will learn more about SIP later in this chapter. IMS's main purpose is to make accessing multimedia and voice applications easier from mobile devices. Figure 9-4 shows the IP Multimedia Subsystem.

IMS can be difficult to understand at first, but the framework basically is separated into four layers:

- **Application Layer**—Contains application servers that provide individual services. Application servers use SIP to communicate with entities in the Control Layer. The Application Layer also contains media servers and gateways.

- **Control Layer**—Contains several components used to control how services are consumed by clients.
  - Authentication information is stored in the home subscriber server (HSS).
  - Call Session Control Function (CSCF)—SIP servers or proxies
- **Transport Layer**—Interface to IP and PSTN networks
- **Device Layer**—Endpoint devices

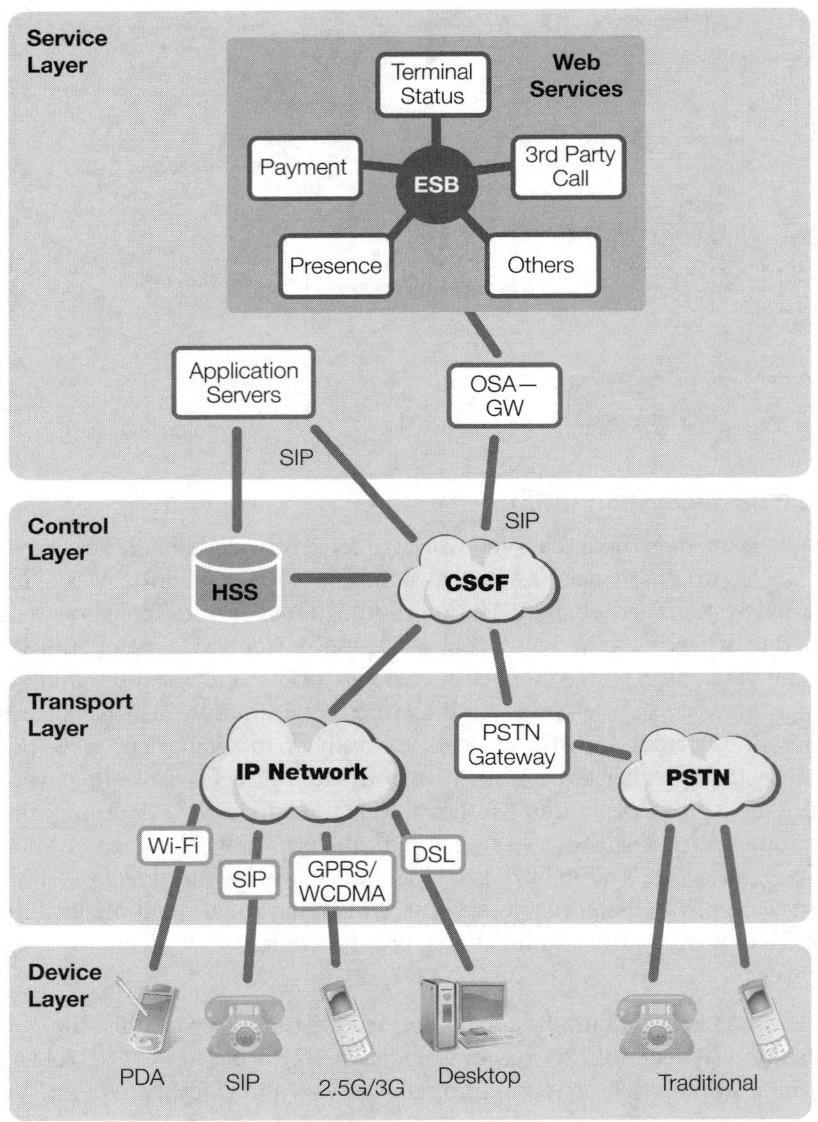

FIGURE 9-4
IP Multimedia Subsystem (IMS).

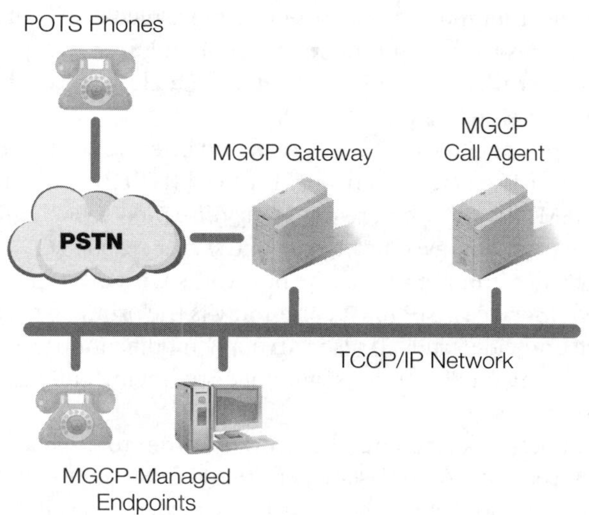

FIGURE 9-5
Media Gateway Control Protocol (MGCP).

Media Gateway Control Protocol (MGCP)

Media Gateway Control Protocol (MGCP) is a protocol for controlling media gateways on networks that include both IP networks and PSTN. MGCP, shown in Figure 9-5, defines both signaling and call control for VoIP. MGCP is most commonly used in VoIP systems that interface with both IP networks and PSTN. The protocol implements a PSTN-over-IP model using a centralized approach. The approach MGCP uses for control is similar to a central office in PSTN. MGCP uses the Session Description Protocol (SDP) to identify and negotiate media streams. It uses Real-Time Transport Protocol (RTP) to frame media streams. You will learn more about SDP and RTP later in this chapter.

MGCP uses a distributed design to handle traffic flowing between the two types of networks. MGCP components include:

- **Call agent (media gateway controller)**—Maintains information on endpoints and gateways. The call agent controls the type of streams to travel to each endpoint.
- **Media gateway**—Performs the media signal conversion between circuit (PSTN) and packets (IP network) and reports endpoint status to the call agent.
- **Signaling gateway**—Often on the same switch as the media gateway. Signaling gateway handles call management details.

Session Initiation Protocol (SIP)

The Session Initiation Protocol (SIP) is a signaling protocol from the Internet Engineering Task Force (IETF) that is widely used to control communication sessions over IP networks. SIP was designed as an alternative to H.323 signaling and is commonly used to control voice and video calls in many of today's VoIP implementations. SIP supports both two-party and multiparty sessions that may consist of one or more media streams. SIP is an Application Layer protocol that is not dependent on lower level protocols. SIP works well with several Transport Layer protocols, including TCP, UDP, and Stream Control Transmission Protocol (SCTP).

SIP is a text-based protocol that is easy to read and interpret. It incorporates many of the elements of Hypertext Transport Protocol (HTTP) and Simple Mail Transport Protocol (SMTP). SIP uses a request/response model. Each SIP transaction consists of a client request, followed by at least one server response.

SIP provides only call signaling and setup, but works with other protocols that provide additional call services. SIP most commonly is the protocol used to set up and tear down voice and video calls. It also can apply modifications to existing calls, such as adding or deleting media streams, adding or removing call participants, or changing addresses or ports.

SIP defines several network elements that work together to provide call signaling and setup/tear down services. A SIP User Agent (UA) is a SIP endpoint that can send and receive SIP messages. SIP UA can be a hardware device or a software program. Each UA can function as a User Agent Client (UAC) or a User Agent Server (UAS) for any transaction. SIP components are identified with Uniform Resource Identifiers (URI). The format of a SIP URI is *sip:username:password@host:port*. When secure transmission is required, the SIP URI takes the form *sips:username:password@host:port*. SIP defines these server elements:

- **Proxy server**—Acts as a server and a client in making requests on behalf of other clients. Proxy servers provide routing and can enforce policy.
- **Registrar**—Server that accepts and stores REGISTRAR requests. The registrar keeps track of all registered UAs.
- **Redirect server**—UAS that creates redirection response to requests. Redirect responses direct a client to contact another set of URIs.
- **Gateway**—Device at the edge of a SIP network that connects to other networks.

SIP uses simple requests and responses. SIP request methods include:

- **REGISTER**—A UA sends its IP address and URLs for which it will receive calls
- **INVITE**—Request to establishes a media session
- **ACK**—Message receipt confirmation
- **CANCEL**—Terminate a pending request
- **BYE**—Terminate a session between two users
- **OPTIONS**—Asks for caller capabilities
- **PRACK (Provisional Response Acknowledgment)**—A receipt response to a provisional response message

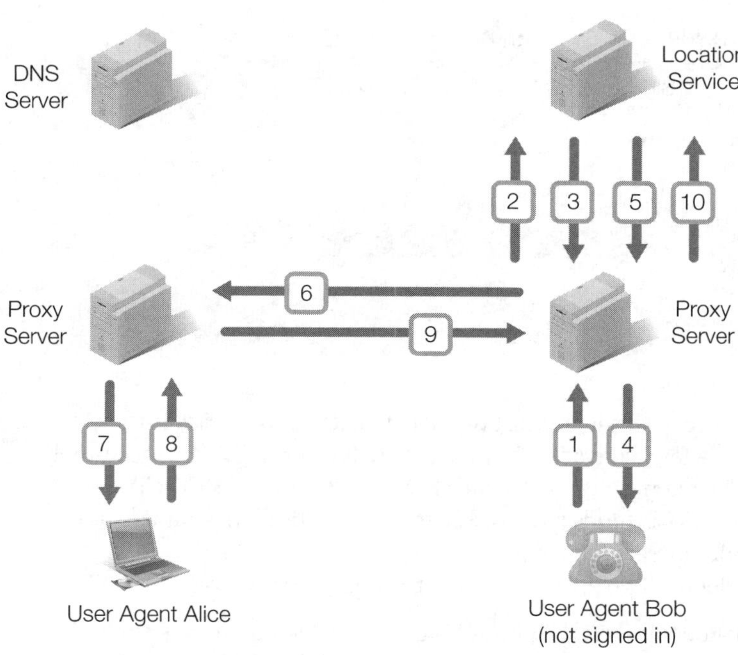

FIGURE 9-6
Session Initiation Protocol (SIP) registration and notification.

1. Register Contact: bob@1.2.3.4
2. Update Database: B=bob@1.2.3.4
3. OK
4. 200 OK
5. Notify <Not Signed In>
6. Notify <Not Signed In>
7. Notify <Not Signed In>
8. 200 OK
9. 200 OK
10. 200 OK

SIP defines the following responses:

- **Provisional (1xx)**—The request was received and is being processed.
- **Success (2xx)**—The action was received, understood, and accepted.
- **Redirection (3xx)**—Additional actions must be taken to complete the request.
- **Client Error (4xx)**—A request contains an error and cannot be completed.
- **Server Error (5xx)**—The server was unable to complete a valid request.
- **Global Error (6xx)**—No server can complete the request.

Figure 9-6 shows an example of how SIP registration and notification works.

SIP's popularity is partially due to its simplicity. It is easy to read and easy to understand. The protocol serves a vital purpose in supporting VoIP.

Real-Time Transport Protocol (RTP)

The **Real-Time Transport Protocol (RTP)** is a standard that defines how to deliver audio and video over IP networks. VoIP uses RTP, along with a signaling protocol such as SIP, to package audio and video streaming content for multimedia communications. RTP handles the issues encountered in transporting media streams across IP networks. Most network issues can cause some packets to be delayed, damaged, or even lost. RTP reassembles packets that arrive out of order and handles retransmission of lost or damaged packets. Real-time streaming media must receive timely delivery of data to present a high-quality stream to the recipient. Any packet delays or losses can impact the stream's quality.

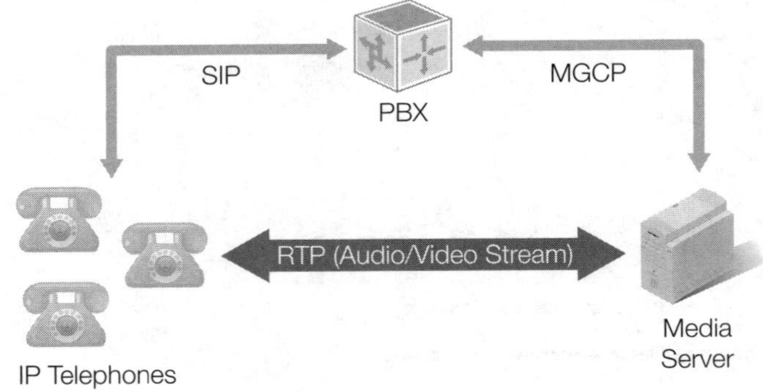

FIGURE 9-7
Real-Time Transport Protocol (RTP).

RTP can cover the loss of a very small amount of packets with error-correcting algorithms, but more than a few delayed or lost packets will be noticeable. Since timely delivery is so important, RTP generally works with UDP, SCTP, or even DCCP. The more common transport protocol, TCP, tends to favor reliability over timeliness and is not the best choice for streaming media transport.

The RTP specification defines two protocols that are collectively referred to as RTP:

- The data transfer protocol is RTP. RTP handles transferring data in real time. RTP includes timestamps, sequence numbers, and the payload format to describe how to deliver and interpret the packet.
- The control protocol is the RTP Control Protocol (RTCP). RTCP sends control and quality of service (QoS) information. RTCP also synchronizes multiple media sessions. RTP creates a separate session for each multimedia stream. RTCP keeps the different sessions synchronized to provide a seamless stream.

RTP was designed from the beginning to work with many multimedia formats. The protocol maintains independence from specific formats by including the format type in the RTP payload header. RTP does not need to know how to interpret each format—just how to transport it. RTP defines profiles and payload formats. Each class of application has a profile definition and one or more defined payload formats. Example application classes include audio and video. The profile defines the supported payload format, and the payload formats define the specific codecs used for the payload. This method makes it possible to define new media formats without changing the RTP specification. Figure 9-7 shows how a media server uses RTP.

Session Description Protocol (SDP)

The **Session Description Protocol (SDP)** defines streaming media attributes and parameters. This IETF standard allows VoIP components to describe multimedia sessions to other VoIP entities. SDP is used by endpoints to negotiate media type, formats, and other variable parameters. SDP is extensible and allows for easy additions of new formats and parameters.

SDP describes each session using fields and values, with one field/value pair on each line. The format for each line in the SDP session description is:

<character>=<value>

A field name (<character>) is a single case-sensitive character. An SDP message can contain three sections. The three SDP message sections are:

- **Session**—Values that describe the session
- **Time**—Length of time a session is active
- **Media**—Information about the media

Table 9-3 lists the SDP fields.

TABLE 9-3 Session Description Protocol (SDP) fields.

SECTION	FIELD	DESCRIPTION
Session	V	Protocol version
	O	Originator and session identifier
	S	Session name
	I	Session information (optional)
	U	URI of description (optional)
	E	E-mail address (optional)
	P	Phone number (optional)
	C	Connection information (optional)
	B	Zero or more bandwidth lines (optional)
		One or more time descriptions
	Z	Time zone adjustments (optional)
	K	Encryption key (optional)
	A	Zero or more session attribute lines (optional)
Time	T	Time the session is active
	R	Zero or more repeat times (optional)
Media	M	Media name and transport address
	I	Media title (optional)
	C	Connection information (optional)
	B	Zero or more bandwidth information lines (optional)
	K	Encryption key (optional)
	A	Zero or more media attribute lines (optional)

VoIP Challenges

You have already learned about some of the challenges of implementing VoIP. This section covers some of the most prevalent challenges when adding VoIP support to an existing network. VoIP is an exciting collection of protocols and technologies that can add substantial value to existing network infrastructure. It is also an added class of traffic that can bring a network to its knees and frustrate users. The difference is in how well the network designers and administrators understand VoIP challenges and how prepared they are to address those challenges.

Quality of Service

Most network applications are tolerant of unreliable transmission. For example, waiting for several seconds for a Web page to load is not uncommon. It is relatively common to see Web pages partially render, then pause for some time before continuing to complete the process. Streaming audio and video is not so forgiving. Most users have encountered buffering waits when playing audio or video streams. This type of waiting is frustrating but tolerable in some cases. However, when participating in a VoIP call or conference, waiting for streams can be extremely frustrating. Interrupted conversations are difficult to follow and sometimes hard to understand.

It is not OK to have any loss of quality when dealing with live streaming data. IP networks are notably less reliable than circuit-switched networks. Packet switching gives up real-time reliability in exchange for scalability. IP networks give their best effort to get a packet to its destination on the first try, but they may have to resort to time-outs and retransmission for lost or late packets. IP networks lack basic **quality of service (QoS)**.

QoS over the WAN

Typically, in most enterprise environments, the cost of bandwidth over the WAN greatly exceeds the respective cost on the LAN. Therefore it is prudent to implement QoS policies on the WAN edge routers. Different vendors often use their own QoS policies; however they are often similar in the fact that they scale. These policies will start with a smaller class model breaking down network traffic into only a small number of classes. Real-time networking such as voice, interactive video, and streaming video, typically will be the highest rated class in the policy and will get dropped last. As the enterprise grows, so can the QoS class model, allowing for multiple classes and marking traffic based on its priority. By marking this traffic, we ensure that real-time networking traffic arrives on time while the lowest priority traffic, such as e-mail or http traffic, is the most susceptible to being dropped.

technical TIP

Propagation delays are the result of fixed transmission times. Excessive propagation delays are normal for some media. For example, any connection that uses satellite links has a fixed delay of nearly one-half second. It takes that long for a signal to travel up to the satellite and back to the earth again. The only way to avoid this type of delay is to replace any satellite links with terrestrial links.

QoS is a measure of how successful a network is at meeting packet delivery timing and error-rate goals. Networks without QoS generally encounter two main issues related to quality: excessive latency and **jitter**. Latency is the amount of time it takes for a packet to travel from one point to another. Jitter is the variable delay that causes gaps in a conversation due to uneven data flow.

During normal operations, the network devices route or forward traffic in the order in which it was received. As volume of traffic increases, routers and switches may take more time to get traffic to the destination than is desired. In such cases, latency causes unacceptable delays. When transporting VoIP traffic, latency that exceeds expectations is unacceptable. Network configuration can affect some latency. This type of latency is a variable and should be a target for optimization. Propagation delays cannot be addressed without infrastructure changes.

Increased network traffic can overload switches to the point that their queues overflow. When that happens, the switch stops accepting traffic, and packets are lost. Protocols such as TCP respond to a situation like this by reducing the transmission rate to allow switches to catch up with the traffic load. This behavior works fairly well for most network applications but not for VoIP. VoIP generally uses UDP to avoid this programmed slowdown under heavy loads. VoIP protocols using QoS can prioritize VoIP traffic to tell switches to transmit the higher-priority packets ahead of lower-priority traffic.

technical TIP

Setting the size of the jitter buffer can have a noticeable impact on network performance. A buffer that is too large will cause a delay that users detect as a delay. If the buffer is set too small, random pauses in the stream will occur. The best setting depends on the network average performance. Continuously sampling the network latency shows the ongoing average latency value. Sampling latency also allows administrators to keep track of the standard deviation of the average, or mean, latency. A good setting for the play-out buffer allows room for two or three standard deviations of packets to accumulate. This setting will reduce jitter in most cases.

When networks are reaching capacity, they often end up transmitting packets out of order due to different QoS priorities. Destination endpoints have to resequence incoming packets to present the stream in the correct order. A high volume of out-of-sequence packets results in jitter. Since jitter is a common occurrence, VoIP receivers often establish small receiving buffers to allow a few out-of-sequence packets to arrive before causing an impact on the stream. The use of these jitter buffers adds a small latency factor to avoid the variable latency of unreliable packet delivery. The compromise between real-time packet delivery and waiting for late packets generally results in a more stable stream.

VoIP and Latency

Phone conversations are inherently sensitive to latency. Enough of a delay in the transmission of the VoIP packet will cause the caller's voice to become jittery, and conversation becomes difficult to understand. Round-trip delays start to become noticeable in phone conversations when they reach 250 mSec. This allows for a one-way latency budget of approximately 150 mSec. The International Telecommunication Union Telecommunication Standardization Sector, more easily remembered as the ITU-T, developed standard G.114, which defines the maximum one-way latency to achieve high-quality voice at 150 mSec.

There are three main components to latency:

- **Network or backbone latency**—In calls over longer geographical distances, geographical calls, VoIP packets typically will traverse several routers, whether it's over a large international enterprise network or over a service provider's network. Traversing this extended path causes delay. It is imperative when designing large-scale networks to be aware of the hop count and try to negotiate the shortest path possible between two sites that will be using VoIP. Service providers also use additional technologies, such as Multi-Protocol Label Switching (MPLS), Dense Wave Division Multiplexing (DWDM), and other services to assist in mapping shorter paths between locations.
- **CODEC latency**—Each codec provides a different level of compression via its own algorithm. The codec used for VoIP packets will determine how much extra delay is added to each additional packet. While some codecs provide efficient compression, they may add too much additional delay in the process. It's important to take this into account when choosing a codec to use while doing VoIP calls over the WAN.
- **Jitter/play-out buffer**—A jitter buffer temporarily stores VoIP packets and holds them for a predetermined amount of time before releasing them for decompression. This buffer is sizable and can be configured based on the network requirements. It's important to note that while the jitter buffer can smooth out the packet flow and assist the codec in processing packets, if configured incorrectly, it can have adverse effects on the latency of the packets arriving at their destination.

The RTCP protocol and MGCP extensions report QoS information and allow network devices to adjust internal settings to decrease the average latency across the network. Several standards, including IEEE 802.1e, IEEE 802.1p, and ITU-T G.hn standards include QoS-type information for Layer 2 devices. These protocols allow lower layer devices to prioritize frames in a similar manner to Layer 3 QoS packet prioritization. Regardless of the mechanism involved, QoS allows network devices to prioritize traffic to ensure media streams do not encounter excessive latency or jitter.

Resiliency

The most prevalent issue related to network resiliency is power. Traditional PSTN calls enjoy power that comes from the circuit. VoIP devices depend on some external power supply. Even when using PoE, intermediate network devices need power. Most network devices in stable networks are connected to UPS devices. These devices can provide uninterrupted power for some period of time during a power failure. Critical networks may include a combination of generators, UPSs, and dual-power feeds to provide more long-term power. Regardless of the method used to provide backup power, alternate devices are mandatory to ensure a power outage does not interrupt the network.

Beyond power issues, network devices and links can fail. Organizations must implement fallback measures to ensure networks do not violate QoS when hardware components fail. One method to continue service is to reroute calls when a primary route fails. Some VoIP service providers even move calls to other networks when their primary routes fail. An organization's routers and switches must be able to survive failures. Redundant hardware and protocols that handle automatic rerouting are essential to consistent VoIP performance.

Security

Since VoIP systems transport conversations using a standard IP network, VoIP calls are susceptible to the same attacks that plague any other IP traffic. It is possible for attackers to compromise insecure passwords and launch DoS attacks or other attacks that can intercept calls or harvest data. Further, attackers can use common attack methods to exploit network vulnerabilities and access users' private information.

VoIP calls require that firewalls and other security devices allow traffic through designated ports. Every additional open range of ports increases the target of potential victims. VoIP providers, such as Skype, that use proprietary protocols increase the attack surface by adding more potential targets. The best defense against any network attack is to enforce strong passwords, use encryption when possible, and carefully control the ports through which traffic flows. Many VoIP implementations opt to not use encryption because of the overhead involved. Although this choice may provide better performance, it may put the entire network as risk. A better choice would be to add more capability to the network media and devices to absorb the small overhead of encryption. A vulnerable network that encounters a DoS attack is far worse than a secure network that carries encryption overhead.

Organizations that implement VoIP solutions also should add multiple layers of defense against any network attacks. Many VoIP software and service providers provide encryption and compression. The use of both techniques can allow VoIP calls to complete with little additional latency. Some organizations, especially those that commonly transmit sensitive conversations, use Voice over Secure IP (VoSIP), Secure Voice over IP (SvoIP), or Secure Voice over Secure IP (SVoSIP) to add layers of encryption to calls. Each of these protocols was developed to address the ongoing security issues of standard VoIP.

Legacy Analog Compatibility

Providing transparent bridging between VoIP and legacy analog telephone networks requires additional effort. Consumers often demand local number portability and mobile number portability. These features allow a subscriber to keep the same telephone number even when switching carriers. This feature requires that the new carrier map new service to an old number. For countries that maintain central databases of numbers, it simply requires a lookup to map a number to a subscriber. The United States Federal Communications Commission (FCC) requires that carriers provide this service. Some countries, such as the United Kingdom, do not maintain central databases of numbers. In these countries, carriers must handle the mapping themselves through per-call network lookups. This feature adds to the setup time for each call.

VoIP providers also must provide methods to route calls between VoIP clients and PSTN devices. Most VoIP software and providers support the E.164 protocol that routes calls between networks. Many VoIP implementations allow users to initiate calls using VoIP-type names instead of remembering telephone numbers. This feature relies on a database of names and numbers that provides the cross-reference at call time.

One of the areas in which VoIP service is still developing is in handling fax transmission. Current voice codecs do not handle fax signals well. The most common solution is to implement the T.38 standard for fax-over-IP. T.38 transmission addresses the codec issues with standard fax transmission and allows standard fax machines to use VoIP networks using an ATA device.

Other telephony devices that commonly use analog telephone lines, such as security alarms and television signal systems, sometimes do not work well with VoIP. These devices originally were designed to connect directly to the PSTN. Even when using an ATA device, they may experience call failures. Newer hardware generally allows the devices to connect to either PSTN or VoIP, but some legacy devices still encounter issues with VoIP.

CHAPTER SUMMARY

VoIP has enjoyed incredible growth over the past 10 years. The many advantages have far surpassed the few drawbacks. Many individuals and organizations have switched to VoIP for their primary telephony needs. For individuals, the key factor is to carefully choose the right service provider. Different providers provide different offerings. Most individuals find a service offering that meets their needs.

Organizations that implement VoIP often find that there are both significant cost savings and additional new costs to using VoIP. VoIP increases the demand on the IP network. It demands an efficient Layer 2 and Layer 3 design. Although many organizations end up adding more hardware to support VoIP, they generally find that the savings far outweigh the new costs. When performance and security issues are addressed, VoIP can provide unparalleled service across entire organizations.

KEY CONCEPTS AND TERMS

Analog telephone adapter (ATA)
Codec
Decode
Encode
H.323
IP Multimedia Subsystem (IMS)
IP telephony
Jitter
Media Gateway Control Protocol (MGCP)
Quality of service (QoS)
Real-Time Transport Protocol (RTP)
Session Description Protocol (SDP)

CHAPTER 9 ASSESSMENT

1. VoIP refers to all systems that implement digital telephony over the IP network.
   A. True
   B. False
2. What is the first step in setting up a VoIP call?
   A. Media channel setup
   B. Signaling
   C. Digitize the analog voice signal
   D. Transmit packets on the IP network
3. Which of the following statements represents one of the main advantages of VoIP?
   A. Overall network usage is decreased
   B. VoIP is more secure than traditional telephone systems
   C. VoIP is designed to run on existing IP network infrastructure
   D. Endpoints are compatible with PSTN and VoIP
4. Which of the following devices allow multiple legacy analog phones to connect to an IP network?
   A. ATA
   B. Gatekeeper
   C. MCU
   D. VoIP gateway
5. Which protocol was the original signaling protocol for VoIP?
   A. SIP
   B. RTP
   C. H.323
   D. IMS
6. At which IMS layer do Call Session Control Function (CSCF) servers operate?
   A. Application
   B. Control
   C. Transport
   D. Device
7. ________ is a signaling protocol from the IETF that is widely used to control communication sessions over IP networks.
   A. SIP
8. The RTP specification defines which two protocols? (Select two).
   A. RTP
   B. SRTP
   C. SDP
   D. RTCP
9. Which protocol defines streaming media attributes and parameters and is used to describe multimedia sessions?
   A. SIP
   B. H.323
   C. UDP
   D. SDP
10. Which of the following terms is a measure of how successful a network is at meeting packet delivery timing and error rate goals?
    A. Latency
    B. Jitter
    C. QoS
    D. Error rate
11. The variable delay that causes gaps in a conversation due to uneven data flow is called ________.
    A. Jitter
12. Which common PSTN traffic do VoIP systems *not* handle well?
    A. Voice
    B. Video
    C. Fax
    D. File transfer

Unified Communications and Session Initiation Protocol

CHAPTER 10

THE TERMS unified communications (UC) and Session Initiation Protocol (SIP) are common in today's networking vocabulary. Despite their popularity, many people do not understand the scope of these terms. The definition of UC varies depending on the person using the term. We will cover those varying perspectives in this chapter. In the case of SIP, it is not a matter of perspective as much as breadth. Most people think that SIP is the best Voice over IP (VoIP) protocol. While this is true, SIP was designed to support all types of sessions. Voice transmission, or more correctly, telephony, over IP was simply its first and most widely recognized application. We will cover the multimedia session aspect of SIP in depth in this chapter as well since it is at the core of UC.

In this chapter you will learn about multimedia traffic on IP networks from a traffic engineering perspective. You also will learn about the importance of quality of [user] experience (QoE), as opposed to the more traditional quality of service (QoS). Understanding this subtlety is important to properly implementing UC applications that users will want to integrate into their lives.

Chapter 10 Topics

This chapter covers the following topics and concepts:

- What the definition of unified communications (UC) is
- What the definition of Session Initiation Protocol (SIP) is
- SIP trunking
- Real-time versus store-and-forward communications
- Big bandwidth versus managed bandwidth
- What quality of service and quality of experience are, and how they compare
- UC applications
- UC and SIP networking

Chapter 10 Goals

When you complete this chapter, you will be able to:

- Explain the fundamental elements and different definitions of UC
- Provide a deeper description of SIP, emphasizing different session types and their application
- Understand how SIP and UC bring the best parts of the traditional telephone network to the World Wide Web, and then improve upon them
- Distinguish between different network design approaches
- Understand the real world issues associated with UC and SIP QoS and QoE
- Apply proper techniques to prioritize and optimize different types of multimedia traffic to maximize use of resources and minimize costs

What Is Unified Communications (UC)?

At a very high level, UC is an umbrella term that includes a large number of communications capabilities. Those capabilities range from services that are nearly as old as the telephone itself, such as direct dialing, to new capabilities such as **presence** and proximity. Presence and proximity can determine the location of persons and nonhuman resources. Locations can be on, above, or below the surface of the earth. These services can also identify how close one resource is to other resources. The new capabilities of UC also include the glue apps. These tie other apps together, such as Facebook and other social networking systems, and make them interesting and useful.

At a more practical level, UC is the next phase in the evolution of IP-based networks. Figure 10-1 shows the major evolutionary phases since the commercialization of the Internet in 1994. The period of 1994 to 1997 was the early adopter period during which time most businesses limited the use of the Internet. At that time, the Internet was perceived as the "great productivity killer." Many organizations limited its use to e-mail. Some prohibited Internet access completely. Following the "hands off" phase, there were three phases of adoption. In Phase 1, the primary focus of IP-network adopters was the reduction of operating expenses (OpEx). Phase 2 saw the main driving force as network simplification. Phase 3 is the current phase, which is being driven by the addition of new capabilities with new benefits, mainly under the banner of UC.

From 1997 to 2001 organizations from the smallest one- and two-person shops to the largest government agencies and companies began to embrace the Internet and private IP networks. They made this shift for a variety of business reasons. During that period, many organizations began to incorporate IP networking into their business plans. The "transport convergence" phase, as it is often called, is when organizations began to exit the restrictive multi-year traditional circuit-switched network contracts and move to all-IP or mainly-IP networks. These allowed organizations to bypass the traditional toll-based phone systems and helped lower the costs of equipment relocations or other changes.

The "service convergence," or virtualization phase, brought with it the network simplification and virtual network resources that are such an important part of UC. Along with them came the first steps toward integrated security and distributed call control. Just as important, if not more so, the first elements of native support for mobility for voice, data, and video soon appeared. This differed from previous models, which provided just cellular voice or voice with very primitive and limited support for data and messaging.

The third phase, "applications convergence," started around 2006 and continues today. This is the phase in which organizations that have made their investments in IP networking and labored through the first two phases are finally beginning to realize a payoff. That long-awaited return on investment (RoI) is in the form of new UC applications that are fundamentally changing the way organizations interact with clients and operate internally. Some of the new capabilities are:

- **Personalized services**—Services that users can personalize or have personalized for them. These services can range from customized ringtones to voice mail greetings in different languages for different callers. Personalized services and self-provisioning are key components of UC.

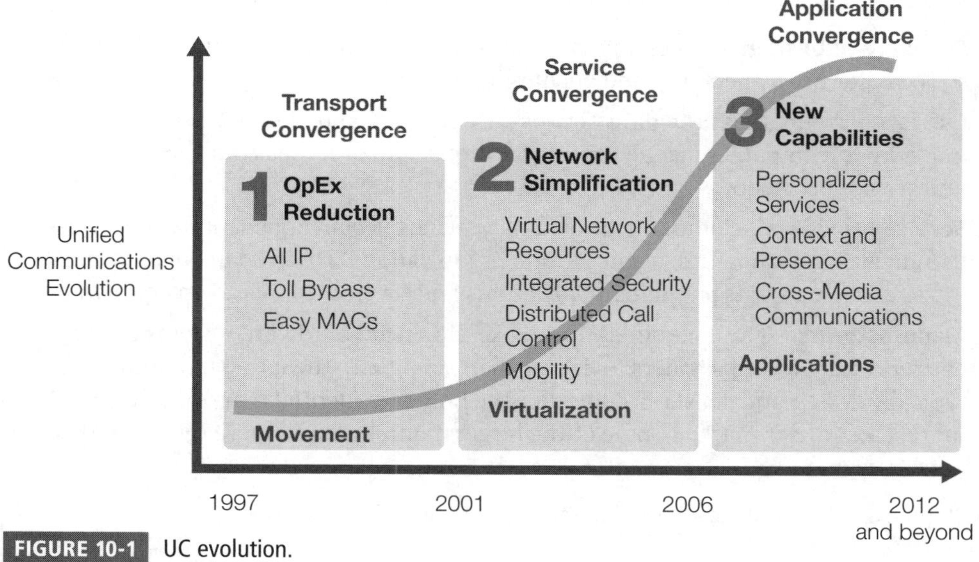

FIGURE 10-1 UC evolution.

- **Presence and context**—Presence is an important element of UC applications. It is the ability to locate an individual or resource geographically. UC presence is particularly valuable when combined with context. Context creates a second level of meaning that makes presence even more valuable. Consider first a presence application: It can find you and put you on a map. But maybe you don't want to be found. With context, you can tell the UC system not to find you, possibly while you are on an airplane or on a conference call). Your particular system may have a "boss override" or "spouse priority," which will allow those important people to find you regardless of what other context features you or your administrator have set.
- **Cross-media communications**—These communications are the capabilities that allow you to move seamlessly from one medium to another. Maybe you just took a voice call, but it would make more sense as a video call. Maybe a two-party video call requires some additional people, such as subject matter experts or family members, to join in. Perhaps it requires a mixture of voice and video. All of these combinations are possible with cross media communications.

Beyond the abstract and evolutionary interpretations, the term UC has many different meanings. The meanings depend upon the role of the person using the term, and the situation in which it is used. While it is possible to adopt a single definition and stick with it, today's telecommunications professionals are better served by understanding the range of definitions and applying the proper definition to the specific situation in which they find themselves. While the number of variations is almost endless, the perspectives, or roles, of persons creating the variations fall into four general categories. End users generally align with the category of their provider. The categories are:

- **Software publishers**—Companies that publish operating system and applications software for use by personal and business end users
- **Carriers**—Companies providing network access and bandwidth for use by individuals, companies, agencies, organizations, and other telecom carriers and service providers
- **Service providers**—Companies providing specific telecom applications or services to individuals, companies, agencies, and organizations. This also includes large internal departments providing applications and services to their own companies.
- **Manufacturers**—The companies that make the actual hardware systems used by carriers and service providers to deliver their services to the market. Manufacturers typically design and deliver products for the home/residential market, enterprise market, or carrier market. Some of the larger manufacturers serve two or all three market segments.

We will take a closer look at all three definitions in the following sections.

Software Publisher's View

Not all software publishers approach UC the same way. But their overall approaches have some common threads. In order to understand UC from the viewpoint of one of the most powerful and influential software publishers, we will begin our tour of the predominant definitions of UC with Microsoft.

Microsoft UC technologies use the power of software to deliver complete communications—messaging, voice, and video—across the applications and devices that people use every day. We're all used to individual experiences. For example, experiences we associate with the telephone include phone calls, voice mail, and conferencing. Experiences we associate with a computer may include documents, spreadsheet, instant messaging, e-mail, and calendars. Integrating the experiences one associates with the telephone into the work done on a computer has the power to fundamentally change the way the world works. Microsoft believes UC will transform business in the coming decade in the same way e-mail changed the business landscape in the 1990s. When phone services become software, are managed by a server, and are delivered to desktop and mobile applications, many interesting things happen.

ISP, MSP, HSP

An Internet service provider (ISP) provides Internet access and basic services such as e-mail. A managed service provider (MSP) or the internal networking department provides a broader, richer set of applications. Examples include Web hosting, database management, VoIP, and UC and network management. This includes the management of routers and firewalls, usually using access provided by the ISP. A **hosting/hosted service provider (HSP)** usually provides services such as UC and VoIP or other applications. It rarely provides access. Most HSP services are considered "cloud services," meaning that they are in the network or Internet cloud. This means they don't require hosting resources or expertise on the part of the user organization. While these definitions have blurred somewhat over the last several years, and will continue to do so, these basic distinctions will be useful in understanding this chapter.

What might be considered to be "missing"? Because Microsoft, and other software publishers, build products for enterprise customers, as opposed to individuals, the Microsoft architecture downplays the importance of social networking tools. For instance, Microsoft applications, such as presence, could be used to locate a friend for a game of tennis. But the enterprise example Microsoft would give would be to locate a technician with the proper set of skills who is closest to a service call and most likely has the proper tools and parts on his or her truck. It is not the tool itself, but instead, it is the application of the tool and by whom. In many cases this distinguishes software publishers from ISPs, MSPs, or even HSPs.

So, what conclusions can we draw from the software publisher's definition of UC? As one might expect, software is the focal point of the solution. The software runs on the widest possible range of platforms and operating systems. This approach is revolutionary—replacing phones—rather than evolutionary—adding functionality or integrating phones into the new paradigms. Note that UC is more than just replacing the traditional "hard" telephone with "soft" phones that run on personal computers and mobile devices. It also includes adding functions to "soft" phones beyond just making and answering phone calls. This ability to extend the definition and use of a telephone is at the heart of the software publisher's definition.

Carrier View

Being the furthest removed from applications in their role and thinking, the carrier has a view of UC that is much closer to network consolidation, or convergence, or transport integration. For an example of carrier UC, we need look no further than AT&T. But do not confuse AT&T, the communications carrier, with their Internet service provider (ISP) or wireless services companies.

AT&T, the carrier, makes little direct mention of UC in its marketing literature or in internal planning. Instead, AT&T talks about enabling UC by providing a bandwidth-rich, reliable, and secure infrastructure that is used by other organizations to provide UC. AT&T considers Layer 1 technologies, such as Dense Wavelength Division Multiplexing, to be its tools of choice for UC. That is because those technologies combine voice, data, and video on a single physical medium. This is usually called transport convergence, rather than UC.

Carriers, Service Providers, and Managed Service Providers

The network universe can be subdivided in many different ways. One of those ways is by the role that an organization plays in the delivery of network services or what parts of the network infrastructure it provides. The bottom level, the OSI Physical Layer (Layer 1), is the realm of the "carrier." According to legal definition, the job of the carrier is to literally carry, or convey, analog or digital information, without modification to any of its physical characteristics such as timing or frequency. As one might expect, the carrier's definition of UC is about as far from the application as possible. The next layer, the OSI Data Link Layer (Layer 2), is the layer where service providers exist. Their services are built upon the underlying circuits provided by the carriers. But service providers add value by reading and interpreting the protocol bits and doing something, such as prioritization or switching. Managed service providers, also known as MSPs or outsourcers, act on behalf of end users or belong to the end user organization and operate at Layer 3. This is the Network Layer using Layer 2 services provided by service providers who, in turn, offer their services on top of the underlying circuits provided by the carriers. The managed service providers are the closest to the applications. They have the most application-oriented view and are most closely aligned to the views of the end users in terms of the definition, usability, and UC value.

Service Provider and Managed Service Provider View

Service Providers and managed service providers exist at or above the Network Layer (Layer 3). This placement allows them to be the most connected to applications. In fact, there are traditional and nontraditional service providers in the marketplace having an impact in UC. For instance, there is the nontraditional managed service provider that Google has either implemented from scratch or purchased a wide range of UC capabilities and made them available to their subscribers. Google's approach has been interesting. It has introduced increasingly specialized UC applications slowly and almost stealthily as the market evolves. Since Google's strategy is still evolving, we will review a more stable set of unified communications-as-a-service (UCaaS) offerings from Cypress Communications (*www.cypresscom.net*). These and additional services will be part of the list of UC applications (apps) from Google and others. An analysis and review of the Cypress Communications offering is currently available for purchase. This analysis will provide an example of the confusion in the definition of UC and the terms and capabilities associated with it. Cypress Communications offers:

- **Advanced collaboration with file sharing, whiteboarding, and chat**—This is considered by many to be a part of UC. Others consider these capabilities, all of which have been available before the term UC was coined, to be a part of conferencing. This arguably may or may not be a part of an organization's UC strategy and tool kit.
- **Real-time presence**—It is noteworthy that Cypress Communications calls this capability "real-time presence." Despite the name, the capability allows one to know who is on the phone or available to take a call at any of the distributed company locations. It requires people to be on a phone at that location or, if on a wireless phone through call forwarding, the individual is identified as being at the office from which their calls are forwarded. This is a traditional telephony centralized switchboard feature. The Cypress Communications application has implemented the feature using VoIP and not the wireless mobility application that locates individuals outside the office.
- **Remote office**—Allows the use of any phone, wired or wireless, as a business phone using call forwarding.
- **Audio/video/Web conferencing**—A traditional conferencing application, as discussed earlier.
- **Account codes for department and client chargeback**—An important capability for business phones, particularly when time is charged to clients, such as an attorney or consultant, or to other departments, as in departments that share employees.
- **Integrated dial plans for multiple locations**—This capability allows the older, structured phone number plan to be migrated to the new VoIP and/or UC environment. Many phone dial plans are disappearing with the move to VoIP and UC. Some companies are slowing or even halting their migration to modern voice communications due to an inability to migrate older, embedded phone numbering plans to a new system.

NOTE

Organizations implementing any new telephony system should audit all existing numbers to be sure that the dial and routing plans can migrate to the new system. At the same time, organizations should resist simply moving an existing dial plan and numbers over to the new system. They first must consider the capabilities of the new system and determine if the old requirements that existed when the old system was developed still exist.

- **Nortel IP phones with advanced features**—The good news is that hard IP phones are available that can consistently and reliably provide a wide range of advanced features. The Nortel IP phone line is an excellent choice for Cypress Communications to offer. The bad news is that hard IP phones are very expensive and tie the client company to a specific vendor. In the Cypress Communications environment, however, the client can choose a range of hard Nortel phones and other mobile and desktop systems. The client then loses the benefits of a single set of features and operating instructions, making support difficult.
- **Direct-dial phone number, voice mail, and e-mail for each employee**—These capabilities, combined with the unified messaging feature described next, are key elements of any UC system. They allow any individual to be uniquely identified and addressed in the same way on stationary, nomadic, and mobile devices. Beginning with a direct-dial 10-digit phone number that will enable all other features is very important.
- **Unified messaging**—Unified messaging is the ability to receive a message in one form and deliver it in another. For instance, a caller leaves a voice mail. A unified messaging system will allow the called party to retrieve the message as a voice mail. Maybe the called party either cannot retrieve a voice mail at that moment, or the preferred delivery form is e-mail. In this case, the unified messaging system might deliver the message as an e-mail with an audio file attachment. It also might perform voice-to-text conversion and deliver the voice e-mail in the body of the e-mail in text format. And, of course, a message originally sent as text can be delivered as a "spoken" voice mail or in some other form. There are also additional features that are being incorporated into UC systems, such as translating the message to a different language.
- **Auto attendant**—Auto attendants are being used more and more often as a destination for a call when the party cannot answer a call or some other procedure needs to be performed by a caller. The auto attendant can be as simple as a recorded or computer voice that asks the caller how they would like their call handled. For example, do they want it forwarded to a mobile number or to voice mail? Or do they want an artificial, intelligence-driven system that can perform complex tasks? Such tasks can include voice registering the caller for an appointment, conference calls, checking account balances, or other activities. While it is true that "auto attendants" have been used for years, UC is expanding their capabilities and providing automation for a range of applications never before considered.

Phone Numbers and URLs

In the late 1880s, telephone pioneer Alexander Graham Bell realized that in order to be truly universal, the telephone must rise above the point-to-point interconnectivity model with which it started. In the beginning, a home-run wire might be strung from the doctor's office to the pharmacy or from the grain elevator to the shipping dock. But it didn't take long for Bell to realize that someone at the grain elevator might need to speak with the pharmacy, or that someone at the shipping dock might need to speak with the doctor. So he developed a five-level hierarchical structure that remained virtually unchanged from the 1880s to the 1980s. A breakthrough element of Bell's innovation was giving each telephone a number. These numbers were initially comprised of a numerical exchange identifier that also had a name, such as 325 or BELvedere, and three or four additional digits. This numbering plan was eventually globally standardized by the **International Telecommunications Union (ITU)** and memorialized in standard E.164.

Today's telephone calls must be able to connect equally well in the traditional telephony environment as in the new, IP-based environment. For this reason, the traditional telephony numbering scheme, and its underlying allocation and management system, has been retained and is as valuable as ever. In cases where telephone calls are placed either from a traditional phone to another traditional phone, on one or different carriers (as in traditional wired or wireless calls or from an IP phone to a traditional phone), the traditional telephone number and traditional telephony network is used to route the call. In instances where a call is placed from an IP phone to another IP phone, and does not traverse the traditional switched telephony network, only a special name called a **uniform resource identifier (URI)** is used. In the special case where a call is routed from an IP phone to a traditional phone or between IP phones, possibly from different providers, the call is also switched across the traditional switched telephony networks. It is necessary to have a traditional telephone number for use in the traditional part of the network when using the traditional switched network.

What about in the IP network? SIP and other Internet telephony technologies do not use phone numbers, per se. A traditional telephone number may be embedded in the addressing structure that SIP/VoIP uses. The addressing structure used by SIP and other VoIP technologies is called a Uniform Resource Identifier (URI). It is a close relative of the URL used to name Web sites and the e-mail address. All of these addressing structures begin with a unique identifier followed by a "@" sign and then a full domain name. The convention that has been adopted by many implementations of SIP/VoIP is to use the traditional telephone number as the unique identifier and, in many cases, use ".phn" as the lowest order element of the domain name, such as *5551112345@phn.company.com*. This allows the phone number to be available when it is needed while adhering to the new IP addressing structure and naming conventions.

- **Call center**—As with many UC systems, particularly UC as a service, the Cypress Communications offering provides a call center that can be customized to the needs of the client. Capabilities include traditional options such as call queuing, basic interactive voice response (IVR), and a wide range of management reports and local and remote agent interfaces. Virtual Call Centers (VCCs) that exist in the cloud are an important tool in most UC offerings. This feature brings the capabilities of advanced call centers, which were formerly available to only the largest organizations, to organizations of any size. There is one additional element that is popular in many UC implementations. It is the ability to originate phone calls from Web pages or even e-mails through a call-to, as opposed to a mail-to, link.
- **Local number portability (LNP) and toll-free numbers**—These are capabilities originating in traditional telephony that are important in making the bridge between the past and future. Local Number Portability (LNP) is the ability to keep numbers that are associated with the client on one carrier and/or system when the client moves to another carrier and/or system. The value of keeping numbers was explained previously. Toll-free numbers allow for a call to the organization that owns the number at no cost to the caller. This remnant from traditional telephony was extremely important in an era where telephone calls, particularly long-distance calls, could cost several cents to over a dollar per minute. It is less important now with low-cost or flat-rate calling plans. But it is still an important component and important to customers or prospective customers in certain economic groups.
- **Dedicated managed routers, e-mail service, Web hosting and domain name services, virtual private networks (VPN)**—A self-explanatory set of options that are clearly part of a **managed service provider (MSP)** service portfolio.

Is this a comprehensive set of UC services? No, it is not, but it comes much closer to meeting the UC need of most companies today than the prior two categories. It should be coming clearer with each example that no one definition is comprehensive. Let's take a look at one final option—the manufacturer's view of UC.

Manufacturer's View

As in the earlier parts of this discussion, we will choose a single manufacturer and allow that company to represent all manufacturers in terms of their view of UC. We will take a look at the UC offerings of Cisco Systems, Inc., which is reasonable from a number of viewpoints. Cisco is among the largest manufacturer of telecommunications systems in the world. They also have products spanning the full range of applications. Their product offerings range from home office/residential to enterprise to service provider to carrier, and everything in between. Cisco has equipment in almost all networks worldwide. But the main reason Cisco is worth considering is that it was one of the earliest manufacturers to provide software specifically for UC.

Stationary, Nomadic, and Mobile

UC is independent of the location status of the individual participating in the UC session. In most cases this is true, except when someone must be in a fixed location such as a broadcast studio. It is beneficial to understand the three distinct location options that can characterize the UC user. The first type of user is stationary. This type of user is always at a fixed location, such as a desk in the office, when participating in UC sessions. This user might be an office worker who uses company UC as a part of his or her job. This is done from a fixed, probably hard-wired video phone. This is the most traditional type of user. The second type of user is the nomadic user, who may participate in UC sessions while at a desk, just like the stationary user. But then that person disconnects, gets up, goes to a different location, and uses UC from that location. It is even possible that he or she connected via a wire in both locations or a wire in one location and wirelessly in the other. An example of this would be a person who uses a laptop computer in a docking station at the office but via WiFi at the airport lounge. That person can participate in UC sessions from each location. The third type of user is the mobile user. The mobile user is completely wireless and is distinguished from a wireless stationary user and a wireless nomadic user in that the mobile user is inclined to move while communicating. In reality, many users fit more than one profile at different times in the day. They might use a stationary computer at home before leaving for work. Then they might use a mobile device on the way to work and be nomadic during the day, moving from one conference room to the other. Stationary, nomadic, or wireless, they can all participate in UC.

How does Cisco look at UC? At Networld Interop in 2007, Cisco CEO John Chambers said "[UC] is the future. It's a hard concept, but it goes right to the issue of increased productivity. But when UC becomes common, it will not only change how we work, but how much we get done. Years ago I predicted that the Internet and now-common ways of communicating would lead to productivity increases of between 3 to 5 percent. Many scoffed at those predictions, but they became true. This will be a replay of that first wave." And so it appears to be.

Cisco's architectural view of UC is consistent with the evolutionary view discussed earlier. In Figure 10-2, the "standards-based solution" and "vendor independence" of components were put in place during the transport convergence phase (Phase 1). They provide the platform upon which the converged voice, video, instant messaging, and applications sharing were built during the service convergence phase (Phase 2). Upon this rest the eight pillars of UC, which support the improved applications, better integration, and, ultimately, improved workflow and capability. A closer investigation of Cisco's eight pillars of UC will highlight many of the important elements that need to be in place for a comprehensive and effective UC solution.

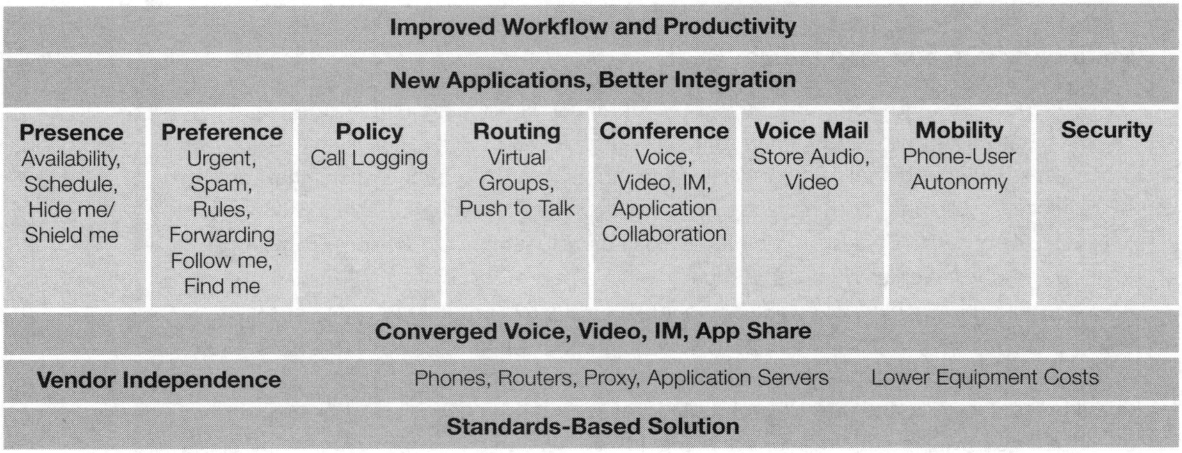

Improved Workflow and Productivity

New Applications, Better Integration

Presence	Preference	Policy	Routing	Conference	Voice Mail	Mobility	Security
Availability, Schedule, Hide me/ Shield me	Urgent, Spam, Rules, Forwarding Follow me, Find me	Call Logging	Virtual Groups, Push to Talk	Voice, Video, IM, Application Collaboration	Store Audio, Video	Phone-User Autonomy	

Converged Voice, Video, IM, App Share

Vendor Independence Phones, Routers, Proxy, Application Servers Lower Equipment Costs

Standards-Based Solution

FIGURE 10-2 Cisco UC architecture.

- **Presence**—As previously discussed, presence allows the geographic location of a person or other resource to be determined. The Cisco model also includes availability, scheduling, and hide me/shield me within its definition of presence, although these characteristics are often considered part of context.
- **Preference**—Preference is Cisco's term for context, part of which is included in presence and the rest is included in policy. Cisco preference includes the ability to apply a set of rules to an incoming communication. Preference can determine if the communication is, for instance, urgent and requires that the called individual be interrupted. Or it can determine if it is spam and can be ignored completely or for the time being. Preference rules also are invoked to determine the operation of such aspects of the UC system as call routing and follow me/find me.
- **Policy**—Policy includes not only the set of rules chosen and implemented by the individual subscriber but any set of overriding rules from "higher authorities," such as a boss or spouse. Policies can be very simple to very sophisticated. They are often the first thing to be reviewed when troubleshooting.
- **Routing**—Although Cisco is known as the "router company," the type of routing that is a pillar of UC is call routing. Call routing is more often determined by a numbering plan and E.164-compliant phone number or the same embedded into the unique descriptor field of a Uniform Resource Identifier (URI) than it is determined by an IP address.

- **Conference**—Conference includes the various media conferencing capabilities, plus the ability to mix and match and move seamlessly between the different call types.
  - **Audio conference**—The ability for two or more persons to share a common voice communication. An **audio conference** is usually implemented via an intermediate phone or a shared conference bridge.
  - **Video conference**—A communication between two or more persons where each may see the other. Optionally, all parties to a **video conference** can see other things such as prerecorded video content or video shown via a camera.
  - **Collaborative conference**—A communication between two or more persons using tools such as shared whiteboards, applications, and computer desktops. The objective of a **collaborative conference** is to accomplish some task between people who are in different geographic locations.
  - **Rich media conference**—A **rich media conference** uses any one of the prior tools, as needed and often in an ad hoc fashion, to accomplish the goals of the conference.
  - **Telepresence**—A real-time video and audio conferencing capability utilizing large-screen and high-definition video so that conference participants appear to be full-size. Conference participants soon lose track of the physical distance between the two or more conference rooms. They then feel more comfortable, as if they are in the same room. Most **telepresence** systems incorporate features that reduce the feeling of being separated. An example is audio that follows an individual as they move around to avoid the audio fade as a person walks away from a single microphone.
- **Voice mail**—The traditional voice mailbox is replaced in UC, and in this instance in Cisco's architecture as well, by a general purpose repository. The new repository allows users to store and retrieve messages in all formats—voice, data, video, image, and fax—and convert from one to another. UC voice mailboxes allow for reading faxes to the subscriber over the phone, e-mailing voice messages, and accommodating all media combinations.
- **Mobility**—Mobility, in Cisco's definition, includes the ability for all type of subscribers to participate in all types of conferencing and information exchange. While voice is the initial application for wireless mobility, it applies to all types of communications: voice, video, image, data, and all hybrids.
- **Security**—Security has become an integral part of virtually everything happening on the Internet, and UC is no different. UC security can apply to communication as it occurs or can apply to stored data to protect it from alteration or disclosure. In many systems, UC security applies to both in-process and stored communication.

Cisco's architecture is often considered the most comprehensive. It includes the features and capabilities that either enable or inhibit the ultimate subscriber and their application software.

You have some idea about the applications that fall under the UC umbrella. Now let's turn our attention to the underlying network technologies that enable UC and their associated applications. Next we will look at the Session Initiation Protocol (SIP).

What Is Session Initiation Protocol (SIP)?

The definition of UC has many possible, even conflicting, elements. It can be problematic and difficult to nail down a specific, usable definition for UC without a clear idea of the context. Not so with Session Initiation Protocol. SIP is a standardized set of procedures for the establishment of a "call," or session, between two endpoints. SIP includes the negotiation of capabilities as well as resources between the two communicating endpoints and the process for taking down, or ending, the call. The rules for applying SIP and its exact structure are clearly spelled out in Internet Engineering Task Force Request for Comments (RFC) 2543. RFC 2543 was later replaced by RFC 3261. We will describe SIP and its operation in the context of multimedia communications in this section.

SIP Versus H.323 (IETF Versus ITU)

In 1994, the people who were doing early work on Telephony over IP (ToIP) applied to the Internet Engineering Task Force (IETF) for assignment of a well-known port number for Telephony over IP/VoIP. The group was made up of Alon Cohen and the inventors and engineers who founded the Israeli company VocalTec in 1989. They wanted a common port for VoIP similar to the well-known port number 80 used uniformly and consistently for most World Wide Web browsers. They were turned down and told that "telephony is not an Internet application." This opinion was based on the fact that the Internet at the time was still largely store-and-forward, while voice is a real-time application.

What the Internet Engineering Task Force neglected to take into account was the fact that the International Telecommunications Union (ITU), the global telephony standards organization and their informal competitor, had been working on a voice over packet for several years. The battle that ensued once the IETF, which shares many members with ITU, realized that telephony and voice could be packet applications is well documented. The result is what is important for today's networking professional to understand. IETF and the Session Initiation Protocol (SIP) won the contest. So today, most applications, with the exception of a few conferencing applications, use SIP and its associated IETF protocols such as Real-Time Transport Protocol (RTP), **Real-Time Control Protocol (RTCP)**, and Real-Time Streaming Protocol (RTSP).

The Internet Engineering Task Force had a specific set of architectural objectives when developing SIP. Their objectives were to develop something that added new capabilities to IP networking while at the same time assuring that SIP conformed to the overall Internet/IP architectural guidelines. The IETF's architectural objectives for SIP were:

- **Services and features are provided end-to-end, when possible**—This is consistent with the overall Internet architectural concept that IP communications are between intelligent endpoints over a network that is as simple as it possibly can be. This is in contrast to the traditional telephony network, where very simple, unsophisticated devices communicate with each other over a highly complex network.
- **Extensions and new features must be generally applicable, not just for certain session types**—This is another architectural requirement of the IETF, which can be observed in a wide variety of examples. For instance, a SIP call can be "redirected," which is the IP equivalent of "forwarded," in the same way that a request for a Web page can be redirected or forwarded to another page or server.
- **Simplicity is the key to success**—One might be left wondering, given the complexity of the Internet, how this could be a guiding design principle. What this really means is that given the choice between two options, the simpler of the two should be selected. An alternative guideline is that the architectures and protocols should be as simple as practical.
- **Reuse of existing IP protocols and architectures and integration with other IP applications is crucial**—Note that while SIP is one of the newer members of the IP family of protocols, it runs on an infrastructure composed of anything that supports the IP itself and TCP and/or UDP. SIP does not require any modifications whatsoever to any underlying protocol.
- **SIP is independent of underlying (lower-layer) protocols**—This is stated as a separate architectural objective, although it is certainly an outcome of adhering to the "reuse of existing IP protocols" rule. SIP certainly complies with this requirement.

SIP is a packet-based communications protocol. It follows some traditional telephony conventions in that there are three distinct stages, or steps, of a UC call. SIP plays a role in two of them. The three stages, or phases, of a UC call are the call set-up phase, the information transfer phase, and the call teardown phase. SIP plays a role in the set-up and teardown phases. The middle phase, information transfer, is carried out by other protocols. The most common information transfer protocol is Real-Time Transport Protocol (RTP). Protocols that are less common are Real-Time Control Protocol (RTCP) and Real-Time Streaming Protocol (RTSP).

FYI

A packet network engineer might find the prior description somewhat unsettling. The description casts SIP in the light of implementation of traditional circuit-based telephony procedures. It also describes the three steps of a call. A packet network engineer would point out that there are two basic types of packet communications—connectionless and connection-oriented. The packet network engineer might note that SIP calls, or sessions as they are more properly called, are of the connection-oriented variety. The characterization in the prior text was written as it was to draw parallels between SIP operation and the operation of traditional telephony. Parallels with traditional telephony are often neglected in the packet context, but realistically, they shouldn't be.

SIP Reference Architecture and Protocol Stack

SIP was designed to operate seamlessly on IP networks. These networks can be the Internet, intranets, extranets, or some hybrid. SIP assumes the characteristics of modern packet networks will be present. Those characteristics include a wide range of delay, delay variation, and packet-loss scenarios, often changing dynamically during a call. SIP will operate best when these characteristics are minimized. In normal operation, SIP will fulfill a basic expectation of Better Than Cell (BTC) performance.

SIP communication occurs between intelligent SIP-enabled endpoints, as shown in Figure 10-3. The physical network in Figure 10-3 appears to be a traditional broadcast Local Area Network (LAN). However, the underlying physical infrastructure is inconsequential because SIP operates over any infrastructure that supports IP. It is possible for endpoint devices to perform more than one function, such as an endpoint and a multimedia controller. Figure 10-3 shows the logical functional element blocks that make up a SIP network. Those functional elements are:

- **SIP User Agent**—SIP UAs (UAs) are the initiators or recipients of call requests. They are also the endpoints of the SIP connection. In other words, the SIP session is established between SIP UAs. The UA is software on a PC, IP phone, tablet device, SIP-enabled camera or video phone, or any other device capable of acting as an endpoint in a SIP session.

FIGURE 10-3
SIP reference architecture.

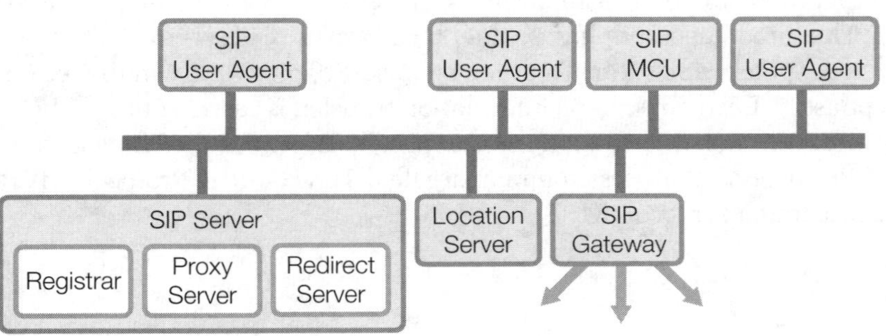

- **SIP server**—The SIP server has three logical components that typically are implemented within the SIP server. It also has one component that may be implemented as a part of the SIP server or on a separate hardware platform. Larger or smaller networks requiring more resiliency and redundancy will implement all four functions on separate, often geographically diverse servers.
- **Registrar**—While it is possible to establish communications directly between two UAs, it is rarely ever done for a variety of reasons. The IP addresses of each device must be known to the other. Also, there is no control over the amount of resources used for that session. For this reason, users register when joining the network. The registrar keeps track of users in the network or domain session status and the amount of resources requested.
- **Proxy server**—The proxy service, when used, is an application layer service that routes SIP requests and replies. It hides the identities of endpoints. It may be redundant because its functions overlap with those of the security/firewall proxy service. Proxy servers are rarely implemented in SIP networks because of the cost, delay, delay variation, and complexity they add to the service.
- **Redirect server**—The redirect service is extremely important. It makes mobile and nomadic users reachable as well as users who have gotten new phone numbers. The redirect server is a part of the availability service as well as geographic location services provided by the location server.
- **Location server**—Geolocation, or location-based services, is among the most exciting and interesting services in mobile networking. They are particularly relevant in the mobile networking aspects of UC. Location services allow identification of the exact location of a human or nonhuman resource. These are the types of services that show available gas stations on GPS devices and restaurant review bubbles on hand-held wireless devices. There are also many applications of location services in law enforcement and public safety, such as pinpointing the location of a 911 caller or the locations of emergency vehicles. Location servers work in cooperation with redirect servers and IP mobility, and provide a geolocation capability to the Domain Name Service (DNS) in an increasing number of cases.
- **SIP multimedia, or multipoint, control unit (MCU)**—In a two-party conference, one of the two parties will be elected to use their internal MCU for the multimedia coordination functions. In a multimedia conference with more than two parties, it is still possible to use the internal MCU in one of the endpoints. But it is far more likely that all of the endpoints will participate in a fully meshed conference by connecting to a separate MCU. The MCU coordinates all conference functions, such as directing audio and video from speakers to listeners and viewers. Its purpose is to give all conference participants the best possible conference experience for the devices from which they are participating.

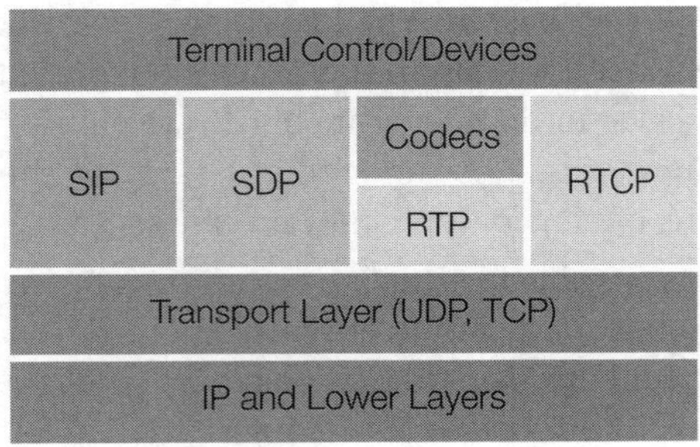

FIGURE 10-4
SIP protocol stack.

- **SIP gateway**—The basic definition of the SIP gateway, like any gateway, is to translate between SIP and "something else." That "something else" can be another identical SIP network. In this case the specific type of gateway would be called a Session Border Controller (SBC). There are dozens of possible SIP gateway types. Some of the most common are trunking gateways, signaling gateways, and service/feature gateways.

Trunking gateways translate between two types of telephony trunking, such as between SIP and traditional, channelized T1 or E1 Options. They also could include SIP-T or maybe a proprietary methodology. SIP-T is discussed in more depth later in the chapter.

Signaling gateways provide a means of connecting two different systems that use different types of signaling, such as a SIP to ISDN gateway or SIP to SS7/CCS7 gateway.

Service/feature gateways allow services or features on a non-SIP network to be delivered on a SIP network, and vice versa. One example is the 411 information service. A 411 gateway would allow 411 calls to be routed from the traditional telephony network to the SIP network. This transfer would be seamless because the translation would be done in the gateway. There would be no change to the originating call.

Now that we have an idea about the logical components and functions within the SIP network, let's take a more-detailed look at the SIP protocol stack.

Figure 10-4 shows the SIP protocol stack. The SIP protocol stack is built on IP and any combination of lower layers that support IP. This is consistent with the prior discussion about the operating characteristics of the underlying network. SIP uses the Transmission Control Protocol (TCP) and/or User Datagram Protocol (UDP) on top of the IP layer. Many IP purists may argue that SIP *should* operate over the simpler, connectionless UDP. But it is common practice that SIP operates over the more reliable connection-oriented TCP. UDP comes into play in most SIP implementations in the information transfer phase (Phase 2). In this phase, the loss of a video frame or a couple of milliseconds of voice is far less disruptive than the loss of a control frame being used to establish a session. That is the case if UDP is used by SIP during the call set-up or teardown phases.

SIP protocol family elements, SIP and Session Description Protocol (SDP), travel over TCP or UDP. Then there are the protocols used for information transfer: Real-Time Transport Protocol (RTP) and Real-Time Control Protocol (RTCP) as well as the coder/decoders (codecs). The codecs translate speech and video to a digital form for transmission. They then translate them back from their digital form for replay at the destination. On top of the SIP-specific layer ride the terminal control functions and endpoint devices between which SIP facilitates communications.

All of these varied elements will come together in the next section, where we will look at an example of how SIP works and a protocol flow diagram.

SIP Session Example

As previously discussed, SIP and related protocols run over IP. That is to say that the SIP messages are placed in the payload of TCP segments or UDP datagrams and then placed in the payload of IP packets. Then they are given IP addresses and other header information and sent on their way. It was also stated previously that UDP is the Layer 4 protocol preferred by the academics. In practical, real-life situations, however, it is the reliable, connection-oriented TCP that is used by SIP for establishing sessions (see Figure 10-5).

SIP is used to perform the first of the three stages of a call, call set-up, and the last of the three stages, call teardown. SIP also uses another protocol to negotiate the capabilities of the devices and to agree on which capabilities and features will be used for this particular session. It is also important to know that an actual connection may be comprised of multiple sessions. For instance, there may be a voice connection from Caller 1 to Caller 2, and a voice connection from Caller 2 to Caller 1. These two connections together provide a two-way voice conversation. Assume there is also a one-way video connection from Caller 1 to Caller 2 because Caller 2 has a screen but not a camera. All of this is negotiated using SDP. It is also important to understand that SIP requires that there be a session description protocol. It does not have to be *the* Session Description Protocol (SDP), though *the* SDP is used in most cases.

Video	Audio	Control	Data
MPEG H.261 H.263 etc. Video Codecs	G.711 G.722 G.723 G.728 G.729 Audio Codecs	SDP Session Description Protocol (or any other session description format)	T.120 Data Sharing
RTP/RTCP			
TCP or UDP (Preferred)			
IP			

FIGURE 10-5
SIP Protocol Reference Model.

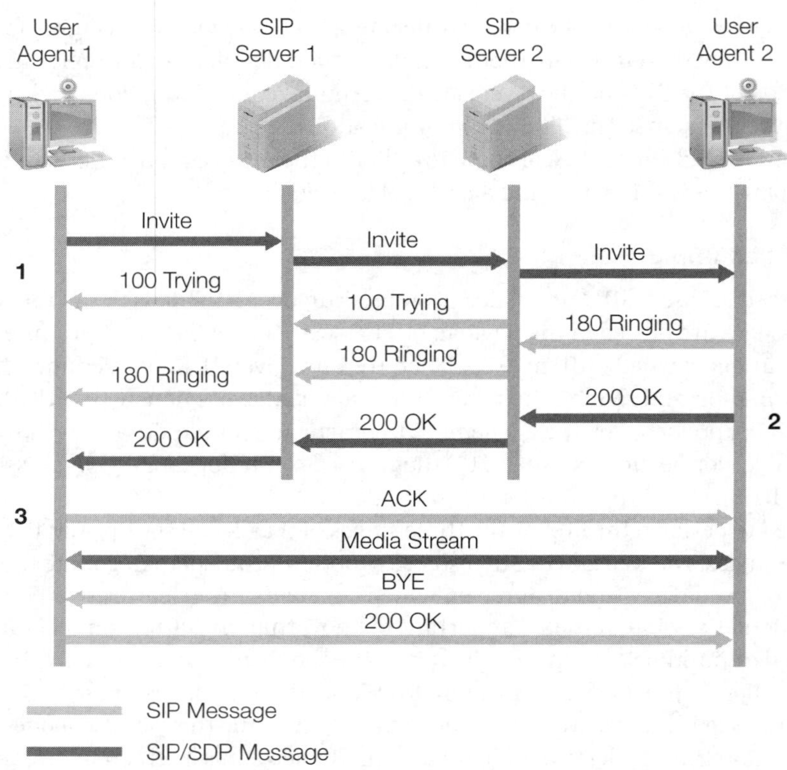

FIGURE 10-6
SIP call flow.

As previously discussed, audio and video content in a variety of possible formats is carried over the Real-Time Transport Protocol (RTP) potentially with the use of the Real-Time Control Protocol. While it is RTP that provides the "containers" to carry the content from sender to receiver, it is RTCP that provides the feedback for the call. This feedback, which travels from receiver to sender, is about a variety of aspects of the status of the call, such as how many voice samples were lost and similar metrics. Collaboration tools are built in SIP using the T.120 protocol. This protocol does not ride in RTP packets and, therefore, adds weight to the argument in favor of using TCP, and not UDP, for transport because T.120 does not have built-in reliability mechanisms.

In Figure 10-6, we begin to see how the elements previously discussed fit together. In this instance User 1, on the left, wishes to establish a SIP session with User 2 on the right. As mentioned previously, it is possible, though unlikely, that the two devices can establish the session without the assistance of a SIP server. In this example there are not one but two SIP servers. In the case of a SIP implementation on a single site, it is likely that they will involve only one SIP server. But the example shown here is very common. In fact, it is even more common to have three SIP servers. In the case of three SIP servers, the SIP servers on the left and right, closest to the SIP UAs, belong to the organizations to which the UAs belong. They negotiate SIP sessions internally, in other words involving only one SIP server and between their local environment. The SIP server owned by their service provider, in turn, communicates to the SIP server owned by the organization of the destination.

In Step 1, User Agent 1 sends an Invite to their local SIP server, SIP Server 1. The Invite contains the Uniform Resource Identifier of the party to whom User Agent 1 wishes to communicate. Something resembling a traditional phone number is probably embedded in the URI, but it is not mandatory. All that matters is that SIP Server 1 be able to resolve the URI to a "next hop," to use router terminology. This is either another SIP server or the destination UA. In our example, the SIP Server 1 responds almost immediately to User Agent 1 with a "Trying" message. This has the dual purpose of acknowledging receipt of the request and placing User Agent 1 in a suspended state while waiting for a status. The Invite is then sent from SIP Server 1 to SIP Server 2 on behalf of User Agent 1. SIP Server 2 then replies, almost immediately, to SIP Server 1 with a "Trying" and then forwards the Invite on to User Agent 2. Almost immediately, User Agent 2 responds to Server 2 with a "Ringing." This performs the same function as the "Trying" messages. It allows all of the participating devices to detect the subtle difference between trying and actually ringing on the destination device. All of these functions are identical in flow to the signaling used in digital telephone systems.

At this point User Agent 2's software actually makes a connection and responds with an "OK." This does not mean that a human actually picked up a telephone handset, although it can mean that. It can also mean that a user has selected a "connect" icon on a tablet computer. Another possibility is that some software task, such as an auto attendant or interactive voice response (IVR), accepted the Invite and will be conducting the call on behalf of the called party who owns the device that User Agent 2 is running. The "OK" message is propagated back along the path from User Agent 2 to User Agent 1, and all of the devices along the path update their state tables.

In Step 3, User Agent 1 now has the IP address of User Agent 2, and vice versa. Direct communication is possible, and the first communication is a positive acknowledgment directly from User Agent 1 to User Agent 2, bypassing the SIP servers. This is the end of the call set-up phase.

At this point, a bidirectional media stream is opened, which is the start of the second stage of the call—information transfer. This stage continues until the session is ended by either party. Then SIP messages may once again flow as a part of the teardown phase (Phase 3) of the call. It is most common that the final exchange is a "BYE/OK" exchange directly between the two UAs. It is also possible that additional messages are sent to the servers so that they can release resources or update call logs.

SIP Message Formats and Options

One of the architectural objectives for SIP, as with all IETF protocols, is that SIP be as similar in format and function as possible to other protocols. For this reason SIP's message structure is similar to that of HTTP, but with different message types and responses.

Protocols Then and Now

Early protocols, such as IBM's Binary Synchronous Communication (BSC), X.25 and even Ethernet, were designed to be extremely efficient in their use of both bandwidth and processing power on the end devices because both were at a premium. The X.25 protocol, for instance, coded each digit of the address into four bits for purposes of efficiency. Protocol developers working in standards committees spent hours arguing the pros and cons of such approaches. Compared to the cost of bandwidth and processing power, their time had virtually no value. Today, however, things are completely reversed. Relative to programmer and software quality assurance engineer's time, the cost of bandwidth and computer power are negligible. Consider the fact that in 1960, there was less than 1 megabyte of computer memory on the planet. Today it is not even possible to purchase a chip that contains *only* 1 megabyte of memory. What this means to modern protocol design is that rather than efficient use of bits that impose a lot more strict programming rules, modern protocols are loosely formatted inefficient text strings that are much easier for less-trained programmers to develop. You need only look as far as HTML and SIP to see examples of this type of messaging.

SIP has two different types of messages: requests and responses. The first line of a request has a method, specifying the type of request and a Request-URI, indicating where the request should be sent. The first line of a response has a response code. The following methods are defined in their respective RFCs, as noted for further reading.

- **INVITE (RFC 3261)**—Indicates a UA is being invited to participate in a session. This is the first step in establishing a session.
- **ACK (RFC 3261)**—Confirms that the destination UA has received a final response to an INVITE request.
- **BYE (RFC 3261)**—Terminates a call and can be sent by either UA.
- **CANCEL (RFC 3261)**—Cancels any pending request.
- **OPTIONS (RFC 3261)**—Queries the capabilities of servers.
- **REGISTER (RFC 3261)**—Registers the address listed in the "To" header field with a SIP server.
- **PRACK (RFC 3262)**—Provisional acknowledgment. PRACK improves network reliability by adding an acknowledgment system to the provisional responses (1xx). PRACK is sent in response to provisional response (1xx).
- **SUBSCRIBE (RFC 3265)**—Subscribes for an event, such as a conference or broadcast, of notification from the notifier
- **NOTIFY (RFC 3265)**—Notify the subscriber of a new event.

- **PUBLISH (RFC 3903)**—Publishes an event to the server.
- **INFO (RFC 6086)**—Sends mid-session information that does not modify the session state.
- **REFER (RFC 3515)**—Asks recipient to issue SIP request (call transfer)
- **MESSAGE (RFC 3428)**—Transports instant messages using SIP
- **UPDATE (RFC 3311)**—Modifies the state of a session without changing the state of the dialog

The SIP response types defined in RFC 3261 fall in one of the following categories. Each category has its own set of specific response messages within the general category:

- **Provisional (1xx)**—Request has been received and is being processed.
  100 Trying
  180 Ringing
  181 Call Is Being Forwarded
  182 Queued
  183 Session Progress
- **Success (2xx)**—The action was successfully received, understood, and accepted.
  200 OK
  202 Accepted: Indicates that the request has been understood but actually can't be processed.
  204 No notification [RFC5839]
- **Redirection (3xx)**—Further action needs to be taken (typically by sender) to complete the request.
  300 Multiple Choices
  301 Moved Permanently
  302 Moved Temporarily
  305 Use Proxy
  380 Alternative Service
- **Client Error (4xx)**—The request contains bad syntax or cannot be fulfilled at the server.
  400 Bad Request
  401 Unauthorized (Used only by registrars or UAs. Proxies should use proxy authorization 407.)
  402 Payment Required (Reserved for future use.)
  403 Forbidden
  404 Not Found (User not found.)
  405 Method Not Allowed
  406 Not Acceptable
  407 Proxy Authentication Required

408 Request Timeout (Couldn't find the user in time.)
409 Conflict
410 Gone (The user existed once, but is not available here anymore.)
412 Conditional Request Failed
413 Request Entity Too Large
414 Request-URI Too Long
415 Unsupported Media Type
416 Unsupported URI Scheme
417 Unknown Resource-Priority
420 Bad Extension (Bad SIP Protocol extension used, not understood by the server.)
421 Extension Required
422 Session Interval Too Small
423 Interval Too Brief
424 Bad Location Information
428 Use Identity Header
429 Provide Referrer Identity
433 Anonymity Disallowed
436 Bad Identity-Info
437 Unsupported Certificate
438 Invalid Identity Header
480 Temporarily Unavailable
481 Call/Transaction Does Not Exist
482 Loop Detected
483 Too Many Hops
484 Address Incomplete
485 Ambiguous
486 Busy Here
487 Request Terminated
488 Not Acceptable Here
489 Bad Event
491 Request Pending
493 Undecipherable (Could not decrypt S/MIME body part)
494 Security Agreement Required

- **Server Error (5xx)**—The server failed to fulfill an apparently valid request.
  500 Server Internal Error
  501 Not Implemented: The SIP request method is not implemented here.
  502 Bad Gateway
  503 Service Unavailable
  504 Server Time-out

505 Version Not Supported: The server does not support this version of the SIP protocol.
513 Message Too Large
580 Precondition Failure

- **Global Failure (6xx)**—The request cannot be fulfilled at any server.
  600 Busy Everywhere
  603 Decline
  604 Does Not Exist Anywhere
  606 Not Acceptable

Before viewing an example of an actual SIP exchange, it is necessary to take a more in-depth look at the Session Description Protocol (SDP). SDP negotiates the parameters for the session and is an integral part of the call set-up exchange between the endpoints.

Session Description Protocol (SDP)

The Session Description Protocol was designed independently from SIP. It is not mandatory to use this particular Session Description Protocol with SIP even though it is used almost universally.

SDP Messages and Options

SDP uses multiple lines of text commands with each line containing a single command. There are three primary sections or divisions in an SDP description: session, timing, and media.

- **Session**—The session part of SDP provides connectivity and context information for the session. Not all of the session descriptors are necessary. Only the particular ones needed to describe this particular session are necessary. The descriptors are:
  `v=` (protocol version)
  `o=` (originator and session identifier)
  `s=` (session name)
  `i=*` (session information)
  `u=*` (URI of description)
  `e=*` (e-mail address)
  `p=*` (phone number)
  `c=*` (connection information-not required if included in all media)
  `b=*` (zero or more bandwidth information lines)
  One or more time descriptions ("`t=`" and "`r=`" lines; see below)
  `z=*` (time zone adjustments)
  `k=*` (encryption key)
  `a=*` (zero or more session attribute lines)
  Zero or more media descriptions

- **Timing**—The timing section contains information regarding the start times for the session. The fields in this section are:
  - `t=` (time the session is active)
  - `r=*` (zero or more repeat times)
- **Media**—The media section describes the media in the session. It is easy to visualize the wide variety of media types and their descriptions that can be constructed using these descriptors.
  - `m=` (media name and transport address)
  - `i=*` (media title)
  - `c=*` (connection information—optional if included at the session level)
  - `b=*` (zero or more bandwidth information lines)
  - `k=*` (encryption key)
  - `a=*` (zero or more media attribute lines)

Although this appears to be a large body of potentially complex information, the box on the facing page, "SIP-T: The Bridge to SIP Signaling," should clear up much of the ambiguity.

SIP Trunking (SIP-T)

SIP-T is an extension to SIP that bridges the gap in the signaling. SIP-T is implemented via a SIP-T gateway where one side of the gateway communicates with the native SIP environment, and the other side of the gateway communicates with the traditional signaling environment. The intricacies of this interface are beyond the scope of this chapter. They are, in fact, an entire industry segment in and of itself. Readers who will be building SIP-only networks need not know any more than what is presented here. Readers worldwide who will be working with SIP-T should study SS7 and/or CCS7. They also should study associated devices, such as mated pairs of Signal Transfer Points (STPs) and similar systems.

Real-Time Versus Store-and-Forward Communications

Earlier in this chapter you read the story of the request for a well-known port number for VoIP/ToIP. To truly understand the ramifications of that important event is to better understand the nature of SIP itself and some of the challenges that come into play in SIP implementation. The Internet Engineering Task Force declined the request for a well-known port number for VoIP/ToIP for one very good reason. The Internet is not well suited to any real-time application. In particular, it is not suited to applications where humans are watching and/or listening and constantly judging quality and, even worse, comparing what they see to TV and what they hear to traditional telephony in real time. The Internet originally was designed for store-and-forward communications. In that regard, it really hasn't changed much since its origins as a National Science Foundation project in the 1960s.

SIP-T: The Bridge to SIP Signaling

The basic telephone is a very simple mechanical device. It contains a spring-loaded mechanism that allows a contact to close. It has a circuit to alert the system to which it is attached that someone wishes to place a call. In the original system, a human saw a light turn on as a result of the closing of the circuit. They attached a patch cord to a switchboard in order to speak live to the person to determine where to insert the other end of the patch cord to complete the call.

This explanation must seem very primitive. Yet it is in fact what happens today by computer chips rather than an operator. The operator also could provide a limited set of special services, such as the time and weather, and eventually collect calls. Eventually a dial was added that automated much of the process by sending a time train of electrical pulses to indicate the "dialed digits" of the desired destination. The time-consuming physical signaling, which required dedicated use of the communications channel, was called in-band signaling.

It eventually was replaced by a set of digital capabilities called out-of-band signaling. This signaling can occur on the access line, as exemplified by the early Integrated Services Digital Network (ISDN). ISDN is also known as Innovation Subscribers Don't Need due to the slow uptake and financial failure of the service. Out-of-band signaling can occur in the backbone of the network as well, using signaling on a separate packet network that runs in parallel with the channelized voice network. The most common protocol for use inside the network is SS7 in North America and CCS7 and its variants in other parts of the world.

Though ISDN was slow to take off and was a financial failure in network access, SS7 and CCS7 were huge successes and generated enormous amounts of revenue. The most common feature enabled by SS7 and CCS7 is caller ID—the ability to show the phone number of the calling party to the called party. Telephone engineers built on that success, or first generation, with something widely known as the Intelligent Network (IN). One of the most visible features of IN was the advent of the name of the calling party along with the phone number, something known as Enhanced Caller ID. It was a huge source of revenue and, along with other capabilities, an enormous success and evolutionary leap for the phone company.

The next, and final, major evolutionary step in network signaling in the traditional telephony network was called the Advanced Intelligent Network (AIN). An example of the huge leap in capability of the AIN are applications, for example, that allows a client of an insurance company to call the same, non-toll free number nationwide and be connected to the geographically closest office to report an accident and file a claim locally. All of these capabilities can be done in IP-based networks using SIP. The real key, however, is to provide a bridge between traditional network signaling and SIP signaling that allows seamless operation of the functionality. That is where SIP-T, or SIP trunking comes into play.

The Store-and-Forward Internet

The author's first exposure to the Internet was in 1976 at the University of North Carolina. At the time, communications via the postal service took a long time. Before the wider use of airmail, a letter to England could take several weeks. So, it was with great joy that results of scientific experiments could be shared by *electronic* mail with British colleagues in Cambridge!

The process was simple but groundbreaking. The results of a scientific experiment were tabulated and entered via a remote terminal to the Triangle University Computation Center at Research Triangle Park near Raleigh, North Carolina. The message would sit on a disk at that facility until midnight local time. At that time, all messages awaiting transmission would be prioritized. Messages for which senders paid more got a higher priority. Messages that had waited longer were also given an advantage in terms of their sending priority. After sorting and prioritizing, a dial-up phone connection was established with another e-mail forwarding point. As many messages were sent as the budget would allow. Messages not sent were reprioritized the next night until they eventually were sent to the next stop on their way to their destination.

In the case of an e-mail bound for Cambridge, England, the dial-up call was to a university near Boston, where the messages would usually sit until the next night. They were then forwarded to London and ultimately to Cambridge. Return messages would follow the reverse path but use the same process. Round trip time? About six days total, and this was considered remarkable at the time. But, today's UC applications are real time on a network in which the architecture has really changed little since the days of only store-and-forward applications, such as e-mail.

What has changed in the Internet is that its reach has expanded from a few colleges, universities, and research institutions. Its size has increased also from several hundred or thousand bits per second (bps) to millions and billions of bps. These two characteristics can make up for a lot of shortcomings in the architecture.

Big Bandwidth Versus Managed Bandwidth

One of the most important factors in the success of UC is the traffic engineering philosophy of the underlying network. This is especially true when it comes to bandwidth-hungry applications, such as rich media conferencing and telepresence. Many have thought the debate of big bandwidth versus managed bandwidth was over a long time ago. The effect of these two very different traffic management philosophies can still be felt, and seen, and heard in the performance of UC applications every minute of every day.

Managed Bandwidth

From the earliest days of networking until the early 1990s, the most expensive elements of a network were bandwidth and computing power as implemented in switches, routers, and other specialized networking devices. The second consideration was the fact that computing power is paid for one time and can be depreciated over time, while bandwidth is a recurring expense with no depreciation schedule. Compared to the cost of equipment and bandwidth, the cost of humans was negligible. Networks were carefully managed by large teams who would assure that they were working at their optimum power level. This was defined as the ratio of what the network delivered to what was possible to deliver. The objective was a 100 percent utilization level that maximized value while minimizing costs. A managed bandwidth approach today seems counterintuitive. In fact, managed bandwidth is still somewhat prevalent in some areas of network operation.

Big Bandwidth

From the early 1990s until today, many innovations have occurred in networking. Most are based on incredible advances in optical communications. They have driven the cost per delivered bit way down. These advances have fostered widespread adoption of technologies ranging from high-definition video to high-speed data applications, virtualization, visualization, and the like. Computer processing power and computer memory have plummeted in price, both in real dollars and in comparison to other costs such as salaries and benefits. For this reason, many networks today are designed around a "bandwidth is free" philosophy where a network is grossly over-configured. The network can then handle any volume of information it is requested to transport while using only a fraction of the network's capacity and never risking an overcapacity situation.

Managed Bandwidth and Big Bandwidth Together

Managed bandwidth networks are expensive to engineer and maintain due to the amount of human effort that is required. They use bandwidth as efficiently as possible, often relying on clever traffic engineering algorithms, prioritization, and oversubscription to accomplish their task. Big bandwidth networks require few human resources to provision and configure. They require even fewer to operate, and they often operate at less than 20 percent of their capacity. Both philosophies are applied in today's networks, but in different areas. The decision of which to use is typically driven by the cost of bandwidth to that organization.

Carrier bandwidth is the foundation upon which all else operates. Carriers almost universally apply a big bandwidth philosophy. After all, carrier bandwidth is least expensive. It also is available in the largest chunks. Provisioning and configuration are simple and inexpensive. Carriers also do not add much value: They simply transport the bits. Service providers pay carriers for bandwidth. They do add value, but service providers are more and more likely with each passing year to minimize staff and apply a big bandwidth philosophy. That leaves MSPs and end user organizations.

Big bandwidth and staff cost reductions are attractive to these organizations, but bandwidth and wireless bandwidth, in particular, are expensive. These organizations are most often the lone holdouts, clinging to managed bandwidth.

Another area in which IP networks are changing, and it is closely related to managed bandwidth versus big bandwidth, is in the area of QoS and how quality is measured by network users. With a shift toward big bandwidth, QoS, as we know it, is no longer needed. This is at least true in the network edge and core—the dominion of carriers and service providers—where type of service (TOS) bits are completely ignored, and everyone's traffic goes first class.

Quality of Service and Quality of Experience

Quality of service is the fabled solution to conflicts for resources in the networks, albeit an unattractive one. When network resources are lightly utilized, the TOS bits in the header of the IP packet are not needed. All traffic flows into the network as it arrives with no "traffic cop" needed to manage the conflicting requests for network resources. When network resources are overburdened, it is the TOS bits that determine which packets go first, which go next, and which packets are discarded. They usually are set by the application in the end system and rarely assured to be compliant with any type of service-level agreement (SLA) or traffic contract. Discarding doesn't solve the problem either. It just delays the problem. In some cases, it compounds the problem if packets from connection-oriented protocols are discarded and then the source resends them as a result of their being discarded. However, any discussion of the value of QoS lacks merit in the era of UC because it is **quality of experience (QoE)**, or more accurately, quality of user experience, that is the new metric of quality.

QoE is not based upon TOS bits or even, effectively, on the treatment of an individual packet within the network. QoE is based on aggregated statistics of packet delivery, delay, delay variation, and service availability. QoE usually is laid out clearly and assured via a SLA. The SLA also has penalties if a certain percentage of the traffic is not delivered within the desirable service window.

QoE usually is calculated in terms of metrics, which can be calculated based upon measurements in the network. They are correlated with a human's opinion of the service, such as the voice Mean Opinion Score, which emulates a human's rating of voice quality based on a variety of factors. A score of 5.0, for instance, is perfect and therefore virtually unobtainable. Most SLAs began charging penalties below an MOS score of 3.6.

QoE is a topic that should receive a lot more attention and depth of coverage than is possible in this chapter. QoE is a subject about which not enough is known, and the value of which is doubted by most in the engineering profession. It is becoming the yardstick by which networks are chosen and judged. QoE is different from QoS in one other important way. A nontechnical network user cannot hear a TOS bit. They can hear the difference, however, between the MOS score of 3.6 and 5.0.

SIP-Enabled Applications Gallery

SIP applications include UC applications and other applications encompassing a wide range of session types. The following gallery of SIP applications is not meant to be comprehensive. It is only to give some ideas of what is possible and to spark new ideas in the mind of the reader.

Multimedia Applications

Multimedia applications use SIP to manage the multiple connections that comprise an application that involves the senses to communicate information about a product or topic. Such applications include everything from virtual test drives to virtual surgery. They range from marketing to educational to gaming applications.

Presence/Availability

Imagine preference settings in your Web profile, maybe from your Facebook page, that know that you love a certain exotic food. Perhaps it is fugu, a rare, expensive fish delicacy. Imagine that a certified sushi restaurant on your way to the airport has posted fugu as the fish of the day. Imagine that your availability shows green for a 45-minute period. All of those pieces of presence and availability information can be combined by an artificial intelligence application that makes a restaurant reservation, puts it on your personal calendar, and informs your GPS system in your car to drive you by the restaurant on the way to the airport. SIP's role? Making all of the connections. Does this application exist yet? Not quite, but all of the pieces are available today and can be glued together with SIP.

IM Chat

As of yet, there is no single universal instant messaging (IM) protocol that allows all IM systems to communicate directly with one another. But thanks to the SIP for Instant Messaging and Presence Leveraging Extensions (SIMPLE), there is a common glue. Any user on an IM system can communicate transparently with any user on any other system because of SIP and SIMPLE. As a result of UC applications, the IM chats are being integrated into other communications applications.

Video and Audio Conferencing

Video and audio conferencing applications have been around in one form or another for decades. What is exciting about the addition of SIP as an enabling technology is that it can manage very complex audio and video sessions, It manages between similar and dissimilar devices and negotiates the common operating ground between them using the Session Description Protocol. SIP helps to lower costs, increase compatibility, and enhance the robustness of conferences. It does so from low bit rate video and audio point-to-point conferences to high bandwidth multilocation telepresence conferences.

Collaboration

Scientists in Huntsville, Alabama, are conferring with their colleagues in Pasadena, California, and Houston, Texas, and with engineers from a manufacturer in Bethesda, Maryland. They are all viewing test results, spreadsheets, and live photographs from a test chamber in Utah. They are using all but one of their senses. They talk to each other and hear what is happing in the test facility. They see the meters, spreadsheet, and test itself in real time. They feel virtual controls using special gloves and feel the vibrations of the sound from the test chamber. They taste the excitement of progress. Except for the engineers, they cannot smell the test—at least not yet.

Digital Signage

Dynamic signs that change their messages periodically, or in rotation, are being seen increasingly on billboards, at movie theaters, and at shopping malls—even at accident sites. But SIP is enabling coordination of sessions involving presence, proximity, preference, and availability to create exciting new applications. Applications are already being demonstrated that adjust the rate of change of digital signage to the speed of traffic and even to the preferences of those persons in the cars. Applications are already being tested that will deliver different billboard messages based upon the preferences of drivers or pedestrians, their direction of travel—toward a business or away, toward home or work, toward lunch or an appointment—and other characteristics. Beyond commercial applications, there are also many public safety and law enforcement applications using digital signage: traffic control for events such as hurricanes, Amber alerts, and other similar applications.

Telepresence

Telepresence is one of the most visually and emotionally engaging applications of the Rich Media/UC era. It allows the ability to interact with other people over a distance, in real time, with the feeling of being there. SIP coordinates the often complex, high bandwidth sessions required for transparent, real-time telepresence. Like most other applications, telepresence is possible without SIP. But SIP makes it much easier and interoperable. Even early telepresence systems based upon earlier standards or proprietary applications are being migrated to SIP.

Your SIP Application

What new, innovative SIP UC application can you think of as we near the end of the chapter? What combination of new knowledge and your existing experience can you create that never previously existed? Give it some thought. This might be your opportunity to make a mark on this new and exciting area of human-to-human communications.

UC and SIP Networking

SIP is capable of establishing the full range of connections needed by UC applications now and in the foreseeable future. UC and SIP are partner technologies, each performing an important part of end-to-end communications. SIP establishes the end-to-end connection that RTP uses to deliver UC's information, assuring that the bandwidth is there. It establishes that the media information and other essential elements are in place. One could not, reasonably, operate without the other.

CHAPTER SUMMARY

UC is without a short, simple, formal definition. For some, it is a unifying technology in their network. For a much larger group of individuals, it is an audio and video conferencing and collaboration capability that seamlessly integrates a diverse set to people and their devices. UC can bring best-of-breed applications and capabilities from the traditional telephone network to a whole new generation of communicators. It also can help humans realize new applications not yet imagined.

SIP may be the winning protocol in the Voice over IP debate. It is the underlying technology that enables UC. It does the serious and specific technical work needed to enable UC and to realize its true potential. Regardless of what they are called, UC and SIP provide two very important elements of one single whole. Together they are paving the way to a future of telecommunications that raises human communications to new heights. They move us closer to realizing our true potential more easily, at lower cost and without regard to location.

KEY CONCEPTS AND TERMS

Audio conference
Collaborative conference
Hosting/hosted service provider (HSP)
International Telecommunications Union (ITU)
Managed service provider (MSP)
Presence
Quality of experience (QoE)
Real-Time Control Protocol (RTCP)
Rich media conference
Service/feature gateway
Signaling gateway
Telepresence
Trunking gateway
Uniform resource identifier (URI)
Video conference

CHAPTER 10 ASSESSMENT

1. The definition of UC is not the same in all situations.
   A. True
   B. False
2. The Session Initiation Protocol (SIP) is documented primarily in which Request for Comments (RFC)?
   A. RFC 2520
   B. RFC 791
   C. RFC 3261
   D. RFC 3265
3. Which of the following are generations of signaling in the traditional telephony network? (Select two.)
   A. Digital Switching
   B. IN
   C. AIN
   D. TIP and RING
4. Which of the following are possible types of SIP gateways? (Select three.)
   A. Dial Plan
   B. Session Border Controller (SIP-SIP)
   C. SIP-Trunking
   D. Domain Name Service (DNS)
   E. Application
5. Which of the following affect the quality of [user] experience?
   A. Grounding
   B. Packet loss
   C. Delay variation
   D. A and B only
   E. None of the above
6. Desired quality of service in IP networks is signaled by ________.
   A. Type of service (TOS) bits
   B. SIP-T
   C. The service-level agreement (SLA)
   D. IPv4
7. Big Bandwidth traffic engineering ________.
   A. Provides "big pipes" resulting in low utilization
   B. Optimizes QoS using TOS bits and prioritization
   C. Manages TOS bits for prioritization and QoE
   D. Does not take QoE into effect
8. Managed bandwidth traffic engineering ________.
   A. Optimizes QoS using TOS bits and prioritization
   B. Provides "big pipes" resulting in low utilization
   C. Is used for Service Level Agreement purposes only
   D. Does not take QoE into effect
9. When a SIP UA is initialized, it usually ________.
   A. Registers with the SIP server/registrar
   B. Uses Address Resolution Protocol to map its URI to a MAC address
   C. Uses Address Resolution Protocol to map its URI to an IP address
   D. Sends an Internet Control Message Protocol request for its URI
10. URI stands for ________.
    A. Uniform resource identifier
    B. Universal resource identifier
    C. Universal record identifier
    D. Uniform record identification
11. Presence in UC means ________.
    A. The geolocation of a human or nonhuman resource
    B. How near one resource is to another
    C. The availability or unavailability of a human or nonhuman resource (such as a conference room)
    D. The way that a subscriber would like their calls to be handled

12. There are three phases of a UC call. They are ________.

A. Call setup, information transfer, and call teardown
B. Initialization, transfer, and de-initialization
C. SS7, IN, and AIN
D. Start phase, transfer phase, and shut-down phase

13. The Layer 4 protocol used most often with SIP is ________.

A. Transmission Control Protocol (TCP)
B. User Datagram Protocol (UDP)
C. Internet Protocol version 4 (IPv4)
D. Internet Protocol version 6 (IPv6)

14. Preference allows ________.

A. A subscriber to direct a UC system on how to handle incoming communications
B. Geolocation of a human or nonhuman resource (such as a conference room) in three-dimensional space
C. Routers to determine the shortest path first for any particular UCUC message
D. None of the above

15. UC is specified in ________.

A. RFC 3621
B. RFC 791
C. RFC 3625
D. None of the above

CHAPTER

11 Layer 3 Networking

"LAYER 3" REFERS TO THE NETWORK LAYER in the Open Systems Interconnection (OSI) Reference Model of the International Standards Organization (ISO). Yes, that's right—the OSI of the ISO. The Network Layer is the core layer of a network engineer's duties and responsibilities. Although it is important to understand the relationship between Layer 3 and the other layers, the vast majority of network protocols, functions, and tasks reside at this layer. In this chapter we will cover these different protocols and how they are used to interact with each other to establish communications over the network. This chapter also will provide an overview of Layer 3 functions, redundancy, and resiliency.

Chapter 11 Topics

This chapter covers the following topics and concepts:

- What the Network Layer routing basics are
- What the Network Layer routing protocols are
- The Internetwork routing functions: LAN to LAN and LAN to WAN
- Routing metrics
- Link-state routing protocols
- Distance-vector routing protocols
- Layer 3 resiliency and redundancy

Chapter 11 Goals

When you complete this chapter, you will be able to:

- Discuss the basic operations of Layer 3 routing
- Describe LAN-to-LAN and LAN-to-WAN routing
- List and describe the link-state protocols that operate on Layer 3
- List and describe the distance-vector protocols that operate on Layer 3
- Explain the purpose of Layer 3 resiliency, and name the protocols used to implement it

Network Layer Basics

The Network Layer of the OSI Reference Model defines the functions and activities that are to occur between the Transport Layer (Layer 4) and the Data Link Layer (Layer 2) to facilitate and ensure the transfer of data from its source to its destination. Included in the functions and actions defined on the Network Layer are:

- **Datagram/packet encapsulation**—Layer 3 functions include encapsulating messages passed from higher layers into datagrams (also called packets) along with Network Layer header information.
- **Error handling and diagnostics**—Layer 3 defines special-purpose protocols that allow logically connected devices to exchange information about the status of a network host or themselves.
- **Fragmentation and reassembly**—Layer 3 passes datagrams to the Data Link Layer, which has limits on the length of some of its frames for transmission. To facilitate the exchange between Layer 3 and Layer 2, the Network Layer breaks up a datagram (packet) into fragments called message transmission units (MTUs) that conform to the size requirements and passes them on to Layer 2. Messages coming from Layer 2 to be eventually passed on to the Transport Layer must be reassembled first. (See the sidebar entitled "IP Fragmentation" for an example of how this works.)
- **Internetwork routing**—The primary function of the Network Layer is to move data across a series of interconnected networks. Therefore, the purpose of the devices and software on the Network Layer is to examine packets from various sources, extract their final destination, and forward them on to the route that is the better path toward that destination.

IP Fragmentation

The Internet Protocol (IP) is the core Network Layer protocol. In order to send messages using IP, higher-layer data must be encapsulated into IP datagrams. Encapsulation means to wrap higher layer data with additional information before passing it to a lower layer. These datagrams are then sent to the Data Link Layer, where they are further encapsulated into frames for the technology in use to carry them physically to their destinations.

On the Network Layer, IP puts Transport Layer messages, including the headers and trailers of all higher layers, into the data field of an IP datagram. On the Data Link Layer, the entire IP datagram is encapsulated into the payload of the applicable frame format. Figure 11-1 shows how data is encapsulated at each layer.

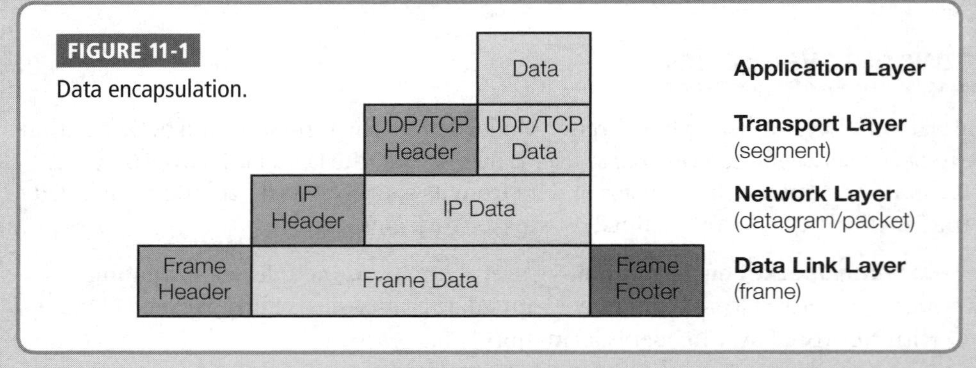

FIGURE 11-1
Data encapsulation.

- **Logical addressing**—Every device on a network has a logical address, which also is called a Layer 3 address. Where the MAC address (Layer 2) is a device's physical address, its corresponding IP address (Layer 3) is a logical address. The main difference between these two addresses is that a logical address is assigned independently to the device. Should the device leave a network, its logical address (IP address) can be assigned to a different network device. One similarity the two addresses share is that they both must be unique addresses on a given network.

Network Layer Protocols

The Network Layer is essentially the routing layer, where the main purpose is to get packets (datagrams) from one network to another. Within the same network (LAN or WLAN), Layer 2 addressing can be used to forward a frame to its destination. However, when a frame is addressed to a host on another network, the frame must be handed up to Layer 3 and prepared for transmission on a LAN, WAN, or the Internet.

Much of the work performed by network administrators and technicians involves IP addressing, sub- or super-netting, routing protocols, firewall rules, access control lists (ACLs), and quality of service (QoS). IP is the best known of the Layer 3 protocols, since it defines internetwork addressing. However, much of what happens on Layer 3 is routing.

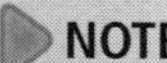

NOTE

See Chapters 3 and 4 for more information on IP addressing.

Router Protocols

First, let's establish that there is a difference between routing and routed protocols. **Routing protocol**s facilitate routers' communication with other routers to advertise their routes, learn of other routes, and make a determination on which routes may be better and more efficient between themselves and other routers. **Routed protocols** prescribe the formatting of the data being routed. A routed protocol can be routed by a routing protocol.

A router is a network appliance that performs the functions and actions of both routing and routed protocols. However, a routing protocol is not the operating system of a router. Routers have distinct operating systems, just like any form of a computer. Cisco routers run the Internetwork Operating System (IOS); Brocade routers run the Ironware OS; Juniper routers run JUNOS; and Alcatel-Lucent routers run the Service Router Operating System (SROS), just to name a few.

Routing Protocols

Routing protocols maintain **routing tables**. Each router has a routing table for each Layer 3 routed protocol it supports. In order to maintain its routing table with the best information available about the conditions of the paths to which it connects, a routing protocol communicates with other routers within its vicinity and uses the information it learns to update its routing table.

FYI

Cisco has owned a large majority of the market share for routers and Ethernet switches for over a decade. As a result of this, as well as the proliferation of Cisco training centers and online training material, there are more network engineers knowledgeable and proficient in Cisco IOS than any other vendor OS. Therefore, to attempt to make an easier sales transition, other vendors have tried to mimic Cisco's IOS as much as possible. This is typically the most difficult pitch for other vendors trying to sell their products into environments that are already occupied by Cisco. Many of them can compete on features and price, but they have to convince the management that their staff will be able to implement and support their product once purchased. Network engineers who are well-versed in multiple operating systems will find themselves more marketable and in higher demand than one having experience with only a single OS.

Routing tables. A router is connected to at least two networks—its own network and at least one external network (such as an ISP's gateway router). The router's primary job is to determine which of its connections would be best to use for a packet to reach its destination most efficiently. Because the network environment is constantly changing, this data must be updated frequently so that it reflects the true and current condition of the network. In a network where a router has only two choices, a routing table is essentially ignored. In a large network where each router is connected to multiple links, the routing table becomes an essential part of the forwarding decision.

Each entry in a routing table specifies one particular route (path or link). All routing tables contain at least one link—a default route. It contains the information of the router's default gateway, which is typically the gateway address of the WAN interface or next hop address of the service provider. However, a default gateway can also be the address where all packets are forwarded if no entry exists in the routing table for its destination.

A routing table entry, which can vary depending on the routed protocol in use, typically will consist of the following information:

- Network ID or host internetwork logical address
- Subnet mask to extract the network ID from the destination IP address
- Forwarding address
- Port number of the interface port associated with the network ID
- Routing metric

If the destination address of the packet to be forwarded matches an entry in the routing table, the metric value is examined to determine whether this route has the lowest **cost** (meaning the lowest metric value of the available routes—more on this later). If multiple routes are available, the route with the lowest cost is chosen, and the packet is forwarded on its link. If only one route is available, it is used.

Entries in a routing table, which is kept in the router's main memory (RAM), reference directly connected networks or remotely connected networks. Directly connected networks are those where one router is linked to another router by a direct connection. A remotely connected network is the opposite of a directly connected network, meaning that there is no direct connection to its router. A message routed to it must pass through an intermediary router.

How a routing table works. When a router receives a forwarded packet, it must extract the packet's destination address and determine from its routing table which of its interface ports the packet should be forwarded to to reach its destination. In the case where a router has only two links, the decision is an either-or. In cases where a router is **multi-homed** (connected to multiple links), the better route for the packet must be determined from the information in the routing table that contains a separate entry for each of the links a router has connected.

Examining the IP Routing Table

The following is an example of a "show ip route" output from a Cisco router. By entering this command on a Cisco router, you are able to see the output display codes to help determine what type of routing protocol a particular network is using. Additionally, the routes could be directly connected routes or static routes, sometimes not using any routing protocols.

```
RouterA#show ip route

Codes: C-connected, S-static, I-IGRP, R-RIP, M-mobile, B-BGP
  D-EIGRP, EX-EIGRP external, O-OSPF, IA-OSPF inter area
  N1-OSPF NSSA external type 1, N2-OSPF NSSA external type 2
  E1-OSPF external type 1, E2-OSPF external type 2, E-EGP
  i-IS-IS, su-IS-IS summary, L1-IS-IS level-1, L2-IS-IS level-2
  ia-IS-IS inter area, *-candidate default, U-per-user static route
  o-ODR, P-periodic downloaded static route

Gateway of last resort is not set

  10.44.0.0/24 is subnetted, 1 subnets
C 10.44.192.0 is directly connected, Ethernet0
  10.108.0.0/24 is subnetted, 1 subnets
C 10.108.99.0 is directly connected, Serial0
S 192.168.1.0/24 [1/0] via 10.44.192.2
```

Some common routing protocols. A few of the more commonly used routing protocols are:

- Routing Information Protocol (RIP/RIPv2)
- Interior Gateway Routing Protocol (IGRP)
- Enhanced IGRP (EIGRP)
- Intermediate System-to-Intermediate System (IS-IS)
- Open Shortest Path First (OSPF)
- Border Gateway Protocol (BGP)

More information is available on each of the above routing protocols later in this chapter.

Routed Protocols

A routed protocol defines the structure and format of the data being forwarded by a router and its routing protocol. Once a packet is formatted in accordance with the packet's routed protocol, the packet can be forwarded by the routing protocol. Examples of routed protocols are Novell IPX (Internetwork Packet Exchange), DECnet, AppleTalk, Banyan Vines, and IP, as well as sub-protocols of IP such as Telnet, Remote Procedure Call (RPC), SNMP (Simple Network Management Protocol), and SMTP (Simple Mail Transport Protocol).

Non-Routable Protocols

There are also protocols that cannot be routed. These protocols assume that all of the hosts to which they must communicate speak the same language and are located on the same network. In order for networks running non-routable protocols to communicate, a network bridge is required. Examples of non-routable protocols are NetBIOS Extended User Interface (NetBEUI), Data Link Command (DLC), Local Area Transport (LAT), and Director Response Protocol (DRP).

Routing Protocols Versus Routed Protocols

It is important to understand the difference between routing protocols and routed protocols. Routing protocols are used to propagate dynamically learned route information from other routers participating in the same process. Routed protocols are responsible for the delivery of the datagram and contain the Network Layer addressing. The routing protocols use this Network Layer information to determine the best path for the packet to take across the network to reach its destination. For example, IP is a routed protocol, and inside the IP packet resides its source and destination network (Layer 3) addresses. A routing protocol, such as RIP, OSPF, or EIGRP, will inspect the destination network address inside the packet. It will make a routing decision on where to forward (route) the packet based on the information in its routing table.

Path Determination

In an IP-based environment, every node, or device, will have its own individual IP address. Devices such as routers, that have an interface on each network involved, will have multiple IP addresses, or an IP address per interface. It is critical when attempting to learn about routing and path determination that you have a solid understanding of subnet masks and how they determine the network and host ID of the IP address, as explained in Chapters 3 and 4.

Before getting into more detailed examples of routing, let's start off with the basics of how routing tables work and how path determination is made. In the example shown in Figure 11-2, we have Router A, which has an interface on Network 1, to which Switch A and Host A belong. Router B has an interface on Network 3, to which Switch B and Host B belong. Network 2 is the transit network, or the network that is used to pass packets between Networks 1 and 3. Each router has an interface on Network 3.

In this example, if we assume Host A needs to talk to Host B, then Host A will forward its packet out its default gateway as Host B does not live on the same network as Host A. The default gateway in this case is the interface of Router A on Network 1. It is important to remember that in topologies such as these, the switch does not act as a Layer 3 device and will just pass packets on to hosts on the same network or to the router. Router A receives the packet and references its routing table. The destination network, Network 3, is not a directly connected network as Networks 1 and 2 are. Instead, it sees Network 3 in its routing table as an external route, known via Router B. Router A knows, via its routing table, that to get to Network 3, it must pass the packet on to the next hop IP address, which is the interface of Router B on the transit network, Network 2. Router B will then check its routing table and determine that it's a directly connected route and forward the packet on to Host B.

In this scenario, Router A originally knows only about its directly connected networks, Network 1 and 2. Router B, likewise knows about its directly connected networks, Network 2 and 3. There are two ways for these routers to communicate to each other. One is to configure a **dynamic routing** protocol, such as one of the examples listed above (RIP, OSPF, EIGRP, etc.). A dynamic routing protocol learns about its directly connected routes and then forwards that information to its directly connected routers, or in more complex environments, to other routers configured in the same process. In Figure 11-2, if we were using a distance vector protocol such as RIP, Router A would forward a copy of its routing table (Network 1 and 2) to Router B. Router B would do the same, passing a copy of its routing table (Network 2 and 3) to Router A. Router A would see that Network 3 is from an external router and install it in its routing table. Any future packet forwarded to Router A, destined to Network 3, it would know to forward to Router B.

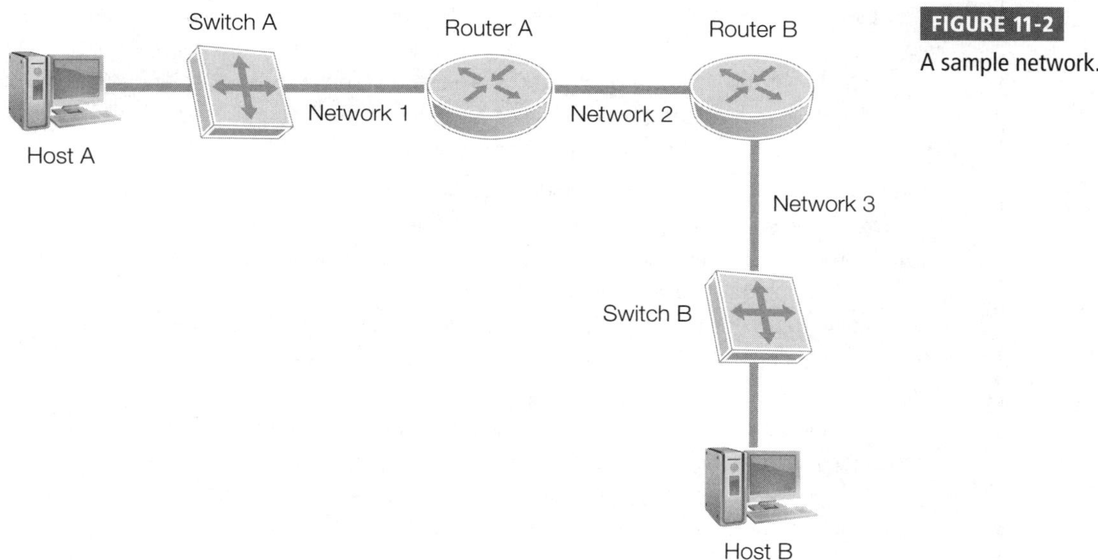

FIGURE 11-2

A sample network.

There is another way to route packets and manipulate path determination without the use of dynamic routing protocols. This method is called **static routing**. Static routing is typically only used in smaller environments with a network that doesn't experience much change. As opposed to dynamic routing protocols that share information with other routers, static routing remains locally significant to the router. Static routing is performed on the router by manually configuring static routes. These routes tell the router which interface or next hop router to use to get to a specific destination network. If a router loses a link to another router, these static routes have to be changed manually as there is no automatic network convergence feature such as is found in dynamic routing protocols.

To show how static routing works, we can reference Figure 11-2. In this example, if Router A needs to be able to get packets to Network 3, then a static route must be installed in Router A that says, "To get to Network 3, forward packets to Router B." If we set up this environment in a lab and configured that previous static route and had sniffers, or network capture devices, on each side, we would see the traffic from Router A reaching Host B. The problem is the return traffic would fail, as Router B would not know how to pass the return traffic. Therefore, a static route also must be configured on Router B that says "To get to Network 1, forward packets to Router A." This would allow full communication between the two hosts.

Static Routing

Static routing is a very simple way to get routers to communicate. While it's true that it's used mostly in smaller networks that don't require much change, you typically will see some form of static routes in almost every network. Static routes can be configured many different ways. They can be set up for use only if another routing protocol process fails. They can also be used to dynamically track an interface or IP address and disappear from the routing table if the interface or IP address is down. There are many ways to use static routes, and they are used for a wide range of functions. Different vendors will deploy them in their own way, but they all have them available to use.

The example of static routing referencing Figure 11-2 brings up an important point that is often overlooked when troubleshooting issues in a network. Whether it's troubleshooting a routing problem or a problem through a firewall, it's important always to remember that we are concerned not only with the packet reaching the destination, but also the return packet reaching the source. This is too often overlooked when troubleshooting routing or firewall problems. There is one way to help isolate this when using routers. It is to debug the Internet Control Message Protocol (ICMP) on both source and destination routers. As you ping the destination router from the source router, if you do not get replies back on the ping, yet the engineer logged into the destination router sees the ICMP debug messages, then the packets are making it to the destination but failing in their return. This scenario assumes that an engineer has eyes locally on the destination device.

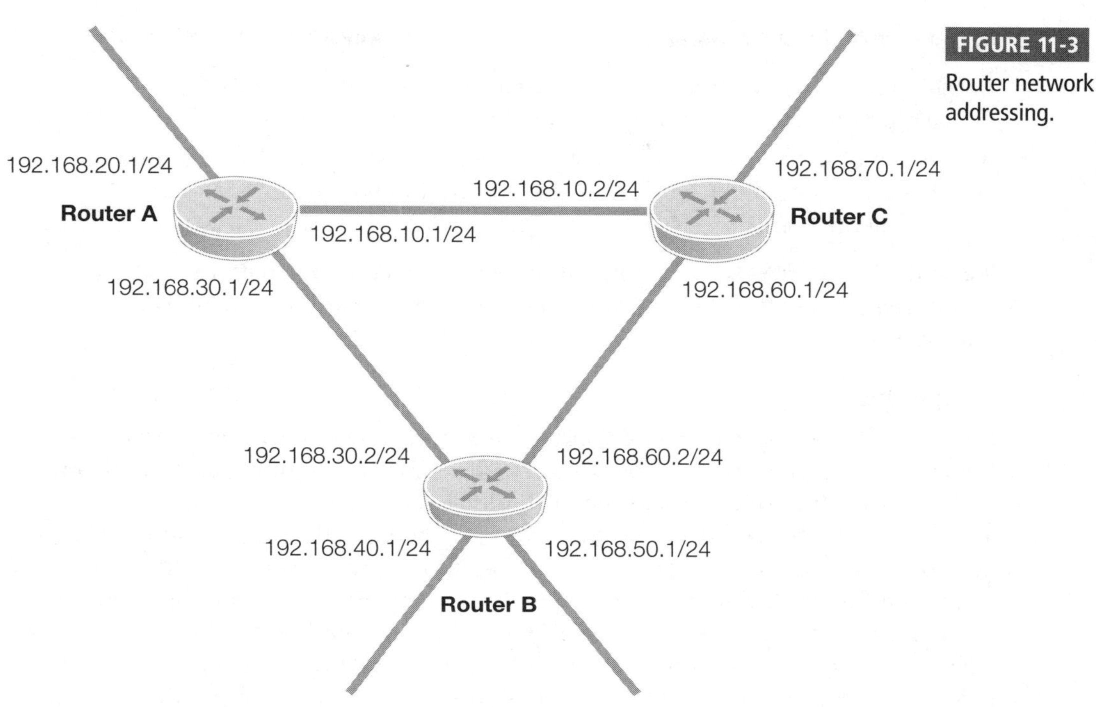

FIGURE 11-3
Router network addressing.

Now that we have learned how routing tables are updated, let's look at an example with multiple paths. Figure 11-3 shows a three-router network with Router A connected to networks 192.168.10.1, 192.168.20.1, and 192.168.30.1; Router B is connected to networks 192.168.30.2, 192.168.40.1, 192.168.50.1, and 192.168.60.2; and Router C is connected to networks 192.168.60.1, 192.168.10.2, and 192.168.70.1. Notice that to each router, the networks to which it is attached is recognized by the IP address assigned to the interface port to which the network is attached. Each interface recognizes and supports the protocols of each link and can therefore determine the state of each network (up or down).

To build its routing table:

1. Router A uses the subnet masks associated with each interface to determine that it is attached to networks 192.168.10.0, 192.168.20.0, and 192.168.30.0.
2. Router A then adds an entry for each network into its routing table along with the information that each network is directly connected.
3. Router A then sends routing update packets to Routers B and C informing them that it is directly connected to these three networks.
4. Routers B and C perform the same steps and send routing updates to Router A informing it of their directly connected networks.
5. Router A updates its routing table with the source address included in each router's routing update packet and the network addresses provided by each router.

However simple this may sound, it can become more complicated and troublesome:

- Both Routers B and C reported being directed connected to 192.168.60.0. Which is the better choice for reaching that network, or are they equals?
- Should Router A update Router C about the networks reported from Router B? What if the connection between them is down? Should Router A pass that information along?

These and other questions concerning the status, availability, and path to various networks require additional information before they can be answered. This is where routing metrics come in.

Routing Metrics

If we assume each router has shared routing information with the other two routers in Figure 11-3, we know that certain networks appear to have multiple paths to them. In order for a router to choose between the multiple routes available to reach a network, some criteria must be used to decide on which is the better path. The criterion used by a router to choose one route over another to a specific network is called a routing metric. A metric is a value calculated for each route that ranks the available routing options. The router then chooses, based on the best metric value, which path to take.

Table 11-1 shows the beginnings of an entry in Router A's routing table. This entry shows that to reach network 192.168.50.0, Router A has two distinct routing options: the directly connected links to each of Router B and Router C.

At this point, the routing table entry contains no information indicating which of the two routing options is the better path to use. A metric stored for each of the routing options that provides a relative ranking is needed. The criteria and meaning of a routing metric vary with each of the different routing protocols. Routing protocols use two metrics primarily: hop count and bandwidth.

Not all routing protocols use the same metrics. The **Routing Information Protocol (RIP)** bases its "best" route decisions strictly on the lowest hop count. Cisco's **Enhanced Interior Gateway Routing Protocol (EIGRP)** uses a metric that is a combination of the bandwidth and **delay** of each route and a few other factors.

TABLE 11-1 A partial entry in a routing table.

DESTINATION NETWORK	ROUTE OPTIONS
192.168.50.0	192.168.30.2/24
	192.168.10.2/24

TABLE 11-2 A routing table with a hop count metric.

DESTINATION NETWORK	ROUTE OPTIONS	HOP COUNT
192.168.50.0	192.168.30.2/24	1
	192.168.10.2/24	2

Hop count. A **hop count** metric indicates the number of intermediary routers a packet will have to pass through to reach a destination network. The hop count is just a count of the number of times a packet must be forwarded by other routers to reach its destination. Each time a packet is forwarded, it counts as a hop.

Looking back at the network in Figure 11-3 and the information in Table 11-1, if hop count is added to the information, the hop count for a packet addressed to a host on the 192.168.50.0 network and passing through Router C is two. One hop is to Router C's 192.168.10.2 interface, and the second hop is to Router B through the 192.168.60.1 interface. The hop count for this packet through Router B is one, a direct connected link, 192.168.30.1.

Therefore, based strictly on the hop count metric, Router A would update its routing table with this information, as shown in Table 11-2. As long as this information remains true and hop count is the only metric in use, Router A will forward packets for the 192.168.50.0 network to Router B.

Bandwidth. Sometimes hop count doesn't really tell the whole story of a link. Perhaps the link from Router A to Router B (see Figure 11-3) is a dial-up line, and the link between Router A and Router C is a dedicated leased T-1 line. In this exaggerated example, it's relatively easy to say that the two-hop link actually may be the better path after all. Bandwidth and the condition of the link is another way to determine the quality of a routing option. A routing protocol that uses a bandwidth metric chooses a path with higher bandwidth over one with lower bandwidth, regardless of the type of link. Bandwidth, all by itself, may not be a single indicator of the condition and quality of a link. It could be that a 56 kbps link is very lightly loaded, and the T-1 link is seeing heavy use at any given moment.

In addition to the bandwidth of a particular link, other metrics can factor in to determine the overall desirability of the link, especially in comparison to other available links. The other metrics that may be included in this determination, when using EIGRP, are:

- **Load**—On any particular route, hop count and bandwidth generally stay the same. However, the amount of traffic or load on the link can fluctuate quickly. A routing protocol that depends too heavily on the line loading for its routing determination may end up with what is called route flapping, rapidly changing the preferred route from one route to another and perhaps back again. However, the idea behind using a load metric is that the best path is the one with the lightest load.

- **Delay**—A delay metric essentially measures a link's throughput or transit time, the duration time for a packet to completely navigate a link end-to-end. A routing protocol using a delay metric favors the link with the least delay. A delay metric can be developed a variety of ways: clocking the time between when a packet is forwarded until the time the packet is acknowledged, for example. Alternatively, it could be the sum of the delay expected from the types of media along the link, and any delay caused by latency of the routers and queuing that occurs along the route. Or delay can be just a time estimate based solely on the link's medium.
- **Reliability**—The **reliability** metric is an indicator of how likely the link may fail during a transmission. Reliability metrics are either variable or fixed. A variable reliability metric may be a count of the actual number of failures that have occurred on a link within a specific time. A fixed reliability metric is a static metric that is typically manually configured by the network administrator and is based on his or her knowledge of a particular link. Of course, the path with the highest indication of reliability would be the preferred link.
- **Maximum transmission unit (MTU)**—It is often referenced in materials that MTU is the fifth factor in deciding the EIGRP metric. The **maximum transmission unit (MTU)** is *not* used in the calculation of the metric. It is, however, tracked through the path to determine the smallest MTU.

Cost. In the context of routing, a cost metric doesn't refer to dollars and cents, but rather to relative metric value that is used to set the condition of a comparison. For example, the route with the lowest cost is likely the link that has the lowest overall value for the metrics included in the path determination method of a protocol. Any path chosen as a preferred route will be the routing option with the lowest cost.

Convergence

Whether a network router is a part of something as large as the Internet (and nearly all gateway or border routers are) or a single gateway router for a two-node network, its routing table must be kept up-to-date with the latest status of the links to which it and its neighboring routers are directly connected. In order to do this, the routing protocol must send out update packets to the other nearby routers whenever a link has failed or its metrics no longer make it a preferred route.

It is critical for neighboring routers to know of the most current condition of the network links so as to avoid routing loops. If two routers determine that each is the best route to a particular network, packets will be forwarded back and forth until either the route condition changes or the message times out and is dropped.

Whenever a major change occurs in the routing table of a router, such as a topology change that involves a new router being added or a router being removed, routing update packets are sent out on all links connected to external networks. Typically, there is a slight delay on the network, and little packet traffic is forwarded until the routing tables of the directly connected devices are once again synchronized, or are in what is called convergence. The time it takes the network to reach convergence is called convergence time.

Load Balancing

Routing protocols may also divide traffic being forwarded to a particular destination address that has two or more paths that can be used. If a particular link has substantial traffic being forwarded on it to reach a particular network, it's more efficient to divide the traffic and forward it alternatively on two or perhaps more links rather than queue it up and wait for a single link.

Internetwork Routing Functions

LAN-to-LAN Routing

When a host on one LAN transmits a message to a host on another LAN connected to the same router, one of two things can happen, depending on the characteristics of the LANs. If the two LANs are running the same network technology, such as Ethernet, it's a simple matter of extracting the destination host's network ID and forwarding the message packets to the link in the routing table.

However, if the two LANs are running different network technologies, such as Ethernet on one and token ring on the second, a new step must be added to the process to preserve the original message for delivery on the second network technology. Layer 3 protocols must be able to interface with the frame formats of different Layer 2 networking technologies.

Let's say we have a case where an Ethernet network is forwarding a message to be delivered on a token ring network. In this case, the router must be relied upon to encapsulate the original message without losing either the data or its Layer 3 logical source and destination addresses, into token ring frame formats. Regardless of which two networking technologies are in use, the translation of higher-level packets into lower-level frames compatible with the network technology is a required Layer 3 function for a router.

LAN-to-WAN Routing

In much the same way as in LAN-to-LAN routing, the Network Layer protocols running on a LAN router must be able to interface with all of the lower layer protocols and methods. It is common that a packet being transmitted to the internetwork will traverse through two or more hops (routers). At each hop, the message packets must process up from the Physical Layer and Data Link Layer to be recognized and analyzed by the hop's Layer 3 protocols. After the router determines the path to which the packet is to be forwarded, the packet is passed down through the lower levels for transmission on that link.

Routing Metrics

Routing protocols can essentially be broken down into two types: link-state routing protocols and distance-vector routing protocols. While both types of routing protocols forward packets, the way they go about it separates them into two distinct groups.

Routing protocols calculate a variety of metrics, values, and indicators to rank available paths to certain logical addresses on a WAN. Each different routing protocol has a unique algorithm that factors a different value or set of values to develop the cost of a link, with the smaller value (lowest cost) indicating the better route choice.

Regardless of the type of routing protocol in use, the metrics and their meanings are relatively constant from protocol to protocol. The metrics used by routing protocols to determine the better path available are:

- **Bandwidth**—The maximum throughput rate available on a link.
- **Cost**—A summary metric that indicates the relative ranking (better or worse) of a link's usability.
- **Delay**—The duration time for a packet to reach its destination on a specific link; delay is measured in ticks, or one-eighteenth of a second.
- **Hop count**—The number of routers (hops) a packet must pass through to reach the network of its destination address.
- **Load**—A measurement for the amount of traffic flowing through a particular router, as expressed in available processing resources.
- **MTU (maximum transmission unit)**—The length in bytes of the longest message unit that can be transmitted on available links that connect a source address to a destination address.
- **Reliability**—A measurement of the amount of downtime on a particular link that indicates the reliability of the link.

Each of the more common routing protocols uses at least one metric to determine the better path to reach a destination. The Routing Information Protocol (RIP), a distance-vector routing protocol, uses hop count as an indicator of distance to a destination. Open Shortest Path First (OSPF), a link-state routing protocol, uses cost to indicate the shortest path to a destination. Enhanced Interior Gateway Protocol (EIGRP), which is a hybrid of both distance-vector and link-state, is based on distance-vector metrics that are more accurate.

Another metric that comes into play is administrative distance (AD). The AD is a relative indication of how trustworthy a particular route is. When a router begins determining the better route for a packet, it first looks at the AD metric of each route available. If the ADs are equal, the protocol proceeds to determine the route using other metrics.

TABLE 11-3 Default administrative distances for Cisco routers.

ROUTE SOURCE/PROTOCOL	DEFAULT AD
Directly connected	0 (Most reliable)
Static route	1
EIGRP	90
IGRP	100
OSPF	110
IS-IS	115
RIP	120
Unknown	255 (Least reliable)

A link that is unavailable is assigned an AD of 255, the highest value (lowest reliability) on the AD scale. The AD is locally significant to the router and is not transmitted in routing updates. Administrative distances vary depending on vendor.

Each link type has a default AD. An example of these values used by Cisco are listed in Table 11-3.

Link-State Routing Protocols

As its name implies, a **link-state routing protocol** is concerned with tracking the status and type of each link to which its router is connected. A link-state routing protocol, like OSPF and IS-IS, calculates a metric, via the use of Dijkstra's shortest path first (SPF) algorithm, that considers the status (state) of a link and its connection type, speed, and delay. This metric indicates that the link is active or inactive, its bandwidth, and the cost of transmitting a packet on the link. The link-state metric also may include some parameters manually configured by the network administrator.

Since a routing protocol can't see beyond the interface ports on a router, in effect a link-state protocol monitors the status of the interface ports available to it. Because link-state routing protocols don't consider metrics like hop count, it is possible that a link-state routing protocol could forward a packet on a faster (shortest) link with more hops over a slower link with fewer hops.

Through its metrics, a link-state routing protocol forms a logical imagery of the topology of its neighboring routers and itself. It then shares this information so that every router has the exact same view of the internetwork. Each router regularly shares information with its neighboring routers on its state and that of any directly connected links it has.

Link-state information is often referred to as an image or snapshot that is passed around for the other routers to capture and record for later use. Link-state routing protocols send update packets only when there is a change in the topology, or rather a change in a link. For example, when OSPF senses a change in the state of a link, a link-state advertisement (LSA) is transmitted as a multicast to the other routers on the topology by the router detecting the change. Each of the other routers uses the information in the LSA to update its state metric on the affected link and then forwards the LSA on to its neighboring devices. Figure 11-4 illustrates how link-state routing protocols react to a link failure in a topology.

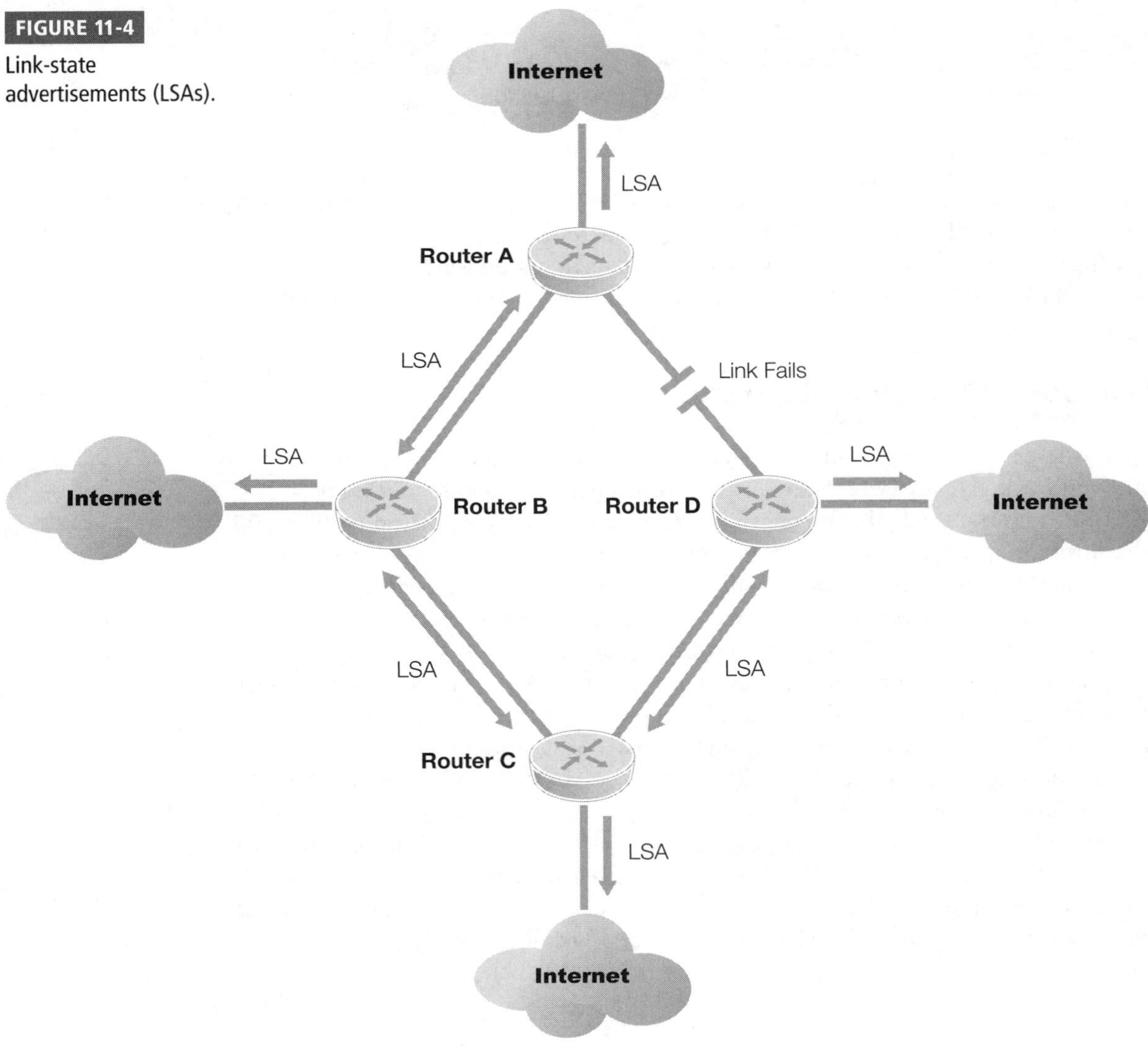

FIGURE 11-4

Link-state advertisements (LSAs).

Distance-Vector Routing Protocols

In the context of routing protocols, distance refers to the number of hops or an accumulated value derived from a set of administrative metrics. Vector is another word for interface, port, or link. Therefore, simplistically, a distance-vector would be the link or interface that has the lowest (shortest) distance and represents the better choice for forwarding a packet. Distance-vector routing is based on the Bellman-Ford algorithm, named after its creators. Like a link-state routing protocol, **distance-vector routing protocols** send updates out to their neighbors when there is a topology change in the network. However, a distance-vector routing protocol doesn't update all of its neighboring devices. In fact, a distance-vector routing protocol only knows the distance and direction (interface port) to neighboring devices that are one hop away.

A distance-vector routing protocol periodically sends out updates that transmit all or most of its router's routing table to nearby neighbors that are running the same distance-vector routing protocol. Once a neighboring router receives this update, it applies it to its own routing table and transmits updates, including its newly updated routing table, on to its neighbors—except the one from which it received the original update message. One of the downsides to distance-vector routing is that there is no way to verify the information used to maintain routing tables, which is why distance-vector routing is referred to as "routing by rumor."

In addition to distance, distance-vector routing protocols use different metrics to determine the better path available. RIP bases its determinations on hop count; IGRP also uses hop count, but considers node delay and bandwidth in its determinations; and **Border Gateway Protocol (BGP)**, a path vector routing protocol, uses path metrics and network policies to determine how reachable a destination address is.

Interior Versus Exterior Routing Protocols

Routing protocols, in general, are divided into two groups based on where they are located in the internetwork, and how they perform routing functions. Both link-state and distance-vector routing protocols are either an interior or exterior gateway protocol.

Interior Routing Protocols

Interior routing protocols, commonly referred to as interior gateway protocols (IGPs), perform routing functions within an **autonomous system (AS)**, which is essentially one routing domain. IGPs are used to perform routing among the routers owned by a single entity or under the control of a single network administrator. Examples of IGP's include RIP, RIPv2, IGRP, EIGRP, OSPF, and IS-IS.

Autonomous Systems

An AS is a grouping of connected IP networks that are managed, maintained, and controlled by a common administrator. The essential purpose of an AS is to implement a common routing policy on an internetwork. Each AS is assigned a unique and registered AS number (ASN) that identifies its routing policy to higher-level routing protocols, such as BGP. BGP uses both public and private ASNs. Private ASNs are used within large enterprise networks and are not known outside the network, whereas public ASNs are used when peering with a service provider network to route public IP addresses onto the Internet. A useful tool for seeing which carrier owns a respective ASN is to use a "looking glass" tool. Many carriers provide these looking glass tools on their Web site. They can be found by simply doing an Internet search for "looking glass."

Exterior Routing Protocols

Exterior routing protocols, also called exterior gateway protocols (EGPs), are used to route messages outside of an AS or between two networks. An EGP, like the BGP, is used to move messages through the Internet cloud. Another common use of EGPs is to facilitate communications on the internetwork for a company or organization that subscribes to services from more than one service provider.

Routing Information Protocol (RIP)

RIP is a distance-vector routing protocol that uses hop count as its routing metric. Essentially, the better available route is the one with the lowest hop count. However, like all distance-vector routing protocols, RIP maintains a routing table that is updated regularly by neighboring routers (running RIP); RIP updates its routing table with unconfirmed information. Because routing updates may not always be up-to-date or provide a complete picture of a network anomaly, errors in a routing table can cause routing loops.

A routing loop is a common routing problem, especially on dynamic routing protocols that operate in essentially a one-hop circumference, like RIP and OSPF. Routing loops can involve many network nodes, but to illustrate this problem, consider a routing loop between two network nodes. As shown in Figure 11-5, networks (routers) A, B, and C are known to each other. Setting routing metrics aside for the time being, Network A believes the route to Network C passes through Network B. Network B believes that the route to Network C passes through Network A. Packets that arrive at either A or B addressed to C will end up in an endless loop between A and B as each forward packets to the other trying to reach C.

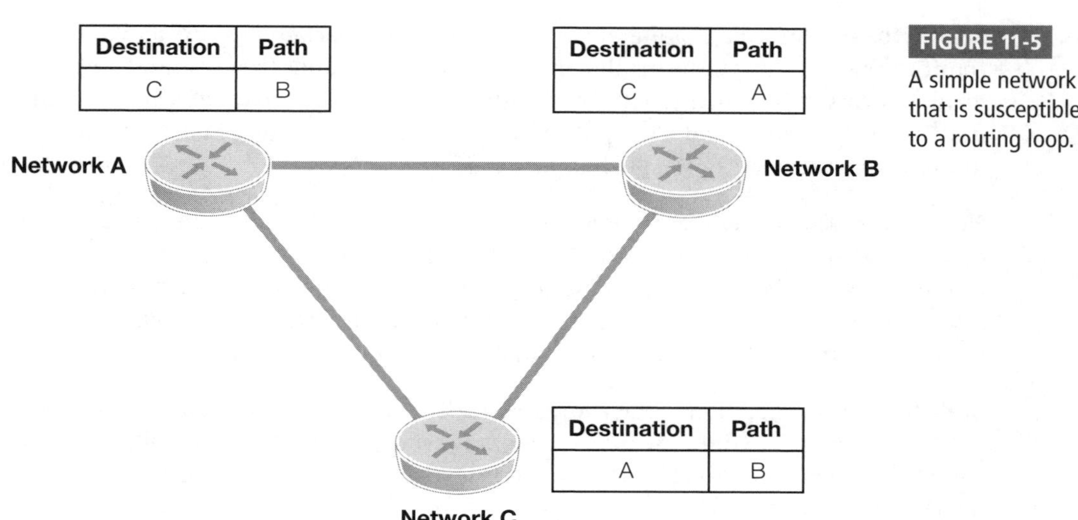

FIGURE 11-5 A simple network that is susceptible to a routing loop.

In an attempt to prevent routing loops from occurring, distance-vector routing protocols employ a variety of timers and mechanisms. These items are discussed below.

Timers and Mechanisms

Hold-down timer. In some distance-vector routing protocols, such as RIP, the hop count is the primary routing metric. The number of hops on the alternative routes between a local router and a distant node determine the better route. The high limit for a reachable node on a remote network is 15 hops, meaning a path requires a packet to pass through fifteen forwarding devices before it reaches the network of its destination node. A hop count of 16 indicates a particular network node is unreachable, at least it was the last time the network was checked, or an update was provided.

Because the topology of the network can change relatively frequently, simply marking a route as unreachable and then forgetting it may limit the capability of the router to use the better route available. On the other hand, if a remote router is truly unreachable, the network needs time to be informed of this and for convergence to be restored. In order to allow time for both or either of these events to take place, when a routing table entry is given the value of 16 (unreachable), it is considered to be in **hold-down** and a hold-down timer begins counting down from 180 seconds (by default). Until the hold-down timer reaches zero, the router will not accept updates on that particular link. The hold-down time also is started when the hop count of a remote device increases or decreases. On many routers, the hold-down timer can be configured by the network administrator. However, this is delicate business; if the hold-down period is too long, normal routing operations may be disrupted; if the timer is set too short, reconvergence most likely didn't occur.

Invalid timer. Immediately after an update arrives for a particular route and the routing table is updated, the invalid timer is set to 180 seconds (by default). If the invalid timer should reach zero before another update is received to refresh the route, the route is marked invalid. The route entry remains in the routing table, but only until an update arrives or the flush timer expires.

Flush timer. The flush timer is set to 240 seconds (by default) at the same time the hold-down timer is set to 180 seconds. The extra 60 seconds provides additional time just in case an update or refresh message arrives for the route. Once a suspect route has completed a hold-down period, the route has another 60 seconds to live before it is removed (flushed) from the routing table.

Update timer. In addition to the above timers, RIP also employs a route update timer (AKA routing update timer), which is generally set to 30 seconds by default. This timer controls the time interval before RIP sends its entire routing table to every enabled interface port running RIP.

Split horizon. When the update timer reaches zero, RIP broadcasts its entire routing table to all of its neighboring routers. Looking back at Figure 11-5, when Router A's update timer reaches zero, Router A broadcasts its routing table to Routers B and C. Because both of the other routers also have update timers (assuming they are running a distance-vector routing protocol such as RIP), the chances are good that much of the information Router A has in its routing table just came from Router B (or Router C, but let's keep this simple) a few seconds ago. In the interest of bandwidth and reducing network traffic, Router A really doesn't need to update Router B with its own information. In fact, every router in Router A's routing table that has a hop count between 0 and 15 most likely received the same information from Router B.

An entry in a routing table that points back to the source of a packet is a reverse route. The **split horizon** mechanism prevents reverse routes between two routers and helps to prevent the possibility of a routing loop. Two levels of split horizon can be implemented on a distance-vector routing protocol:

- **Simple split horizon**—This version of split horizon does not send information or update packets about a route through the interface port used to reach that route. An example is if Router B tells Router A that it is on path 10.50.100.200, there is no need for Router A to tell Router B that it is on path 10.50.100.200.
- **Split horizon with poisoned reverse**—On larger networks, simple split horizon may not prevent routing loops between more distant routers. So, instead of simply not advertising a route to its source, split horizon with **poisoned reverse** keeps these routes in its routing table, but marks (poisons) all information that came from a particular interface with an infinite distance metric before broadcasting its routing table to the network. While poisoned reverse is most commonly used with split horizon, it also can be implemented with hold-down timers.

FYI

RIP is one of the easiest routing protocols to deploy, configure, and troubleshoot, as the protocol is fairly simple. However, while it may be easy to deploy, it does not scale well and should not be used beyond smaller-scale networks. Typically, most all routers, small to large from any vendor, have support in their OS for RIP. In addition, because of the added features in RIPv2, it is always preferable to use RIPv2 over RIP.

RFC 2080 defines RIP next generation (RIPng), which adds support for IPv6 and the requirement for IPSec for authentication.

RIP Version 2 (RIPv2)

The original version of RIP had its share of problems and limitations. Therefore, in 1998, RIP version 2 (RIPv2) was standardized. The new release of RIP included the capability to carry subnetwork information and support CIDR. Another difference in the RIPv2 technology over RIP is that RIPv2 multicasts its routing table to its neighboring routers on a standard multicast address (224.0.0.9), where RIP simply broadcasted its information with unicast addressing. RIPv2 also includes the capability to tag routes as internal or external redistribution routes from edge and border gateway protocols.

Interior Gateway Routing Protocol (IGRP)

Like RIP, the **Interior Gateway Routing Protocol (IGRP)** is an interior distance-vector routing protocol, but that's where the similarities end. IGRP was developed by Cisco Systems to improve on the limitations of RIP, especially the use of a single routing metric. IGRP exchanges its routing information with other routers within its AS.

IGRP uses multiple metrics to characterize routes, including hop count, bandwidth, delay, load, MTU length, and reliability. These metrics are distilled down to a single metric that is used for comparison purposes in choosing the better router available. IGRP raises the maximum hop count to a maximum of 255. IGRP routing updates are broadcast every 90 seconds, by default.

IGRP is a classful routing protocol in that it doesn't apply a subnet mask directly. IGRP assumes that all addresses within an IP address class, whether Class A, B, or C, share the subnet mask of the interface port through which they are reached.

Enhanced Interior Gateway Routing Protocol (EIGRP)

The Enhanced Interior Gateway Routing Protocol (EIGRP), another Cisco proprietary protocol, is a hybrid interior routing protocol that combines the shortest-path considerations of a link-state routing protocol with the metrics of IGRP into what is called Diffusing-Update Algorithm Finite-State Machine (DUAL FSM). DUAL, its short name, dynamically adjusts routing table entries based on changes in the network topology.

EIGRP adds a feasibility condition to its routing metrics that is intended to make sure that only loop-free routing is ever used. If no route is feasible (loop-free), DUAL uses a diffusing computation to purge any references to a problem network from the routing tables of the AS. In normal operation, two routers running EIGRP establish a neighbor relationship and begin exchanging route information. To ensure that its neighbors know of its condition, EIGRP routers multicast "hello" or "keepalive" UDP datagrams to their neighbors regularly. Should a keepalive packet not arrive on time, a router knows that its neighbor or its link is down.

Intermediate System-to-Intermediate System (IS-IS)

IS-IS was originally defined in International Organization for Standardization (ISO) 10589 as an international standard within the Open Systems Interconnection (OSI) Reference Model. The IETF published IS-IS as an Internet Standard in RFC 1142. IS-IS is a link-state routing protocol and operates by flooding link-state information to all other routers within an area participating in the IS-IS process. It was originally developed to support routing of datagrams using the OSI protocol stack called Connectionless Network Service (CLNS). CLNS is the service provided by Connectionless Network Protocol (CLNP) and used by Transport Protocol Class 4 (TP4). This is similar to the widely used TCP/IP protocol.

IS-IS was later extended to provide support for IP. This version of IS-IS is referred to as Integrated IS-IS or Dual IS-IS. In today's networks, it is just referred to as IS-IS. As a link-state routing protocol, IS-IS uses the Dijkstra shortest path first (SPF) algorithm, as does OSPF, to calculate the best path through the network. It sends out link state protocol data units (LSPs), also referred to as link-state packets, to other IS-IS routers in the area. These LSPs contain information regarding the connected links, neighbor routes, IP subnets, and metric information. The routers build and synchronize a link-state database (LSDB) so that they all have the same topology representation of the network.

The biggest advantage of IS-IS is its ability to scale. Therefore, it is most commonly seen in large ISPs. In ISP networks, it is critical for the network architect to be able to manipulate traffic based on network requirements. An example of these requirements might be something like having one path to a destination routing through the north side of the United States while another path routes traffic through the south side. IS-IS has extensions for traffic engineering, which allow the protocol to manipulate traffic flow across the network in a way that is not possible in most other protocols.

Open Shortest Path First (OSPF)

Open Shortest Path First (OSPF) is a link-state routing protocol and is considered an Interior Gateway Protocol (IGP) as it distributes routing information to other routers within the same AS. It has enhanced features such as support for Variable Length Subnet Masks (VLSM), route summarization, and the use of authentication for routing updates.

Each OSPF router shares an identical link-state database. This database acts as a topology of all of the routers in an area. Routing tables are then built by referencing this database and constructing a shortest-path tree using Dijkstra's shortest path first (SPF) algorithm. These routing tables dictate the paths to reach others routers within the AS via mapping metrics to each path. These metrics are called cost.

OSPF uses hello packets to verify link information between routers. On broadcast networks, such as Ethernet, these packets are generated every 10 seconds, and on non-broadcast multiple access (NBMA) networks, such as X.25 and Frame Relay, every 30 seconds.

The recalculation of routes is performed very quickly with OSPF, and convergence happens much quicker than RIP. The reason for this is because link-state information is flooded to all routers whenever a change occurs as opposed to RIP, which processes this information per hop. If a change has not occurred, OSPF sends out link-state information once every 30 minutes, compared to every 30 seconds with RIP. OSPF uses the term "areas" to define groups of routers that share the same LSDB. "Area 0" is referred to as the backbone area, and all other areas must connect to Area 0. In smaller networks, it is typical to see just one area used. As the network grows larger, it is useful to split up the network into different areas to help limit routing traffic updates and to allow for a more manageable network environment.

The number of areas that are set up in the OSPF network, and whether the network will be connected to other routers using different routing protocols, will determine the different types of OSPF routers. OSPF classifies four different router types:

- **Internal router**—A router with all directly connected interfaces in a single area.
- **Area border router**—An area border router (ABR) has at least one interface in Area 0 and another interface in another area. These routers advertise routes from the backbone into other non-backbone areas and vice versa. An ABR also can advertise summary routes from one area into another. An ABR contains a LSDB for every area to which it has an interface.
- **Backbone routers**—A router with at least one interface in the backbone area, Area 0. A router can be both an internal router and a backbone router if all of its interfaces reside in Area 0. Likewise, an area border router is also considered a backbone router.
- **Autonomous system boundary router**—When connecting an OSPF area to another AS and distributing information from another exterior gateway protocol (EGP), or AS, the ASBR is used to help disseminate this routing information into the OSPF area.

FYI

While an extensive study of any one of these protocols referenced is out of the scope of this chapter, it is helpful to know the key points to study and master. In regard to OSPF, it is important to understand the different router types as shown above, as well as the different LSA types (LSAs 1–7). It's also important to understand the different area types: backbone, stub, not-so-stubby area (NSSA), totally stubby, NSSA totally stubby (yes, that's correct), and transit. Entire books have been published on single routing protocols such as OSPF. If you want to get an in-depth understanding, these books are highly recommended.

Border Gateway Protocol (BGF)

The BGP is a path vector routing protocol that routes messages between networks and autonomous systems. The routing table of BGP contains a prefix code for each IP network and its reachability. This type of routing is called path vector routing, and its routing decisions are based on network policies (configured by its administrators), path information (prefixes), and routing rule sets. BGP is also commonly referred to as a reachability protocol. Perhaps the most common application of BGP is between Internet service providers (ISPs) and, although it is an exterior routing protocol, BGP is used as an interior protocol within the very large networks of corporations and governments.

A unique autonomous system number (ASN), numbered 1–64511, is allocated to each public AS that participates in routing on the Internet. A private ASN, numbered 64512–65535, can be used for corporations wishing to use BGP internally within their network. Another example is a customer who may choose to run a private ASN when peering to its ISP. In this scenario, the private ASN is not distributed to the Internet,

Routing Protocols in the Real World

This chapter covers a wide range of both distance-vector and link-state protocols. However, in the real world, some of these protocols are used much more than others. A perfect example is both RIP and IGRP. With the enhancements of RIP to RIPv2, there is no reason to use the original version of RIP. RIP doesn't support discontiguous networks or variable length subnet masks (VLSM). IGRP functions in much of the same way and is now unsupported by Cisco in their latest IOS releases. EIGRP is Cisco's replacement protocol and is widely used in Cisco-only networks.

The most common protocols seen on medium-to-large enterprise networks are OSPF and EIGRP. If the network is using any combination of vendor devices other than Cisco, then the choice to use OSPF is simple, as EIGRP is only supported on Cisco devices. IS-IS is not seen much in enterprise networks but is quite prevalent in service provider networks. IS-IS works well with MPLS and Traffic Engineering. This allows you more granular flexibility with the protocol to adjust routes and traffic patterns.

BGP can be used in association with any of these protocols. It is most commonly used to connect to service provider networks to gain access to the Internet. BGP is the core protocol used to route Internet traffic. In smaller networks, a network engineer might decide to only receive default routes via BGP. This setup forwards all unknown destinations out to the Internet. Larger networks that want more visibility into the Internet and have servers themselves that they want advertised on the Internet often will receive full BGP tables from the service provider. This means that the customer edge router will have a view into the entire route table of the Internet. The current Internet routing table size, at the time of this writing, contains almost 380,000 entries. Therefore, it requires a robust router with a large amount of resources.

and the ISP handles the distribution of network prefixes on the customer's behalf. Prefixes are used within BGP to advertise a network block of IP addresses.

Typically, companies that have a requirement to have public IP addresses for Web servers, etc., will receive a block of publicly routable IP addresses from their ISP. The ISP takes that block of network addresses, or network prefix, and combines it into a larger prefix to advertise to other ISPs. This way when someone outside the network needs to browse to the companies' Web server, the packet will traverse the ISP that owns, and is advertising, that larger block of addresses. From there the ISP knows to route the packet down to the specific customer. In these types of environments, it is typical for the customer to receive only a default route from the ISP as they are only using one connection to the Internet.

In larger networks that require the use of multi-homed circuits, or have more than one ISP, it is often necessary to receive full BGP tables from the ISPs. In this scenario, Customer A will apply for its own address space from an Internet registry. An Internet registry is an entity that manages the assignment of public IP addresses to both ISPs and corporations. Customer A has a multi-homed connection to two different ISPs. Each ISP will advertise out Customer A's IP prefix via BGP to their upstream ISPs. These ISPs then readvertise the IP prefix out to other ISPs that they peer with. A customer outside of this network that needs to browse to the Web server will route out to its own respective ISP. From there, this ISP generally will see two different paths. It will look at which route has the shortest AS path, and it will forward the traffic on to the ISP, which will then forward it to Customer A's Web server.

Network and Router Resilience

A network's capability to maintain a certain level and quality of service at all times, regardless of faults and interruptions, is **resilience**. In other words, the network is resilient to failure. In order for the network to be resilient, its Physical Layer media, its Layer 2 network access functions, and its Layer 3 forwarding and addressing functions must have hot-swap redundancy ready to take over when there is a network or system failure. However, please understand that redundancy and resiliency are not the same thing.

Configuring Resilience

Redundancy can provide resiliency, but only through the installation of additional devices, systems, or links that are able to come online when the primary device, system, or link fails. Redundant devices also can be used in a load sharing situation, which means they are already online and ready to take on the entire load, if needed. However, when certain devices fail, for example, a power supply unit (PSU) installed in a router as a backup to its main PSU, the backup devices must be configured or have the power to fully replace the failed part. Too often, the backup device cannot support the load of the primary device, which means the backup part is worthless.

Creating resiliency on a network makes that network fault-tolerant. However, just having redundant devices or links won't create resiliency unless you have configured your routers to make use of it should the primary link or device fail.

The first steps in configuring a resilient network are to determine how resilient the network needs to be and just where in the network resilience is needed. For the most part, adding resilience to a network can be accomplished at virtually no cost, since most network switches and routers already support the basic tools. Remember that on a resilient network, a short delay, which used to be acceptable, is no longer good. In fact, users shouldn't know that an interruption occurred.

The easiest steps to take are to run redundant links between the switches and routers and implement Spanning Tree Protocol (STP) or Rapid Spanning Tree (RST) to avoid loops and configure the timer settings to eliminate delays. Technology such as Cisco's EtherChannel, which configures link aggregation, allows the network devices and protocols to believe that the multiple links between devices are just one link. When one link fails, to the network services there was seemingly no failure at all. This is true even if the failure is a connection on the router or switch. Cisco IOS has a resilient configuration feature, that when enabled, allows the router to keep a current copy of its configuration to guard against attacks that attempt to erase its memory.

Routing Protocol Resilience

Routing protocols also can support the resilience of a network, but the ability of the router and its routing protocol to recover quickly is dependent on the configuration of the router, the routing protocol, and the links connected to the router. Configuring the router for **load balancing** can add to the resilience of the network, but only if the router is connected to equal-cost links of equal capabilities. Otherwise, if a lower-cost link (bandwidth) fails, the higher-cost link may not be able to carry the entire **load**. It may need to be configured to carry only the most vital traffic when the primary link fails.

There are two routing protocols designed specifically to support and provide network resilience: the Hot Standby Routing Protocol (HSRP) and the **Virtual Router Redundancy Protocol (VRRP)**.

Hot Standby Routing Protocol (HSRP)

In computing, the word "hot" means that a device or service is powered, running, and ready to replace another device or service should it fail—as in "hot swap." In configuring a network for resilience, this meaning carries forward. The purpose of HSRP, which is a Cisco proprietary protocol, is to provide a hot swappable IP gateway to end devices, such as desktop PCs, laptops, and servers, without installing another physically redundant device. HSRP provides for a constant, virtual gateway to end devices.

What HSRP does is assign an IP address to a virtual router and then link the virtual router to the primary physical router. All other available routers to which it has links

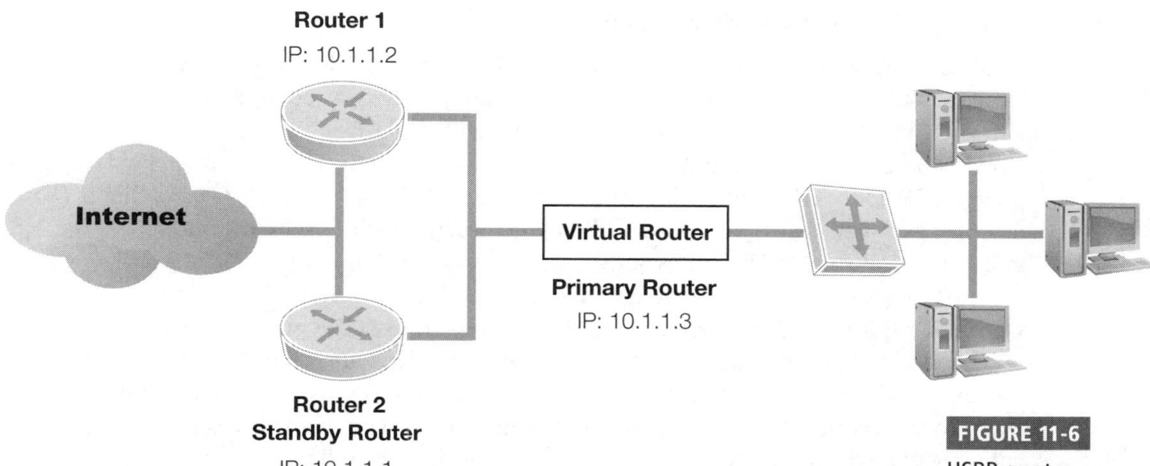

FIGURE 11-6
HSRP creates a virtual router that is the primary router for its network.

are listed as hot standbys. The end devices on the network reference only the IP address of the virtual router and don't know, and don't have to care, if the primary router fails because the hot standby router is now servicing traffic through the virtual router link.

As illustrated in Figure 11-6, the end devices are switched to the virtual router, which isn't a real device. Instead, they are switched to a virtual IP address that is linked to the primary router. Should the link to or the primary router itself fail, the same virtual address now links to the standby router. This applies only to outbound traffic.

The level of resiliency provided by HSRP is dependent on how fast the standby router is able to assume the role of primary router. If there is any downtime for the end devices, it amounts to only the time needed for the switchover. There also could be some convergence time involved as well. When the standby router becomes the primary router, for a short time the internetwork will still see the failed primary router as the gateway to its network. However, HSRP broadcasts its hello datagrams in milliseconds, and convergence should occur within a second or two.

Virtual Router Redundancy Protocol (VRRP)

VRRP is the standard redundancy protocol with functions similar to HSRP. VRRP routers cooperate to create a VRRP virtual router. A network may have several virtual routers using different combinations of the devices. In effect, VRRP routers hold an election based on priority values and select one router to be the master router. Each virtual router is designated with a virtual router identifier (VRID). Using the VRID arrangement, VRRP also can provide load balancing on each router's links.

Global Load Balancing Protocol (GLBP)

GLBP is a Cisco proprietary router that improves on the functionality of HSRP. While HSRP is useful for setting up a virtual IP address to be used as a redundant gateway, it lacks some features. The main feature that GLBP adds is the ability to load balance traffic over multiple routers. HSRP uses an active/standby model where a virtual IP address is managed by one router, the active router, and is always the primary gateway unless the router or link goes down, in which case a standby takes over that role and becomes active.

With GLBP, we are able to load balance cross multiple routers using a single virtual IP address and multiple virtual MAC addresses. A GLBP group is created, and each member is configured with the same virtual IP address, and all of the routers participate in forwarding packets. The members use hello messages, sent every three seconds, to communicate with one another. The members elect one gateway to be the active virtual gateway (AVG) for the group. The AVG then assigns a virtual MAC address to each group member (router). This mapping allows each router to act as active virtual forwarders (AVFs) for their virtual MAC address.

The AVG answers Address Resolution Protocol (ARP) requests for the virtual IP address. The AVG then load balances by replying to the ARP requests with different virtual MAC addresses of the respective AVFs. The AVFs then forward on the packets.

CHAPTER SUMMARY

In this chapter, we have discussed the basic operations of the OSI Reference Model's Layer 3 (Network Layer) routing, the way routing is used to forward messages to different network topologies and technologies, distance-vector and link-state routing protocols and their functions, the reasons for and the functions of Layer 3 resiliency, and the protocols used to implement it.

The routing capabilities of any network or internetwork provide its effectiveness as a facilitator in accessing information and resources within or external to a local network. The reliability of any network is dependent on how resilient the network is to faults and failures. A truly resilient network is able to switch to hot standby devices and services without the end user knowing it occurred.

KEY CONCEPTS AND TERMS

Autonomous system (AS)
Border Gateway Protocol (BGP)
Cost
Delay
Distance-vector routing protocol
Dynamic routing
Enhanced Interior Gateway Routing Protocol (EIGRP)
Exterior routing protocol
Hold-down
Hop count
Interior Gateway Routing Protocol (IGRP)
Interior routing protocols
Link-state routing protocol
Load
Load balancing
Maximum transmission unit (MTU)
Multi-homed
Poisoned reverse
Reliability
Resilience
Routed protocols
Routing Information Protocol (RIP)
Routing protocols
Routing tables
Split horizon
Static routing
Virtual Router Redundancy Protocol (VRRP)

CHAPTER 11 ASSESSMENT

1. Which of the following is/are Layer 3 functions or services?

A. Logical link management
B. Logical addressing
C. Physical addressing
D. Frame encapsulation

2. Routing occurs on the ________ Layer of the OSI Reference Model.

A. Data Link
B. Transport
C. Network
D. Session

3. A routing protocol maintains a routing table on which path determination is based.

A. True
B. False

4. Which routing protocol is used to route traffic on the Internet?

A. OSPF
B. BGP
C. RIPv2
D. EIGRP

5. The two forms of routing entries are dynamic and ________.

A. Logical
B. Metric
C. Multi-homed
D. Static

6. Which one of the following is a routed protocol?

A. RIP
B. SMTP
C. OSPF
D. IGRP

7. The routing metric that indicates the number of intermediary routers a packet must pass through to reach the network of its destination address is called the ________.

A. Delay
B. Hop count
C. Cost
D. Load

8. The bandwidth of a link is never used as a routing metric.

A. True
B. False

9. The condition that exists when the routing tables of neighboring routers are in synchronization is called ________.

A. Resiliency
B. Convergence
C. Confluence
D. Balance

10. The action in which a router divides and forwards incoming or outbound message traffic to multiple links is known as ________.

A. Convergence
B. Resiliency
C. Redundancy
D. Load balancing

11. The two types of dynamic routing protocols are link-state and distance-vector.

A. True
B. False

12. The length of the longest data unit that can be transmitted on an available link is the ________.

A. Hash count
B. Maximum transmission unit
C. Distance-vector
D. Link-state

13. Which distance-vector routing protocol bases its routing decisions solely on hop count?

A. OSPF
B. EIGRP
C. RIP
D. BGP

14. What methodology is used on networks to prevent routing loops?

A. Resilience
B. Split horizon
C. Redundancy
D. Spanning tree

15. HSRP is a routing protocol that can be used to configure resilience on a network.

A. True
B. False

PART THREE

Network Management—Fault, Configuration, Accounting, Performance, Security (FCAPS)

CHAPTER

12

Fault Management and the Network Operations Center

YOU HAVE LEARNED about the necessary components to build a network that meets an organization's advanced communications needs. You know about how important it is that well-trained individuals, a good network design, and the right network devices work together to provide a solid solution. Building a great network is a challenge. Once everything is up and running, keeping that network running smoothly is a new challenge. Both part-time and full-time network administrators must understand how to proactively manage a network. In the remaining chapters of this book, you will learn how to establish and follow procedures that will keep your network running smoothly.

Chapter 12 Topics

This chapter covers the following topics and concepts:

- What network fault management is
- What the primary approaches to network fault management are
- Which protocols network fault management uses
- What a network operations center is
- Which best practices enable solid network fault management

Chapter 12 Goals

When you complete this chapter, you will be able to:

- Define network fault management
- Describe the primary approaches to network fault management
- List the common protocols used in network fault management
- Describe a network operations center
- Discuss network fault management best practices

Network Fault Management

Far too many organizations approach network management as a fire-fighting activity. They do not invest very many resources until there is a problem that cannot be ignored. Organizations like this only react to problems. Reactive network management really is not management at all. This approach wastes resources and often fails to address the root causes of problems. A much better approach to network management is to be proactive. Proactive network management means planning ahead for issues and attempting to avoid them instead of fixing problems.

One of the first steps in moving from a reactive to a proactive management style is to learn what to expect from network operations. Managing malfunctions is one part of the complete picture. Any malfunction of a network hardware or software component is called a **fault**. **Fault management** is the collection of procedures, devices, software programs, and actions that enable network administrators to detect and respond to faults. Fault management includes several activities:

- Defining fault conditions
- Developing plans to respond to each fault type
- Recognizing when a fault occurs
- Communicating the fault to the appropriate people
- Responding to the fault
- Making necessary configuration changes to avoid future faults

Fault Response

Actually responding to the fault is only one part of the process. In environments that only react to problems, this may be the only step in the process of fault response. Each new fault results in a new response. In a proactive environment, the majority of the faults encountered already have planned response procedures. The importance of fault management is that responses are well planned and repeatable. Planned responses make it easy to spot trends and allow an organization to make necessary changes to avoid future faults.

technical TIP

Planned responses and documentation procedures make it easy to identify recurring problems. Suppose a review of recent faults shows that four switches, all of the same model, have failed in the past three months. Each switch has had to be replaced to make the network fully operational again. Keeping accurate documentation of faults and responses would make this information readily available. This type of information could cause the organization to investigate problems with this type of switch. The staff could proactively replace the switches or use resilience techniques to ensure that failures do not disrupt network operations.

You will learn about approaches to the overall fault management process in the next section. For now, just consider what happens when a fault occurs. Of course, lots of planning has already occurred before this point, and network administrators and operators already know what to do. When a fault occurs, the software or device that encounters the fault generates an alarm. An alarm can be a special protocol message, an entry in a log file, or another method of getting a message to an operator. Different types of faults result in messages of different types and severity. For example, an application server that loses its connection to the main database is a higher priority than a workstation encountering an occasional network timeout. Some alarms are immediately important. Others become a higher priority if they last for longer periods of time. Alarms generally receive a severity ranging from debug (low) to emergency (extremely high). Other severity classifications may rank alarm severity from warning (low) to critical (extremely high).

> **NOTE**
> An enterprise-wide network fault management system is not just for enterprise organizations. Any organization that has more than one network device can benefit from a network fault management system. Smaller organizations may need simpler systems, but a fault management system will help keep a network of any size running smoothly.

Regardless of the type and severity of the alarm, network administrators should be able to view a current list of alarms. This list tells the administrator what problems are currently being reported. The administrator also should be able to see recently cleared alarms. The recently cleared alarms list tells the story of how the network performed in the recent past. Both of these lists can help the network administrator develop a clear picture of the network's health. The fault management system should provide easy access to alarm lists from multiple systems and devices. Ideally, an enterprise-wide network fault management system should provide easy access to current and recent faults across the entire network.

Each alarm should have some type of action associated with it. Some actions may involve notification only while others may require additional immediate steps. Many network fault management systems allow alerts to run other scripts or programs to automatically respond. It is practically impossible for a human to monitor and identify all network faults. One important feature of a good fault management system is its ability to filter normal events from faults. Faults should be the only events that trigger alarms. Normal events should not create alarms that would just add to the noise an administrator has to analyze. Most fault management systems require some configuration to reduce the number of false alarms.

Passive Versus Active

The two main methods of detecting faults are passive and active. **Passive fault detection** involves waiting for some indication that a fault has occurred. Indications can include log file entries or receipt of an alarm message. The fault management system in passive mode does little more than wait until it receives some notification. **Active fault detection** involves taking action to determine if everything is working properly. Active detection can include actions such as sending a message to a device asking for status information.

technical TIP

Do not rely exclusively on active or passive fault detection. Neither method is best in all cases. A solid fault detection strategy should include both types of detection actions. A mixed approach will return the most accurate status picture for all devices in a network.

Passive techniques depend on each device being able to send messages indicating fault conditions. This type of monitoring doesn't work well for total device failures. Active monitoring can detect failed devices. Failed devices will not be able to return status inquiries. A status inquiry that doesn't return indicates a fault with the destination device.

Active fault detection also can detect situations that aren't total failures. For example, an active fault detection system could send a status inquiry to a device every five seconds. Failure to return indicates a failed device. However, failure to return in under a half second may indicate a potential performance problem. Most fault management systems do not immediately trigger alarms on every event sample. In the case of a potential performance problem, the system may wait for three consecutive slow message returns before triggering an alarm.

Primary Approaches to Network Fault Management

Early network adopters realized there was a need to monitor network health and take action when faults occurred. Network devices were supposed to participate in network communications and make networking possible. Checking on device health was something network administrators did on a per-device basis. In many cases, they would simply respond to complaints of network application failures. It did not take long for organizations with networks to realize a need for a standard approach to monitoring network health and handling issues.

As more network administrators studied the problem, they realized that managing network faults was a recurring cycle of tasks. The process is similar to many other ongoing plan-monitor-react cycles. A common body of knowledge began to emerge that defined the basic steps involved in managing network faults. The generally agreed-upon fault management steps include the following, as shown in Figure 12-1:

- **Predict**—Predict which faults are most likely for a given network environment, and develop or modify plans to detect and respond to faults.
- **Detect**—Monitor network operation and use known information to identify faults, and notify the appropriate people when faults occur.
- **Recover**—Take necessary action to clear the fault, and return the network to normal operation.
- **Analyze**—Examine the process of detecting and responding to faults, along with any new information, and identify any suggested procedural changes.

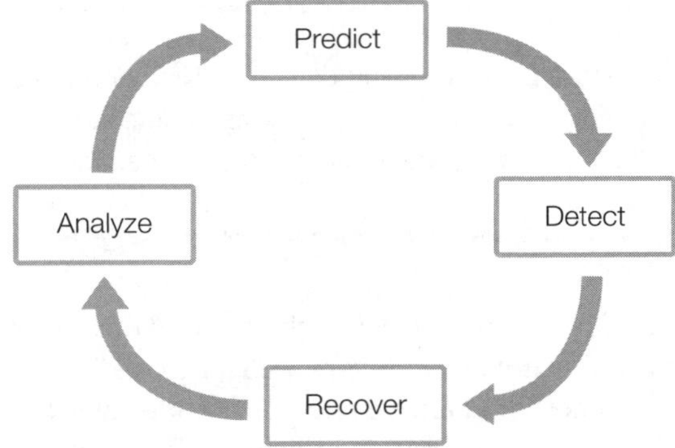

FIGURE 12-1
Network fault management process.

Once organizations began to understand the process, they started to develop tools and frameworks to formally define the process and make it repeatable.

Using Simple Network Management Protocol

One of the first standard approaches was to use **Simple Network Management Protocol (SNMP)** to collect and process information about network devices. SNMP is a standard protocol designed to help manage devices on an IP network. You will learn more about SNMP in the next section. While the approach using SNMP provided an easy way to query devices, it lacked structure. Many organizations developed their own frameworks that used SNMP to monitor their networks.

A typical SNMP-based system has three main components, as shown in Figure 12-2:

- One or more devices to monitor
- A software agent that runs on each monitored device
- Software that communicates with the agents to identify and respond to faults

The SNMP standard provided all of the components, but there was still a need for a larger framework to define how the components worked together in a larger system.

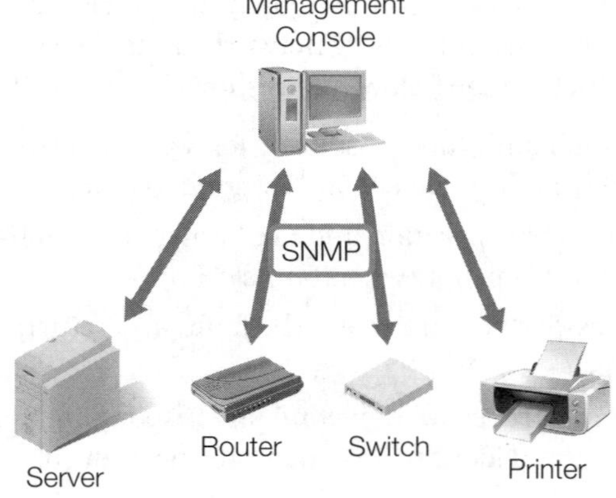

FIGURE 12-2
Typical SNMP fault management system components.

FCAPS

The International Telecommunication Union (ITU-T) introduced Recommendation M.3010, a protocol model for managing open systems in a communication network. This model was called the **Telecommunications Management Network (TMN)**.
TMN defines four layers:

- Business management
- Service management
- Fault and performance management
- Element and configuration management

The main purpose of TMN was to provide a framework to align telecommunications assets to business goals. ITU-T realized that the basic model was solid but could be modified to provide a generic framework for any networked environment. In 1997, the ITU-T refined the TMN model to focus on five functionally different areas of tasks. The refined model was named **FCAPS**. FCAPS stands for the five types of tasks it defines (Figure 12-3):

- **Fault management**
- **Configuration management**
- **Accounting management**
- **Performance management**
- **Security management**

FCAPS was incorporated into the ISO/IEC 10040 standard that was released in 1998. In fact, the term FCAPS appeared in an early draft of ISO 10040 in the early 1980s. FCAPS quickly became a recognized standard for understanding and expressing the services necessary to proactively manage networks. The remainder of this book will follow the FCAPS approach to network management. You will learn about fault management in this chapter and the remaining management task in later chapters.

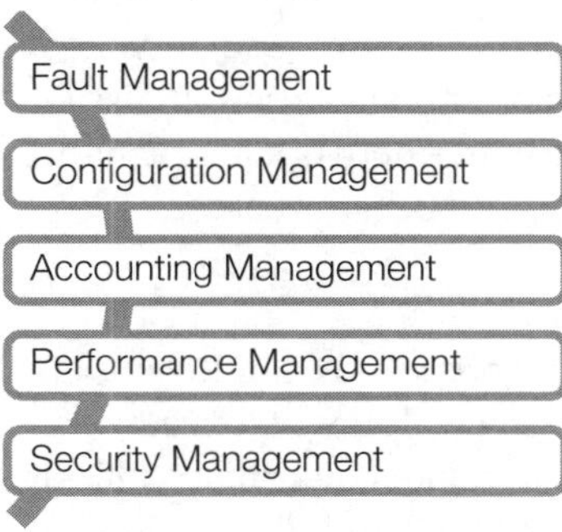

FIGURE 12-3
FCAPS management categories.

Fault Management

The goal of fault management is to detect faults, correct them, and protect the network from future occurrences of similar faults. A solid fault management system should be able to provide information to help predict faults before they occur and help to protect the network and keep it running smoothly. Fault management means more than just predicting and detecting faults. It also covers the planning process prior to detection. The plans developed prior to detection help personnel and systems respond to faults in a prescribed manner. Fault management allows organizations to respond to faults in a way that is repeatable and helps to avoid future faults.

Configuration Management

Network devices and software are generally very configurable. This means they have many settings that alter the way they operate. A device can only perform well when it is configured properly. Many faults or other performance issues are directly related to configuration changes or incorrect settings. Configuration management is a process of making configuration simpler and more stable. Configuration management helps to do the following:

- Document device and software configurations
- Control and track changes made to configurations
- Provide a path for configuration changes

Accounting/Asset/Administration Management

Accounting management tracks network resource use. Examples of resources include disk usage, CPU time, and network link utilization. Accounting management also can be called billing management since collected information is often used to bill customers for network use. Some organizations bill internal users for network use. This practice allows an organization to spread the network costs fairly across multiple departments.

> **NOTE**
> RADIUS, TACACS, and Diameter are examples of protocols commonly used for accounting.

In some applications of FCAPS, "administration" or "asset" replaces "accounting." Networks that do not bill for use can still find value in tracking use. In many cases, use tracking can help validate network device and bandwidth allocation. It also can point out when changes would produce better network performance. As in all FCAPS activities, there is overlap with other areas.

Performance Management

Performance management is the process of monitoring how well the network meets performance standards and taking action when necessary. Networks that support unified communication (UC) and related real-time traffic are very sensitive to performance fluctuations. It is important to carefully monitor network performance and quickly address any issues. In many cases, being proactive can keep small problems from becoming larger ones.

Performance management is concerned mainly with the speed and integrity with which packets are delivered. Any latency or dropped packets above a reasonable level should trigger an alarm and some action. This area of FCAPS should ensure the organization's network is providing the highest throughput with the lowest response time and error rate. Meeting or exceeding these goals should provide the best user experience.

Security Management

Security management is the process of ensuring that the three main tenets of security are protected:

- **Confidentiality**—Only authorized users can access sensitive data and resources.
- **Integrity**—Only authorized users can change sensitive data or configurations.
- **Availability**—Data and resources are available to all authorized users when they request them.

Protocols

Getting devices from different manufacturers to communicate is often difficult. The only way so many of today's networks operate with a mix of vendor hardware is due to standards. Standards define how devices should communicate with one another. Fault management systems rely on the ability to communicate. The only way a fault management system can determine a device's status is to exchange information with it. In some cases, a successful exchange indicates that everything is okay, and a communication failure means that a problem exists. In other cases, the device may successfully communicate the presence of a fault. Standards define how a fault management system and its monitored devices should interact.

Common Management Information Protocol

OSI published a protocol for network management called **Common Management Information Protocol (CMIP)**. This protocol defines an implementation for communicating between management applications and their agents. This protocol, along with its accompanying service description, Common Management Information Service (CMIS), was defined in ITU-T X.700 recommendations.

CMIS/CMIP describes a robust method of management communication. It has more flexibility and functionality than its rival protocol, SNMP. CMIS/CMIP supports the definition of any type of actions. This added flexibility makes it somewhat more difficult to configure and manage. Most of today's IP network devices support SNMP.

Simple Network Management Protocol

The SNMP is both a protocol and a framework used for network management. SNMP supports remote monitoring and configuration of network devices. It was developed to provide a simple method to monitor and manage network devices from a variety of manufacturers. The SNMP framework supports network-wide management from a central location.

The central SNMP Network Management Server (NMS) receives notifications from monitored devices. These notifications are called SNMP traps. You will learn about SNMP traps later in this chapter. Each SNMP-enabled device allows administrators to define conditions that create SNMP traps. Any time the preconfigured conditions occur, the device creates an SNMP trap.

SNMP allows any number of devices to communicate regardless of their manufacturer. Any SNMP-enabled devices can interact with any SNMP-enabled NMS. In fact, multiple NMSs can manage each device to provide extra layers of protection for critical resources. SNMP's flexibility and simplicity has made it the most popular choice for IP network management.

SNMP supports more than just monitoring devices and triggering alarms. SNMP also can update device configurations. This ability allows organizations to store device configurations in a central location and update devices remotely. Central configuration management can ease the burden on administrators as the network grows. It can help control configuration changes and protect the settings from alteration or loss. Regular backup procedures can easily include centrally stored device configurations.

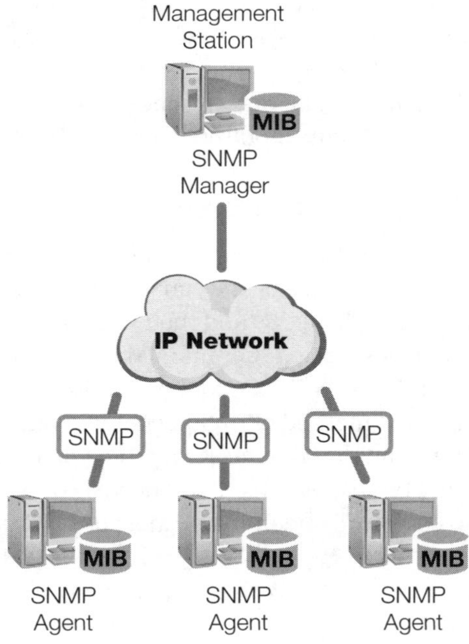

FIGURE 12-4 SNMP devices with MIBs.

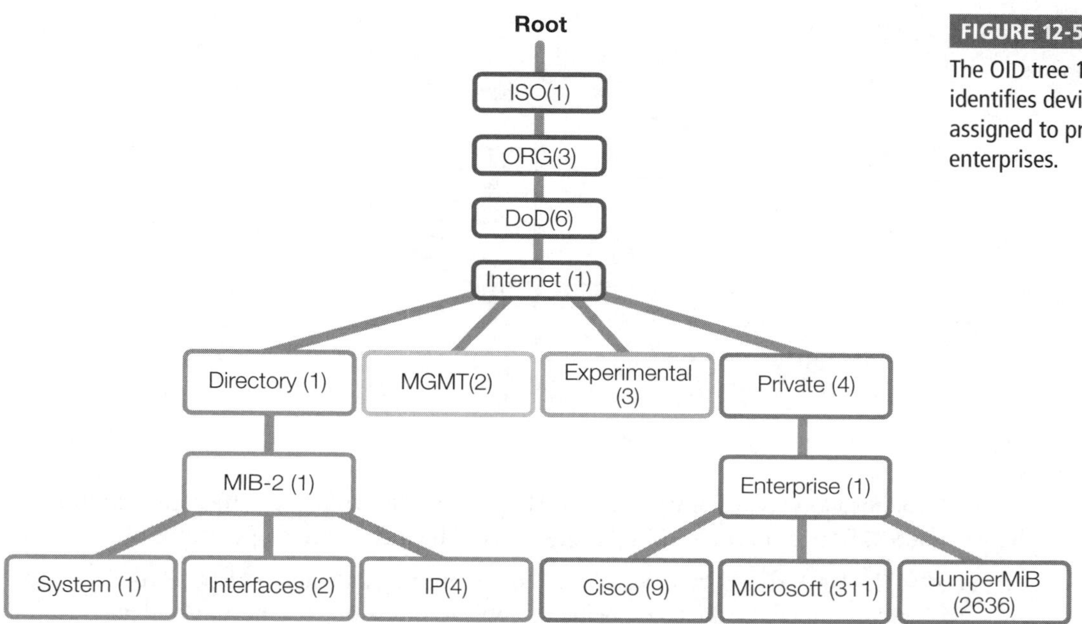

FIGURE 12-5 The OID tree 1.3.6.1.4 identifies devices assigned to private enterprises.

MIBs

SNMP does not define specific device characteristics to monitor. Instead, the protocol and framework allows extensions to reference external databases of device characteristics. This design makes SNMP able to manage new devices without having to change the protocol. A **management information base (MIB)** is a small database of characteristics for a specific type of device. Individual settings in a MIB are called **MIB variables**. All MIB variables that describe a single device are called a **MIB module**. Each MIB module represents a specific device. Loading a MIB module into the NMS identifies the device as a managed device (Figure 12-4).

Each MIB module gets a unique identifier called its **object ID (OID)**. The Internet Assigned Numbers Authority (IANA) manages OIDs to ensure uniqueness between manufacturers. Each OID is represented by a string of numbers separated by dots, similar to IPv4 address dot notation. Each separate number in the OID represents a different level in the OID tree. For example, IANA defines OIDs for private enterprises as 1.3.6.1.4.1. Figure 12-5 shows the OID tree for private enterprises. Any OIDs for devices assigned to private enterprises would start with 1.3.6.1.4.1.

technical TIP

Most device manufacturers provide preconfigured MIB modules for their devices. They generally come with the device, or you can download them from the device or from the manufacturer's Web site.

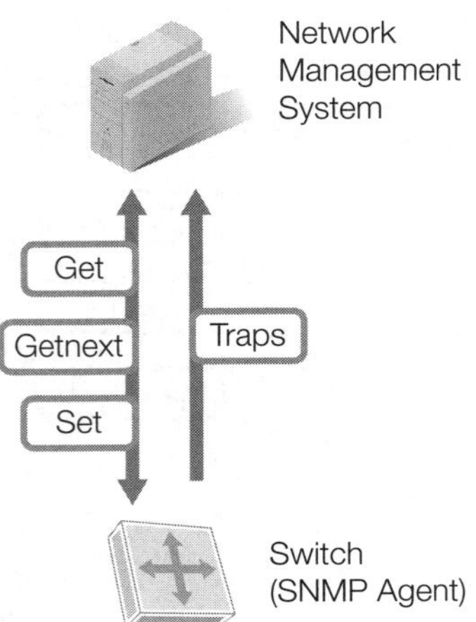

FIGURE 12-6
SNMP operations.

SNMP defines four types of operations. These operations make up the conversations between a SNMP agent and a NMS (Figure 12-6). The four defined operations are:

- **Get**—The NMS requests information from a managed device. The NMS uses a complete OID to locate the specific variable in question. The managed device responds with the value of the requested variable.
- **Getnext**—Similar to the get operation, getnext gets information from the next variable in the tree. In other words, the getnext operation gets the value of the next variable in the same device as the previous get or getnext request.
- **Set**—The set operation changes the value of a device variable to a value supplied by the NMS.
- **Trap**—A message to the NMS from the agent. Traps are most commonly used to notify the NMS of alert conditions.

SNMP on Network Devices

Configuring SNMP on network devices and tuning it appropriately can be a tricky procedure. For example, in a switch infrastructure, it is common to disable SNMP on access level ports for phones and workstations. At the same time, it is imperative to have SNMP enabled on all uplink ports and critical server ports. If all ports on a switch are SNMP-enabled by default, the result will be a flooding of SNMP traps to the NMS. Too many traps sent to the NMS as a result of misconfigured devices will often lead to important alerts being missed. It is also important to set severity levels depending on the status of a link. An administrator might configure a SNMP trap to automatically e-mail the server administrator when a specific server port goes down while separately sending an e-mail to the network operations center (NOC) and management to open a critical bridge in the event that the link to the Internet goes down.

SNMP Traps

An SNMP trap is the only type of message the agent initiates. It requires no response. An SNMP trap is a message sent to the NMS any time a preconfigured condition is met. The trap contains the agent OID and the value of the variable. An agent will only generate traps for conditions currently configured. In other words, the NMS must tell the agent which conditions should generate a trap before the condition occurs.

The agent also needs to know where to send the trap. Some networks have multiple NMSs to provide resilience in case a NMS fails. The only responsibility an agent has in the fault management process is to send the trap to the correct location when a defined condition occurs. The NMS is responsible for handling the trap. The NMS has a range of options it can follow. Once it receives a trap it can:

- Ignore the trap
- Log the trap
- Notify someone
- Instruct the agent to modify a variable
- Take a predefined action, such as shutting down the device
- Launch a program or script to respond to the trap

The correct option depends on the type of device, the nature of the fault, and the capability of the NMS. Each organization must carefully define appropriate actions for each defined fault. Aggressive and well-planned responses are the core of good fault management.

Syslog

Syslog is a standard for logging messages from programs and devices. While not specifically designed for network management, it does play a part in a total management system. Syslog messages are unidirectional. Messages flow only from managed devices to the syslog server. The central sever stores the log file messages in a secure location. There are several advantages to using syslog over local log file storage:

- **Security**—Central log file storage on a secure server makes it harder to modify logs.
- **Log correlation**—Syslog makes it easier to combine log file messages from multiple devices. In many situations, faults involve more than a single device. Syslog allows searching through combined logs for events.
- **Standard log format**—Although most vendors have their own log file formats, sending log messages to syslog allows the different formats to be stored in similar formats.

technical TIP

There is no single syslog format. Although there is a general format for syslog messages, different vendors' products use slightly different formatted messages when sending log file information to syslog. Make sure the syslog server software you choose can understand the formats your devices use.

Syslog in the Network Environment

Syslog messages can be an extremely useful tool for helping determine a reason for outage (RFO). If a network device fails and is unrecoverable, or comes back up with no local log files remaining, it can be useful to review the syslog data stored on the syslog server to find what messages the device was sending out before its failure. If it is determined that it's something that can be remedied, such as adding additional memory, then a change can be put in place to upgrade the device before putting it back into production. Syslog messages likewise can help determine if a configuration change caused a device outage and can help pinpoint who was logged into the device to make that change.

Network Operations Center

A **network operations center (NOC)** is a central location used to monitor and control networks. Small- and medium-sized organizations generally have only a single NOC. Very large enterprises may maintain a separate NOC for each region. Multiple NOCs may even be prescribed to provide redundancy in case of disaster.

The heart of any NMS is the management console. This collection of programs provides administrators and operators with a view of alerts, alarms, and operational metrics. Many management consoles summarize the most important information into visual indicators that use colors and graphics to convey the network's health.

NOCs provide the ability for multiple troubleshooters and analysts to be in the same room. A control room philosophy encourages a team approach to solving problems. The open forum allows problems to be identified and communicated with the network management team. The team responsible for responding to faults also can include business analysts as well as technical analysts. Some faults have wider impact than others. Mobilizing a response team that includes business and technical representatives can help contain damage and avoid more-serious impact on the business operation.

Historically, network management was a technical concern. Today's organizations are realizing the importance of reaching beyond the technical aspects of networks. Networks exist to satisfy business requirements. More precisely, they exist to support technical solutions to business requirements. It makes sense to have business analysts in the NOC when network issues may impact business functions.

Many NOCs have similar layouts. They typically have several rows of desks that all face a video wall. The video wall generally has multiple monitors or screens that show significant events and overall network performance. The video wall often includes a current display of news and weather conditions at operational sites. The video wall, along with the individual technician displays, gives a complete picture of the network's health.

NASA Mission Control

A NOC, pronounced like "knock," is similar to NASA's famous Mission Control Center (MCC) in Houston, Texas. MCC is responsible for monitoring and controlling every aspect of a United States manned space flight once the launch vehicle clears the launch tower. MCC is the hub of information and activity during a flight. MCC has representatives from every aspect of a flight, including flight hardware manufacturers, medical personnel, astronaut representatives, and many other areas. They convene in the open setting to be able to exchange information freely and work on problems as they develop. This setting has proved to be a very effective way to ensure things operate as planned and to solve any problems that occur. NOCs provide the same advantages, albeit with a little less drama.

Many NOCs also have adjacent rooms to hold team meetings. These are sometimes oriented in such a way that occupants can still see the video wall and monitor ongoing issues while they meet to work on specific problems.

NOCs are more than just desks and displays. The real heart of any NOC is its procedures. Having the critical resources in one place only makes effective response possible. It does not guarantee effective response. Most NOCs have clear procedures for handling faults. Each fault generally passes through several layers, starting from the bottom. As each attempt to resolve the fault is unsuccessful, the fault rises to the next level of severity. Full attention of the NOC staff is reserved for critical faults that have an immediate impact on the business operation.

A growing trend with enterprise NOCs is to outsource the operation. Instead of building a NOC within an organization, some enterprises are hiring companies that specialize in network management. These organizations set up their own NOC, often at remote locations, to manage the customer's network. The customer avoids having to maintain network expertise. The service provider gets to focus only on network management. Some enterprise organizations are finding that outsourcing network management makes good business sense.

Best Practices

Many organizations implement network management systems. They try many different approaches. Some work well, and others do not. The practice of sampling the approaches that have worked well for other organizations helps to avoid costly mistakes. In this section you will learn about some network management practices that have produced positive results in multiple organizations. These approaches are not the only effective approaches. Nor are they the "best" solution for any situation. However, they do provide positive guidance for implementing a good network management system.

Preventive Measures

The best faults are the ones that never occur. These are the easiest ones to handle. The best way to avoid faults or to keep small faults from getting worse is to enact preventive measures. Here are best practices in the area of prevention:

- **Ensure all documentation is current**—Update diagrams, inventory manifests, procedures, and configurations.
- **Discard out-of-date documentation**—Old documentation can cause confusion.
- **Identify all single points of failure**—Change infrastructure to ensure that there are no single points of failure.
- **Ensure all software is up-to-date**—Update computers and devices with the latest software patches and firmware.

Communication

Another common place to identify best practices is in the area of team and organizational communication. Making sure the right message gets to its destination is not just a technical network issue. Here are best practices in the area of communication:

- **Define clear roles and responsibility descriptions**—Make sure everyone knows his or her assignments.
- **Make communication easy**—Ensure team members have access to phones and radios at all times, especially during events.
- **Make policies and procedures available**—Publish all documents related to policy, and make team members aware of them.
- **Set up a chain of command**—Avoid letting issues fall through the cracks.
- **Train the team**—Hold recurring training and simulations to keep everyone current.
- **Document each action**—Keep a record of everything done during fault response.
- **Always debrief**—After a fault resolution, debrief participants to collect vital experience.

Reacting to Faults

One of the central ongoing activities for the network management team is reacting to faults. Here are best practices in the area of fault response:

- **Limit the false positives**—Use filters and priorities to suppress and diminish less important events.
- **Avoid reporting uncorroborated events**—Attempt to correlate multiple events among several devices.

- **Identify scope of fault**—Determine what the fault affects.
- **Choose the appropriate level of response**—Develop clear guidelines to determine how the team should respond to each type of fault.
- **Establish a response time line**—Know how long a response should take.

Escalation

Knowing when to escalate is important when responding to faults. Once the decision has been made to escalate—to involve more people, including people at higher levels within the organization, in solving the problem—it is important to know how to escalate and whom to contact. Here are best practices in the area of issue escalation:

- **Establish escalation guidelines**—Know what criteria indicate a need to escalate.
- **Set specific escalation time goals**—Escalate if the team misses resolution time goals.
- **Determine when to call for extreme action**—Define when to take extreme action.
- **Avoid "protectionism"**—Resist the urge to "save face." Always take necessary action, and call for help when needed.

Being Proactive

Finally, take every opportunity to be proactive, not reactive. Here are best practices in the area of being proactive:

- **Automate**—Use automation whenever possible to detect and resolve faults.
- **Predict faults**—Use the information at your disposal to predict likely faults before they occur.
- **Recognize anomalies**—Study normal operation to recognize behavior that is not normal (use automation).
- **Query intelligently**—Avoid the excessive overhead of active polling where possible. Use related events to trigger polling activity.

CHAPTER SUMMARY

Fault management is the initial activity in the FCAPS framework. It addresses the preparation for, identification of, and response to network faults. A network fault is an indication that the network is not performing as intended. Fault management provides network administrators with the ability to plan for expected faults and respond to any faults that occur. Planned responses are repeatable and more effective than those without forethought.

Organizations with well-planned fault management systems have more stable networks. They enjoy smoother operation and less disruption when faults do occur. Implementing the FCAPS framework helps to ensure the network resources are available to support business functions.

KEY CONCEPTS AND TERMS

Active fault detection
Common Management Information Protocol (CMIP)
Fault
Fault management
FCAPS
Management information base (MIB)
MIB module
MIB variable
Network operations center (NOC)
Object ID (OID)
Passive fault detection
Simple Network Management Protocol (SNMP)
Syslog
Telecommunications Management Network (TMN)

CHAPTER 12 ASSESSMENT

1. A fault is any malfunction of a network hardware or software component.
   A. True
   B. False

2. Which type of fault management is generally ineffective?
   A. FCAPS
   B. Outsourced
   C. Reactive
   D. Planned

3. Which of the following best describes an alarm?
   A. A network fault
   B. A message generated when a fault occurs
   C. An event that causes a fault
   D. The programmed response to clear a fault

4. Which term describes scanning log files for indications of faults?
   A. Passive fault detection
   B. Alarm detection
   C. Active fault detection
   D. Detective analysis

5. Which of the following methods include polling devices?
   A. Passive fault detection
   B. Alarm detection
   C. Active fault detection
   D. Detective analysis

6. ________ is a common protocol used to collect and process information about network devices.

7. Which of the following management areas are included in FCAPS? (Select two.)
   A. Proactive management
   B. Configuration management
   C. Security management
   D. Provenance management

8. What is a SNMP notification called?
   A. Trap
   B. Notification
   C. Agent message
   D. Agent response

9. What is a database of characteristics for a specific type of device called?
   A. Trap
   B. Module
   C. Variable
   D. MIB

10. An ________ uniquely identifies each MIB module.

11. Which of the following is a standard for logging messages from programs and devices?
    A. SNMP
    B. Syslog
    C. CMIP
    D. Snort

12. Which SNMP is the only operation that the agent initiates?
    A. Get
    B. Getnext
    C. Set
    D. Trap

CHAPTER 13

Configuration Management and Accounting

MODERN NETWORKs are composed of many parts. Each part makes a contribution to a complex process. That process facilitates the movement of information from a source to a destination. It is also possible that information will flow in the other direction as well. The process, communication, has been going on for millennia, but it has never been as rich and complex, and has never occurred over such a long distance, as it does today. One of the primary tasks of today's network architect, engineer, technician, or manager is to make the operation of the complex network as transparent as possible to the user. The greatest steps in the evolution of networks have come when the network operation has been simplified. The simpler a network is to use, the more useful it is to a wider range of people. This chapter is about making the network as useful as possible by assuring that it is available as much as possible, and that it is as easy to use as possible. The tools that will be applied to this task are configuration management and change control.

In a similar textbook in the 1980s about the story of configuration management and change control, this chapter would have been very different. A major change has occurred since the late 1980s and early 1990s. Before the 1990s, most, if not all, components in a computer network were owned and operated by the single enterprise. That enterprise had information that moved across the network links. That is not true today. Managing the various hardware and software components, from a variety of sources, has become one of the most problematic areas of configuration and change management. A discussion of this point is central to this chapter.

Chapter 13 Topics

This chapter covers the following topics and concepts:

- What change control is
- What configuration management and the change control board are
- What best practices for configuration management are
- How to manage physical hardware changes
- How to manage software changes
- What asset management and inventory control are
- What loss control is
- What interruption control is

Chapter 13 Goals

When you complete this chapter, you will be able to:

- Manage the change control process of both hardware and software
- Perform configuration management; understand the value and role of the change control board (CCB)
- Explain configuration management best practices and apply them in enterprise networking situations
- Manage physical hardware changes
- Apply asset management and inventory control procedures
- Understand the value and processes of business continuity planning and disaster recovery planning

Change Control

Once a network has been installed and is "up and running," the normal operating state of the network should be documented. From that point forward, every effort should be made to maintain the network in that state. Any deviation from the normal state should either be a carefully planned and executed upgrade or a carefully planned and executed response to a network failure. Nothing else should be allowed. This is how networks were operated until the late 1980s and early 1990s. Since then, a major shift has been occurring in how networks are managed and operated. The shift is occurring in who owns the different network components and who controls the software.

The first generation of computer networks connected large mainframe computers to each other. The mainframe computers sat in air-cooled vaults that most people never saw. They had very particular and specialized power requirements. The mainframes, and their interconnections, were controlled by one or two companies. All of the components were purchased from a single manufacturer. The single manufacturer tested, assured, and guaranteed the interoperation of all components. In the case of any failure, the manufacturer dispatched a team of experts to solve the problem. The company who owned the computers and networks did not have to be too technical to keep everything up and running. The company was technical, in many cases, but was not required to be.

The second generation was not a complete replacement of the first generation. Many remnants of the first generation survived, though in specialized applications. The second generation featured minicomputers. Minicomputers breathed the same air that we do. Their power requirements were much more those of copiers and refrigerators. The minicomputer was often a part of the office landscape, as were the large shared printers that accompanied the minicomputers. More companies provided components. All of the components were assembled, tested, assured, and guaranteed by a single company. But in the second generation, the company was not the manufacturer. The company was the integrator. It is very unlikely that the integrator actually manufactured any of the components. The good news was that the customer rarely understood the difference between the first and second generations. If a second-generation system had a failure, the integrator dispatched a team of experts to solve the problem. The company who owned the computers and networks did not have to be too technical to keep everything up and running. The company was technical, in many cases, but was not required to be.

The third generation is where the complexity of configuration management, change control, and related areas began to rise steeply. It included some mainframes and other components from the first generation. The third generation included many minicomputers and components from the second generation. But the predominant devices in the third generation were personal computers. They were small and inexpensive enough, even from the beginning, for departments, small companies, and individuals to purchase. In most cases, at least early in the third generation, there was no centralized control of the devices and their software. Much worse was that there was no control over the management of the information stored on those devices.

The Radio Shack TRS-80 personal computer, one of the earliest models of PC, began to show up, without the invitation of the data processing department, in many companies in the late 1970s and early 1980s. The original device had an 8-bit processor and 4 kb of memory. Input/output, or I/O as it was termed, was via a standard analog audio tape recorder. By the end of the third generation in the early 1990s, most companies had at least reined in the independent souls who wanted their own personal capability to crunch the company's numbers and manage their portion of the company's data.

If a third-generation system had a failure, no one dispatched a team of experts to solve the problem. In many cases the owner of the personal computer was required to solve the problem. That took time and energy away from that person's primary job. The company who owned the computers and networks in Generation 3 required a lot more personal knowledge of the computers' operation. The company couldn't always rely on the data processing department. In many cases the data processing department did not have the expertise. In many cases that department's employees resented the individuals wresting control away from them within their own kingdom. In most cases it was a combination of the two. When things went really wrong in the third generation, it was often the accounting or research department that suffered most. Their accountants and researchers looked for software bugs and upgraded print drivers while they should have been accounting or researching.

The fourth generation, which is the current generation, is really a free-for-all in many ways. As a result of a precipitous decline in telecom service and hardware costs and a steep rise in the capabilities of these systems, many companies are no longer providing employees with even basic phone service. Mobile and small office/home office (SOHO) workers are often left to select their own telephone and network service providers, service plans, and devices. This is true even in many companies that support secure **virtual private networks (VPNs)** for employee, contractor, and supplier connectivity. This approach has led to an entirely different set of obstacles, though the objectives for network availability and network resiliency remain largely unchanged from the first generation. In many cases, network uptime and availability requirements are even more stringent today than ever. This raises the question: What are the objectives? What can be done to meet, or even exceed, the requirements? What are the penalties if the objectives are not met? What roles do change management and change control play?

Service-Level Agreements

The first and second generations were managed, in fact, very stringently. The first two generations had various and nonstandardized performance objectives and tracking methods. Each company seemed to have its own. But eventually it became possible to develop metrics for industry-wide comparisons. The financial industry, for instance, had performance statistics based upon the number of credit card transactions performed per hour, day, or month. Automotive manufacturers' statistics often measured how quickly a **computer-aided design (CAD)** drawing could be retrieved from an archive, or how quickly a spare part could be located in inventory. Regardless of specific performance measures, all industries had availability numbers even though there were some slight differences in how they were calculated. Also, these networks were based upon fixed circuits. Their metrics were somewhat easier to calculate and substantially more expensive to replicate or provide alternate paths for.

The Origin of the Service-Level Agreement

The origin of the network service-level agreement can be traced to **British Telecom (BT)** in the early 1980s. BT was one of the largest and most powerful **PTT (postal, telephone, and telegraph) agencies** on earth. It was a part of the British government until its privatization in 1984. Before that time, competing with BT was illegal. Service-level agreements were a contractual tool used by BT to lock in customers and set a standard so high that the fledgling Mercury Communications, a subsidiary of the British overseas carrier Cable & Wireless, could never even hope to meet it. Many people with inside knowledge of BT in its early days as a private company will tell you that this "crackerjack move" on the part of BT is what kept Mercury Communications from ever establishing a strong foothold, even though they provided a much less expensive alternative to BT.

To understand BT's early SLAs was to understand their incredible power. For instance, if BT did not meet contracted service levels, there were substantial penalties paid by BT, refunds of service fees, and changes of account management and engineering teams. For not meeting service levels across more than two billing cycles, BT even committed to move the customer, at BT's cost, to a competitor—though there is nothing but anecdotal evidence to document that this ever really happened. In any case, the SLA cemented customer loyalty. It made it clear who the dominant carrier was and set an unachievable standard for Mercury Communications and all other up-and-comers.

The wisdom of SLAs was also not lost on the American telecommunications juggernaut MCI. BT and MCI began merger negotiations and sharing of strategies and tactics under nondisclosure agreements as early as 1992. MCI brought the SLA to the United States but lacked the market trust and respect and network quality to bring value to their SLAs. Sprint took MCI's lead. It was the first US network services provider or carrier to make widespread use of SLAs both as a competitive and network measurement tool. Today the SLA is standard fare on virtually every network services contract.

The broad spectrum of measurements and reporting systems used by different companies in the first and second generations of networks was replaced in the third generation by something called a service-level agreement (SLA) with underlying compliance software. In keeping with the Internet/IP packet theme of the third and fourth generations, network SLAs were based entirely on packet metrics. Interestingly, SLAs were initially as varied and nonstandard as their disparate first- and second-generation counterparts. But pressure from individuals procuring network services caused some de facto standards to emerge. There are, of course, various subtleties and points of differentiation. But most SLAs include, at minimum, four important metrics: packet delivery or discard, delay, delay variation, and availability.

Packet Delivery/Discard

Is the glass half empty or half full? The first, and most common, SLA metric is either "packet delivery" or "packet discard." Packet delivery is a measure of the percentage of packets that make it to the destination point in the network compared with the number of packets given to the network to deliver. For example, if 100 packets are delivered to the network to transmit, and 95 make it to their destination, then the packet delivery rate is 95 percent. This also could be measured as a packet discard rate of 5 percent. By the way, this example is simplified to make a point. Numbers this large rarely occur, and are never, ever service-level targets in an SLA.

Packet delivery metrics impact different services in different ways. Losing a single packet containing a single syllable of voice, for instance, is rarely a problem because the human brain can "fill in the blank." Losing a packet containing even a single byte of a financial transaction, on the other hand, could be considered catastrophic and usually triggers a retransmission of the financial transaction. For this very reason, packet delivery targets are often specified in SLAs by type of service. They also are often tied to the handling of packets that have specific **type of service (TOS)** bit settings in their IP headers. This is often counted and managed only for contractual reasons because, as it was pointed out in Chapter 10, most large networks adhere to the Big Bandwidth design philosophy and treat all packets equally. One would hope that "equally" would mean "equally well." It usually does.

Delay

A second key characteristic is delay. Unlike in circuit-only networks with a constant, fixed clock rate, packets are variable in length. Packets may occupy the circuit for different periods of time, may be delayed at intermediate relaying points, such as routers, or may be discarded. Delay, therefore, may vary within a range. And, because packets traverse underlying circuits, the delay characteristics of the circuit also must be taken into account. For these reasons delay, and the following metric, delay variation, are often tiered; that is to say the carrier or service provider will commit to different delay and delay variation metrics based upon the distance. Very often tiers such as "in country," "on continent," "transoceanic," etc., are utilized.

Delay Variation

The third metric common to virtually all SLAs is delay variation. Many different causes of delay variation exist. Delay variation also will grow with the total end-to-end distance. This usually means that a packet traversing the much longer networks will encounter more intermediate relaying equipment. This might delay the packet more, or less, as it makes its long journey.

Measurement Points and Directionality for SLA Metrics

There are two substantial considerations when comparing SLAs from different providers. It is not of particular importance what is included and what is not included. Rather what matters is that the points of measurement and directionality are the same. For example, most ISP metrics are measured at the point where packets enter and leave the ISP **point of presence (POP)**. ISPs don't think they should have to include the carrier access lines in their measurements. It is usually fine if they don't for purposes of comparison. It must be understood, however, that the delay figures will not even closely approach the real delay numbers the application user will experience.

Managed service providers and end user organizations usually include the network delay in their calculations, *in both directions*, and the access line delay. It is noteworthy that many services have a different delay in each direction for a variety of reasons. The most common reason is that a small request packet traverses the network in one direction very quickly. Packets going back the other direction in response to the request, for a large video file, for instance, take much longer. What is often not included is the server processing time. It is a part of the total delay that the user experiences. It must be considered, although it is often outside the scope of a network SLA.

Availability

Many people think that availability is a mandatory characteristic of any network or network service. This is not really so. It is the definition of availability and the importance, or lack of importance, of availability that indicates the difference between the Internet and traditional telephony. When the Internet or cellular phone service is down, it is no real cause for alarm. But people can get annoyed if they lift the handset of a telephone instrument without immediately hearing a dial tone. Availability is becoming a core metric of network service quality.

Availability: Component, Network, and Service

"Availability" used to mean "Is the circuit up, or is it down?" In the packet era, and to a lesser degree in the circuit world, it is not that simple. SLA targets for "availability" usually mean service availability. The user does not care if a given router is working or not, or if a packet is traveling over a slightly longer, or shorter, path on a different fiber. That is because the usual route is down as long as the packets are arriving within the allowable range of the SLA. Inside the network itself, however, in order to assure the service availability, the network also must also have availability targets for the network components and the network itself.

Circuit SLA Metrics

SLAs began in the packet era. That does not mean, however, that standalone circuits, or even circuits carrying packets, can't have their own SLA metrics. Circuits do have SLA metrics, as do call centers, dial-in and dial-out services, telco trunks, and other aspects of telecommunications and nontelecom services. The metrics are just different. There is a rough equivalent of packet delivery/discard in the circuit world: **bit error rate (BER)**. The big difference is that BER measures errors in individual bits. This metric is, of course, only a rough approximation. It can measure only disruptions that change a 1 bit to a 0 bit or a 0 bit to a 1 bit. It cannot, however, measure disruptions that change a 1 bit to a 1 bit or a 0 bit to a 0 bit. And a packet may be discarded in a packet network if there is a single bit error, or multiple bit errors. Or it may not be discarded if there are bit errors—depending upon the protocol and other factors.

Circuits have delay, too, which is a function of the time it takes an electron to travel its length. For a given circuit, delay never changes. There is no delay variation. Yes, of course, there is also availability. This is much easier to calculate for a circuit because a circuit is either on or off. Also, there is no measure of congestion with a circuit because the bits flow at a constant, clocked rate all day every day, whether they are utilized or not.

Availability may seem simple, and it can be—deceptively so. Because availability is the metric out of all four of the primary SLA metrics that can be observed most readily by a user, it is often the one that gets the most vocal complaints. It is also the metric that is most often pointed to in determining if a service is "good" or "bad" because it is most visible to the user. When determining a suitable availability calculation, it is also important to remove scheduled outages and service windows from the calculation. It is only fair that a network with a planned service window that never exceeds its service window and is otherwise up and running 99.97 percent of the time get a 99.97 percent availability score.

Other SLA Metrics

There are other SLA metrics, such as **mean time between failures (MTBF)**, **mean time to repair (MTTR)**, **mean time to install (MTTI)**, and a list of others. But packet delivery/discard, delay, delay variation, and availability are the most important ones.

SLAs: Not Just for Carriers and Service Providers

While SLAs began as competitive tools in the carrier world and evolved into useful engineering performance metrics, SLAs are not just for "outside" carriers and service providers. Many telecom and IT departments have their own internal SLAs for their internal customers. Just remember, an internal SLA cannot deliver better performance than the SLA upon which it is based. Usually, it must have a lower value.

SLAs and Change Control

This chapter has so far devoted a lot of space to SLAs, and for a very good reason. Regardless of what network we are talking about, or who runs it, it is the SLA that provides the baseline for operation. What this means to change control is if a change is going to cause the network to operate at a level below the SLA, then the change must not be made. If an outage or failure causes the network's performance to fall below the SLA, the network must be restored again as quickly as possible. A network can operate below a given threshold for only so long. After some point, average performance will never rise above the SLA target metrics. And, because financial incentives and penalties are tied to SLA compliance, or noncompliance, these are very important considerations. In the next section we will discuss the process of configuration management and the entity responsible for controlling change within the network.

Configuration Management and the Change Control Board

We will leave the response to outages, failures, and other unplanned events to another chapter. Here we will focus on managing planned changes to the network configuration. We will discuss best practices in the next section. Most organizations, large and small, have processes and procedures in place that govern the way that configuration changes are requested, reviewed, and either declined or implemented. Some processes are very formal, particularly in larger organizations, where a change can impact many people, or where a mistake can be costly, such as in a financial services organization. Other processes can be very informal, such as making sure changes are made only on weekends, and every conceivable combination in between. Most organizations also have a change control manager or even a Change Control Board, which must debate and approve or disapprove change requests. There is always an override procedure for handling exception conditions. The override procedure should be written and implemented in such a way that it is only used in true emergency situations and not as a vehicle for bypassing the approval process.

Change Control Board Membership

Though the change control board in many organizations is a "board" of one, it makes sense that several different entities be represented. There should, of course, be a management representative who can make or recommend the ultimate decisions and individuals representing both the hardware and software areas who can bring specific knowledge of those areas. Increasingly, someone representing the network security and, possibly, corporate security areas are represented on change control boards. The most savvy management teams put someone from the finance and possibly procurement departments on the change control board as well. These two related areas are critical to project success. Having them on the team from the earliest stages increases the chances of success. How many times does a project progress to a mature state of development only to find that it is not budgeted or that needed components are not available from the manufacturer or distributor until weeks or months after the date they are needed? A quick check at the earliest stages of a project can help avoid disappointment.

One individual often neglected in the planning process is the actual user. Some organizations meet this requirement by having a staff person in the network operations area play the role of User Ambassador or User Ombudsman. The ambassador knows the network operations side of the organization and the user needs of multiple user profiles. These include desktop PC basic user, desktop PC power user, mobile laptop user, and tablet computer user. They simply cycle through the list of users when considering any change or configuration option. This approach has worked well for some organizations in the past. But it leaves the change control board without the guidance and input from the ultimate users. Actually asking users about their needs and the positive or negative impact of changes is the only way of really knowing, in advance, what their requirements are.

It has been controversial, to say the very least. But this author strongly recommends that representatives of hardware vendors and network services providers also be on the change control board. It can be argued that this is akin to letting a hungry wolf keep an eye on the chickens while the farmer goes to town. But suppliers often bring a different perspective, and keen insights, that are simply unavailable to anyone else. This is not to say that a vendor, or even an outside consultant, should be placed in a leadership role on a change control board. As a matter of policy, they should not be. But their input can be very valuable.

Change Control Board Function

In most organizations, the change control board's function is to review requests for changes to the network configuration and approve or disapprove the change. They compare requests to policy, budget, and SLA target performance levels. If budget is the issue, they may return a request for funding or have some other mechanism. In the case of policy conflicts or noncompliance with SLAs, particularly internal SLAs, they are usually required to decline a request. The real value of the change control board, however, is in weighing multiple, potentially conflicting requests.

One example might be a change control board that is reviewing a request for an additional block of IPv4 addresses. One department is expanding the IPv4-based virtual private network (VPN) due to company growth. Another department is requesting that the network be upgraded to IPv6. The change control board must, as a group, have the knowledge to determine the best outcome for the organization. What might they do? They could take a “ships in the night” approach and upgrade network equipment software to handle both IPv4 and IPv6 traffic. They might use IPv6-to-IPv4 tunneling through the backbone. They might cap the growth of the IPv4 VPN and institute an IPv6 upgrade. They might approve a move to IPv6 for the one department, use tunnels across the IPv4 backbone, and recover the IPv4 addresses block or blocks for use in the growing IPv4 network. There are other possibilities as well. But, the change control board will have to examine the intersection of the two requests and the impact on organizational policy and operations.

Change Control Board Policies and Practices

There are two ways to set policies and practices for a change control board. The reader can decide which is the “right” way and which is the “wrong” way. Each has its own pluses and minuses. The first way, and a very common way, is to start with a “clean piece of paper” and wait for requests to come in. As requests come in, the merits debated, and decisions issued, the decisions are recorded on that blank piece of paper and represent policies and practices. With each new request, the first step is to see if there is a policy or practice already in the book to cover the request. If not, render a new decision, and record it in the growing library of policies and practices. The second approach is to make an attempt to anticipate what may be required and to fill a book with policies and practices ahead of time. This approach can be based upon the hard-won battles of policy and practice from other organizations from books, white papers, consultants, or other sources. It can allow an organization the time to make determinations about legal, security, and operational aspects of certain policies and practices. In either case, the policies and procedure document must be a living, dynamic document that can change as requirements change.

Before we leave this potentially vexing subject, let’s consider an analogy—raising children. It is possible that the reader is raising children. But the fact is irrefutable that the reader has been *raised*, so everyone will have an opinion on this topic. The analogy of the first example is to just have a child and see what happens. Does the child cry? Why? If the parents determine that the child is hungry, they should feed the child. If, as inexperienced new parents with no policies and practices, they misdiagnose the crying to mean that the child is cold and simply turn up the heat, then the outcome might be grim. If, on the other hand, the parents have a clearly written policy and practice manual based on behavior of other children in similar circumstances, then they are much more likely to make the right decision. They will feed the child and get a much more desirable outcome.

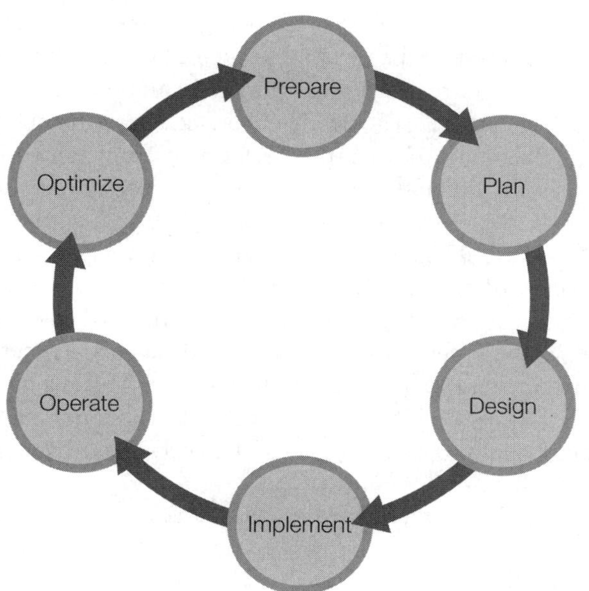

FIGURE 13-1
Life cycle management.

Configuration Management Best Practices

Because this is a chapter and not an entire book of its own, it is impossible to cover all of the subtle aspects and nuances of this topic in sufficient depth. However, as in the prior example, it is possible to look at configuration management best practices of several organizations and choose one as an example. For our example, we will look at Cisco Systems, Inc.'s Life Cycle Management. This is also known as Prepare, Plan, Design, Implement, Operate, and Optimize (PPDIOO), as shown in Figure 13-1. Configuration management best practices exist, and are applied somewhat differently, at each of the phases in the lifecycle of a network. In the following subsections, we will consider the impact of configuration management best practices in each of these phases.

 TIP

Best Practice: Assign a single individual, or two, with sole responsibility for configuration change management. Ideally, change management should be their only job. At minimum, it should be a specific responsibility with time allocated to it on a regular basis.

Prepare

The preplanning preparation phase is where configuration management best practices begin. The best practices must evolve along with the plan. If using an existing set of guidelines, they can be applied from the very beginning. If a set of best practices will be evolved, they can be started here during the prepararation phase.

TIP

Best Practice: Perform formal modeling of the network, and test "what-if" assumptions. Start that process in the Prepare Phase. This effort will support the Plan Phase.

If a new network is being created, then this is the time to set up the templates and file layouts. These will be used to capture baseline network information that will later be used to model requested network changes and determine network impact. If the project is for an existing network, then this would be the time to do a complete network audit and update existing files. In a perfect world, complete with actual budgets, this also would be the time to purchase or upgrade a network modeling tool or to engage a service. All modern network modeling tools allow traffic to be gathered from an existing, operating network. Or they should be generated based upon certain assumptions so that "what if" scenarios can be tested. Many modern network modeling tools also allow policy and security assumptions to be tested. This is a lot of effort for a very large network. It is well worth the effort. In lower budget situations, suitable results can be achieved with properly built tools using Microsoft Excel spreadsheets and well-crafted and well-thought-through what-if scenarios.

Once the Prepare Phase is complete, the network moves on to the Plan Phase.

TIP

Best Practice: Use detailed scripts. Test and test the scripts in varying environments and with different personnel. Ask testers to try to propose scenarios where the script will not work. Improve the script, and test, test, test.

TIP

Best Practice: Involve users in the Plan Phase whenever possible. If you ask their opinion, be willing to take it into account in the plan. This is particularly important now because in the current phase, it is often the user who chooses the device and service provider. Consider, for example, an employee who makes her own decision on a service provider and a mobile device, which she will then use in her work as well as her personal life.

Plan

The Plan Phase could be a formal plan for a new network, for a migration or evolution, or maybe just a phase in testing a what-if scenario for a network modification or upgrade. In any case, the Prepare Phase sets the stage. The Plan Phase is where the real work begins.

In terms of configuration management best practices, the Plan Phase is where detail-level project or program management plans are created. In many cases, the creation of scripts will reveal issues, both positive and negative. The process begins by visualizing the steps and discussing them among experienced individuals and, in many cases, going as far as actually stepping through the process in a controlled, or lab, environment.

A final aspect of the Plan Phase is to consider the needs of the user, both on an individual level and a macro level. Very often network planning groups are so focused on maintaining the network and its planned evolutionary path that they miss concepts that are completely revolutionary. They are caught off guard by industry or technology trends that seem perfectly clear to others. Keeping in close communication with actual users inside and outside the company, with market trends and new technology and product developments, is a key to good planning.

The Value of Scripts

In the network context, scripts are pre-written sets of instructions, created by knowledgeable individuals in a lab or other controlled environment. Scripts are not created under the pressure of restoring a down service. Rather, like the plans, policies, and procedures discussed elsewhere in this chapter, they are written with input from several sources. They have the benefit of time and resources. The very best networking organizations use scripts. They use scripts to assure that changes are applied uniformly by any and all personnel.

The creation process of scripts is begun in the Plan Phase and should not be relegated to a later step. In many cases, the creation of detailed, command-level, or step-by-step level scripts reveals problems that might not be revealed until a much later phase of the project when it is far more complicated and expensive to fix the problem. A specific example involving this author was an upgrade of a bank's modem network in the mid-1980s. A somewhat antiquated example, admittedly, but it will illustrate the point.

A regional bank invested a substantial amount of money in modem upgrades so that information from the central mainframe in Atlanta could be transmitted between its remote branches all over the Southern region at a higher rate. Customer transactions then could be completed more quickly. The bank realized the potential downtime, and costs, associated with the upgrades. In order to minimize both, the bank used routing software, developed by soft drink companies, to develop optimum car routes for the installation techs to minimize the techs' time in the field. A tech would arrive at the bank branch, install the new modem, and test the new line. If that step passed, the bank's system, including local ATMs, would be shut down quickly. The bank would be moved to the new line and tested, and the branch would be back online within 30 minutes. If not, the branch was put back on its old line, and the installation was escalated. The first step was planning the upgrades. This involved creating a "clean area" that represented a bank branch and then scrutinizing each and every step of the process. At that point, all scripts had been written, tested, and retested. And all specialized tools, spare modems, and almost every other contingency had been considered. Only then was a final check done prior to going out for the first installation near the data center in Atlanta, "just in case."

A final walkthrough by a seasoned engineer revealed the fact that the new modems required a new and rather hard to find fuse. The cost of the fuse, in a big box from a local supplier, was less than $1. Even though Federal Express had been operating at that point for over a decade, the cost of shipping the fuse to a bank branch was over $30. Driving one out was even more expensive. It was clearly more cost-effective to supply extra fuses with the modems upfront than to try to get replacements for fuses once they had blown. The scripts were updated to include the step of taping a pair of fuses to the back of each modem at install time, showing bank personnel the proper way to determine if a fuse was blown, and how to install the new fuse. This is an example of the value of command level or step-by-step scripts in configuration and change management.

TIP

Best Practice: Check the planned configuration changes at every step to assure that the planned change does not cause the network to operate outside the bounds of the SLA. If it is determined at any step that the SLA requirements cannot be met, the requirements need to be changed or the network needs to be modified in some way. Otherwise, the configuration or change request must be abandoned.

After developing confidence that a plan is nearly complete, it is time to move to the Design Phase. The Design Phase will reveal flaws in the plan and require some reworking. But it is impossible to develop a good plan without putting it to the test.

Design

At this point in the process, a specific new configuration or change to an existing configuration may be requested. It may have been approved or received a conditional approval and put into the PPDIOO process. The initial research and preparations have been done, and a plan has been crafted and tested, or at least bench-checked. Now it is time to make the actual network design changes that will be required to implement the planned change.

This is another point at which a network modeling tool can be used. It is also important to use a lab or test environment to validate design changes, if at all possible.

Implement

Some design changes can be implemented within the network while it is operating. But some changes will require a maintenance window or planned downtime. This can be very costly and almost impossible in many networks. Some networks, for instance, cross many time zones or might even be global in scope. They may have users who are traveling outside their regular time zone. Many manufacturers allow software to be downloaded to a second processor or CPU blade in a switch or router within the network. A flash cut can be performed with the ability to roll back to the prior software very quickly. As enticing as these types of features are, they should be utilized when the network is at a lower capacity for a variety of reasons. One reason is that the network will not be stressed. It will be more likely to operate in the capacity range. This will allow a sufficient number of CPU cycles and enough network bandwidth to allow the flash cut and roll-back to work. Another reason is that a catastrophic outage will expose fewer users to potential damage.

TIP

Best Practice: Determine the potential impact of implementation problems. Notify all potentially impacted users in advance of any implementation changes. Besides being a good public relations move for the network engineering team, a prior notification can reduce the risk and potential liabilities of a "surprise" failure.

Observe the network in operation once changes or new features have been implemented and all needed changes have been made to network documentation.

Operate

If all prior steps have been done properly, the Operate Phase should be uneventful. Of course, in today's complex networks, many different configuration changes, updates, and upgrades may be occurring simultaneously. Their interactions might conflict. Consider all of these contingencies in prior steps, particularly in Plan and Design. Keep in mind that it is possible that conditions exist in the network that are not possible to predict.

Configuration changes are requested. The changes are modeled. The results are compared, determining the change. Improvements are kept. Degradations are discarded. This is a simple way to optimize network performance.

TIP

Best Practice: If multiple new configurations and/or changes are going to be implemented within the same timeframe, implement them one at a time, in some predetermined order and timing. This will allow problems to be isolated easily. Never make multiple changes simultaneously. Treat network changes the same way that a doctor would treat drug interactions. Try to predict the results of the multiple changes, and make them one at a time—monitoring and testing at each step.

Optimize

Network performance optimization is an ongoing, almost constant effort—or at least it should be. Changes can occur in the live network due to planned configuration changes, unplanned events such as the normal ebb and flow of traffic, or malicious intervention by hackers. Network performance also can be impacted by shifts in traffic loads and application mix. All of these need to be simultaneously considered. PPDIOO and similar models are cyclical. The optimization steps themselves, because they represent changes to the network, must go back through the complete life cycle process—from the very beginning.

The network configuration and change management process is ongoing. Whether you and your organization favor the PPDIOO process or something different, chances are that the steps will be roughly the same, encompass the same considerations, and be in the same general order. Now that the overall process is better understood, we will take a deeper look at the process of managing physical hardware changes.

TIP

Best Practice: Any change required to optimize the network or otherwise modify the network design to accommodate configuration changes in a manner that was not anticipated in the formal planning process must go back through the life cycle or change management process. Networks are often modified in ways that produce undocumented aspects or inexplicable changes as a result of even small, unplanned modifications to the network's hardware and/or software.

Managing Physical Hardware Changes

Hardware and software are inextricably interwoven: You cannot have one without the other. However, the jobs of managing physical hardware and software changes are usually performed by two different people with two different specialties.

The first step in managing physical hardware changes is to establish policies and to assure that those policies are followed in day-to-day operation. For instance, is it the policy of the organization that certain components be repaired in the field? Should they be swapped out completely? What tools and spares should technicians carry with them? To what extent should an organization standardize on equipment, tools, and spares? Which departments, roles, or job functions are responsible for making decisions that vary from standard policy and practice? All of these policies and procedures, and potentially hundreds of others, should be considered well in advance so they may be implemented without delay when they are required.

"Legacy" Equipment

There is a joke among network managers: Your current network equipment is everything that you have purchased, while the legacy gear is everything your predecessor purchased. This may have some ring of truth for network managers who change jobs every eighteen months or so. Any manager who stays in his or her job for any period of time will certainly accumulate an inventory of legacy equipment. What savvy organizations understand is that one person's boat anchor is another person's gold nugget. That is as true in networking as it is in any other industry. Many organizations have policies regarding reselling of used equipment that has outlived its useful life in the network. There is a thriving secondary market for a wide variety of used equipment, and sometimes of the oldest vintages or quirkiest configurations, simply because it is so rare or so unusual. In some cases, a sale can be made directly to another company. In most cases, it is made to some equipment broker or middleman who cleans it up, marks it up, and resells it. They may wait for someone who really needs it to ask a more exorbitant amount based on the laws of supply and demand. Another option is to make a donation to a trade school or charity for a tax deduction.

One aspect of the legacy equipment situation is that two different divisions within the same corporation may have two different sets of needs. They may have two approaches to the same needs and one may have a requirement for equipment the other is trying to get rid of. In one example, this author helped multiple divisions of a global energy conglomerate establish a refurbishing, cataloging, warehousing, and distribution center for old analog telephone key sets. These were needed by some divisions to delay an expensive move to VoIP using equipment that was being discarded or abandoned by other divisions in their aggressive planned migration to VoIP.

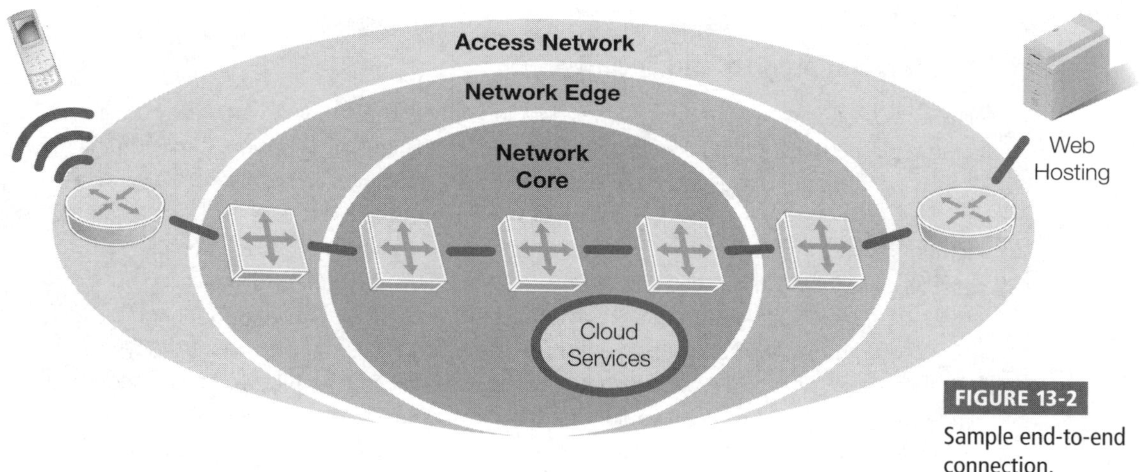

FIGURE 13-2
Sample end-to-end connection.

Granularity of Hardware Change Management

The level of components, and the policies regarding how hardware changes involving those components are managed, vary greatly with the type of device and its role in the network. Let's look at some basics of an end-to-end connection in order to demonstrate this concept.

Figure 13-2 shows a wireless user on the far left who accesses the network via either 802 wireless Ethernet standards and protocols or cellular packet protocols. The details are not important in this example. The wireless antenna is connected to an edge router, which is then connected to intermediate routers and/or switches through the inner tiers of the network. Ultimately, this allows connectivity to cloud services or hosted Web services. Many other variations are possible. But this simple example will suffice for the purposes of illustrating a point.

What is meant by "granularity?" If the user mobile device in this example is damaged, or even stolen, the general policy would be to replace the device completely and not even attempt a repair. The level of "granularity" in this case would be "unit" or "device."

Moving from left to right, if the antenna in Figure 13-2 represents a wireless access point built into a router in the user's home, or in a small office, the replacement policy, or granularity, likewise would probably be "unit" or "device." Again, because of the low cost of the device relative to the value of the time spent waiting for a repair, and the time spent making the repair, a swap-out would be done very quickly. The new device would be tested, and the service ticket or repair order would be closed. This is also where the difference between component availability and service availability comes into play. If the user's mobile devices fail at a rate of one per month, the component availability statistics are not good. But if a replacement, possibly a standby device with batteries charged and ready to go, takes less than a minute, the overall service availability is very high.

Mobile Data Integrity and Security

Hardware change management overlaps data integrity and security. A hardware device being replaced may contain critical data of importance to the organization. It may be the only place that data is available. Mobile phones, personal digital assistants (PDAs), iPhones, and similar devices are excellent examples of these types of devices. Over time, small data elements such as contact information, calendars, serial numbers, photos of completed projects or installations, and a wide variety of other information that is not backed up anywhere else accumulates in the device. In some cases, user/password information or access codes must be reset, causing a disruption to work. Clear policies about the type of information stored and how it is managed are essential. In a perfect world, the people who replace hardware devices would simply be able to check a log file and tell the owner of the device (a mobile phone, for instance) that the last backup was seven hours and nine minutes ago. They would then load the new replacement device with information from the backup and leave it to the user to use whatever process is in place to recover the missing data. But this is rarely the case because personal and business users rarely follow a disciplined backup regime. Most of the time losing a device means losing the data. If the device is damaged beyond repair, and you cannot retrieve the data, you will lose valuable information. Backing up data is always better than trying to react to a loss.

Moving further toward the core of the network, the first router may be a part of the customer premise equipment or may represent a shared router inside the ISP. If it is a customer premise router, the granularity might be a unit for the very same reasons stated before. If, on the other hand, this is a shared access router in the ISP, then maybe the granularity is "blade" because this router is but one blade in a shelf—possibly even a hot standby blade. In the case of a hot standby, a failure of a blade in a shelf causes traffic to be handled by another blade. This is another case where the device availability statistics for the specific device, and the type of device, are reduced but without any impact on service availability. It is also worth noting that during the switch-over, a packet or two may be retransmitted. But there will be no noticeable impact on the service.

Moving further into the network, there are more and more connections aggregated on the shared devices until ultimately cloud or Web servers are reached. Depending upon the service itself, it is possible that services such as e-mail are load balanced across multiple physical servers in diverse geographic locations, and that the granularity of these systems is "server." In other words, an entire hot standby server is put in place in the case of a failure of any aspect of a server. This would also likely be the case in instances such as a **storage area network (SAN)** and similar groupings, or clusters, of servers.

Accessories and Supplies

Each and every piece of hardware has its own associated supplies and accessories as well as the supplies and accessories needed to properly service the hardware. A major part of proper physical hardware change management involves being certain that all of these key pieces are at the location where they are needed when they are needed. The most senior and professional technicians always take it upon themselves to be certain that they have everything that they need. But even the newest rookie techs should have all of the parts needed, and that is the job of management.

Accessories and supplies range widely, depending upon a variety of factors, but include things such as power cords, proper drill bits to screw and unscrew certain fasteners, color-coded wire ties of different length to match organizational standards, test equipment, power supplies, fans, and all such related items.

Firmware

Many installations and repairs are thwarted by the software that is burned into chips not being proper for the installation, or repair, being performed. Firmware controls how the hardware operates. It is the first suspect if components are not operating as they should. Firmware management is a critical part of good hardware change management. Yes, it is software, technically, but it is the responsibility of the hardware change management group. If that is not a part of the written policies and procedures, it should be made so.

Hardware Spare Management

Hardware spare management is covered in more detail in a following section. That section speaks more to the financial aspects of this issue. There are technical aspects that need to be considered as well. For instance, whenever possible:

- Spare hardware should be kept powered up.
- The spare's firmware revision levels should be maintained at a level consistent with the devices that will be replaced.
- Antistatic bags always should be used in transporting cards.
- Static discharge wrist bands always should be used when handling hardware.
- Power sources always should be checked for proper voltage levels.
- Grounding should be checked.
- Many other related items should be covered.

There are far too many items to cover here, but this will provide a representative list.

Managing Software Changes

Managing hardware is not simple, but it is simple compared to managing software changes. With the exception of firmware, everything about hardware can be physically touched, unlike software. Software is the way that certain bits are set and the way those bits cause the hardware to operate. The same software will interact differently with slightly different hardware and firmware. Take the somewhat unstable operating system and application software that inhabits all devices in a network. Add to that malicious software introduced for a variety of reasons, and you have a broad picture of the complexity. Once the base software has been installed, there is an almost constant process of customization. These range from data in contact lists to favorites lists in browsers to preferred programs to launch when certain file types are encountered. Everything with a computer chip and memory is a computer, including iPhones, VoIP phones, PDAs, cell phones, and all similar devices. They are all, therefore, subject to attack by malicious software. While all of this background information is critical to understand, we have not yet begun to address the question of how to manage software changes.

In the first and second generations, as discussed earlier, all of the software and hardware was purchased, installed, and managed by the organization itself for its own internal needs. This model is still followed in some organizations. Managing software changes in those organizations is reasonably straightforward: Propose changes to the change control board or other authority, get permission, go through whatever testing exercise is deemed appropriate for that instance, and update the software using the means available to you. These include floppy disks, network-based upgrades, swapping out devices with new software versions for devices with old software versions, or whatever is needed.

In the third and fourth generations, organizations are adopting software change management models that are much more like service providers than bosses. The same initial steps occur in third and fourth generation networks as in first and second generation networks in terms of proposed changes, change control board, or other management approvals, testing, etc. The difference in third- and fourth-generation networks is that instead of pushing the software changes out to all users on some management-determined schedule, the users are made aware of the availability and the problems it will solve and introduce. They are allowed to opt-in and download the new software and upgrade at their own initiative. In many organizations, most notably organizations with powerful users such as attorney firms or stock trading firms, the software upgrade notices read more like sales pitches than edicts: *"This change will allow you to securely access the database from your PDA over any public access point. Users not upgrading will continue with their limited access and will not be able to assist customers in the field using wireless access."* The cycle of "optional" upgrades is repeated over a series of minor release levels. It only becomes a mandate, and even then an "optional" one, for major releases or if an update involves security or liability. At that point, the organizational users are told, just as an ISP customer might be told, *"We regret that if you do not upgrade to version x.y.z that we will no longer be able to support you as a user on our network. For additional information, please contact your system administrator."*

A final item that must be considered is personal software that resides on a device used for business. In the first and second generations, this was simply not allowed by most companies, although many employees and contractors routinely broke the rules. Some organizations, such as schools, got around the problem by reimaging computers, sometimes nightly, with a baseline standard set of operating system options and applications. This is not practical in an environment where a device may be a personal one and where the device might have both business and personal applications and data. Related topics include liability for pirated software on the shared device and malicious software that may have been introduced via personal use, but which makes its way into the organizational environment via the organization's network connections.

Asset Management/Inventory Control

Asset management and inventory control have both a financial component and an operational component. The financial component includes the ability to determine the present value of all tangible assets owned by an organization and to account for the assets' whereabouts. Reporting systems allow cross-tabulation of reports by various categories and reports on depreciation and other financial aspects of assets. The primary role of network management personnel is to be able to locate all of the network components down to the level of detail that management has determined is required for proper accounting. For instance, inventory might be maintained by a laptop computer serial number with each laptop containing the same components, or three grades or classes of laptops for different levels of users. However, a network traffic capture system might be based upon the same hardware as the super-user laptop and only be distinguishable by its serial number or even by opening the case and looking at the components inside.

Radio Frequency Identification

One of the most promising technologies for asset tracking is radio frequency identification (RFID). Small chips, some smaller than the head of a pin, are attached in some manner to an asset so that it can be detected when it passes a reader. Not only are RFID chips small enough to go virtually undetected, readers are also getting smaller and stealthier and can be installed in door frames and other points where assets with RFID chips might reside. It is also possible to have RFID readers installed in mobile systems that can inventory an entire warehouse, equipment storage facility, ISP point of presence (POP), or carrier **central office (CO)** in a matter of minutes without touching a single thing.

As will be discussed in the next section, RFID chips can be as valuable in loss control, acting much like electronic fingerprints for assets, as they are in asset management. Due to their small size and low cost, virtually anything can be tracked using RFID. Clever organizations are finding new applications all the time.

A Quick History of RFID

There are several different stories about the invention of RFID, But there is only one certain early application. RFID was used by the British Royal Air Force (RAF) in World War II to inventory incoming and outgoing fighter planes and bombers. Each plane was outfitted with a radio device that allowed the plane to be checked out when it left the airfield and checked in upon return. The implementation of RFID was then as it is now: A radio source is required that is unique to each object being tracked, and the object being tracked has to pass by a reader.

RFID applications are divided into categories. The first two categories are passive or active. Passive RFID systems have no power of their own. The RFID chips emit a signal when excited by an external wave of electromagnetic power. Passive systems can be made very inexpensively and very small: One application is to embed passive RFID chips in the paper packaging of food to manage inventories in the store and even in the home. This type of system also can be applied to computer hardware, computer cards, and computer tools. It is well-suited to these applications because no power is required. Active systems have their own power source. Examples of active systems are the large toll tracking boxes that adhere to vehicle windshields, allowing them to keep moving through toll points and to be billed electronically. The second categories are fixed and mobile. These categories apply to systems whereby the readers are fixed or mobile. RFID systems can be passive and mobile, passive and fixed, active and mobile, or active and fixed. RFID holds great promise in the future for tracking the location of just about anything-or anybody. More and more humans every day are having RFID chips implanted-from Mexican Drug Enforcement to persons at risk of kidnapping. RFID technology also is being used to identify and track cattle, race horses, and valued pets.

Loss Control

All asset management systems have mechanisms for dealing with the loss of assets. In some cases assets are completely depreciated. They have reached a financial value of zero and must be removed from the accounting books and disposed of. This is the normal and desirable course of events. There are, however, other situations that are far less desirable and can cost an organization a lot of money because an asset is taken out of service before it has reached a financial value, or "book value," of zero.

Damage

An asset can become damaged beyond repair. The car insurance business uses the word "totaled." In this case, the damaged asset is available for inspection and verification. Appropriate accounting steps are taken to remove the asset from the books completely or, in the case of an asset that is still needed, to replace the asset.

Theft

The outright theft of organizational assets is fairly common. It can have some remarkably dire consequences. When we think of theft of assets in a telecommunications network, we think about schemes to divert network devices, such as routers and switches, to the black market. Another example is stealing cell phones or iPads and sending them to a foreign country at a profit. All of these scenarios do occur every day. One often neglected area is called "harvesting." It involves theft of the metallic lines, and often fiber, used to carry the electronic signals. Harvesting is just as common in the US today as it is in other countries due to the high price being paid for copper on the global market. In fact, much of the copper being stolen today has been abandoned by old telephone companies. Its removal is nondisruptive to telecommunications. On the other hand, theft of copper-connecting cell towers to communications points, for example, can be very disruptive and costly. The thieves cannot tell one from the other, and, frankly, they don't care. They sell the wire by the pound to scrap yards and recyclers.

Conversion

Conversion is a term that has been around forever in the asset management vocabulary. It simply means to take something that was designed and purchased for one use, and use it for another. It is not always a bad thing. Increasingly since September 11, 2001, conversion has taken on a more sinister meaning. It is most often applied to the conversion of an asset by criminals or terrorists for their own use. The most visible

PC: Phone Home

There are many clever security mechanisms available for PCs and other high-value devices, especially ones that accompany traveling workers. The value in a security mechanism as a deterrent is often as high as, or higher than, its value in actually preventing theft. This is much like residential alarm systems. The sign out front saying that you are protected by ABC Security Company will cause a robber to choose to rob the neighbor's house, bypassing yours. In any case, you are more secure as a result of having the sign. One approach that has a deterrent value is to mark PCs clearly and permanently in some way. This deters theft for resale and allows easier recovery when the devices are stolen. Another approach that has a high recovery value is the use of security systems that allow PCs to notify a command center of their whereabouts when they are eventually reconnected to the Internet. There are a range of solutions such as hardware-based systems and software that embeds itself in the boot software or operating system kernel. They protect a wide range of operating systems and devices. Whatever specific approach and products are eventually chosen, this is a class of security system that is well worth investigating. It is also useful in locating devices for purposes of inventory when they have been merely mislaid.

example of conversion by terrorists is taking over commercial airliners intended to deliver passengers safely to their destination, and using them as guided missiles against key US targets. Conversion is a very real issue. It cannot be completely eliminated. The risk can be reduced, however, with a comprehensive employee suspicious activity reporting program. Such a program is based upon the assets an organization owns and/or has access to, and the possible terrorist or criminal uses to which they could be applied.

Cannibalization

Cannibalization is a term that conjures up a number of bad mental pictures. It is the proper term applied to the process of dismantling one asset for the value of its components parts. For instance, suppose two switches were ordered, and both arrived damaged. One appears to be intact completely except for its power supply. The other appears to have a good power supply, but many of its cards are damaged. Cannibalization occurs when parts are taken from one to make the other operational without the proper inventory management approvals and tracking. With the proper inventory management process, cannibalization is reduced to a series of transactions that allow all assets to be tracked. Without following the proper procedures it is ... cannibalization.

Interruption Control

Business continuity planning (BCP) and **disaster recovery planning (DRP)** are related but different disciplines. Organizations need both. In a broad sense, business continuity planning can be thought of more as the policy, or soft side, of surviving a disaster. Disaster recovery planning is more aligned with hard assets, although there are crossovers between the two.

Business Continuity Planning

To be most effective, BCP should be performed the same way the US federal government does Continuity of Government planning: It should be done with an organizational chart, because business continuity is mainly about people.

Essential Functions

Essential functions is a more politically correct way of saying “essential people.” In continuity of government, not only is extensive planning done to ensure the safety of the US President and top officials, it is done to ensure that they stay in communication with each other and the American people, and that they are visibly in charge. This is of particular importance in the early phases of a disaster.

Nonessential Functions

Nonessential functions, in effect nonessential people, must be clearly identified in advance of a disaster. They must know exactly what their roles are in case of a disaster. In many cases, the job of a nonessential person is simply to leave the premises. It is critical that when an organization shifts from its normal operational mode to disaster response that nonessential personal not place a burden on what might be limited resources.

Policies, Procedures, Priorities, and Practice

Every organization must plan in advance for response to a variety of foreseeable disasters. They also must plan for disasters of a more mysterious nature that cannot be specifically anticipated. Building this type of resiliency into a business continuity plan is often the difference between emerging from the disaster as a working business and being a case study in a "why businesses fail" textbook.

A key element of success is being sure that all personnel understand exactly what they are supposed to do, how to do it, and under what circumstances. Maybe a nonessential software coder becomes a floor marshal to direct others to exits and assemble in the parking lot for a head count. Maybe a nonessential database administrator only has to find an exit and assemble in the parking lot. The president of the organization may be in the middle of an important conference call in his office on the 18th floor. But he knows he must stop the call immediately, without letting anyone know there is a disaster, and make it down the 22 flights of stairs—and not via elevator—to the secure "war room" in the sub-basement.

The Role of Tabletop Exercises

Emergency response training and exercises are the lifeblood of emergency preparation and readiness. It has been a part of every culture for years. Think, for instance, about school fire drills or, in earlier years, air raid drills. Businesses, just like public safety and emergency management agencies, can have periodic group meetings to discuss scenarios and contingencies and plan responses or test existing policy and plans.

A tabletop exercise generally starts with a written scenario, which may or may not be known to exercise participants. All participants talk about their readiness and responses as the scenario unfolds. The "lessons learned" are published in after action reports (AARs). These reports guide modifications to policy or creation of new policy and plans. Tabletop exercises can be conducted periodically as standalone events or as a part of other meetings. They can be based on completely fictional scenarios or on scenarios drawn from the experiences of the organization, from news headlines, or from consultants who specialize in tabletop exercises, disaster recovery, and business continuity planning.

Business Continuity: Practice Makes Perfect

Every person alive with access to live television on September 11, 2001, remembers where they were and what they were doing on that day. In much the same way, many people recall the Challenger explosion or the assassination of John F. Kennedy or Martin Luther King, Jr. This author witnessed a second memorable event only minutes after it was verified that the September 11 attacks were of terrorist origin. I was in a secure long-distance telephone company data center in central Florida to teach a class, which was just getting under way, when the first plane hit the first tower. Minutes later, a cryptic announcement was made over the intercom system. Every single one of the several hundred persons in that facility rose to their feet in unison and went about their previously assigned business continuity tasks. The facilities' management personnel went to a secure operations area. Essential personnel either continued their tasks or assumed new, still-essential roles. Nonessential personnel either assumed essential roles or quietly left the facility. I was located by my designated point of contact and escorted, almost wordlessly, out of the facility. What I witnessed is the rare performance of an organizational dance that had clearly been choreographed well in advanced. Every participant was well-trained and well-rehearsed.

Disaster Recovery Planning

To be most effective, disaster recovery planning should be performed the same way networks are designed and implemented. It should be performed with the OSI or IETF models, because disaster recovery planning is primarily about technology and hardware. Because most networks today are packet-based, this discussion will use the Internet Engineering Task Force (IETF) five-layer model. The process is fundamentally a checklist approach. The first step is to determine if a specific component, service, or capability is required during disaster recovery. If it is required, one should determine how to make it available during the emergency.

Physical Layer

In disaster recovery planning, Physical Layer planning includes all of the concerns that are usually included. It also must take into account concerns such as electricity, water, and other basic services that may be needed to make the Physical Layer components operational. One example of bad planning is the National Guard unit that arrived at a flood disaster relief site with a mobile cellular antenna on a trailer, referred to as cellular on wheels (COW), with no source of power and without the proper cable to connect it to any generators brought by other agencies or relief organizations. No detail is too small.

Data Link Layer

Data Link Layer planning includes the normal Layer 2 devices, such as bridges and switches. In most cases, it will not require complete redundancy because the number of essential personnel working through a disaster may be substantially less than those needing service under normal conditions.

Network Layer

The same issues impacting switch redundancy will impact routers as well. One thing to consider, well in advance, is how connectivity can be maintained to the Internet if that connectivity is required for normal business operation. If an organization is utilizing cloud-based services for essential functions, assuring the Internet connectivity is critical.

Transport Layer

Transport Layer protocols will work if the applications work and the Network Layer is working.

Applications Layer

It may be advisable to block or limit access to certain applications during disaster recovery operations to lessen the burden on network resources. Organizations should enforce policies regarding essential and nonessential applications in much the same way that distinctions are made between essential and nonessential personnel. A further distinction could and should be made between essential and nonessential access and users to reduce the load on servers and applications during disaster recovery.

Intersection of BCP and DRP

Business continuity planning and disaster recovery planning are both important functions and, when used together, address most issues that an organization will encounter. Both functions need to be done before the disaster, require the involvement and support of upper management, and cross the divide between management and operations.

CHAPTER SUMMARY

This chapter covers a wide range of related topics—from configuration management and its role to function and composition of the change control board. Asset management and inventory control are discussed, as are business continuity planning and disaster recovery planning. For many readers, this chapter may have lacked the excitement of Request for Comments or detailed ladder diagrams of how session initiation protocol works. It is a very important chapter, nonetheless, because it discussed many important functions of the management of networks that are required knowledge for engineers who aspire to get into management.

KEY CONCEPTS AND TERMS

Bit error rate (BER)
British Telecom (BT)
Business continuity planning (BCP)
Central Office (CO)
Computer-aided design (CAD)
Disaster recovery planning (DRP)
Mean time between failures (MTBF)
Mean time to install (MTTI)
Mean time to repair (MTTR)
Point of presence (POP)
PTT (postal, telephone, and telegraph) agency
Storage area network (SAN)
Type of service (TOS)
Virtual private network (VPN)

CHAPTER 13 ASSESSMENT

1. One of the first steps in change control is determining a normal baseline from which changes will be made.

A. True
B. False

2. Which of the following is not a generation of networking as outlined in this chapter?

A. First generation: mainframe computers owned and operated by the organization
B. Second generation: minicomputers owned and operated by the organization
C. Third generation: personal computers owned and operated by individuals
D. Fourth generation: PCs and mobile devices owned and operated by individuals
E. Fifth generation: mobile devices, including Droids and tablets linked to social networking sites such as Facebook

3. Which of the following is not a usual parameter in a network Service Level Agreement?

A. Availability
B. Delay variation
C. Frequency response
D. Delay
E. Packet delivery

4. The use of service-level agreements in networking originated in ________.

A. the US by MCI
B. Britain by BT
C. Britain by Mercury Communications
D. France by France Telecom
E. Germany by the Deutsch Bundespost

5. Packet deliver/discard ________.

A. Are two very different measurements
B. Is enforced by the PDD algorithm
C. Is enforced based on IP TOS bits
D. Impacts certain applications more than others
E. None of the above

6. Delay ________ .

A. Occurs in both circuit and packet networks
B. Occurs only in circuit networks
C. Occurs only in packet networks
D. Occurs in neither circuit nor packet networks

7. Delay variation ________.

A. Occurs only in packet networks
B. Occurs only in circuit networks
C. Occurs in both circuit and packet networks
D. Occurs in neither circuit nor packet networks

8. SLA metrics from different carriers and service providers ________ . (Mark all that apply.)

A. Are possibly measured in different places in the network
B. May or may not represent round-trip delay
C. Are measured and calculated per RFC 2109
D. Are measured and calculated per TIA 1405
E. None of the above

9. Availability calculations are differentiated based upon ________ availability.

A. Network, component, and service
B. Day, month, and year
C. IETF, ITU, and telco
D. End system, intermediate system, and server

10. MTBF stands for ________.

A. Mean time between failures
B. Maximum time between failures
C. Minimum time between failures
D. Mean time before failures

11. Internal service-level agreements ________. (Mark all that apply.)

A. Replace external service agreements
B. Can never be better than external SLAs
C. Often promise different levels of service to different applications or traffic types
D. Often tiered delay and delay variation metrics based on distance between the communicating end points

12. Change control boards are technical bodies and do not need to consider policy, finance, or other nontechnical aspects of proposed changes.

A. True
B. False

13. BCP stands for ________.

A. Business continuity planning
B. Business career planning
C. Business continuity policy
D. Business continuity practices

14. DRP stands for ________.

A. Disaster recovery planning
B. Disaster recovery procedures
C. Design recommendation policy
D. Design review policy

15. An organization must choose between BCP and DRP as an approach for dealing with unplanned events affecting their telecommunications infrastructure.

A. True
B. False

CHAPTER

14 Performance Management

NETWORKS EXIST to increase productivity and offer services not previously available prior to connecting devices together. The usefulness of any network is based entirely on its ability to perform well enough to meet its goals. The overall goal of any network is to support business operations. Workers must be able to use the network to accomplish tasks and conduct business. A network that routinely makes it difficult to complete tasks is not useful. Every organization encounters network issues occasionally, but it is the recurring problems that need attention. In this chapter you will learn about maintaining good network performance. You will learn about how to measure, analyze, and affect network performance.

There are many ways to set network performance goals. At the highest level, a network is operating well when it supports all of the workers in completing their tasks. But what if they are not able to complete their tasks efficiently? How do you measure network performance? Once you measure it, what is good and what is bad? Once you determine that performance is bad, what do you do about it? You will learn the answers to these questions in this chapter. You will learn how important network performance is to each organization, and how to ensure that the network is performing well.

Chapter 14 Topics

This chapter covers the following topics and concepts:

- What network performance factors are
- How to measure network performance
- How to monitor network performance
- What network performance protocols are
- How to respond to network performance issues

Chapter 14 Goals

When you complete this chapter, you will be able to:

- Describe network performance issues
- Explain how to measure network performance
- Describe how to monitor network performance
- List common network performance monitoring protocols
- Describe how to respond to network performance issues

Network Performance Factors

Performance management is the fourth component of FCAPS—the five-part concept of fault, configuration, accounting, performance, and security management. It is the collection of activities that work together to identify performance problems and address them. FCAPS defines each of the main five components at the same level. That means each of the five areas of tasks is equal in importance to the others. Although performance management is a separate group of tasks, it exists as a subset of fault management. Any negative event in a network is a fault. Performance that does not meet minimum standards can be viewed as a fault as well. Looking at it this way, every performance issue is a special type of fault. In most cases, performance problems that are not critical may go unnoticed and unreported for a long period of time.

Faults and Performance

The main difference between most standard types of faults and network performance issues is that standard faults generally result from failed devices. All faults do not indicate failed equipment, but many do. Most performance issues exist on networks where all devices are still working. The network's performance becomes a problem when user productivity is affected. A slow network makes it harder to get work done. One of the biggest challenges to performance management is that performance problems can exist long before they become critical. Organizations that rely only on users to report performance problems often find out about problems only when they become critical. An important aspect of performance management is finding the problems before they degrade productivity.

One of the most important pieces of information when managing a network's performance is what "normal" looks like. Abnormal network performance is always characterized in terms of normal performance. Regardless of the metrics used, different networks will perform well when exhibiting different numbers. Always know what "normal" looks like before starting to evaluate performance. One of the best ways to document normal performance is to create one or more **baselines**. A baseline is a collection of performance measurements against a system at a particular point in time. In other words, it is a snapshot of how a system is performing. The best baseline is one that was created during normal operation.

Baselines provide the ability to compare current performance measurements to a known "normal" system. The measurements in the baseline make it easy to see any differences. These differences provide a starting point to investigate the cause of a performance problem. To get a better understanding of baselines and assessing performance, it is necessary to look at performance factors.

Factors That Affect Performance

Network performance is a measure of how well packets travel from their source to their destination. There is not a single number that represents a measure of performance. In fact, performance is a collection of measurements. Each measurement shows the state of one of several performance factors. Overall network performance is actually a combination of these factors. You will use each of these factors in measuring and assessing network performance. Here are the most common network performance factors:

- **Latency**—How long it takes a packet or frame to travel from one node to another. When using protocols that acknowledge receipt, it is possible to calculate the round-trip time. For protocols that do not acknowledge receipt, a one-way latency value represents the time it takes to travel from a source to a destination. Layer 2 devices can track frame latency, while Layer 3 devices can track packet latency.
- **Packet loss**—The number or percent of packets that do not reach their intended destination. Packet loss may be caused by a network device or link failure, excessive congestion, security filtering, or dropping traffic to enforce a specific service level.
- **Retransmission**—This is related to packet loss. Any time a packet is lost when using a reliable protocol, the sender must retransmit it. **Retransmission** delays measure the amount of time required to retransmit a packet (or frame).
- **Throughput**—A measure of the amount of traffic a network can handle. **Throughput** is normally expressed as kilobits, megabits, or gigabits per second.

These four factors are the most common network performance metrics. There are others as well. Other factors that contribute to network performance include compression, encryption, and format translation and can all affect how well a network performs. The rest of this chapter will focus on the four primary performance factors.

Network performance management includes the activities that measure, analyze, and optimize each of the performance factors. Contrary to popular belief, the main purpose of performance management is not to optimize the numbers. The numbers only provide indications as to what is really happening. The real goal of performance management is to ensure the network supports high productivity. Never forget that networks exist to support business functions. They can have great performance numbers, but if a network does not support business operations, then great performance numbers do not matter.

Measuring Performance

One of the first tasks in identifying performance problems is to measure the nature of the problem. In many cases, users describe performance problems as "The network is really slow." That phrase does not tell you very much. You cannot tell what the cause could be with so little information. You do not know what "slow" really means, and you do not know exactly what it is that is slow. A good approach to uncovering the facts would be to compare current overall performance to a baseline to show how the network is performing differently.

Baselines

The previous section introduced the idea of a baseline. Creating a baseline is the first step in measuring performance in any context. A good baseline gives you the ability to compare current performance with normal performance. Of course, that assumes you created the baseline during a period of normal performance. Since perceptions can change over time, it is important to create a snapshot of performance when things are going well. That baseline then helps you, when you have a problem in the future, determine how bad things really are.

There are two main steps that are necessary to create a good baseline. First, create a set of documents that fully describe your network. This document should include topology diagrams, inventory lists, and a description of how each device is configured. Configuration details are an important part of a baseline. Many network management server (NMS) tools provide the ability to automatically discover network devices and connections between them. Effective tools are a crucial part of a solid performance management system. A poorly connected network will never perform to its potential. Creating baselines that reflect a network's current topology is an important part of the overall performance process.

The second part of the baseline is a performance assessment of the network and its most important applications. The combination of the network description, configuration, and performance assessment provides a complete picture of how a network is performing.

Creating a baseline is not the final activity. Although the baseline serves as a historical record of a network's performance, it has additional value. A baseline can help organizations understand their network and how it is being used. They also can study baselines to identify areas of the network where they may need to add more capacity. The real value of creating baselines is in comparing them over time to develop trending information. Trends can help network designers identify areas that are likely to cause problems. Predicting problems allows time to take proactive measures. For example, analyzing several baselines may show that a network's backbone is reaching its capacity. Adding redundant links or incorporating link aggregation to increase **bandwidth** could alleviate a problem before it occurs.

Check the Cables

This author was once asked to participate in a project to identify and fix a critical network performance problem. One of the world's largest manufacturers of construction equipment had a problem. The company had just implemented redundant hardware to protect its enterprise resource planning (ERP) servers and databases. The two failover cluster servers were connected with two high-speed fiber optic cables. One connection served as a control channel, and the other transmitted data between the two servers. The problem was that after a few hours, the connection would fail and the two servers would stop communicating. This was a critical issue for the company. The problem rendered their investment in redundant hardware worthless.

After listening to a thorough review of the problem, each team member was asked for input. Each could ask a question or request more information. One team member asked for a verified map of the connections between the two servers. The client had chosen not to send technicians to trace cables. As it turned out, the second day of the meeting started with a report from the technical team. They had decided to trace the cables late the previous night. They found that the two cables were crossed. The two cables were not connected properly. Cables were then swapped at one end, and everything worked perfectly. Never underestimate the value of correct physical cabling.

Chain of Events

Poor network performance does not just happen. In many cases, it does not have a single cause. However, there are some situations in which a single device can cause an entire network to perform poorly. With today's network designs, packets make several hops as they travel from source to destination. Each hop represents a potential point that could slow a packet down on its journey. Most network performance metrics are actually cumulative values as a packet travels toward its destination. Passing through each device is a new event in the life of a packet. Each event is a new opportunity for delay or disruption.

A packet's journey from source to destination is actually a chain of transmission events. Since each hop adds time to each packet's transit time, each step needs to be optimized. It takes only one misconfigured device in the chain to cause performance problems. Although a single device with a bad configuration can be a source of performance problems, many problems result from several devices and links. A device that suddenly sends a high volume of traffic may cause congestion in other parts of the network. When looking for network problems, always look at the big picture. Try not to focus on individual devices too early.

Part of a good baseline is a sample of normal times to traverse the network. That involves timing packets at each device as they travel through the network. Collecting timing information when the network is working well can provide several useful statistics.

Saving performance information in a format that is easy to access makes it possible to create reports and calculate trends on the network as a whole or for individual segments. Many NMS tools provide the ability to store and analyze performance data.

A study of how traffic moves through a network is called a **network readiness assessment (NRA)**. Such studies include sending packets to network devices to record various characteristics such as latency, loss, and jitter. Understanding each of these characteristics helps to create a network environment that performs well and provides a positive user experience. The information collected during an NRA can help identify potential trouble spots in a network and possible areas that need to be reinforced.

Key Metrics

Part of creating a baseline is taking measurements of a network's performance. Once you have one or more baselines in place, the process of comparing them to current performance also involves taking measurements. Measuring network performance is critical to all aspects of managing performance. Without measurements, there is no way to really know how a network is performing. There are four main steps to taking performance measurements. These steps include:

- **Decide what to measure (and why)**—The best standard of measurement, or **metric**, should most accurately describe what you are trying to measure. It is also important that you know why you are measuring something. A measurement by itself does not mean much. It is important that you define the reasons and the context for each measurement. For example, if you want to measure the current speed your vehicle is traveling, you would likely measure miles per hour (mph) or kilometers per hour (kph). Assume that you are trying to determine if you are exceeding the speed limit.
- **Select the best measuring tool**—Select a tool that accurately and efficiently measures the metric you chose. Be careful to avoid using tools that alter what you are trying to measure. A good tool should not affect what it is measuring. When measuring speed, you could use a speedometer, an external radar detection device, or a known distance and a stopwatch. In most cases, the speedometer is the easiest tool to use.
- **Take the measurement**—Use the tool to take a measurement, and record the results. Know how to use the tool to read its results. Always record any readings, and add sufficient documentation to explain the context of the measurement. The minimal context includes date and time of the reading, the scale or the measurement, and the target measured.
- **Interpret the results**—Compare the results to a standard or guideline to determine its meaning. A number or category value is not much good without a standard against which you can compare it. In the case of measuring a vehicle's speed, the measurement only makes sense when compared to another value. To determine if you are speeding, you must compare your speed to the current speed limit. If you are traveling at 54 mph in a zone where the speed limit is 60 mph, then you are obeying the speed limit law. If the current road's speed limit is 40 mph, you are speeding. The vehicle's speed is the same in both scenarios. Only the context is different.

Warm or Cool?

Suppose you want to take a measurement of the air temperature. You select a thermometer as the best measuring tool for the job. The thermometer shows that the air temperature is 60 degrees Fahrenheit. Is that warm or cool? There are several important items missing. First, what is the reason for taking the measurement? What is the context? What values determine warm or cold?

Look at this example in two different contexts. First, assume it is early spring. You have just endured several months of temperatures that were below freezing. Today the sun is out, and the temperature is 60 degrees Fahrenheit. In this context, 60 degrees feels warm. Now, assume the time is late summer. You are on vacation and have enjoyed several days of 80 degree weather. Today is cloudy and 60 degrees. It feels cool. Interpreting measurements always depends on context and trends. Be careful to avoid placing too much emphasis on individual numbers.

Deciding what to measure to assess network performance involves examining key performance factors. There are five main metrics commonly used to measure network performance. There are many more than these five, but these are the most common. The first two measure how traffic flows throughout the network. The last three measure how the network hardware handles the traffic. These common network performance metrics include:

- Throughput
- Network latency
- Device errors and discards
- Network hardware resource utilization
- Buffer usage

Highway Bandwidth or Throughput?

For a comparison of the two terms, consider an interstate highway. The bandwidth of a stretch of the highway would be a measure of the maximum number of cars that could pass a certain point traveling at maximum speed for a specific amount of time. No real highway ever achieves this maximum. In real life, there is a gap between vehicles. Also, some vehicles do not travel uniformly at the maximum speed. (Assume vehicles cannot physically exceed the maximum speed.) To make the example even more realistic, highway traffic flow also suffers from congestion, accidents, and construction closures. When planning a morning commute, the current throughput is far more valuable than the highway's bandwidth. The throughput shows how slowly the highway's traffic is moving right now.

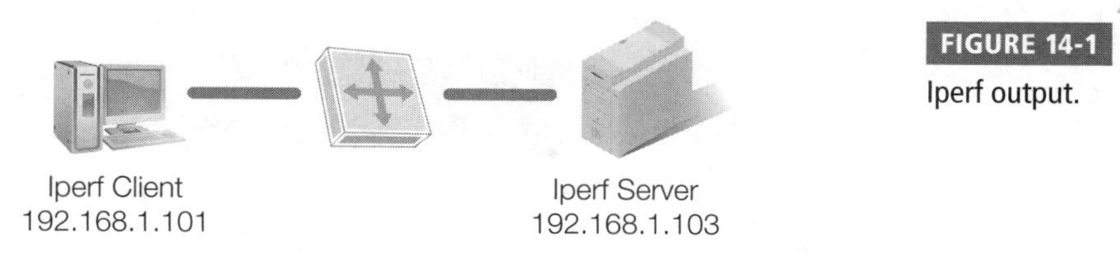


```
------------------------------------------------------
Client connecting to 192.168.1.103, TCP port 5001
TCP window size: 16.0 KByte (default)
------------------------------------------------------
[ 3] local 192.168.1.101 port 59291 connected with 192.168.1.103 port 5001
[ID] Interval      Transfer     Bandwidth
[ 3] 0.0-10.0 sec     113 MBytes   94.5 Mbits/sec
```

FIGURE 14-1
Iperf output.

Throughput

Network throughput is the measure of how much data a network carries in a specific period of time. Many people use the term bandwidth interchangeably with throughput. These two terms are very different. Bandwidth refers to a theoretical maximum capability of a specific physical medium. Ethernet technology uses a baseband transmission method that uses all of the medium's bandwidth. The throughput measurement returns a much more realistic measure of network performance.

The relationship between throughput and bandwidth is important. Think of bandwidth as the maximum amount of data you can push through a network segment. Throughput is the actual amount of data that you are pushing through a network segment. Network planners often want to see these two metrics together. When throughput approaches bandwidth, it is time to increase the bandwidth. Insufficient bandwidth means the device or the media may need to be upgraded or augmented to support more traffic.

The Iperf tool is a good free tool to measure network throughput. See Table 14-1 for more information on Iperf and other performance measuring tools. Iperf measures bandwidth, packet loss, and delay jitter. It provides various options to include additional network performance characteristics. Figure 14-1 shows the output of Iperf.

Network Latency

Latency is often one of the primary causes of network performance problems. Unless a network's throughput is near the bandwidth, capacity is not the problem. Latency is a measure of how long a packet takes to travel from one node to another. Latency in today's networks can vary from less than one millisecond on LANs to a half second (500 milliseconds) for satellite connections. Latency is a good measure of network performance because it samples how well the network is doing its job at a specific point in time. It is a good snapshot of current performance.

Latency typically increases as conditions slow the network down. Conditions could include congestion, hardware failure, or malicious attacks. When network latency is high, it generally helps to start measuring latency between individual nodes in the

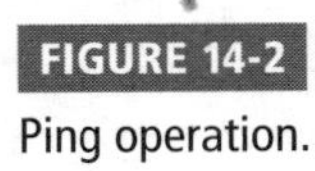

FIGURE 14-2

Ping operation.

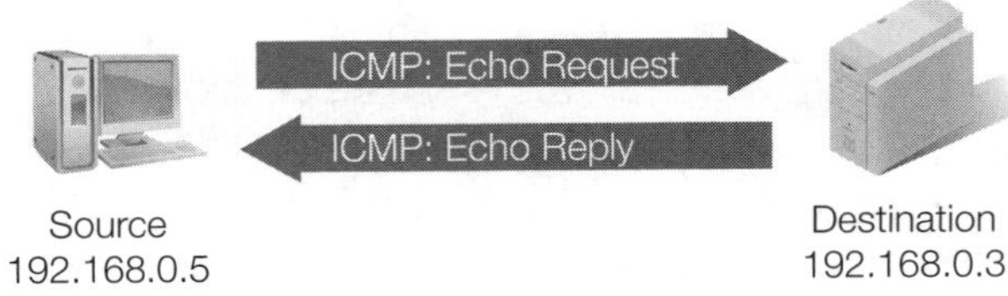

network. This process can help identify the problem and help direct recovery efforts. An NMS that monitors an entire network can help automate the performance problem identification process.

One of the most popular tools to measure latency is ping, also known in extended format as Packet Internet Groper. The ping tool is available in most operating systems. See Table 14-1 for more performance measuring tools. The name came from the early days of using sonar to find submarines. Sonar operators would send a single signal, called a "ping," to search for any submarines. The "ping" would bounce off any objects and return to the sending station. The ping network tool operates in a similar fashion.

The sending node creates an Internet Control Message Protocol (ICMP) echo request packet. You will learn more about ICMP and its different packet types later in this chapter. The sending node sends the packet to a target system and starts a timer. The target system receives the packet and returns it to the sender. The sender reports the elapsed time as the **round trip time (RTT)** for the path between the two nodes. Figure 14-2 shows how the ping tool works.

This simple tool provides a lot of information. Receiving a returned message allows ping to report the following characteristics:

- That the target node is connected to the network
- That the target node is alive
- That the target node is reachable
- A measure of the amount of time a message takes to travel to the target and back again
- Average RTT and dropped packet percent values as the result of a sequence of ping messages

A ping timeout does not give as much information. Any number of problems could have prevented the message from making its round trip. The target node could be unavailable, or a network device between the sender and the target could drop all ping messages. Firewalls are often configured to restrict ICMP traffic. Therefore, if you are pinging a device that is on the other side of a firewall, and that firewall is restricting ICMP traffic, the ping will not be successful.

Device Errors and Discards

Network devices that introduce errors can cause packets to become corrupted or dropped. Although device errors are technically faults, they can have a direct impact on network performance. Devices that introduce errors cause nodes to retransmit damaged or missing packets. The additional impact to performance is that the source nodes do not magically retransmit damaged or missing packets. Some other node has to request retransmission. This occurs either after a timeout or detecting a damaged packet. Device errors can help explain why a network starts performing poorly.

The best way to measure device errors for multiple devices is to let the NMS do it. Configure the NMS to passively listen for error reports and periodically poll for status updates for all devices on the network. Simple Network Management Protocol (SNMP) makes communicating and managing this type of information possible in a large environment.

Discards are not normally causes for network performance problems. In many cases, they are a result of performance issues. A network **discard** is a situation in which a device drops one or more packets. The two main reasons for discards are:

- **Security policy**—A device discards a packet based on a security policy. Security policies often instruct devices to filter traffic.
- **QoS policy**—A device discards a packet to allow packets with higher priorities to pass.

In the case of QoS discards, the action occurs because the network did not have sufficient capacity to handle all of the traffic. Frequent QoS discards may indicate that the network needs to expand to handle more traffic. Excessive security discards may indicate that the device is overworked. It may make sense to add another device closer to the source of the filtered traffic to filter out the bad packets earlier. The NMS is the best place to measure discard frequency.

Network Device Utilization

Each network device is an electronic hardware device that processes network traffic. Some devices are very sophisticated, and some are simple. Regardless of how complex they are, they all have limited processing capabilities. When the frequency and volume of network traffic exceed any device's ability to process it, the device increases latency to each packet. To keep a network running smoothly, each device should be processing traffic at less than 100 percent of its utilization. An NMS can use SNMP to query devices to ensure each one has some idle time.

A network device can become over-utilized when it is unable to respond quickly to all of the inbound traffic it receives. The fix for this situation is not always to make the device more powerful. The problem could be due to a failure of another device or connection.

One device failure may result in much more traffic having to travel through a limited number of devices. Figure 14-3 shows how one failed device can substantially increase the traffic for other devices.

Other causes for saturated devices could include DoS attacks, configuration setting changes, or excessive network use. Detecting a saturated device is the responsibility of the NMS. An NMS can monitor the values of several device characteristics to determine if the device has any idle time. Three of the most common statistics for any processing devices, including network devices, are:

- **CPU usage**—What percentage of the CPU's time is spent on work, and what percentage is idle. Consistent idle time means the device is not completely saturated.
- **Memory usage**—How much of the device's memory is in use.
- **Buffer usage**—How efficiently is the device able to use its buffers to avoid introducing additional latency.

Buffer Usage

Network devices use memory buffers to temporarily store frames before forwarding them to their destinations. Store-and-forward devices store the entire frame in memory before forwarding it. Cut-through devices only store part of the frame. Once the cut-through receives enough of the frame to determine its destination, it starts transmitting the frame to that destination.

FIGURE 14-3

One failed device may overrun another device.

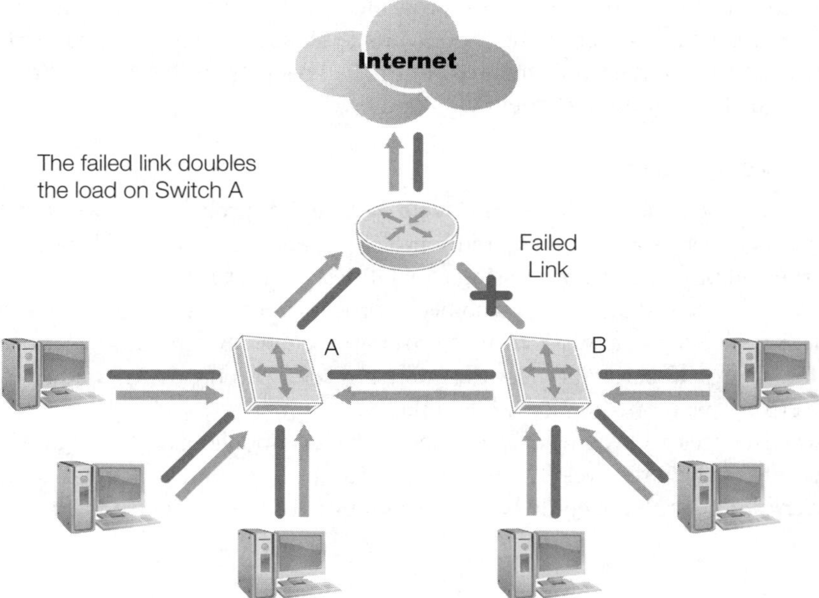

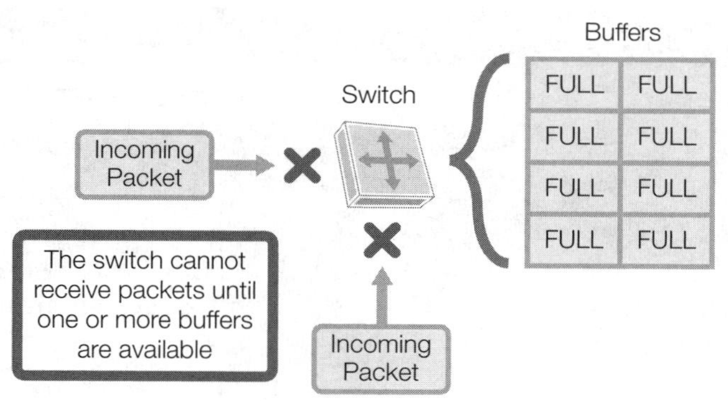

FIGURE 14-4
The impact of no free buffers.

The whole buffering process should keep the network running smoothly. However, if a device runs out of available buffers, it has to stop receiving traffic until it can empty a buffer (see Figure 14-4). Any wait time increases latency. NMS device utilization management should include measuring at least these buffer-related metrics:

- **Total number of buffers**—A count of input and output buffers
- **Free buffers**—Buffers that are available for use
- **Buffer activity**—Buffer hits, misses, add buffers, remove buffers

Just as with any other device-specific metric, buffer metrics may only reflect external problems. A device that reports no available buffers may be suffering from a large amount of traffic caused by another device. Pay attention to buffer statistics, but always view them in a larger context.

Measuring Tools

The overall goal for good performance is to maximize throughput and minimize each of the remaining key metrics. There are many tools available to measure various network performance metrics. The best set of tools will be different for each organization. Choose the tools that fit your budget and give you what you need to know. Table 14-1 lists some of the common network performance measuring tools.

Table 14-1 is not a comprehensive list of performance measurement tools. Many more tools are available. Some tools are simple, while others are actually collections of tools brought together into one software package. Use the tools that fit best in your organization. The important aspect of measuring network performance is that you understand what the numbers represent. Thousands of numbers do not help unless you understand their context and meaning.

TABLE 14-1 Network performance measuring tools.

TOOL	DESCRIPTION	LICENSE	WHERE TO GET IT
Httping	Similar to ping, but for HTTP requests—measures latency of Web server and network	Free	*http://www.vanheusden.com/httping/*
Iperf	Measures maximum TCP and UDP bandwidth performance	Free	*http://sourceforge.net/projects/iperf/*
Layer Four Traceroute (LFT)	Similar to traceroute, but works faster and in more environments	Free	*http://pwhois.org/lft/index.who*
Mtr	Tool that combines traceroute and ping	Free	*http://www.bitwizard.nl/mtr/*
Netperf	Benchmark network performance	GPLv2 (free)	*http://www.netperf.org/netperf/*
Paris Traceroute	Enhanced traceroute tool that provides accurate measurements in networks that use load balancing	Free	*http://www.paris-traceroute.net/*
Ping	Measures round-trip time and packet loss	In operating system	Included in operating system
PingPlotter	Graphical representation of ping and traceroute output	Free and paid versions available	*http://www.pingplotter.com/*
Synack	Stanford tool to measure client-server connection round-trip time (RTT)	Free	*http://www-iepm.slac.stanford.edu/tools/synack/*
tcpdump/Windump	Shows packets traveling between nodes (hosts)	BSD (free)	*http://www.tcpdump.org/*
Traceroute (tracert)	Measures round-trip time, and reports path taken to destination	In operating system	Included in operating system
Ttcp/nttcp (Test TCP)	Measures throughput between hosts using TCP or UDP	Free	*http://www.pcausa.com/Utilities/pcattcp.htm*

Monitoring Performance

Measuring network performance is like taking a patient's temperature. Taking a single measurement can provide good information, but it does not tell the whole picture. For example, is a patient's temperature of 100.5 degrees Fahrenheit good or bad? If the temperature is rising, it is generally bad. If the patient has had a very high temperature for several days and it is coming down to 100.5 degrees, it would be good news. Always remember that context is often more important than any single measurement. The same wisdom applies to managing network performance. Measuring performance is good, but monitoring it is even better.

Monitoring performance means to take individual measurements at scheduled times, and record each measurement. The stored measurements provide a historical reference and a context for new measurements. Monitoring also implies action in some cases. One of the purposes of monitoring is to determine whether measurements are in normal ranges. When a measurement falls outside a normal range of the monitoring software, the NMS should take some action. NMS actions may include notifying an attendant or running a predefined set of instructions to react to a specific measurement.

The NMS should analyze all SNMP traps for abnormal performance. It also should send periodic probing requests to retrieve updated performance metrics for network devices. Both the active probing and the passive SNMP trap receipts should give the NMS sufficient information to assess the network. The NMS is looking for anything out of the ordinary. If it identifies any unusual activity, it will take action.

Don't Overload the Network

Carefully consider the difference between passive and active network monitoring. Most networks include a mixture of the approaches. Active polling can give better results in some cases, but it requires that you add traffic to the network. An overactive NMS sending out frequent queries can cause a network to slow down. New monitoring of hardware or software may fail and can cause network disruptions. Remember that the purpose of monitoring a network is to maintain good performance, not decrease performance. Always assess network performance before and after adding new polling actions. Ensure that any new devices do not create single points of failure. If new polling messages degrade the network's performance, then investigate alternative methods to get the information you need. In many cases, just reducing the polling frequency can reduce its impact on normal network traffic.

Collecting Data

A good NMS should collect and store important network performance information. There are many different measurements the NMS could store. Which ones are important? The answer varies between organizations, but the most important performance characteristics include:

- **Bits received or transmitted per second**—Shows how much work a node is doing
- **Response time**—The current and average response time shows how well the network is operating
- **Device errors and discards**—Shows how well each device is handling traffic
- **Packet loss**—Describes how well the network is delivering packets between endpoints

Each of these individual characteristics is important to assessing a network's performance. A good NMS allows users to view the network's performance characteristics in the context of other characteristics and historical measurements. The ability to easily compare characteristics makes it easier to identify unusual activity. Long-term trending can help administrators identify slowly developing problems or unusual activity that is not easy to see in individual measurements.

Reporting Information

A good NMS has several roles to fill. It must provide accessible methods to identify and monitor network components. It also must define action thresholds and take action when activity exceeds thresholds, as well as helping analyze collected data. Reporting and presentation capabilities are important to a comprehensive NMS.

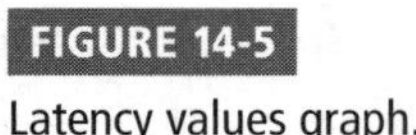

FIGURE 14-5

Latency values graph.

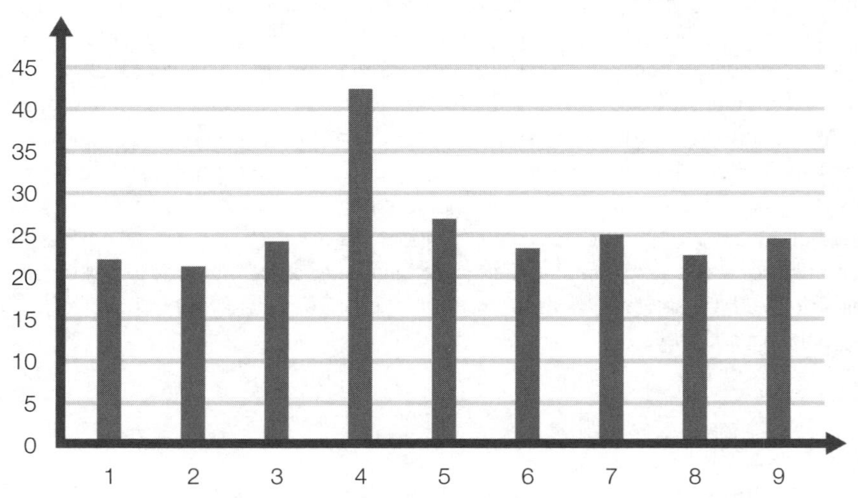

TABLE 14-2 Network performance monitoring tools.

TOOL	DESCRIPTION	LICENSE	WHERE TO GET IT
IxChariot	Robust network performance management tool	Commercial	*http://www.ixchariot.com/products.html*
Multi Router Traffic Grapher (MRTG)	Monitors the traffic load on network links. Works with many network devices.	GNU GPL (free)	*http://oss.oetiker.ch/mrtg/*
Nagios	Comprehensive IT infrastructure monitoring	Open source and commercial versions	*http://www.nagios.org/*
Net-SNMP	Software suite for using the SNMP protocol	Open source	*http://www.net-snmp.org/*
PRTG Network Monitor	Complete network monitoring	Commercial	*http://www.paessler.com/prtg*
QCheck	Network troubleshooting tool	Free	*http://www.ixchariot.com/products.html*
RRDTool	Data logging and graphing	GNU GPL (free)	*http://oss.oetiker.ch/rrdtool/*
SolarWinds	Complete network monitoring	Commercial	*http://www.solarwinds.com*

Most good NMS products for enterprise application provide multiple reporting methods. They provide the ability to align performance statistics with the current network map and help isolate trouble spots. Although formatted reports can be valuable, graphical visualizations of network performance ease the process of analysis. Explore the reporting capabilities of any NMS before adopting it.

Graphs are common visual tools that help show measurements that stand out from normal processing. Figure 14-5 shows a graph of latency measurements. The higher-than-normal latency measurement clearly stands out in the graph.

There is a wide range of network performance monitoring tools available. Capabilities can vary substantially between products. As with any network performance measuring tools, evaluate each monitoring tool, and select the ones that best fit your requirements. Table 14-2 lists some of the common network performance monitoring tools.

technical TIP

There are several resources on the Internet that list many more network performance tools and information. Take a look at these three sites for information on tools and techniques for nearly any environment:

- **Network Performance Tools**—*http://www.wcisd.hpc.mil/tools/*
- **Measuring IP Network Performance (Cisco)**—*http://www.cisco.com/web/about/ac123/ac147/archived_issues/ipj_6-1/measuring_ip.html*
- **Stanford Linear Accelerator Center Network Monitoring Tools**—*http://www.slac.stanford.edu/xorg/nmtf/nmtf-tools.html*

Performance Protocols

Network performance management uses two different types of protocols. The first protocol group helps to identify performance issues. The second type of protocol helps to avoid performance issues or respond to issues that occur. Simple network performance measuring tools and comprehensive NMS suites use both types in normal operation. You have already seen most of these protocols in earlier chapters or sections. This section will highlight each protocol's use in network performance management.

Performance Measurement Protocols

Two protocols are the most popular for measuring network performance. Most tools either use these protocols or higher-layer protocols to simulate their behavior. The following sections cover each of these two protocol's details.

Internet Control Message Protocol

One of the best-known network performance measurement tools is ping. Ping uses the **Internet Control Message Protocol (ICMP)** to discover information about networks and routes through the networks. ICMP is a protocol that defines how control messages are exchanged between nodes in a network. ICMP does not normally transport any user data. It transmits only messages that describe the network's current characteristics.

ICMP messages consist of a header and data sections. The header is 8 bytes in length and the data section is variable length. The ICMP header includes:

- **Type**—1 byte value for the ICMP message type
- **Code**—1 byte value for the ICMP message subtype
- **Checksum**—2 byte checksum for the entire ICMP message
- **Remaining header**—Remaining 4 bytes value depends on ICMP message type

ICMP supports many control messages that are useful for discovering network performance information, as shown in Table 14-3.

TABLE 14-3 Common ICMP message types and codes (first two bytes in the ICMP header).

ICMP TYPE	CODE	DESCRIPTION
0—Echo reply	0	Echo reply used by ping
1–2		Reserved
3—Destination unreachable	0	Destination network unreachable
	1	Destination host unreachable
	2	Destination protocol unreachable
	3	Destination port unreachable
	4	Fragmentation required (DF flag set)
	5	Source route failed
	6	Destination network unknown
	7	Destination host unknown
	8	Source host isolated
	9	Network administratively prohibited
	10	Host administratively prohibited
	11	Network unreachable for TOS
	12	Host unreachable for TOS
	13	Communication administratively prohibited
4—Source quench	0	Congestion control-source quench
5—Redirect message	0	Redirect datagram for the network
	1	Redirect datagram for the host
	2	Redirect datagram for the TOS and network
	3	Redirect datagram for the TOS and host
6		Alternate host address
7		Reserved
8—Echo request	0	Echo request (used by ping)
9—Router advertisement	0	Router advertisement
10—Router solicitation	0	Router discovery
11—Time exceeded	0	Time to live (TTL) expired during transit
	1	Time exceeded to reassemble fragments
12—Parameter problem: bad IP header	0	Pointer indicates the type of error
	1	Required option missing
	2	Bad length

TABLE 14-3 Common ICMP message types and codes, *continued.*

ICMP TYPE	CODE	DESCRIPTION
13—Timestamp	0	Timestamp
14—Timestamp reply	0	Timestamp reply
15—Information request	0	Information request
16—Information reply	0	Information reply
17—Address mask request	0	Address mask request
18—Address mask reply	0	Address mask reply
19–29		Reserved
30—Traceroute	0	Information request
31		Datagram conversion error
32		Mobile host redirect
33		Where-Are-You (introduced for IPv6)
34		Here-I-Am (introduced for IPv6)
35		Mobile registration request
36		Mobile registration reply
37		Domain name request
38		Domain name reply
39		Simple key-management for IP (SKIP) discovery
40		Session key management failure
41		ICMP for experimental products
42–255		Reserved

technical TIP

The ping and traceroute tools used to be common in nearly every network administrator's list of favorite tools. Attackers recognized how much the tool was used and devised several attacks that use the ICMP protocol. Since administrators wanted to benefit from the information that the ping and traceroute tools could provide, they often allowed ICMP messages to travel their networks freely. Attackers found methods to construct invalid ICMP messages that would flood network devices and render parts of a network unusable. To protect from such attacks, many network devices now block ICMP traffic. Administrators had to develop other ways to measure their networks' performance. That is why there are so many alternatives to the ping and traceroute tools.

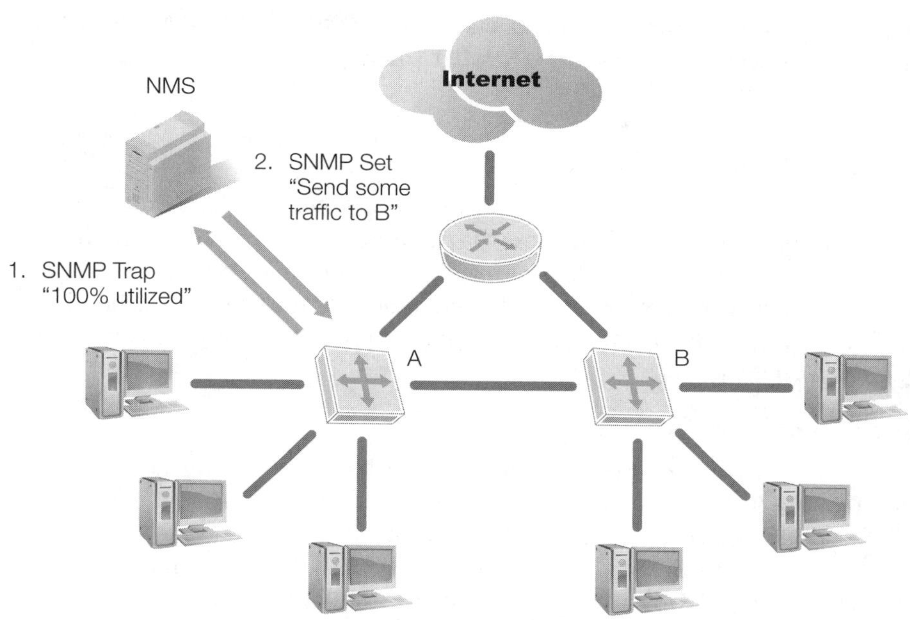

FIGURE 14-6
SNMP messages can help identify and address performance problems.

Simple Network Management Protocol

You learned about SNMP in Chapter 12. Recall that SNMP is a standard protocol designed to help manage devices on an IP network. It is not a protocol dedicated to performance characteristics, but it is a fundamental protocol in collecting performance-related information from devices. SNMP provides a central NMS with the information to assess individual device and overall network performance. Polling devices through SNMP allow the NMS to collect ongoing performance data and identify potential problems.

One of the basic metrics for any device is its usage characteristics. The NMS can poll devices periodically for the latest byte counts of traffic each device handles. Periodic polls allow the NMS to create a picture of how busy devices are over time. They can detect periods of high usage and trigger alarms when usage exceeds predefined thresholds. Since the NMS polls multiple devices, it can use the network map to isolate links that may be experiencing heavy loads. Other important performance metrics SNMP queries can reveal are the number of dropped packets, buffer usage, and device memory usage. Each of these metrics paints a partial picture. But put together, the SNMP-supplied data can help the NMS identify problems and even suggest solutions in some cases. An intelligent NMS that identifies a heavily loaded link can identify an alternate path for some traffic. The NMS could then send configuration updates to devices to use the alternate link and relieve the traffic bottleneck. Figure 14-6 shows how SNMP can help detect and address performance problems.

Net-SNMP is just one example of an application suite based on SNMP. Net-SNMP provides a simple collection of tools to use SNMP to manage a network. For more information on Net-SNMP, see Table 14-2.

Performance Modification Protocols

The protocols in this section differ from the previous protocols. These are protocols primarily used to transport user data across the network. These protocols contain characteristics or actions that can affect performance. Some characteristics just allow the protocols to operate more efficiently, and some alter the way devices handle the traffic. Either way, the following protocols can alter their behavior to modify a network's performance.

Transmission Control Protocol

TCP is an OSI Layer 4 protocol used to provide reliable data delivery from one node to another. The TCP header contains an options section that can contain many various TCP options. Figure 14-7 shows a TCP header.

The options section of a TCP header has a variable length. The size can vary from 0 to 320 bits in increments of 32 bits. Each option contains 1 to 3 fields.

- **Field 1: Option-Kind (8 bits)**—Defines the type of option
- **Field 2: Option-Length (8 bits)**—Length of the option data (optional, depending on option kind)
- **Field 3: Option data (variable length)**—Value of the option

Table 14-4 lists the kinds of options supported in the TCP header.

FIGURE 14-7

TCP header.

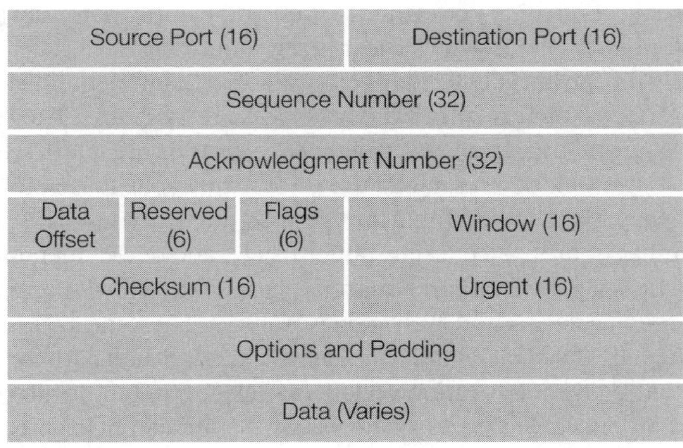

TABLE 14-4 TCP header option kinds.

OPTION KIND	OPTION LENGTH (BYTES)	DESCRIPTION
0	N/A	End of option list
1	N/A	No-operation (NOP)
2	4	Maximum segment size
3	3	WSOPT—Windows scale
4	2	SACK permitted
5	Variable	SACK
8	10	TSOPT—Timestamp option
18	3	Trailer checksum option
20	N/A	SCPS capabilities
21		Selective negative acknowledgments
22		Record boundaries
23		Corruption experienced
24		SNAP
26		TCP compression filter
27	8	Quick-start response
28	4	User time-out option
29		TCP authentication option (TCP-AO)

Several of these options can directly affect performance. These options include:

- **Maximum segment size (2)**—Maximum size of each TCP segment. This option should be set to the network maximum transmission unit (MTU) during connection negotiation. This setting allows TCP to send the largest amount of data in each segment without fragmenting.
- **Windows scale (3)**—Allows TCP to use a Windows size of up to 2^{30}, as opposed to the default maximum of 2^{16}. The Windows size allows senders to send more data without receiving acknowledgments. Increasing the Windows scale option helps TCP work more efficiently in high-bandwidth, high-delay networks.
- **SACK permitted (4), SACK (5)**—The Selective ACKnowledgments (SACK) option allows the receiver to acknowledge segments received out of order. The default behavior (with SACK) is to only acknowledge the highest segment received. This behavior can lead to a high number of packet transmissions, which increase overall congestion.

Quality of Service

You learned about QoS in Chapter 10. Although quality of user experience (QoE) is a newer metric used to measure performance, QoS is still in use to affect performance. In short, QoS provides a plan of action when a network's performance falls below desired thresholds. Many types of streaming media require specified levels of service to avoid poorly performing applications. Network devices attempt to achieve the stated level of service by delaying or even dropping traffic that gets in the way of higher priority traffic.

There are several protocols that provide QoS. Each one allows set performance standards to dictate which traffic should supersede other traffic. These protocols include:

- Type of Service (ToS) in IPv4 headers
- IP differentiated services (DiffServ)
- IP integrated services (IntServ)
- Resource Reservation Protocol (RSVP) & RSVP-TE
- Multiprotocol label switching (MPLS)
- IEEE 802.1p, 802.1q, 802.11e

Responding to Issues

Monitoring networks for performance problems can reveal many types of issues before they become critical. Of course, some issues occur so quickly that they may become critical before there is a chance to respond. The next step in the performance management process is to respond to identified issues. Responding to a performance issue means to take action to address the cause of the problems and restore the network to normal operation.

The actions you should take depend on the nature of the performance problem. In some cases, adding additional devices or capacity to existing devices may sufficiently increase the network's capacity. If the network is able to dynamically use the new devices or capacity, you may not need to take further action. Other situations may require configuration changes as well. Performance problems that include WAN connections may benefit from using a different routing design. The goals in addressing any performance problems include some, or all, of the following:

- Remove the problem
- Add more capacity to alleviate the problem
- Route traffic around the problem
- Change the network's architecture

Responding to performance problems is more than just keeping users happy. As more business functions rely on network communications, productivity is linked more closely to network performance. When performance suffers, productivity suffers. Network performance problems translate directly to quantifiable business losses. Keeping networks running smoothly and efficiently is a key business objective.

Once individual tools or NMS software identifies a performance issue, a graduated series of actions should be pursued to resolve the problem. Performance resolution steps should explore ways to implement the items in the list above. Although each organization will have different approaches, here are some general steps to resolve performance problems:

1. Explore configuration changes to address the problem. Configuration changes can often be implemented with little or no downtime. Configuration changes could include protocol characteristics, device settings, or routing tables. Solving problems with configuration changes has the least impact on the network.
2. Determine if the performance problem is due to failed or failing hardware. If this is the case, replace the faulty hardware.
3. Examine the traffic to identify unauthorized or excessive traffic. When possible, modify policies and security controls to reduce unauthorized or unexpected traffic.
4. Explore how adding additional devices, device capacity, or additional media bandwidth could resolve the performance problem.
5. Analyze your existing network and its performance problems to see if any architectural changes would allow the network to perform more efficiently. Architectural changes could include flattening the network to rely more on Layer 2 switches instead of Layer 3 routers.

Regardless of the type of response you choose, document each step involved. Performance resolution documentation should include all options considered and the rationale behind each decision. Formally monitoring a network's performance and responding to each issue can keep a network running smoothly. An efficient network supports worker productivity and contributes to an organization's success.

CHAPTER SUMMARY

Organizations rely on networks to support critical and noncritical operations. Any decrease in response time directly translates into a decrease in worker productivity. Good network performance is mandatory for organizations to operate efficiently. Slow networks cost money and can cause organizations to fall behind competitors. There are many tools and strategies to help ensure that network performance problems either do not happen or do not last very long. Proactively monitoring a network and responding to issues is much more than just an IT concern. It is a concern for the entire organization.

Effective NMSs can empower an organization's IT department to aggressively manage the network and ensure it is performing efficiently. These actions directly relate to any organization's viability and success in the marketplace.

KEY CONCEPTS AND TERMS

Bandwidth
Baseline
Discard
Internet Control Message Protocol (ICMP)
Metric
Network readiness assessment (NRA)
Retransmission
Round trip time (RTT)
Throughput

CHAPTER 14 ASSESSMENT

1. The first step in measuring performance is to sample current latency.
   A. True
   B. False

2. Which term describes the amount of time it takes for a packet to travel from one node to another?
   A. Latency
   B. Bandwidth
   C. Throughput
   D. Jitter

3. A ________ is a collection of performance measurements against a system at a particular point in time.

4. What is the average latency of satellite links?
   A. 10 milliseconds
   B. 100 milliseconds
   C. 500 milliseconds
   D. 1,000 milliseconds

5. Why might a network device discard a packet? (Select two.)
   A. Security policy
   B. Link failure
   C. QoS policy
   D. Time-out

6. What action does a network device take when its buffers are full?
   A. Returns packets to their source
   B. Stops accepting packets
   C. Reduces time-to-live (TTL) value
   D. Drops packets in buffers

7. Which protocol does ping and traceroute use to measure performance?
   A. SNMP
   B. RTP
   C. TCP
   D. ICMP

8. Which protocol is used to set device characteristics?
   A. SNMP
   B. RTP
   C. TCP
   D. ICMP

9. Which TCP option should be set to the network MTU?
   A. Windows scale
   B. Maximum segment size
   C. SACK permitted
   D. Quick-start request

10. What describes a plan of action when a network's performance falls below desired thresholds?
   A. QoE
   B. RTP
   C. QoS
   D. RTCP

CHAPTER

15 Security Management

SECURITY IS A MAJOR CONCERN for every organization. The news is full of stories about attackers who disrupt security measures and wreak havoc. Today's linked networks provide new ways to launch attacks. They are most often against an organization's most valuable asset—its information. In recent years, computer attackers have stolen credit card data, for example, and even damaged control systems in factories. Links to the outside world made these attacks possible.

In this chapter you will learn about how vulnerable networked information systems are, and how to protect them from attack. You will learn what makes networks attractive to attackers. You will also learn what organizations can do to reduce the probability of being attacked. No network is completely secure. But strategies exist that can help your organization address the many threats to its network. You will learn how to put proven strategies into play that will increase your network's overall security and protect your organization's assets.

Chapter 15 Topics

This chapter covers the following topics and concepts:

- What security concerns apply to networks
- What the motivations for securing networks are
- Which approaches make networks more secure
- How to use multilayered defense
- What network security controls are
- How to manage network security controls

Chapter 15 Goals

When you complete this chapter, you will be able to:

- Describe network security concerns
- Discuss the motivations for securing networks
- List approaches that make networks more secure
- Describe multilayered defense
- Explain network security controls
- Describe how to manage network security controls

Security Concerns

As information systems become more powerful and networks connect more resources, the opportunities for attackers increase. A whole new industry has developed over the past 20 years to address concerns of information security. This new industry helps organizations of all sizes keep their data secure. One main goal is to do this without making data inaccessible. But what does it mean for information to be secure? And how is secure data related to networks?

The CIA Triad

Secure information exhibits three main properties. These properties are also called the basic tenets of security, or the **security triad**. Securing data involves providing assurance that each of the three properties is satisfied. The three properties of secure information are confidentiality, integrity, and **availability**:

- **Confidentiality**—Only authorized users can access sensitive information.
- **Integrity**—Only authorized users can modify sensitive information.
- **Availability**—Information is available to authorized users when they want it.

These three properties are basic to an understanding of information security. Each one is related to, and affects, the other two properties. To show that they are all related, the three are often shown as a triangle called the CIA triad. (It's also known as the A-I-C triad, which sounds less cloak-and-daggerish.) The acronym CIA represents the three properties of confidentiality, integrity, and availability. Figure 15-1 shows the CIA triad.

FIGURE 15-1
The CIA triad.

Greater reliance on information makes that data valuable to organizations. Attackers also put a high value on the same information. There are two main reasons why it is so attractive to attackers. First, organizations depend on it to conduct business. Think of what would happen to your organization if all of your data were unavailable. Most users do not consider how much they rely on information systems. Here are just a few places information influences daily activity:

- E-mail messages provide a primary means of communication. Many people use e-mail to record conversations. They use it to store notes and background information for tasks, meetings, and other activities.
- Calendars organize personal and professional activities.
- Online contact databases store contact methods and numbers or addresses.
- Personal workstations and shared storage servers store documents, spreadsheets, presentations, local databases, and project plans. There are many other stored files as well that are necessary for daily tasks.
- Databases contain customer and partner information. They also have detailed information needed for normal operation.
- VoIP systems contain information used to conduct regular telephone calls and advanced teleconferences.

The list above only presents general types of information. Each organization uses specific types of information to conduct their operations. Loss of this data could be catastrophic. The realization that information is that important makes it valuable. Clearly, organizations must act to protect their data. And attackers know that controlling an organization's information gives them power and influence over it. One common motive is to harm an organization or disrupt regular operation. One method is to make information inaccessible. Consider large online retailers, such as Amazon.com. Making Amazon.com's Web site unavailable would cause large financial losses for the company. Some attackers who want to harm organizations use information attacks to do so. This type of attack compromises information availability.

Another method for attackers is the use of information against an organization or a person to disclose private data. Although attackers use different methods, the motive is still to harm the organization. This type of attack can embarrass an organization or a person and hurt their public image. Such an attack also can cause prospective customers, partners, and investors to question the organization's stability. Individuals generally suffer embarrassment and damage to their good name. An example of this type of attack occurred during the 2008 United States presidential race. Someone hacked into vice-presidential candidate Sarah Palin's e-mail account and disclosed personal e-mails. This type of attack compromises the information's confidentiality.

The second motive for an attack is greed. This type of attacker does not just want to hurt an organization. It also wants to profit from it. Consider the widely publicized TJX Companies' loss of private information. The company owns T.J. Maxx, Marshalls, and several other clothing retailers. The attacker was able to steal millions of credit and debit card numbers. Consumer confidence in the company plummeted. TJX ended up spending over $200 million in breach-related fines and expenses. The attack damaged TJX's reputation, but the attacker's real motive was to profit from the sale of the data. This type of attack also focused on the information's confidentiality, even though the attacker's motive differed from the previous attacks.

Network Security

Up to this point, you have seen how important it is to secure information. But how does this relate to networks? Networks just make it easier to attack an organization's infrastructure and information. The collection of all opportunities for attackers to compromise a system is called the system's **attack surface**. In other words, the attack surface is a collection of all of the vulnerable points of a system. A network connects resources. This makes it easier for an attacker to access many more resources than would be possible with a closed system. Networks increase the attack surface of all connected resources. In many cases, this increase is substantial.

This means that many more vulnerable components of a typical IT infrastructure are accessible. Attackers can use vulnerabilities in network components to reach other sensitive resources on the network. For example, an attacker that can compromise a Web server or an application server could use that server to reach a database server that stores confidential data. In this situation, the network provided the connections to allow the attack.

Types of Attacks

Today's organizations routinely spend substantial resources trying to prevent attacks on their networks and data. Regardless of how well a network is protected, attackers sometimes get through. Any event that results in a violation of any of the CIA security properties is called a **security breach**. Some security breaches interrupt business functions on purpose. Others are accidental. They may result from hardware or software failures. Regardless of whether a security breach is accidental or intentional, it can affect an organization's ability to conduct business.

There are three main categories of attacks that primarily involve networks. These types are reconnaissance, eavesdropping, and denial of service. Each type has a different impact on the confidentiality, integrity, and availability of the data a network carries. You will learn about each of them in the following sections.

Reconnaissance

The purpose of network reconnaissance is for attackers to gather information about a network to use in a future attack. Such activities are not always direct attacks. Because their purpose is to provide intelligence for impending attacks, they are treated as attacks. An attacker conducting reconnaissance on a network likely will gather information that includes:

- IP addresses used on the network
- Types of firewalls and other security systems and devices
- Remote access techniques in use
- Operating system(s) of computers on the network
- Identification of network devices
- Services in use and open ports
- Weaknesses in network software

Much of this information makes it easier to plan an attack. Suppose reconnaissance reveals that there is a vulnerable version of Microsoft Internet Information Services Web server running in your network. An attacker will likely use that information to select an attack that is often successful against similar software.

Eavesdropping

Network eavesdropping is what happens when an attacker accesses the network between a sender and receiver. An external attacker generally must either compromise access controls or eavesdrop on remote users connecting from the Internet. Local attackers that can connect to your LAN have an easier time eavesdropping. These attacks violate the privacy end of security.

Eavesdropping is easy on an unprotected network. All an attacker needs is access to the network and unencrypted packets. The easiest countermeasure is to encrypt any sensitive communications. Most communication software provides the ability to use encryption. Securing network access is a little more challenging. It requires limiting physical access to network media and carefully controlling access to wireless connections. You will learn more about countermeasures later in this chapter.

Denial of Service

The last major type of network attack is a denial of service (DoS) attack. These attackers are not interested in accessing data. They just want to create a situation in which no authorized users can access data or network services. This type of attack can be a very effective method to disrupt business operations. There are two main strategies to conducting a DoS attack. The attacker can flood the network (or key devices) with traffic or attempt to shut down a single point of failure.

The simplest method is to flood the network with more traffic than it can handle. There are several known DoS attacks that use specially crafted packets to confuse network devices. These attacks can slow network devices down to a point that they cannot handle normal traffic. This has the effect of dramatically slowing down or even stopping network traffic.

Classic DoS attack packets come from a single source. These types of attacks are fairly easy to stop. All a security device must do is block all traffic from the identified attacker. One variation of the DoS is a distributed denial of service (DDoS) attack. A DDoS attack uses many compromised computers or devices to launch the attack. They are far more difficult to stop because the attack source keeps changing from one address to another.

Threats and Vulnerabilities

One of the first steps to securing a network is to understand the threats to the network. A **threat** is any action that could damage an asset. A **vulnerability** is any weakness in a system that makes it possible for a threat to cause harm. Threats often exploit one or more known vulnerabilities.

If a vulnerability exists in a network, so does the possibility of a threat. Any threat against a vulnerability creates a risk that a negative event may occur. There is no way to eliminate threats. But you can protect a network against vulnerabilities. That way, even though a threat still exists, the threat cannot exploit the vulnerability. The key to protecting assets from the risk of attack is to eliminate or address as many vulnerabilities as possible.

A threat is significant from a security viewpoint. The goal of network security is to provide insights, methodologies, and ways to deal with threats. You can achieve this with policies that help network system administrators, designers, developers, and users avoid undesirable network quirks and weaknesses.

You can identify threats and rank them according to their importance and impact. You can rank threats by dollar loss, negative reputation created, monetary liability, or how often they are likely to occur. Each organization may rank a threat higher or lower than another organization, based on its importance to them. A threat's rank depends on its potential impact.

The most common threats, in no particular order, include the following:

- Malicious software
- Hardware or software failure
- Internal attackers
- Equipment theft
- External attackers
- Natural disaster
- Industrial espionage
- Terrorism

Not all threats are malicious. Although some threats may be intentional, others may be accidental. Accidental threats might include hardware failure or a software problem caused by a lack of controls. The results of accidental threats can be just as damaging as malicious threats, however. You must make every effort to minimize all security breaches, whether they are malicious or accidental. The overall goal is to protect the network from any attack, and to prevent the theft, destruction, and corruption of individual or organizational assets. Meeting this goal protects an organization's information confidentiality, integrity, and availability.

Motivations for Securing Networks

Successful network attacks impact an organization's ability to conduct normal business operations. Either directly or indirectly, attacks cost money. Organizations that survive for long periods of time must manage the costs of conducting business. They want to know how expensive attacks could be, and how much it costs to prevent them. No organization can protect itself from every attack. Some attacks are more likely or more dangerous than others. So which ones should organizations focus on first? It turns out that there is no simple answer.

Business Impact Analysis

The first step in determining how to protect an organization from security attacks is to know what is really important to the organization. A common method to uncover important processes is to conduct a **business impact analysis (BIA)**. A BIA is a process that results in a list of activities necessary for an organization to conduct business operations. The analysis defines the impact to the organization if any critical activity stops. The BIA provides critical input for several functions, including business continuity planning (BCP), disaster recovery planning (DRP), and security planning.

Risk Assessment

The BIA provides a starting point for determining what to protect. Each process or activity in the BIA is necessary for the organization to operate. Any threat that can exploit a vulnerability within a critical business function poses a danger to the organization. **Risk** is the likelihood that an attack will successfully exploit a vulnerability. An important planning activity is to consider the most important risks and take measures to manage them. Some attacks are more likely than others. For example, it is possible that your data center will catch fire and destroy all of the computers and devices it contains. If you assume this event will happen once every 10 years, there is a 10 percent chance this risk will be realized each year. If you estimate the loss would be $1.4 million, the annual expected loss to a data center fire risk would be 10 percent × $1.4 million = $140,000.

The process of identifying and addressing all risks is called **risk management**. There is no way to address all risks. Every organization has limited budgets. No one can foresee all risks. However, organizations can attempt to identify as many risks as possible and analyze each risk. One method to do this is called **quantitative risk analysis**. This analysis associates a dollar value, or cost, with each risk. The example of the data center fire risk used quantitative risk analysis. This approach requires more information and analysis work, but produces cost values that make it easy to compare with other risks.

The other main method of analyzing risks is called **qualitative risk analysis**. This analysis ranks risks relative to one another. Each risk receives a qualitative rating, such as "critical," "moderate," and "low." Each rating takes the probability and impact into account. Risks that are likely to occur and would cause substantial impact would be given a "critical" rating. Organizations normally attempt to address the most critical risks first.

The main purpose of any type of risk analysis is to help organizations determine which risks they should address first. Since budgets are limited, it is important to invest money where it will make the most impact. It makes sense to spend money to protect from the most serious risks first.

Risk Management

Risk management defines the procedures needed to identify, assess, and remediate risks. Since risks carry costs, risk management is part of cost management. Managing risks well leads directly to lower costs and higher profits. That reason alone is sufficient motivation. Security is not an added focus. It must be a core focus of every organization. Regardless of the sophistication of any security plan, no organization is safe from all attacks. Risk management's focus is not to avoid all risks. It addresses each risk using at least one of the following methods:

- **Mitigate**—Employ countermeasures to reduce the risk to an acceptable level. Countermeasures may be policies, hardware or software, or physical devices. For example, a locked door is a physical device that prevents unauthorized access to the server room.
- **Assign or transfer**—Transfer the risk to another person or entity. The most common way to assign or transfer risk is to purchase insurance. Fire insurance transfers the risk of loss due to a fire to the insurance company. The organization pays a premium for the protection. If a fire results in a loss, the insurance company covers the loss.
- **Accept**—Decide to accept the consequences of the risk. Some risks may be realized but only result in a modest loss. In such cases, the cost to mitigate or assign the risk may be higher than the expected loss. Acceptance is the best choice when it results in the lowest cost.
- **Avoid**—Avoiding a risk generally means choosing not to engage in an activity that makes the risk possible. For example, an organization may choose not to offer a new product line because of the risk it would pose. They can avoid the risk by not selling the products.

The best risk management technique depends on the risk and the costs associated with each option. In spite of the best risk management strategy, some threats will be realized. Every realized threat has some impact on the target organization. Some result in direct costs. Some result in indirect costs. Quantitative risk analysis attempts to associate a cost value with each risk. Regardless of the risk analysis method used, all risks carry costs. The cost incurred from realized threats can include the following:

- **Direct costs**—Any costs directly associated with recovering lost or damaged assets. Examples can include replacing damaged hardware, labor costs for entering lost data, or fees to pay external firms for cleanup activities.
- **Loss of business**—Security breaches can cause customers to cancel orders or drop stated plans to purchase products or services in the near future. Customers may doubt the organization's ability to withstand further attacks and continue normal business operations.

- **Loss of prospective business**—Security breaches often cause prospective customers to choose to conduct business with competitors. This cost is difficult to determine. It represents a loss of expected potential business, and expectation of lower profits.
- **Loss of reputation**—This loss is closely related to the previous two loss categories. Organizations that suffer security breaches often experience a loss of short-term sales and perhaps even long-term confidence. A loss of reputation or confidence lowers sales, increases customer complaints, and causes an increased load on all customer service activities. A poorly handled security breach can have long-lasting effects in the press and the public's perception of the organization. Such negative perceptions can decrease sales for long periods of time.
- **Fines and penalties**—One of the fastest rising categories of security breach costs is fines and penalties. Legislation, regulation, and commercial requirements have stated security standards and fines or penalties for violations. The Payment Card Industry Data Security Standard (PCI DSS) imposes fines for violations involving payment card information. The Health Insurance Portability and Accountability Act (HIPAA) sets fines for violations involving patient health care information. These are just two of the many ways an organization can incur fines or penalties for security breaches.

Regulations and Legislation

An increase in the use of networked resources over the last 20 years has created many new chances for attack. Information-related crime has grown. So have legislation and regulation to protect organizations and people from criminal acts.

Today's organizations are subject to laws that protect the privacy of electronic data. Each organization must comply with laws and regulations. The specific requirements depend on where the organization is located and the type of information it handles.

The following list summarizes some of the most important laws and regulations that affect how organizations conduct IT operations:

- **Sarbanes-Oxley Act (SOX)**—Sarbanes-Oxley became law in July of 2002. It introduced sweeping changes on the regulation of corporate governance and financial practices. SOX established the Public Company Accounting Oversight Board (PCAOB). This board is responsible for overseeing, regulating, inspecting, and disciplining accounting firms in their roles as auditors of public companies. SOX also dictates policies that address auditor independence, corporate governance, internal control assessment, and enhanced financial disclosure.
- **Health Insurance Portability and Accountability Act (HIPAA)**—HIPAA took effect on April 14, 2006. It governs how doctors, hospitals, and other health care providers handle personal medical data. HIPAA requires that all medical records, billing, and patient information be handled in ways that maintain the patient's privacy. HIPAA also guarantees that all patients be able to correct errors or omissions, and be informed about how personal information is shared and used. HIPAA requires that every patient receive notification of privacy procedures any time they submit medical information.

- **Federal Information Security Management Act (FISMA)**—FISMA officially recognizes the importance of information security to the national security and economic health of the US. FISMA requires every federal agency to develop and maintain formal information-security programs. These include security-awareness efforts, secure access to computer resources, strict acceptable-use policies, and formal incident response and contingency planning.
- **Gramm-Leach-Bliley Act (GLBA)**—GLBA addresses information-security concerns in the financial industry. It requires that financial institutions provide their clients with a privacy notice that explains what data the company gathers about the client. The notice must also inform clients where it is shared, and how the company protects it. Companies must provide clients with this privacy notice prior to entering into a business agreement.
- **Payment Card Industry Data Security Standard (PCI DSS)**—Although not a law, PCI DSS affects any organization that processes or stores credit card information. The founding payment brands of the PCI Security Standards Council include American Express, Discover Financial Services, Japan Credit Bureau (JCB), MasterCard Worldwide, and Visa International. These members developed PCI DSS to foster consistent global data-security measures. It is a comprehensive security standard that includes requirements for security management, policies, procedures, network architecture, software design, and other critical protective measures.
- **The Family Educational Rights and Privacy Act (FERPA)**—This federal law protects the privacy of student education records. It applies to all schools that receive funds under an applicable program of the US Department of Education. Under FERPA, schools must receive written permission from a parent or eligible student before releasing any information contained in a student's education record.

It's the duty of each organization to understand which laws and regulations apply to them and to employ necessary countermeasures to comply. Fiscal responsibility is the single most compelling reason to address security. In simple terms, failure to secure an organization's network exposes it to multiple costs. Suffering a severe security breach can impact an organization so much that it may not recover. Security is a preservation activity. It is a necessity in today's business world.

Approaches to Securing Networks

Risk management means deciding how to handle each type of risk. Assigning, accepting, and avoiding risks generally require nontechnical solutions. The remaining risks are the ones that will be mitigated. Mitigating risks requires some countermeasure to reduce the risks. Taking countermeasures to mitigate network risks is often referred to as securing or hardening the network. The two main approaches to securing any network are:

- Removing network connectivity to sensitive resources.
- Adding countermeasures to protect the network and any sensitive resources.

The easiest option is to simply unplug sensitive resources from the network. Of course, this makes the resource unavailable. Remember that availability is a property of secure information. That means in almost all cases, the only viable option is to add appropriate countermeasures to protect sensitive resources. At the network level, the countermeasures of greater interest are those that protect the organization from the network attacks discussed earlier.

There are many different approaches to securing a network. Just as there is no completely secure network, there is no single "most correct" way to secure a network. The best choice for any network is the collection of countermeasures that satisfy cost and protection goals. They must protect what they are supposed to protect and should not cost more than the expected loss of a realized threat.

The main idea in securing a network is to protect it from various types of attacks. The attacks of greatest concern should come from the risk analysis process. Once you know the attacks that most threaten your organization, where do you start placing countermeasures? Which ones will be the most effective? Approaches to securing any network generally focus on countermeasure number, type, and placement. Most approaches fall into one or more of the following categories:

- **A centralized device to protect the entire network**—All network traffic flows through a single security device. It examines every packet for malicious intent.
- **A dedicated countermeasure for each device or resource**—Each device or resource connected to the network has an embedded security device. Or it has a security device between the resource and the network.
- **A countermeasure for each type of threat**—This approach is a compromise between the previous two approaches. Several security devices are attached to the network that filter traffic associated with one particular type of attack. For instance, one device may protect from DoS and DDoS attacks. Another protects from unauthorized reconnaissance.
- **Strict least privilege policy**—The principle of **least privilege** means allowing users only the minimum access privileges they need to complete their assigned tasks. Under this policy, users cannot carry out any task except those needed for their direct responsibilities.
- **Multilayered defense**—Multiple countermeasures that an attacker must compromise to reach any protected resource. This approach is often described as a series of concentric rings around protected resources. It is often called **defense in depth**.

Each of these approaches has both advantages and disadvantages. Most of the approaches are deceptive. They look good at first. But they have serious potential drawbacks when examined in detail. Table 15-1 lists the most important advantages and disadvantages of each approach.

The most secure approach by far is a multilayered approach. You will learn more about this approach in the next section.

TABLE 15-1 Approaches to securing a network.

APPROACH	ADVANTAGES	DISADVANTAGES
Single centralized device	• Single device • Central management • Easy to add to the network	• Single point of failure • Compromising the single device means compromising the entire network • Likely negative impact on performance—all traffic must flow through single device
Separate security device for each resource	• Device has to protect only one resource • Each device can be customized • Traffic pattern does not have to change	• Difficult to install and manage—many new devices • Must use strict configuration management • Compromising the single device means the resource is compromised
Separate security device for each attack type	• Each security device can focus on one type of attack • Fewer security devices than one for each resource	• Traffic must flow through each device • Many new added hops for each network message • Must change network topology to include new devices in all links
Least privilege policy	• Minimal network topology change • Puts burden of security on authentication/authorization • Limits impact of malicious user	• Difficult to manage—lots of users and specific permissions • Users' needs often demand privilege changes • Attackers that compromise authentication/authorization can own the network
Multilayered defense	• Time tested • Protects resources even when one or more countermeasures are compromised • Good balance between isolation and performance • Superior overall protection	• Requires careful planning • More administration than simpler approaches

technical TIP

Always remember: There is no completely secure network. A determined attacker with sufficient resources will eventually succeed. Your goal is to place enough obstacles in the attacker's way that he gives up or runs out of resources to continue.

Multilayered Defense

Protecting important resources with a single countermeasure is not a good idea. For thousands of years, armies and security forces have explored ways to protect high-value targets. Protecting network resources is just a twenty-first century version of protecting anything of value. The lessons learned throughout the years still apply to networks.

Hundreds of years ago, important people and items needed protection from more than just one person. Kings and treasures normally stayed in a fortified castle for protection. The castle was built with a secure central group of buildings surrounded by a wall. There might have been several additional groups of buildings with additional walls enclosing the central buildings. Traveling away from the secure center would eventually take you to the outer city wall. This wall would be a tall fortified wall with a large gate that could be closed to seal the city. There might have been a moat or other obstacle outside the city wall and an army camped nearby to defend the city.

The point is that the king did not depend on just one bodyguard or a group of soldiers for defense. He felt secure behind layers of defense. An attacker would have to fight his way through many soldiers and break through many physical barriers to reach the king. This approach to security is called multilayered defense or defense in depth.

Changing Attacks

Attackers are becoming more and more sophisticated. The earliest network attacks were generally simple and carried out by amateurs. Most of the original attackers launched attacks out of curiosity. The following waves of attacks have each become more serious and sophisticated. Attackers today generally belong to one of these categories:

- **Amateur**—Mostly students who are curious
- **Hackers**—More sophisticated amateurs interested in notoriety
- **Professional hackers**—Individuals and organized criminals interested in monetary gain
- **Spies and cyberterrorists**—Agents acting on behalf of national interests or nonstate actors such as terrorist groups

The increase in sophistication and impact of attacks means that network defenses must be refined enough to defend from the best attackers. A multilayered defense is more flexible than a fixed approach. It can react to changing situations and provide continuous protection. The main idea behind defense in depth is that all of the parts work together to be stronger than the whole. An individual countermeasure may fail but should not compromise the overall network's security.

Blended Response

Increasingly sophisticated attackers mean traditional targeted defense will not always protect the network. The best defense uses the model of multiple layers of defense. It also uses different resources. Attackers use a combination of attack methods. It then makes sense for defenders to do the same. A good defense-in-depth approach to security does not rely on technology alone. A great firewall cannot secure an entire network alone. A broad defense plan must include personnel and strong policies. Combining these three components provides the base for a strong blended response.

One way to look at multilayered defense is to consider multiple layers of countermeasures that protect each resource. A common way to describe the concept is a set of concentric rings around a protected resource. Figure 15-2 shows how an attacker must compromise multiple layers of countermeasures to reach a protected resource.

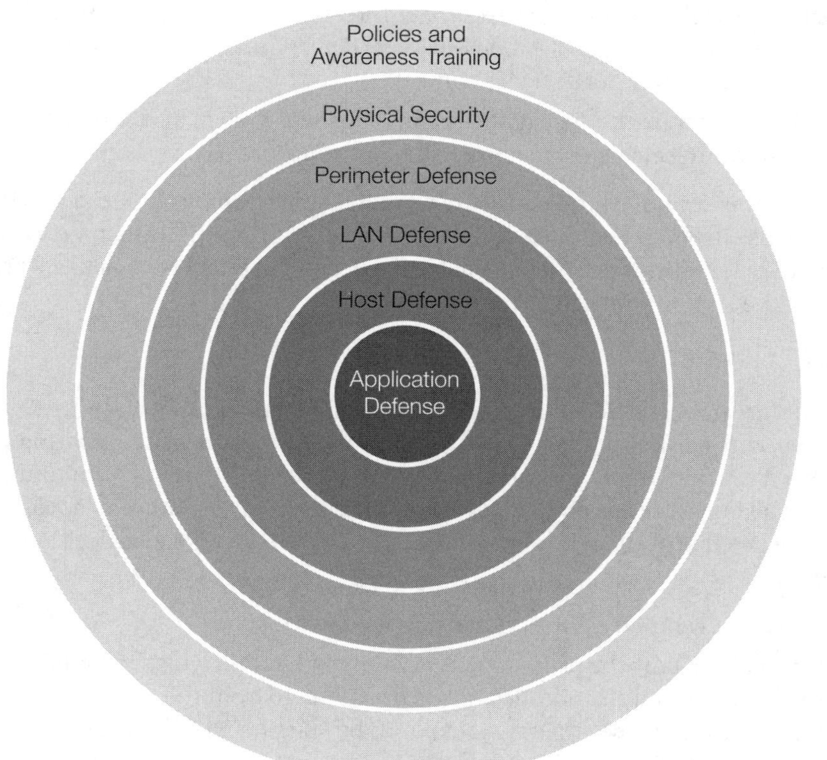

FIGURE 15-2 Multilayered defense.

For example, suppose you want to protect a database server that is connected to your network. The layers that protect the database server are:

- **Security policies and procedures**—Administrative countermeasures that define what actions are allowed, disallowed, and mandatory. Policies and procedures that tell users what to do and what not to do.
- **User awareness and training**—Ensuring all network users understand the security policies and procedures, and comply with them.
- **Physical security**—Physical barriers, such as locked doors to the server room. This keeps unauthorized users from accessing the physical devices.
- **Perimeter defense**—Devices and software that sits between the internal LANs and the external WAN (often the Internet). A common perimeter defense method includes firewalls, intrusion detection/prevention systems, and separated subnetworks.
- **LAN defense**—Countermeasures that protect the internal LANs from network attacks. Internal intrusion detection/prevention systems and firewalls are common LAN security devices.
- **Host defenses**—Countermeasures that protect the host (server) from malicious attacks. These include host-based intrusion detection/preventions systems, access controls, and port/service control.
- **Application defenses**—The database management system also should include internal countermeasures to ensure that only authorized users can access data.

This list contains several countermeasures, but it is still incomplete. The idea is that a broad defense in depth approach requires an attacker to get through many countermeasures to reach the target. All but the most determined attackers will likely give up long before they reach your sensitive resources.

Firewalls

All firewalls are not created equal. In fact, there can be such a wide disparity of functions and features between two firewalls that it would be like comparing a beat-up old car that barely runs to a new Ferrari. The first step in determining which firewall fits the needs of your organization is to create a requirements list. An example of some of the requirements needed to make an informed decision could be:

- **Budget**—How much is the organization willing to spend?
  - Budget is usually the primary factor. A lot of bells and whistles sound really nice. But if the organization is unwilling to front the cost of the purchase, then it becomes a moot point. By starting with a budget, we can immediately refine our focus.

- **Quantity**—How many firewalls are going to be purchased?
    - Many firewalls come with features built into them. They can work as an active/standby or even active/active pair. This allows for redundancy in the event that one firewall fails, and an active/active pair can help split the load.
- **Placement**—Where is the firewall going to logically reside?
    - Is it going to act as a perimeter firewall or application firewall? Maybe it needs to sit in front of some critical systems. Determining where the firewall logically fits into the network will help in finding the correct features.
- **Data**—What data are you trying to protect?
    - Not all data, and not all servers, are the same. For example, a Web server that many external users access would most likely sit in a separate protected network segment. These require firewalls that can handle a very high number of simultaneous sessions. They must be able to thwart DoS and DDoS attacks, since they have public IP addresses and are known to the outside world. Database servers, on the other hand, typically sit deeper in the network. They are protected by an additional layer of firewalls. These firewalls allow tight controls on access. Another example is for the user segment, or LAN, where the requirement might be for the firewall to also perform URL filtering, anti-spam and anti-malware, as well as data loss prevention (DLP).
- **Capabilities**—What features and capabilities are you asking the firewall to perform?
    - Some firewalls act as very simple stateful packet filter (SPF) firewalls. They basically have a trusted network on one side of the firewall and an untrusted network on the other side. In its simplest form, the firewall allows all traffic to flow from the trusted side (LAN) to the untrusted side (Internet). At the same time it denies any traffic flow initiated from the other direction. These firewalls keep a state table that allows the return traffic inbound after a session has been initiated from the inside. More specific rules can be put in place to further restrict access.
    - Other newer and more expensive firewalls have the ability to do a higher level of packet inspection into higher layers of the packets. These firewalls can set rules denying Skype traffic or other IM traffic that typically flows over port 80 (the common http port used for most Web traffic). So depending on what type of data you are trying to protect, it makes a huge difference what type of firewall you consider.
- **Users**—How many users will be accessing data behind the firewalls?
    - Almost all firewalls have limits on user sessions. As the session capacity rises, so does the cost of a firewall. Typically, firewall vendors will list out how many sessions each of the models of their respective firewall can handle.

Physical Security

Physical security is an important aspect around the security of a network. Restricting the perimeter reduces the chance of unauthorized access for malicious purposes. By securing and watching the perimeter of a facility, personnel can easily and effectively control who enters and leaves. There are layers of physical security that should be provided when protecting a network. This allows logical access to be controlled by a number of "barriers." Securing the perimeter simply means physically limiting access to the facility. Both the internal and external perimeter are protected.

For example, strong physical security includes but is not limited to:

- Perimeter fence line
- Landscaping that creates a natural barrier
- Hand geometry units
- Iris scanners
- Access control systems, as well as levels of access within an access control system
- Armed security onsite
- Barrier systems
- IP cameras along with infrared cameras for night vision
- Digital video recorders (DVRs) onsite to view and record camera footage and retain the footage for a designated length of time

A perimeter fence line creates a physical barrier from the outside community. It gives the ability to close all entries and exits during a heightened security event. Monitoring the perimeter speaks to the need to have an area awareness of the perimeter. This includes the areas immediately beyond the perimeter as well as the areas inside the perimeter. Effective monitoring can be done by electronic surveillance systems and intrusion detection systems that are part of these surveillance systems. It is vital to have on-site security, whether armed or unarmed, to detect and deter possible unauthorized entry. Barriers are a means of a perimeter line. This includes berms, bollards, and natural landscaping barriers. These types of barriers control and also restrict the facility. They provide a channeled entry and controlled entry points.

The access control system is a key feature in the protection of cyber assets. Most facilities place the critical cyberassets within a six-wall barrier with badge access and more security measures. These consist of hand geometry units or iris scanners as a second level of access control. A camera system that monitors internal and external features allows the facility to monitor access on and within the site at all times of the day. Video recordings allow review after the fact to confirm access. These cameras also allow monitoring of areas that cannot be watched by the human eye at all times.

- **Speed**—What are the network connectivity requirements?
  - The physical placement in the network and the speeds of the uplink network ports need to be known. Some firewalls may come with 100 Mb links. Others offer 1 Gb or even 10 Gb port speeds. If the firewall is placed at the Internet edge or used as a site-to-site VPN for data center connectivity, a throughput analysis is needed. This will determine how much network traffic will be traversing the firewall.
- **Greenfield or brownfield**—What kind of deployment is the firewall to be?
  - Is the firewall part of a larger greenfield deployment—one where a new network is being deployed from scratch? Or is the firewall part of a brownfield deployment—integrating, in other words, into an existing network? If it's a greenfield deployment, then a network architecture needs to be created first as well as a forecast of the needs of the network. It is critical to involve the different groups in IT, such as the server team, the network team, and the security team, to help accomplish this.
- **Support**—Who is going to support the device?
  - Firewalls often have vastly different operating systems and management consoles. It is important to research the skill level of the staff who will be supporting them. You also should determine what type of background they have. In a larger enterprise environment, it will be much simpler to manage multiple firewalls if they are all from a single vendor.

These are only a few of the requirements that need to be answered before starting to look at different firewall choices. Once some of them are determined, we can start to look at model offerings from several vendors. Vendors are more than willing to come to customers to pitch their products. However, it's important to read through the sales pitch and compare them each to your set of requirements.

Demilitarized Zone (DMZ)

Nearly anyone can connect to the Internet. In fact, many are connected to the Internet often or continuously. In spite of being convenient, connecting to the Internet causes a security problem. Connecting a home or corporate network makes accessing internal resources much easier for attackers. Many attackers frequently scan networks that are connected to the Internet for known vulnerabilities. The problem network designers have is one of competing goals. Organizations want to allow their users to connect to the Internet and make their resources available to Internet users. But they also want to separate the organization's internal resources from malicious Internet users.

Firewalls can separate internal networks from external networks (the Internet). But sometimes resources need to be connected to both types of networks. For example, Web servers need to be accessed from the Internet and also be connected to internal resources. Organizations that host Web applications that provide access to their information often run into this problem. One of the most successful strategies used to protect an internal network from external attacks is called a **demilitarized zone (DMZ)**.

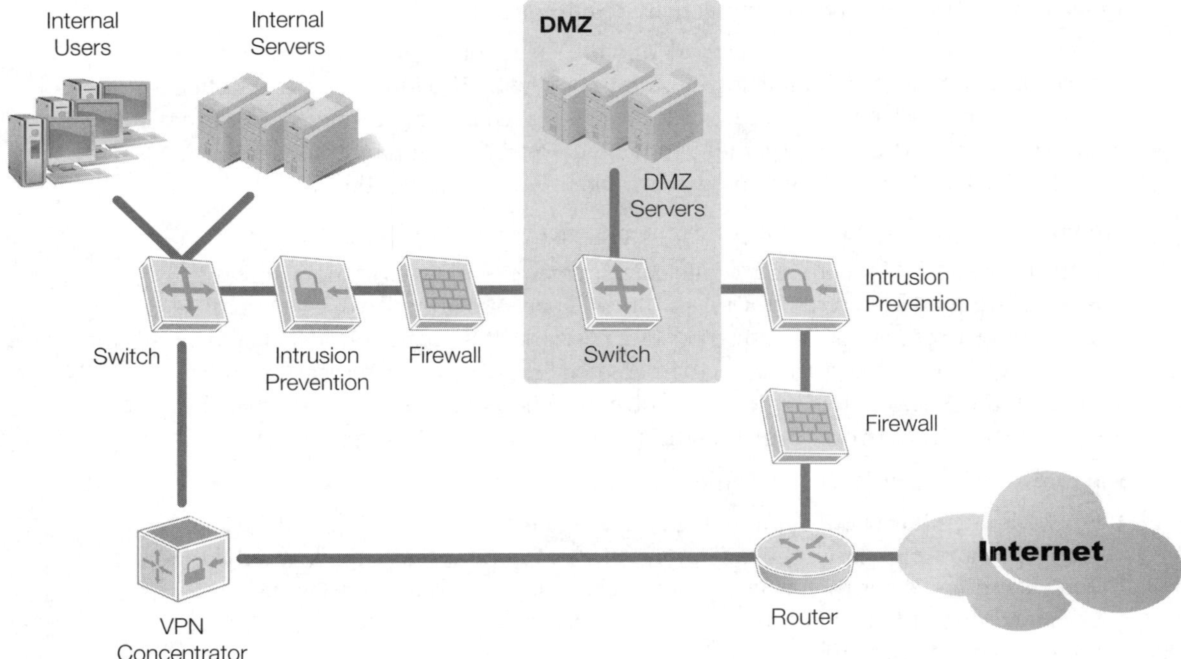

FIGURE 15-3 DMZ design.

A DMZ is a separate network that allows connections from external networks and internal LANs (Figure 15-3). In most cases, it is separated from each network by a firewall. A firewall sits between the Internet and the DMZ, and another firewall sits between the DMZ and the internal LAN. These firewalls control the traffic that flows through it and keeps anonymous users from connecting directly to the internal LAN. This approach allows organizations to place servers in the DMZ and expose them to the Internet without having to expose the whole internal network.

Security Controls

Continuing the discussion from the multilayered defense section, there are no simple measures to protect your organization from network attacks. You must focus on countermeasures that detect vulnerabilities, prevent attacks, and respond to the effects of successful attacks. This is not easy, but it is better than the alternative. Dealing with network attacks is a cost of doing business in today's business world.

The most sophisticated attackers continue to invent new methods of attacking network resources. Many are well-known and can be defeated with a variety of available tools. The best strategy is to identify vulnerabilities and reduce them to avoid attacks in the first place.

Avoiding attacks should be the highest priority. Unfortunately, you cannot avoid all attacks. Some attacks will succeed. Your response to attacks should be as aggressive as the attack itself. You can respond to attacks by developing plans to rapidly restore network resources if they are attacked. You can close holes in your organization's defenses and obtain evidence for prosecution of offenders. Of course, you should use the lessons learned from an attack to protect the network from similar attacks.

Responding to attacks involves planning, policy, and detective work. Fortunately, law-enforcement agencies, forensic experts, security consultants, and independent response teams are available to assist you in responding to a security incident as well as prosecuting the offender. In addition, many organizations have a special team to handle security incidents when they occur. An **incident response team (IRT)** knows how to recognize incidents and respond to them in a way that minimizes damage and preserves evidence for later action.

A countermeasure that protects resources from attack is called a **security control**. Security controls are classified into different categories. In fact, they can be classified at least two different ways—by their nature or by their timing. Classifying security controls by their nature defines the following categories:

- **Physical control**—Any device or object that protects a resource, such as doors, fences, or fire extinguishers.
- **Administrative control**—Administrative actions that affect personnel behavior, such as training, procedures, and policies.
- **Technical control**—Any technical measures to protect resources, such as encryption, authentication, firewalls, and access control lists (ACLs).
- **Regulatory/compliance control**—Regulation, legislation, and high-level policies that state minimum standards and requirements for security.

The other common method to classify security controls is by their timing in relation to an attack. These categories include:

- **Preventive control**—Any control designed to prevent a threat from being realized. Locked doors and firewalls with closed ports are examples of these controls.
- **Detective control**—Any control designed to detect either an attack or the results of an attack. These include motion detectors, intrusion detection systems, and log file analyzers.
- **Corrective control**—Any control that corrects, or repairs, the damage caused by an attack. They also may act to change the current environment and become a preventive control against further damage from the same type of attack. An example of a purely corrective control is restoring a backup copy of information after the primary copy is damaged. An extended corrective control also could be an intrusion prevention system function that blocks an identified attacker after the first successful attack.

Regardless of which method you use to classify security controls, a network should exhibit security controls from each category. Multilayered defense applies to the types of controls as well as their placement. An attacker should encounter a chain of security controls regardless of the path he takes to a resource. Always remember that the idea behind multilayered defense is to ensure every resource has multiple security controls protecting it. A **firewall** is what most people think of when they think of network security. A firewall is a program or dedicated hardware device that inspects network traffic passing through it. It then denies or permits that traffic based on a set of rules determined from a stored configuration. A firewall's basic task is to regulate the flow of traffic between computer networks of different trust levels. For example, a firewall can regulate network traffic flow between the Internet domain and the LAN domain. While firewalls are important, they are not the only type of network security control.

Secure networks should have controls of various types protecting them from any known attack route. Common network controls can include any of the following:

- Clear and complete security policies
- Complete security awareness training
- Firewall
- Intrusion detection/prevention system
- User access control
- Network access control
- Encryption
- Change/configuration control
- Log and file integrity monitoring
- Software updating procedure
- Workstation, server, and device-hardening procedures
- Malware prevention, detection, and eradication
- Formal incident response procedures

As you can see from this sample list, security controls require coordination from multiple domains. A network can be secure only if the organization leads its people to plan and execute strong policies and procedures. Everyone who accesses the network plays a part in its security. In most environments, the weakest links in security are the people. That is why policies and training are listed first. Clear policies and well-trained people are crucial to ensuring that your network is secure. Regardless of how good your technical controls are, they cannot keep the network secure with sloppy users. Effort expended in making users aware of the importance of security will always pay off in a more secure system.

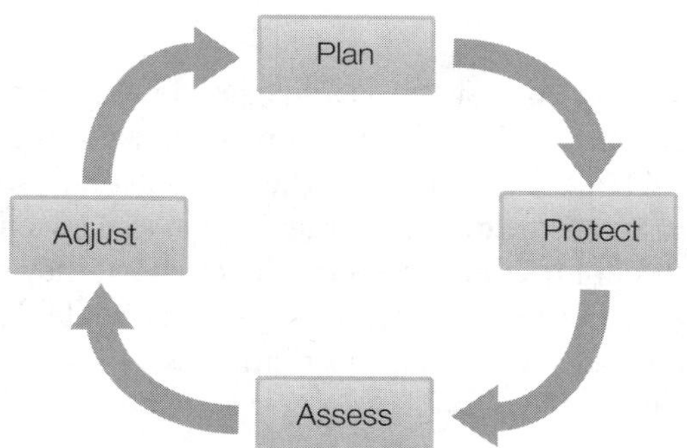

FIGURE 15-4
Managing security controls.

Managing Security Controls

The process of managing security controls is an ongoing endeavor. It ensures that your controls are current and effective. Managing security controls involves the same procedures you followed to put the initial security controls in place. As soon as a security control set is put into place, it begins to age and become less effective. Attack methods change over time. Users are added, removed, and modified. Network configurations routinely change to reflect current conditions. All of these changing conditions alter the network's security requirements. It is important that the security controls are reviewed and updated as necessary. This maintains the most effective security posture.

Effectively managing network security controls involves a cycle of four related activities, shown in Figure 15-4:

- **Plan**—Conduct a BIA and risk analysis to identify the highest priority risks. Organizations and their environments are dynamic. Risks to the organization continually change. They should be reflected in the security plan.
- **Protect**—Use the risk analysis to identify and deploy the best security controls for your environment.
- **Assess**—Periodically determine the vulnerabilities present in your network. Assess the effectiveness of existing security controls.
- **Adjust**—Make any necessary changes to existing security controls to increase their effectiveness. Drop ineffective controls. Add new controls where needed.

Each step in the security management process is a set of activities and warrants more explanation. The next four sections provide more details of each integral part of security management.

Plan

Conducting a business impact analysis (BIA) and risk analysis is not a one-time event. They should be regularly scheduled activities. Many organizations conduct these activities annually. They also should take place any time the organization's structure changes, the network layout changes significantly, or the organization suffers a major security breach. Although the BIA and risk analysis may require a lot of effort, they ensure the organization is focusing on handling the most important risks. An out-of-date risk analysis may miss an emerging threat. That could result in a substantial loss. Up-to-date risk information is the base of a solid security plan.

Protect

A security team receives an updated risk analysis. It then should review how well existing controls align with the ranked risks. Note that this is not the place to evaluate each security control's effectiveness. During the protect phase, the goal is just to ensure that every risk on the risk analysis has the proper security controls deployed. Of course, each organization has to determine which controls are properly based on each risk's severity.

Assess

Assessment is closely related to protection. Assessment includes at least two distinct task groups. First, the security team should assess the current state of the network. This can include vulnerability assessments and security audits. These processes should identify network vulnerabilities and any existing security controls to address them. A security audit examines existing security policies to find out how well the policies meet security goals and needs.

The second group of tasks assesses how well existing controls protect the network. The team should review each security control to find out if it is successfully protecting the network from known and potential threats. These two groups of tasks should align security protection controls with known and potential vulnerabilities. The result should identify any known vulnerabilities for which there are no security controls in place. This type of analysis is called a **security gap analysis**.

The "assess" activity identifies any needs for additional security controls. It also validates the effectiveness of existing security controls.

Adjust

Adjustment seeks to remedy any security gaps found in previous steps. The security gap analysis should identify any gaps between known and existing security controls. The best remedy may not be a new control. Existing controls may just need changes to close any gaps.

This should occur within the borders of the organization's configuration management practices. The security gap analysis does not authorize changes or new security controls. It only requests and recommends the changes via the change control board. Strict configuration management is in itself another security control. It should not be bypassed.

CHAPTER SUMMARY

Network security is a large concern that covers a wide range of topics. This chapter provides a brief overview of the important topics in network security. The main focus of securing networks is to understand the importance of following a formal approach to a complete solution. Each step of the process described in this chapter is important to the overall security of any network. Start with an understanding of what processes are critical to your organization. Next, identify and assess the risks to these critical processes. Identify the best security controls to mitigate the risks. Then deploy a system of multilayered defense to best protect your network. This approach is one that many large organizations use to build an effective network security program.

KEY CONCEPTS AND TERMS

Attack surface
Availability
Business impact analysis (BIA)
Defense in depth
Demilitarized zone (DMZ)
Firewall
Incident response team (IRT)
Least privilege
Qualitative risk analysis
Quantitative risk analysis
Risk
Risk management
Security breach
Security control
Security gap analysis
Security triad
Threat
Vulnerability

CHAPTER 15 ASSESSMENT

1. The right mix of security controls can make a network completely secure.

A. True
B. False

2. The CIA triad includes which three security properties?

A. Consistency, integrity, authorization
B. Confidentiality, isolated, authorization
C. Confidentiality, integrity, availability
D. Consistency, isolated, availability

3. Which security property assures that only authorized users can modify sensitive information?

A. Confidentiality
B. Integrity
C. Consistency
D. Isolated

4. Which term describes the cumulative opportunities for attackers to compromise a system?

A. Risks
B. Present threats
C. Known vulnerabilities
D. Attack surface

5. A ________ is any event that results in a violation of any of the CIA security properties.

6. An eavesdropping attack violates which CIA property?
   A. Confidentiality
   B. Integrity
   C. Consistency
   D. Isolated

7. Which term best describes any event that could damage an asset?
   A. Event
   B. Threat
   C. Risk
   D. Vulnerability

8. Which term best describes any weakness in a system that can allow an attack to cause harm?
   A. Event
   B. Threat
   C. Risk
   D. Vulnerability

9. A ________ risk assessment ranks risks relative to one another.

10. Which of the following courses of action is best if the cost to mitigate a risk exceeds the expected loss if the risk is realized?
    A. Mitigate
    B. Assign
    C. Accept
    D. Avoid

11. Insurance is a common form of which type of risk handling?
    A. Mitigate
    B. Assign
    C. Accept
    D. Avoid

12. Which of the following best describes the principle of least privilege?
    A. Allow users only the minimum access required to complete assigned tasks.
    B. Allow users the maximum access allowed for their job function.
    C. Restrict users from accessing any data they do not need to know.
    D. Ensure users have at least the minimum access required to complete assigned tasks.

APPENDIX A

Answer Key

CHAPTER 1 Today's Personal and Business Communication Requirements

1. A 2. C 3. B 4. B 5. B 6. B 7. B 8. A 9. Store and forward/ real-time 10. A 11. E 12. E 13. C 14. C 15. A

CHAPTER 2 Solving Today's Business Communication Challenges

1. B 2. B and D 3. C 4. B 5. Just in time (JIT) 6. D 7. C 8. B 9. B 10. Business problem

CHAPTER 3 Circuit-Switched, Packet-Switched, and IP-Based Communications

1. A 2. B 3. B 4. C 5. B 6. Destination 7. Destination IP 8. Cut-through 9. D 10. A

CHAPTER 4 The Evolution of Ethernet

1. A 2. C 3. D 4. C 5. B 6. A 7. B 8. C 9. A 10. A 11. B 12. D 13. B

CHAPTER 5 TCP/IP and Networking

1. B 2. A 3. C 4. B 5. Network Layer 6. C 7. Network Address 8. A 9. C 10. D 11. B and C 12. B 13. B 14. A and D 15. D

CHAPTER 6 Wireless LAN Standards

1. C 2. D 3. A 4. C 5. B 6. B 7. D 8. A 9. C 10. C 11. A 12. B 13. A 14. A 15. C

CHAPTER 7 Layer 2 Networking

1. C 2. A 3. C 4. D 5. Router (Layer 3 device) 6. C 7. A 8. A 9. C 10. A

CHAPTER 8 Layer 2 Networking VLANs

1. B 2. D 3. B 4. C 5. A 6. D 7. Trunk 8. A 9. Root bridge 10. B 11. B and D 12. Link Aggregation Control Protocol (LACP)

CHAPTER 9 Voice over Internet Protocol (VoIP)

1. B 2. B 3. C 4. D 5. C 6. B 7. SIP 8. A and D 9. D 10. C 11. Jitter 12. C

CHAPTER 10 Unified Communications and Session Initiation Protocol

1. A 2. C 3. B and C 4. B, C, and E 5. D 6. A 7. A 8. A 9. A
10. A 11. A 12. A 13. A 14. A 15. D

CHAPTER 11 Layer 3 Networking

1. B 2. C 3. A 4. B 5. D 6. B 7. B 8. B 9. B 10. D 11. A
12. B 13. C 14. B 15. A

CHAPTER 12 Fault Management and the Network Operations Center

1. A 2. C 3. B 4. A 5. C 6. Simple Network Management Protocol (SNMP)
7. B 8. A 9. D 10. Object ID (OID) 11. B 12. D

CHAPTER 13 Configuration Management and Accounting

1. A 2. E 3. C 4. B 5. D 6. A 7. A 8. A and B 9. A 10. A
11. B, C, and D 12. B 13. A 14. A 15. B

CHAPTER 14 Performance Management

1. B 2. A 3. Baseline 4. D 5. A and C 6. B 7. D 8. A 9. B 10. C

CHAPTER 15 Security Management

1. B 2. C 3. B 4. D 5. Security breach 6. A 7. B 8. D 9. Qualitative
10. C 11. B 12. A

List of Abbreviations

B

3DES	triple DES
AAA	authentication, authorization, and accounting
ACL	access control list
AES	Advanced Encryption Standard
ARP	Address Resolution Protocol
ATM	asynchronous transfer mode
ATP	AppleTalk Transaction Protocol
BCP	business continuity planning
BER	bit error rate
BGP	Border Gateway Protocol
BPDU	bridge protocol data unit
bps	bits per second
CA	certificate authority
CIDR	classless inter-domain routing
CLNP	Connectionless Network Protocol
CLNS	Connectionless Network Service
CSMA/CD	carrier sense multiple access with collision detection
DCE	data circuit-terminating equipment
DDoS	distributed denial of service
DES	Data Encryption Standard
DHCP	Dynamic Host Configuration Protocol
DMZ	demilitarized zone
DNS	Domain Name Service
DoS	denial of service
DRP	disaster recovery planning
DTE	data terminal equipment
DWDM	dense wave division multiplexing
EAP	Extensible Authentication Protocol
EGP	Exterior Gateway Protocol
EIA	Electronic Industries Alliance
EIGRP	Enhanced Interior Gateway Routing Protocol
ERP	enterprise resource planning
FDM	frequency division multiplexing
FTP	File Transfer Protocol
GSM	Global System for Mobile
HSRP	Hot Standby Routing Protocol
HTTP	Hypertext Transport Protocol
IANA	Internet Assigned Numbers Authority
ICMP	Internet Control Message Protocol
IEEE	Institute of Electrical and Electronics Engineers
IETF	Internet Engineering Task Force
IGRP	Interior Gateway Routing Protocol
IMAP	Internet Message Access Protocol
IOS	Internetwork Operating System
IP	Internet Protocol
IPSec	Internet Protocol Security
IRF	intelligent resilient framework
ISDN	Integrated Services Digital Network
ISO	International Standards Organization
ISP	Internet service provider
ITU	International Telecommunications Union
IVR	interactive voice response
L2TP	Layer 2 Tunneling Protocol
LACP	Link Aggregation Control Protocol
LAN	local area network
LEAP	Lightweight Extensible Authentication Protocol
LLC	logical link control
LSA	link-state advertisement
LSPs	link state protocol data units
MAC	Media Access Control
MAU	multistation access unit
Mbps	megabits per second
MD5	message-digest algorithm
MGCP	Media Gateway Control Protocol
MIB	management information base

MIME multipurpose Internet mail extensions
MPLS Multi-Protocol Label Switching
MSTP Multiple Spanning Tree Protocol
MTBF mean time between failures
MTTI mean time to install
MTTR mean time to repair
MTU maximum transmission unit or message transmission unit
NAT Network Address Translation
NDP Neighbor Discovery Protocol
NetBEUI NetBIOS extended user interface
NetBIOS Network Basic Input/Output System
NIC network interface controller
OSPF Open Shortest Path First
OSI Open Systems Interconnection
PEAP Protected Extensible Authentication Protocol
PKI Public Key Infrastructure
PoE Power over Ethernet
POP point of presence
POTS plain old telephone service
PPP Point-to-Point Protocol
PPTP Point-to-Point Tunneling Protocol
PSTN public switched telephone network
PVST Per-VLAN Spanning Tree
QoS quality of service
RADIUS Remote Authentication Dial-In User Service
RC4 Rivest Cipher 4
RFC Request for Comments
RFP request for proposal
RIP Routing Information Protocol
RPC remote procedure call
RSVP Resource Reservation Protocol
RTP Real-Time Transport Protocol
SACK Selective ACKnowledgments
SAN storage area network
SCTP Stream Control Transmission Protocol
SDP Session Description Protocol
SES Symmetric Encryption System
SIP Session Initiation Protocol
SKA shared key authentication
SLA service-level agreement
SOA service-oriented architecture
SOHO small office/home office
SMS short message service
SMTP Simple Mail Transport Protocol
SNMP Simple Network Management Protocol
SPF shortest path first
SRP Stream Reservation Protocol
SSH Secure Shell
SSL Secure Sockets Layer
STP Spanning Tree Protocol
SVoSIP Secure Voice over Secure IP
TCN topology change notification
TCO total cost of ownership
TCP Transmission Control Protocol
TCP/IP Transmission Control Protocol/Internet Protocol
TFTP Trivial File Transfer Protocol
TKIP Temporal Key Integrity Protocol
TLS Transport Layer Security
ToIP Telephony over IP
TOS Type of Service
TTL time to live
TTLS Tunneled Transport Layer Security
UPS uninterruptible power supply
URL uniform resource locator
UDP User Datagram Protocol
UTP unshielded twisted pair
VID VLAN identifier
VLAN Virtual LAN
VLSM variable length subnet masking
VoIP Voice over IP
VoSIP Voice over Secure IP
VPN virtual private network
VRID virtual router identifier
VRRP Virtual Router Redundancy Protocol
WAN wide area network
WEP Wired Equivalent Privacy
WMAN Wireless MAN
WPA Wi-Fi Protected Access
WPA2 Wi-Fi Protected Access 2
WRAP Wireless Robust Authenticated Protocol

Seven Domains of a Typical IT Infrastructure

APPENDIX C

An Overview of the Seven Domains

The concepts presented in this book focus on the various components found in many of today's networks. Whether in a small business, large government body, or publicly traded corporation, most IT infrastructures consist of the seven domains shown in Figure A-1.

User Domain

The User Domain defines the people who access an organization's information systems.

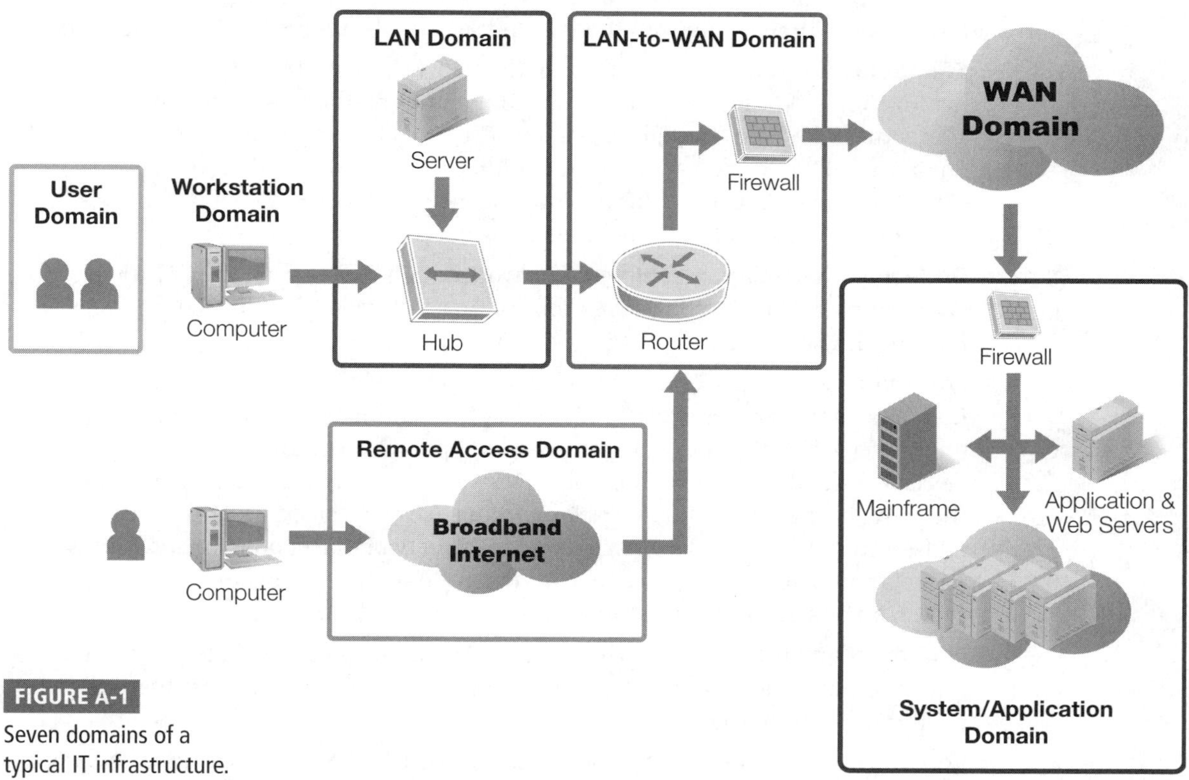

FIGURE A-1
Seven domains of a typical IT infrastructure.

Workstation Domain

The Workstation Domain is where most local users connect to the IT infrastructure. A workstation can be a desktop computer, laptop computer, or any other device that connects to the network. Other devices might include a personal data assistant (PDA), a smartphone, or a special-purpose terminal. You can find more details about mobile devices in the Remote Access Domain section.

LAN Domain

A local area network (LAN) is a collection of computers that are connected to one another or to a common connection medium. Network connection mediums can include wires, fiber-optic cables, or radio waves. LANs are generally organized by function or department. Once connected, your computer can access systems, applications, possibly the Internet, and data.

The physical part of the LAN Domain consists of the following:

- **Network interface card (NIC)**—The interface between the computer and the LAN physical media. The NIC has a unique 6-byte Media Access Control (MAC) layer address that is unique to the NIC and serves as a unique hardware identifier.
- **Ethernet LAN**—LAN solution based on the IEEE 802.3 CSMA/CD standard for 10/100/1000Mbps Ethernet networking. Ethernet is the most popular LAN standard. Today's LAN standard is the Institute of Electrical and Electronics Engineers (IEEE) 802.3 carrier sense multiple access/collision detection (CSMA/CD) specification. Ethernet is available in 10 Mbps, 100 Mbps, 1 Gbps, 10 Gbps, 40 Gbps, and 100 Gbps speeds.
- **Unshielded twisted-pair cabling**—The workstation cabling that uses RJ-45 connectors and jacks to physically connect to a 100 Mbps/1 Gbps/10 Gbps Ethernet LAN switch.
- **LAN switch**—The device that connects workstations into a physical Ethernet LAN. A switch provides dedicated Ethernet LAN connectivity for workstations and servers. This provides maximum throughput and performance for each workstation. There are two kinds of LAN switches. A Layer 2 switch examines the MAC layer address and makes forwarding decisions based on MAC layer address tables. A Layer 3 switch examines the network layer address and routes packets based on routing protocol path determination decisions. A Layer 3 switch is the same thing as a router.
- **File server and print server**—High-powered computers that provide file sharing and data storage for users within a department. Print servers support shared printer use within a department.
- **Wireless access point (WAP)**—For wireless LANs (WLANs), radio transceivers are used to transmit IP packets from a WLAN NIC to a WAP. The WAP transmits WLAN signals for mobile laptops to connect. The WAP connects back to the LAN switch using unshielded twisted-pair cabling.

Ethernet switches typically provide 100 Mbps or 1 Gbps connectivity for each workstation. Ethernet switches are also equipped with modules that support 1 Gbps or 10 Gbps Ethernet backbone connections. These backbone connections commonly use fiber optic cabling.

The logical part of the LAN Domain consists of the following:

- **System administration**—Setup of user LAN accounts with login ID and password access controls (that is, user login information).
- **Design of directory and file services**—The servers, directories, and folders to which the user can gain access.
- **Configuration of workstation and server TCP/IP software and communication protocols**—IP addressing, IP default gateway router, subnet mask address, etc. The IP default gateway router acts as the entry/exit to the LAN. The subnet mask address defines the IP network number and IP host number.
- **Design of server disk storage space, backup, and recovery of user data**—Users can store data files on LAN disk storage areas where data is backed up and archived daily. In the event of data loss or corruption, data files can be recovered from the backed-up files.
- **Design of virtual LANs (VLANs)**—With Layer 2 and Layer 3 LAN switches, you can configure Ethernet ports to be on the same virtual LAN (VLAN), even though they may be connected to different physically connected LANs. This is the same thing as configuring workstations and servers to be on the same Ethernet LAN or broadcast domain.

Users get access to their department's LAN and other applications according to what their jobs call for.

LAN-to-WAN Domain

The LAN-to-WAN Domain is where the IT infrastructure links to a wide area network and the Internet. Network applications use two common transport protocols: Transmission Control Protocol (TCP) and User Datagram Protocol (UDP). Both TCP and UDP use port numbers to identify the application or function; these port numbers function like channels on a TV, which dictate which station you're watching. Examples of common TCP and UDP port numbers include the following:

- **Port 80: Hyper Text Transfer Protocol (HTTP)**—The communications protocol between Web browsers and Web sites with data in clear text.
- **Port 20: File Transfer Protocol (FTP)**—A protocol for performing file transfers. FTP uses TCP as a connection-oriented data transmission but in clear text. "Connection oriented" means individual packets are numbered and acknowledged as being received to increase integrity of the file transfer.

- **Port 69: Trivial File Transfer Protocol (TFTP)**—A protocol for performing file transfers. TFTP utilizes UDP as a connectionless data transmission but in clear text. This is used for small and quick file transfers given that it does not guarantee individual packet delivery.
- **Port 23: Terminal Network (Telnet)**—This is a network protocol for performing remote terminal access to another device. Telnet uses TCP and sends data in clear text.
- **Port 22: Secure Shell (SSH)**—This is a network protocol for performing remote terminal access to another device. SSH encrypts the data transmission for maintaining confidentiality of communications.

A complete list of well-known port numbers from 0 to 1023 is maintained by the Internet Assigned Numbers Authority (IANA). The IANA helps coordinate global domain name services, IP addressing, and other resources. Well-known port numbers are on the IANA Web site at this location: *http://www.iana.org/assignments/port-numbers*.

WAN Domain

The Wide Area Network (WAN) Domain connects remote locations. As network costs drop, organizations can afford higher-speed Internet and WAN connections. Today, telecommunication service providers sell the following:

- **Nationwide optical backbones**—Optical backbone trunks for private optical backbone networks.
- **End-to-end IP transport**—IP services and connectivity using the service provider's IP networking infrastructure.
- **Multisite WAN cloud services**—IP services and connectivity offered for multisite connectivity such as multi-protocol label switching (MPLS) WAN services. MPLS uses labels or tags to make virtual connections between endpoints in a WAN.
- **Metropolitan Ethernet LAN connectivity**—Ethernet LAN connectivity offered within a city's area network.
- **Dedicated Internet access**—A broadband Internet communication link usually shared within an organization.
- **Managed services**—Router management and security appliance management 24×7×365—continuously, in other words.
- **Service level agreements (SLAs)**—Contractual commitments for monthly service offerings such as availability, packet loss, and response time to fix problems.

WAN services can include dedicated Internet access and managed services for customers' routers and firewalls. Management agreements for availability and response time to outages are common. Networks, routers, and equipment require continuous monitoring and management to keep WAN service available.

Some organizations use the public Internet as their WAN infrastructure. While it is cheaper than a private network, the Internet does not guarantee delivery or security. Telecommunication service providers sell WAN connectivity services. Some providers now also provide security-management services.

Remote Access Domain

The Remote Access Domain connects remote users to the organization's IT infrastructure. Remote access is critical for staff members who work in the field or from home—for example, outside sales reps, technical support specialists, or health care professionals. Global access makes it easy to connect to the Internet, e-mail, and other business applications anywhere you can find a wireless fidelity (Wi-Fi) hotspot. The Remote Access Domain is important to have but dangerous to use. It introduces many risks and threats from the Internet.

Today's mobile worker depends on the following:

- **Highly available cell-phone service**—Mobile workers need cell-phone service to get in touch with office and support teams.
- **Real-time access for critical communications**—Use of text messaging or IM chat on cell phones provides quick answers to short questions and does not require users to completely interrupt what they are doing.
- **Access to e-mail from mobile device**—Integration of e-mail with cell phones, smartphones, personal data assistants (PDAs) or other smart devices provides quick response to important e-mail messages.
- **Broadband WiFi Internet access**—Some nationwide service providers now offer WiFi broadband access cards. They allow wireless access in major metro areas.
- **Local Wi-Fi hotspot**—Wi-Fi hotspots are abundant, including in airports, libraries, and coffee shops. While most are free, some require that users pay for access.
- **Broadband Internet access to home office**—Staffers who work from home require broadband Internet access. This is usually bundled with VoIP telephone service and digital TV service.
- **Secure remote access to a company's IT infrastructure**—Remote workers require secure VPN tunnels to encrypt all IP data transmissions through the public Internet. This is critical if private data is being accessed remotely.

The scope of this domain is limited to remote access via the Internet and IP communications. The logical configuration of the Remote Access Domain requires IP network engineering and VPN solutions. This section addresses individual remote access and large-scale remote access for many remote users.

System/Application Domain

The System/Application Domain holds all the mission-critical systems, applications, and data. Authorized users may have access to many components in this domain. Secure access may require second-level checks.

Examples of applications that may require second-level authentication include the following:

- **Human resources and payroll**—Only staff who work on payroll services need access to this private data and confidential information.
- **Accounting and financials**—Executive managers need access to accounting and financial data to make sound business decisions. Securing financial data requires unique security controls with access limited to those who need it. Publicly traded companies are subject to Sarbanes-Oxley (SOX) compliance law requiring security.
- **Customer relationship management (CRM)**—Customer-service reps need real-time access to information that includes customer purchasing history and private data.
- **Sales-order entry**—Sales professionals need access to the sales-order entry and order-tracking system. Private customer data must be kept safe.
- **U.S. military intelligence and tactics**—United States military commanders who make decisions on the battlefield use highly sensitive information. Access to it must meet U.S. Defense Department data classification standards.

Exclusive OR (XOR) Binary Operator

APPENDIX

D

The "exclusive OR" (XOR) binary operation is a common operation used in encryption algorithms. Also called exclusive disjunction, this operation provides a quick and convenient method to flip bits in a memory value, to tell whether two bits are equal, and whether there are an odd number of bits with a value of 1 in a memory value. The XOR operator makes it possible to implement encryption algorithms that rely on one or more of these features.

The XOR operation is simple. For any two bits, the result of the XOR operation on the two bits is 1 if either of the bits is 1 (but not both). The result is 0 if neither of the input bits is 1, or if both the input bits are 1.

Here are the possible values for the XOR operation:

- 0 XOR 0 = 0
- 0 XOR 1 = 1
- 1 XOR 0 = 1
- 1 XOR 1 = 0

For data values that contain multiple bits, the XOR operation is a bitwise operation. That means it applies the XOR operation to each corresponding pair of bits in the two operands. For example, what would the result of 17 XOR 35 be?

The first step in understanding how XOR works is to convert the operands, 17 and 35, into their binary representations:

17 in decimal notation is 10001 in binary notation.
35 in decimal notation is 100011 in binary notation.

Starting from the right side of each number (the least significant digit) and working our way to the left, apply the XOR operation to each pair of bits (10001 is on the left side and 100011 is on the right side below):

17 XOR 35 is the same as:
1 XOR 1 = 0
0 XOR 1 = 1
0 XOR 0 = 0
0 XOR 0 = 0
1 XOR 0 = 1
0 XOR 1 = 1 (We added a leading 0 to the left hand number to make the operands the same length.)

So, 010001 XOR 100011 = 110010.
In decimal notation, 17 XOR 35 = 50.

Encryption algorithms routinely apply the bitwise XOR operation to bytes, words, or even longer blocks of equal length operands.

APPENDIX E

IPv4 Subnet Addressing

You learned about IP addresses in Chapter 5. Many organizations need more flexibility to define logical groups of nodes within a LAN. There are many reasons to create subsets of LANs, or subnets. These reasons include:

- **Separate network segments that use different technologies**—Subnets allow Ethernet, token ring, and other LAN technologies to have groups of addresses within the organization's address space.
- **Create security groups**—Subnets make it easy to logically group nodes together by functional use or type of access needed. This feature allows security administrators to limit permissions to nodes within a particular subnet address range.
- **Increase performance**—Nodes that frequently communicate with one another can be grouped into a subnet. Subnets provide the ability to separate traffic among related nodes from other unrelated nodes.

Just as Layer 2 switches separate LANs into separate collision domains, Layer 3 routers can separate networks into subnetworks using IP addressing to logically group related nodes. Nodes in the same subnet do not have to be physically near one another. A subnet is a function of each device's IP address.

Layer 3 devices use IP addresses and subnet masks to determine the boundaries of subnets. IPv4 separates an IP address into two variable-length parts: the network address and the node address. Since an IPv4 address is 32 bits, the length of the node address depends on the length of the network address. The separate subnet mask defines how much of the IP address is the network portion and how much is left over for the node address. A subnet mask is a 32-bit number in which the bits are set to 1 for the corresponding bits in the IP address that represent the network address. In other words, if the first 24 bits in an IP address represent the network address, the subnet mask for that network would have the first 24 bits all set to 1 and the remaining bits set to 0.

technical TIP

IPv6 addresses have fixed network address lengths and do not need subnet masks.

The subnet address in the previous example would be: 11111111.11111111.1111 1111.00000000, or 255.255.255.0. This addressing scheme corresponds to a Class C subnet mask. This strategy of using subnet masks provides the ability to address many types of subnets. In fact, organizations can design their subnets based on their own needs.

Layer 3 devices use the subnet mask to determine to which subnet an IP address belongs. To determine the subnet network address, the device performs a bitwise *and* operation on the IP address and the subnet mask. (The logical *and* operation results in a 1 if both input bits are 1, and results in a 0 otherwise.)

Suppose a node has an IP address of 192.168.12.88 and is using a subnet mask of 255.255.255.0. Here is how to calculate the network address (the subnet to which this node belongs):

(A) IP Address:	110000 10101000 00001100 01011000	(192.168.12.88)
(B) Subnet mask:	11111111 11111111 11111111 00000000	(255.255.255.0)
Network address: (A *and* B)	11000000 10101000 00001100 00000000	(192.168.12.0)

Another way to show the combined network address and subnet mask is to list the network address, followed by a slash character, "/," followed by the number of binary 1 digits in the subnet mask. The combined address notation for the network address in the previous example would be 192.168.12.0/24.

For a slightly more complex subnet, consider the following IP address and subnet mask:

IP Address:	192.168.12.88 (Same IP address as in the previous example)
Subnet mask:	255.255.224.0 (Different subnet mask—not a Class C network)

(A) IP Address:	110000 10101000 00001100 01011000	(192.168.12.88)
(B) Subnet mask:	11111111 11111111 11100000 00000000	(255.255.224.0)
Network address: (A *and* B)	11000000 10101000 00000000 00000000	(192.168.0.0)

The combined address notation for the network address in the previous example would be 192.168.0.0/19.

The range of usable addresses for 192.168.0.0/19 is 192.168.0.0–192.168.31.255. The last address, 192.168.31.255, is the broadcast address for that subnet.

technical TIP

If you want more practice with IP addresses and subnets, try out this online IP address calculator: *http://jodies.de/ipcalc*

Glossary of Key Terms

10Base2 "Thinnet" | IEEE 802.3a Ethernet standard that defines communication at 10 Mbps using thin coaxial cable.

10Base5 "Thicknet" | IEEE 802.3 Ethernet standard that defines communication at 10 Mbps using thick coaxial cable.

10BaseT | IEEE 802.3i Ethernet standard that defines communication at 10 Mbps using unshielded twisted-pair cable.

100BaseTX | IEEE 802.3u Ethernet standard that defines communication at 10 Mbps using unshielded twisted-pair cable.

1000BaseT (GigE) | IEEE 802.3ab Ethernet standard that defines communication at 10 Mbps using unshielded twisted-pair cable.

3270 terminal emulation | Software that is used for PCs and workstations to mimic an IBM SNA mainframe terminal device.

A

AAA server | A server that provides authentication, authorization, and accounting for a network.

Active fault detection | A fault detection technique that involves taking action to determine if everything is working properly.

Address resolution | The process of finding an IP address for a host name.

Address Resolution Protocol (ARP) | A communications protocol that network devices use to find a Link Layer address (MAC address) from a Network Layer address (IP address).

Analog | Transmission method that uses a continuously variable signal, as opposed to digital transmission that uses two distinct signal values.

Analog telephone adapter (ATA) | A device that converts an analog voice signal from the analog telephone into a digital signal for the IP network.

Answering machine | Device to automatically answer a telephone call, play a recorded message, and then record the caller's message.

Asymmetric encryption system | A system that uses a public key to encode data and a private key to decrypt data.

Attack surface | A collection of all of the vulnerable points of a system.

Attenuation | Loss or degradation of electrical signal.

Audio conference | The ability for two or more persons to share a common voice communication, usually implemented via an intermediate phone or a shared conference bridge.

Automated teller machine (ATM) | A computerized telecommunications device that allows bank customers access to financial transactions.

Autonomous system (AS) | A grouping of connected IP networks that are managed, maintained, and controlled by a common administrator.

Availability | The security requirement that information be available to authorized users when they want it.

B

Backbone | A topology used to connect several smaller networks to create a larger, segregated network.

Bandwidth | The rate of data transfer or throughput; a theoretical maximum capability of a specific physical medium.

Baseline | A collection of performance measurements against a system at a particular point in time.

Basic Service Set (BSS) | A WLAN network that includes an access point.

Beeper | Device that generates a sound or effect when a caller calls a specific telephone number; also called a pager. Some beepers support sending short messages, either numeric, or voice, to the device.

Bit error rate (BER) | The ratio of the total number of bits transmitted to the bits that were modified in transmission.

Border Gateway Protocol (BGP) | An exterior hybrid routing protocol that routes messages between networks and AS.

British Telecom (BT) | A primary global telecommunications carrier building upon its strong global connections and former monopoly role.

Broadband | Telecommunications signal of greater bandwidth than normal signals.

Broadcast domain | The collection of all nodes that are connected to the same set of repeaters, hubs, switches, and bridges.

Broadcast storm | A situation in which broadcast messages get forwarded and replicated to a point that the network cannot handle all of the traffic.

Broadcasting | Sending a packet to a complete range of IP addresses.

Brouter | A network device that combines the functionality of a switch/bridge and a router. The device uses MAC addresses for local devices and IP addresses for remote devices.

Bus topology | A network layout that starts with a central high-speed cable. The main cable runs throughout the organization's physical space and provides accessible connections anywhere along its length.

Business continuity planning (BCP) | Planning primarily for the people response to a disaster. The elements that would be included in BCP are policy related to the continuation of business during and immediately following a disaster.

Business impact analysis (BIA) | Process that results in a list of activities necessary for an organization to conduct business operations.

Business process management (BPM) | A process of aligning business process and mapping each one to software applications and IT solutions.

Business to Business (B2B) | E-commerce model that describes activities that involve doing business with other businesses.

Business to Consumer (B2C) | E-commerce model that describes business activities that involve providing products or services directly to end consumers.

Business to Government (B2G) | E-commerce model that describes activities that support business activities between commercial organizations and government agencies, also called public sector organizations (PSO).

C

Campus backbone | A backbone that connects other backbones to create a larger network.

Capacity | The number of nodes and the amount of shared bandwidth available to each node and coverage.

Central Office (CO) | A facility owned and operated by a telecommunications carrier where all its common switching equipment is located.

Checksum | A mathematical calculation that verifies the length and integrity of the transmitted Ethernet frame to a destination.

Circuit-switched | Refers to a network that sets up a circuit for each conversation. All messages during the conversation follow the same path from source to destination.

Classful network | The original addressing architecture used for the Internet.

Classless Inter-Domain Routing (CIDR) | A strategy that allows IANA to segment any IPv4 address space to define larger or smaller networks as needed.

Codec | A software program or hardware device that converts an analog signal to digital and a digital signal to analog.

Collaboration | An application that allows multiple users to communicate online as a group.

Collaborative conference | A communication between two or more persons, often in different geographic locations, using tools such as shared whiteboards, applications, and computer desktops.

Collapsed backbone | A network topology that minimizes traffic flowing between departmental LANs by replacing a bus with one or more central switches.

Collision | Any time two or more network nodes transmit messages at the same time. A collision results in a garbled message.

Collision domain | The collection of nodes that exchange unfiltered traffic with other nodes.

Common Management Information Protocol (CMIP) | A protocol that defines an implementation for communicating between management applications and their agents.

Complementary code keying (CCK) | A modulation scheme defined in the IEEE 802.11b standard.

Computer-aided design (CAD) | Computer software used to prepare mechanical or engineering drawings. CAD software is used widely in creating network diagrams and "as built" documentation of equipment racks and data centers.

Confidentiality | The security requirement that only authorized users be allowed to access sensitive information.

Connection medium | Physical method to link network devices together.

Connection-oriented protocol | A communication protocol that sets up a connection with the remote node before exchanging messages with it. Both participants in the conversation use the same connection for the duration of the conversation.

Connectionless protocol | A communication protocol that does not require a predefined connection and treats each packet as a separate entity.

Convergence | The amount of time it takes for a network to find and initiate a backup or redundant link in the event of failure of a primary link.

Cost | A relative metric value used to set the condition of comparison.

Coverage | The attempt to provide the same level of signal strength to all network nodes.

CSMA/CD (carrier sense multiple access with collision detection) | The media access control mechanism for how network-attached devices listen to the network before transmitting with collision detection.

D

Data circuit-terminating equipment (DCE) | A device located between a DTE device and a data transmission circuit. The DCE device converts a DTE signal into a transmission format for the attached circuit. A modem is a common DCE device.

Data terminal equipment (DTE) | A device that converts user input to signals, and converts received signals into user output. DTE devices normally allow users to interact with computer systems.

Datagrams | Layer 3 protocol units of data sent to a destination node, also called network packets.

Decode | To convert a digital signal to an analog signal.

Defense in depth | Multiple countermeasures that an attacker must compromise to reach any protected resource. It is often described as a series of concentric rings around protected resources.

Demilitarized zone (DMZ) | A separate network that allows connections from external networks and internal LANs; in most cases, it is separated from each network by a firewall.

Designated port (DP) | The port to a network segment with the lowest root path cost.

Digital | Transmission method that uses two distinct signal values, high and low, or 0 and 1, as opposed to analog transmission that uses a continuously variable signal.

Digital signature | Application used to verify that the sender of a document, image, or message is a trusted source.

Direct sequence spread spectrum (DSSS) | A modulation technique included in the IEEE 802.11x standards.

Disaster recovery planning (DRP) | Planning primarily for the technical response to a disaster.

Discard | A situation in which a network device drops one or more packets.

Distance-vector routing protocol | A type of routing protocol that maintains a routing table containing route metrics provided by neighboring routers on which routing decisions are made.

Domain Name System (DNS) | A hierarchical naming system that allows organizations to associate host names with IP address name spaces.

Dot notation | Standard notation for IPv4 addresses.

Dual IP stack | A network software implementation in which the operating system supports both IPv4 and IPv6 using two separate network stacks for the Internet Protocol.

Dumb terminal | A terminal device that does little more than send and receive sequences of characters to and from a host computer.

Dynamic Host Configuration Protocol (DHCP) | An automatic configuration protocol used to assign device attributes to devices on IP networks.

Dynamic rate shifting (DRS) | Adapts the nominal bit rate of a wireless node to better use a communication channel.

Dynamic routing | Using links determined by a routing protocol through information from other routers.

E

E-commerce | The practice of doing business with remote customers over the Internet.

Edge network | A network at the last 100 meters or 300 feet from a wiring closet, where desktops physically connect to the network.

Electronic Industries Association (EIA) | An alliance of standards and trade organizations for electronics manufacturers in the United States. EIA changed its name to the Electronic Industries Alliance in 1997. EIA ceased operations as a unified organization as of February 11, 2011, but its member organizations still operate independently.

Encapsulation | The process of adding the IP header data to a network packet.

Encode | To convert an analog signal to a digital signal.

Enhanced Interior Gateway Routing Protocol (EIGRP) | A hybrid interior routing protocol that combines the shortest-path considerations of a link-state routing protocol with the metrics of IGRP.

Enterprise business | An organization with more than 500 employees.

Ethernet | A family of networking technologies that define how computers and devices communicate on a LAN.

Ethernet tagging | Same as IEEE 802.1q, where Ethernet Frames are "labeled" with a "tag number" to designate a specific VLAN.

Extended Service Set (ESS) | A WLAN that links together two BSS networks with a common linking device.

Extensible Authentication Protocol (EAP) | An authentication method that is used in WLANs and point-to-point connections.

Exterior routing protocol | A protocol that routes messages outside an AS or between two networks.

Extranet | A remotely accessible network that an organization makes accessible to its business partners and suppliers through the public Internet. An extranet is a secure network that requires proper access controls and authentication before granting access.

F

Facsimile device | Connection to a standard telephone line that allows a user to scan one or more pages of documents and send the scanned images to a fax machine connected to a telephone line in another location.

Fault | Any malfunction of a network hardware or software component.

Fault management | The collection of procedures, devices, software programs, and actions that enable network administrators to detect and respond to faults.

Fault tolerance | The ability to encounter a fault, or error, of some type and still support critical operations.

FCAPS | A model that focuses on five primary areas of network management: fault management, configuration management, accounting management, performance management, and security management.

Firewall | A program or dedicated hardware device that inspects network traffic passing through it. It then denies or permits that traffic based on a set of rules determined from a stored configuration.

Flat topology | A network layout that uses Layer 2 switching only and has no addressing hierarchy.

Fragmentation | Process in which IP software chops packets into smaller packets, allowing computers to send large packets across a network that can only handle smaller packets.

Frame | A term used to describe a Data Link Layer frame format such as Ethernet v2.0 or IEEE 802.3 CSMA/CD, etc.

Full duplex | A mode of operation in which both ends of a connection between computers can communicate simultaneously.

Fully connected mesh | A network topology in which all nodes are directly connected to every other node.

G

Gateway | A network device that connects two networks that use different protocols.

Graph | A mathematical representation of a set of objects.

H

H.323 | A VoIP packet-based standard that supports audio, video, and data communications across IP networks.

Half duplex | A mode of operation in which both ends of a connection between computers can communicate, but only one at a time.

Hold-down | A period of time during which a particular path is suspended.

Hop count | The number of routers (hops) a packet must pass through to reach the network of its destination address.

Host-based | Refers to a computer system that consists of a central powerful computer with many users that connect directly to it.

Hosting/hosted service provider (HSP) | A company that usually provides services such as UC, VoIP, or other applications.

Hub | A simple network device with multiple ports that echoes every message it receives to all ports.

Hybrid topology | A network layout that contains several different topologies.

Hyperconnectivity | The state of being in close proximity to multiple devices that are perpetually connected to the Internet.

IEEE 802.1q | Standard for VLAN tagging.

IEEE 802.3 | A collection of standards that define the Data Link Layer protocol for accessing wired Ethernet.

IEEE 802.3 CSMA/CD | Standard for the Ethernet LAN specification.

IEEE 802.3af–2003 | Power over Ethernet standard and specification up to 15.4 watts of electrical power.

IEEE 802.3at–2009 | Power over Ethernet standard and specification up to 25.5 watts of electrical power.

IEEE 802.5 token ring | Standard for 4Mbps/16Mbps token ring LANs.

Incident response team (IRT) | A special team formed to handle security incidents when they occur.

Independent Basic Service Set (IBSS) | A peer-to-peer WLAN designation for each node in an ad hoc mode network.

Industrial, scientific, and medical (ISM) bands | The 2.4 GHz bandwidth allocated to unlicensed use and used for 802.11b/g/n.

Instant message (IM chat) | A real-time communication application supported by SIP; it offers text messaging between users.

Institute of Electrical and Electronics Engineers (IEEE) | A global association that defines and publishes standards for many aspects of electronic components and communication.

Integrity | The security requirement that only authorized users be allowed to modify sensitive information.

Interior Gateway Routing Protocol (IGRP) | An interior distance-vector routing protocol that exchanges routing information with other routers within its AS.

Interior routing protocols | Protocols that perform routing functions among the routers owned by a single entity or under the control of a single network administrator.

International Telecommunications Union (ITU) | The agency within the United Nations responsible for global standardization of telecommunications practices and procedures.

Internet | A global network made up of interconnected networks that all use the standard Internet Protocol Suite (TCP/IP).

Internet Assigned Numbers Authority (IANA) | The organization responsible for coordinating IP addresses and resources around the world.

Internet Control Message Protocol (ICMP) | A protocol that defines how control messages are exchanged between nodes in a network.

Internet Engineering Task Force (IETF) | A global volunteer organization that develops and promotes Internet standards.

Internet Protocol (IP) | The primary protocol, or set of communication rules, used to transmit messages across the Internet and similar networks.

Internet Protocol Suite | See TCP/IP suite.

Internet service provider (ISP) | An organization that provides access to the Internet.

Internetworking | The interconnecting of two or more LANs or networks.

Intranet | An internal network, generally only accessible from locations in an organization's physical space.

IP address | A numeric label assigned to each computer or device connected to a network that uses the Internet Protocol.

IP Multimedia Subsystem (IMS) | A framework for delivering multimedia services over IP networks.

IP telephony | All systems that implement digital telephony over IP networks.

J

Jitter | The variable delay that causes gaps in a conversation due to uneven data flow.

Just in time (JIT) | A production strategy in which finished goods are completed and available to a subsequent process in the supply chain when they are needed, and not before.

L

Latency | The amount of time required for a message to reach its destination, measured in milliseconds (mSec).

Layer 2 | A term used to represent the OSI model Data Link Layer.

Layer 3 | A term used to represent the OSI model Network Layer.

Least privilege | The security principle that users possess only the minimum access privileges they need to complete their assigned tasks.

Lightweight Extensible Authentication Protocol (LEAP) | Cisco Systems' version of EAP. It supports dynamic key encryption and mutual authentication.

Link aggregation | A method to combine multiple physical links together that can be used as a single logical link.

Link Aggregation Control Protocol (LACP) | The protocol that defines how dynamic link aggregation operates.

Link bundling | A method to combine multiple physical links together that can be used as a single logical link.

Link-state routing protocol | A type of routing protocol that calculates the status (state) of a link and its connection type, speed, and delay.

Load | The amount of bandwidth in use on a particular link.

Load balancing | Routing protocols that divide message traffic over two or more links.

Logical topology | A picture of how networks transfer data between nodes.

M

MAC layer bridge | A network device that creates the MAC address table by learning where all the MAC layer addresses are of other devices.

Managed service provider (MSP) | Provides a broad, rich set of applications, such as Web hosting, database management, VoIP, and UC and network management, such as management of routers and firewalls, usually using access provided by the ISP.

Management information base (MIB) | A small database of characteristics for a specific type of device.

Manufacturer | Organization that takes raw materials and/or components and fabricates or assembles them to create a new product.

Maximum transmission unit (MTU) | The length in bytes of the longest message unit that can be transmitted on available links that connect a source address to a destination address.

Mean time between failures (MTBF) | A measurement or calculated number for the mean amount of time between equipment failures. MTBF was measured in years, or even decades, in the traditional telco network, while it may be measured in weeks, days, or even hours in modern IP networks.

Mean time to install (MTTI) | A measurement or estimate of the time required to install a specific piece of equipment or an entire service.

Mean time to repair (MTTR) | A measurement or calculated number for the mean amount of time required to repair a specific piece of failed equipment. MTBF and MTTR are important parts of network reliability calculations.

Media Access Control (MAC) layer address | The unique address of a specific device's NIC on the network.

Media Gateway Control Protocol (MGCP) | A protocol for controlling media gateways on networks that include both IP networks and PSTN.

Mesh topology | A network layout in which all nodes are directly connected to most, or all, other nodes.

Message integrity check (MIC) | Prevents an attacker from intercepting, modifying, and retransmitting message packets by checking the integrity of a packet using the ICV.

Metcalfe's law | The number of connections required in a fully connected network is proportional to the square of the number of devices. The formula to calculate the number of wires you need to connect all devices in a network with n devices is: $n(n - 1)/2$.

Metric | A standard of measurement.

MIB module | All MIB variables that describe a single device.

MIB variable | An individual setting in an MIB that stores the value of a single device characteristic.

Mobile phone | Telephone that connects to the telephony network using radio transmission instead of wires.

Multi-homed | Refers to a device with connections to multiple links.

Multipath | The propagation that results in RF signals reaching the receiving antenna at different times and by two or more different paths.

Multiple-input and multiple-output (MIMO) | An antenna technology that uses multiple antennas (to receive and transmit) at both ends of a transmission.

Multiple spanning tree (MST) | A spanning tree that maps to one or more VLANs.

Multiple spanning tree instance (MSTI) | Each group of VLANs that are assigned to an instance of a multiple spanning tree.

Multiple Spanning Tree Protocol (MSTP) | A protocol that defines several data structures to create and maintain spanning trees.

N

Neighbor Discovery Protocol (NDP) | Protocol used by IPv6 networks to provide a similar service as ARP.

Network adapter | See network interface controller.

Network Address Translation (NAT) | The process of replacing a private IP address with a public IP address, or vice versa.

Network interface card | See network interface controller.

Network interface controller (NIC) | A hardware device that connects a computer or other device to network media.

Network operations center (NOC) | One or more central locations used to monitor and control networks.

Network readiness assessment (NRA) | A study of how traffic moves through a network.

Network topology | A map of the network that shows how devices connect to one another and how they use connection medium to communicate.

O

Object ID (OID) | A unique identifier that refers to a specific MIB module.

Open System Authentication (OSA) | A process through which a node gains access to a wireless network running WEP and access files that are not encrypted.

Open Systems Interconnection (OSI) Reference Model | An internationally accepted framework of standards that governs how separate computer systems communicate using networks.

Optimistic transmission | The transmitting node assumes its transmissions will all be successful.

Orthogonal Frequency Division Multiplexing (OFDM) | A frequency-division multiplexing (FDM) scheme that applies a digital multi-carrier modulation method.

P

Packet | A small, easily managed chunk of a network message. Networks often chop up messages and transmit each chunk separately.

Packet jitter | A measure of how much network latency changes over time. This measure is often expressed as an average of the deviation from the mean latency of a network.

Packet loss | The percentage of packets sent that do not reach the intended destination.

Packet-switched | Refers to a network that chops up network messages into smaller chunks and sends each chunk, or packet, separately. Each packet can take a different path from source to destination.

Pager | Device that generates a sound or effect when a caller calls a specific telephone number, also called a beeper. Some pagers support sending short messages, either numeric, or voice, to the device.

Partially connected mesh | A network layout in which network nodes connect to only some of the other nodes.

Passive fault detection | A technique that involves waiting for some indication that a fault has occurred.

Path length | The number of steps a message takes to get from the sender to the receiver.

Personal digital assistant (PDA) | Personal devices that provide the ability to store and manage personal information. Many PDAs have the ability to connect to the Internet.

Personally identifiable information (PII) | Data that can uniquely identify a specific person.

Physical topology | A picture of the actual network devices and the medium the devices use to connect to the network.

Plain old telephone service (POTS) | Voice-grade telephone service network. POTS generally refers to the analog predecessor of today's telecommunication networks.

Point of presence (POP) | A facility operated by an ISP where all its common routing equipment, and very often servers, are located.

Point-to-point | Refers to a network layout in which computers or devices are directly connected to one another.

Poisoned reverse | Prevents information from a particular interface from being repeated to that interface.

Power over Ethernet (PoE) | An IEEE standard for providing electrical power to an IP phone from an Ethernet switch in the wiring closet.

Presence | Technology that allows the geographic location of a human or non-human resource (such as a conference room) to be determined.

Private IP address | An IP address in the reserved ranges (10.0.0.0 to 10.255.255.255, 172.16.0.0 to 172.16.255.255, or 192.168.0.0 to 192.168.255.255) used for devices in a private network. Private IP addresses are not visible to external Internet devices.

Protocol | A set of rules that define a particular aspect of communication.

PTT (postal, telephone, and telegraph) agency | A term for government-owned telecommunications monopolies outside the US. Traditionally these functions were housed in a single government ministry.

Public Switched Telephone Network (PSTN) | Voice-grade telephone service network. POTS generally refers to the analog predecessor of today's telecommunication networks.

Q

Quadrature amplitude modulation (QAM) | A technique that can modulate both analog and digital transmissions.

Qualitative risk analysis | A method that ranks risks relative to one another.

Quality of experience (QoE) | Users' perceptions or measurements and calculations approximating user's perceptions of the quality of a real-time voice or video communication.

Quality of service (QoS) | A measure of how successful a network is at meeting packet delivery timing and error rate goals.

Quantitative risk analysis | A method that associates a dollar value, or cost, with each risk.

R

Radio frequency identification (RFID) | A technology that exchanges data through a wireless connection between a reader and a tag attached to a product to track the movement of the product.

Rapid Spanning Tree Protocol (RSTP) | A Layer 2 resiliency standard that provides a faster convergence time than STP.

Real-time applications | Network applications that rely on immediate traffic delivery, such as streaming audio or video.

Real-time communication | A communication method in which messages are sent directly to the recipient immediately (in real time).

Real-Time Control Protocol (RTCP) | The protocol used by Real Time Protocol to provide feedback from the recipient of RTP-transported information to the sender regarding traffic management metrics, such as number of packets received, delay, delay variation, and Mean Opinion Scores (MOSs).

Real-Time Transport Protocol (RTP) | A standard that defines how to deliver audio and video over IP networks. Also known as real-time protocol.

Reliability | A measurement of the amount of downtime on a particular link that indicates the reliability of the link. An indicator of how likely a link is to fail during transmission.

Reliable communication | A communication process in which senders have verification that recipients received all sent messages.

Request for proposal (RFP) | A formal document requesting that interested vendors submit proposals to meet a specific organizational requirement.

Resilience (resiliency) | Another term for redundancy or failover; specifically, a condition in which a network can "bounce back" from failures because its Physical Layer media, Layer 2 network access functions, and Layer 3 forwarding and addressing functions have hot-swap redundancy.

Retailer | An organization that sells products and/or services to consumers.

Retransmission | The amount of time required to retransmit a packet.

Rich media conference | A conference that uses such tools as audio, video, and shared whiteboards and desktops to accomplish its goals.

Ring topology | A network layout in which each computer connects to two other computers. The computers connect to one another in a virtual ring.

Risk | The likelihood that an attack will successfully exploit a vulnerability.

Risk management | The process of identifying and addressing all risks.

Root bridge | The first node in a spanning tree.

Root path cost | The accumulated cost of all the links in a path leading to the root bridge.

Root port (RP) | The port on any switch that leads to the root bridge and also has the lowest root path cost.

Round trip time (RTT) | The amount of time it takes to send a packet to another node and have that node return the packet to the sender.

Routed protocols | Protocols that define the formatting and structure of data being routed.

Router | A device that operates at OSI Layer 3 (Network Layer) to determine the destination address for network messages.

Routing Information Protocol (RIP) | An interior distance-vector routing protocol that uses hop count as its routing metric.

Routing protocols | Communicates with other routers to maintain routing information with which path determination can be made.

Routing tables | Maintained by a routing protocol to store metrics about the addresses available through each interface port of a router.

RS-232 | A set of EIA standards for serial binary data and control signals that connect DTE and DCE devices. RS-232 is a common standard used for computer serial ports.

S

Security breach | Any event that results in a violation of any of the "CIA" (confidentiality, integrity, and availability) security properties.

Security control | A countermeasure that protects resources from attack.

Security gap analysis | An analysis that identifies known vulnerabilities for which there are no security controls in place.

Security triad | The three basic properties of information security: confidentiality, integrity, and availability.

Serial communications | A communication method in which a device sends individual characters, one at a time.

Service/feature gateways | Gateways allowing services or features on a non-SIP network to be delivered on a SIP network, and vice versa. One example is the 411 information service.

Session Description Protocol (SDP) | A protocol that defines streaming media attributes and parameters.

Session Initiation Protocol (SIP) | A signaling protocol commonly used to control multimedia communication sessions.

Shared Key Authentication (SKA) | A process through which a node gains access to a WLAN running the WEP protocol.

Signaling gateway | A gateway that provides a means of connecting two different systems that use different types of signaling, such as a SIP to ISDN gateway or SIP to SS7/CCS7 gateway.

Simple Network Management Protocol (SNMP) | A protocol used to collect and process information about network devices.

Simplex | A mode of operation for communication between computers in which only the source can send data to the destination, and the destination cannot respond.

Single point of failure (SPOF) | A single piece of hardware or software that must operate for the larger system or network to operate.

Small- and medium-sized business (SMB) | The sector made up of organizations with fewer than 500 employees.

Small office/home office (SOHO) | An office or location with fewer than 10 employees.

Snail mail | A communication method in which the sender delivers a message to a recipient using standard mail delivery services.

Spanning tree | A path that starts at one node and visits all of the other nodes exactly once.

Spanning Tree Protocol (STP) | A network protocol that identifies infinite loops in switched networks and helps devices direct packets around loops.

Split horizon | A feature or distance-vector routing protocol that prevents reverse routes between two routers and helps to prevent the possibility of a routing loop.

Star-wired topology | A network layout in which a central network device connects to all other network devices.

Static routing | Using fixed links configured manually.

Storage area network (SAN) | A special version of local area network where all devices connected to the SAN are storage devices or servers required to manage storage devices.

Store-and-forward communication | A communication method in which the sender sends a message to an agent that stores the message until the recipient retrieves it from the agent.

Structured cabling system | A collection of standard components that connect with one another to provide a complete cabling solution.

Subnet mask | A binary number that contains all 1's in the leftmost prefix length positions, and all other bits are 0's.

Switch | A network device that receives a message, examines the destination address, and sends the message directly to the destination (or directly to the next device nearest to the destination).

Switching loop | Switches linked together in a loop or ring topology.

Symmetric encryption system | A system of encryption that applies the same exact key to encrypt and decrypt data.

Syslog | A standard for logging messages from programs and devices.

T

TCP/IP Reference Model | See Transmission Control Protocol/Internet Protocol (TCP/IP) Reference Model.

TCP/IP suite | By far the most popular set of standards used today to communicate over networks, this suite of protocols takes its name from the most common two protocols at its core: Transmission Control Protocol (TCP) and Internet Protocol (IP). Also known as Internet Protocol Suite.

Telecommunications Management Network (TMN) | A protocol model for managing open systems in a communication network.

Telepresence | A real-time video and audio conferencing capability utilizing large-screen and high-definition video such that conference participants appear to be full-size.

Temporal Key Integrity Protocol (TKIP) | A security protocol used in the IEEE 802.11x wireless standard.

Terminal | A device that has a keyboard and a monitor that connects to a computer system and interacts with it.

Threat | Any action that could damage an asset.

Throughput | A measure of the amount of traffic a network can handle.

Time-sensitive protocols | Network communication protocols that guarantee delivery within a specified amount of time.

Token | A special message that authorizes a device to transmit.

Topology | The logical layout of a network.

Total cost of ownership (TCO) | An estimate of the total direct and indirect financial costs associated with a product or service.

Transmission Control Protocol (TCP) | A network protocol that guarantees the delivery of a reliable stream of data between two computer programs. TCP operates at OSI Layer 4.

Transmission Control Protocol/Internet Protocol (TCP/IP) Reference Model | a descriptive framework for computer network protocols, created by the US Department of Defense in the 1970s. This model is often called the TCP/IP Model.

Trunk link | A link that connects to trunk ports on separate switches.

Trunk port | A port on a switch that allows VLAN traffic to pass through it.

Trunking gateway | A type of gateway that translates between two types of telephony trunking.

Type of service (TOS) | Usually refers to a specific set of bits in the header of IP packets that indicate what type of priority treatment the packet expects from intermediate relaying systems (routers). TOS can also refer to the desirable treatment, and not specifically to the bits themselves.

U

Unicast addresses | IPv6 addresses that specify a unique device.

Unified communications (UC) | A process of combining multiple technologies to provide the most effective real-time and non-real-time communication with the correct target or destination.

Uniform resource identifier (URI) | An identifier, formatted much like an e-mail address, that identifies a user in the SIP realm.

Unique local address (ULA) | A private (non-routable) IPv6 device address. IPv6 ULAs are in the range fc00:/7, or fc00:0:0:0:0:0:0:0 to fdff:ffff:ffff:ffff:ffff:ffff:ffff:ffff.

Unlicensed National Information Infrastructure (UNII) | The 5 GHz frequency band used by IEEE-802.11a devices.

V

Variable Length Subnet Masking (VLSM) | A strategy to allow IPv4 networks to be fragmented into any size subnetwork.

Video conference | A communication between two or more persons where each may see the other and, optionally, all parties can see other things such as pre-recorded video content.

Virtual LAN (VLAN) | A group of network nodes that are logically grouped together to form a single broadcast domain.

Virtual private network (VPN) | A network built using public/shared network services, but which has the appearance to the users of a private network. VPN users, for instance, cannot reach the Internet directly from their VPN nor can Internet users reach the VPN without special client software. VPNs almost universally use some sort of cryptography to protect the integrity of VPN information.

Virtual Router Redundancy Protocol (VRRP) | An IEEE standard redundancy protocol that clusters multiple routers into a single virtual router.

VLAN trunking | The process of forwarding traffic within a VLAN from one switch to another.

Voice over IP (VoIP) | A collection of communication protocols and technologies to deliver voice communication and sessions over IP networks.

Vulnerability | Any weakness in a system that makes it possible for a threat to cause it harm.

W

Wholesaler | An organization that purchases products or services from a supplier and resells them to other organizations, often retailers.

Wireless fidelity (Wi-Fi) | A standard developed by the Wi-Fi Alliance to certify protocols, software, and equipment standards.

Workgroup | A group of people and the devices they use to perform related job functions.

World Wide Web | A collection of hypertext documents that are interlinked and accessible via the Internet.

References

Alpern, Naomi J., Matthew Shepherd, and Robert Shimonski. *Eleventh Hour Network+: Exam N10-004 Study Guide*. Waltham, MA: Syngress, 2010.

Andriole, Stephen J. *Best Practices in Business Technology Management*. Boca Raton, FL: CRC Press, 2009.

Angelescu, Silviu. *CCNA Certification All-In-One for Dummies*. Hoboken, NJ: Wiley, 2010.

Banzal, Shashi. *Data and Computer Network Communication*. Bangalore: Firewall Media/ Laxmi Publications Pvt. Ltd., 2007.

Barnes, David, and Basir Sakandar. *Cisco LAN Switching Fundamentals*. Indianapolis: Cisco Press, 2004.

Bowman, Ronald H. *Business Continuity Planning for Data Centers and Systems: A Strategic Implementation Guide*. Hoboken, NJ: John Wiley and Sons, 2008.

Carpenter, Colman, David Duffett, Nik Middleton, and Ian Plain. *Asterisk 1.4: The Professional's Guide: Implementing, Administering, and Consulting on Commercial IP Telephony Solutions*. Birmingham, England: Packt Publishing, Ltd., 2009.

Cavanagh, James P. *The Definitive Guide to Successful Deployment of VoIP and IP Telephony*. San Francisco: Realtime Publishers, 2004.

Chesbrough, Henry William. *Open Services Innovation: Rethinking Your Business to Grow and Compete in a New Era*. San Francisco: Jossey-Bass, 2011.

Cole, Eric. *Network Security Bible*, 2nd ed. Indianapolis: Wiley, 2009.

Coleman, David D., and David A. Wescott. *CWNA Certified Wireless Network Administrator Official Study Guide: Exam PW0-104*. Boston: Sybex, 2009.

Collins, Daniel. *Carrier Grade Voice Over IP*, 2nd ed. New York: McGraw Hill, 2002.

Corbitt, Brian J., and Nabeel A.Y. Qirim. *E-Business, e-Government & Small & Medium-Size Enterprises: Opportunities and Challenges*. Hershey, PA: Idea Group Inc. (2004).

Davies, Joseph. *Understanding IPv6*, 2nd ed. Redmond, Wash.: Microsoft Press, 2008.

Dean, Tamara. *CompTIA Network+ 2009 In Depth*. Cambridge: Course Technology, 2009.

Donoso, Yezid. *Network Design for IP Convergence*. Boca Raton, FL: CRC Press, 2009.

Farrel, Adrian. *Network Management: Know It All*. Burlington, MA: Morgan Kaufmann/ Elsevier, 2009.

Frey, Robert S. *Successful Proposal Strategies for Small Business: Using Knowledge Management to Win Government, Private-Sector, and International Contracts*, 4th ed. Boston: Artech House. (2005).

Froom, Richard, Balaji Sivasubramanian, Erum Frahim, and Geoff Tagg. *Implementing Cisco IP Switched Networks (SWITCH) Foundation learning for SWITCH 642-813*. Indianapolis: Cisco Press, 2010.

Geier, Jim. *Designing and Deploying 802.11n Wireless Networks*. Indianapolis: Cisco Press, 2010.

Gilster, Ron. Cisco *Networking For Dummies*, 2nd ed. Indianapolis: Wiley, 2002.

Goralski, Walter. *The Illustrated Network: How TCP/IP Works in a Modern Network*. Amsterdam: Elsevier/Morgan Kaufmann, 2009.

Graziani, Rick, and Allan Johnson. *Routing Protocols and Concepts, CCNA Exploration Companion Guide*, Indianapolis: Cisco Press, 2007.

Hattingh, Christina, Darryl Sladden, and Zakaria Swapan. *SIP Trunking*. Indianapolis: Cisco Press, 2010.

Keogh, James Edward. *The Essential Guide to Networking*. Upper Saddle River, NJ: Prentice Hall PTR, 2001.

Khasnabish, Bhumip. *Implementing Voice over IP*. New York: Wiley-Interscience, 2003.

King, Brett. *Bank 2.0: How Customer Behavior and Technology Will Change the Future of Financial Services*. Singapore: Marshall Cavendish Business, 2010.

Krawetz, Neal. *Introduction to Network Security*. Rockland, MA: Charles River Media, 2007.

Lee, In. *E-Business Innovation and Process Management*. Hershey, PA: CyberTech Publishing, 2007.

Lee, Sang M., and David Louis Olson. *Convergenomics: Strategic Innovation in the Convergence Era*. London: Gower, 2010.

Manzuik, Steve, André Gold, and Chris Gatford. *Network Security Assessment: From Vulnerability to Patch*. Norwich, CT: Syngress Publishers, 2007.

McCabe, James D. *Network Analysis, Architecture, and Design*, 3rd ed. Amsterdam: Elsevier/Morgan Kaufmann Publishers, 2007.

McQuerry, Stephen. *Interconnecting Cisco Network Devices Part 2*. Indianapolis: Cisco Press, 2008.

Meyers, Michael, Scott Jernigan, Alec Felh, and Christopher A. Crayton. *CompTIA Network+ All-in-One Exam Guide*, 4th ed. New York: Osborne/McGraw-Hill, 2009.

Odom, Wendell. *CCNA ICND2 Official Exam Certification Guide*. Indianapolis: Cisco Press, 2007.

Price, Ron. *Fundamentals of Wireless Networks*. New York: McGraw Hill, 2006.

Qian, Yi, David Tipper, Prashant Krishnamurthy, James Joshi. *Information Assurance: Dependability and Security in Networked Systems*. Amsterdam: Elsevier/Morgan Kaufmann, 2008.

Ranjbar, Amir. *Troubleshooting and Maintaining Cisco IP Networks (TSHOOT) Foundation Learning Guide: Foundation Learning for CCNP TSHOOT 642-832*. Indianapolis: Cisco Press, 2010.

Riggs, Cliff. *Network Perimeter Security: Building Defense In-Depth*. Chicago: Auerbach Publications, 2004.

Seifert, Rich, and James Edwards. *The All-New Switch Book: The Complete Guide to LAN Switching Technology*, 2nd ed. Indianapolis: Wiley, 2008.

Shepard, Steven. *Voice over IP Crash Course*. New York: McGraw-Hill, 2005.

Sherif, Mostafa Hashem. *Handbook of Enterprise Integration*. Boca Raton, FL: Auerbach Publications/CRC Press, 2010.

Sinnreich, Henry, Alan B. Johnston, Robert J. Sparks, and Vinton G. Cerf. *SIP Beyond VoIP: The Next Step in the IP Communications Revolution*. Melville, NY: VON Publishing LLC, 2005.

Snedaker, Susan. *Business Continuity and Disaster Recovery Planning for IT Professionals*. Burlington, MA: Syngress Publishing, 2007.

Sosinsky, Barrie. *Networking Bible*. Indianapolis: Wiley, 2009.

Tanenbaum, Andrew S., and D. Wetherall. *Computer Networks*, 5th ed. Boston: Pearson Prentice Hall, 2011.

Zemke, Ron, and Thomas K. Connellan. *E-Service: 24 Ways to Keep Your Customers—When the Competition Is Just a Click Away*. New York: AMACOM, 2001.

Index

Figures and tables are indicated by an "f" or a "t" following the page number.

A

B

C

INDEX

F

J

K

L

N

Q

R

S

T

U

INDEX

V